CASES AND MATERIALS

A WOMAN'S PLACE IS IN THE MARKETPLACE:

GENDER AND ECONOMICS

by

EMMA COLEMAN JORDAN
Professor of Law
Georgetown University Law Center

ANGELA P. HARRIS
Professor of Law
Boalt Hall–School of Law, University of California, Berkeley

FOUNDATION PRESS

NEW YORK, NEW YORK

2006

Foundation Press, of Thomson/West, has created this publication to provide you with accurate and authoritative information concerning the subject matter covered. However, this publication was not necessarily prepared by persons licensed to practice law in a particular jurisdiction. Foundation Press is not engaged in rendering legal or other professional advice, and this publication is not a substitute for the advice of an attorney. If you require legal or other expert advice, you should seek the services of a competent attorney or other professional.

© 2006 By FOUNDATION PRESS
        395 Hudson Street
        New York, NY 10014
        Phone Toll Free 1–877–888–1330
        Fax (212) 367–6799
        fdpress.com
Printed in the United States of America
ISBN 13: 978–1–58778–956–4
ISBN 10: 1–58778–956–6

TEXT IS PRINTED ON 10% POST CONSUMER RECYCLED PAPER

For the late E. W. Coleman and M. H. Coleman,
my daughters Kristen and Allison and my sisters Betty, Jean and Earlene

*

INTRODUCTION

The civil law, as well as nature herself, has always recognized a wide difference in the respective spheres and destinies of man and woman. Man is, or should be, woman's protector and defender. The natural and proper timidity and delicacy which belongs to the female sex evidently unfits it for many of the occupations of civil life. The constitution of the family organization, which is founded in the divine ordinance, as well as in the nature of things, indicates the domestic sphere as that which properly belongs to the domain and functions of womanhood. The harmony, not to say the identity, of interests and views which belong, or should belong, to the family institution is repugnant to the idea of a woman adopting a distinct and independent career from that of her husband. * * * The paramount mission and destiny of women are to fulfill the noble and benign offices of wife and mother. This is the law of the Creator.

So wrote Justice Joseph Bradley in 1873, in his famous concurrence in the case of Bradwell v. Illinois. In that decision the Supreme Court rejected a Fourteenth Amendment challenge to the state of Illinois' decision to deny admission to the state bar to Myra Bradwell because she was a woman. In the view of the Illinois state bar, permitting women to practice law threatened what social historians now name "domesticity," that social order (according to Justice Bradley, originally set in place by God Himself) within which women belonged in the home and men in the marketplace.

In the twenty-first century, the right of women in the United States to participate in the marketplace on equal terms with men is protected by the Constitution. But the ideology of domesticity has not entirely disappeared. Today, women struggle with the tension between "work" and "family." An enormous popular and scholarly literature counsels women on how to juggle home life and family life, and how manage the "second shift," the term sociologist Arlie Hochschild coined to describe the duty of running the home and taking care of children that women are expected to fulfill after coming home from a full day of working for wages. Women are sometimes told, as well, that they can't "have it all": high-paid C.E.O.s and Hollywood celebrities smilingly tell reporters of the joy of quitting one's rat-race job to take care of children. The "joy of childlessness," however, does not get similar attention. If job and family are incompatible, women are expected to sacrifice the marketplace.

Is domesticity still with us? What is the relationship between the family and the marketplace? As the ideology of domesticity suggests, family and market are often treated as opposites: the market is "public" and the family "private." But both "family" and "market" are treated as "private" spaces when compared to the public world of the state and politics. As critical theorists have pointed out, it is commonplace to hear complaints about the state "intervening" in the market, and those complaints sound very much like complaints about the state "intervening" in the family. These theorists would respond that the state, through law, shapes both the market and the family. Rather than being private spaces removed from politics, then, family and market are already political.

This book explores the relationship between these different social spaces—state, market, family—and the gender order. As Justice Bradley's opinion suggests, domesticity explains the relationship between the family and the market by keying it to gender: the family is a feminine space, the market is a masculine space. But the American gender order has changed in dramatic ways since 1873, and to a great extent it was the marketplace that gave rise to these changes. The "family wage" associated with union jobs in the industrial economy—which enabled wives to stay at home with children while their husbands took on the role of "breadwinner"—has largely disappeared. Many manufacturing jobs have moved overseas or disappeared as technological capacity expands, and unions play an increasingly marginalized role in determining wages and benefits. In the new economy, high-paying careers demand steep investments of education and training, while jobs accessible to those without college and post-graduate training increasingly tend to be "McJobs": jobs that offer flexibility, but little in the way of high wages, good benefits, stability, or access to a progressive career ladder. In order to pursue the good life, women as well as men now expect to be in the marketplace for much of their adult lives.

How should the family, and the state, respond to these changes? Has the imperative pushing all adults into the marketplace created a crisis in the family? Who should take care of the children while Mom and Dad work full-time? A government-subsidized day care? An immigrant woman without citizenship papers? If the reciprocal relationship between the family and the market has broken down, what about the relationship between male and female? Is heterosexuality itself—or, at least, the binary gender order—becoming a nineteenth-century anachronism?

As well as posing these substantive questions about the family, the market, the state, and the gender order, this book provides a variety of analytic tools for thinking about them. We are used to talking about gender in legal and moral terms, with words like "fairness," "difference," and "equality." We are used to thinking about the family in emotional and psychological terms with words like "love" and "care." What might the language of economics bring to the analysis of family and gender? The Chicago economist Gary Becker caused a stir when he began to analyze the family as a site of bargaining and negotiation. Was he right that the family is a place of economic power struggle, not just a place where one goes to recover from the harsh world of the market? If the family is an economic institution, how does that change our picture of its relationship to the "market" as traditionally conceived?

Juxtaposing moral, legal, and economic analyses in this way might also change the way we think about economics. Does an economic analysis of gender and the family require greater attention to social norms and to questions of power? Do certain economic practices—like using the "household" as the basic unit of analysis—become problematic when we recognize that a household can contain power struggles? Can economic analysis effectively recognize and take account of family structures not recognized by law, such as same–sex partnerships and support systems that transcend blood relations?

Chapter 1 of this book sets the stage for considering these questions by introducing the student to basic concepts and data concerning wealth and inequality. What is wealth, and how is it measured? How is wealth different from income? What is economic inequality, and how is it measured? Chapter 2 adds personal voices to the data, providing narratives from individuals on different rungs in the American class structure and illustrating the influence of material culture on the rich, the poor, and those in the middle. Chapter 3 focuses on the family as an institution shaped by history and economic pressures as well as by ideology and basic human needs. Chapter 4 explores questions of the relationship between culture and identity. Chapter 5 provides resources with which to think about not only the "formal" economy, but also "underground" and "informal" economies. Each of these economies, we will see, is gendered.

At this moment in history, the "family" has been placed at the center of economic and political controversies and upheavals. We hope this book will help students think about what we mean when we talk about the family, and we hope its focus on gender and the family will show how law, culture, and economics are intertwined.

*

ACKNOWLEDGEMENTS

The idea for creating teaching materials to introduce law students to a systematic examination of the interdisciplinary dimensions of increasing economic inequality and the role of identity in the distribution of wealth first occurred to me more than ten years ago. My decision to create this casebook arose from my mounting frustration with the conceptual limitations of the consumer protection features of commercial law and banking, the two traditional areas in which I had been working over the course of my career. I deeply appreciate the contributions of Nancy Ota who came to Georgetown Law Center in 1992–93 as a graduate Fellow in the Future Law Professor Program to work with me. She invested her unique imagination and commitment to assist me in creating the first set of teaching materials for the first course on Economic Justice.

This casebook owes much to the confidence and support I enjoyed from my publisher, Steven Errick. His enthusiasm and shared vision for the innovations of this effort and his never-failing generosity in responding to and initiating additional publishing opportunities for the Economic Justice topic were important at critical points in the process. Steve's departure in the weeks before this book went to press was a real personal loss. I look forward to working with the new publisher, John Bloomquist in future editions.

I especially want to thank the many Georgetown University Law Center students who enrolled in the early courses in Economic Justice, and who became my most enthusiastic cheering section (offering rap and pop lyrics, African proverbs, Equal Access to Justice/E.A.T. Justice, a socially conscious business venture and strong counterarguments) as this project moved forward to completion. I learned so much from our intense classroom investigations of some of my then forming hypotheses about educational capital, wealth and income inequalities, intergenerational economic effects, linguistic differences, the relationship of the Constitution to economic outcomes, and the limits of conventional market theory. The richness and complexity of this project owe much to my students.

From my Georgetown law students, I chose outstanding research assistants who worked with passion and conviction on the research for this book. They found many truly important additions to the materials. They designed the critical copyright accounting system, chased elusive copyright holders with the zeal of a "repo" man/woman. They kept me laughing when I might have otherwise turned grouchy. They discussed this newly emerging field with me with intelligence and energy. My special thanks go to Angela

Ahern '05, Rashida Baskerville '06, Katherine Buell '04, Cassandra Charles '05, Kenneth Leichter '06, William Morriss '05, Michael Radolinski '06, and Joshua Soszynski '07.

Shaping the boundaries of this project required many hours of conversation with colleagues. Steven Salop was exceptionally generous with his time and the contents of his library on economics. The time we spent talking about economics and shuttling from my office to his across the hall, undoubtedly accelerated my understanding of the intellectual framework of modern economics. I benefited greatly from the expertise and gentle prodding of several colleagues: Alex Aleinikoff, William Braxton, Jerry Kang (during his visit in 2004–5), Carrie Menkel-Meadow, Michael Seidman, Gerry Spann, Rebecca Tushnet, Kathy Zeiler and the colleagues who participated in the Georgetown Law Center Summer Faculty Workshop in 2004. If there are any errors in what follows, it must be because I didn't listen to their sage advice.

This project could not have been finished without the superb institutional arrangements in place at Georgetown University Law Center to support faculty manuscripts. Georgetown enjoys an organizational structure that would be the envy of most casebook writers. I received several summer research grants to allow me to devote time to developing and completing the project. In their capacities as lead manuscript editor and faculty services librarian for this book, Zinta Saulkans and Jennifer Locke and her staff were truly indispensable to achieving a high technical quality for the final manuscript. Diane McDonald, my faculty assistant, Derreck Brown, Sylvia Johnson, Toni Patterson, Ronnie Reese, and Anna Selden in the Office of Faculty Support were always optimistic in the face of frustrations and the unexpected nightmares of formatting, and other technical meltdowns. They were responsive to my many requests during the development of this book. Finally, the Office of Information Systems and Technology introduced me to new equipment and software for managing the project. My special thanks go to Dianne H. Ferro Mesarch, Dimo Michailov, Pablo Molina and Barry Wileman.

In 2001, Angela Harris visited at Georgetown from Boalt Hall at the Univ. of California at Berkeley. As we discussed her work on class and race, it became clear that I could benefit from working with her on this casebook. When she agreed to join the project, I could not know then what a terrific contributor she would be. Her intelligence and humor made the work flow effortlessly to conclusion. We truly had fun doing this work; my only regret is that I didn't think to ask her to join me sooner.

Finally, I want to thank my dear friends Gail, Audrey, Fay and Marta for their support, as well as my two daughters Kristen and Allison for their patience and understanding during the many hours I devoted to completing this project.

EMMA COLEMAN JORDAN

Washington, D.C. August, 2005

I would like to thank my students at Boalt and at Georgetown (Wealth and Class Relations, fall 2000; Wealth and Class Relations, fall 2001; and Law, Markets, and Culture, fall 2004) for their excitement, hard work, and insight as we tried to think through the complicated mutual entanglements of "fairness," "efficiency," "markets," "culture," and "law," and as we struggled toward an institutional theory of human flourishing.

I would like to thank my assistant, Ayn Lowry, for her skill and dedication at tracking down copyright holders across the globe, and for her enthusiasm for this project despite the many last-minute headaches it caused.

I owe a huge debt to my co-author, Emma Coleman Jordan, for talking me into joining and then sticking with the project, and for her wonderful combination of brilliant vision, sisterly solidarity, and can-do spirit.

Last, but not least, I would like to thank my amazing research assistants, Tucker Bolt Culbertson and Naomi Ruth Tsu, for everything: research, pep talks, proofreading, formatting, article suggestions, critical feedback, and, of course, cookies.

ANGELA HARRIS

Berkeley, California
August 2005

*

SUMMARY OF CONTENTS

INTRODUCTION	v
ACKNOWLEDGEMENTS	ix
TABLE OF CASES	xix

CHAPTER 1. Wealth and Inequality — 1

A. Defining "Class"	2
B. The Constitution: Wealth and Class	16
C. Class and Inequality—Historical Perspectives	24
• Income Inequality	24
D. Wealth, Class and Economic Mobility—The Intergenerational Effects	36
• Wealth Inequality.	54

CHAPTER 2. Life in a Class Society — 83

A. Down and Out	83
B. Relations of (Re)production	98
C. Class and Consumption	155

CHAPTER 3. Defining Family — 183

A. Nuclear Family vs. Extended Family	184
B. Unmarried Heterosexual Couples	200
C. Same–Sex Couples	212
D. Sex Between Consenting Adults	221
E. A Family Based on Same Sex Marriage	238

CHAPTER 4. Culture and Identity — 247

A. Culture and Identity	248
B. Racial Discrimination: Two Competing Theories and Empirical Evidence of Disparate Racial Impact	321
1. A Rational Choice Theory of Racial Discrimination in the Marketplace	321
2. A Sociological Theory of Racial Discrimination in the Marketplace	325
3. An Empirical Study of Racial Discrimination	357

xiii

CHAPTER 5. Cash and Carry ... 380

A. The Underground Economy ... 380

COPYRIGHT PERMISSIONS & FURTHER ACKNOWLEDGMENTS ... 407
INDEX ... 411

TABLE OF CONTENTS

INTRODUCTION	v
ACKNOWLEDGEMENTS	ix
TABLE OF CASES	xix

CHAPTER 1. Wealth and Inequality 1

Introduction 1
A. Defining "Class" 2
    Class-Based Affirmative Action: Lessons and Caveats 2
    Notes and Questions 14
B. The Constitution: Wealth and Class 16
    San Antonio Independent School District v. Rodriguez 16
    Notes and Questions 24
C. Class and Inequality—Historical Perspectives 24
    • Income Inequality 24
        Economic Development in Indian Country: Will Capitalism or Socialism Succeed? 24
        Black Wealth/White Wealth: New Perspectives on Racial Inequality 29
        Race, Gender & Work: A Multicultural Economic History of Women in the United States 33
D. Wealth, Class and Economic Mobility—The Intergenerational Effects 36
    The Sticky Ladder 37
    Economic Scene; The Apple Falls Close to the Tree, Even in the Land of Opportunity 38
    The Sons Also Rise 41
    For Richer 42
    Notes and Questions 53
    • Wealth Inequality 54
        Wealth and Inequality in America 54
        The 1980s and Beyond Bigger Shares for the Wealthy 55
        Access to Assets 59
        Notes and Questions 62
        Hidden Cost of Being African American 63
        The Price of Segregation—Unconventional Wisdom: New Facts From the Social Sciences 64
        The Failures of Integration, How Race and Class are Undermining the American Dream 65
        Notes and Questions 66
        Your Stake in America 71
        Notes and Questions 81

CHAPTER 2. Life in a Class Society 83

A. Down and Out 83
    Number of People Living in Poverty Increases in U.S. 83
    Just Trying to Survive 86

A. Down and Out—Continued

Mathematics	92
Homelessness and the Issue of Freedom	93
Notes and Questions	95

B. Relations of (Re)production ... 98

The Working Poor: Invisible in America	98
Down and Out in Discount America	104
Notes and Questions	110
Nanny Diaries and Other Stories: Imagining Immigrant Women's Labor in the Social Reproduction of American Families	112
The Hidden Injuries of Class	124
Notes and Questions	128
The Overworked American: The Unexpected Decline of Leisure	131
Life.com	135
The Law and Economics of Critical Race Theory	140
Notes and Questions	153

C. Class and Consumption ... 155

The Overspent American: Why We Want What We Don't Need	155
No Scrubs	158
Dress As Success	159
Notes and Questions	165
Advertising At the Edge of the Apocalypse	167
Uneasy Ryder! Jury Finds Winona Guilty in Shoplift Case	180
Notes and Questions	181

CHAPTER 3. Defining Family ... 183

Introduction ... 183

A. Nuclear Family vs. Extended Family ... 184
Moore v. City of East Cleveland, Ohio ... 184
Notes and Questions ... 198

B. Unmarried Heterosexual Couples ... 200
Marvin v. Marvin ... 200
Notes and Questions ... 210

C. Same–Sex Couples ... 212
Whorton v. Dillingham ... 212
Domestic Partner Ordinance Quashed: Atlanta to Appeal in Second Defeat ... 219
Notes and Questions ... 220

D. Sex Between Consenting Adults ... 221
Lawrence v. Texas ... 221
Notes and Questions ... 236

E. A Family Based on Same Sex Marriage ... 238
Goodridge v. Department of Public Health ... 238
Notes and Questions ... 245

CHAPTER 4. Culture and Identity ... 247

Introduction ... 247

A. Culture and Identity ... 248
Economics and Identity ... 248
Identity in Mashpee ... 265

A. Culture and Identity—Continued
   Whiteness as Property 295
   Notes and Questions 318
B. Racial Discrimination: Two Competing Theories and Empirical Evidence of Disparate Racial Impact 321
   1. A Rational Choice Theory of Racial Discrimination in the Marketplace 321
      The Forces Determining Discrimination in the Market Place 321
   2. A Sociological Theory of Racial Discrimination in the Marketplace 325
      Cooperation and Conflict: The Economics of Group Status Production and Race Discrimination 325
      Notes and Questions 356
   3. An Empirical Study of Racial Discrimination 357
      Fair Driving: Gender and Race Discrimination in Retail Car Negotiations 357

CHAPTER 5. Cash and Carry 380

A. The Underground Economy 380
   Cashing in on Domestic Help 381
   Notes and Questions 383
   The Diamonds As a Business Enterprise 386
   Notes and Questions 394
   Carole, Interview with Barbara, in Sex Work: Writings By Women in the Sex Industry 396
   Phyllis Luman Metal, One for Ripley's, in Sex Works: Writings by Women in the Sex Industry 402
   Notes and Questions 404

COPYRIGHT PERMISSIONS & FURTHER ACKNOWLEDGMENTS 407
INDEX 411

TABLE OF CASES

Principal cases are in bold type. Non-principal cases are in roman type. References are to Pages.

Bowers v. Hardwick, 478 U.S. 186, 106 S.Ct. 2841, 92 L.Ed.2d 140 (1986), 236

Dukes v. Wal–Mart, 222 F.R.D. 137 (N.D.Cal. 2004), 111

Erlanger, In re Estate of, 145 Misc. 1, 259 N.Y.S. 610 (N.Y.Sur.1932), 211

FW/PBS, Inc. v. City of Dallas, 493 U.S. 215, 110 S.Ct. 596, 107 L.Ed.2d 603 (1990), 199

Goodridge v. Department of Public Health, 440 Mass. 309, 798 N.E.2d 941 (Mass.2003), **238**

Griswold v. Connecticut, 381 U.S. 479, 85 S.Ct. 1678, 14 L.Ed.2d 510 (1965), 198

In re (see name of party)

Jones v. Daly, 122 Cal.App.3d 500, 176 Cal. Rptr. 130 (Cal.App. 2 Dist.1981), 220

Lawrence v. Texas, 539 U.S. 558, 123 S.Ct. 2472, 156 L.Ed.2d 508 (2003), **221,** 236, 237, 238

Marvin v. Marvin, 134 Cal.Rptr. 815, 557 P.2d 106 (Cal.1976), **200,** 210, 211, 212, 220

Moore v. City of East Cleveland, Ohio, 431 U.S. 494, 97 S.Ct. 1932, 52 L.Ed.2d 531 (1977), **184,** 198, 199, 200, 211, 236

People v. _____ (see opposing party)

Rosenstock v. Board of Governors of University of North Carolina, 423 F.Supp. 1321 (M.D.N.C.1976), 69

San Antonio Independent School Dist. v. Rodriguez, 411 U.S. 1, 93 S.Ct. 1278, 36 L.Ed.2d 16 (1973), **16**

Smith v. Organization of Foster Families, 431 U.S. 816, 97 S.Ct. 2094, 53 L.Ed.2d 14 (1977), 199

Snyder v. Massachusetts, 291 U.S. 97, 54 S.Ct. 330, 78 L.Ed. 674 (1934), 198

Stanley v. Illinois, 405 U.S. 645, 92 S.Ct. 1208, 31 L.Ed.2d 551 (1972), 199

Superior Court of Alameda County, People v., 138 Cal.Rptr. 66, 562 P.2d 1315 (Cal. 1977), 405

Whorton v. Dillingham, 202 Cal.App.3d 447, 248 Cal.Rptr. 405 (Cal.App. 4 Dist. 1988), **212,** 220

CASES AND MATERIALS

A Woman's Place is in the Marketplace:
Gender and Economics

*

CHAPTER 1

WEALTH AND INEQUALITY

Introduction

As Deborah Malamud has observed:

Class is all but invisible in contemporary American social discourse. At most, it is a fleeting image, a rarely detected underlayer to the complex texture of race, ethnicity, and gender that captures our society's attention. For many, America stands as the model of the classless society, one in which most people think of themselves as middle class (or at least as potentially so, with hard work and a little luck) and in which middle-classness is the socioeconomic face of "American-ness." The recognized exception, the chronic poor, is seen as an aberration rather than evidence of a general system of class in the United States.

Similarly, American law does not recognize class. Constitutional equal protection doctrine and antidiscrimination statutes are the major mechanisms through which American law recognizes and redresses hierarchy in American society. Both are silent on the question of class. Welfare law advocates have utilized litigation and other mechanisms to argue that "the poor" is a legally significant group, that "poverty" is a suspect classification, and that welfare benefits are "new property" entitled to protection. Scholars have exhibited interest in addressing the question of how the law contributes both to the creation of cycles of poverty and to the social construction of poverty. But the very location of this work within poverty advocacy and theory has meant that it has drawn attention not to class as a general social phenomenon but to the aberrational nature of poverty and our social tolerance for it. Thus poverty is marked, middle-classness unmarked; poverty is figure, middle-classness ground. Poverty needs social, culture, and legal explanation. Middle-classness does not.

Deborah C. Malamud, *"Who They Are—Or Were": Middle–Class Welfare in the Early New Deal*, 151 U. PA. L. REV. 2019, 2019 (2003).

In this chapter, we will attempt to make visible the invisible category of class. Part A examines the difficulties in conceptualizing and measuring "class." Part B provides some historical perspectives on the law's role in shaping the class structure and relations we have today. Part C looks at income and wealth inequality at present and points at future trends.

A. Defining "Class"

Martha Mahoney notes that social and political theory has been dominated by two different concepts of class. One concept of class—"status-class"—draws on the work of sociologist Max Weber, and "analyzes economic participation through a focus on distribution and the market and emphasizes status as an important aspect of structural inequality."[a] In contrast, economist and theorist Karl Marx's concept of class "emphasizes class relations in a system of production and the exploitation of labor by capital."[b] A class analysis in the Weberian tradition, then, might divide American society into upper, middle, and lower classes (looking for indicia of stratification); a class analysis in the Marxist tradition might divide American society into capitalists and workers (looking for relations of power and exploitation). Another way to distinguish the two theories of class is to note that Weberian theories take a "snapshot" of existing class relations; Marxist theories attempt to explain historically how classes emerge and evolve.

To the extent that Americans are comfortable thinking about class relations at all, they usually focus on status. The excerpt that follows points out some of the difficulties in measuring and analyzing status-class.

Class–Based Affirmative Action: Lessons and Caveats
74 Tex. L. Rev. 1847, 1852–93 (1996).

■ Deborah C. Malamud

Two basic models of economic inequality compete in the American ideological marketplace, each with two major versions. * * *

One view—which I will call economic individualism—depicts the American economic order as completely open to economic mobility for those individuals with the gumption to pursue it. The economic individualist view admits (as it must) that at any given moment individuals occupy a wide range of positions on a continuum of economic attainment. But this distribution is seen as a result of, rather than a constraint on, free market forces. So long as there is sufficient mobility by individuals, the inequalities in the rewards accorded to different positions are of no theoretical or political importance.

A more moderate version of economic individualism—and the only form of economic individualism that an advocate of class-based affirmative action could embrace—is what one might call pro-interventionist economic individualism. Here, it is admitted that past economic position is a con-

---

a. Martha R. Mahoney, 76 S. Cal. L. Rev. 799, 817 (2003). **b.** *id.*

straint on future economic position; for example, that lack of economic resources can interfere with an individual's capacity to make the investments in human capital necessary for advancement. It is thus perceived as necessary to make a modest level of economic assistance available on the basis of need at certain key junctures of personal economic development—financial aid for college, for example. Once modest assistance is given, previous experiences of economic disadvantage are deemed no longer relevant to future success.

The other major perspective on economic inequality posits the existence of class—a structured system of inequality (as opposed to a simple unequal distribution of economic outcomes among individuals) that is intrinsic to the economic realm and that is not fundamentally altered by the economic mobility of individuals. What distinguishes class perspectives from individualist perspectives on economic inequality is that class perspectives are inherently social (as opposed to individual) and diachronic (as opposed to synchronic). Class is social in the dual sense that the class system is inherent in and perpetuated by the structure of economic relations in the society and that shared class position has the potential for being mobilized as the basis for both group identity and political action. Class is diachronic in the triple sense that class position is (1) intergenerationally transmitted, (2) mediated through the strategic behavior of social actors over time, and (3) incapable of being understood without reference to patterns of change in the economic organization of the society.

Finally, there is an alternative version of a belief in class, which builds on the meaning of class just described, but goes beyond it. In this view, class is said to interact with race, gender, and ethnicity (and perhaps other elements of social identity, such as place of residence) in interlocking and mutually defining structures, and it is their interaction that is seen to shape both consciousness and life chances. * * *

II. MEASURING ECONOMIC INEQUALITY

A. *The Shape of Economic Inequality: Continua, Categories, and Conflicts*

On the broadest level, economic inequality can be represented in one of three ways. Under one view, relative economic advantage is represented as *gradational*: as a continuous sliding scale of relative economic position, rank ordered according to one or more specified criteria. The continuum may then be divided for convenience into categories (such as "lower class," "lower middle class," "upper middle class," etc.) by assigning labels to certain ranges on the continuum. But the validity of the gradational model does not turn on any notion that the theorist's groupings identify groups of people with similar patterns of consciousness and action.

Under the *categorical* approach, economic space is divided in a noncontinuous manner on the basis of the criterion that is, according to the relevant theory, the most significant indicator of economic status. The classic example of a categorical approach is the importance placed by some scholars on the distinction between blue-collar (manual) and white-collar (nonmanual) employment. It is generally contended that the theorists' categories capture "native" distinctions—in other words, that they describe patterns of affinity and difference that motivate social action. Thus, the fact that the values and behavior patterns of some skilled blue-collar workers appear to be closer to those of white-collar workers than to those of their unskilled blue-collar brethren is, for a categorical theorist (but not for a gradational theorist), a challenge to the theory or evidence of a flaw in methodology.

Finally, under what [Erik Olin] Wright calls the *relational* approach, the groups that matter for the analysis of economic inequality are identified not merely by patterns of affinity and difference, but also by their intrinsically antagonistic social relations with other economic groups. Just as the elements within such classic pairings as "parent and child" and "master and servant" take their meaning only in relationship to each other, relational perspectives see each economic grouping as existing only with reference to and in tension with the others. Different terms are used to describe the field in which economic groups operate (for example, "the market" or "relations of production") and the nature of the tension among them (for example, "domination," "hegemony," "exploitation," or "exclusion")—terminologies that often do a better job of identifying putative alliances with Weberian, neo-Marxist, or classical Marxist social theory than of describing different social realities. But what identifies an approach as relational is its emphasis on the structured nature of group relations and on the intrinsically antagonistic nature of group interests. * * *

B. *Whose Economic Inequality?: Individual Versus Household or Family as the Relevant Unit of Analysis*

In discussing economic inequality, one cannot go far without confronting the question of whose economic position is to be measured. Many studies use the individual worker as the unit of analysis. But in any household or family with more than one worker, each worker's economic position is potentially modified by that of the others—not only as to the availability of second (or third) incomes, but in *all* the many ways in which economic position affects life chances. Indeed, the household or family is the most appropriate unit of analysis without regard to the number of income earners in the household. This is demonstrated by the work of sociologist Greg J. Duncan, who has shown on the basis of longitudinal data that changes in household composition account for much of the intragenerational economic change in the status of families.

Family and *household* are not the same concept. Family may or may not involve blood or marital ties, as work on gay and lesbian kinship demonstrates. Divorce creates families and households of numerous shapes, and decision rules must be developed to determine the economic saliency of noncustodial parents, of custodial stepparents, of the subsequent spouses of noncustodial parents, and so forth. Even in the absence of divorce (or widowhood), families may not fit the nuclear family image: family-based households often include other relatives whose economic experiences can be quite salient to all members of the household well beyond the effects of any income-sharing that may take place. Substituting the "traditional" nuclear family for the isolated individual as the unit for measuring class position is thus only a small step in the right direction, and it creates myriad problems of its own. Furthermore, class not only is shaped by family and household composition, but at times also shapes family and household composition. Measuring class position with reference to the nuclear family mirrors middle class kinship ideology, but fails both to accord validity to other classes' conceptions of family life (a flaw on the level of cultural adequacy) and to make available for measurement the wide range of relationships upon which individuals are empowered to draw for resources under these alternative conceptions (a flaw on the level of technical adequacy).

Furthermore, household or family is important in the dimension not only of space (the sharing of the space of a common household), but also in the dimension of time. For example, it is undisputed that at least to some extent, the economic characteristics of a person's family of origin shape that person's economic prospects and attainment over the life span. There is room for debate over the extent to which this is true, the length of time for which it is true, and the mechanisms that cause it to be true. But for our present purposes, what matters is the existence of *"intergenerational inertia,"* because of which the intergenerational family is the appropriate unit for understanding a family's economic status.

The complexity of "family" as a unit existing in time and space is well demonstrated by an example used by Frank Parkin. Picture two families, in each of which the father is a blue-collar worker and the mother is a high school graduate who is not employed outside the home. In one family, the mother is the child of a blue-collar worker: she has married within her own class. In the other, the mother is the child of a white-collar worker, meaning that she has "married down." According to a study cited by Parkin, the son of the within-class marriage has a forty-two percent chance of going to college, while the son of the mother who "married down" has an eighty percent chance of going to college. In the dimension of space, it is the child's interaction with his nonworking mother that is determinative of his college prospects. In the dimension of time, the key to understanding the child's life chances lies in the grandparental generation. Without considering the economic status of the high school boys in light of their families viewed in the dimensions of time and space, the boys would appear to be similarly situated. In reality, they are not.

C. *Trajectory*

Sophisticated analyses of economic inequality take into consideration not merely a *snapshot* of an individual's (or household's or family's) economic circumstances, but a longer view. Jobs that require significant investments in human capital tend to have rising trajectories. In contrast, some occupations are quintessential "young man's (or woman's) games"— such as sports, dance, or physically dangerous service or industrial jobs—in which work opportunities and earnings decline over time. Furthermore,

Pierre Bourdieu correctly points out that in periods of economic change, there exists a "collective trajectory"—the mobility of an entire occupation, class fragment, or class—that does much to shape both political attitudes and the class's capacity to maintain its socioeconomic position. At the extreme, rising or falling group trajectories can destabilize basic elements of the class structure. In all of these aspects, economic position must be understood as playing out over time. There can be doubt as to whether the downwardly mobile family (intra- or inter-generational) is better or worse off than the upwardly mobile family at the point at which their trajectories cross. But it is clear that a snapshot is an oversimplification of the true position of economically mobile families.

D. Measuring Relative Economic Status: The Constituent Elements of Economic Inequality

Up to this point, I have mentioned in passing a number of factors that shape the economic situations of individuals and families: occupation, income, education, orientation toward educational attainment, and numerous extra-economic characteristics (including race and gender). When I have asked students to identify their "class," they have referred to a good number of these factors and some others. But each factor raises its own problems of definition and measurement, and their interactions are complex. I am pessimistic about the capacity of the legal system to capture enough of these complexities to achieve anything resembling a culturally adequate account; and even technical adequacy may be beyond its reach.

1. Wealth.—I mention wealth first precisely because it is so invisible in most studies of economic inequality: indeed, it is common to think of "socioeconomic status" as a product of earned income, occupation, and education, with no regard to wealth at all. Perhaps wealth is ignored because Americans are far more private about their wealth than about their incomes. As one working man said to Paul Fussell, classes "can't be [defined by] money, ... because nobody ever knows that about you for sure."

"Wealth" in the sense of ownership of productive assets is no longer at the core of theories of economic inequality. But that is no justification for ignoring wealth as an element of economic status. Wealth is "distributed far less equally than income" in American society. Wealth barriers are strongly resistant to intergenerational mobility, and inequalities in wealth have greatly increased in the United States since the mid–1970s.

Wealth has a major impact on life chances, in that it diminishes the dependency of an individual's economic well-being upon occupation, income, educational attainment, or any of the other conventionally measured elements of relative economic position. Even the expectation of future wealth is highly significant in assessing an individual's economic circumstances. For example, a recent college graduate who expects to inherit wealth in the near future can accept a "meaningful" low-paying job in social services, the humanities, or the arts and can even create the appearance that he is living on his salary. But he knows that if he ever wants to buy a house, he need not save in advance for a down payment (an obstacle that would be insurmountable for nonwealthy people of his income); he knows that he need not save money for retirement, limit himself to jobs that provide health benefits, or worry that his choices will render him unable to afford to raise children. Wealth is thus a source of personal economic freedom in a broader sense: it is the freedom to take risks, to make mistakes, to be cushioned from market forces. To fail to consider wealth is to understate the extent both of economic inequality in the United States and of its intergenerational transmission. * * *

2. *Occupation.*—Occupation is of central importance to the sociological study of class; indeed, it is common for studies that claim to be about "social mobility" to in fact be solely concerned with occupational mobility. For classical Marxist theory, class is largely determined by position in relations of production, and the locus of attention is therefore on occupation. Marxism is not alone in stressing occupation: so do numerous other neo-Weberian, neo-Marxist, and structuralist theories. Where these theories disagree is on *why* occupation is so central to class. For classical Marxists, occupation matters because the all-important exploitative relationship between capital and labor is most clearly experienced through work. For social scientists in a Weberian tradition, occupation plays an important role in shaping life chances, although it may well not be the central line of political cleavage in a society. For any number of social scientists, in contrast, there is no perceived necessity to theorize the centrality of occupation; instead, occupation is used as a convenient proxy for other important criteria (for example, income, human capital investment, or likelihood of participation in internal labor markets) or for their combined effects.

The central tool of occupation-based class analysis is some sort of scheme for grouping and ranking occupations. These scales are works of social construction on a number of different levels, in which some principled basis must be found for decisionmaking—from the level of deciding how many occupational "classes" there are, to defining and labeling them, to assigning "jobs" to them.

Occupations might be ranked according to one or more of a number of criteria, some of which are the "social prestige" or honor they command, the quantity and quality of credentials or training necessary to perform them, the degree of supervisory or managerial authority they involve, the amount of autonomy they afford, and their income-earning potential. Shortcuts might be used—such as the white-collar versus blue-collar distinction—on the theory that they capture interrelationships of a number of the important criteria. The rankings can be designed to give priority to one criterion (for example, white-collar versus blue-collar employment) and then consider other criteria for purposes of secondary fine-tuning. But unless the ranking system is to be unworkably complex, choices must be made that are bound to produce unnuanced results. Indeed, the results often seem counterintuitive or downright wrong to lay sensibilities (and perhaps to expert sensibilities as well). For example, where collar color plays a central role in the occupational hierarchy, it is considered "upward mobility" to move, via deindustrialization, from a position as a skilled machinist to one as a file clerk. * * *

The picture within categories is no more compelling. Take, for example, the category "service class"—the "top" category—in the occupational scheme of Erikson and Goldthorpe. The category is defined not in terms of the "service sector," but rather in terms of the authors' distinction between "service relationships" and relationships governed by labor contracts—with the former involving the exercise of "delegated authority or specialized knowledge and expertise" and therefore requiring the employees to be accorded a fair measure of autonomy. This means, of course, that the category is (as it should be) theory-driven, based on the view that autonomy and discretion are central to the definition of class relations. But even given the authors' theoretical approach, the category includes occupations that vary widely in respects that are theory-relevant. For example, it includes "supervisors of non-manual workers" in the same category as "large proprietors" and "higher-grade professionals"—meaning that Bill Gates of Microsoft is grouped together with the Microsoft employees who have the power to hire and fire secretaries. All professionals and high-level technicians are included in the top category as well (meaning, for example, that a high school teacher and a physician would be in the same category).

These problems of aggregation have important consequences. Frank Parkin has observed that "there is what might be called a social and cultural 'buffer zone' " between classes and that "[m]ost mobility, being of a fairly narrow social span, involves the movement into and out of th[ese] zone[s] rather than movement between the class extremes." This means that the ability to detect mobility between groups crucially depends on where the lines between the groups are drawn.

Even after "occupations" have been defined and ranked, the work of social construction continues. The "occupations" found in social scientific occupational scales are not necessarily the "jobs" that people are hired to do, which are in turn not necessarily the "jobs" that people actually do. The process of assigning a person's "job" (in either sense) to one of a restricted number of "occupational" categories is a complex process, one that produces inevitable distortions. Take the job of "secretary," routinely classified in occupational scales as "white-collar clerical." Then consider the differences between a member of a secretarial pool in a medium-sized company and a secretary for a Supreme Court Justice or for the CEO of a major corporation. Or, for another example, consider the job of "professor," likely to be classified as "professional/managerial" in most scales. Then examine the differences between a professor who strings together part-time and temporary teaching jobs and a tenured professor at a major research university. In both of these comparisons, both individuals in the pair would be classified as having the same "occupation," but there are likely to be gaps between them in prestige, autonomy, job-related social networks, job benefits, and other aspects of life and work (beyond differences in income) that would go uncaptured by their occupational classification. The latter example points, in particular, to the dangers of occupational schemes that do not reflect the important concerns of segmented labor market theory.

Finally, the problems inherent in systems of occupational classification go far deeper than mere problems of measurement. As Frank Parkin notes,

> Sociological models are almost bound to take on something of the imprint of the age in which they are put together; and the model of class recommended in a period of general affluence and economic growth is likely to look a strange and awkward thing in a period haunted by the anxieties of inflation, recession, and economic stagnation.

Many of the leading occupational frameworks have an anachronistic quality to them: they are based on theories that no longer match the realities of work. With the demise of private-sector unions, there are likely to be fewer reasons in the future to be concerned about the class placement of good blue-collar jobs. Privatization is putting pressure on the line between public and private employment. Overseas outsourcing and decreasing stability of tenure in white-collar work, including such highly trained "knowledge" work as computer programming, is increasing the commonality of job conditions across the collar color line. Cost-containment pressures are limiting the autonomy of the traditional professions. The middle classes are far from becoming an undifferentiated proletariat. But the field is wide open for social scientists to theorize the emerging economic order (or orders)—and, in particular, to theorize the elements of comparative advantage among the different segments of the middle classes. * * *

3. *Income.*—Many scholars focus on income rather than on occupation as the major force in determining relative economic advantage. So do many lay people. For a number of reasons, income-based measures are particularly compatible with the economic individualist perspective. A stress on income suggests that the "goodies" that constitute relative economic advantage (for example, knowledge, education, cultural refinement, residence in safe suburbs, etc.) are commodities that can be purchased with money. An income measure is (at least potentially) agnostic as to the source of income and therefore tacitly rejects the theoretical position that the labor process is at the center of economic relations. Finally, mobility studies that focus on income tend to show higher rates of intergenerational economic mobility in the United States than do occupation-based studies.

Income-based measures also have the practical advantage that the measurement of income is more straightforward than the construction and implementation of occupational hierarchies. But income measurement presents a number of methodological problems that are capable of generating troublesome inaccuracies, both in measuring individual cases and in depicting economic mobility.

First among the issues in income measurement is the question of whose income it is appropriate to measure. Many studies of income inequality look solely at the incomes of individual earners—in part because this information is easily obtained (from employers and from tax returns, for example). But households routinely pool income, so that the more accurate measure of economic position is "family" or "household" income—the measurement of which is complex. Even at the level of the individual, conventional measures of income tend to understate the economic position of high-income individuals and families by excluding the value of employee benefits (for example, pensions and health benefits). And high-income taxpayers have the greatest opportunities to shelter income from taxation, which means that relying on tax returns as the source of income data understates their economic advantage.

Once a measure of income is agreed upon, there remains the question of how (if at all) to determine which income levels correspond to meaningful "breaks"—whether for purposes of a gradational or a categorical scheme. The first question is whether the breaks are to be determined in absolute terms, in relative terms, or in terms of the purchasing power of the income. Another important question is the number of groupings to use. A fairly common approach is to divide individuals into quintiles according to income and then study mobility between quintiles. But mobility between two adjacent quintiles—the most common form of mobility—may not be much mobility at all: it may simply represent a trading of positions between those with income locations at the quintile boundaries. As is the case with occupations, aggregation is necessary for the sake of simplicity, but the data loss inherent in aggregation makes the data harder to interpret—and may well overstate the degree of income mobility in this country. * * *

* * * Education is most often quantified as the number of years studied or the highest degree attained. But to treat education as a commodity in this fashion is to miss differences that are palpably relevant in work and in life. On the college level, for example, educational attainment is routinely judged in real life by type of school (four-year college versus community college, accredited versus unaccredited, day versus night program, and so forth); quality of school (often measured by selectivity or by academic reputation); content of study (with superiority of attainment measured for different purposes along a number of potentially conflicting dimensions ranging from raw difficulty to likelihood of producing cultural literacy); grades and honors; outside enrichment activities (overseas studies, for example); and numerous other more subjective judgments about the student's "character" as reflected through her curricular choices. * * *

5. *Consumption.*—It was turn-of-the-century economist Thorstein Veblen who most colorfully pointed to patterns of consumption as definitive of class aspiration and class position. Just as inflation can be measured by the relative cost of a fixed "basket" of food items, middle class status is often described as the possession of a "basket" of middle class goods. When middle class status is so defined, mobility into the middle classes is made easier to the extent that the items in the basket are easy to identify (through advertising, popular culture, and so forth) and easy to afford (as the Levittowns democratized suburbanization for white urbanites).

At first glance, it would seem easy to create a quick material index to capture the key elements of middle class material consumption. The consumption choice that most defines ascent into the middle classes is home ownership—which is why federal tax policy subsidizes home ownership and why the fact that young people cannot afford homes is viewed as a breach of faith with the middle class. A conventional consumption index might include such elements as home ownership; type of home (stand-alone versus townhouse versus mobile home); location (with suburban rating highest, except for the most exclusive city homes); home size; the ownership of cars (divided by old and new); the purchase of private primary or secondary education; number and kind of home electronics (with class ascending as the ratio of computers and cellular phones to televisions increases); the eating of meals outside of the home; and perhaps the nature of preferred leisure activities. Such a list—reworked as required by location (for example, the lack of home ownership and cars for many affluent New Yorkers)—could provide broad brush strokes to draw a line between lower and middle classes.

But as anyone with a good ear for the culture knows, these elements of consumption are not so much measures of class unity as they are fields for the social process (and processing) of distinction. Houses can be large because they have many bedrooms (for many children) or because they offer grand spaces for entertaining. Their grounds can be groomed "just right," too poorly, or too well ("If there's no crabgrass at all, we can infer an owner who spends much of his time worrying about slipping down a class or two...."). The living room can be furnished from antique markets or from Sears. Cars can be utilitarian objects or displays of wealth and taste; they can be old in order to demonstrate patrician nonconcern with material values or because the family cannot afford new. Food cooked at home can be traditional or gourmet. The gulfs in consumption within the "middle class" category are, in short, huge. The advertising industry knows this, and it markets goods not to some broad aggregate "middle class," but to very carefully defined segments within it, defined as much by class aspiration and cultural orientation as by income.

The literature on consumption-based markers of class identity always generates laughter because it so sharply points out the anxiety of our attempts to manipulate social status. But consumption is no laughing matter. The material world is a minefield for the class-mobile, and every dollar spent a potentially fatal misstep. Consumption choices shape opportunities for conversation and for the formation of friendships and professional networks. (If tennis is the game of choice at your office, being a top-notch bowler does you no good; and try inviting your boss to dinner if your only table is in the kitchen.) They are, at the very least, the most easily observed markers of who you are and where you fit into the social hierarchy; they may in fact be an important part of the constitution of the self.

In sum, consumption is central to our (often unarticulated) cultural understandings of class. * * *

6. *Consciousness.*—Categorical and relational models of class are built upon the claim that the "classes" they describe have the potential for some degree of consciousness of themselves as classes. Class consciousness is important to students and practitioners of politics and for Marxist theorists, for whom the capacity of groups to organize and take action on the basis of class is all-important. It is also important to culturally oriented class theorists, for whom the system of *beliefs* about economic inequality is an important component of the system of economic inequality. And understanding the consciousness of social actors is necessary if their dignity is to be respected. * * *

7. *Interactions Among the Elements of Economic Inequality.*—The various measures of economic inequality I have reviewed are not independent of one another, but cannot freely substitute for one another. The acquisition of credentials may have some value in and of itself, but its greatest value is in securing a job that utilizes those credentials (or purports to utilize them) and brings one into contact with coworkers who have attained similar or greater educational levels. Access to high culture is limited by lack of income, but high income alone does not guarantee the "right" kind of understanding and the entree into cultured circles that goes with it. Within prestigious occupations, status declines in relation to the relative status of one's clients. Impressive attainments of cultural capital are of little use without the income and occupation to put them to work and the education to announce their presence on the surface of a resume. Resources can be rendered far less meaningful in their impact by coming too early or too late in the lifespan. Yet there is *some* measure of tolerance for gaps in the personal economic armor, *some* capacity for substitution.

What this means is that the relationships among the elements of economic privilege are not simply additive or multiplicative. They are structural. The factors contributing to relative economic advantage exist in a delicate balance and interact in space and time, as is generally true of the elements of society and culture. Their effects are likely to be nonhomogenous—meaning that the analysis of important socioeconomic factors and their interrelationships must be "disaggregated," with an eye to spotting relevant discontinuities. No easily administered, quantitative, composite index of the elements of economic inequality can capture their complex interrelationships.

To the extent that social scientific studies can simultaneously recognize and order the complexities of class, theory allows them to do so. At some point, it is necessary to stress one element and de-emphasize the others—to decide, for example, whether class or economic inequality is or is not fundamentally grounded in the realm of work. That is the role of theory. But the corollary of the centrality of theory is that in shopping for a measurement method and in deciding which factors form the core of relative economic advantage, the legal system will be buying a social theory—whether it admits it or not, and whether it wants one or not. * * *

8. *Outside Interactions: Race, Gender, and the Danger of False Claims of "Holding Class Constant."*—Up until this point, we have discussed class

as though it were a hermetically sealed category, impervious to other forms of inequality. But it is not. Just as economic variables interact, there are important interactions between each of those elements (and their interactions) and "outside" elements, such as race and gender.

Gender issues in class analysis are obscured (or perhaps underscored) by the fact that studies of social mobility commonly look only at the experience of men. The reason is that one of the most vexing problems in research on class and economic inequality is how to determine the economic position of women—both their individual status and their contributions as wage-earners and domestic producers to the economic status of their households and families. It should be obvious that ignoring the economic participation of women distorts the picture of household or family economic status in important ways. * * * Indeed, there is ample evidence that the interactions among economic factors differ for men and women, that women are less able than men to take personal advantage of inherited and earned economic and social capital, and that occupational schemes developed for men are less accurate for women.

Theorizing and measuring the economic status of members of racial and ethnic minority groups pose problems of equal magnitude. I will limit myself to only a few illustrations of the many ways in which strategies for the transmission of economic advantage from parents to children have historically been less successful for blacks than for whites.

Part of the problem is that black upward mobility is so recent a phenomenon for many black families. In a study of intergenerational elements of educational attainment in the black middle class, Zena Smith Blau found that when black and white families of seemingly similar socioeconomic status (measured by the occupational status of the higher ranking parent and both parents' educational attainment) were compared, black families "in fact, possess fewer resources than those white families." The key difference was that white parents' own socioeconomic status translated into a more privileged social milieu. This means, Blau concluded, that parental occupational and educational gains in white families "are more readily translated into access to middle-class influences and role models than is usually the case for black families." There is also evidence, from Coleman, that although "black parents ... show a greater interest in their child's education and greater aspirations for his success in education than do white parents of the same economic level," the interests of black, Hispanic, and Native American parents do not translate as well into improved academic performance for the child.

More generally, the past and present effects of discrimination mean that blacks and whites who appear to have the same occupation, education, or residential situation when a simple metric is used may well not occupy the same status in reality. When black families live in the suburbs, they tend to live in predominantly black suburbs that lie closer to the inner city and that are less advantaged in their public and private services. Blacks are more likely to be employed in the public sector, where civil-service employment rules diminish the ability of parents to use their influence to provide jobs for children in their community. Although patterns of segregation are breaking down, black professionals are historically more likely to serve within the black community, which means that having professionals in the family opens up a less advantaged social network for blacks than for whites. Blacks in the professions remain more likely than whites to be employed in occupations at the lower end of the category in credentials, prestige, and income. Blacks have less wealth than whites of the same income level. And skin color remains a powerful obstacle to the translation of wealth, occupation, income, education, and cultural capital into even the most basic dignity in public life. As one Jewish carpenter explained to an ethnographer in Brooklyn, New York, my hometown: "The problem is that we see blacks as a mass. It is unfortunate. We can't tell the difference between a black pimp and a black mailman. When I look at a white man, I can tell what social class he is, but if he is colored, I can't tell." There is little gain to be had from class mobility if its public indicia are overwhelmed by the more socially salient reality of race.

These examples demonstrate that if an overly simplistic measurement of class is used, systematic differences in the present and historical economic condition of blacks will be ignored, and the socioeconomic privilege of middle class blacks will be overstated. It is highly likely, given the complexity of the phenomenon, that even the most earnest efforts at designing an adequate metric will fail. And the result of failure will likely be that the law's official discourse will falsely proclaim that in the contest for economic equality, class has been "held constant"—and that if blacks still lose, their loss must be because of some postulated lack of individual or collective merit. That is a significant danger for anyone concerned with racial justice in this country.

NOTES AND QUESTIONS

1. Class position. How would you describe your class position? What was your parents' class position when you were growing up? Has it changed over time? Of the factors Malamud lists as relevant to the determination of a person's "class," which do you think are the most determinative? Is class a relevant category in American life?

2. The American Dream. A central ideology of American democracy and markets is that economic mobility is fully open to all citizens with talent and a strong work ethic. The asserted classlessness of American society remains a cherished characterization of the opportunity structure here. Americans venerate our tradition of individual achievement. Opposition to the accumulation of great wealth and the hereditary privileges associated with such concentrations of political, social and economic power have been a feature of American political rhetoric since the founding of the nation.

Political scientist Jennifer Hochschild uses a quote from former President Bill Clinton to encapsulate the "American Dream":

> The American Dream that we were all raised on is a simple but powerful one—if you work hard and play by the rules you should be given a chance to go as far as your God-given ability will take you.

President Bill Clinton, Speech to Democratic Leadership Council, 1993.

> In one sentence, President Clinton has captured the bundle of shared, even unconsciously presumed, tenets about achieving success that make up the ideology of the American Dream. Those tenets answer the questions: *Who* may pursue the American Dream? In *what* does the pursuit consist? *How* does one successfully pursue the dream? *Why* is the pursuit worthy of our deepest commitment?
>
> The answer to "who" in the standard ideology is "everyone, regardless of ascriptive traits, family background, or personal history." The answer to "what" is "the reasonable anticipation, though not the promise, of success, however it is defined." The answer to "how" is "through actions and traits under one's control." The answer to "why" is "true success is associated with virtue."

JENNIFER L. HOCHSCHILD, FACING UP TO THE AMERICAN DREAM: RACE, CLASS, AND THE SOUL OF THE NATION 18 (1995). How does belief in the American Dream shape attitudes toward class?

3. The immigrant story. Related to the American Dream is another central ideology in American life, one that relates to the possibility of group rather than individual class mobility. The United States is a nation of immigrants, and many Americans can tell stories of a great-grandfather or grandfather who came to this country with "nothing" and was able to "work his way up," eventually passing wealth along to his children. Nathan Glazer puts this kind of story into a larger framework:

> [T]he American polity has * * * been defined by a steady expansion of the definition of those who may be included in it to the point where it now includes all humanity; * * * the United States has become the first great nation that defines itself not in terms of ethnic origin but in terms of adherence to common rules of citizenship; * * * no one is now excluded from the broadest access to what the society makes possible; and * * * this access is combined with a considerable concern for whatever is necessary to maintain group identity and loyalty.

Nathan Glazer, *The Emergence of an American Ethnic Pattern, in* FROM DIFFERENT SHORES: PERSPECTIVES ON RACE AND ETHNICITY IN AMERICA 13, 14 (Ronald Tataki ed., 1987).

Is the immigrant story of individual and group social and economic mobility despite ethnic difference a story that can be told about all groups? Robert Blauner argues that there is a key historical difference between "colonized" and "immigrant" minorities. As he sets forth his argument, he identifies three assumptions on which it rests:

The first assumption is that racial groups in America are, and have been, colonized peoples; therefore their social realities cannot be understood in the framework of immigration and assimilation that is applied to European ethnic groups. The second assumption is that the racial minorities share a common situation of oppression, from which a potential political unity is inferred. The final assumption is that there is a historical connection between the third world abroad and the third world within.

Robert Blauner, *Colonized and Immigrant Minorities, in* FROM DIFFERENT SHORES: PERSPECTIVES ON RACE AND ETHNICITY IN AMERICA 149, 149 (Ronald Takaki ed., 1987).

4. *San Antonio Independent School District v. Rodriguez.* Malamud is pessimistic about American law's ability to adequately deal with issues of class. As you read *San Antonio Independent School District v. Rodriguez*, think about how Justice Powell is trying to conceptualize wealth discrimination. Does he adequately distinguish this case from the precedents he discusses? Does "class" fit into the ways lawyers think about "discrimination"? How might Malamud conceptualize the issues faced by the litigants in the case?

B. THE CONSTITUTION: WEALTH AND CLASS

San Antonio Independent School District v. Rodriguez
411 U.S. 1 (1973).

■ MR. JUSTICE POWELL delivered the opinion of the Court.

This suit attacking the Texas system of financing public education was initiated by Mexican–American parents whose children attend the elementary and secondary schools in the Edgewood Independent School District, an urban school district in San Antonio, Texas. They brought a class action on behalf of schoolchildren throughout the State who are members of minority groups or who are poor and reside in school districts having a low property tax base. * * *

I

The first Texas State Constitution, promulgated upon Texas' entry into the Union in 1845, provided for the establishment of a system of free schools. Early in its history, Texas adopted a dual approach to the financing of its schools, relying on mutual participation by the local school districts and the State. As early as 1883, the state constitution was amended to provide for the creation of local school districts empowered to levy ad valorem taxes with the consent of local taxpayers for the "erection ... of school buildings" and for the "further maintenance of public free schools." Such local funds as were raised were supplemented by funds distributed to each district from the State's Permanent and Available School Funds. * * *

Until recent times, Texas was a predominantly rural State and its population and property wealth were spread relatively evenly across the State. Sizable differences in the value of assessable property between local school districts became increasingly evident as the State became more industrialized and as rural-to-urban population shifts became more pronounced. The location of commercial and industrial property began to play a significant role in determining the amount of tax resources available to each school district. These growing disparities in population and taxable property between districts were responsible in part for increasingly notable differences in levels of local expenditure for education.

In due time it became apparent to those concerned with financing public education that contributions from the Available School Fund were not sufficient to ameliorate these disparities. * * *

Recognizing the need for increased state funding to help offset disparities in local spending and to meet Texas' changing educational requirements, the state legislature in the late 1940's undertook a thorough evaluation of public education with an eye toward major reform. In 1947, an 18-member committee, composed of educators and legislators, was appointed to explore alternative systems in other States and to propose a funding scheme that would guarantee a minimum or basic educational offering to each child and that would help overcome interdistrict disparities in taxable resources. The Committee's efforts led to the passage of the Gilmer–Aikin bills, named for the Committee's co-chairmen, establishing the Texas Minimum Foundation School Program. Today, this Program accounts for approximately half of the total educational expenditures in Texas.

The Program calls for state and local contributions to a fund earmarked specifically for teacher salaries, operating expenses, and transportation costs. The State, supplying funds from its general revenues, finances approximately 80% of the Program, and the school districts are responsible—as a unit—for providing the remaining 20%. The districts' share, known as the Local Fund Assignment, is apportioned among the school districts under a formula designed to reflect each district's relative taxpaying ability. * * *

In the years since this program went into operation in 1949, expenditures for education—from state as well as local sources—have increased steadily.

* * *

The school district in which appellees reside, the Edgewood Independent School District, has been compared throughout this litigation with the Alamo Heights Independent School District. This comparison between the least and most affluent districts in the San Antonio area serves to illustrate the manner in which the dual system of finance operates and to indicate the extent to which substantial disparities exist despite the State's impressive progress in recent years. Edgewood is one of seven public school districts in the metropolitan area. Approximately 22,000 students are enrolled in its 25 elementary and secondary schools. The district is situated in the core-city sector of San Antonio in a residential neighborhood that has little commercial or industrial property. The residents are predominantly of Mexican–American descent: approximately 90% of the student population is Mexican–American and over 6% is Negro. The average assessed property value per pupil is $5,960—the lowest in the metropolitan area—and the median family income ($4,686) is also the lowest. At an equalized tax rate of $1.05 per $100 of assessed property—the highest in the metropolitan area—the district contributed $26 to the education of each child for the 1967–1968 school year above its Local Fund Assignment for the Minimum Foundation Program. The Foundation Program contributed $222 per pupil for a state-local total of $248. Federal funds added another $108 for a total of $356 per pupil.

Alamo Heights is the most affluent school district in San Antonio. Its six schools, housing approximately 5,000 students, are situated in a residential community quite unlike the Edgewood District. The school population is predominantly "Anglo," having only 18% Mexican–Americans and less than 1% Negroes. The assessed property value per pupil exceeds $49,000, and the median family income is $8,001. In 1967–1968 the local tax rate of $.85 per $100 of valuation yielded $333 per pupil over and above its contribution to the Foundation Program. Coupled with the $225 provided from that Program, the district was able to supply $558 per student. Supplemented by a $36 per-pupil grant from federal sources, Alamo Heights spent $594 per pupil.

* * *

The District Court held that the Texas system discriminates on the basis of wealth in the manner in which education is provided for its people.[1] Finding that wealth is a "suspect" classification and that education is a "fundamental" interest, the District Court held that the Texas system could be sustained only if the State could show that it was premised upon some compelling state interest.[2] On this issue the court concluded that "[n]ot only are defendants unable to demonstrate compelling state interests ... they fail even to establish a reasonable basis for these classifications."[3]

Texas virtually concedes that its historically rooted dual system of financing education could not withstand the strict judicial scrutiny that this Court has found appropriate in reviewing legislative judgments that interfere with fundamental constitutional rights or that involve suspect classifications. If, as previous decisions have indicated, strict scrutiny means that the State's system is not entitled to the usual presumption of validity, that the State rather than the complainants must carry a "heavy burden of justification," that the State must demonstrate that its educational system has been structured with "precision," and is "tailored" narrowly to serve legitimate objectives and that it has selected the "less drastic means" for effectuating its objectives, the Texas financing system

1. 337 F. Supp., at 282.
2. *Id.*, at 282–284.
3. *Id.*, at 284.

and its counterpart in virtually every other State will not pass muster. The State candidly admits that "[n]o one familiar with the Texas system would contend that it has yet achieved perfection." Apart from its concession that educational financing in Texas has "defects" and "imperfections," the State defends the system's rationality with vigor and disputes the District Court's finding that it lacks a "reasonable basis."

This, then, establishes the framework for our analysis. We must decide, first, whether the Texas system of financing public education operates to the disadvantage of some suspect class or impinges upon a fundamental right explicitly or implicitly protected by the Constitution, thereby requiring strict judicial scrutiny. If so, the judgment of the District Court should be affirmed. If not, the Texas scheme must still be examined to determine whether it rationally furthers some legitimate, articulated state purpose and therefore does not constitute an invidious discrimination in violation of the Equal Protection Clause of the Fourteenth Amendment.

II

The District Court's opinion does not reflect the novelty and complexity of the constitutional questions posed by appellees' challenge to Texas' system of school financing. In concluding that strict judicial scrutiny was required, that court relied on decisions dealing with the rights of indigents to equal treatment in the criminal trial and appellate processes, and on cases disapproving wealth restrictions on the right to vote. Those cases, the District Court concluded, established wealth as a suspect classification. Finding that the local property tax system discriminated on the basis of wealth, it regarded those precedents as controlling. It then reasoned, based on decisions of this Court affirming the undeniable importance of education, that there is a fundamental right to education and that, absent some compelling state justification, the Texas system could not stand.

We are unable to agree that this case, which in significant aspects is *sui generis*, may be so neatly fitted into the conventional mosaic of constitutional analysis under the Equal Protection Clause. Indeed, for the several reasons that follow, we find neither the suspect-classification nor the fundamental-interest analysis persuasive.

A

The wealth discrimination discovered by the District Court in this case, and by several other courts that have recently struck down school-financing laws in other States, is quite unlike any of the forms of wealth discrimination heretofore reviewed by this Court. Rather than focusing on the unique features of the alleged discrimination, the courts in these cases have virtually assumed their findings of a suspect classification through a simplistic process of analysis: since, under the traditional systems of financing public schools, some poorer people receive less expensive educations than other more affluent people, these systems discriminate on the basis of wealth. This approach largely ignores the hard threshold questions, including whether it makes a difference for purposes of consideration under the Constitution that the class of disadvantaged "poor" cannot be identified or defined in customary equal protection terms, and whether the relative—rather than absolute—nature of the asserted deprivation is of significant consequence.

* * *

The case comes to us with no definitive description of the classifying facts or delineation of the disfavored class. Examination of the District Court's opinion and of appellees' complaint, briefs, and contentions at oral argument suggests, however, at least three ways in which the discrimination claimed here might be described. The Texas system of school financing might be regarded as discriminating (1) against "poor" persons whose incomes fall below some identifiable level of poverty or who might be characterized as functionally "indigent," or (2) against those who are relatively poorer than others, or (3) against all those who, irrespective of their personal incomes, happen to reside in relatively poorer school districts. Our task must be to ascertain whether, in fact, the Texas system has been shown to discriminate on any of these possible bases and, if so, whether the resulting classification may be regarded as suspect.

The precedents of this Court provide the proper starting point. The individuals, or groups of individuals, who constituted the class discriminated against in our prior cases shared two distinguishing characteristics: because of their impecunity they were completely unable to pay for some desired benefit, and as a consequence, they sustained an absolute deprivation of a meaningful opportunity to enjoy that benefit. In *Griffin v. Illinois*[4] and its progeny, the Court invalidated state laws that prevented an indigent criminal defendant from acquiring a transcript, or an adequate substitute for a transcript, for use at several stages of the trial and appeal process. The payment requirements in each case were found to occasion *de facto* discrimination against those who, because of their indigency, were totally unable to pay for transcripts. And the Court in each case emphasized that no constitutional violation would have been shown if the State had provided some "adequate substitute" for a full stenographic transcript.

* * *

Likewise, in *Douglas v. California*,[5] a decision establishing an indigent defendant's right to court-appointed counsel on direct appeal, the Court dealt only with defendants who could not pay for counsel from their own resources and who had no other way of gaining representation. *Douglas* provides no relief for those on whom the burdens of paying for a criminal defense are relatively speaking, great but not insurmountable. Nor does it deal with relative differences in the quality of counsel acquired by the less wealthy.

Williams v. Illinois[6] and *Tate v. Short*[7] struck down criminal penalties that subjected indigents to incarceration simply because of their inability to

4. 351 U.S. 12 (1956).
5. 372 U.S. 353 (1963).
6. 399 U.S. 235 (1970).
7. 401 U.S. 395 (1971).

pay a fine. Again, the disadvantaged class was composed only of persons who were totally unable to pay the demanded sum. Those cases do not touch on the question whether equal protection is denied to persons with relatively less money on whom designated fines impose heavier burdens. The Court has not held that fines must be structured to reflect each person's ability to pay in order to avoid disproportionate burdens. Sentencing judges may, and often do, consider the defendant's ability to pay, but in such circumstances they are guided by sound judicial discretion rather than by constitutional mandate.

Finally, in *Bullock v. Carter*[8] the Court invalidated the Texas filing-fee requirement for primary elections. Both of the relevant classifying facts found in the previous cases were present there. The size of the fee, often running into the thousands of dollars and, in at least one case, as high as $8,900, effectively barred all potential candidates who were unable to pay the required fee. As the system provided "no reasonable alternative means of access to the ballot",[9] inability to pay occasioned an absolute denial of a position on the primary ballot.

Only appellees' first possible basis for describing the class disadvantaged by the Texas school-financing system—discrimination against a class of defineably "poor" persons—might arguably meet the criteria established in these prior cases. Even a cursory examination, however, demonstrates that neither of the two distinguishing characteristics of wealth classifications can be found here. First, in support of their charge that the system discriminates against the "poor," appellees have made no effort to demonstrate that it operates to the peculiar disadvantage of any class fairly definable as indigent, or as composed of persons whose incomes are beneath any designated poverty level. Indeed, there is reason to believe that the poorest families are not necessarily clustered in the poorest property districts. A recent and exhaustive study of school districts in Connecticut concluded that "[i]t is clearly incorrect ... to contend that the 'poor' live in 'poor' districts.... Thus, the major factual assumption of *Serrano*—that the educational financing system discriminates against the 'poor'—is simply false in Connecticut." Defining "poor" families as those below the Bureau of the Census "poverty level," the Connecticut study found, not surprisingly, that the poor were clustered around commercial and industrial areas—those same areas that provide the most attractive sources of property tax income for school districts. Whether a similar pattern would be discovered in Texas is not known, but there is no basis on the record in this case for assuming that the poorest people—defined by reference to any level of absolute impecunity—are concentrated in the poorest districts.

Second, neither appellees nor the District Court addressed the fact that, unlike each of the foregoing cases, lack of personal resources has not occasioned an absolute deprivation of the desired benefit. The argument here is not that the children in districts having relatively low assessable property values are receiving no public education; rather, it is that they are

---

8. 405 U.S. 134 (1972).   9. *Id.*, at 149.

receiving a poorer quality education than that available to children in districts having more assessable wealth. Apart from the unsettled and disputed question whether the quality of education may be determined by the amount of money expended for it, a sufficient answer to appellees' argument is that, at least where wealth is involved, the Equal Protection Clause does not require absolute equality or precisely equal advantages. Nor indeed, in view of the infinite variables affecting the educational process, can any system assure equal quality of education except in the most relative sense. Texas asserts that the Minimum Foundation Program provides an "adequate" education for all children in the State. * * *

For these two reasons—the absence of any evidence that the financing system discriminates against any definable category of "poor" people or that it results in the absolute deprivation of education—the disadvantaged class is not susceptible of identification in traditional terms.

As suggested above, appellees and the District Court may have embraced a second or third approach, the second of which might be characterized as a theory of relative or comparative discrimination based on family income. Appellees sought to prove that a direct correlation exists between the wealth of families within each district and the expenditures therein for education. That is, along a continuum, the poorer the family the lower the dollar amount of education received by the family's children. * * *

If, in fact, these correlations could be sustained, then it might be argued that expenditures on education—equated by appellees to the quality of education—are dependent on personal wealth. Appellees' comparative-discrimination theory would still face serious unanswered questions, including whether a bare positive correlation or some higher degree of correlation is necessary to provide a basis for concluding that the financing system is designed to operate to the peculiar disadvantage of the comparatively poor, and whether a class of this size and diversity could ever claim the special protection accorded "suspect" classes. These questions need not be addressed in this case, however, since appellees' proof fails to support their allegations or the District Court's conclusions. * * *

This brings us, then, to the third way in which the classification scheme might be defined—*district* wealth discrimination. Since the only correlation indicated by the evidence is between district property wealth and expenditures, it may be argued that discrimination might be found without regard to the individual income characteristics of district residents. Assuming a perfect correlation between district property wealth and expenditures from top to bottom, the disadvantaged class might be viewed as encompassing every child in every district except the district that has the most assessable wealth and spends the most on education. Alternatively, as suggested in Mr. JUSTICE MARSHALL's dissenting opinion, * * * the class might be defined more restrictively to include children in districts with assessable property which falls below the statewide average, or median, or below some other artificially defined level.

However described, it is clear that appellees' suit asks this Court to extend its most exacting scrutiny to review a system that allegedly discriminates against a large, diverse, and amorphous class, unified only by the common factor of residence in districts that happen to have less taxable wealth than other districts. The system of alleged discrimination and the class it defines have none of the traditional indicia of suspectness: the class is not saddled with such disabilities, or subjected to such a history of purposeful unequal treatment, or relegated to such a position of political powerlessness as to command extraordinary protection from the majoritarian political process. * * *

[The Court turns to the question of whether education is a fundamental right protected by the Constitution.]

Lindsey v. Normet,[10] decided only last Term, firmly reiterates that social importance is not the critical determinant for subjecting state legislation to strict scrutiny. The complainants in that case, involving a challenge to the procedural limitations imposed on tenants in suits brought by landlords under Oregon's Forcible Entry and Wrongful Detainer Law, urged the Court to examine the operation of the statute under "a more stringent standard than mere rationality."[11] The tenants argued that the statutory limitations implicated "fundamental interests which are particularly important to the poor," such as the "need for decent shelter" and the "right to retain peaceful possession of one's home."[12] MR. JUSTICE WHITE'S analysis, in his opinion for the Court is instructive:

> "We do not denigrate the importance of decent, safe and sanitary housing. But the Constitution does not provide judicial remedies for every social and economic ill. We are unable to perceive in that document any constitutional guarantee of access to dwellings of a particular quality or any recognition of the right of a tenant to occupy the real property of his landlord beyond the term of his lease, without the payment of rent.... *Absent constitutional mandate*, the assurance of adequate housing and the definition of landlord-tenant relationships are legislative, not judicial, functions."[13]

Similarly, in *Dandridge v. Williams*,[14] the Court's explicit recognition of the fact that the "administration of public welfare assistance ... involves the most basic economic needs of impoverished human beings,"[15] provided no basis for departing from the settled mode of constitutional analysis of legislative classifications involving questions of economic and social policy. * * *

[The Court concludes that education is not a fundamental right and that the Texas system survives the rational basis test.]

■ MR. JUSTICE MARSHALL, with whom MR. JUSTICE DOUGLAS concurs, dissenting.

10. 405 U.S. 56 (1972).
11. *Id.*, at 73.
12. *Ibid.*
13. *Id.*, at 74 (emphasis supplied).
14. 397 U.S. 471 (1970).
15. *id.*, at 485.

* * * In my view, * * * it is inequality—not some notion of gross inadequacy—of educational opportunity that raises a question of denial of equal protection of the laws. I find any other approach to the issue unintelligible and without directing principle. Here, appellees have made a substantial showing of wide variations in educational funding and the resulting educational opportunity afforded to the schoolchildren of Texas. This discrimination is, in large measure, attributable to significant disparities in the taxable wealth of local Texas school districts. This is a sufficient showing to raise a substantial question of discriminatory state action in violation of the Equal Protection Clause.

NOTES AND QUESTIONS

1. **Economic inequality.** One issue that bears both on how we measure class and on our understanding of the American Dream is the issue of economic inequality. In this section, we look at readings that investigate economic inequality along two of the dimensions of class described by Malamud—income and wealth.

2. **The right to education under state constitutions.** Forty-eight out of fifty states have education clauses in their state constitutions. *See* Michael Heise, *State Constitutions, School Finance Litigation, and the "Third Wave": From Equity to Adequacy*, 68 Temple L. Rev. 1151, 1163 (1995). *See* Paul L. Tractenberg, *Using the Law to Advance the Public Interest: Rutgers Law School and Me*, 51 Rutgers L. Rev. 1001, 1011–12 (Rutgers Law Review Symposium 1999); Susan H. Bitensky, *Theoretical Foundations for a Constitutional Right to Education Under the U.S. Constitution: A Beginning to the End of a National Education Crisis*, 86 Nw. U. L. Rev. 550 (1992); Molly McUsic, *The Use of Education Clauses in School Finance Reform Litigation*, 28 Harv. J. on Legis. 307 (1991); James S. Liebman, *Three Strategies for Implementing Brown Anew*, in Race in America: The Struggle for Equality 112, 120–21 (Herbert Hill & James E. Jones, Jr. eds., 1993).

C. Class and Inequality—Historical Perspectives

- Income Inequality

Economic Development in Indian Country: Will Capitalism or Socialism Succeed?

80 Oreg. L. Rev. 757 (2001).

■ Robert J. Miller

* * * European settlers and early Americans misunderstood tribal economies and property rights. Even today, there seems to be an almost universal misunderstanding that American Indian cultures had and still have little or no appreciation or understanding of private property ownership and private, free market, capitalist economic activities. This mistaken idea could not be further from the truth. It appears to be based almost exclusively on the idea that most American Indian tribes did not consider that land could be privately owned but instead thought that tribal lands were communally owned. Thus, the European and American colonists came to believe that Indians did not believe in or understand private property and capitalist principles.

In contrast, as in all societies, Indians and their governing bodies had to provide for the daily needs of their families and their tribes. Hence, Indians were continuously involved in the production of food, tools, clothing, shelter and all sorts of objects for personal use. Indians also regularly traded goods with other peoples from near and far both for survival and to make life as comfortable as possible. The majority, if not all, of this trade was conducted in free market situations where private individuals voluntarily came together to buy and sell items they had manufactured for sale and which they exchanged by barter and sometimes even sold for money. Startlingly, perhaps, it appears that the only way in which Indian principles of economics and private property differed from the European/American concepts was in the conflicting views these societies had on the private ownership of land. The actual purpose for the European and American settlers to discount or intentionally to ignore how Indians viewed and used private property may have been to provide justification for stealing Indian property rights with a clear conscience. * * *

From its inception, the United States copied the long-standing English political and economic policies towards tribes. The economic goal of the English government had been to make Indians dependent on English goods by integrating them into the colonial marketplace. Politically, England wanted to keep the peace with tribes by preventing the colonists and traders from provoking the tribes to warfare through the colonists' uncontrolled trade and land grabs. Thus, England and the American colonial governments established regulations and bonding and licensing schemes to control who traded with Indians and how the trade was conducted. * * *

* * * Government trading houses were operated at twenty-eight locations all across the frontier from 1795–1822. This process assisted in making Indians dependent on the federal government as they bought their supplies at the federal stores, and it also contributed to shutting the door to free trade and free markets in Indian country.

The federal control of free trade and economic activities in Indian country inhibited the operation of a free capitalist market and most economic development in Indian country. In essence, Congress preempted the American free market and became "a surrogate for Indian decision making in ... economic relations with the settlers." The federal executive branch also participated in this isolation of Indian country from the American capitalist economy. Most treaties with tribes required that the tribe limit their previous trading habits or only trade with the United

States government. Many tribes later realized that they were suffering from an absence of access to trade and they negotiated in subsequent treaties to take steps to increase trade and to gain better access to goods.

One result of the Trade and Intercourse Era policy, intentional or not, was to start the process of shutting Indians, tribes, and their lands and resources out of the American capitalist economy and free trade market. Congress caused this result by refusing to allow any use of tribal assets, such as for leasing land for grazing or farming, or for mineral or timber development, by imposing strict limits on traders interacting with Indians, and by creating the federal trading houses which dominated the early American trade with Indians. The policy had the concrete impact of cutting Indian and tribal assets out of the American economy. Indians were thus severely limited if not totally prevented from participating in the American capitalist economy to whatever extent they might have wished to participate. Consequently, Indians have lived in governmentally controlled, quasi-socialist economies since 1790.

* * *

For decades preceding the 1880s, liberal thinkers, politicians, "Friends of the Indians," and Christian reformers had been closely examining federal Indian policy. The predominant idea on how to deal with tribes was to civilize and christianize individual Indians and liberate them from the control and communal living of tribal life. This policy was designed to bring Indians into the American "melting pot" by assimilating them into mainstream society. This era in federal Indian policy also had the explicit goals of breaking up tribal ownership of land, ending tribal existence, and, most importantly, opening reservation lands to non-Indian settlement. In fact, the desire of non-Indians to own reservation lands and to open tribal lands and assets to the American economy may have been the prime motivation behind the allotment policy.

The allotment aspect of the policy was designed to break up the communally owned tribal lands into individual plots, or allotments, to be owned by individual Indians and operated as farms. The General Allotment Act and the tribal-specific allotment acts that followed during 1890–1910, generally provided for the division or allotment of reservations into 160 or 80 acre plots to be given to individual tribal members who could later become U.S. citizens. To protect economically unsophisticated Indians, the United States retained legal ownership of these allotments by holding the land in trust for twenty-five year periods during which the land was inalienable and not taxable by the states. The idea was that Indians over time would become astute in business affairs and farming and could eventually handle their own business matters. Significantly, reservation land not allotted to Indians was considered "surplus" and was sold for non-Indian settlement. Most tribes did not have sufficient populations to allot their entire reservation to just tribal members. Hence, the United States sold the surplus lands to non-Indians and today many reservations have much higher non-Indian than Indian populations.

In the 1890s, Congress also began opening reservation assets to the American economy, which had been closed by the Trade and Intercourse policy, by allowing the development of minerals and timber in Indian country and the leasing of reservation land to non-Indians for grazing and farming. Congress also utilized Indian lands for other purposes for the U.S. economy, such as for telephone, telegraph, and railroad rights of ways. Indian lands have also often been used for dams and reclamation and irrigation projects that benefitted non-Indians.

An important aspect of the Allotment Era policy did provide for individual Indians to gain private ownership of land free from tribal and federal governmental restraints. It appears, however, to be an exaggeration to state that the policy had the economic goal to make Indians and tribal economies capitalist in nature. Rather than having economic goals, the purpose of allotment was to turn Indians into "civilized" and "christianized" American citizens and small scale farmers based on the model of white Americans. In regard to its effect on the economy in Indian country, the Allotment policy ultimately created long-term problems that have stifled individual Indian and tribal economic activity to this very day.

Subsequent events severely limited any private benefits accruing to Indians from the allotment and ownership of ex-tribal lands. Many Indians quickly sold or lost their allotments to tax foreclosures once they received alienable patents or deeds to their land. Thus, the lands are no longer in Indian ownership to help Indians or tribal governments with economic development. Another problem, which was not foreseen, is the "fractionalization" of ownership of the individual allotments that remain in Indian ownership, which occurred because the original allottees died and their property passed intestate to ever larger numbers of heirs. Many individual allotments on reservations today have hundreds of Indian owners. This has led to a serious lack of coordinated ownership and decision making over allotments and a nightmare of record keeping and legal work to manage and utilize these lands for tribal and federal governments. In this situation, many Indians today have severe problems putting together and operating viably sized pieces of real property to make economic endeavors feasible. It is often easier for Indians passively to lease these properties than to gain consensus on projects or to consolidate enough land to develop a business or project involving allotments on reservation. * * *

The Indian Reorganization Era of Federal Indian policy ran from the early 1930s to about 1945 and was marked by passage of the Indian Reorganization Act (IRA) in 1934. Under the IRA, the United States completely reversed its allotment policy of breaking up reservations and attempting to destroy tribal governments and instead decided to support tribal governments. By the 1930s, it had become obvious that allotment of tribal lands and the attempt to assimilate Indians had led to disaster. A two-year study of Indian country showed that reservation Indians were living in far worse economic and social conditions after four decades of allotment and assimilation than they had been in 1887. Consequently, among many other goals, the IRA ended the federal policy of allotting tribal lands to individuals and placed a freeze on the sale or loss of any remaining trust allotments still held by individual Indians.

The federal government now actively encouraged and assisted tribes to organize governments and adopt constitutions and bylaws. The IRA also had a very explicit goal to increase economic activity and development in Indian country. The IRA attempted to accomplish this goal by providing for the formation of federally chartered tribal corporations to engage in economic development and business. This provision is very significant to the modern day predominant role of tribal governments in reservation economies.

The IRA allowed tribes to apply to the Secretary of the Interior for federal charters to create tribal corporations through which they could operate businesses, hire attorneys, enter contracts, and engage in litigation. The official policy of the IRA was to encourage tribal business and economic development to be undertaken by tribal governments and tribal institutions even if it worked to exclude individual Indians from the economic activity. The tribal corporations formed under section 17 of the IRA were granted the power to manage their own property, to buy and sell and manage any property, and "such further powers as may be incidental to the conduct of corporate business...." Tribal corporations could also borrow money from a ten million dollar revolving loan fund authorized by Congress for tribal economic development purposes. The loan fund was created primarily to serve tribal economic enterprises although tribes could transfer loans to tribal members. The IRA arguably had a significant socialistic impact on the economic life on reservations because the federal and tribal efforts and concentration on economic development became focused on the tribal government as the entity to start and operate reservation businesses, even to the exclusion of individuals.

For this very reason, when the IRA was proposed it encountered virulent opposition by groups claiming that it promoted socialism and communism. The various opponents of the IRA thought, among other things, that assimilation of Indians should continue, that Indians were inhibited in their liberty and citizenship rights by being subject to tribal governmental control, and that reservation lands and assets should continue to be available to the American market. The charges of communism and socialism that were used to fight and later to reverse the IRA might have only been a form of "red-scare" politics in the 1930s. However, many different groups and persons described the IRA and the alleged intention to keep Indian people segregated from white society and living in a communal, tribal society as being the start of communism and socialism in America. Even Congresspersons opposed the Act and worked to amend and repeal it because of concerns about socialism.

Notwithstanding any "red scare" claims of socialism, and the serious doubts about the IRA in the 1930s, it is certain that the IRA established strong tribal governments in Indian country that today have pervasive control over the economic life and economies of reservations. Modern day observers contend that the IRA imposed tribal governments, tribally controlled economies, and artificial economies on Indian country. In fact, the IRA had such an all encompassing tribal business orientation that many of the tribal governmental entities that were formed under the IRA are today officially called the tribal business committee or tribal business council. This is no surprise since the IRA encouraged tribes "to organize along the lines of modern business corporations" and demanded that economic development proceed with a "tribal approach." Tribal governments and their role in operating tribal businesses have become so intertwined that even the federal government and others have often confused and failed to distinguish between the activities and identity of the tribal governments formed under IRA section 16 and the tribal corporations formed under IRA section 17. Commentators agree that the IRA has led to tribal governments starting and operating businesses, something they are ill-equipped to do.

The economic aspects of the IRA have led to problems for tribes and individual Indians with regard to economic development in Indian country. The primary problem beyond leading tribal governments to becoming the main economic force on reservations is that the IRA also helped create pervasive federal bureaucratic control over Indian economic activity. For example, while tribes could now hire their own attorneys, the "choice of counsel and fixing of fees [was] subject to the approval of the Secretary of the Interior." Furthermore, federal control of tribal economic activity had already been greatly increased in 1871 when Congress enacted a statute that required the Secretary of the Interior to approve all contracts tribes might sign "relative to their lands." The 1871 act and the IRA's creation of new tribal governments and businesses led to extensive federal agency oversight and direction of tribal governments in their political and business decisions. The federal control and direction of tribes became overwhelming in the IRA Era and for decades afterwards. It is universally accepted, however, that federal bureaucratic review and approval authority over tribal economic activities is a death knell to effective and efficient business decision making, yet this is the situation tribal economic development found itself in during the IRA Era and thereafter. It is no surprise, then, that tribal economies did not develop well under the IRA and the subsequent federal control over tribal decisions, assets and resources. Tribal and federal management of reservation economies and direct control over most of the reservation jobs and economic activity since the IRA Era has not created economic success. Indeed, the IRA has almost prevented the success on reservations of individual entrepreneurship and free market capitalism and instead has created governmentally controlled economies that do not function very well.

Black Wealth/White Wealth: New Perspectives on Racial Inequality
■ MELVIN L. OLIVER & THOMAS M. SHAPIRO 12–13, 13–16, 16–18 (1995).

Disparities in wealth between blacks and whites are not the product of haphazard events, inborn traits, isolated incidents or solely contemporary individual accomplishments. Rather, wealth inequality has been structured over many generations through the same systemic barriers that have hampered blacks throughout their history in American society: slavery, Jim Crow, so-called de jure discrimination, and institutionalized racism. How these factors have affected the ability of blacks to accumulate wealth, however, has often been ignored or incompletely sketched. * * *

The close of the Civil War transformed four million former slaves from chattel to freedmen. Emerging from a legacy of two and a half centuries of legalized oppression, the new freedmen entered Southern society with little or no material assets. With the north's military victory over the South freshly on the minds of Republican legislators and white abolitionists, there were rumblings in the air of how the former plantations and the property of Confederate soldiers and sympathizers would be confiscated and divided among the new freedmen to form the basis of their new status in society. The slave's often-cited demand of "forty acres and a mule" fueled great anticipation of a new beginning based on land ownership and a transfer of skills developed under slavery into the new economy of the South. Whereas slave muscle and skills had cleared the wilderness and made the land productive and profitable for plantation owners, the new vision saw the freedmen's hard work and skill generating income and resources for the former slaves themselves. W.E.B. DuBois, in his *Black Reconstruction in America*, called this prospect America's chance to be a modern democracy.

Initially it appeared that massive land redistribution from the Confederates to the freedmen would indeed become a reality. Optimism greeted Sherman's March through the South, and especially his Order 15, which confiscated plantations and redistributed them to black soldiers. Such wartime actions were eventually rescinded and some soldiers who had already started to cultivate the land and build new lives were forced to give up their claims. Real access to land for the freedman had to await the passage of the Southern Homestead Act in 1866, which provided a legal basis and mechanism to promote black landownership. In this legislation public land already designated in the 1862 Homestead Act, which applied only to non-Confederate whites but not blacks, was now opened up to settlement by former slaves in the tradition of homesteading that had helped settle the West. The amount of land involved was substantial, a total of forty-six million acres. Applicants in the first two years of the Homestead Act were limited to only eighty acres, but subsequently this amount increased to 160 acres. The Freedmen's Bureau administered the program, and there was every reason to believe that in reasonable time slaves would be transformed from farm laborers to yeomanry farmers.

This social and economic transformation never occurred. The Southern Homestead Act failed to make newly freed blacks into a landowning class or to provide what Gunnar Myrdal in *An American Dilemma* called "a basis of real democracy in the United States." Indeed, features of the legislation worked against its use as a tool to empower blacks in their quest for land.

First, instead of disqualifying former Confederate supporters as the previous act had done, the 1866 legislation allowed all persons who applied for land to swear that they had not taken up arms against the Union or given aid and comfort to the enemies. This opened the door to massive white applications for land. One estimate suggests that over three-quarters (77.1 percent) of the land applicants under the act were white. In addition, much of the land was poor swampland and it was difficult for black or white applicants to meet the necessary homesteading requirements because they could not make a decent living off the land. What is more important, blacks had to face the extra burden of racial prejudice and discrimination along with the charging of illegal fees, expressly discriminatory court challenges and court decisions, and land speculators. While these barriers faced all poor and illiterate applicants, Michael Lanza has stated in his *Agrarianism and Reconstruction Politics* that "The freedmen's badge of color and previous servitude complicated matters to almost incomprehensible proportions."

Gunnar Myrdal's *An American Dilemma* provides the most cogent explanation of the unfulfilled promise of land to the freeman in an anecdotal passage from a white Southerner. Asked, "Wouldn't it have been better for the white man and the Negro" if the land had been provided?

The old man remarked emphatically:

> "No, for it would have made the Negro 'uppity.' " ... and "the real reason ... why it wouldn't do, is that we are having a hard time now keeping the nigger in his place, and if he were a landowner, he'd think he was a bigger man than old Grant, and there would be no living with him in the Black District.... Who'd work the land if the niggers had farms of their own?"

Nevertheless, the extent of black landowning was remarkable given the economically deprived backgrounds from which the slaves emerged. * * *

The suburbanization of America was principally financed and encouraged by actions of the federal government, which supported suburban growth from the 1930s through the 1960s by way of taxation, transportation, and housing policy. Taxation policy, for example, provided greater tax savings for businesses relocating to the suburbs than to those who stayed and made capital improvements to plants in central city locations. As a consequence, employment opportunities steadily rose in the suburban rings of the nation's major metropolitan areas. In addition, transportation policy encouraged freeway construction and subsidized cheap fuel and mass-produced automobiles. These factors made living on the outer edges of cities both affordable and relatively convenient. However, the most important government policies encouraging and subsidizing suburbanization focused on housing. In particular, the incentives that government programs gave for the acquisition of single-family detached housing spurred both the development and financing of the tract home, which became the hallmark of suburban living. While these governmental policies collectively enabled over thirty-five million families between 1933 and 1978 to participate in homeowner equity accumulation, they also had the adverse effect of constraining black Americans' residential opportunities to central-city ghettos of major U.S. metropolitan communities and denying them access to one of the most successful generators of wealth in American history—the suburban tract home.

This story begins with the government's initial entry into home financing. Faced with mounting foreclosures, President Roosevelt urged passage of a bill that authorized the Home Owners Loan Corporation (HOLC). According to Kenneth Jackson's *Crabgrass Frontier*, the HOLC "refinanced tens of thousands of mortgages in danger of default or foreclosure." Of more importance to this story, however, it also introduced standardized appraisals of the fitness of particular properties and communities for both individual and group loans. In creating "a formal and uniform system of appraisal, reduced to writing, structured in defined procedures, and implemented by individuals only after intensive training, government appraisals institutionalized in a rational and bureaucratic framework a racially discriminatory practice that all but eliminated black access to the suburbs and to government mortgage money." Charged with the task of determining the "useful or productive life of housing" they considered to finance, government agents methodically included in their procedures the evaluation of the racial composition or potential racial composition of the community. Communities that were changing racially or were already black were deemed undesirable and placed in the lowest category. The categories, assigned various colors on a map ranging from green for the most desirable, which included new, all-white housing that was always in demand, to red, which included already racially mixed or all-black, old, and undesirable areas, subsequently were used by Federal Housing Authority (FHA) loan officers who made loans on the basis of these designations.

Established in 1934, the FHA aimed to bolster the economy and increase employment by aiding the ailing construction industry. The FHA ushered in the modern mortgage system that enabled people to buy homes on small down payments and at reasonable interest rates, with lengthy repayment periods and full loan amortization. The FHA's success was remarkable: housing starts jumped from 332,000 in 1936 to 619,000 in 1941. The incentive for home ownership increased to the point where it became, in some cases, cheaper to buy a home than to rent one. As one former resident of New York City who moved to suburban New Jersey pointed out, "We had been paying $50 per month rent, and here we come up and live for $29.00 a month." This included taxes, principal, insurance, and interest.

This growth in access to housing was confined, however, for the most part to suburban areas. The administrative dictates outlined in the original act, while containing no antiurban bias, functioned in practice to the neglect of central cities. Three reasons can be cited: first, a bias toward the financing of single-family detached homes over multifamily projects favored open areas outside of the central city that had yet to be developed over congested central-city areas; second, a bias toward new purchases over repair of existing homes prompted people to move out of the city rather than upgrade or improve their existing residences; and third, the continued use of the "unbiased professional estimate" that made older homes and communities in which blacks or undesirables were located less likely to receive approval for loans encouraged purchases in communities where race was not an issue.

While the FHA used as its model the HOLC's appraisal system, it provided more precise guidance to its appraisers in its *Underwriting Manual*. The most basic sentiment underlying the FHA's concern was its fear that property values would decline if a rigid black and white segregation was not maintained. The *Underwriting Manual* openly stated that "if a neighborhood is to retain stability, it is necessary that properties shall continue to be occupied by the same social and racial classes" and further recommended that "subdivision regulations and suitable restrictive covenants are the best way to ensure such neighborhood stability. The FHA's recommended use of restrictive covenants continued until 1949, when, responding to the Supreme Court's outlawing of such covenants in 1948 (*Shelley v. Kraemer*), it announced that 'as of February 15, 1950, it would not insure mortgages on real estate subject to covenants.'"

Even after this date, however, the FHA's discriminatory practices continued to have an impact on the continuing suburbanization of the white population and the deepening ghettoization of the black population. While exact figures regarding the FHA's discrimination against blacks are not available, data by county show a clear pattern of "redlining" in central-city counties and abundant loan activity in suburban counties.

The FHA's actions have had a lasting impact on the wealth portfolios of black Americans. Locked out of the greatest mass-based opportunity for wealth accumulation in American history, African Americans who desired and were able to afford home ownership found themselves consigned to central-city communities where their investments were affected by the "self-fulfilling prophecies" of the FHA appraisers: cut off from sources of new investment their homes and communities deteriorated and lost value in comparison to those homes and communities that FHA appraisers deemed desirable. One infamous housing development of the period—Levittown—provides a classic illustration of the way blacks missed out on this asset-accumulating opportunity. Levittown was built on a mass scale, and housing there was eminently affordable, thanks to the FHA's and VHA's accessible financing, yet as late as 1960 "not a single one of the Long Island Levittown's 82,000 residents was black."

Race, Gender & Work: A Multicultural Economic History of Women in the United States
(1991)

■ Teresa Amott & Julie Matthei

Chapter 4—The Soul of the *Tierra Madre*: Chicano Women

Much of the complex economic history of the Chicana/o people centers on struggles over land and national boundaries. The earliest ancestors of today's Chicanas were members of many different Indian nations who inhabited the lands now known as Mexico and the U.S. Southwest, including the Aztec, Pueblo, and Tlaxcalán. Beginning in the sixteenth century, these indigenous peoples were conquered by Spanish invaders. Sexual relations, many of them forced, between Spanish men and indigenous (and African slave) women soon produced a *mestiza/o* population. Through colonization and settlement, the Spanish extended their territories north. The vast country of Mexico was formed after independence from Spain in 1821, stretching from what we know today as Guatemala up through Texas, California, Arizona, Colorado, New Mexico, and Nevada, and even into parts of Oregon, Utah, and Idaho.

In the early nineteenth century, Anglo settlers from the deep South migrated to Texas, sowing the seeds for a war between Mexico and the United States that eventually led to the annexation of almost half of Mexico's territories in 1848. From then up until the present, Mexican citizens have migrated to the United States in search of work, and many have become U.S. citizens. * * *

As a result of this history, the economics and politics of the U.S. Chicana population are inextricably linked to those of Mexico. * * *

* * * [In Mexico, t]he period between 1834 and 1846 has been called the "Golden Age of the ranchos" because land became increasingly concentrated in the hands of a few wealthy ranchers, all of them of Spanish ancestry (or claiming to be). Next in the class hierarchy were *mestiza/o* small ranchers and farmers. Following them were *mestiza/o* artisans, skilled workers, laborers, and seasonal workers in the cattle industry. Lowest of all were the Indians, the chief source of manual labor.

The new country quickly became engaged in a bitter struggle with Anglo settlers in what we know now as Texas, culminating in the Mexican–American War of 1846. Anglo settlers began arriving in Mexico's northern territories in the early 1800s, granted land first by the Spanish government and later by Mexico, which encouraged migration to the sparsely settled area. Most anglo settlers came to farm or raise cattle, but starting in 1829, an increasing number brought slaves from the deep South to work cotton plantations. Although there were some landed Mexicans in Texas, by the 1830s, Anglo Texans outnumbered Mexicans by five to one. To discourage slavery and stem further Anglo immigration, Mexico prohibited importation of slaves in 1830. In 1835, Anglo Texans, chafing under these restrictions, began the Texas Revolt to free themselves from Mexican rule. After losses at the Alamo and Goliad, they defeated Mexican forces in 1837 and set up the Lone Star Republic. In 1845, Texas became part of the United States. One researcher documented the transfer of land ownership from Mexicans to Anglos in Nueces County, Texas in the 1800s: "at the beginning of the Texas Revolt in 1835 every foot of land in Nueces County was held under

Mexican land grants, two years prior to the Civil War all but one had passed out of Mexican hands, and by 1883 none was held by Mexicans."

* * * The [Mexican–American] war ended with the Treaty of Guadalupe Hidalgo in 1848, in which Mexico was forced to give up more than half her territory—including California, New Mexico, Utah, Nevada, Colorado, and Arizona—in exchange for $15 million. In the annexation, the United States acquired lands populated by over 80,000 Spanish-speaking people, most of them *mestiza/o* and *criolla/o*. The quarter of a million Indian peoples in these lands now faced U.S. rather than Mexican efforts to subordinate or exterminate them.

While the language of the Treaty contained protections for Mexican land titles and water rights, the United States government made no attempt to safeguard these rights. Thus the annexation of Mexican territories placed annexed Mexicans in a vulnerable position. As Anglo settlers flooded into the Southwest, they took over the lands and wealth of the Mexican inhabitants, reducing most of the Mexican population in the Southwest to a landless, politically disempowered group.

Some of the *ricos* were able to protect their landholdings by intermarrying with Anglo newcomers. In San Antonio, for instance, marriage records between 1837 and 1860 show that one daughter from almost every *rico* family had married an Anglo. Such marriages were attractive to Anglo men since daughters as well as sons inherited property in Mexican families.

But many other Mexicans, particularly those with smaller landholdings or subsistence plots, lost their lands through a variety of devices familiar to us from the history of American Indians. Anglo domination of the political and judicial systems, along with the use of force and violence, ensured Anglo economic domination. For instance, when floods, drought, or economic downturns made it difficult for Mexican ranchers to pay taxes imposed by the Anglo-controlled government, their lands were quickly sold to Anglos. California passed a law in 1851 that encouraged squatters to take over Mexican lands. Lynching was also a common tool employed by Anglos to terrorize Mexicans into leaving their lands. Some estimate that more Mexicans were lynched between 1850 and 1930 than African Americans during the same period.

* * *

During the second half of the nineteenth century, the southwestern economy expanded rapidly. Subsistence farming began to give way to huge ranches and cash crops as railroads made it possible for southwestern products to reach eastern markets. Displaced Mexicans found jobs as seasonal agricultural workers, domestic workers, or miners in isolated, company-controlled towns.

* * *

Chapter 7—Climbing Gold Mountain: Asian American Women

From 1840 through World War II, Asian immigrants—first Chinese, then Japanese, and finally Filipinas/os—were recruited as a low-wage second-class labor force by employers in the western United States and Hawaii. The U.S. legal system denied Asian immigrants the legal rights which had been accorded their European counterparts, relying on the 1790 naturalization law that restricted the privilege of citizenship to "free white persons." When the law was revised after the Civil War to make African Americans eligible for citizenship, the phrase "persons of African descent" was added, and the law continued to bar Asian immigrants from naturalizing. Unable to become citizens, Asian immigrants remained permanent "aliens" (non-citizens), and whites were able to pass numerous laws which restricted their rights simply by referring to their alien status. For example, in the early twentieth century California passed laws which prevented Asian immigrants from purchasing land. However, children of immigrant Asians were allowed to become citizens and escape these restrictions if they were born in the United States.

On the West Coast, where the vast majority of Asians lived, whites bolstered their own relative economic status at the expense of Asian immigrants. White employers achieved higher profits by using Asians as low-wage replacements for white workers and as strikebreakers. White workers resented the threat Asians appeared to pose to wages and unionizing efforts. Self-employed whites felt threatened by Asian successes in small business.

To defend their economic positions, whites formed broad-based movements to restrict Asian immigration and even to send migrants back to Asia. Filipino historian Paul Valdez wrote of the anti-"Oriental" movement of the 1920s, "They used to pass out leaflets saying that the Japanese were taking the lands from the Americans, the Chinese were taking the businesses, and the Filipinos were taking the women." Under these pressures, white-controlled federal and state governments passed close to 50 laws specifically aimed at restricting and subordinating Asian immigrants between 1850 and 1950. These sentiments culminated in laws excluding further immigration. Chinese immigration was cut off in 1882 and 1892; Japanese in 1907–08 and 1924; Indian in 1917; and Filipina/o in 1934.

Whites also discriminated against second-generation Asians who, unlike white ethnics, could not disguise their ethnicity by speaking English and adopting European American ways. These barriers to upward mobility in the labor market compelled many Asian Americans to seek advancement through self-employment in family-based businesses—for the Chinese, laundries and restaurants; for the Japanese, truck farming; and for the Koreans, grocery stores.

D. WEALTH, CLASS AND ECONOMIC MOBILITY—THE INTERGENERATIONAL EFFECTS

In what follows, three writers: two influential Princeton economists, Alan B. Krueger and Paul Krugman, as well as conservative *New York Times* columnist, David Brooks, explore the emerging problem of decreasing economic mobility and pinched opportunity structures arising from inherited economic status across all socio-economic groups. This research and argument poses a direct challenge to that part of our national story that depends on belief in the power of individual effort, merit, and achievement. If parent-child wealth correlations are as strong as these economists argue, it reveals a largely hidden force that will preserve economic inequality for a long time. This force could be described as the new "invisible hand," shaping markets and posing a threat to the democratic distribution of political power.

The Sticky Ladder
N.Y. TIMES, Jan. 25, 2005, at A19.

■ DAVID BROOKS

>In his Inaugural Address President Bush embraced the grandest theme of American foreign policy—the advance of freedom around the world. Now that attention is turning to the State of the Union address, it would be nice if he would devote himself as passionately to the grandest theme of domestic policy—social mobility.

>The United States is a country based on the idea that a person's birth does not determine his or her destiny. Our favorite stories involve immigrants climbing from obscurity to success. Our amazing work ethic is predicated on the assumption that enterprise and effort lead to ascent. "I hold the value of life is to improve one's condition," Lincoln declared.

>The problem is that in every generation conditions emerge that threaten to close down opportunity and retard social mobility. Each generation has to reopen the pathways to success.

>Today, for example, we may still believe American society is uniquely dynamic, but we're deceiving ourselves. European societies, which seem more class driven and less open, have just as much social mobility as the United States does.

>And there are some indications that it is becoming harder and harder for people to climb the ladder of success. *The Economist* magazine gathered much of the recent research on social mobility in America. The magazine concluded that the meritocracy is faltering: "Would-be Horatio Algers are finding it no easier to climb from rags to riches, while the children of the privileged have a greater chance of staying at the top of the social heap."

>Economists and sociologists do not all agree, but it does seem there is at least slightly less movement across income quintiles than there was a few decades ago. Sons' income levels correlate more closely to those of their fathers. The income levels of brothers also correlate more closely. That suggests that the family you were born into matters more and more to how you will fare in life. That's a problem because we are not supposed to have a hereditary class structure in this country.

But we're developing one. In the information age, education matters more. In an age in which education matters more, family matters more, because as James Coleman established decades ago, family status shapes educational achievement.

At the top end of society we have a mass upper-middle class. This is made up of highly educated people who move into highly educated neighborhoods and raise their kids in good schools with the children of other highly educated parents. These kids develop wonderful skills, get into good colleges (the median family income of a Harvard student is now $150,000), then go out and have their own children, who develop the same sorts of wonderful skills and who repeat the cycle all over again.

In this way these highly educated elites produce a paradox—a hereditary meritocratic class.

It becomes harder for middle-class kids to compete against members of the hypercharged educated class. Indeed, the middle-class areas become more socially isolated from the highly educated areas.

And this is not even to speak of the children who grow up in neighborhoods in which more boys go to jail than college, in which marriage is not the norm before child-rearing, in which homes are often unstable, in which long-range planning is absurd, in which the social skills you need to achieve are not even passed down.

In his State of the Union address, President Bush is no doubt going to talk about his vision of an ownership society. But homeownership or pension ownership is only part of a larger story. The larger story is the one Lincoln defined over a century ago, the idea that this nation should provide an open field and a fair chance so that all can compete in the race of life.

Today that's again under threat, but this time from barriers that are different than the ones defined by socialists in the industrial age. Now, the upper class doesn't so much oppress the lower class. It just outperforms it generation after generation. Now the crucial inequality is not only finance capital, it's social capital. Now it is silly to make a distinction between economic policy and social policy.

We can spend all we want on schools. But if families are disrupted, if the social environment is dysfunctional, bigger budgets won't help.

President Bush spoke grandly and about foreign policy last Thursday, borrowing from Lincoln. Lincoln's other great cause was social mobility. That's worth embracing too.

Economic Scene; The Apple Falls Close to the Tree, Even in the Land of Opportunity

N.Y. TIMES, Nov. 14, 2002, at C1.

■ ALAN B. KRUEGER

It seems increasingly apparent that the secret to success is to have a successful parent. Consider some prominent examples: George H. W. Bush

D. WEALTH, CLASS AND ECONOMIC MOBILITY—THE INTERGENERATIONAL EFFECTS

and George W. Bush; Bobby Bonds and Barry Bonds; Henry Fonda and Jane Fonda; Estee Lauder and Ronald Lauder; Julio Iglesias and Enrique Iglesias; Sam Walton and Jim, John, S. Robson and Alice Walton.

As more recent and better data have become available, economists have marked up their estimate of the impact of parents' socioeconomic status on their children's likelihood of economic success.

It turns out that the famous line attributed to Andrew Carnegie—"from shirt-sleeves to shirt-sleeves in three generations"—is an understatement. Five or six generations are probably required, on average, to erase the advantages or disadvantages of one's economic origins.

This represents a marked departure from past thinking. In the 1980s, when Gary S. Becker of the University of Chicago pioneered the economic theory of intergenerational transmission of economic status, it was believed that the correlation between a father's and son's income was only around 0.15—less than half the correlation between fathers' and sons' heights.

The early studies suggested that if a father's income was twice the average, his son's expected income would be 15 percent above average, and his grandson's just 2 percent above average. This is fast "regression to the mean," a concept Sir Francis Galton used to describe the progression of offspring toward the average height.

Landmark studies published by Gary Solon of the University of Michigan and David J. Zimmerman of Williams College in The American Economic Review a decade ago, however, led economists to revise substantially upward the estimate of the similarity of fathers' and sons' incomes. They noted that income fluctuated for idiosyncratic reasons from year to year—an employee could lose a job, for example—so estimates that depended on a single year were based on "noisy" data. Also, the samples previously analyzed represented only a narrow slice of the population at different points in individual careers. These factors caused the correlation in annual incomes to understate the correlation in "lifetime" incomes.

Averaging earnings over five years produced a correlation of around 0.40 for fathers' and sons' earnings—the same as the correlation between their heights. If people's incomes were represented by their heights, the similarity in income between generations would resemble the similarity observed in the heights of fathers and sons.

New studies by Bhashkar Mazumder of the Federal Reserve Bank of Chicago suggest that the similarity in income is even greater. Using Social Security records, he averaged fathers' earnings over 16 years (1970 through 1985) and sons' earnings over four years (1995 through 1998), and found that around 65 percent of the earnings advantage of fathers was transmitted to sons. The wider window provides a better reflection of lifetime earnings.

Also, the samples previously analyzed represented only a narrow slice of the population at different points in individual careers. These factors caused the correlation in annual incomes to understate the correlation in "lifetime" incomes.

The relationship between fathers' and daughters' earnings was just as strong.

So that grandson (or granddaughter) mentioned previously could expect to earn 42 percent more than average. After five generations, the earnings advantage would still be 12 percent.

Furthermore, the degree of persistence across generations is strong for both rich and poor. Thomas Hertz of American University finds that a child born in the bottom 10 percent of families ranked by income has a 31 percent chance of ending up there as an adult and a 51 percent chance of ending up in the bottom 20 percent, while one born in the top 10 percent has a 30 percent chance of staying there and a 43 percent chance of being in the top 20 percent.

In another study, David I. Levine of Berkeley and Dr. Mazumder found that the impact of parental income on adult sons' income increased from 1980 to the early 1990s.

Why is there such a strong connection between parents' socioeconomic status and their children's? A large part of the answer involves intergenerational transmission of cognitive ability and educational level.

But these factors can "explain at most three-fifths of the intergenerational transmission of economic status," Samuel Bowles and Herbert Gintis of the University of Massachusetts wrote in the latest issue of The Journal of Economic Perspectives. They suggest that the intergenerational transmission of race, geographical location, height, beauty, health status and personality also plays a significant role.

Arthur S. Goldberger of the University of Wisconsin has long questioned whether knowledge of the "heritability" of income is of much use. Even if the father-son correlation is high because traits that affect earning power are inherited, well-designed interventions could still be cost effective and improve the lot of the disadvantaged.

To take an extreme example, the correlation in incomes between fathers and sons was high in South Africa under apartheid because race is an inherited trait. The abolition of apartheid reduced the correlation. The organization of society matters.

Perhaps the only legitimate use of the intergenerational correlation in income is to characterize economic mobility. The data challenge the notion that the United States is an exceptionally mobile society. If the United States stands out in comparison with other countries, it is in having a more static distribution of income across generations with fewer opportunities for advancement.

Anders Bjorklund of Stockholm University and Markus Jantti of the University of Tampere in Finland, for example, find more economic mobility in Sweden than in the United States. Only South Africa and Britain have as little mobility across generations as the United States.

Luke Skywalker and Darth Vader are an unusual father-son pair; in most families, the apple does not fall so far from the tree.

The Sons Also Rise
N.Y. TIMES, Nov. 22, 2002, at A27.

■ PAUL KRUGMAN

America, we all know, is the land of opportunity. Your success in life depends on your ability and drive, not on who your father was.

Just ask the Bush brothers. Talk to Elizabeth Cheney, who holds a specially created State Department job, or her husband, chief counsel of the Office of Management and Budget. Interview Eugene Scalia, the top lawyer at the Labor Department, and Janet Rehnquist, inspector general at the Department of Health and Human Services. And don't forget to check in with William Kristol, editor of The Weekly Standard, and the conservative commentator John Podhoretz.

What's interesting is how little comment, let alone criticism, this roll call has occasioned. It might be just another case of kid-gloves treatment by the media, but I think it's a symptom of a broader phenomenon: inherited status is making a comeback.

It has always been good to have a rich or powerful father. Last week my Princeton colleague Alan Krueger wrote a column for The Times surveying statistical studies that debunk the mythology of American social mobility. "If the United States stands out in comparison with other countries, he wrote, 'it is in having a more static distribution of income across generations with fewer opportunities for advancement.'" And Kevin Phillips, in his book "Wealth and Democracy," shows that robber-baron fortunes have been far more persistent than legend would have it.

But the past is only prologue. According to one study cited by Mr. Krueger, the heritability of status has been increasing in recent decades. And that's just the beginning. Underlying economic, social and political trends will give the children of today's wealthy a huge advantage over those who chose the wrong parents.

For one thing, there's more privilege to pass on. Thirty years ago the C.E.O. of a major company was a bureaucrat—well paid, but not truly wealthy. He couldn't give either his position or a large fortune to his heirs. Today's imperial C.E.O.'s, by contrast, will leave vast estates behind—and they are often able to give their children lucrative jobs, too. More broadly, the spectacular increase in American inequality has made the gap between the rich and the middle class wider, and hence more difficult to cross, than it was in the past.

Meanwhile, one key doorway to upward mobility—a good education system, available to all—has been closing. More and more, ambitious parents feel that a public school education is a dead end. It's telling that Jack Grubman, the former Salomon Smith Barney analyst, apparently sold his soul not for personal wealth but for two places in the right nursery school. Alas, most American souls aren't worth enough to get the kids into the 92nd Street Y.

Also, the heritability of status will be mightily reinforced by the repeal of the estate tax—a prime example of the odd way in which public policy and public opinion have shifted in favor of measures that benefit the wealthy, even as our society becomes increasingly class-ridden.

It wasn't always thus. The influential dynasties of the 20th century, like the Kennedys, the Rockefellers and, yes, the Sulzbergers, faced a public suspicious of inherited position; they overcame that suspicion by demonstrating a strong sense of noblesse oblige, justifying their existence by standing for high principles. Indeed, the Kennedy legend has a whiff of Bonnie Prince Charlie about it; the rightful heirs were also perceived as defenders of the downtrodden against the powerful.

But today's heirs feel no need to demonstrate concern for those less fortunate. On the contrary, they are often avid defenders of the powerful against the downtrodden. Mr. Scalia's principal personal claim to fame is his crusade against regulations that protect workers from ergonomic hazards, while Ms. Rehnquist has attracted controversy because of her efforts to weaken the punishment of health-care companies found to have committed fraud.

The official ideology of America's elite remains one of meritocracy, just as our political leadership pretends to be populist. But that won't last. Soon enough, our society will rediscover the importance of good breeding, and the vulgarity of talented upstarts.

For years, opinion leaders have told us that it's all about family values. And it is—but it will take a while before most people realize that they meant the value of coming from the right family.

TABLE 2.1. "Like Parent, Like Child—Recent Studies Find That There Is Less Income Mobility from One Generation to Another than Previously Believed."

	Chance of Children Attaining Each Income Level		
Parent's Income	*Top Quintile*	*Middle Quintile*	*Bottom Quintile*
Top 20%	42.3%	16.5%	6.3%
Middle 20%	15.3%	25.0%	17.3%
Bottom 20%	7.3%	18.4%	37.3%

SOURCE: *Thomas Hertz, American University.*

For Richer

N.Y. TIMES, Oct. 20, 2002, § 6 (magazine), at 62.

■ PAUL KRUGMAN

I. THE DISAPPEARING MIDDLE

When I was a teenager growing up on Long Island, one of my favorite excursions was a trip to see the great Gilded Age mansions of the North

Shore. Those mansions weren't just pieces of architectural history. They were monuments to a bygone social era, one in which the rich could afford the armies of servants needed to maintain a house the size of a European palace. By the time I saw them, of course, that era was long past. Almost none of the Long Island mansions were still private residences. Those that hadn't been turned into museums were occupied by nursing homes or private schools.

For the America I grew up in—the America of the 1950's and 1960's—was a middle-class society, both in reality and in feel. The vast income and wealth inequalities of the Gilded Age had disappeared. Yes, of course, there was the poverty of the underclass—but the conventional wisdom of the time viewed that as a social rather than an economic problem. Yes, of course, some wealthy businessmen and heirs to large fortunes lived far better than the average American. But they weren't rich the way the robber barons who built the mansions had been rich, and there weren't that many of them. The days when plutocrats were a force to be reckoned with in American society, economically or politically, seemed long past.

Daily experience confirmed the sense of a fairly equal society. The economic disparities you were conscious of were quite muted. Highly educated professionals—middle managers, college teachers, even lawyers—often claimed that they earned less than unionized blue-collar workers. Those considered very well off lived in split-levels, had a housecleaner come in once a week and took summer vacations in Europe. But they sent their kids to public schools and drove themselves to work, just like everyone else.

But that was long ago. The middle-class America of my youth was another country.

We are now living in a new Gilded Age, as extravagant as the original. Mansions have made a comeback. Back in 1999 this magazine profiled Thierry Despont, the "eminence of excess," an architect who specializes in designing houses for the superrich. His creations typically range from 20,000 to 60,000 square feet; houses at the upper end of his range are not much smaller than the White House. Needless to say, the armies of servants are back, too. So are the yachts. Still, even J.P. Morgan didn't have a Gulfstream.

As the story about Despont suggests, it's not fair to say that the fact of widening inequality in America has gone unreported. Yet glimpses of the lifestyles of the rich and tasteless don't necessarily add up in people's minds to a clear picture of the tectonic shifts that have taken place in the distribution of income and wealth in this country. My sense is that few people are aware of just how much the gap between the very rich and the rest has widened over a relatively short period of time. In fact, even bringing up the subject exposes you to charges of "class warfare," the "politics of envy" and so on. And very few people indeed are willing to talk about the profound effects—economic, social and political—of that widening gap.

Yet you can't understand what's happening in America today without understanding the extent, causes and consequences of the vast increase in inequality that has taken place over the last three decades, and in particular the astonishing concentration of income and wealth in just a few hands. To make sense of the current wave of corporate scandal, you need to understand how the man in the gray flannel suit has been replaced by the imperial C.E.O. The concentration of income at the top is a key reason that the United States, for all its economic achievements, has more poverty and lower life expectancy than any other major advanced nation. Above all, the growing concentration of wealth has reshaped our political system: it is at the root both of a general shift to the right and of an extreme polarization of our politics.

But before we get to all that, let's take a look at who gets what.

II. THE NEW GILDED AGE

The Securities and Exchange Commission hath no fury like a woman scorned. The messy divorce proceedings of Jack Welch, the legendary former C.E.O. of General Electric, have had one unintended benefit: they have given us a peek at the perks of the corporate elite, which are normally hidden from public view. For it turns out that when Welch retired, he was granted for life the use of a Manhattan apartment (including food, wine and laundry), access to corporate jets and a variety of other in-kind benefits, worth at least $2 million a year. The perks were revealing: they illustrated the extent to which corporate leaders now expect to be treated like *ancien régime* royalty. In monetary terms, however, the perks must have meant little to Welch. In 2000, his last full year running G.E., Welch was paid $123 million, mainly in stock and stock options.

Is it news that C.E.O.'s of large American corporations make a lot of money? Actually, it is. They were always well paid compared with the average worker, but there is simply no comparison between what executives got a generation ago and what they are paid today.

Over the past 30 years most people have seen only modest salary increases: the average annual salary in America, expressed in 1998 dollars (that is, adjusted for inflation), rose from $32,522 in 1970 to $35,864 in 1999. That's about a 10 percent increase over 29 years—progress, but not much. Over the same period, however, according to Fortune magazine, the average real annual compensation of the top 100 C.E.O.'s went from $1.3 million—39 times the pay of an average worker—to $37.5 million, more than 1,000 times the pay of ordinary workers.

The explosion in C.E.O. pay over the past 30 years is an amazing story in its own right, and an important one. But it is only the most spectacular indicator of a broader story, the reconcentration of income and wealth in the U.S. The rich have always been different from you and me, but they are far more different now than they were not long ago—indeed, they are as different now as they were when F. Scott Fitzgerald made his famous remark.

That's a controversial statement, though it shouldn't be. For at least the past 15 years it has been hard to deny the evidence for growing inequality in the United States. Census data clearly show a rising share of income going to the top 20 percent of families, and within that top 20 percent to the top 5 percent, with a declining share going to families in the middle. Nonetheless, denial of that evidence is a sizable, well-financed industry. Conservative think tanks have produced scores of studies that try to discredit the data, the methodology and, not least, the motives of those who report the obvious. Studies that appear to refute claims of increasing inequality receive prominent endorsements on editorial pages and are eagerly cited by right-leaning government officials. Four years ago Alan Greenspan (why did anyone ever think that he was nonpartisan?) gave a keynote speech at the Federal Reserve's annual Jackson Hole conference that amounted to an attempt to deny that there has been any real increase in inequality in America.

* * * Meanwhile, politically motivated smoke screens aside, the reality of increasing inequality is not in doubt. In fact, the census data understate the case, because for technical reasons those data tend to undercount very high incomes—for example, it's unlikely that they reflect the explosion in C.E.O. compensation. And other evidence makes it clear not only that inequality is increasing but that the action gets bigger the closer you get to the top. That is, it's not simply that the top 20 percent of families have had bigger percentage gains than families near the middle: the top 5 percent have done better than the next 15, the top 1 percent better than the next 4, and so on up to Bill Gates.

Studies that try to do a better job of tracking high incomes have found startling results. For example, a recent study by the nonpartisan Congressional Budget Office used income tax data and other sources to improve on the census estimates. The C.B.O. study found that between 1979 and 1997, the after-tax incomes of the top 1 percent of families rose 157 percent, compared with only a 10 percent gain for families near the middle of the income distribution. Even more startling results come from a new study by Thomas Piketty, at the French research institute Cepremap, and Emmanuel Saez, who is now at the University of California at Berkeley. Using income tax data, Piketty and Saez have produced estimates of the incomes of the well-to-do, the rich and the very rich back to 1913.

The first point you learn from these new estimates is that the middle-class America of my youth is best thought of not as the normal state of our society, but as an interregnum between Gilded Ages. America before 1930 was a society in which a small number of very rich people controlled a large share of the nation's wealth. We became a middle-class society only after the concentration of income at the top dropped sharply during the New Deal, and especially during World War II. The economic historians Claudia Goldin and Robert Margo have dubbed the narrowing of income gaps during those years the Great Compression. Incomes then stayed fairly equally distributed until the 1970's: the rapid rise in incomes during the first postwar generation was very evenly spread across the population.

Since the 1970's, however, income gaps have been rapidly widening. Piketty and Saez confirm what I suspected: by most measures we are, in fact, back to the days of "The Great Gatsby." After 30 years in which the income shares of the top 10 percent of taxpayers, the top 1 percent and so on were far below their levels in the 1920's, all are very nearly back where they were.

And the big winners are the very, very rich. One ploy often used to play down growing inequality is to rely on rather coarse statistical breakdowns—dividing the population into five "quintiles," each containing 20 percent of families, or at most 10 "deciles." * * * For example, a conservative commentator might concede, grudgingly, that there has been some increase in the share of national income going to the top 10 percent of taxpayers, but then point out that anyone with an income over $81,000 is in that top 10 percent. So we're just talking about shifts within the middle class, right?

Wrong: the top 10 percent contains a lot of people whom we would still consider middle class, but they weren't the big winners. Most of the gains in the share of the top 10 percent of taxpayers over the past 30 years were actually gains to the top 1 percent, rather than the next 9 percent. In 1998 the top 1 percent started at $230,000. In turn, 60 percent of the gains of that top 1 percent went to the top 0.1 percent, those with incomes of more than $790,000. And almost half of those gains went to a mere 13,000 taxpayers, the top 0.01 percent, who had an income of at least $3.6 million and an average income of $17 million.

A stickler for detail might point out that the Piketty–Saez estimates end in 1998 and that the C.B.O. numbers end a year earlier. Have the trends shown in the data reversed? Almost surely not. In fact, all indications are that the explosion of incomes at the top continued through 2000. Since then the plunge in stock prices must have put some crimp in high incomes—but census data show inequality continuing to increase in 2001, mainly because of the severe effects of the recession on the working poor and near poor. When the recession ends, we can be sure that we will find ourselves a society in which income inequality is even higher than it was in the late 90's.

So claims that we've entered a second Gilded Age aren't exaggerated. In America's middle-class era, the mansion-building, yacht-owning classes had pretty much disappeared. According to Piketty and Saez, in 1970 the top 0.01 percent of taxpayers had 0.7 percent of total income—that is, they earned "only" 70 times as much as the average, not enough to buy or maintain a mega-residence. But in 1998 the top 0.01 percent received more than 3 percent of all income. That meant that the 13,000 richest families in America had almost as much income as the 20 million poorest households; those 13,000 families had incomes 300 times that of average families.

And let me repeat: this transformation has happened very quickly, and it is still going on. * * *

III. UNDOING THE NEW DEAL

In the middle of the 1980's, as economists became aware that something important was happening to the distribution of income in America, they formulated three main hypotheses about its causes.

The "globalization" hypothesis tied America's changing income distribution to the growth of world trade, and especially the growing imports of manufactured goods from the third world. Its basic message was that blue-collar workers—the sort of people who in my youth often made as much money as college-educated middle managers—were losing ground in the face of competition from low-wage workers in Asia. A result was stagnation or decline in the wages of ordinary people, with a growing share of national income going to the highly educated.

A second hypothesis, "skill-biased technological change," situated the cause of growing inequality not in foreign trade but in domestic innovation. The torrid pace of progress in information technology, so the story went, had increased the demand for the highly skilled and educated. And so the income distribution increasingly favored brains rather than brawn.

Finally, the "superstar" hypothesis—named by the Chicago economist Sherwin Rosen—offered a variant on the technological story. It argued that modern technologies of communication often turn competition into a tournament in which the winner is richly rewarded, while the runners-up get far less. The classic example—which gives the theory its name—is the entertainment business. As Rosen pointed out, in bygone days there were hundreds of comedians making a modest living at live shows in the borscht belt and other places. Now they are mostly gone; what is left is a handful of superstar TV comedians.

The debates among these hypotheses—particularly the debate between those who attributed growing inequality to globalization and those who attributed it to technology—were many and bitter. I was a participant in those debates myself. But I won't dwell on them, because in the last few years there has been a growing sense among economists that none of these hypotheses work.

* * *

The Great Compression—the substantial reduction in inequality during the New Deal and the Second World War—also seems hard to understand in terms of the usual theories. During World War II Franklin Roosevelt used government control over wages to compress wage gaps. But if the middle-class society that emerged from the war was an artificial creation, why did it persist for another 30 years?

Some—by no means all—economists trying to understand growing inequality have begun to take seriously a hypothesis that would have been considered irredeemably fuzzy-minded not long ago. This view stresses the role of social norms in setting limits to inequality. According to this view, the New Deal had a more profound impact on American society than even its most ardent admirers have suggested: it imposed norms of relative equality in pay that persisted for more than 30 years, creating the broadly middle-class society we came to take for granted. But those norms began to unravel in the 1970's and have done so at an accelerating pace.

Exhibit A for this view is the story of executive compensation. In the 1960's, America's great corporations behaved more like socialist republics than like cutthroat capitalist enterprises, and top executives behaved more like public-spirited bureaucrats than like captains of industry. I'm not exaggerating. Consider the description of executive behavior offered by John Kenneth Galbraith in his 1967 book, "The New Industrial State": "Management does not go out ruthlessly to reward itself—a sound management is expected to exercise restraint." Managerial self-dealing was a thing of the past: "With the power of decision goes opportunity for making money.... Were everyone to seek to do so ... the corporation would be a chaos of competitive avarice. But these are not the sort of thing that a good company man does; a remarkably effective code bans such behavior. Group decision-making insures, moreover, that almost everyone's actions and even thoughts are known to others. This acts to enforce the code and, more than incidentally, a high standard of personal honesty as well."

Thirty-five years on, a cover article in Fortune is titled "You Bought. They Sold." "All over corporate America," reads the blurb, "top execs were cashing in stocks even as their companies were tanking. Who was left holding the bag? You." As I said, we've become a different country.

Let's leave actual malfeasance on one side for a moment, and ask how the relatively modest salaries of top executives 30 years ago became the gigantic pay packages of today. * * * The key reason executives are paid so much now is that they appoint the members of the corporate board that determines their compensation and control many of the perks that board members count on. So it's not the invisible hand of the market that leads to those monumental executive incomes; it's the invisible handshake in the boardroom.

* * * That is, the explosion of executive pay represents a social change rather than the purely economic forces of supply and demand. We should think of it not as a market trend like the rising value of waterfront property, but as something more like the sexual revolution of the 1960's—a relaxation of old strictures, a new permissiveness, but in this case the permissiveness is financial rather than sexual. * * *

How did this change in corporate culture happen? Economists and management theorists are only beginning to explore that question, but it's easy to suggest a few factors. One was the changing structure of financial markets. In his new book, "Searching for a Corporate Savior," Rakesh Khurana of Harvard Business School suggests that during the 1980's and 1990's, "managerial capitalism"—the world of the man in the gray flannel suit—was replaced by "investor capitalism." Institutional investors weren't willing to let a C.E.O. choose his own successor from inside the corporation; they wanted heroic leaders, often outsiders, and were willing to pay immense sums to get them. The subtitle of Khurana's book, by the way, is "The Irrational Quest for Charismatic C.E.O.'s"

* * *

Economists also did their bit to legitimize previously unthinkable levels of executive pay. During the 1980's and 1990's a torrent of academic papers—popularized in business magazines and incorporated into consultants' recommendations—argued that Gordon Gekko was right: greed is good; greed works. In order to get the best performance out of executives, these papers argued, it was necessary to align their interests with those of stockholders. And the way to do that was with large grants of stock or stock options.

* * *

What economists like Piketty and Saez are now suggesting is that the story of executive compensation is representative of a broader story. Much more than economists and free-market advocates like to imagine, wages—particularly at the top—are determined by social norms. What happened during the 1930's and 1940's was that new norms of equality were established, largely through the political process. What happened in the 1980's and 1990's was that those norms unraveled, replaced by an ethos of "anything goes." And a result was an explosion of income at the top of the scale.

IV. THE PRICE OF INEQUALITY

It was one of those revealing moments. Responding to an e-mail message from a Canadian viewer, Robert Novak of "Crossfire" delivered a little speech: "Marg, like most Canadians, you're ill informed and wrong. The U.S. has the longest standard of living—longest life expectancy of any country in the world, including Canada. That's the truth."

But it was Novak who had his facts wrong. Canadians can expect to live about two years longer than Americans. In fact, life expectancy in the U.S. is well below that in Canada, Japan and every major nation in Western Europe. On average, we can expect lives a bit shorter than those of Greeks, a bit longer than those of Portuguese. Male life expectancy is lower in the U.S. than it is in Costa Rica.

Still, you can understand why Novak assumed that we were No. 1. After all, we really are the richest major nation, with real G.D.P. per capita about 20 percent higher than Canada's. And it has been an article of faith in this country that a rising tide lifts all boats. Doesn't our high and rising national wealth translate into a high standard of living—including good medical care for all Americans?

Well, no. Although America has higher per capita income than other advanced countries, it turns out that that's mainly because our rich are much richer. And here's a radical thought: if the rich get more, that leaves less for everyone else.

That statement—which is simply a matter of arithmetic—is guaranteed to bring accusations of "class warfare." If the accuser gets more specific, he'll probably offer two reasons that it's foolish to make a fuss over the high incomes of a few people at the top of the income distribution. First, he'll tell you that what the elite get may look like a lot of money, but it's still a small share of the total—that is, when all is said and done the rich aren't getting that big a piece of the pie. Second, he'll tell you that trying to do anything to reduce incomes at the top will hurt, not help, people further down the distribution, because attempts to redistribute income damage incentives.

These arguments for lack of concern are plausible. And they were entirely correct, once upon a time—namely, back when we had a middle-class society. But there's a lot less truth to them now.

First, the share of the rich in total income is no longer trivial. These days 1 percent of families receive about 16 percent of total pretax income, and have about 14 percent of after-tax income. That share has roughly doubled over the past 30 years, and is now about as large as the share of the bottom 40 percent of the population. That's a big shift of income to the top; as a matter of pure arithmetic, it must mean that the incomes of less well off families grew considerably more slowly than average income. And they did. Adjusting for inflation, average family income—total income divided by the number of families—grew 28 percent from 1979 to 1997. But median family income—the income of a family in the middle of the distribution, a better indicator of how typical American families are doing—grew only 10 percent. And the incomes of the bottom fifth of families actually fell slightly.

Let me belabor this point for a bit. We pride ourselves, with considerable justification, on our record of economic growth. But over the last few decades it's remarkable how little of that growth has trickled down to ordinary families. Median family income has risen only about 0.5 percent per year—and as far as we can tell from somewhat unreliable data, just about all of that increase was due to wives working longer hours, with little or no gain in real wages. * * *

Still, many people will say that while the U.S. economic system may generate a lot of inequality, it also generates much higher incomes than any alternative, so that everyone is better off. That was the moral Business Week tried to convey in its recent special issue with "25 Ideas for a Changing World." One of those ideas was "the rich get richer, and that's O.K." High incomes at the top, the conventional wisdom declares, are the result of a free-market system that provides huge incentives for performance. And the system delivers that performance, which means that wealth at the top doesn't come at the expense of the rest of us.

A skeptic might point out that the explosion in executive compensation seems at best loosely related to actual performance. Jack Welch was one of the 10 highest-paid executives in the United States in 2000, and you could argue that he earned it. But did Dennis Kozlowski of Tyco, or Gerald Levin of Time Warner, who were also in the top 10? A skeptic might also point out that even during the economic boom of the late 1990's, U.S. productivity growth was no better than it was during the great postwar expansion, which corresponds to the era when America was truly middle class and C.E.O.'s were modestly paid technocrats.

* * *

Many Americans assume that because we are the richest country in the world, with real G.D.P. per capita higher than that of other major advanced countries, Americans must be better off across the board—that it's not just our rich who are richer than their counterparts abroad, but that the typical American family is much better off than the typical family elsewhere, and that even our poor are well off by foreign standards.

But it's not true. Let me use the example of Sweden, that great conservative bete noire.

A few months ago the conservative cyberpundit Glenn Reynolds made a splash when he pointed out that Sweden's G.D.P. per capita is roughly comparable with that of Mississippi—see, those foolish believers in the welfare state have impoverished themselves! Presumably he assumed that this means that the typical Swede is as poor as the typical resident of Mississippi, and therefore much worse off than the typical American.

But life expectancy in Sweden is about three years higher than that of the U.S. Infant mortality is half the U.S. level, and less than a third the rate in Mississippi. Functional illiteracy is much less common than in the U.S.

How is this possible? One answer is that G.D.P. per capita is in some ways a misleading measure. Swedes take longer vacations than Americans, so they work fewer hours per year. That's a choice, not a failure of economic performance. Real G.D.P. per hour worked is 16 percent lower than in the United States, which makes Swedish productivity about the same as Canada's.

But the main point is that though Sweden may have lower average income than the United States, that's mainly because our rich are so much richer. The median Swedish family has a standard of living roughly comparable with that of the median U.S. family: wages are if anything higher in Sweden, and a higher tax burden is offset by public provision of health care and generally better public services. And as you move further down the income distribution, Swedish living standards are way ahead of those in the U.S. Swedish families with children that are at the 10th percentile—poorer than 90 percent of the population—have incomes 60 percent higher than their U.S. counterparts. And very few people in Sweden experience the deep poverty that is all too common in the United States. One measure: in 1994 only 6 percent of Swedes lived on less than $11 per day, compared with 14 percent in the U.S.

The moral of this comparison is that even if you think that America's high levels of inequality are the price of our high level of national income, it's not at all clear that this price is worth paying. The reason conservatives engage in bouts of Sweden-bashing is that they want to convince us that there is no tradeoff between economic efficiency and equity—that if you try to take from the rich and give to the poor, you actually make everyone worse off. But the comparison between the U.S. and other advanced countries doesn't support this conclusion at all. * * *

And we might even offer a challenge from the other side: inequality in the United States has arguably reached levels where it is counterproductive. That is, you can make a case that our society would be richer if its richest members didn't get quite so much.

I could make this argument on historical grounds. The most impressive economic growth in U.S. history coincided with the middle-class interregnum, the post-World War II generation, when incomes were most evenly distributed. But let's focus on a specific case, the extraordinary pay packages of today's top executives. Are these good for the economy?

* * *

It's easy to get boggled by the details of corporate scandal—insider loans, stock options, special-purpose entities, mark-to-market, round-tripping. But there's a simple reason that the details are so complicated. All of these schemes were designed to benefit corporate insiders—to inflate the pay of the C.E.O. and his inner circle. That is, they were all about the "chaos of competitive avarice" that, according to John Kenneth Galbraith, had been ruled out in the corporation of the 1960's. But while all restraint has vanished within the American corporation, the outside world—including stockholders—is still prudish, and open looting by executives is still not acceptable. So the looting has to be camouflaged, taking place through complicated schemes that can be rationalized to outsiders as clever corporate strategies.

Economists who study crime tell us that crime is inefficient—that is, the costs of crime to the economy are much larger than the amount stolen. Crime, and the fear of crime, divert resources away from productive uses: criminals spend their time stealing rather than producing, and potential victims spend time and money trying to protect their property. Also, the things people do to avoid becoming victims—like avoiding dangerous districts—have a cost even if they succeed in averting an actual crime.

The same holds true of corporate malfeasance, whether or not it actually involves breaking the law. Executives who devote their time to creating innovative ways to divert shareholder money into their own pockets probably aren't running the real business very well (think Enron, WorldCom, Tyco, Global Crossing, Adelphia ...). Investments chosen because they create the illusion of profitability while insiders cash in their stock options are a waste of scarce resources. And if the supply of funds from lenders and shareholders dries up because of a lack of trust, the economy as a whole suffers. Just ask Indonesia.

* * *

VI. PLUTOCRACY?

* * *

D. WEALTH, CLASS AND ECONOMIC MOBILITY—THE INTERGENERATIONAL EFFECTS

America in the 1920's wasn't a feudal society. But it was a nation in which vast privilege—often inherited privilege—stood in contrast to vast misery. It was also a nation in which the government, more often than not, served the interests of the privileged and ignored the aspirations of ordinary people.

Those days are past—or are they? Income inequality in America has now returned to the levels of the 1920's. Inherited wealth doesn't yet play a big part in our society, but given time—and the repeal of the estate tax—we will grow ourselves a hereditary elite just as set apart from the concerns of ordinary Americans as old Horace Havemeyer. And the new elite, like the old, will have enormous political power.

Kevin Phillips concludes his book *Wealth and Democracy* with a grim warning: "Either democracy must be renewed, with politics brought back to life, or wealth is likely to cement a new and less democratic regime—plutocracy by some other name." It's a pretty extreme line, but we live in extreme times. Even if the forms of democracy remain, they may become meaningless. It's all too easy to see how we may become a country in which the big rewards are reserved for people with the right connections; in which ordinary people see little hope of advancement; in which political involvement seems pointless, because in the end the interests of the elite always get served.

Am I being too pessimistic? Even my liberal friends tell me not to worry, that our system has great resilience, that the center will hold. I hope they're right, but they may be looking in the rearview mirror. Our optimism about America, our belief that in the end our nation always finds its way, comes from the past—a past in which we were a middle-class society. But that was another country.

NOTES AND QUESTIONS

1. **Other factors influencing income inequality.** Besides intergenerational economic position, what are other factors that could explain income inequality in America?

2. **Intergenerational economic mobility: racial implications.** The above-cited study by Charles and Hurst portrays the strong correlation between individuals' parents' incomes and their own economic futures. Are such findings consistent for all demographic groups? In other words, are members of one ethnic or racial group more likely to break free of their parents' economic status than members of another demographic group?

American University professor of economics Tom Hertz encountered this question in a study of economic mobility. Using data compiled from the Panel Study of Income Dynamics, consisting of a sample of 6,723 black and white families observed over thirty two years and in two generations, Hertz found that African Americans are more likely to remain in lower income brackets than their white counterparts. The study revealed that blacks' rate of persistence at low-income levels was 42 percent, while their rate of persistence at high income levels was only 4 percent. On the other hand, for whites, the rate of persistence at the bottom was approximately half that at the top (17 percent versus 30 percent). Adjusted for age, the study revealed blacks' persistence to remain in a lower income bracket was 41 percent, while whites' persistence to remain at the bottom was 25 percent. Also, for white families, extreme upward mobility is more likely than downward mobility (14 percent versus 9 percent), but the reverse is true for blacks—blacks have a 35 percent chance of substantially sliding down the income scale, and only have a 4 percent chance of substantially moving up the scale. These findings all point to the conclusion that black families have a significantly lower rate of upward mobility from the bottom income bracket than do whites. Tom Hertz, *Rags, Riches and Race: The Intergenerational Mobility of Black and White Families in the United States*, under review for inclusion in: UNEQUAL CHANCES: FAMILY BACKGROUND AND ECONOMIC SUCCESS (Samuel Bowles, et al. eds., forthcoming).

What are the reasons for income differences among demographic groups?

- WEALTH INEQUALITY

Wealth and Inequality in America
BLACK WEALTH/WHITE WEALTH: A NEW PERSPECTIVE ON RACIAL INEQUALITY 53–90 (1997).

■ MELVIN L. OLIVER & THOMAS M. SHAPIRO

[A] thorough analysis of economic well-being and social and racial equality must include a wealth dimension. A lack of systematic, reliable data on wealth accumulation, however, partly explains the general absence of such an analysis until now. * * *

The bulk of our analysis and discussion of wealth is drawn from the Survey of Income and Program Participation. SIPP is a sample of the U.S. population that interviews adults in households periodically over a two-and-a-half-year period. A new panel is introduced every year. Data for this study came from the 1987 Panel. Household interviews began in June 1987, and the same households were reinterviewed every four months through 1989. The full data set of eight interviews was available for 11,257 households. * * *

What is wealth? How does one define it? What indicators of wealth are the best ones to use? Definitional and conceptual questions about wealth have produced a diverse and sometimes confusing set of approaches to the topic. Indeed, a major difficulty in analyzing wealth is that people define it in different ways with the result that wealth measures lack comparability. After working with the literature for several years, we decided to measure wealth by way of two concepts. The first, *net worth* (NW) conveys the straightforward value of all assets less any debts. The second, *net financial assets* (NFA), excludes equity accrued in a home or vehicle from the calculation of a household's available resources.

Net worth gives a comprehensive picture of all assets and debts; yet it may not be a reliable measure of *command over future resources* for one's self and family. Net worth includes equity in vehicles, for instance, and it is not likely that this equity will be converted into other resources, such as prep school for a family's children. Thus one's car is not a likely repository in which to store resources for future use. Likewise, viewing home equity as a reasonable and unambiguous source of future resources for the current generation raises many vexing problems. Most people do not sell their homes to finance a college education for their children, start a business, make other investments, buy medical care, support political candidates, or pay lobbyists to protect their special interests. Even if a family sells a home, the proceeds are typically used to lease or buy replacement housing. An exception to the general rule may involve the elderly. Mortgage payments, especially in times of high housing inflation, may be seen as a kind of "forced savings" to be cashed in at retirement or to pass along to one's children.

* * * The specific differences between net worth and net financial assets is that equity in vehicles and homes is excluded from the latter, although debts are subtracted from NFA. In contrast to net worth, net financial assets consists of more readily liquid sources of income and wealth that can be used for a family's immediate well-being. Because the distinction between net worth and net financial assets is somewhat controversial and still open to debate, we usually present both measures. Generally, in our view, however, net financial assets seem to be the best indicator of the current generation's command over future resources, while net worth provides a more accurate estimate of the wealth likely to be inherited by the next generation.

Let us now turn to the substantive questions at the heart of our study. How has wealth been distributed in American society over the twentieth century? What about the redistribution of wealth that took place in the decade of the eighties? And finally, what do the answers to these questions imply for black-white inequality?

The 1980s and Beyond Bigger Shares for the Wealthy

Available information concerning wealth in the twentieth century, until very recently, comes mainly from national estate-tax records for the very wealthy collected between 1922 and 1981, and from sporadic cross-sectional household surveys starting in 1953. Drawing from these data bases, we track trends in the distribution of wealth, paying particular attention to whether inequality is falling, remaining stable, or rising, into the late 1980s and early 1990s.

Estate-tax data show consistently high wealth concentrations throughout the early part of the twentieth century. According to Edward Wolff's "The Rich Get Increasingly Richer," the top 1 percent of American households possessed over 25 percent of total wealth between 1922 and 1972. Beginning in 1972, however, the data indicate a significant decline in wealth inequality. The share of the top percentile declined from 29 percent to 19 percent between 1972 and 1976. While this decline was unexpected, it was not permanent. In fact in the next five-year period, from 1976 to 1981, a sharp renewal of wealth inequality occurred. Between 1976 and 1981 the share of the richest 1 percent expanded from 19 to 24 percent.

The standard theory explaining wealth inequality associates the phenomenon with the process of industrialization. Stable, low levels of inequality characterize preindustrial times; the onset of modern economic growth is characterized by rapid industrialization, which ushers in a sharp increase in inequality; and then advanced, mature industrial societies experience a gradual leveling of inequality and finally long-term stability. This explanation highlights industrialization as a universal, master trend in the evolution of market economies. The twentieth century in particular is said to represent a clear pattern, specifically from 1929 on, when, according to Jeffrey Williamson's and Peter Lindert's *American Inequality*, wealth imbalance "seems to have undergone a permanent reduction." One must question the persistence of this reduced inequality into the 1990s, especially in light of growing income inequalities.

Estimates of household wealth inequality from two relatively consistent sources of household survey data, the 1962 Survey of Financial Characteristics of Consumers and the Surveys of Consumer Finances conducted in the 1980s, furnish more recent information. Responses to these surveys indicate that wealth inequality remained relatively fixed between 1962 and 1983. The top 3 percent of wealth holders held 32 percent of the wealth in 1962 and 34 percent in 1983. The Gini coefficient, which measures equality over an entire distribution rather than as shares of the top percentile, rose slightly, from 0.73 in 1962 to 0.74 in 1983. The Gini ratio is a statistic that converts levels of inequality into a single number and allows easy comparisons of populations. Gini figures range from 0 to 1. A low ratio indicates low levels of inequality; a high ratio indicates high levels of inequality. Thus Ginis closer to 0 illustrate more distributional equality, while figures closer to 1 indicate more inequality. While the Gini coefficient is a very useful summary measure of inequality, it is probably most helpful and meaningful as a way of comparing distributions of wealth between time periods, given its sensitivity to small changes and its clear indication of the direction of change.

What happened during the 1980s? Quite simply, the very rich increased their share of the nation's wealth. One leading economist dubbed the resulting wealth imbalance an "unprecedented jump in inequality to Great Gatsby levels." Notably, inequality had risen very sharply by 1989, with the wealthiest 1 percent of households owning 37.7 percent of net worth. An examination of net financial assets suggests even greater levels of inequality. In 1983 the top 1 percent held 42.8 percent of all financial assets, a figure that increased to 48.2 percent in 1989. The Gini coefficient reflects this increase in inequality, rising 0.04 during the period. Wealth inequality by the end of the 1980s closely approximated historically high levels not seen since 1922.

Our review of other wealth indicators and studies corroborates the finding that wealth is reconcentrating. It also goes a way toward revealing the relationship between trends toward wealth concentration and growing inequality and [a] lower standard of living * * *. The evidence presented by Edward Wolff in "The Rich Get Increasingly Richer" and by others using [Survey of Consumer Finances] data suggests that while the concentration of wealth decreased substantially during the mid–1970s, it increased sharply during the 1980s. In particular the *mean* net worth of families grew by over 7 percent from 1983 to 1989. However, *median* net worth grew much more slowly than mean wealth, at a rate of 0.8 percent. According to Wolff, this discrepancy "implies that the upper-wealth classes enjoyed a disproportionate share [of wealth]" between 1983 and 1989. Wolff's median net financial assets declined 3.7 percent during this period. Thus the typical family disposed of fewer liquid resources in 1989 than in 1983. In stark contrast, the wealth of the "superrich," defined as the top one-half of 1 percent of wealth-holders, increased 26 percent from 1983 to 1989. Over one-half (55 percent) of the wealth created between 1983 and 1989 accrued to the richest one-half of one percent of families, a fact that vividly illustrates the magnitude of the 1980s increase in their share of the country's wealth. Not surprisingly, the Gini coefficient increased sizably during this period, from 0.80 to 0.84. Indeed, U.S. wealth concentration in 1989 was more extreme than at any time since 1929.

SIPP as well as SCF data confirm that the wealth pie is being resliced, and that the wealthy are getting larger pieces of it. In a 1994 update on its ongoing SIPP study, the Census Bureau reports that the median net worth of the nation's households dropped 12 percent between 1988 and 1991. The drop in median wealth is associated with a sharp decline in the middle classes' largest share of net worth: home equity. The median home equity declined by 14 percent between 1988 and 1991 as real estate values fell.

The trends of increasing income and wealth inequality have disrupted long-standing post-World War II patterns. The movement toward income equality and stability expired by the mid–1970s, while the trend toward wealth equality extended into the early 1980s. By 1983 wealth inequality began to rise. The time lag in these reversals is important. Along with declining incomes, a growth in debt burden, and fluctuations in housing values and stock prices, the actions of government—and the Reagan tax cuts of the early 1980s—can only be viewed as prime causes of the increase in wealth inequality.

How has this redistribution of wealth in favor of the rich affected the middle class? Examining wealth groups by ranking all families into wealth fifths provides one way to get at this question. The average holdings of the lower-middle and bottom wealth groups (fifths) declined in real terms by 30 percent. The wealth of the middle group remained unchanged, while that of the upper-middle group increased by slightly less than 1 percent a year. The average wealth of the top group increased by over 10 percent. Combining this with previous information showing a decline in median net financial assets strengthens the argument that the economic base of middle-class life is becoming increasingly fragile and tenuous.

During the 1980s the rich got much richer, and the poor and middle classes fell further behind. One obvious culprit was the Reagan tax cuts. These cuts provided greater discretionary income for middle-and upper-class taxpayers. However, most middle-class taxpayers used this discretionary income to bolster their declining standards of living or decrease their debt burden instead of saving or investing it. Although Reagan strategists had intended to stimulate investment, the upper classes embarked on a frenzy of consumer spending on luxury items. Wolff's "The Rich Get Increasingly Richer" explains the redistribution of wealth in favor of the rich during the 1980s as resulting more from capital gains reaped on existing wealth than from increased savings and investment. He attributes 70 percent of the growth in wealth over the 1983–1989 period to the appreciation of existing financial assets and the remaining 30 percent to the creation of wealth from personal savings. Led by rapid gains in stocks, financial securities, and liquid assets, existing investments grew at an impressive rate at a time when it was difficult to convert earnings into personal savings.

One asset whose value grew dramatically during the eighties was real estate. Home ownership is central to the average American's wealth portfolio. Housing equity makes up the largest part of wealth held by the middle class, whereas the upper class and wealthy more commonly own a greater degree of their wealth in financial assets. The percentage of families owning homes peaked in the mid–1970s at 65 percent and has subsequently declined by a point or two. Forty-three percent of blacks own homes, a rate 65 percent lower than that of whites. Housing equity constitutes the most substantial portion of all wealth assets by far. SIPP results clearly demonstrate this assertion: housing equity represented 43 percent of median household assets in 1988. It is even more significant, however, in the wealth portfolios of blacks than of whites, accounting for 43.3 percent of white wealth and 62.5 percent of black assets. This initial glance at the role of housing in overall wealth carries ramifications for subsequent in-depth analysis. Thus, owning a house—a hallmark of the American Dream—is becoming harder and harder for average Americans to afford, and fewer are able to do so. The ensuing analysis of racial differences in wealth requires a thorough investigation of racial dynamics in access to housing, mortgage and housing markets, and housing values.

The eighties ushered in a new era of wealth inequality in which strong gains were made by those who already had substantial financial assets. Those who had a piece of the rock, especially those with financial assets, but also those with real estate, increased their wealth holdings and consolidated a sense of economic security for themselves and their families.

Others, a disproportionate share of them black, saw their financial status improve only slightly or decline.

In *Warm Hearts and Cold Cash* Marcia Millman notes that for most of this century, the primary legacy of middle-class parents to children has been "cultural" capital, that is, the upbringing, education, and contacts that allowed children to get a good start in life and to become financially successful and independent. Now some parents have more to bestow than cultural capital. In particular, middle-class Americans who started rearing families after World War II have amassed a huge amount of money in the value of their homes and stocks that they are now in the process of dispatching to the baby boom generation through inheritances, loans, and gifts. Millman says this money is "enormously consequential in shaping the lives of their adult children."

Much of this wealth was built by their parents between the late 1940s and the late 1960s when real wages and saving rates were higher and housing costs were considerably lower. For the elderly middle class, the escalation of real estate prices over the last twenty years has been a significant boon. * * *

Access to Assets

The potential for assets to expand or inhibit choices, horizons, and opportunities for children emerged as the most consistent and strongest common theme in our interviews. Since parents want to invest in their children, to give them whatever advantages they can, we wondered about the ability of the average American household to expend assets on their children. This section thus delves deeper into the assets households command by (1) considering the importance of home and vehicle equity in relation to other kinds of assets; (2) inspecting available financial assets for various groups of the population; and (3) looking at children growing up in resource-deficient households. We found a strong relationship between the amount of wealth and the composition of assets. Households with large amounts of total net worth control wealth portfolios composed mostly of financial assets. Financial investments make up about four-fifths of the assets of the richest households. Conversely, home and vehicle equity represents over 70 percent of the asset portfolio among the poorest one-fifth of American households, one in three of which possesses zero or negative financial assets.

Table 4.5 reports households with zero or negative net financial assets for various racial, age, education, and family groups. It shows that one-quarter of white households, 61 percent of black households, and 54 percent of Hispanic households are without financial resources. A similar absence of financial assets affects nearly one-half of young households; circumstances steadily improve with age, however, leaving only 15 percent of those households headed by seniors in a state of resource deficiency. The educational achievement of householders also connects directly with access to resources, as 40 percent of poorly educated household heads control no financial assets while over 80 percent of households headed by a college graduate control some NFA. Findings reported in this table also demonstrate deeply embedded disparities in resource command between single and married-couple parents. Resource deprivation characterizes 62 percent of single-parent households in comparison to 37 percent of married couples raising children.

TABLE 4.5 Who is on the Edge?

	Households with 0 or Negative NFA*	Households without NFA* for 3 months**	Households without NFA* for 6 months**
Sample	31.0%	44.9%	49.9%
Race			
White	25.3	38.1	43.2
Black	60.9	78.9	83.1
Hispanic	54.0	72.5	77.2
Age of Householder			
15–35	48.0	67.0	72.8
36–49	31.7	45.0	50.7
50–64	22.1	32.0	36.2
65 or older	15.1	26.4	30.6
Education			
Less than high school	40.3	55.5	60.0
High school degree	32.2	48.0	63.2
Some college	29.9	45.3	61.4
College degree	18.9	26.8	31.2
Family Type* * *			
Single parent	61.9	79.2	83.2
Married Couple	36.9	53.8	59.9

* Net financial worth
** NFA reserves to survive at the poverty line of $968 per month
*** Includes only households with children

Besides looking at resource deprivation, table 4.5 also sets criteria for "precarious-resource" circumstances. Households without enough NFA reserves to survive three months at the poverty line ($2,904) meet these criteria. Nearly 80 percent of single-parent households fit this description. Likewise 38 percent of white households and 79 percent of black households live in precarious-resource circumstances.

Among our interviewees, parents with ample assets planned to use them to create a better world for their children. Those without them strategized about acquiring some and talked about their "wish list." Parents talked about ballet lessons, camp, trips for cultural enrichment or even to Disney World, staying home more often with the children, affording full-time day care, allowing a parent to be home after day care. The parents discussed using assets to provide better educational opportunities for their children. Kevin takes great pride in paying for his son's college and being able to offer him advanced training. Stacie wants to be able to afford private school for Carrie. Ed and Alicia told us about the private school choices and dilemmas facing their children.

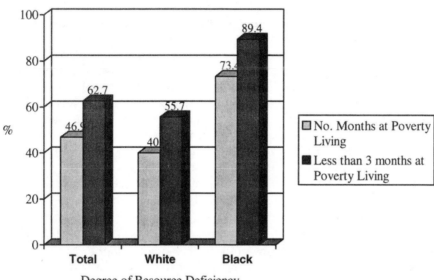

FIGURE 4.2 Percent of Children in Resource-Deficient Households, by Race

Figure 4.2 looks at the percentage of children in resource-poor households by race. It provides information both on households with no net financial assets and on those with just enough assets to survive above the poverty line for at least three months. Close to one-half of all children live in households with no financial assets and 63 percent live in households with precarious resources, scarcely enough NFA to cushion three months of interrupted income.

A further analysis of this already disturbing data discloses imposing and powerful racial and ethnic cleavages. For example, 40 percent of all white children grow up in households without financial resources in comparison to 73 percent of all black children. Most telling of all perhaps, only 11 percent of black children grow up in households with enough net financial assets to weather three months of no income at the poverty level. Three times as many white kids live in such households.

According to Richard Steckel and Jayanthi Krishnan, cross-sectional measures of wealth acquisition and inequality may disguise underlying changes in wealth status. Analyzing surveys from 1966 and 1976, Steckel and Krishnan found that changes in marital status were associated with changes in wealth. The largest increase in wealth occurred for single women who later married. Other groups who experienced increases in wealth included households headed by the young, those with at least twelve years of schooling, and individuals who married. The greatest loss in wealth occurred among households headed by older individuals, single men, and those experiencing marital disruption.

SUMMARY

Financial wealth is the buried fault line of the American social system. The wealth distribution portrait drawn in this chapter has disclosed the existence of highly concentrated wealth at the top; a pattern of steep resource inequality; the disproportionate asset reserves held by various demographic groups; the precarious economic foundation of middle-class life; and how few financial assets most American households can call upon. This chapter has also provided documentation concerning the relationship between income inequality and wealth inequality. At one level, income makes up the largest component of potential wealth. At the same time, however, distinctive patterns of income and wealth inequality exist. Put another way, substituting what is known about income inequality for what is not known about wealth inequality limits, and even biases, our understanding of inequality. A thorough understanding of inequality must therefore pay more attention to resources than has been paid in the past.

Perhaps no single piece of information conveys the sense of fragility common to those on the lowest rungs of the economic ladder as the proportion of children who grow up in households without assets. Reducing all life's chances for success to economic circumstances no doubt overlooks much, but resources nonetheless provide an accurate measure of differential access to educational, career, health, cultural, and social opportunities. In poignantly reciting the hopes they have for their children, parents recognize the importance of resources. Our interviews show how parents use assets to bring these hopes to life, or wish they had ample assets so they could bring them to life. Nearly three-quarters of all black children, 1.8 times the rate for whites, grow up in households possessing no financial assets. Nine in ten black children come of age in households that lack sufficient financial reserves to endure three months of no income at the poverty line, about four times the rate for whites.

NOTES AND QUESTIONS

1. Some data on poverty rates. During the era of Gunnar Myrdal's classic study of American society, *An American Dilemma*, the majority of African Americans in the United States lived in the South; white supremacy relegated blacks to an inferior socioeconomic status; and social, political, and economic opportunity for African Americans was virtually non-existent. Ronald F. Ferguson, *Shifting Challenges: Fifty Years of Economic Change Toward Black-White Earnings Equality*, in AN AMERICAN DILEMMA REVISITED: RACE RELATIONS IN A CHANGING WORLD 76 (Obie Clayton, Jr. ed., 1996). Though almost sixty years have passed since Myrdal's commentary on the socioeconomic status of African Americans during the period between the Great Depression and World War II, grave economic inequalities continue to plague minorities, maintaining a systematic socioeconomic hierarchy in society. *Id.,* at xxiii.

Sociologists Melvin L. Oliver and Thomas M. Shapiro conclude that several variables account for wealth differences among racial and ethnic communities, including geographic region, educational attainment, the number of workers in the household, marital status, gender, and age.[16] As we have just discussed, intergenerational wealth effects are stronger than was once thought to be the case. For the poor this economic and social immobility creates brutal traps in a world of disadvantage. A study by Thomas Hertz of American University found that a child born to a family in the bottom 10 percent income bracket has a 31 percent chance of remaining in that same caste as an adult and a 51 percent chance of moving into the bottom 20 percent. However, a child born in the top 10 percent has a 30 percent chance of remaining in that income bracket and a 43 percent chance of moving into the top 20 percent.[17]

Hidden Cost of Being African American

HIDDEN COST OF BEING AFRICAN AMERICAN 141 (2004).

■ THOMAS M. SHAPIRO

In the 20 largest metropolitan areas, where 36 percent of all African Americans live, segregation pervades basic dimensions of community life. The residential color line means that blacks have greater difficulty overcoming problems associated with poor communities, especially crime, violence, housing abandonment, unstable families, poorer health and higher mortality, environmental degradation, and failing schools. No other group experiences segregation to the extent that blacks do. In many geographical areas, two decades of rising income inequality and budget cuts have produced a concentration of poverty that further compounds problems of segregation. Poor black neighborhoods are crowded, highly concentrated, and isolated far more severely than neighborhoods where poor whites, Latinos, or Asians live.

---

16. MELVIN L. OLIVER & THOMAS M. SHAPIRO, *Wealth and Inequality, in* BLACK WEALTH/ WHITE WEALTH: A NEW PERSPECTIVE ON RACIAL INEQUALITY 67–90 (1997).

17. Alan B. Krueger, *Economic Scene; The Apple Falls Close to the Tree, Even in the Land of Opportunity,* N.Y. TIMES, Nov. 14, 2002, at C1.

TABLE 2.2.

1984 Residence	1994 Residence			
	Predominately White Area	Racially Mixed Area	Predominately Black Area	TOTAL
WHITE FAMILIES				
Predominately White Area	95.6%	4.4%	-	100.0% (456)
Racially Mixed Area	40.2%	58.8%	1.0%	100.0% (97)
Predominately Black Area	-	-	-	100.0%
TOTAL	85.9% (475)	13.9% (77)	0.2% (1)	100.0% (553)
BLACK FAMILIES				
Predominately White Area	66.7%	33.3%	-	100.0% (21)
Racially Mixed Area	6.5%	79.0%	14.5%	100.0% (214)
Predominately Black Area	8.5%	56.4%	66.3%	100.0% (166)
TOTAL	8.5% (34)	56.4% (226)	35.2% (141)	100% (401)

SOURCE: *Id.* at 138.

Sheryll Cashin argues that "housing [is] the last plank in the civil rights revolution ... [s]egregated residential housing contributes to pervasive inequality in this country."[18]

The Price of Segregation—Unconventional Wisdom: New Facts From the Social Sciences
WASH. POST, Dec. 28, 1997, at C5.

■ RICHARD MORIN

THE PRICE OF SEGREGATION

FOR SALE: Three-bedroom, two-bath ranch-style house. Near good schools and good neighbors. Low taxes, low crime. Located in a white neighborhood.

How much would you pay for this house? If you're white, a new study of housing prices suggests that you'll pay, on average, about 13 percent more than if the same house were located in a racially integrated part of town.

That's the premium that whites appear to be willing to pay to live in the typical segregated white neighborhood, say Harvard economists David Cutler, Edward Glaeser and Jacob Vigdor.

And it's this extra cost that's now primarily either responsible for keeping America's neighborhoods predominantly black or white decades after legal segregation officially ended, Cutler argues.

---

18. SHERYLL CASHIN, THE FAILURES OF INTEGRATION: HOW RACE AND CLASS ARE UNDERMINING THE AMERICAN DREAM 3 (2004) infra at 484.

To measure just how much whites will pay to live in white neighborhoods, Cutler and his colleagues collected a mountain of data on every neighborhood in three American cities: Cleveland, Atlanta and Sacramento. They selected these cities because they were "representative of the urban experience of the past century." The information they gathered included Census data, neighborhood characteristics and federal reports on housing prices back to 1940, the first year such information was collected.

They found that the whiter the neighborhood, the higher the housing prices. "We can say that the premium that a white pays in a segregated city (such as Cleveland) in 1990 is 18 percent, while the premium that a white pays in a relatively integrated city (such as Sacramento) in 1990 is 12 percent," Glaeser said.

These researchers also said [they] were able to track the shifting patterns of residential segregation, from a system enforced by laws to one sustained by market forces.

Through the 1950s, segregation was enforced by law and the "collective actions taken by whites to exclude blacks from their neighborhoods."

Real estate covenants written into deeds in some neighborhoods barred homeowners from selling or renting to blacks (or Jews or sometimes even unmarried people). When laws and covenants didn't work, Cutler said "whites took bats, broke some windows and threw things at the house to run off black families who dared to move into white neighborhoods, as well as to warn other African–Americans to stay out. You can't do that any more."

Now, Cutler said it's sticker shock that is keeping many African-Americans out.

The Failures of Integration, How Race and Class are Undermining the American Dream
Public Affairs, New York, at 4 (2004).

■ SHERYLL CASHIN

"Housing—where we live—is fundamental in explaining American separatism. Housing was the last plank in the civil rights revolution, it is the realm in which we have experienced the fewest integration gains. When it comes to integration, housing is also the realm in which Americans most seem to agree that separation is acceptable. We may accept, even desire, integrated workplaces and integrated public spheres. But when it come to our private life space, more visceral personal needs of comfort and security take precedence-especially for families with children. In this context, for many, integration is simply irrelevant or perceived as a threat to more fundamental concerns...."

"How do you decide where to live? Eleven years ago, I bought a lovely bungalow in Shepherd Park, in integrated, albeit a majority-black, upper-middle-class neighborhood in the northwest quadrant of Washington, D.C. My goal at the time was to acquire a house in the best and safest neighborhood I could afford. The race or class of my would-be neighbors was not at the forefront of my thinking. But many communities were beyond consideration. As a committed urbanite and a hater of traffic living outside the Beltway was out of the question. As a black woman with a strong racial identity, I found the overwhelmingly white neighborhoods west of Rock Creek Park, such as Georgetown, American University Park, and Bethesda, inherently unattractive. I was not prepared, even if investment wisdom counseled otherwise, to make the profound personal sacrifice of living totally among 'others' with who I could not identify and who likely could not identify with me. Implicit in my choice about where to live was the understanding that I wanted to be among more than just a smattering of black people. If I had been forced to describe my ideal neighborhood, I suppose I would have said it was an integrated one."

NOTES AND QUESTIONS

1. Note on wealth and income inequalities. Why do parents and children have similar wealth? Availability of economic resources accounts for some of the correlation, but Charles and Hurst conclude spending patterns and comparable portfolio investment decisions between parents and their children have a considerable impact on the relationship between parents' wealth and their offspring's. They argue that when parents make investment choices, they set an example for their children to follow. For example, a mother who owns a company can advise her children on the tools necessary to succeed in running an enterprise and may pass on the company to her children. In addition, a wealthy parent may allow his children to take on investment decisions, such as stock ownership early in life. Kerwin Kofi Charles & Erik Hurst, *The Correlation of Wealth Across Generations* (National Bureau of Economic Research (NBER), Working Paper 9314, Oct. 2002), *at* http://www.nber.org/papers/w9314. *See also* DALTON CONLEY, THE PECKING ORDER: WHICH SIBLINGS SUCCEED AND WHY (2004).

Can Charles and Hurst's conclusion be extended to a large demographic group? For example, is it possible for children to learn about and mimic spending patterns and investment decisions, from not only their parents, but also from members of their own ethnic community? The Federal Reserve Board issued a Survey of Consumer Finances in 1998, reporting that the net wealth of the typical African American household was $15,500 that year; this figure is less than one-quarter that of the net wealth of the typical American household (including blacks)—$71,000. The study also revealed considerable differences in self-reported financial behavior between African American families and all families about investments, spending and income, savings tendencies, and risk aversion. Black households are much more likely than all households to have a shorter fiscal planning perspective, spend more rather than less of their earnings, not save and not save consistently, and be less willing to take monetary risks when saving or investing.

Is it possible for African Americans to persistently remain in the lower wealth brackets because members of the black community share similar ill-advised spending behaviors? Other factors influence the difference in wealth between black families and other families; for example, fewer African American households reported having received an inheritance, and black inheritors reported receiving lower bequests. Stephen Brobeck, Executive Director of the Consumer Federation of America, believes financial education is needed to aid the black community in revamping their financial behavior in order to increase wealth. However, he maintains that financial education should be shaped to meet the cultural needs of the African–American community:

> [F]inancial education needs to recognize important ethnic and cultural differences. Obviously, this education can be most effective if it uses language with which targeted populations are comfortable. But it also may be more effective if the education appeals to unique ethnic identities. For example, a Black American Saves initiative may well have more appeal to African Americans than does a more generalized America Saves initiative. Stephen Brobeck, *Black American Personal Wealth: Current Status* (Consumer Federation of America, Aug. 2002), at http://www.americasaves.org/back_page/BlackWealthReport082902.doc.

A recent study, "The Lives and Times of the Baby Boomers" by Duke sociology professors Angela M. O'Rand and Mary Elizabeth Hughes, suggests that the children of African American "baby boomers" are not doing as well as their parents. *See* Darryl Fears, *Black Baby Boomers' Income Gap Cited; Study Says That, Economically, Generation Has Not Improved Over Its Parents'*, WASH. POST, Dec. 17, 2004, at A02.

2. Wealth distribution and residential segregation. Though segregation is no longer enforced by explicitly racist laws, residential segregation is still prevalent. Due to the stark differences in wealth among racial groups, richer white families live in more affluent areas, while poorer minorities often live in meager surroundings. Though this proposition logically makes sense, it fails to consider other implications, like the dependency of housing prices on the racial makeup of the neighborhood. Harvard economists David Cutlen, Edward Glaeser, and Jacob Vigdor performed a study in 1997 and found that on average a white individual is willing to pay thirteen percent more for a house not located in a racially integrated part of town. The study intimated that because whites are willing to pay a premium to live in the typical segregated white neighborhood, housing prices are higher in white areas. In turn, residential segregation continues to prevail, standing as a clear reminder that socioeconomic inequalities based on background still exist.

3. College admissions. Educational attainment is one variable that aids in determining an individual's socioeconomic position in American society. For this reason, the prominence of one's college background plays an influential role in developing cultural capital. Parents invest tremendous amounts of time and resources in preparing their children for college by sending them to prestigious secondary schools, hoping their children's academic excellence will ensure them a prosperous lifestyle in the future.

One impressive institution, the Groton School in Massachusetts, sends countless students to prestigious colleges and universities each year. One would assume that remarkable achievement at such a school would ensure successful results in the college admissions process. However, in a society where familial status and networking are significant factors in attaining success, scholastic honors do not always guarantee a ticket to a top university. Several affluent children of universities' alumni and celebrities often have lower academic scores and still have the opportunity to study at the nation's top colleges. These students have what college admissions officers call a "hook"—criteria for preferential treatment. Henry Park, a 1998 graduate of Groton, had no "hook" to get accepted to several leading institutions. Park's parents, middleclass Korean immigrants from New Jersey, went to college in Korea and sacrificed their finances to pay Groton's $33,000 per year tuition and room and board. However, Mr. Park was ranked fourteenth in his class, earned a 1560 on his SAT, and demonstrated mathematical prowess. How do schools like those that rejected Mr. Park—Harvard, Yale, Brown, and Columbia—justify their choices in admitting less qualified students? Some assert that favoring children of alumni and prospective donors helps to ensure the growth of their institutions through the funding of scholarships, faculty salaries, and other projects by alumni parents. They further contend that children of celebrities "enhance an institution's visibility." Daniel Golden, *For Groton Grads, Academics Aren't Only Keys to Ivy Schools*, WALL ST. J., Apr. 25, 2003, at A1.

The college admissions process has serious implications for low-income and minority students. Considering most prestigious universities have relatively few minority alumni and low-income families do not have the means to contribute to colleges, many promising students are excluded from the elite academic realm. Consequently, they will attend less prestigious schools and have trouble attaining prominent occupations in the job market. In turn, these students will fail to pass to their children the capital necessary to succeed and the socioeconomic caste in society will endure through time. Economic distribution will continue to dwindle and wealth inequalities will consistently prevail.

Is it unjust for colleges to use legacy or donation criteria in deciding to offer a student admission? Some deem that the legacy preference unfairly favors wealthy applicants:

> The reason for the legacy preference appears to be primarily economic. Harvard and Yale, along with many other academic institutions, argue that the financial support provided by alumni is critical to their fiscal health. The assumption is that alumni will stop donating to fundraising campaigns if colleges reject their children. If economics were the primary basis for admission, however, why should the wealthiest applicants always not be accepted over all others? The very purpose of a need-blind admissions policy as expounded by both Harvard and Yale is to admit students regardless of their ability to pay or their financial background. Yet by preferring legacies over other applicants based

upon economic reasons, both schools are admitting that the financial resources of an applicant's family do matter. Thus, need-blind admissions are a misnomer, for economic considerations apparently are of great importance in the admissions process. John D. Lamb, *The Real Affirmative Action Babies: Legacy Preferences at Harvard and Yale*, 26 COLUM. J.L. & SOC. PROBS. 491, 517–18 (1993).

Do you agree with Lamb that admissions are not truly need-blind because admissions officers take financial issues into account when evaluating applications?

Are the legacy preferences unconstitutional? Can students like Mr. Park bring an equal protection claim against schools like Harvard and Yale for denying them admission and admitting lesser qualified students whose parents donated a gymnasium to the institution? Though no cases address the legitimacy of a private institution's admissions preference for children of alumni, a North Carolina court upheld a preference for out-of-state legacies at the University of North Carolina at Chapel Hill. There, the plaintiff asserted that she was denied equal protection when the school rejected her while accepting legacies and in-state applicants. Because the plaintiff was not part of a suspect class and no fundamental criteria were involved, the state was only required to show a rational basis for its preferential treatment. The court held that because out-of-state alumni offer considerable financial support for the school, the university's preferential treatment was a rational basis and not unconstitutional. *Rosenstock v. Governors of Univ. of N.C.*, 423 F.Supp. 1321, 1322–27 (M.D.N.C. 1976).

4. Estate tax. The estate tax, also referred to by opponents as the death tax, is a means of limiting the impact of intergenerational transmission of wealth and redistributing wealth through government spending. Only about 2 percent of deaths result in estate tax liability due to exemptions and other provisions, and the average estate paid taxes of 17 percent. Iris J. Lay & Joel Friedman, *Estate Tax Repeal: A Costly Windfall for the Wealthiest Americans* (Center on Budget and Policy Priorities, rev. Feb. 6, 2001), *available at* http://www.cbpp.org/5-25-00tax.htm.

People in the highest 20 percent of the income distribution at the time of their death pay 99 percent of estate taxes. And 91 percent of decedents had annual incomes over $190,000. *Id.* Opponents to the estate tax claim that farms and small businesses bear the weight of the tax, but these estates in fact make up a small proportion of taxable estates and could be given additional relief without repealing the entire estate tax. *Id.* The complete repeal of the estate tax will cost the government about $60 billion annually; the wealthiest people in the country would receive windfalls, often in the millions of dollars; and income such as unrealized capital gains would never be taxed. *Id.*

Despite the potentially devastating effects, there is bipartisan political support for repealing the estate tax. The Economic Growth and Tax Relief Reconciliation Act of 2001 phases out the estate tax between 2002 and 2009, but it includes a sunset provision that would reinstate the estate tax in 2011 unless further legislation extends the repeal. Agnes C. Powell, *Hocus-Pocus: The Federal Estate Tax—Now You See It, Now You Don't*, Nat'l Bus. Ass'n Mag. 21 (Oct. 2001).

The repeal of the estate tax would greatly increase the intergenerational transmission of wealth, further restraining economic mobility, and leading to cutbacks of government funded programs. What could prevent further legislation limiting redistribution of wealth? What alternative means of wealth redistribution could close the economic gap between rich and poor, and between black and white?

5. **Race and taxes.** Thomas and Mary Edsall argue in *Chain Reaction: The Impact of Race, Rights and Taxes on American Politics* that political party voting alignment with regards to tax policy is linked to issues of race. Specifically, they contend that "race has become a powerful wedge, breaking up what had been the majoritarian economic interests of the poor, working, and lower-middle classes in the traditional liberal coalition." Thomas Byrne Edsall & Mary D. Edsall, Chain Reaction: The Impact of Race, Rights and Taxes on American Politics 4 (1991). The general polarization between the two parties that has taken place on issues of race has been reflected in the fashioning of a "Republican populism" in which conservative politicians have devised a strategy "to persuade working and lower-middle class voters to join an alliance with business interests and the affluent." *id.* at 13. Central to this strategy has been opposition to programs designed to benefit racial minorities, such as busing and affirmative action, along with a commitment to reduced spending and curtailed government programs, and rejection of welfare and social programs which have been portrayed as benefiting minorities to the detriment of working-class whites. *Id.* at 13–19. The Edsalls detect a new definition of taxes, in which they are not understood as resources for the funding of government, but rather as a hand-out from those who work to those who do not, the latter group implicitly being racial minorities. *id.* at 214. *See also*, Woojin Lee & John Roemer, *Racism and Redistribution in the United States: A Solution to the Problem of American Exceptionalism*, Cowles Foundation for Research in Economics, Discussion Paper No. 1462 (2004).

In a progressive tax system, tax burdens rise with incomes. Dana Milbank & Jonathan Weisman, *Middle Class Tax Shares Set to Rise: Studies Say Burden of Rich to Decline*, Wash. Post, Jun. 4, 2003, at A1. Although progressivity is evident in much of the tax system, cuts on dividends, capital gains, and estate taxes lower the burden on the wealthiest Americans, actually increasing the burden on the middle class. *Id.* How will the tax cuts affect economic equality? Will those households identified by Oliver and Shapiro as "on the edge," and therefore least equipped to handle the economic downturn, benefit from the tax cuts? Is a progressive tax system fair, or should the poor and wealthy contribute comparable portions of their income?

6. **Financial behavior.** A thriving couple in *Wealth and Inequality in America* credited their financial success to the values instilled in them by their families. Could differences in financial behaviors (such as financial

planning horizons, spending compared to income, saving habits, and financial risk taking in investments) explain the wealth disparities between African Americans and other Americans? Stephen Brobeck, *Black American Personal Wealth: Current Status* (Consumer Federation of America, Aug. 2002), *available at* http://www.americasaves.org/back_page/Black-WealthReport082902.doc. According to the Consumer Federation of America, differences in financial behaviors between black Americans and all other Americans "virtually disappear" when comparing similar wealth levels. *Id.* Discrepancies in financial behavior between African Americans and the nation as a whole can be attributed to the concentration of wealth-poor people—45 percent of black Americans compared with 25 percent of all Americans. While education efforts should continue to recognize ethnic and cultural differences, effective financial education should focus on the behavior of the wealth-poor. *Id.*

Your Stake in America
41 Ariz. L. Rev. 249 (1999).

■ Bruce Ackerman & Anne Alstott

America has become a three-class society. More than twenty-five percent of its children now graduate from a four-year college and move into the ranks of the symbol-using class. Their increasing prosperity stands in sharp contrast to the grim picture of life at the bottom. The lowest twenty percent inhabit a world of low wages, dead-end jobs, and high unemployment despite the economic boom.

Then there is the vast majority. Over the past quarter century, they have endured a long period of economic stagnation. Despite optimistic rhetoric from the right, economic growth has bypassed these forgotten Americans. The richest twenty percent has captured virtually all of the growth in the nation's wealth since the early 1980s. While income trends have been somewhat less extreme, family income for the vast middle is only modestly higher than in 1973. Even treading water has been tough. Real wages for men have declined by nearly fifteen percent, and it is only the massive entry by women into the workplace that has taken up the slack.

Trickle-down economics has utterly failed and will continue to fail in the globalizing economy of the future. The past is prologue: By 1995, the top one percent owned 38.5% of the nation's disposable wealth, up from 33.8% in 1983. During the 1990s, the share of total income earned by the top twenty percent has risen to its highest point since 1947.

Our politics has not caught up with this three-class reality. On the one hand, we heap large subsidies on the college-bound. On the other, we target the underclass with diminishing amounts of assistance. However, we have done little to aid the vast middle. While the rich have been showered with tax breaks, the middle has been treated to a series of symbolic gestures signifying nothing. The 1997 "middle-class tax cut" hid a darker agenda.

The average family took home a few hundred dollars in new tax credits for children and education, but the rich gained thousands of dollars from the capital gains tax cut and other goodies.

The result is simmering resentment and a ready reception of the protectionist nostrums of Ross Perot and Pat Buchanan. The current boom will hold these economic nationalists in check for a while, but it is past time to search for a more constructive response to economic inequality. How can we use the benefits of globalization to ensure that every American gets a fair start in life?

This is the question we set for ourselves in our new book The Stakeholder Society. Stakeholding seeks justice by rooting it in capitalism's preeminent value: the importance of private property. It points the way to a society that is more democratic, more productive, and more free. Bear with us, and you will see how a single innovation once proposed by Tom Paine can achieve what a thousand lesser policies have failed to accomplish.

The basic proposal is straightforward. As young Americans rise to maturity, they should claim a stake of $80,000 as part of their birthright as citizens. This stake should be financed by an annual wealth tax, equal to two percent of every individual's wealth in excess of $80,000. The tie between wealth-holding and stake-holding expresses a fundamental social responsibility. Every American has an obligation to contribute to a fair starting point for all.

Stakeholders are free. They may use their money for any purpose they see fit: to start a business or pay for higher education, to buy a house or raise a family or save for the future. But they must take responsibility for their choices. Their triumphs and blunders are their own.

At the end of their lives, stakeholders have a special responsibility. Since the $80,000 was central in starting them off in life, it is only fair for them to repay it at death if this is financially possible. The stakeholding fund, in short, will be enriched each year by the ongoing contributions of property-owners, and by a final payback at death.

There are many possible variations on the stakeholding theme, but we have said enough to suggest its broad political appeal. How many young adults start off life with $80,000? How many parents can afford to give their children the head-start that this implies?

Stakeholding liberates college graduates from the burdens of debt, often with something to spare. It offers unprecedented opportunities for the tens of millions who do not go to college and have often been short-changed by their high school educations. For the first time, they will confront the labor market with a certain sense of security. The stake will give them the independence to choose where to live, whether to marry, and how to train for economic opportunity. Some will fail, but fewer than today.

We should, of course, structure the program to maximize the successes. For starters, no stakeholder should be allowed free use of his $80,000 without completing high school and passing a state or national qualifying examination. High-school dropouts would have their stakes held in trust,

D. WEALTH, CLASS AND ECONOMIC MOBILITY—THE INTERGENERATIONAL EFFECTS

and would have access only to the annually accruing interest. Since only three-quarters of American teenagers have high school degrees, this single requirement will prevent massive "stakeblowing" by those least capable of handling adult responsibilities. It will also provide a beacon of hope to kids locked in rural poverty or urban ghettos. Stay in school and graduate, and you will not be forgotten. You will get a solid chance to live out the American dream of economic independence.

Timing is also crucial. High school graduates should get immediate access to their money if they want to spend their $80,000 on college. Those choosing other paths should be obliged to learn a few lessons in the school of hard knocks before they can get their stakes—in $20,000 annual payments between the ages of twenty-one and twenty-four. The result will change the way young people think about themselves, their options, and their obligations to society.

Begin with the college-bound. Poor kids confront hardships unknown to their better-off peers—juggling schoolwork and jobs in ways that easily overwhelm self-confidence. The endless rounds of scholarship applications, and intermittent failures to pay tuition, take a toll by themselves. Statistics confirm that students in two-year colleges are even harder-pressed: a much higher percentage live at home, hold a job, and work more hours. It should be no surprise, then, that lower-class kids are much more likely to delay enrollment, and less likely to earn a degree, than their richer peers. At the end of the day, fifty-one percent of students from the top quarter earn bachelor's degrees, compared to twenty-two percent of middle-status students, and only 7.2% in the lowest socioeconomic quartile. For this large group of college-bound students, stakeholding will work a genuine revolution. It would allow all young men and women to focus their energies on academic work and compete with their peers on relatively equal terms.

Stakeholding would also inaugurate a new era of healthy competition in higher education. While colleges might try to raise tuition, they would face countervailing market pressures to keep costs low. Every student would enter the market with significant resources and an incentive to shop carefully. No longer would state universities or community colleges have a captive pool of in-state or low-income students without other options. These people could now choose a school in another community, or across the country, or even overseas.

This option will be especially valuable to people interested in a two-year college degree. At present, these colleges provide much smaller subsidies to their students than do more traditional universities. However, under the new system, students at two-year colleges will have the same buying power as their more academically inclined age-mates. To be sure, they will be utterly unwilling to spend their entire $80,000 on a couple of years of post-high school education. However, their stakes will create new incentives for serious programs directed at their distinctive concerns. Over time, two-year colleges will emerge from the shadow of their bigger brothers, and build their students' skills and self-confidence with increasing imagination and vigor.

We have left the best for last. Consider the millions of Americans who decide that college—even a two-year college—is not for them. These are today's forgotten Americans. Many of them have already been denied the decent high school education that should be every citizen's birthright. Now they are tossed unaided into the marketplace, while their upwardly mobile peers are given federal scholarships and state-subsidized tuitions.

This is just plain wrong. Joe Sixpack is every bit as much of an American as Joe College. And for the first time, his claim to equal citizenship will be treated with genuine respect. Since these high-school graduates are not going to college, they will have to wait until their early twenties to gain access to their stakes. Indeed, some may want to require young adults to wait until twenty-five or so before they get any of their money. We would be happy to compromise so long as the basic principle of universal stakeholding remains intact. The decision to go to college should not be required for an American to gain his country's support for the pursuit of happiness. All Americans have a fundamental right to start off as adults with a fair chance at making a decent life for themselves.

For all our precautions, some will fail to make good use of their stakes, and in ways they will bitterly regret. But the predictable failures of some should not deprive millions of others of *their* fair chance to pursue happiness. Each individual citizen has a right to a fair share of the patrimony left by preceding generations. This right should not be contingent on how others use or misuse their stakes.

Some poor Americans do face multiple social problems—inadequate education, drug or alcohol abuse, a propensity to violence—that leave them ill-equipped to handle financial responsibility for their stake. Despite pervasive media images, the size of the so-called "underclass" is quite tiny—less than four percent of the population. Most of these people would be excluded from full control of their stake by the requirement of high-school graduation.

In addition, we propose a cautious use of stakeholding as a sanction in the criminal law justice system. At the present time, the only way we have to punish young adults is to deprive them of their personal liberty. Stakeholding will, however, for the first time, also allow us to use financial sanctions against youth crime. For example, we would put nineteen year olds on notice that participation in the drug-trade would mean the loss of all or part of their stakes. For many people of eighteen or nineteen, such a threat might have more deterrence value than a prison term.

In any event, the important point is this: We should not allow trendy talk of "underclass" pathologies to divert our attention from the central problem posed by our emerging three-class society. Quite simply, there are tens of millions of ordinary Americans who are perfectly capable of responsible decision making in a stakeholding society, but are now becoming the forgotten citizens of our globalizing economy. We should confront this problem now before the wealth gap widens to Latin American proportions.

D. WEALTH, CLASS AND ECONOMIC MOBILITY—THE INTERGENERATIONAL EFFECTS

In our many conversations on the subject, somebody invariably suggests the wisdom of restricting the stake to a limited set of praiseworthy purposes—requiring each citizen to gain bureaucratic approval before spending down his $80,000. Would not this allow us to redistribute wealth and make sure the money is well spent?

This question bears the mark of the bureaucratic mindset that has haunted so much policymaking in the twentieth century. Our goal is to transcend the welfare state mentality, not transform stakeholding into another exercise in paternalistic social engineering. The point of stakeholding is to liberate each citizen from government, not to create an excuse for a vast new bureaucracy intervening in our lives. To be sure, the construction industry, the university sector, and the brokerage houses would prefer a plan that limited stakeholders' choices to home-buying, education, or investment. But if stakeholders want advice, they can buy it on the market. If people in their twenties can not be treated as adults, when will they be old enough?

We do not deny the need for a "social safety net" for Americans who make particularly bad choices, but this is not our primary focus. We are concerned with providing a fair opportunity for success for all Americans, and not only those lucky enough to be born to parents of the symbol-using classes. It is one thing to make a mess out of your life; quite another, never to have had a fair chance.

Indeed, the real problem with stakeholding is that it does not go far enough to redeem America's promise of an equal opportunity society. Does not the $80,000 come too late for all those who have been shortchanged as children?

Our short answer is yes. As a consequence, we certainly favor more spending on better versions of Head Start and the like. Nonetheless, we are skeptical of the egalitarian potential of enormous new investments in primary and secondary education. So long as suburbs can insulate themselves from central cities, there is only so much that money alone can accomplish. And, the upper classes have proven themselves adept in channeling federal aid for the disadvantaged into their own local school systems. Worse yet, school decentralization and privatization seem to be the order of the day—rather than a movement toward metropolitan-wide school systems and greater national efforts to provide poorer regions of the country with greater educational resources.

By contrast, it would be relatively easy to realize the goals of a stakeholder society. To a very large degree, the institutional infrastructure is already in place. We already have an Internal Revenue Service and a Social Security Administration. Although it is fashionable to denigrate these "bureaucracies," both agencies are full of competent people whose tasks might easily be broadened to encompass the jobs of identifying eligible stakeholders and paying out benefits. Unlike a comparable educational reform, stakeholding will not require a massive reorganization of the existing institutional framework. It builds on what we already have.

Americans could, in relatively short order, actually achieve the massive step toward equality of opportunity that stakeholding makes possible. This breakthrough, in turn, would give the lie to neo-conservative banalities about the inevitability of government failure. Having established that Americans *can* succeed in redeeming their fundamental ideals by inaugurating stakeholding, many other seemingly impossible initiatives may seem within our grasp.

Of course, real freedom and equal opportunity do not come cheap. Using conservative assumptions, the annual cost of stakeholding today would be about $255 billion—a little less than we spend on national defense. This is a big number, but we have made comparable commitments in the past: Would America have been a better place after the Second World War without the GI Bill of Rights? At that time, wealthy taxpayers were a lot poorer than they are today. They were paying far heavier taxes, and yet they did not seek to evade their obligation to give the rising generation a fair start in adult life.

The GI Bill represented the payment of a debt for the sacrifices that our soldiers made during the war. Today the ties that bind older to younger are less obvious—but no less important. Day after day, our society demands countless small acts of voluntary cooperation, as well as many larger personal sacrifices. If the younger generation is denied a fair start, how can the rest of us expect them to reciprocate as the need requires?

For the rest of their lives, stakeholders will endlessly consider how their $80,000 contributed to their individual pursuits of happiness—and at the same time reflect on their good fortune in enjoying this precious right of economic citizenship. Except for the most hardened cynics, this will lead to a deep and sustaining loyalty to the country that made stakeholding a concrete reality. Rather than dismissing the Declaration of Independence as boastful words on paper, stakeholders will hear in Jefferson's proud phrases a description of their own lives, and seek, as best they can, to repay their own debt by passing on their great American heritage on to the future.

We have talked enough about the potential benefits of stakeholding. Let us move to the revenue-raising side of the equation: How are we going to come up with the necessary quarter of a trillion dollars a year?

Well, there is never a good time for a tax hike, but now is the best time we will have for a long time. To be sure, we would not bet the ranch on the optimistic budgetary projections coming out of Washington right now. Since both Bill Clinton and Congressional Republicans are happy to take credit for restoring the nation to fiscal health, neither side emphasizes how much a sharp recession or two might dent their happy predictions of multi-trillion dollar surpluses over the next decade or so. More importantly, short-term surpluses will be swamped in the longer run. Depending on what we do with Medicare, the deficits looming by mid-century may well be horrific. Nevertheless, the happy numbers of the next decade should provide us a much-needed pause for reflection on our long-run fiscal responsibilities.

Stakeholding makes an initial intellectual contribution by exposing a question-begging assumption behind the emerging debate surrounding the budget surplus. Too often, the talk proceeds as if the only serious question is how much of the surplus should be used to save Social Security and Medicare. This begs the question whether our only exigent fiscal priority is aid to the elderly or whether the time has not come to emphasize the competing claim of the generation only now rising to maturity.

In raising stakeholding as a serious alternative, we do not suggest that it should automatically trump the claims of the older generation to a decent level of income and medical care. But we do believe that both social justice and social peace require America to redeem its promise of equal opportunity to the young no less than its promise of decency to the old. If we can not afford to do both, it is not obvious that we should entirely ignore stakeholding and lavish the lion's share of the surplus on the old.

America *is* rich enough to do both. Despite the fog of anti-tax rhetoric, our taxes remain far lower than those imposed by other rich Western nations, and they would remain so after we have paid the quarter-of-a-trillion-dollar annual bill for stakeholding. Obviously, there are lots of different ways of raising the money. For example, we would favor a hike in the income tax or a new national consumption tax whose revenues were dedicated to the stakeholding fund. But, so far as we are concerned, the best way to proceed is through a new comprehensive tax on wealth similar to the ones currently imposed by twelve other countries in the elite club of first-world nations called the Organization for Economic Cooperation and Development.

We have built many conservative assumptions into our economic analysis of the revenue-raising potential of such a tax. We have also allowed every American an $80,000 personal exemption, thereby eliminating the bottom sixty percent of the population from all liability. Nevertheless, our analysis reveals that an annual tax of two percent would be enough to fund the entire program.

Even when we focus on the top forty percent, this tax would have a vastly different impact on different groups. So far as the households falling between the sixtieth and eightieth percentile, the average tax would be $1100 a year, and the entire group would contribute only seven percent of the total fund. The big tax burden would be borne at the top, with thirty-nine percent of the total tax contributed by the top one percent of American households, whose median wealth in 1995 was $4.6 million.

The disproportionate impact of the tax on the rich strikes us as entirely fair. Since wealth is correlated with age, Americans over the age of fifty or sixty will bear the brunt of the burden. But it is precisely these people who have participated fully in the great post-war economic boom. The wealthy man or woman who is sixty in the year 2000 was born in 1940—just in time to avoid the agonies of the Great Depression and the Second World War, but just in time to reap the harvest. Graduating from college about 1960, the typical up-and-comer was in a perfect position to take advantage of the rich array of opportunities made possible by America's rise to world power. The best universities, the most advanced companies, the biggest pool of capital—all of these were available for Americans who seized the moment. To be sure, nobody could become wealthy without some combination of effort, insight, and luck. It would be blind for any sixty-year-old to ignore the role played by the simple fact that he was an American in an American age—and thereby gained the enormous advantages created at great sacrifice by his parents' generation. Given their existing balance of generational advantage, it is especially appropriate to ask this group of elder Americans to make a sacrifice to sustain the Republic's political and economic equilibrium.

We are calling upon older Americans to remember that they themselves were the beneficiaries of similar acts of statesmanship by earlier generations. During the New Deal and Great Society, Americans recognized the elderly as a group that was particularly threatened by the inegalitarian operation of market forces. By responding with Social Security and Medicare, our predecessors ensured a decent life for millions of elderly Americans today. Without these programs, the distribution of wealth would be even more unequal than it already is. Is it not time, then, for the elder generation to reciprocate when the market threatens to undermine the promise of economic opportunity for millions of younger Americans?

This commitment should not come at the cost of retirees who depend on their monthly Social Security checks. Rather than leading a raid on Social Security revenues, we simply urge prosperous older Americans to recognize the moral claim of younger Americans who will otherwise live out lives of quiet despair.

Or not so quiet despair. After all, the prison population has soared over the last quarter century. About 100 Americans in every 100,000 were in the nation's prisons in 1975; that number is now over 400. Young males, and increasingly females, are the prime targets for prison—men and women who might find it within themselves to take a different path in a stakeholding society. If inequality increases over the next century, are we really prepared to lock up more and more young Americans who react with rage at a system that has never delivered on its promises? If those with the greatest stake in the system do not take heed, who is supposed to?

It is time for the wealthy to accept stakeholding as part of the social compact. While wealth taxes are unfamiliar in America, they are a fixture of public finance in most other industrialized nations. Of course, every new tax generates the same old cry that it will kill the economy. Rich people are always happy to tell you the story of the goose that lays the golden eggs, but is it just a fairy tale?

Not only has our economy boomed, and busted, under very different levels of taxation, recent empirical research suggests that the link between tax rates and growth is far weaker than implied by the prevailing political rhetoric. Moreover, stakeholding will itself unleash the energies of millions of youthful entrepreneurs—while many will fail, many others will succeed in ways that will enrich the lives of us all.

D. Wealth, Class and Economic Mobility—The Intergenerational Effects

Two hundred years ago, Tom Paine surveyed the revolutionary world he helped create, and sensed something missing: "A revolution in the state of civilization is the necessary companion of revolutions in the system of government." This could be accomplished, he was convinced, only through stakeholding. Every citizen, Paine insisted, had a right to a stake of fifteen pounds Sterling "when arrived at the age of twenty-one years." In a remarkable gesture for the eighteenth century, Paine argued that this expanded stake should go to every man *and* woman. Regardless of his or her claims on private wealth, each should be accorded an economic stake in the commonwealth.

Tom Paine was not alone. Our leading Founders acknowledged a deep relationship between property and citizenship. When Madison viewed "the merits alone," it was clear to him that "the freeholders of the Country would be the safest depositories of Republican liberty," and that the propertyless should be excluded from the suffrage. Standing before the Constitutional Convention, he did not conceal his anxiety as he glimpsed the dread day when the "great majority of the people will not only be without landed, but any other sort of, property."

But in 1787, this grim prospect could be deferred to the remote future. The Founders treated the problem of propertylessness in the way they dealt with the curse of slavery. They did not seek a definitive solution, leaving it to some later generation to confront the crisis when it became acute.

This seemed sensible enough. A vast frontier beckoned to generations of yeomen farmers. So long as the government sold virgin land at low prices, the link between property and citizenship could be more or less preserved. But as the nineteenth century moved on, this Jeffersonian vision of a farmer-republic became increasingly obsolete. By the time of the great Homestead Act of 1863, the statute's provision of free land on the frontier was already out of sync with the needs of the rising urban masses of the East. If the link between property and citizenship were to be sustained, provision of free land would no longer suffice. With the closing of the frontier, something like Tom Paine's vision of stakeholding was required to guarantee each citizen a property interest in America.

By then Paine's voice had become a muffled memory. The mainstream of reform was flowing in other directions: Populists, Progressives, New Dealers, and the partisans of the Great Society sought to regain control over the market economy, but none moved in the direction of citizen-stakeholding. Rather than broadening the property-owning base, their overriding aim was to regulate property more intensely in the public interest.

We think that the intellectual climate really is changing today. Nationalization of industry is on nobody's agenda anymore. People are slowly recognizing that "capitalism" is a Marxist label concealing the vast differences between economic systems built on private property and competitive markets—some bitterly unjust, and others striving for a world worthy of a free and equal citizenry. It is time to stop dreaming about the abolition of private property and get to work creating a commonwealth in which all citizens are property owners.

This intuition has been behind some major initiatives attempted by leading politicians of our age. They have gained great followings through initiatives that bear a family resemblance to our proposal. When Margaret Thatcher became Prime Minister, thirty-two percent of all housing in England was publicly owned. Though bent on sweeping privatization, Thatcher refused to sell off these vast properties to big companies. She invited residents to buy their own homes at bargain rates. With a single stroke, she created a new class of property-owning citizens, and won vast popularity in the process.

A more sweeping initiative took place in the Czech Republic in the aftermath of 1989. The Prime Minister, Vaclav Klaus, was confronting a much larger task than Thatcher's: the state sector contained 7000 medium and large-scale enterprises, 25,000 to 35,000 smaller ones. How to distribute this legacy of Communism? Klaus saw his problem as an opportunity to create a vast new property-owning class.

The mechanism was the ingenious technique of "voucher privatization." Each Czech citizen was encouraged to subscribe to a book of vouchers that he could use to bid for shares in state companies as they were put on the auction block. An overwhelming majority—8.5 out of 10.5 million—took up Klaus' offer, and claimed their fair share of the nation's wealth as they moved into the free-market system. Klaus' creative program helped cement his position as the leading politician of the Republic. More importantly, the broad involvement of citizen-stakeholders played a central role in legitimating the country's transition to liberal democracy.

Thatcher and Klaus conceived their initiatives as one-shot affairs. However, the citizens of Alaska have made stakeholding a regular part of their political economy. Once again, the occasion was the distribution of a major public asset, in this case the revenues from North Slope oil. Rather than using it all for public expenditures, the Republican leadership designed a stakeholding scheme that is now distributing about a $1000 a year to every Alaskan citizen. Once again, the system has become broadly popular, with politicians of both parties regularly pledging that they will not raid the symbolically-named Permanent Fund.

There is no good reason to limit stakeholding to physical assets like housing or factories or oil. Americans have created other assets that are less material, but have even greater value. Most notably, the free enterprise system did not drop from thin air. It has emerged only as the result of a complex and on-going scheme of social cooperation. The "free market" requires heavy public expenditures on police, courts, and much else besides. But without billions of voluntary decisions by Americans to respect the rights of property in their daily lives, the system would collapse overnight. All Americans benefit from this cooperative activity—some much more than others. Those who benefit the most have a duty to share some of their wealth with fellow citizens whose cooperation they require to sustain the market system. This obligation is all the more exigent when the operation of the global market threatens to split the country more sharply into haves and have-nots.

This view gives our proposal a different ideological spin from those pioneered by Margaret Thatcher and Vaclav Klaus. Surely there will be some on the Right who will blanch at the implications of our proposal. But we hope that many others will come to see its justice. We expect a similar split on the Left. Some will be deeply suspicious of liberating stakeholding assets from the grip of the regulatory state, leaving each citizen free to make their own decisions. Others will be more impressed by the justice of empowering all Americans to share in the pursuit of happiness.

Stakeholding also holds out the promise of political renewal. Nobody we have met has the slightest problem grasping the idea of $80,000—or the possibility of funding the program by taxing wealth. Lots of people do not like the initiative, but at least they know what they are disagreeing with— and this is absolutely essential for a rebirth of democratic politics in this country. Unless progressives come up with projects that are transparent to the common understanding, the politics of scandal will have no real competitor. The general public has no patience for a policy debate that speaks a technocratic language accessible only to people with advanced degrees.

If Beltway babble is the alternative, ordinary Americans will turn with relief to news of the latest personal indiscretion by leading politicos. Only a program like stakeholding can focus the public mind on the prospects for real change. It raises—in a straightforward and concrete way—the leading questions of our age: Is America more than a libertarian marketplace? Can we preserve a sense of ourselves as a nation of free and equal citizens?

Stakeholding really does bring power back to the people. It marks a radical break with the elitist tradition of social engineering. We do not need a host of experts to minister to ordinary Americans. Give citizens their stakes and let them inaugurate a new age of freedom.

This call can unify a badly fractured nation. Even many Americans in the top twenty percent may recognize its power. Do they really want their own children to live in gated communities locked away from the rest of American life?

The stakeholder society is no utopia, but it does provide an alternative to our current moral drift. Perhaps we will never fully realize the American Dream of equal opportunity. But without that dream, this country will become a very ugly place.

NOTES AND QUESTIONS

1. Ackerman & Alstott's proposal. Do you think the stakeholder idea effectively addresses the problems of inequality outlined in this section? Will it do what the authors think it will? Is it politically feasible?

2. **The stakeholder society and African American reparations.** Does Ackerman & Alstott's proposal address racialized disparities in wealth? What can minority groups do to overcome obstacles to economic opportunity? Claud Anderson of The Harvest Institute (a think tank whose goal is to reform the social and economic aspects of African American life) offers several suggestions to African Americans to escape financial inequality, including mastering the principles of capitalism and group economics, vertically integrating industries and businesses, expanding business in minority communities, and increasing black leadership. CLAUD ANDERSON, BLACK LABOR WHITE WEALTH: THE SEARCH FOR POWER AND ECONOMIC JUSTICE 188 (1994). Another notable recommendation by Anderson is for African Americans to ask the government for reparations: "Reparation payments should be directed into black communities ... to repair the socioeconomic damages that the dominant society and government have inflicted in 16 generations of black Americans." *Id.* at 182. Is Anderson's request too radical? If only five or six generations are needed to eradicate the indicia of slavery, why is Anderson asking for *sixteen* generations to be compensated? *See* Emma Coleman Jordan, *A History Lesson: Reparations for What?*, 58 N.Y.U. ANN. SURV. AM. L. 1,557 (2003). *See also*, ROY L. BROOKS, ATONEMENT AND FORGIVENESS: A NEW MODEL FOR BLACK REPARATIONS (2004).

3. **Stakeholding and inequality.** Why do income and wealth inequality matter? After all, capitalism is premised on the notion of competition, and not everyone can be a winner. Do Ackerman and Alstott explain why we should care about rising inequality?

CHAPTER 2

LIFE IN A CLASS SOCIETY

A. DOWN AND OUT

Number of People Living in Poverty Increases in U.S.
N.Y. TIMES, Sept. 25, 2002, at A1.

■ ROBERT PEAR

The proportion of Americans living in poverty rose significantly last year, increasing for the first time in eight years, the Census Bureau reported today. At the same time, the bureau said that the income of middle-class households fell for the first time since the last recession ended, in 1991.

The Census Bureau's annual report on income and poverty provided stark evidence that the weakening economy had begun to affect large segments of the population, regardless of race, region or class. Daniel H. Weinberg, chief of income and poverty statistics at the Census Bureau, said the recession that began in March 2001 had reduced the earnings of millions of Americans.

The report also suggested that the gap between rich and poor continued to grow.

All regions except the Northeast experienced a decline in household income, the bureau reported. For blacks, it was the first significant decline in two decades; non-Hispanic whites saw a slight decline. Even the incomes of Asians and Pacific Islanders, a group that achieved high levels of prosperity in the 1990's, went down significantly last year.

"The decline was widespread," Mr. Weinberg said.

The Census Bureau said the number of poor Americans rose last year to 32.9 million, an increase of 1.3 million, while the proportion living in poverty rose to 11.7 percent, from 11.3 percent in 2000.

Median household income fell to $42,228 in 2001, a decline of $934 or 2.2 percent from the prior year. The number of households with income above the median is the same as the number below it.

A family of four was classified as poor if it had cash income less than $18,104 last year. The official poverty levels, updated each year to reflect changes in the Consumer Price Index, were $14,128 for a family of three, $11,569 for a married couple and $9,039 for an individual.

The bureau's report is likely to provide fodder for the Congressional campaigns. The White House said the increase in poverty resulted, in part, from an economic slowdown that began under President Bill Clinton. But Democrats said the data showed the failure of President Bush's economic policies and his tendency to neglect the economy.

Mr. Bush said today that he remained optimistic. "When you combine the productivity of the American people with low interest rates and low inflation, those are the ingredients for growth," Mr. Bush said.

But Senator Paul S. Sarbanes, Democrat of Maryland, said the administration should "start paying attention to the economic situation." Richard A. Gephardt of Missouri, the House Democratic leader, expressed amazement that Mr. Bush, after being in office for 20 months, was still blaming his predecessor.

Rudolph G. Penner, a former director of the Congressional Budget Office, said: "The increase in poverty is most certainly a result of the recession. The slow recovery, the slow rate of growth, has been very disappointing. Whether that has a political impact this fall depends on whether the election hinges on national conditions or focuses on local issues."

Although the poverty rate, the proportion of the population living in poverty, rose four-tenths of a percentage point last year, it was still lower than in most of the last two decades. The poverty rate exceeded 12 percent every year from 1980 to 1998. As the economy grew from 1993 to 2000, the rate plunged, to 11.3 percent from 15.1 percent, and the poverty rolls were reduced by 7.7 million people, to 31.6 million.

The latest recession showed an unusual pattern, seeming to raise poverty rates among whites more than among minority groups, Mr. Weinberg said.

Increases in poverty last year were concentrated in the suburbs, in the South and among non-Hispanic whites, the Census Bureau said. Indeed, non-Hispanic whites were the only racial group for whom the poverty rate showed a significant increase, to 7.8 percent in 2001, from 7.4 percent in 2000.

Poverty rates for minority groups were once much higher. But last year, the bureau said, they remained "at historic lows" for blacks (22.7 percent), Hispanics (21.4 percent) and Asian Americans (10.2 percent).

With its usual caution, the Census Bureau said the data did not conclusively show a year-to-year increase in income inequality. But the numbers showed a clear trend in that direction over the last 15 years.

The most affluent fifth of the population received half of all household income last year, up from 45 percent in 1985. The poorest fifth received 3.5 percent of total household income, down from 4 percent in 1985. Average income for the top 5 percent of households rose by $1,000 last year, to $260,464, but the average declined or stayed about the same for most other income brackets.

Robert Greenstein, executive director of the Center on Budget and Policy Priorities, a liberal research institute, said, "The census data show that income inequality either set a record in 2001 or tied for the highest level on record."

Median earnings increased 3.5 percent for women last year, but did not change for men, so women gained relative to men.

"The real median earnings of women age 15 and older who worked full time year-round increased for the fifth consecutive year, rising to $29,215—a 3.5 percent increase between 2000 and 2001," Mr. Weinberg said. The comparable figure for men was unchanged at $38,275. So the female-to-male earnings ratio reached a high of 0.76. The previous high was 0.74, first recorded in 1996.

Democrats said the data supported their contention that Congress should increase spending on social welfare programs, resisted by many Republicans. But Wade F. Horn, the administration's welfare director, said the number of poor children was much lower than in 1996, when Congress overhauled the welfare law to impose strict work requirements.

Of the 32.9 million poor people in the United States last year, 11.7 million were under 18, and 3.4 million were 65 or older. Poverty rates for children, 16.3 percent, and the elderly, 10.1 percent, were virtually unchanged from 2000. But the poverty rate for people 18 to 64 rose a half percentage point, to 10.1 percent.

Median household income for blacks fell last year by $1,025, or 3.4 percent, to $29,470. Median income of Hispanics, at $33,565, was virtually unchanged. But household income fell by 1.3 percent for non-Hispanic whites, to $46,305, and by 6.4 percent for Asian Americans, to $53,635.

The Census Bureau report also included these findings:

There were 6.8 million poor families last year, up from 6.4 million in 2000. The poverty rate for families rose to 9.2 percent, from a 26-year low of 8.7 percent in 2000.

The rate in the South rose to 13.5 percent, from 12.8 percent in 2000. The South is home to more than 40 percent of all the nation's poor, and it accounted for more than half of the national increase in the number of poor last year.

The poverty rate for the suburbs rose to 8.2 percent last year, from 7.8 percent in 2000. The number of poor people in suburban areas rose by 700,000, to 12 million. There was virtually no change in the rates in central cities (16.5 percent) and outside metropolitan areas (14.2 percent).

The bureau said the number of "severely poor" rose to 13.4 million last year, from 12.6 million in 2000. People are considered to be severely poor if their family incomes are less than half of the official poverty level.

Just Trying to Survive

ROSA LEE: A MOTHER AND HER FAMILY IN URBAN AMERICA 39–47 (1996).

■ LEON DASH

Rosa Lee guided her eleven-year-old grandson through the narrow aisles of a thrift shop in suburban Oxon Hill, Maryland, past the crowded racks of secondhand pants and shirts, stopping finally at the row of children's jackets and winter coats. Quickly, the boy selected a mock-leather flight jacket with a big number on the back and a price tag stapled to the collar.

"If you want it," Ross Lee said, "then you're going to have to help me get it."

"Okay, Grandmama," he said nervously. "But do it in a way that I won't get caught."

Like a skilled teacher instructing a new student, Rosa Lee told her grandson what to do. "Pretend you're trying it on. Don't look up! Don't look around! Don't laugh like it's some kind of joke! Just put it on. Let Grandma see how you look."

The boy slipped off his old, coat and put on the new one. Rosa Lee whispered, "Now put the other one back on, over it." She pushed down the new jacket's collar so that it was hidden.

"What do I do now?" he asked.

"Just walk on out the door," Rosa Lee said. "It's your coat."

Four days later, Rosa Lee is recounting this episode for me, recreating the dialogue by changing her voice to distinguish between herself and her grandson. It is January 1991. By now, I have spent enough time with Rosa Lee that her shoplifting exploits no longer surprise me.

The previous November, Rosa Lee took her eight-year-old granddaughter into the same thrift shop on a Sunday morning to steal a new winter coat for the girl one week after they were both baptized in a Pentecostal church. On the Sunday of the shoplifting lesson, Rosa Lee had decided she did not want to take her granddaughter back to the church because her winter coat was "tacky and dirty."

In the thrift shop, Rosa Lee told her granddaughter to take off her coat and hang it on the coatrack. Next, she told the grinning child to put on the attractive pink winter coat hanging on the rack.

"Are we going to take this coat, Grandma?" asked the skinny little girl.

"Yes," Rosa Lee told her. "We are exchanging coats. Now walk out the door."

A month later, a week before Christmas, Rosa Lee was searching for something in a large shopping bag in her bedroom and dumped the contents onto the bed. Out spilled dozens of bottles of expensive men's cologne and women's perfume, as well as leather gloves with their sixty-dollar price tags still attached. She leaves the tags on when she sells the goods as proof of the merchandise's newness and quality.

"Did you get all this in one trip?" I ask.

"Oh, no," she says. "This is a couple of weeks' worth."

In Rosa Lee's younger years especially, shoplifting was a major source of income, supplementing her welfare payments and the money she made during fifteen years of waitressing at various nightclubs. With eight children to feed and clothe, stealing, she says, helped her survive. Later on, when she began using heroin in the mid-1970s, her shoplifting paid for drugs.

She stole from clothing stores, drugstores, and grocery stores, stuffing items inside the torn liner of her winter coat or slipping them into one of the oversized black purses that she carries wherever she goes. When her children were young—the ages of the grandson and granddaughter—she taught them how to shoplift as well.

"Every time I went somewhere to make some money, I would take my children," she said. "I would teach them or they would watch me. 'Just watch what Mama does. I'm getting food for y'all to eat.'"

In supermarkets, she could count on her children "to distract the security guard while I hit the meat freezer. The guards would always watch groups of children before they'd watch an adult."

Her favorite targets were the department stores. One of her two older brothers, Joe Louis Wright, joked with me one day that Rosa Lee "owned a piece" of Hecht's and had put Lansburgh's out of business. "Man, she would get coats, silk dresses," he recalled. "A cloth coat with a mink collar. She got me a mohair suit. Black. Three-piece. I don't know how the hell she'd get them out of there."

Her stealing has caused divisions and hard feelings in her family, and is one reason why Rosa Lee's relationships with several of her brothers and sisters are strained. They see Rosa Lee's stealing as an extreme and unjustified reaction to their impoverished upbringing. And her sons Alvin and Eric have always refused to participate in any of their mother's illegal activities.

Rosa Lee has served eight short prison terms for various kinds of stealing during the past forty years, dating back to the early 1950s. Her longest stay was eight months for trying to steal a fur coat from a Maryland department store in 1965. She says that she went to prison rehabilitation programs each time but that none had much of an effect on her. "I attended those programs so it would look good on my record when I went before the parole board," she says. "What they were talking about didn't mean anything to me. I didn't have the education they said would get me a job. I couldn't read no matter how many programs I went to."

Nothing seems to deter her from shoplifting, not even the specter of another jail term. On the day she directed her grandson in stealing the flight jacket, she was four days away from sentencing at the city's Superior Court for stealing the bedsheets from Hecht's the previous summer.

"I'm just trying to survive," she says.

Rosa Lee had chosen her clothes carefully for her appearance before Commissioner John Treanor in November. She wanted to look as poor as possible to draw his sympathy.

She wore an ill-fitting winter coat, gray wool overalls and a white wool hat pulled back to show her graying hair. She had removed her upper dental plate to give herself a toothless look when she smiled. "My homey look," she calls it. "No lipstick. No earrings. No nothing!"

Rosa Lee did not expect to go home that day. She saw a heavyset female deputy U.S. marshal move into place behind the defense table when the courtroom clerk called her name. It was a certain sign that Treanor had already decided to "step her back" and send her to jail. She hastily handed me her purse with all her documents.

"Hold on to these papers for me, Mr. Dash," she whispered. "Looks like I'm going to get some jail time. Tell my children where I'm at. You better come see me!"

Her lawyer's statements matched her downtrodden look. Rosa Lee's life was a mess, Elmer D. Ellis told Treanor. She was addicted to heroin, a habit she had developed in 1975. She was HIV positive. She was caring for three grandchildren because their mother was in jail.

Rosa Lee told Treanor that she was trying hard to turn herself around. She was taking methadone every day to control her heroin addition and had turned again to the church. "I got baptized Sunday, me and my three grandchildren," she said, her voice breaking. "And I'm asking you from the bottom of my heart, give me a chance to prove that I'm taking my baptize seriously, 'cause I know I might not have much longer."

Tears ran down her cheeks. "I'm asking you for a chance, please," she begged Treanor. "I know I have a long record."

Rosa Lee was stretching the truth. Yes, she had been baptized, and yes, she was taking methadone. But no, she wasn't caring for her grandchildren alone. Their mother's jail term had ended in July, and she had returned to Rosa Lee's two-bedroom apartment to take care of the children, with help from Rosa Lee.

Treanor looked unimpressed with Rosa Lee's performance. He glowered at her, and Rosa Lee braced for the lecture she knew was coming. Both had played these roles before.

"Every time you pump yourself full of drugs and spend money to do it," he said, "you're stealing from your grandchildren. You're stealing food from their plates, clothes from their backs, and you're certainly jeopardizing their future. You're going to be the youngest dead grandmother in town. And you're going to have three children that will be put up for adoption or going out to some home or some junior village or someplace."

That had been Rosa Lee's opening. "Can I prove to you that my life has changed?"

"Yeah, you can prove it to me, very simply," Treanor answered. "You can stay away from dope. Now I'll make a bargain with you.... You come back here the end of January and tell me what you've been doing, and then we'll think about it. But you're looking at jail time. You're looking at the cemetery."

Rosa Lee had won. Treanor postponed the sentencing. The marshal, who had moved in closer behind Rosa Lee at the start of Treanor's lecture, moved back. Treanor, red-faced with anger, called a ten-minute recess and hurriedly left the bench. Ellis shook Rosa Lee's hand.

Rosa Lee came over to me, her cheeks still tearstained but her face aglow. "Was I good?" she asked.

"Yeah," I said, startled at her boldness.

"Thank you," she said, smiling.

The marshal walked up to Rosa Lee. She too was smiling. She had escorted Rosa Lee and her daughters to the jail several times in the not-so-distant past. "You were going to jail, honey," she said to Rosa Lee. "You stopped him with those three grandchildren. He didn't want to have to deal with making arrangements for those children if he had sent you to jail. Is their mama still over the jail?"

"Yes, she is," Rosa Lee lied, putting on a sad face.

Five days before the hearing Rosa Lee was teaching her grandchild how to shoplift. Through most of November and December, Rosa Lee stole cologne, perfume, gloves, and brightly colored silk scarves to sell to people who used them as Christmas presents. The day before her court appearance, she and a fellow drug-clinic patient, Jackie, were shoplifting in a drugstore one block from the Superior Court building shortly after they had drunk their morning meth.

When she returns for sentencing on January 22, a transformed Rosa Lee enters the courthouse. She looks good. She has a clean report from the methadone clinic. She stopped injecting heroin and cocaine in November, after her last seizure. She seems to have done everything Commissioner Treanor asked.

She always dresses well, but she has outdone herself today: she's wearing a two-piece, white-and-gray cotton knit suit with tan leather boots and a tan pocketbook. A gold-colored watch on a gold-colored chain hangs around her neck, both items she stole from the drugstore.

Before they enter Treanor's courtroom, Elmer Ellis has a word with Rosa Lee. "Please don't cry, Mrs. Cunningham," her lawyer says gently. "If you start crying again, you're only going to make Treanor angry." Rosa Lee laughs and agrees not to cry.

"What would you like to say, Mrs. Cunningham?" Treanor asks Rosa Lee when she stands in front of him.

"Well, Your Honor, I know I haven't been a good person. I know it," she begins.

Treanor cuts her off. His demeanor is softer, his words more sympathetic than in November. "Wait a minute, now. Why do you say that? . . . You're taking care of those three grandchildren, isn't that right?"

"Yes, Sir," Rosa Lee says, keeping up the pretense.

"All right," he says. "Now you've raised one family, and now you have another one."

"Yes, Sir," she says.

"Which is really too much to ask of anybody, so I don't think you should sell yourself short. You're doing the Lord's work. Your daughter's in jail for drugs, right?"

"Yes, sir," Rosa Lee says.

"And you have or have had a bad drug problem yourself."

"Yes, Sir."

Then Treanor launches into another lecture about drugs. He doesn't ask Rosa Lee why she steals. "You steal to support your habit," he says. "It's as plain as the nose on your face."

But it isn't that plain. Rosa Lee began stealing long before she became a drug addict.

Finally, Treanor announces his decision: no jail. Instead, he gives her a suspended sentence and one year of probation with drug counseling. "Now, don't come back here," he says.

Rosa Lee sometimes puts on a public mask, the way she wants the world to see her. She fudges a little here, omits a little there, even when she is trying to be candid about her behavior. By her account, her stealing started when she was a teenager. It was her eldest brother, Ben Wright, who told me that Rosa Lee's stealing started when she was nine years old. Her target: the lunch money that her fourth-grade classmates at Giddings Elementary School kept in their desks.

"JESUS, BEN!" Rosa Lee shouts when I ask her about it.

"What's the matter?" I laugh. "You said I could interview Ben."

It is a late afternoon in January, not long after her court appearance. We are talking in my car, which is parked outside Rosa Lee's apartment. We watch the teenage crack dealers come and go, making the rounds of the low-rent housing complex. Two of Rosa Lee's grandchildren are playing nearby on a patch of dirt where the grass has been worn away. The sun is beginning to sink behind the buildings as she tells me about her first theft.

The year was 1946, and Giddings's imposing red-brick building at Third and G streets, S.E., was a bustling part of the District's then-segregated education system. The school served black children living in Capitol Hill neighborhoods; some, like Rosa Lee, came from poor sharecropping families who had moved to Washington during the Depression, and they did not have the new clothes and spending money that their better-off classmates did.

Rosa Lee's father, Earl Wright, never made much money. He worked for a paving contractor as a cement finisher but he was never given that title; instead, he was always classified as a "helper" and paid a lower wage. Eventually, drinking became the primary activity of his life. Rosa Lee's mother, Rosetta Lawrence Wright, brought in most of the family's money, working as a domestic on Capitol Hill during the day.

"She used to call it 'day work,'" remembers Rosa Lee. "That's what she used to do down in the country" in North Carolina. "Clean white people's houses."

Rosetta also sold dinners from the family's kitchen in the evening and on weekends, always for cash. "She wanted cash because she was getting a welfare check for us," says Rosa Lee. The welfare payments began several years before her father's death because he spent all his time drinking and did not work. After he died, Rosetta had four additional children by another man. "Back in those days, they gave you a check for each child. Seventeen dollars a check. You never want the welfare to know how much money you got. They'll cut the check."

Ben contends that his sister's memory is faulty, that the family did receive monthly deliveries of surplus government food in this period, as did all of the poorest families in Washington, but his mother did not receive a monthly welfare stipend.

Whatever the truth, Rosa Lee and Ben agree that their family—there were eleven children in all—was poor. For much of her childhood, they lived in a ramshackle wooden row house within a mile of the Capitol, since replaced with a public housing project. None of the houses they rented over the years had electricity. The toilet for each dwelling was an outhouse along the edge of the property in the back yard. Water came from a standpipe spigot in the center of the yard.

"I hated them!" says Rosa Lee of the houses, her mouth turning down in a grimace. "No privacy. People knew what you were doing when you went into" the outhouse. "No bathtub. I was always afraid of the kerosene lamps. I was scared they'd turn over and we'd all burn up in those houses."

Other girls came to school with change to buy "brownie-thins"— penny-a-piece cookies that the teachers sold to go with free milk at lunch. Rosa Lee's family was too poor to spare even a few pennies. Rosa Lee was determined to steal her classmates' money so she too could buy cookies. And she did. She knew it was wrong to steal from her classmates' desks, she says. But she couldn't stand being poor, either.

Rosa Lee soon found that she had plenty of opportunities to steal, if she were daring enough. During the summer of 1948, a sinewy Rosa Lee was the only girl among the many "roughneck" boys selling the *Baltimore-Washington Afro–American* newspaper door-to-door on Tuesday and Thursday evenings. She was eleven. The newspaper sales were timed to catch middle-class black people—low-level federal and city civil servants—when they had just come from work.

Rosa Lee was not concerned about tough neighborhood bullies taking her money or trying to force her off the blocks where an *Afro* seller was sure to be successful. "Rosa Lee would fight quick," remembers Ben. "Fight anybody! Beat up most girls and a good many boys. I don't remember ever having to stick up for her."

Selling the *Afro* also gave Rosa Lee a chance to slip into neighborhood row houses and rifle through the pocketbooks that women often left on the dining room table or the living room couch. Washington was a safer place in those days, and Rosa Lee discovered that many families would leave their front screen doors unlatched while they chatted in their back yards, trying to cool off on hot summer evenings after returning home from work.

"I would walk down Fourth Street," says Rosa Lee, in front of the row houses across from Mount Joy Baptist Church, where her family worshipped. "I would go and knock on their screen door. '*Afro!* Anybody want an *Afro?*' I would open the screen door and if no one answered, I'd go in. I could look through the house and see them out back," she remembers. "Some people would leave their pocketbooks on the chair in the front room or on their table. I would go into so many peoples' houses." * * *

Mathematics
BLACK ON BOTH SIDES (Priority Records 1999).

■ MOS DEF

* * *

Yo, it's one universal law but two sides to every story

Three strikes and you be in for life, mandatory

* * *

Young soldiers tryin' to earn they next stripe

When the average minimum wage is $5.15

You best believe you gotta find a new ground to get cream

The white unemployment rate, is nearly more than triple for black

so frontliners got they gun in your back

Bubblin' crack, jewel theft and robbery to combat poverty

and end up in the global jail economy

Stiffer stipulations attached to each sentence

Budget cutbacks but increased police presence

And even if you get out of prison still livin'

join the other five million under state supervision

This is business, no faces just lines and statistics
from your phone, your zip code, to S-S-I digits
The system break man child and women into figures
Two columns for who is, and who ain't niggaz
Numbers is hardly real and they never have feelings
but you push too hard, even numbers got limits
Why did one straw break the camel's back? Here's the secret:
the million other straws underneath it—it's all mathematics.

* * *

Homelessness and the Issue of Freedom
39 UCLA L. Rev. 295, 299–302 (1991).

■ Jeremy Waldron

Estimates of the number of homeless people in the United States range from 250,000 to three million. A person who is homeless is, obviously enough, a person who has no home. One way of describing the plight of a homeless individual might be to say that there is no place governed by a private property rule where he is allowed to be.

In fact, that is not quite correct. Any private proprietor may invite a homeless person into his house or onto his land, and if he does there *will* be some private place where the homeless person is allowed to be. A technically more accurate description of his plight is that there is no place governed by a private property rule where he is allowed to be whenever *he* chooses, no place governed by a private property rule from which he may not at any time be excluded as a result of someone else's say-so. As far as being on private property is concerned—in people's houses or gardens, on farms or in hotels, in offices or restaurants—the homeless person is utterly and at all times at the mercy of others. And we know enough about how this mercy is generally exercised to figure that the description in the previous paragraph is more or less accurate as a matter of fact, even if it is not strictly accurate as a matter of law.

For the most part the homeless are excluded from *all* of the places governed by private property rules, whereas the rest of us are, in the same sense, excluded from *all but one* (or maybe all but a few) of those places. That is another way of saying that each of us has at least one place to be in a country composed of private places, whereas the homeless person has none.

Some libertarians fantasize about the possibility that *all* the land in a society might be held as private property ("Sell the streets!") This would be catastrophic for the homeless. Since most private proprietors are already disposed to exclude him from their property, the homeless person might discover in such a libertarian paradise that there was literally *nowhere* he was allowed to be. Wherever he went he would be liable to penalties for trespass and he would be liable to eviction, to being thrown out by an owner or dragged away by the police. Moving from one place to another would involve nothing more liberating than moving from one trespass liability to another. Since land is finite in any society, there is only a limited number of places where a person can (physically) be, and such a person would find that he was legally excluded from all of them. (It would not be entirely mischievous to add that since, in order to exist, a person has to be *somewhere*, such a person would not be permitted to exist.)

Our society saves the homeless from this catastrophe only by virtue of the fact that some of its territory is held as collective property and made available for common use. The homeless are allowed to *be*—provided they are on the streets, in the parks, or under the bridges. Some of them are allowed to crowd together into publicly provided "shelters" after dark (though these are dangerous places and there are not nearly enough shelters for all of them). But in the daytime and, for many of them, all through the night, wandering in public places is their only option. When all else is privately owned, the sidewalks are their salvation. They are allowed to *be* in our society only to the extent that our society is communist.

This is one of the reasons why most defenders of private property are uncomfortable with the libertarian proposal, and why that proposal remains sheer fantasy. But there is a modified form of the libertarian catastrophe in prospect with which moderate and even liberal defenders of ownership seem much more comfortable. This is the increasing regulation of the streets, subways, parks, and other public places to restrict the activities that can be performed there. What is emerging—and it is not just a matter of fantasy—is a state of affairs in which a million or more citizens have no place to perform elementary human activities like urinating, washing, sleeping, cooking, eating, and standing around. Legislators voted for by people who own private places in which they can do all these things are increasingly deciding to make public places available only for activities other than these primal human tasks. The streets and subways, they say, are for commuting from home to office. They are not for sleeping; sleeping is something one does at home. The parks are for recreations like walking and informal ball-games, things for which one's own yard is a little too confined. Parks are not for cooking or urinating; again, these are things one does at home. Since the public and the private are complementary, the activities performed in public are to be the complement of those appropriately performed in private. This complementarity works fine for those who have the benefit of both sorts of places. However, it is disastrous for those who must live their whole lives on common land. If I am right about this, it is one of the most callous and tyrannical exercises of power in modern times by a (comparatively) rich and complacent majority against a minority of their less fortunate fellow human beings.

NOTES AND QUESTIONS

1. Illicit activity as means for survival. Traditionally, the majority of African American women have been obliged, by necessity, to work outside the home to support their families. LEITH MULLINGS, ON OUR OWN TERMS: RACE, CLASS, AND GENDER IN THE LIVES OF AFRICAN AMERICAN WOMEN 90 (1997). Due to severe levels of unemployment of black men, the labor force participation rate of black females has become approximately equal to that of black males. *Id.* Though black women comprise a considerable proportion of the labor force, women like Rosa Lee still face several obstacles to achieve economic stability and must therefore resort to either government assistance and/or illicit activity to support their families. In a study performed in Central Harlem in 1990, for example, 54.7 percent of women eligible to work were not in the labor force, with 28.9 percent of individuals residing in Harlem receiving Aid to Families with Dependent Children. *Id.* at 91 (citing *Persons 16 Years and Over by Labor Force Status and Sex, New York City, Boroughs and Community Districts.* (New York: Department of City Planning, no. 317, 1990)). Furthermore, that study found that more than half of all households in Harlem headed by females that include children under age eighteen have incomes below the poverty line. *Id.* (citing *Socioeconomic profiles: A Portrait of New York City's Community Districts from the 1980 and 1990 Census of Population and Housing* (New York: Department of City Planning)). Faced with poor odds of achieving economic stability, and in "just trying to survive," what can women like Rosa Lee do but break the law to support their families?

University of Pennsylvania Professor of Law Regina Austin explains that though illegal activity may be disparaged, it may be the only means for underprivileged African Americans to survive in America:

> [F]or some poor blacks, breaking the law is not only a way of life: it is the only way to survive. Thus, what is characterized as economic deviance in the eyes of a majority of people may be viewed as economic resistance by a significant number of blacks. Regina Austin, *"An Honest Living": Street Vendors, Municipal Regulation, and The Black Public Sphere*, 103 YALE L.J. 2119, 2119 (1994).

Austin reaches this conclusion based on her study of black street vendors in major cities like New York, Washington, D.C., and Philadelphia. These vendors are part of an informal economy where merchants work without a license and in violation of applicable regulations and sales tax laws. Though illegal, street vending by black workers gives people jobs, supplies African Americans with their preferred products, contributes to the maintenance of African American culture, and assists individuals in gaining the necessary capital and knowledge to operate a business in the formal sector. Because of street vending's benefits for afflicted black communities, Austin stresses that such activity should not immediately be written off, and should instead be respected:

> As blacks in America, we must not fall into the trap of automatically equating legitimacy with legality. Just because an enterprise is small,

informal, and illegal does not mean that it is not valuable or that it should be disparaged. *Id.* at 2130.

Based on her comments, how do you think Austin would react to Rosa Lee's illegal behavior? Would she disagree with Rosa Lee's actions because stealing, like street vending, does not achieve legitimate objectives such as promoting African American black entrepreneurial activity?

2. Sociology of deviance. Are lawbreakers innately inclined to transgress social norms, or are they simply reacting to society's imposed institutions? In other words, are individuals like Rosa Lee instinctively prone to deviate from societal standards, or are they simply products of their insolvent, unstable environments? Howard S. Becker addressed these questions in *Outsiders: Studies in the Sociology of Deviance*, and proposed the premise that deviant peoples violate rules because social groups establish laws whose breach constitutes deviance, and by applying those laws and penalties to an "offender." Becker defines an outsider as an individual who others deem deviant and therefore unworthy of inclusion in society's "normal" social functions.

Would Howard Becker maintain that Rosa Lee is an outsider—one who is judged by law-abiders and stands outside of conventional social groups? Is she more likely to be labeled as an outsider because she is an African American? Becker elaborates on the implications of being an outsider:

> The degree to which an act will be treated as deviant depends also on who commits the act and who feels he has been harmed by it. Rules tend to be applied more to some persons than others. Studies of juvenile delinquency make the point clearly. Boys from middleclass areas do not get as far in the legal process when they are apprehended as do boys from slum areas. The middle-class boy is less likely, when picked up by the police, to be taken to the station; less likely when taken to the station to be booked; and it is extremely unlikely that he will be convicted and sentenced. This variation occurs even though the original infraction of the rule is the same in the two cases. Similarly, the law is differentially applied to Negroes and whites. It is well known that a Negro believed to have attacked a white woman is much more likely to be punished than a white man who commits the same offense; it is only slightly less well known that a Negro who murders another Negro is much less likely to be punished than a white man who commits murder.

HOWARD S. BECKER, OUTSIDERS: STUDIES IN THE SOCIOLOGY OF DEVIANCE 12–13 (1973).

Consider Becker's proposition and Rosa Lee's case. Recall that Rosa Lee was acquitted when she returned to court for a shoplifting charge. Though she is African American and a "deviant outsider," she was able to receive approval from the judge and continue to maintain her freedom. However, was Rosa Lee not trying to portray herself as an "insider" by wearing more respectable attire and emotionally appealing to the judge?

3. **"Underclass" and "culture of poverty."** Since the 1970s, conservative scholars and critics have attempted to highlight the role of "culture" in maintaining poverty, arguing that poverty becomes intergenerational when poor people lack self-discipline, initiative, and "soft skills" required for success in the working world. These arguments played a large part in welfare reform from the 1970s through the turn of the twenty-first century. A similar debate has gone on about the so-called "underclass," identified as a group of people (Marx would have called them an "industrial reserve army") so chronically lacking regular employment that they can be seen as having effectively been marginalized from the economy altogether. In the late 1980s, the media spent a lot of time worrying about the "underclass," which was said to epitomize all the cultural deviance (lack of initiative, dependency, and so on) exhibited by the poor more generally, and which was thought to be a breeding ground for street crime. For scholarly discussions of the "underclass," *see, e.g.*, WILLIAM JULIUS WILSON, THE TRULY DISADVANTAGED: THE INNER CITY, THE UNDERCLASS, AND PUBLIC POLICY (1987); CHRISTOPHER JENCKS, RETHINKING SOCIAL POLICY: RACE, POVERTY, AND THE UNDERCLASS (1992).

Is it "culture" or material conditions that account for the large gaps that remain in family income, wages, and employment between African Americans and whites? For a "cultural" explanation, *see, e.g.*, STEPHEN THERNSTROM & ABIGAIL THERNSTROM, *America in Black and White* (1997); for a "material" explanation, *see, e.g.*, MICHAEL K. BROWN, ET AL., WHITEWASHING RACE: THE MYTH OF A COLOR-BLIND SOCIETY 66–103 (2003). Does a material explanation account for the behavior of people like Rosa Lee?

4. ***"Underclass"* and prison industrial complex.** Some might argue that to the extent that an underclass exists, it is, ironically, the effect as much as the cause of state policy. The "war on drugs" and the "war on crime" more generally have created an incarceration crisis for many poor communities. African American and Latino men are incarcerated for long periods at dramatic rates, which creates a social ripple effect of poverty: ex-felons find it difficult to get jobs when they get out of prison; the removal of these men from families and neighborhoods places extra economic and social stress on the people left behind. This social disorganization, in turn, leads to more crime in the increasingly impoverished and dangerous neighborhoods of inner cities. *See* Tracey Meares, *Social Organization and Drug Law Enforcement*, 35 AM. CRIM. L. REV. 191 (1998); Dorothy Roberts, *The Social and Moral Cost of Mass Incarceration in African American Communities*, 56 STAN. L. REV. 1271 (2004).

Some scholars argue that this vicious circle is coupled with another vicious circle: the increasing dependency of strapped towns and counties on prisons as economic engines, which leads to the increased political power of prison guards and prison officials unions, which leads in turn to a continuation of punitive criminal justice policies. *See* Stephen C. Thaman, *Is America a Systematic Violator of Human Rights in the Administration of Criminal Justice?* 44 ST. LOUIS L.J. 999 (2000). Another element in the continuing appeal of punitive policies, some scholars argue, is the declining influence of criminal justice experts: criminal justice policy today tends to be seen as a populist issue and not an issue about which experts should have any particular say. In this environment, politicians promising to be "tough on crime" and prosecutors dominate the legislative process. *See* Franklin Zimring, *Populism, Democratic Government, and the Decline of Expert Authority: Some Reflections on "Three Strikes" in California*, 28 PAC. L.J. 243 (1996); William Stuntz, *The Pathological Politics of Criminal Law*, 100 MICH. L. REV. 505 (2001).

5. **Crime, class, and race**. The United States mass incarceration policy does not seem to have been either effective at stopping crime nor economically efficient. Why, then, has it persisted? Some scholars argue that punitive criminal justice policy serves ideological functions that are more powerful than their economic or social functions. *See, e.g.*, JEFFREY REIMAN, THE RICH GET RICHER AND THE POOR GET PRISON: IDEOLOGY, CLASS, AND CRIMINAL JUSTICE (7TH ED. 2003); MICHAEL TONRY, MALIGN NEGLECT: RACE, CRIME, AND PUNISHMENT IN AMERICA (1996); DAVID COLE, NO EQUAL JUSTICE: RACE AND CLASS IN THE AMERICAN CRIMINAL JUSTICE SYSTEM (2000).

6. **Homelessness and criminal justice policy.** Like "the underclass," "the homeless" are frequently a target of fear and loathing in American culture; like the poor generally, some make an effort to distinguish the innocent or involuntary homeless from those who have "chosen" their situation; and like poverty generally, homelessness and crime are closely connected in the public mind, resulting in, ironically, more criminalization. *See* CHRISTOPHER JENCKS, THE HOMELESS (1995); PETER H. ROSSI, DOWN AND OUT IN AMERICA: THE ORIGINS OF HOMELESSNESS (1991). For a lively discussion of how not only law but architecture and urban planning are affected by the desire to make homeless people invisible in city spaces, see MIKE DAVIS, CITY OF QUARTZ: EXCAVATING THE FUTURE IN LOS ANGELES (1992).

B. RELATIONS OF (RE)PRODUCTION

The Working Poor: Invisible in America
39–44 50, 64–67 (2004).

■ DAVID K. SHIPLER

Christie did a job that this labor-hungry economy could not do without. Every morning she drove her battered '86 Volkswagen from her apartment in public housing to the YWCA's child-care center in Akron, Ohio, where she spent the day watching over little children so their parents could go to work. Without her and thousands like her across the country, there would have been fewer people able to fill the jobs that fueled America's prosperity. Without her patience and warmth, children could have been harmed as well, for she was more than a baby-sitter. She gave the youngsters an emotionally safe place, taught and mothered them, and sometimes even rescued them from abuse at home.

For those valuable services, she received a check for about $330 every two weeks. She could not afford to put her own two children in the day-care center where she worked.

Christie was a hefty woman who laughed more readily than her predicament should have allowed. She suffered from stress and high blood pressure. She had no bank account because she could not keep enough money long enough. Try as she might to shop carefully, she always fell behind on her bills and was peppered with late fees. Her low income entitled her to food stamps and a rental subsidy, but whenever she got a little pay raise, government agencies reduced the benefits, and she felt punished for working. She was trapped on the treadmill of welfare reform, running her life according to the rules of the Personal Responsibility and Work Opportunity Reconciliation Act of 1996. The title left no doubt about what Congress and the White House saw as poverty's cause and solution.

Initially the new law combined with the good economy to send welfare caseloads plummeting. As states were granted flexibility in administering time limits and work requirements, some created innovative consortiums of government, industry, and charity to guide people into effective job training and employment. But most available jobs had three unhappy traits: They paid low wages, offered no benefits, and led nowhere. "Many who do find jobs," the Urban Institute concluded in a 2002 report, "lose other supports designed to help them, such as food stamps and health insurance, leaving them no better off—and sometimes worse off—than when they were not working."

Christie considered herself such a case. The only thing in her wallet resembling a credit card was a blue-green piece of plastic labeled "Ohio" and decorated with a drawing of a lighthouse projecting a beam into the night. Inside the "O" was a gold square—a computer chip. On the second working day of every month, she slipped the card into a special machine at Walgreen's, Save-A-Lot, or Apple's, and punched in her identification number. A credit of $136 was loaded into her chip. This was the form in which her "food stamps" were now issued—less easy to steal or to sell, and less obvious and degrading in the checkout line.

The card contained her first bit of income in every month and permitted her first expenditure. It could be used for food only, and not for cooked food or pet food. It occupied the top line in the balance sheet she kept for me during a typical October.

"2nd Spent 136.00 food stamps," she wrote. So the benefit was all gone the day she got it. Three days later she had to come up with an additional $25 in cash for groceries, another $54 on October 10, and $15 more on the twelfth. Poor families typically find that food stamps cover only one-half to three-quarters of their grocery costs.

Even the opening balance on the card was chipped away as Christie inched up in salary. It makes sense that the benefit is based on income: the less you need, the less you get. That's the economic side. On the psychological side, however, it produces hellish experiences for the beneficiaries.

Every three months Christie had to take half a day off from work (losing half a day's wages) and carry an envelope full of pay stubs, utility bills, and rent receipts to be pawed over by her ill-tempered caseworker, who applied a state-mandated formula to figure her food stamp allotment and her children's eligibility for health insurance. When Christie completed a training course and earned a raise of 10 cents an hour, her food stamps dropped by $10 a month.

That left her $6 a month ahead, which was not nothing but felt like it. Many former welfare recipients who go to work just say good riddance to the bureaucracies that would provide food stamps, medical coverage, and housing. Some think wrongly that they're no longer eligible once they're off welfare; others would rather forfeit their rights than contend with the hassle and humiliation. Quiet surrender ran against Christie's grain, however. She was smart and insistent, as anyone must be to negotiate her way through the system. She never flinched from appealing to higher authority. When she once forgot to put a utilities bill in her sheaf of papers, her caseworker withheld her food stamps. "I mailed it to her the next day," Christie said. Two weeks passed, and the card remained empty. Christie called the caseworker. "She got really snotty," Christie remembered. " 'Well, didn't I tell you you were supposed to send some documentation?' "

"I was like, 'Have you checked your mail?' " No, as it turned out, the caseworker's mail had piled up unread. "She was like, 'Well, I got people waiting up to two, three months on food stamps.' And she didn't get back with me. I had to go to her supervisor." The benefits were then restored.

It is easy to lose your balance having one foot planted tentatively in the working world and the other still entwined in this thicket of red tape. Managing relations with a boss, finding reliable child care, and coping with a tangle of unpaid bills can be daunting enough for a single mother with little such experience; add surveillance by a bureaucracy that seems more prosecutor than provider, and you have Christie's high blood pressure.

While she invoked the system's rules to get her due, she also cheated—or thought she did. Living with her surreptitiously was her boyfriend, Kevin, the father of her son. She was certain that if the Housing Authority knew, she would be evicted, either because he was a convicted felon (two years for assault) or because his earning power, meager though it was, would have lifted her beyond eligibility. So slight are the margins between government assistance and outright destitution that small lies take on large significance in the search for survival.

Kevin looked like a friendly giant—a solid 280 pounds, a shaved head, and a small earring in his right ear. His income was erratic. In decent weather he made $7.40 an hour working for a landscaper, who rewarded him with a free turkey to end the season at Thanksgiving—and then dumped him onto unemployment for the winter. He wanted to drive a truck or cut meat. He had received a butcher's certificate in a training course during imprisonment, but when he showed the document from the penitentiary, employers didn't rush to put a knife in his hand.

The arithmetic of Christie's life added up to tension, and you had to look hard through her list of expenditures to find fun or luxury. On the fifth she received her weekly child support check of $37.66 from Kevin (she got nothing from her daughter's father, who was serving a long prison sentence for assault). The same day, she put $5 worth of gas in her car, and the next day spent $6 of her own money to take the day-care kids to the zoo. The eighth was payday, and her entire $330 check disappeared in a flash. First, there was what she called a $3 "tax" to cash her check, just one of several such fees for money orders and the like—a penalty for having no checking account. Immediately, $172 went for rent, including a $10 late fee, which she was always charged because she never had enough to pay by the first of the month. Then, because it was October and she had started to plan for Christmas, she paid $31.47 at a store for presents she had put on layaway, another $10 for gasoline, $40 to buy shoes for her two kids, $5 for a pair of corduroy pants at a secondhand shop, another $5 for a shirt, $10 for bell-bottom pants, and $47 biweekly car insurance. The $330 was gone. She had no insurance on her TVs, clothes, furniture, or other household goods.

Utilities and other bills got paid out of her second check toward the end of the month. Her phone usually cost about $43 a month, gas for the apartment $34, electricity $46, and prescriptions between $8 and $15. Her monthly car payment ran $150, medical insurance $72, and cable TV $43. Cable is no longer considered a luxury by low-income families that pinch and sacrifice to have it. So much of modern American culture now comes through television that the poor would be further marginalized without the broad access that cable provides. Besides, it's relatively cheap entertainment. "I just have basic," Christie explained. "I have an antenna, but you can't see anything, you get no reception." And she needed good reception because she and Kevin loved to watch wrestling.

One reason for Christie's tight budget was the abundance of high-priced, well-advertised snacks, junk food, and prepared meals that provide an easy fallback diet for a busy working mother—or for anyone who has never learned to cook from scratch. Besides the staples of hamburgers, and chicken, "I buy sausages," Christie said, "I buy the TV dinners 'cause I might be tired some days and throw it in the oven—like Salisbury steaks and turkey and stuff like that. My kids love pizza. I get the frozen pizzas.... I buy my kids a lot of breakfast things 'cause we're up early and we're out the door. You know, those cereal bars and stuff like that, they're expensive! You know? Pop Tarts, cereal bars, Granola." The cheaper breakfasts, like hot cereal, came only on weekends, when she had time. "They eat the hot cereal, but during the week we're on the go. So I give them cereal in the bag. My son likes to eat dry cereal, so I put him some cereal in the lunch bag. Cocoa Puffs. They got Cocoa Dots." She laughed. "Lucky Charms. He's not picky. My daughter's picky." Those candylike cereals soak up dollars. At my local supermarket, Lucky Charms cost dearly: $4.39 for a box of just 14 ounces, while three times as much oatmeal goes for nearly the same price, $4.29. * * *

Her mother, "Gladys," had dropped out of high school, spent years on welfare, and nurtured the fervent dream of seeing her three children in college. The ambition propelled two of them. Christie's brother became an accountant, and her sister, a loan officer. But Christie never took to higher education. She began reluctantly at the University of Akron, lived at home, and finally got fed up with having no money. The second semester of her sophomore year, she went to work instead of to school, a choice that struck her then as less momentous than it turned out to be.

"She didn't take things as serious as they really were," Gladys complained. "Now she sees for herself how serious this is." Just how serious depended on what she wanted to do. She loved working with children but now discovered that without a college degree she would have trouble getting hired at a responsible level in the Head Start preschool program, much less as a teacher in a regular school; she was limited to a YWCA day-care center whose finances were precarious. Since 95 percent of the Y's children came from low-income families, the fees were essentially set by the center's main source of income, Ohio's Department of Human Services, which paid $99 to $114 a week for full-time care. Given the center's heavy expenses, the rates were not enough to pay teachers more than $5.30 to $5.90 an hour.

Christie's previous jobs had also imprisoned her close to the minimum wage as a hostess-cashier at a Holiday Inn, a cashier at Kmart, a waitress in a bar, a cook and waitress and cashier in various restaurants. She had become a veteran of inadequate training programs designed to turn her into a retail salesperson, a bus driver, and a correctional officer, but the courses never enabled her and her classmates to pass the tests and get hired. She had two words to explain why she had never returned to college. "Lazy. Lazy."

It was strange that she thought of herself as lazy, because her work was exhausting, and her low wage required enormous effort to stay afloat.
* * *

The new millennium arrived in a crescendo of American riches. The nation wallowed in luxury, burst with microchips, consumed with abandon, swaggered globally. Everything grew larger: homes, vehicles, stock portfolios, life expectancy. Never before in the sweep of human history had so many people been so utterly comfortable.

Caroline Payne was not one of them. A few weeks after New Year's Day, she sat at her kitchen table and reflected on her own history. Two of her three goals had been achieved: She had earned a college diploma, albeit just a two-year associate's degree. And she had gone from a homeless shelter into her own house, although it was mostly owned by a bank. The third objective, "a good-paying job," as she put it, still eluded her. Back in the mid–1970s, she earned $6 an hour in a Vermont factory that made plastic cigarette lighters and cases for Gillette razors. In 2000, she earned $6.80 an hour stocking shelves and working cash registers at a vast Wal-Mart superstore in New Hampshire. * * *

Anyone who walked all the way around the outside of the Wal-Mart superstore on Route 103 would walk a mile, Caroline said. The place was immense. It sold everything from lawn mowers to ground beef, underpricing smaller stores that were struggling to survive in the center of town. Its 300 to 330 employees, who came and went seasonally, wore Wal-Mart's uniform of blue smocks and friendly smiles, trained as they were to be surprisingly helpful to customers.

Mark Brown, the manager, could pay his people more without raising prices, he conceded. He sat at a table in the store's snack bar, watching the part of the grocery section he could see, listening to the public address system's call for help at the registers, his eyes darting around this corner of his fiefdom like a school principal waiting for the next catastrophe. He was thirty-one, but he looked as young as a college kid and spoke with the twang of his native southeast Missouri. He had come from another store in Georgia and was learning to ski here in New Hampshire.

His employees started at $6.25 an hour, earned an extra dollar at night and another 25 cents "for going to the front end," which meant working one of the twenty-four cash registers. And if he started them at $8 an hour, say, instead of $6.25, how would that change the economics of the store? "Hmmmm. I don't think it would change at all." He wouldn't have to raise prices? "No. We've got a corporate pricing structure. And the way we do things, we go out and we check our competition every single week. Every department manager in this store goes out once a week and checks competition, and that's what determines our prices. We have a core price structure that we set regionally, by areas. Definitely the base price here would be probably higher than what it is in Arkansas, where there's a cheap cost of living. So it would be higher here, but it would still be standard to this area. And then after they give us that base, then we go out and check our competition, and if we're gettin' beat, we lower our prices."

So there's enough profit to absorb an increase from $6.25 to $8? "There would be, because if we were having to raise our wages, then evidently everybody else would be too, and if we make sure we're low enough, our competitors' customers are gonna shop with us." Would wage increases have any effect at all? "We'd have to cut corners on other things like, you know, we may not be able to put all the pretty balloons up all over the store. The non-necessities we'd have to cut back on."

Three days later Wal-Mart Stores, Inc., announced a net income of $5.58 billion for 1999, up 26 percent from the previous year.

Caroline was bouncing from one department to another, from one shift to another, but her pay stayed within a narrow range, beginning at $6.25, going to $6.80, sometimes up to $7.50 if she worked at night. So unpredictable were her hours that she couldn't work a second job, which would have helped her cash flow. She kept applying to higher positions and kept hearing that she needed a bit more experience. * * *

In more depressed parts of the country and during recessions,* * * some Wal-Mart managers were accused of forcing employees to work before punching in or after punching out to avoid paying overtime as required by law. "Wal-Mart management doesn't hold itself to the same standard of rectitude it expects from its low-paid employees," wrote Barbara Ehrenreich, who worked at a Wal-Mart in Minnesota while researching her book *Nickel and Dimed*. "When I applied for a job at Wal-Mart in the spring of 2000, I was reprimanded for getting something 'wrong' on this test: I had agreed only 'strongly' to the proposition, 'All rules have to be followed to the letter at all times.' The correct answer was 'totally agree.' Apparently the one rule that need not be slavishly adhered to at Wal-Mart is the federal Fair Labor Standards Act, which requires that employees be paid time and a half if they work more than forty hours in a week." Workers were warned against "time theft," which meant "doing anything other than working during company time, anything at all," she reported. "Theft of *our* time is not, however, an issue."

Caroline never had the overtime problem in her New Hampshire store, but in six Southern states employees filed a class-action suit against the company for ordering them off the clock as their weekly time approached forty hours. Their attorney calculated the benefits to the firm: If each of 250 hourly wage "associates" in a single store worked just one hour of unpaid overtime a week, that would total 250 unpaid hours a week, 1,000 a month, 12,000 a year—and there were over 300 Wal-Mart stores in Texas, producing savings in that state alone of more than $30 million that should have been paid to employees.

Caroline did not suffer from any violations of law, as far as she could tell, but her career went nowhere. Mark Brown, the manager who liked her, got transferred to Pennsylvania, dimming her prospects for advancement. So after a year and a half at Wal-Mart, she signed up with a temp agency, which found her a $7.50–an-hour daytime job Monday through Friday assembling wallpaper sample books. And she had the pleasure of telling Wal-Mart's assistant manager that she was leaving for higher pay.

Down and Out in Discount America

The Nation, Dec. 16 2004, http://www.thenation.com/doc.mhtml?i=20050103&s=featherstone.

Liza Featherstone

On the day after Thanksgiving, the biggest shopping day of the year, Wal-Mart's many progressive critics—not to mention its business competitors—finally enjoyed a bit of schadenfreude when the retailer had to admit to "disappointing" sales. The problem was quickly revealed: Wal-Mart hadn't been discounting aggressively enough. Without low prices, Wal-Mart just isn't Wal-Mart.

That's not a mistake the big-box behemoth is likely to make again. Wal-Mart knows its customers, and it knows how badly they need the discounts. Like Wal-Mart's workers, its customers are overwhelmingly female, and struggling to make ends meet. Betty Dukes, the lead plaintiff in *Dukes v. Wal-Mart*, the landmark sex-discrimination case against the company, points out that Wal-Mart takes out ads in her local paper the same day the community's poorest citizens collect their welfare checks. "They are promoting themselves to low-income people," she says. "That's who they lure. They don't lure the rich.... They understand the economy of America. They know the haves and have-nots. They don't put Wal-Mart in Piedmonts. They don't put Wal-Mart in those high-end parts of the community. They plant themselves right in the middle of Poorville."

Betty Dukes is right. A 2000 study by Andrew Franklin, then an economist at the University of Connecticut, showed that Wal-Mart operated primarily in poor and working-class communities, finding, in the bone-dry language of his discipline, "a significant negative relationship between median household income and Wal-Mart's presence in the market." Although fancy retailers noted with chagrin during the 2001 recession that absolutely everybody shops at Wal-Mart—"Even people with $100,000 incomes now shop at Wal-Mart," a PR flack for one upscale mall fumed—the Bloomingdale's set is not the discounter's primary market, and probably never will be. Only 6 percent of Wal-Mart shoppers have annual family incomes of more than $100,000. A 2003 study found that 23 percent of Wal-Mart Supercenter customers live on incomes of less than $25,000 a year. More than 20 percent of Wal-Mart shoppers have no bank account, long considered a sign of dire poverty. And while almost half of Wal-Mart Supercenter customers are blue-collar workers and their families, 20 percent are unemployed or elderly.

Al Zack, who until his retirement in 2004 was the United Food and Commercial Workers' vice president for strategic programs, observes that appealing to the poor was "Sam Walton's real genius. He figured out how to make money off of poverty. He located his first stores in poor rural areas and discovered a real market. The only problem with the business model is that it really needs to create more poverty to grow." That problem is cleverly solved by creating more bad jobs worldwide. In a chilling reversal of Henry Ford's strategy, which was to pay his workers amply so they could buy Ford cars, Wal-Mart's stingy compensation policies—workers make, on average, just over $8 an hour, and if they want health insurance, they must pay more than a third of the premium—contribute to an economy in which, increasingly, workers can only afford to shop at Wal-Mart.

To make this model work, Wal-Mart must keep labor costs down. It does this by making corporate crime an integral part of its business strategy. Wal-Mart routinely violates laws protecting workers' organizing rights (workers have even been fired for union activity). It is a repeat offender on overtime laws; in more than thirty states, workers have brought wage-and-hour class-action suits against the retailer. In some cases, workers say, managers encouraged them to clock out and keep working; in others, managers locked the doors and would not let employees go home at the end of their shifts. And it's often women who suffer most from Wal-Mart's labor practices. *Dukes v. Wal-Mart*, which is the largest civil rights class-action suit in history, charges the company with systematically discriminating against women in pay and promotions. * * *

SOLIDARITY ACROSS THE CHECKOUT COUNTER

Given the poverty they have in common, it makes sense that Wal-Mart's workers often express a strong feeling of solidarity with the shoppers. Wal-Mart workers tend to be aware that the customers' circumstances are similar to their own, and to identify with them. Some complain about rude customers, but most seem to genuinely enjoy the shoppers.

One longtime department manager in Ohio cheerfully recalls her successful job interview at Wal-Mart. Because of her weight, she told her interviewers, she'd be better able to help the customer. "I told them I wanted to work in the ladies department because I'm a heavy girl." She understands the frustrations of the large shopper, she told them: " 'You know, you go into Lane Bryant and some skinny girl is trying to sell you clothes.' They laughed at that and said, 'You get a second interview!' "

One plaintiff in the *Dukes* lawsuit, Cleo Page, who no longer works at Wal-Mart, says she was a great customer service manager because "I knew how people feel when they shop, so I was really empathetic."

Many Wal-Mart workers say they began working at their local Wal-Mart because they shopped there. "I was practically born in Wal-Mart," says Alyssa Warrick, a former employee now attending Truman State University in Missouri. "My mom is obsessed with shopping.... I thought it would be pretty easy since I knew where most of the stuff was." Most assumed they would love working at Wal-Mart. "I always loved shopping there," enthuses *Dukes* plaintiff Dee Gunter. "That's why I wanted to work for 'em."

Shopping is traditionally a world of intense female communication and bonding, and women have long excelled in retail sales in part because of the identification between clerk and shopper. Page, who still shops at Wal-Mart, is now a lingerie saleswoman at Mervyn's (owned by Target). "I do enjoy retail," she says. "I like feeling needed and I like helping people, especially women."

Betty Dukes says, "I strive to give Wal-Mart customers one hundred percent of my abilities." This sentiment was repeated by numerous other Wal-Mart workers, always with heartfelt sincerity. Betty Hamilton, a 61-year-old clerk in a Las Vegas Sam's Club, won her store's customer service award last year. She is very knowledgeable about jewelry, her favorite department, and proud of it. Hamilton resents her employer—she complains about sexual harassment and discrimination, and feels she has been penalized on the job for her union sympathies—but remains deeply devoted to her customers. She enjoys imparting her knowledge to shoppers so "they can walk out of there and feel like they know something." Like Page, Hamilton feels she is helping people. "It makes me so happy when I sell something that I know is an extraordinarily good buy," she says. "I feel like I've done somebody a really good favor."

The enthusiasm of these women for their jobs, despite the workplace indignities many of them have faced, should not assure anybody that the company's abuses don't matter. In fact, it should underscore the tremendous debt Wal-Mart owes women: This company has built its vast profits not only on women's drudgery but also on their joy, creativity and genuine care for the customer.

Why Boycotts Don't Always Work

Will consumers return that solidarity and punish Wal-Mart for discriminating against women? Do customers care about workers as much as workers care about them? Some women's groups, like the National Organization for Women and Code Pink, have been hoping that they do, and have encouraged the public not to shop at Wal-Mart. While this tactic could be fruitful in some community battles, it's unlikely to catch on nationwide. A customer saves 20–25 percent by buying groceries at Wal-Mart rather than from a competitor, according to retail analysts, and poor women need those savings more than anyone.

That's why many women welcome the new Wal-Marts in their communities. *The Winona* (Minnesota) *Post* extensively covered a controversy over whether to allow a Wal-Mart Supercenter into the small town; the letters to the editor in response offer a window into the female customer's loyalty to Wal-Mart. Though the paper devoted substantial space to the sex discrimination case, the readers who most vehemently defended the retailer were female. From the nearby town of Rollingstone, Cindy Kay wrote that she needed the new Wal-Mart because the local stores didn't carry large-enough sizes. She denounced the local anti-Wal-Mart campaign as a plot by rich and thin elites: "I'm glad those people can fit into and afford such clothes. I can barely afford Shopko and Target!"

A week later, Carolyn Goree, a preschool teacher also hoping for a Winona Wal-Mart, wrote in a letter to the *Post* editor that when she shops at most stores, $200 fills only a bag or two, but at Wal-Mart, "I come out with a cart full top and bottom. How great that feels." Lacking a local Wal-Mart, Goree drives over the Wisconsin border to get her fix. She was incensed by an earlier article's lament that some workers make only $15,000 yearly. "Come on!" Goree objected. "Is $15,000 really that bad of a yearly income? I'm a single mom and when working out of my home, I made $12,000 tops and that was with child support. I too work, pay for a mortgage, lights, food, everything to live. Everything in life is a choice.... I am for the little man/woman—I'm one of them. So I say stand up and get a Wal-Mart."

Sara Jennings, a disabled Winona reader living on a total of $8,000, heartily concurred. After paying her rent, phone, electric and cable bills, Jennings can barely afford to treat herself to McDonald's. Of a recent trip to the LaCrosse, Wisconsin, Wal-Mart, she raved, "Oh boy, what a great treat. Lower prices and a good quality of clothes to choose from. It was like heaven for me." She, too, strongly defended the workers' $15,000 yearly income: "Boy, now that is a lot of money. I could live with that." She closed with a plea to the readers: "I'm sure you all make a lot more than I. And I'm sure I speak for a lot of seniors and very-low-income people. We *need* this Wal-Mart. There's nothing downtown."

From Consumers to Workers and Citizens

It is crucial that Wal-Mart's liberal and progressive critics make use of the growing public indignation at the company over sex discrimination, low pay and other workers' rights issues, but it is equally crucial to do this in ways that remind people that their power does not stop at their shopping dollars. It's admirable to drive across town and pay more for toilet paper to avoid shopping at Wal-Mart, but such a gesture is, unfortunately, not enough. As long as people identify themselves as consumers and nothing more, Wal-Mart wins.

The invention of the "consumer" identity has been an important part of a long process of eroding workers' power, and it's one reason working people now have so little power against business. According to the social historian Stuart Ewen, in the early years of mass production, the late nineteenth and early twentieth centuries, modernizing capitalism sought to turn people who thought of themselves primarily as "workers" into "consumers." Business elites wanted people to dream not of satisfying work and egalitarian societies—as many did at that time—but of the beautiful things they could buy with their paychecks.

Business was quite successful in this project, which influenced much early advertising and continued throughout the twentieth century. In addition to replacing the "worker," the "consumer" has also effectively displaced the citizen. That's why, when most Americans hear about the Wal-Mart's worker-rights abuses, their first reaction is to feel guilty about shopping at the store. A tiny minority will respond by shopping elsewhere—and only a handful will take any further action. A worker might call her union and organize a picket. A citizen might write to her congressman or local newspaper, or galvanize her church and knitting circle to visit local management. A consumer makes an isolated, politically slight decision: to shop or not to shop. Most of the time, Wal-Mart has her exactly where it wants her, because the intelligent choice for anyone thinking as a consumer is not to make a political statement but to seek the best bargain and the greatest convenience.

To effectively battle corporate criminals like Wal-Mart, the public must be engaged as citizens, not merely as shoppers. What kind of politics could encourage that? It's not clear that our present political parties are up to the job. Unlike so many horrible things, Wal-Mart cannot be blamed on George W. Bush. The Arkansas-based company prospered under the state's native son Bill Clinton when he was governor and President. Sam Walton and his wife, Helen, were close to the Clintons, and for several years Hillary Clinton, whose law firm represented Wal-Mart, served on the company's board of directors. Bill Clinton's "welfare reform" has provided Wal-Mart with a ready workforce of women who have no choice but to accept its poverty wages and discriminatory policies.

Still, a handful of Democratic politicians stood up to the retailer. California Assemblywoman Sally Lieber, who represents the 22nd Assembly District and is a former mayor of Mountain View, was outraged when she learned about the sex discrimination charges in *Dukes v. Wal-Mart*, and she smelled blood when, tipped off by dissatisfied workers, her office discovered that Wal-Mart was encouraging its workers to apply for public assistance, "in the middle of the worst state budget crisis in history!" California had a $38 billion deficit at the time, and Lieber was enraged that taxpayers would be subsidizing Wal-Mart's low wages, bringing new meaning to the term "corporate welfare."

Lieber was angry, too, that Wal-Mart's welfare dependence made it nearly impossible for responsible employers to compete with the retail giant. It was as if taxpayers were unknowingly funding a massive plunge to the bottom in wages and benefits—quite possibly their own. She held a press conference in July 2003, to expose Wal-Mart's welfare scam. The Wal-Mart documents—instructions explaining how to apply for food stamps, Medi-Cal (the state's healthcare assistance program) and other forms of welfare—were blown up on posterboard and displayed. The morning of the press conference, a Wal-Mart worker who wouldn't give her name for fear of being fired snuck into Lieber's office. "I just wanted to say, right on!" she told the assemblywoman.

Wal-Mart spokespeople have denied that the company encourages employees to collect public assistance, but the documents speak for themselves. They bear the Wal-Mart logo, and one is labeled "Wal-Mart: Instructions for Associates." Both documents instruct employees in procedures for applying to "Social Service Agencies." Most Wal-Mart workers I've interviewed had co-workers who worked full time for the company and received public assistance, and some had been in that situation themselves. Public assistance is very clearly part of the retailer's cost-cutting strategy. (It's ironic that a company so dependent on the public dole supports so many right-wing politicians who'd like to dismantle the welfare state.)

Lieber, a strong supporter of the social safety net who is now assistant speaker pro tempore of the California Assembly, last year passed a bill that would require large and mid-sized corporations that fail to provide decent, affordable health insurance to reimburse local governments for the cost of providing public assistance for those workers. When the bill passed, its opponents decided to kill it by bringing it to a statewide referendum. Wal-Mart, which just began opening Supercenters in California this year, mobilized its resources to revoke the law on election day this November, even while executives denied that any of their employees depended on public assistance.

Citizens should pressure other politicians to speak out against Wal-Mart's abuses and craft policy solutions. But the complicity of both parties in Wal-Mart's power over workers points to the need for a politics that squarely challenges corporate greed and takes the side of ordinary people. That kind of politics seems, at present, strongest at the local level.

Earlier this year, labor and community groups in Chicago prevented Wal-Mart from opening a store on the city's South Side, in part by pushing through an ordinance that would have forced the retailer to pay Chicago workers a living wage. In Hartford, Connecticut, labor and community advocates just won passage of an ordinance protecting their free speech rights on the grounds of the new Wal-Mart Supercenter, which is being built on city property. Similar battles are raging nationwide, but Wal-Mart's opponents don't usually act with as much coordination as Wal-Mart does, and they lack the retail behemoth's deep pockets.

With this in mind, SEIU president Andy Stern has recently been calling attention to the need for better coordination—and funding—of labor and community anti-Wal-Mart efforts. Stern has proposed that the AFL-CIO allocate $25 million of its royalties from purchases on its Union Plus credit card toward fighting Wal-Mart and the "Wal-Martization" of American jobs. * * *

Such efforts are essential not just because Wal-Mart is a grave threat to unionized workers' jobs (which it is) but because it threatens all American ideals that are at odds with profit—ideals such as justice, equality and fairness. Wal-Mart would not have so much power if we had stronger labor laws, and if we required employers to pay a living wage. The company knows that, and it hires lobbyists in Washington to vigorously fight any effort at such reforms—indeed, Wal-Mart has recently beefed up this political infrastructure substantially, and it's likely that its presence in Washington will only grow more conspicuous.

The situation won't change until a movement comes together and builds the kind of social and political power for workers and citizens that can balance that of Wal-Mart. This is not impossible: In Germany, unions are powerful enough to force Wal-Mart to play by their rules. American citizens will have to ask themselves what kind of world they want to live in. That's what prompted Gretchen Adams, a former Wal-Mart manager, to join the effort to unionize Wal-Mart. She's deeply troubled by the company's effect on the economy as a whole and the example it sets for other employers. "What about our working-class people?" she asks. "I don't want to live in a Third World country." Working people, she says, should be able to afford "a new car, a house. You shouldn't have to leave the car on the lawn because you can't afford that $45 part."

NOTES AND QUESTIONS

1. **Wal-Mart as avatar of new economy.** Simon Head notes the phenomenal success of Wal-Mart:

> Within the corporate world Wal-Mart's preeminence is not simply a matter of size. In its analysis of the growth of U.S. productivity, or output per worker, between 1995 and 2000—the years of the "new economy" and the high-tech bubble on Wall Street—the McKinsey

Global Institute has found that just over half that growth took place in two sectors, retail and wholesale, where, directly or indirectly, Wal-Mart "caused the bulk of the productivity acceleration through ongoing managerial innovation that increased competition intensity and drove the diffusion of best practice." This is management-speak for Wal-Mart's aggressive use of information technology and its skill in meeting the needs of its customers.

In its own category of "general merchandise," Wal-Mart has taken a huge lead in productivity over its competitors, a lead of 44 percent in 1987, 48 percent in 1995, and still 41 percent in 1999, even as competitors began to copy Wal-Mart's strategy. Thanks to the company's superior productivity, Wal-Mart's share of total sales among all the sellers of "general merchandise" rose from 9 percent in 1987 to 27 percent in 1995, and 30 percent in 1999, an astonishing rate of growth which recalls the rise of the Ford Motor Company nearly a century ago. McKinsey lists some of the leading causes of Wal-Mart's success. For example, its huge, ugly box-shaped buildings enable Wal-Mart "to carry a wider range of goods than competitors" and to "enjoy labor economies of scale."

McKinsey mentions Wal-Mart's "efficiency in logistics," which makes it possible for the company to buy in bulk directly from producers of everything from toilet paper to refrigerators, allowing it to dispense with wholesalers. McKinsey also makes much of the company's innovative use of information technology, for example its early use of computers and scanners to track inventory, and its use of satellite communications to link corporate headquarters in Arkansas with the nationwide network of Wal-Mart stores. Setting up and fine-tuning these tracking and distribution systems has been the special achievement of founder Sam Walton's (the "Wal" of Wal-Mart) two successors as CEOs, David Glass and the incumbent Lee Scott.

Simon Head, *Inside the Leviathan,* 51 N.Y. REV. BOOKS 80 (2004), *available at* http://www.nybooks.com/archives. Wal-Mart's success has also, however, crucially relied on its ability to keep wages and benefits low. Like Featherstone, Head argues for stronger and better enforced labor laws, asserting that "Wal-Mart has reached back beyond the New Deal to the harsh, abrasive capitalism of the 1920s." *id.*

2. Wal-Mart and gender discrimination. In the summer of 2004, a federal district court certified a sex discrimination class action against Wal-Mart on behalf of 1.6 million women who had worked at Wal-Mart since December 26, 1998. The plaintiffs in *Dukes v. Wal-Mart,* 222 F.R.D. 137 (N.D. Cal. 2004), the largest private civil rights case in United States history, alleged that Wal-Mart discriminated against its female employees in making promotions, job assignments, pay decisions and training, and retaliated against women who complained about such practices. *See* http://www.walmartclass.com.

3. Markets in poverty. Many services as well as goods are targeted to the poverty market. As David Shipler describes in his book, *The Working*

Poor: Invisible in America (2004), tax preparers, check-cashing outlets, credit card companies, and mortgage and other loan providers often market their services to poor people. Services to the poor, however, tend to cost more money than the same services to the middle-class or the wealthy. The "subprime" market is a lucrative one because the customers have few options, urgent need, and often little information about their rights. Shipler offers an example of how poverty costs money:

> Say you're short of cash, and the bills are piling up, along with some disconnection notices. Payday is two weeks away, and your phone and electricity will be shut off before then. The guy at the local convenience store, who has a booth for cashing checks, throws you a lifeline. If you need $100 now, you write him a check for $120, postdated by two weeks. He'll give you the $100 in cash today, hold your check until your wages are in your bank account, and then put the check through. Or you can give him the $120 in cash when you get it, and he'll return your check. Either way, 20 percent interest for two weeks equals 1.438 percent a day, or 521 percent annually. * * *
>
> Furthermore, the loans are not technically loans in some states, because there's a check. And if a check bounces, more severe penalties apply than those for unrepaid loans. Borrowing $300, for instance, an Indiana woman paid a $30 fee and wrote a check for $330. When the check bounced, her bank and the payday loan establishment charged $80 in fees. Then the lender took her to court, won triple damages of $990, lawyer's fees of $150, and $60 in court costs. The total charge on the $300 loan: $1,310.

SHIPLER, THE WORKING POOR, *supra* at 18–19.

4. **Health care and bankruptcy.** A recent study found that about half of personal bankruptcy filers interviewed cited "medical causes" as the reason for their filing bankruptcy. Among those whose illnesses led to bankruptcy, out-of-pocket costs averaged $11,854 since the start of illness; 75.7 percent had insurance at the onset of illness. David U. Himmelstein et al., *Market Watch: Illness and Injury as Contributors to Bankruptcy*, HEALTH AFFAIRS, Feb. 2, 2005, http://content.healthaffairs.org/cgi/content/full/hlthaff.w5.63/DC1. The authors of the study concluded that "Even middle-class insured families often fall prey to financial catastrophe when sick." *Id.*

Nanny Diaries and Other Stories: Imagining Immigrant Women's Labor in the Social Reproduction of American Families[a]

52 809, 813, 814–22, 832–47 (2003).

■ MARY ROMERO

> *Wanted: One young woman to take care of four-year-old boy. Must be cheerful, enthusiastic, and selfless—bordering on masochistic. Must*

---

a. For further discussion of the racial, national and class dimensions of the U.S. domestic labor market, see chapter 5 at 381.

relish sixteen-hour shifts with a deliberately nap-deprived preschooler. Must love getting thrown up on, literally and figuratively, by everyone in his family. Must enjoy the delicious anticipation of ridiculously erratic pay. Mostly, must love being treated like fungus found growing out of employer's Hermes bag. Those who take it personally need not apply.

INTRODUCTION

Two former nannies employed on the Upper East Side of Manhattan offer this want advertisement as an illustration of employers' expectations and working conditions awaiting potential employees. Although it is a fictionalized account of their total six-year experience as nannies while attending college, Emma McLaughlin and Nicola Kraus's *The Nanny Diaries: A Novel* has spurred significant attention from the media. * * *

* * *

II. *THE NANNY DIARIES*: REALITY OR FANTASY?

Given the media attention and public discourse generated by the novel, it is worth asking the question: How representative is *The Nanny Diaries?* * * *

Given the large number of undocumented immigrants and United States workers employed "off the books," workers with temporary or permanent visas, and the broad category that the Department of Labor and the Census classify as domestic service, precise numbers of domestics and nannies are difficult to obtain. Assessing the United States Bureau of Labor Statistics, Human Rights Watch estimates that 800,000 private household workers were officially recorded in 1998, of which 30% were immigrant women. Regions exporting the largest number of women to labor as domestic servants are Asia, Africa, Latin America, and Eastern Europe. Research conducted on domestics in the United States include immigrants from Latin America, the Caribbean, and the Philippines.

A distinctive characteristic of domestic service in the United States is the race and ethnic differences between employer and employee. The intersection of class, race, and ethnicity has been a prominent component to the study of African-American, Chicana and Japanese-American domestics. Racial distinctions remain a striking feature identifying caregivers from their charges and employers. Reflecting on the playground scene in Central Park depicted in *The Nanny Diaries*, one onlooker contrasted the faces of children and caretakers:

> There are also adults there, but curiously, the faces of the two groups (adults and children) don't match. For every white child in a stroller, there is a black woman leaning down, to guide a juice box into their mouth. If she isn't black, she is Hispanic or Asian. The women are the

children's nannies. In many cases, they are stepping in for white parents, who are working full-time.

Apparent differences between native-born and immigrant women of color employed as maids and nannies are education and previous work experience. African-American, Chicana and Japanese-American women rarely have more than a high school education. A growing number of Latina and Caribbean immigrants are high school and college graduates, and some have held white-collar positions in their homeland. Helma Lutz noted the international trend toward older and better educated third-world immigrant women in her survey of research on the globalization of domestic service. Unlike younger and single European immigrant women at the turn of the twentieth century, these women work to cope with financial crisis, to support families, and to educate their children. Thus, Nan's race, marital status, and citizenship are not characteristic of many women employed as nannies in the United States. With the exception of European women immigrating to the United States with J-1 visas to work as *au pairs* while pursuing their education, most immigrant women are not part-time college students. Nan's career trajectory is obviously destined for a professional or managerial position; whereas, older immigrant working mothers find little if any social mobility. For these women, domestic service is best described as a ghetto occupation rather than a bridging occupation.

Nan informs the reader of the existing continuum of childcare arrangements which she designates as three types of nanny gigs: (1) "a few nights a week for people who work all day and parent most nights;" (2) " 'sanity time' a few afternoons a week to a woman who mothers most days and nights;" and (3) "provide twenty-four/seven 'me time' to a woman who neither works nor mothers." Embedded in this classification are live-in positions (twenty-four hours a day, seven days a week) and day workers that might work solely for one employer full-time or for a number of employers. Employers make arrangements with agencies, franchises, collectives, or directly with the employee. Employees working on their own include some that are bonded and considered self-employed, and others working in the underground economy. However, the actual distinctions are reflected in the working conditions: hours of employment, wages, lack of benefits, and the inclusion of all household work alongside childcare.

Researchers and labor advocates reporting wages for immigrant women over the last decade point to the variability in the market. Grace A. Rosales found wages ranging from $100 to $400 a week in Los Angeles. In her study of immigrant women employed as domestics and nannies in Los Angeles, Pierrette Hondagneu-Sotelo states that many Latina live-in workers do not receive minimum wage, whereas day workers averaged a higher wage of $5.90 an hour. Doreen Mattingly interviewed current and former Latina domestics in San Diego during the same period and found the average hourly rate for day workers was $8.02 and for live-ins was $2.72. Rhacel Salazar Parreñas reports that Filipina women migrating to Los Angeles earned an average of $425 a week for providing elderly care and $350 a week for live-in housekeeping and childcare. In a survey conducted in 2000, the Center for the Childcare Workforce in Washington, D.C., found that half of childcare providers earned less than $4.82 an hour and worked 55 hours a week. Human Rights Watch reviewed 43 egregious cases among domestic workers with special visas in the United States, and found a median hourly rate of $2.14.

Variation in wages and working conditions among employees points to the hierarchical structure in domestic service reinforced by employers' preferences. Obviously the hierarchy was not completely lost by McLaughlin and Kraus. In a reading at a Barnes & Noble bookshop, Kraus acknowledged the privileged subject position she and her colleague experienced: "We were the Hermès bags of nannies.... [A]s white, middle-class and university-educated nannies they [she and McLaughlin] were able to avoid the seamier elements of the industry." Latina and Caribbean immigrants are more vulnerable in the labor market than European immigrants. Skills do appear to be taken into consideration under certain circumstances. For instance, in her study of language between nannies and children in Los Angeles, Patricia Baquedano–López concluded that speaking English and a high school education were assets that domestics used in their negotiations with employers.

McLaughlin and Kraus portray a typical day of nanny tasks as "spent schlepping Grayer to French class, music lessons, karate, swimming, school and play dates." Although consistent with the image of Maria Rainer, the governess that Captain Von Trapp hired to care for his children in the film *The Sound of Music*, most employers with a live-in nanny assign employees a wide range of household tasks. While the distinction between housekeepers and nannies is frequently used to distinguish workers employed primarily to care for children, housekeepers may occasionally be asked to assist in childcare and nannies may be expected to cook, wash dishes, "pick-up," and do other household work directly related to the care of children. A consistent complaint among nannies is the expectation that they do housework and cook, alongside caring for children. Distinctions between domestic workers or private household workers and nannies are blurred in the everyday reality of employees as they engage in a broad range of household and caregiving activities, including cleaning, cooking, laundry, nursing the sick, supervising, playing with children, and grocery shopping.

Obviously, the most lucrative and sought after positions are the ones that make a clear distinction between tasks and recognize employees' skills, expertise, and experience. Immigrant women, particularly those who are undocumented, are more likely to be hired for live-in, as well as day work, positions that do not have clearly defined job descriptions. These nannies are unlikely to have much authority over the children or in planning activities. Instead, they find themselves at the beck and call of children as they serve and wait on them. Given the number of immigrant women nannies that McLaughlin and Kraus saw in the park, it is not surprising that they wrote, "[E]very playground has at least one nanny getting the shit kicked out of her by an angry child." *San Francisco Chronicle* reporter Adair Lara differentiated job descriptions offered to non-immigrant women:

"At the other end of the spectrum, a professional nanny often works weekends, engages the child in imaginative play, knows CPR.... She will want her hours guaranteed, will expect a bonus, and might be persnickety about doing more than the dishes and the baby's laundry."

Nan's life implies that work as a nanny is filled with new learning opportunities and adventures, from learning to cook exotic foods for Grayer to vacationing among the rich and famous. This depiction does not capture the overwhelming sense of isolation reported by immigrant women, particularly among live-in workers. Since Lucy Salmon's sociological study at the turn of the century, extreme isolation continues to be cited among live-in workers as one of the worst aspects of the job. Isolation from relatives, friends, and other domestic workers removes them from gaining resources to find employment elsewhere. Separation from their own children is frequently identified as a major force in developing strong emotional attachment to their charges. Domestics' loneliness is not countered by stimulating tasks. In the transformation of domestic labor from the unpaid work of mothers to low-wage work, physical demands are increased and more creative aspects are eliminated. The transformation from unpaid to paid childcare results in assigning immigrant nannies to the least pleasant tasks. Childcare advocates Suzanne W. Helburn and Barbara R. Bergmann describe the division as follows: "The parents try to reserve the more interesting child-rearing tasks for themselves. They do the storytelling and reading, supervise homework, and organize outings and parties in order to spend 'quality time' with their children."

Like the public discourse generated by the Nannygate scandals over the last decade, *The Nanny Diaries* examined the impact on employers and their children rather than on the employees and their children. Editorials and book reviews focus on employer rights to privacy, poor parenting, and the suffering and deprivation of "the poor little rich boy, Grayer." Since the novel's fictionalized couple who hired the nanny was portrayed as a cheating husband and an unemployed trophy wife, the stage is set against a public debate over the needs of working parents. Labor issues are contexualized as interpersonal gender relationships between women (and their competing expectations and emotions in doing "women's work") and the difficulty of employees identifying as a servant. Reference to immigrant nannies are curtailed to discussions concerning the impact that their limited English skills and cultural differences have on children under their care.

However, when immigrant women speak for themselves, the following list of labor issues are similar to the concerns expressed by workers in the United States: low wages, unpaid hours, lack of decent standards, absence of health insurance and other employee benefits, and constant supervision. In the case of live-in domestics, employer abuses include violations of their human rights. Grievances reported in Bridget Anderson and Philzacklea's international study that are also found in the United States include:

> denial of wages in cases of dismissal following trial or probation periods, refusal by employers to arrange legal resident status (for tax

reasons, etc.); control and sexual harassment; pressure to do additional work (for friends and colleagues); excessive workloads, especially where in addition to caring for children and elderly people they are responsible for all other household chores; and finally the very intimate relationship between the domestic helpers and their employers.

Human Rights Watch cites the following additional employer abuses in the United States: "basic telephone privileges, prohibiting them from leaving employers' homes unaccompanied, and forbidding them to associate or communicate with friends and neighbors." "To prevent domestic workers from leaving exploitative employment situations, employers confiscate the workers' passports and threaten them with deportation if they flee. In the most severe cases of abuse, migrant domestic workers—both live-in and day workers—have reported instances of sexual assault, physical abuse, and rape." Health hazards posed by cleaning chemicals "causing everything from skin irritation and rashes to serious respiratory problems from inhaling toxic fumes" is another grievance reported by human rights and labor advocates.

* * *

IV. Immigrant Nanny Care and the Reproduction of Privilege

Globalization of childcare is based on income inequality between women from poor countries providing low-wage care work for families in wealthier nations. Even with the low wages and variability in the market cited above, hiring a nanny is recognized as the most expensive childcare option. Researchers recognize this reality: "The grim truth is that some women's access to the high-paying, high-status professions is being facilitated through the revival of semi-indentured servitude. Put another way, one woman is exercising class and citizenship privilege to buy her easy way out of sex oppression." The largest number of domestic workers are located in areas of the country with the highest income inequality among women. In regions with minimal income inequality, the occupation is insignificant. Particular forms of domestic labor that affirm and enhance employers' status, shift the burden of sexism to low-wage women workers, and relegate the most physically difficult and dirty aspects of domestic labor. However, little attention has been given to the ways that privilege is reproduced through childcare arrangements and the significance that third-world immigrant women's labor plays in the reproduction of privilege.

Intensive and competitive mothering revolves around individuality, competition, and the future success of their children. Competition and individualism are values embedded in children's activities. Annette Lareau refers to this version of child rearing as "concerted cultivation" geared toward "deliberate and sustained effort to stimulate children's development and to cultivate ... cognitive and social skills." Concerted cultivation aims to develop children's ability to reason by negotiating with parents and placing value on children's opinions, judgments, and observations. Family leisure time is dominated by organized children activities, such as sports, clubs, and paid lessons (e.g., dance, music, tennis). Most children's time is adult-structured rather than child-initiated play. "Play is not just play anymore. It involves the honing of 'large motor skills,' 'communication skills,' 'hand-eye coordination,' and the establishment of 'developmentally appropriate behavior.'"

Qualities of intensive and competitive mothering are at odds with demanding careers. Everyday practices of intensive mothering [require] immense emotional involvement, constant self-sacrificing, exclusivity, and a completely child-centered environment. These mothering activities are financially draining and time-consuming. Mothers with disposable income use commodities to fulfill areas of intensive and competitive mothering that they find themselves falling short of. In *The Mother Puzzle*, Judith D. Schwartz argues that advertising companies use guilt as significant child leverage:

> Companies who are marketing to our guilt inevitably start marketing the guilt itself in order to keep us shopping. This toy will help your child develop motor skills (implicit message: his motor skills will suffer without it). This line of clothing is made of the softest cotton (implicit message: other, less expensive fabrics may be abrasive).

By the 1990s, "babies and children were firmly entrenched as possessions that necessitated the acquisition of other commodities (and that became more valuable with further investment in goods and services)." Advertisers targeted the new "Skippies" market (*s*chool *k*ids with *i*ncome and *p*urchasing *p*ower). Quoting *People* magazine, Schwartz characterizes parents of these "gourmet children" as "rapaciously grabbing kudos for their kids with the same enterprise applied to creating fortunes on Wall Street." She suggests that, "Teaching values to our children has been replaced by building value into them ... by preparing them to compete and giving them what we think they need to do so."

Hiring a live-in immigrant worker is the most convenient childcare option for juggling the demands of intensive mothering and a career. Purchasing the caretaking and domestic labor of an immigrant [woman] commodificates reproductive labor and reflects, reinforces, and intensifies social inequalities. The most burdensome mothering activities (such as cleaning, laundry, feeding babies and children, and chauffeuring children to their various scheduled activities) are shifted to the worker. Qualities of intensive mothering, such a sentimental value, nurturing, and intense emotional involvement, are not lost when caretaking work is shifted to an employee. Employers select immigrant caretakers on the basis of perceived "warmth," "love for children," and "naturalness in mothering." Different racial and ethnic groups are stereotyped by employers as ideal employees for housework, childcare, or for live-in positions. Stereotyping is based on a number of individual characteristics—race, ethnicity, class, caste, education, religion, and linguistic ability—and results in a degree of "otherness" for all domestic servants. However, such a formalization of difference does not always put workers in the subordinate position, and employers' preferences can vary from place to place. Janet Henshall Momsen notes that, "Professionally-trained British nannies occupy an élite niche in Britain and North America." Interviewing employers in Los Angeles and New York City, Julia Wrigley observed Spanish-speaking nannies were identified by employers for their ability to broaden the cultural experience of their children, particularly in exposing them to a second language in the home. Employers referenced the growing Latino population in their community and the long-term benefits of their children learning Spanish. However, the socialization to race and culture politics may be the most significant consequence of the current commodification of reproductive labor.

The primary mission of reproductive labor in contemporary mothering is to assure their children's place in society. This is partially accomplished through socialization into class, gender, sexual, ethnic and race hierarchies. Employment of immigrant women as caregivers contributes to this socialization. Reinforced by their parents' conceptualization of caretaking as a "labor of love," children learn a sense of entitlement to receiving affection from people of color that is detached from their own actions. Children learn to be "consumers of care" rather than providers of caregiving. Caretaking without parental authority does not teach children reciprocal respect but rather teaches that the treatment of women of color as "merely means, and not as ends in themselves." The division of labor between mother and live-in caretaker domestic stratifies components of reproductive labor and equates burdensome, manual and basic maintenance labor with immigrant women of color. This gendered division of labor serves to teach traditional patriarchal privilege. Privilege is learned as they acquire a sense of entitlement to having a domestic worker always on call to meet their needs.

Stratified reproductive labor of a live-in immigrant domestic assures "learned helplessness and class prejudice in the child," and teaches "[dependence], aggressiveness, and selfishness." Systems of class, racial, ethnic, gender and citizenship domination are taught to children by witnessing "the arbitrary and capricious interaction of parents and servants or if they are permitted to treat domestic servants in a similar manner." As children move from their homes located in class (and frequently racially) segregated neighborhoods to schools (also likely to be segregated), power relationships and the larger community's class and racial etiquette are further reinforced. "As care is made into a commodity, women with greater resources in the global economy can afford the best-quality care for their family." If mothering is directed toward assuring their child's social and economic status in society—a society that is racist, capitalist, and patriarchal—then her goals are strengthened by employing a low wage, full-time or live-in immigrant woman. Conditions under which immigrant women of color are employed in private homes is structured by systems of privilege and, consequently, employers' children are socialized into these norms and values.

V. Prolongation of Immigrant Women Subordination

Paid reproductive labor in the United States is structured along local, national and international inequalities, positioning third-world immigrant women as the most vulnerable workers. Careworkers are sorted by the degree of vulnerability and privilege. Consequently, paid domestic labor is not only structured around gender but is stratified by race and citizenship status, relegating the most vulnerable worker to the least favorable working conditions and placing the most privileged in the best positions. A major initiative in the American childcare movement is addressing low wages in the childcare industry. However, the plight of live-in caregivers and immigrant women as a specific group is rarely addressed. The solution of hiring a live-in domestic, used by a relatively privileged group, is a component of reproductive labor in the United States, and serves to intensify inequalities between women: first, by reinforcing childcare as a private rather than public responsibility; and second, by reaping the benefits gained by the impact of globalization and restructuring on third-world women. The globalization of domestic service contributes to the reproduction of inequality between nations in transnational capitalism and cases reported of domestic servitude is increasingly characterized as global gender apartheid.

Devaluation of immigrant women in the international division of labor begins in the home as unpaid labor; then is further devalued in the segregated labor forces within third-world countries used by wealthier nations for cheap labor. Women are relegated to low-wage factory work in textiles and electronics industries with no opportunities available for better-paid positions. Migrating and working as domestics becomes the primary strategy for sustaining households for both poor and middle-class women. The demand for low-wage migrant workers expands the pool of cheap labor that unemployment and welfare regulations are unable to maintain. Theorists have traditionally argued that women's unpaid domestic labor in the home served as a reserve labor force. Applying this qualification to immigrant domestic workers, the employment of third-world women becomes a significant source for reproducing a labor reserve, similar to the function of the unemployed and underemployed. Saskia Sassen states this proposition in the following question: "Does domestic service—at least in certain locations—become one of the few alternatives and does it, then, function, as a privatized mechanism for social reproduction and maintenance of a labor reserve?" The transnational export of women from global south to the rich industrialized countries of the north has resulted in promoting domestics as a major "export product." Transnational division of labor is determined "simultaneously by global capitalism and systems of gender inequality in both sending and receiving countries of migration."

A prominent feature of globalized reproductive labor is commodification. Parreñas argues that, "Commodified reproductive labor is not only low-paid work but declines in market value as it gets passed down the international transfer of caretaking." However, Anderson argues that the commodification process in globalization is not limited to the labor but is extended to the worker. In her work on the global politics of domestic labor, she points out that employers "openly stipulate that they want a particular type *person* justifying this demand on the grounds that they will be working in the home." Having hired the preferred racialized domestic caretaker on the basis of personal characteristics rather than former experience or skills, the emotional labor required is not recognized by the employer but the worker's caring "brings with it no mutual obligations, no entry into a community, no 'real' human relations, only money."

Employers' hiring preferences for employees who are a particular race, ethnicity, and nationality contributes to the hierarchical chain of domestic caretakers. Hondagneu-Sotelo notes that African Americans are no longer the preferred employee in Los Angeles homes because [they] are portrayed as "bossy" and with "terrifying images associated with young black men." Similar images are applied to Caribbean women in New York and are cautioned against coming "across in interviews as being in any way aggressive." Latina immigrants in Los Angeles are perceived as "responsible, trustworthy, and reliable" workers as well as "exceptionally warm, patient, and loving mothers." In the case of Filipina women, Dan Gatmaytan argues that their labor is distinctively featured in international division of labor as "docile and submissive," and thus, ideally packaged to be imported "by other countries for jobs their own citizens will not perform and for wages domestic citizens would not accept." Parreñas's findings suggest that employers view Filipinas as providing a "higher-quality" service because they speak English and generally have a higher education than Latina immigrants.

However, without state regulations of labor and immigration policies, employers' preferences are irrelevant in the racialization of reproductive labor in the United States. Joy Mutanu Zarembka, director of the Campaign for Migrant Domestic Workers' Rights, argues that the estimated four thousand special visas issued annually for third-world immigrant women contributes to commodification of these workers into a "maid to order" in the United States. Three visas perpetuating the subordination of immigrant women of color as live-in domestic workers are:

> A-3 visas to work for ambassadors, diplomats, consular officers, public ministers, and their families; G-5 visas to work for officers and employees of international organizations or of foreign missions to international organizations and their families; and B-1 visas to accompany U.S. citizens who reside abroad but are visiting the United States or assigned to the United States temporarily for no more than four years, or foreign nations with nonimmigrant status in the United States.

In contrast to special visas given primarily to third-world immigrant women, the J-1 visa is increasingly used to bring young and middle-class European immigrant women as nannies or *au pairs* with "educational and cultural exchange" their primary purpose. Under this visa, each nanny receives an orientation session and is placed in geographical locations near other nannies. After her placement, she attends an orientation session and "receives information on community resources, educational opportunities and contacts for a local support network." Counselors have monthly sessions with each employer and nanny to "report any problems and resolve disputes." "In contrast, with the G-5, A-1 and B-1 domestic worker programs, there are no official orientations, no information, no contact numbers, no counselors, and no educational programs. In practice, as well, there is often no freedom—many are systematically (though illegally) forbidden from contacting the outside world."

Human Rights Watch further asserts that special visas intensify workers' vulnerability to abuse and facilitate the violation of other human rights. Procedures, guidelines, laws, and regulations governing special domestic worker visas construct circumstances that tolerate and conceal employer abuses, and restrict workers' rights. Among the problems cited by Human Rights Watch are the lack of INS follow-up monitoring or investigations to verify employer compliance with employment contracts, and the Department of Labor's lack of involvement with administrating these visas. Consequently, no governmental agency is responsible for enforcing contracts. Zarembka asserts that the secrecy of the whereabouts of G-5, A-3 and B-1 workers makes "them some of the most vulnerable and easily exploited sectors of the American workforce" and violation of human rights is silenced by their invisibility. In addition to low wages, long hours, and the lack of both privacy and benefits that are common among live-in conditions, immigrant women experience other abuses. They include passport confiscation, limited freedom of movement and ability to communicate with others, employer threats of deportation, assault and battery, rape, servitude, torture, and trafficking. Changing employers under live-in conditions has always been difficult for workers, and for women with employment-based visas, they are faced with weighing "respect for their own human rights and maintaining their legal immigration status." For similar reasons, women are reluctant to report abuse because they fear losing their jobs, deportation, unfamiliarity with the American legal system, social and cultural isolation, and fear that "their retaliation powerful employers will retaliate against their families in their countries of origin."

Exclusion from a number of labor policies contribute to the hardships immigrant women experience as live-in domestics. They are excluded from overtime provisions provided in the Fair Labor Standard Act, from the right to organize, strike, and bargain collectively in the National Labor Relations Act, and from regulations in the Occupational Safety and Health Act. "In practice, too, live-in domestic workers are rarely covered by Title VII protections against sexual harassment in the workplace, as Title VII only applies to employers with fifteen or more workers."

Third-world immigrant domestics experience first hand the inequalities of caregiving as they provide labor for parents in rich industrialized countries while leaving their own children. Sarah Blaffer Hrdy equates mothers leaving their children with relatives in their homelands to European infants left in foundling homes or sent to wet nurses during the eighteenth century: "Solutions differ, but the tradeoffs mothers make, and the underlying emotions and mental calculations, remain the same." Anderson notes that immigrant women's care for their children is limited "in the fruits of hard labour, in remittances, rather than in the cuddles and 'quality time' that provide so much of the satisfaction of care." Transnational mothering cannot provide the "physical closeness, seen as healthy and 'normal' in the Western upbringing of a child, are not given, because most of the women are not allowed to take their children with them." These conditions reduce mothering to the basic function of economic support. In her research on Filipina women in Rome and Los Angeles, Parrenas observed the impact of economic ties rather than affective ties between mother and child departed from each over a long period of time. The use of material good, financial assistance, and school tuition result in commodifying family relationships and motherhood. Inequalities in the distribution and quality of domestic labor and caregiving is a cost borne by the children of live-in workers. The absence of retirement benefits pension assures that workers will not be able to contribute financially to their children's future, but rather will need their assistance.

VI. Conclusion

Before the September 11 attacks, the Federation for American Immigration Reform (FAIR), Patrick Buchanan, Pete Wilson and others vilified immigrants as the cause of all problems in the United States. Homeland security has further fanned the flames of xenophobia and support for vilifying immigrants. Yet, within the intimacy of many American homes, immigrant women (primarily Latina and Caribbean immigrants) continue to provide assisted reproductive labor that fulfills the basic tasks of maintaining families of dual career couples and contribute to middle-upper- and upper-class lifestyles. Popular culture functions to normalize the hiring of immigrant women by depicting domestic service as a bridging occupation that offers social mobility, opportunities to learn English, and other cultural skills that assist in the assimilation process. The characterization of nannies and private household workers in *The Nanny Diaries*, as well as in films and sitcoms, serves to reduce the significance of immigrant women in fulfilling childcare needs in the United States and to erase issues of employee rights from the American imagination. Instead, employers are classified as good or bad: good employers who are benevolent and provide immigrant women with a modernizing experience, or bad employers who are rich couples ignoring their children. Popular culture does not contextualize paid reproductive labor. Economic, political and legal structures surrounding the migration of Latina, Caribbean and Filipina women are ignored along with the circumstances that relegate their labor to low-wage dead-end jobs. Consequently, we can maintain our illusions of Latina domestics as sexually out of control and utterly colorful spitfire, the self-deprecating accented smart-mouthed, or the rosary-praying maid. We can continue to see these images and sing out, "Yes, that's what maids are like."

* * *

Centering immigration on questions of "belonging" (and related concepts, e.g., assimilation, ethnic differences, and ethnic loyalty) blinds us to inquiries into the role of immigration in sustaining systems of privilege and perpetuating myths and ideologies central to national identity. Immigration and labor regulations reproduce race, class, gender and citizenship inequalities and privileges. In the case of immigrant women employed as private household workers or caregivers, the social reproduction of inequalities begins in the employer's home. Managing the contradictions of intimacy and vilification of immigrants through cultural images that falsify employee-employer relationships, allows Americans to reap the benefits of retaining a vulnerable labor force unprotected from exploitation while arguing humanitarian positions. The popular version of nannies depicted in *The Nanny Diaries* assists in normalizing privilege and erases issues of economic injustice. Our complacency in the subordination of immigrant women is once again obtained by our fascination with chatty gossip on sex, drugs, money, and family values of the wealthy on Park Avenue. Moreover, our illusion that there is no greater state of being than Americans is further enhanced by denying the privileges gained by third-world assisted social reproduction.

The Hidden Injuries of Class
79–87 (1972).

■ RICHARD SENNETT & JONATHAN COBB

Josiah Watson Grammar School is an old red-brick building with a simple but well-kept playground. It is a large school, in the midst of an urban neighborhood of mostly three-decker houses. In the community surrounding the school live groups of Irish, Italian, and old-stock New Englanders, but almost all are manual laborers. The median family income in the neighborhood is about $8000—neither poor nor affluent.

The rooms at the Watson School evoke the interiors of the children's homes: old, rather run down, and yet clean, almost austere. In each schoolroom the only decorations consist of an American flag, a bound set of maps, and a plaque with the Pledge of Allegiance. The school desks are new—tubular steel legs holding up flat wooden boxes. In them, children's supplies are neatly arranged, even for the littlest children. The teachers take a certain pride in this, but they apologize to the visitor for the tops scratched with the obscene words, drawings, and initials that children always seem to inflict on such objects.

The classes in Watson School, even as low as the second grade, jolt the outsider who has lost touch with the institutional life of children. Everything that goes on in the second-grade class, from reading preparedness to play with toys, is directed by the teacher. She takes great pains to see that the children act "good and proper." The visitor who is aware of his own presence in these classrooms at first thinks this show of discipline, this constant commanding and watching, is the teacher's response to that presence. After the teacher relaxes and forgets he is there, however, the discipline continues. It varies among the teachers from harsh to loving; but all those in charge of classrooms at the Watson School act like conductors who must bring potentially unruly mobs of musicians under their direction.

As the principal remarks, "It is by establishing authority that we make this school work."

In Watson School, teachers restrict the freedom of the children because these figures of authority have a peculiar fear of the children. It is the mass who seem to the teachers to threaten classroom order, by naughty or unruly behavior; only a few are seen as having "good habits" or the right attitude. As one teacher explained, "These children come from simple laborers' homes where the parents don't understand the value of education." Yet in the early grades the observer noticed few examples of disruptive behavior. He sensed among the six-and seven-year olds a real desire to please, to accept the teacher's control and be accepted by her. One pathetic incident, although extreme, stands out. In the middle of a reading-preparedness class, a child wet his pants because he was absorbed in his lesson. "What can you do with children like that?" the teacher later remarked in a tone of disgust.

What happens is that the teachers act on their expectations of the children in such a way as to *make* the expectations become reality. Here is how the process worked in one second-grade class at Watson School—unusual in that it was taught by a young man. In this class there were two children, Fred and Vincent, whose appearance was somewhat different from that of the others: their clothes were no fancier than the other children's, but they were pressed and seemed better kept; in a class of mostly dark Italian children, these were the fairest-skinned. From the outset the teacher singled out these two children, implying that they most closely approached his own standards for classroom performance. He never praised them openly by comparison to the other children, but a message that they were different, were better, was spontaneously conveyed. As the observer watched the children play and work over the course of the school year, he noticed these two boys becoming more serious, more solemn, as the months passed. Obedient and never unruly from the first, by the end of the year they were left alone by the other children.

By then they were also doing the best work in the class. The other children had picked up the teacher's hidden cues that their performance would not be greeted with as much enthusiasm as the work of these two little boys. "It's not true of the other children that they generally have less potential," the teacher remarked. "It's a question of not developing their ability like Fred and Vincent. I know you're right, I tend to encourage them more despite myself, but I—it's obvious to me these little boys are going to make something of themselves."

In the Watson School, by the time the children are ten or eleven the split between the many and the few who are expected to "make something of themselves" is out in the open; the aloofness developing in the second grade has become open hostility by the sixth. Among the boys, this hostility is expressed by images which fuse sex and status. Boys like Fred and Vincent are described by the "ordinary" students as effeminate and weak, as "suck-ups." The kids mean by this both that the Freds and Vincents are getting somewhere in school because they are so docile, and that only a homosexual would be so weak; the image of a "suck-up" crystallizes this self-demeaning, effeminate behavior that to them marks off a student whom the institution can respect.

What has happened, then, is that these children have directed their anger at their schoolmates who are rewarded as individuals rather than at the institution which is withholding recognition of them. Indeed, the majority of boys in the fifth and sixth grades are often not consciously in conflict with the school at all. Something more complex is happening to them.

These "ordinary" boys in class act as though they were serving time, as though schoolwork and classes had become something to wait out, a blank space in their lives they hope to survive and then leave. Their feeling, apparently, is that when they get out, get a job and some money, *then* they will be able to begin living. It is not so much that they are bored in school—many in Watson School like their classes. It is rather that they have lost any expectation that school will help them, that this experience will change them or help them grow as human beings.

One teacher in this school, an enthusiastic young woman who liked to work with "ordinary" students, said her greatest problem was convincing the students that they could trust her. The other teachers and the principal disapprove of her because she runs her class in an informal manner. They feel she lets the students "get away with anything," "that she can't keep discipline." Permissiveness is a vice, order a necessity, in the minds of the other teachers; they believe that most of their charges, due to family class background and past school performances, will resist following the rules which to an educated adult seem so logical and beneficial. It is not that these teachers are intentionally mean, but that they unwittingly set in motion in the classroom a vicious circle that produces exactly the kind of behavior they expect.

There is a counterculture of dignity that springs up among these ordinary working-class boys, a culture that seeks in male solidarity what cannot be found in the suspended time that comprises classroom experience. This solidarity also sets them off from the "suck-ups." Hanging around together, the boys share their incipient sexual exploits, real and imagined; sex becomes a way to compete within the group. What most cements them as a group, however, is the breaking of rules—smoking, drinking, or taking drugs together, cutting classes. Breaking the rules is an act "nobodies" can share with each other. This counterculture does not come to grips with the labels their teachers have imposed on these kids; it is rather an attempt to create among themselves badges of dignity that those in authority can't destroy.

A full circle: outsider observers—parents, teachers, and others—who see only the external aspects of this counterculture, are confirmed in their view that "hanging around" is destructive to a child's self-development. Dignity in these terms exacts a toll by the standards of the outer world.

The division of children, in schools like Watson, into groups with a shared sense of loyalty and individuals alone but "getting somewhere," characterizes many levels of education; it is not something unique to, say, college-bound youth as opposed to vocational school boys. Studies of trade schools show the same phenomenon occurring: boys who are good at car mechanics in school start to feel cut off from others, even though the possession of those skills might make them admired by their less-skilled peers outside of school. It is an institutional process that makes the difference, a question of mere toleration versus active approval from those in power.

The drama played out in the Watson School has as its script the assigning and the wearing of badges of ability like those described earlier, worn by adults. The teachers cast the Freds and Vincents into the role of Andrew Carnegie's virtuous man. Ability will make these children into individuals, and as individuals they will rise in social class. The mass find themselves in a role similar to that which Lipset assigns to adult workers: their class background allegedly limits their self-development, and the counterculture of compensatory respect they create reinforces, in a vicious circle, the judgments of the teachers.

The teacher has the *power* to limit the freedom of development of his or her students through this drama. But why is he or she moved to act in this repressive way? This question is really two questions: it is first a matter of a teacher legitimizing in his own mind the power he holds, and second, a matter of the students taking that power as legitimate.

The teachers are in a terrible existential dilemma. It is true that they are "prejudiced" against most of their students; it is also true that they, like all human beings, want to believe in the dignity of their own work, no matter how difficult the circumstances in which they have to work seem to them. If a teacher believed that every single student would perpetually resist him, he would have no reason to go on teaching—his power in the classroom would be empty. A teacher needs at least a responsive few in order to feel he has a *reason* to possess power. The few will confirm to him that his power to affect other people is real, that he can truly do good. To sort out two classes of ability, then, in fear of the "lower" class of students, is to create a meaningful image of himself as an authority rather than simply a boss.

It is true that an analysis at this level of teachers, or other power figures dealing with working-class people, is by itself inadequate. A teacher may be having an existential crisis, but that doesn't explain why images of social class and classes of ability have come to fuse in his mind, nor does it explain how useful, how convenient, this crisis of self-legitimacy is in keeping the present class structure going. Still, it is important to keep before ourselves the experiential reality facing a person who has power over others. The teachers at Watson did not think of themselves as tools of capitalism, or even as repressive. They felt they had to legitimize their own work's dignity in the face of working-class students; and making a moral hierarchy on the basis of ability—however artificially and unjustifiably—was the natural means they used.

The perceptions the children had of the teachers similarly concerned not their power, but their legitimacy.

The observer is playing marbles with Vinny, a third-grader, described by his teacher as an "unexceptional average student who tolerates school," and Vinny begins absentmindedly to arrange the marbles in sets by color. The observer points out to him that he is doing something like what the teacher had asked him to do in arithmetic hour and he hadn't then been able to do. Vinny replies, "I didn't want to give her no trouble"—an answer the observer notes without, at the time, understanding what Vinny meant. In a class on grammar, Stephanie gives a past participle incorrectly; the teacher asks her to try again, but while she is thinking, one of the bright children interrupts with the right answer. The teacher—the experimental and "permissive" woman already described—tells the bright child to shut up and gives Stephanie another answer to work out. Stephanie looks at her in total surprise, wondering why the teacher should still care about whether *she* can learn to do it, if the right answer has already been provided. Max, an obnoxious fifth-grade bully, has somehow formed an interest in writing doggerel rhymes. During a composition hour he reads one, but when he finishes, the teacher makes no reply, merely smiles and calls on the next pupil. Asked later how he felt, Max looks a little crestfallen and says with characteristic grace, "Lookit, shithead, she ain't got time to waste on me."

NOTES AND QUESTIONS

1. "Globalization" at top and bottom of economy. Saskia Sassen argues that "globalization" has produced both transnational marginalized labor classes and transnational privileged classes: while the elite of "global cities" such as New York, Hong Kong, and Paris are increasingly intertwined through networks of education and training, the "underclass" in such cities are also intertwined, through networks of migration and the demand for low-end service work. Saskia Sassen, *Toward a Feminist Analytics of the Global Economy*, 4 IND. J. GLOBAL LEGAL STUD. 7 (1996). Sassen argues that migration (legal and illegal), which is often treated as only a problem for the government sector to be solved through immigration law, should be seen as intimately connected to trade policy and economic policy more generally.

How might the increasing income and wealth inequality brought about by globalization affect women as a group? Sassen is hopeful that the globalizing economy, as it pulls more women into wage work, will empower them within their families and in the public sector. *id.*, at 27. At the same time, she acknowledges that women are "constituted as an invisible and disempowered class of workers in the service of the strategic sectors constituting the global economy." *id.*, at 26.

2. Modern-day slavery. The very lowest caste of contemporary workers is made up of those whose labor power is forcibly expropriated by others. Kevin Bales argues that slavery is alive and well today, although it takes different legal and social forms than the "old" slavery:

> *My best estimate of the number of slaves in the world today is 27 million.*
>
> This number is much smaller than the estimates put forward by some activists, who give a range as high as 200 million, but it is the number I feel I can trust * * *. The biggest part of that 27 million, perhaps 15 to 20 million, is represented by *bonded labor* in India, Pakistan, Bangladesh, and Nepal. Bonded labor or debt bondage happens when people give themselves into slavery as security against a loan or when they inherit a debt from a relative * * *. Otherwise slavery tends to be concentrated in Southeast Asia, northern and western Africa, and parts of South America (but there are some slaves in almost every country in the world, including the United States, Japan, and many European countries). There are more slaves alive today than all the people stolen from Africa in the time of the transatlantic slave trade. Put another way, today's slave population is greater than the population of Canada, and six times greater than the population of Israel.
>
> These slaves tend to be used in simple, nontechnological, and traditional work. The largest group work in agriculture. But slaves are used in many other kinds of labor: brickmaking, mining or quarrying, prostitution, gem working and jewelry making, cloth and carpet making, and domestic service; they clear forests, make charcoal, and work in shops. Much of this work is aimed at local sale and consumption, but slave-made goods reach into homes around the world. Carpets, fireworks, jewelry, and metal goods made by slave labor, as well as grains, sugar, and other foods harvested by slaves, are imported directly to North America and Europe. In addition, large international corporations, acting through subsidiaries in the developing world, take advantage of slave labor to improve their bottom line and increase the dividends to their shareholders.

KEVIN BALES, DISPOSABLE PEOPLE: NEW SLAVERY IN THE GLOBAL ECONOMY 8–9 (1999).

Bales argues that the new slavery differs from the old slavery in several ways. Among these differences are the following: slaveholders no longer assert legal ownership over their slaves; slaveholders do not contribute to the maintenance costs of their slaves; ethnic differences between slaveholding and slave classes are less important than they were in, for example, American slavery; slaves produce very high profits; the relationship between slaveholder and slave tends to be short-term rather than long-term; and there is a surplus rather than a shortage of potential slaves. *id.*, at 15.

The International Labor Organization defines "forced labor" as "all work or service which is exacted from any person under the menace of any penalty and for which the said person has not offered himself voluntarily." International Labor Organization, Convention Concerning Forced Labor (No. 29). Using this definition, a team of researchers at the University of California at –Berkeley, working with a nonprofit antislavery organization, examined the nature and scope of forced labor in the United States from January 1998 to December 2003. According to their report:

> Over the past five years, forced labor operations have been reported in at least ninety U.S. cities. These operations tend to thrive in states with large populations and sizable immigrant communities, such as California, Florida, New York, and Texas—all of which are transit routes for international travelers.
>
> Forced labor is prevalent in five sectors of the U.S. economy: prostitution and sex services (46%), domestic service (27%), agriculture (10%), sweatshop/factory (5%), and restaurant and hotel work (4%) * * *. Forced labor persists in these sectors because of low wages, lack of regulation and monitoring of working conditions, and a high demand for cheap labor. These conditions enable unscrupulous employers and criminal networks to gain virtually complete control over workers' lives.

HUMAN RIGHTS CENTER & FREE THE SLAVES: FORCED LABOR IN THE UNITED STATES 1 (2004), *available at* http://www.hrcberkeley.org/download/hidden-slaves_report.pdf. (posted September 2004) (last visited, Mar. 6, 2005). The researchers estimated that approximately 10,000 people are working as forced laborers in the United States at any given time. *id.*, at 10.

In the United States, slavery and human trafficking are subject to the federal Victims of Trafficking and Violence Protection Act of 2000, § 107, 22 U.S.C. §7105 (2004). The act, among other things, establishes mandatory restitution from convicted traffickers, and an amendment allows survivors to sue their captors for civil damages for violations of the statute. See Trafficking Victims Protection Reauthorization Act of 2003, 18 U.S.C. § 1595 (2004) (civil damages provision). The act also provides social services and immigration status to victims of a "severe form of trafficking" who cooperate with law enforcement to prosecute the traffickers.

3. Women, prostitution and sex work: abolitionists versus labor activists. Feminists have long argued over whether prostitution and other forms of sex work should be abolished as forms of violence against women, or legalized and regulated as just another kind of labor. Jane Larson argues that the dichotomy is unhelpful and that prostitution, like sweatshop labor, child labor, and various forms of bonded and indentured labor, should be examined more closely to help us think more generally about what kinds of labor are acceptable and why:

> Instead of fruitless debates about the "essential nature" of the commodity relation of prostitution, I urge instead a common project aimed at defining the material, moral, and legal differences between free and unfree labor, describing with empirical depth and range what conditions of work characterize commercial sex in its various forms and

locales, and measuring the sex industry against the free labor standard. What is force and compulsion in the sex labor setting? Is the definition of force such that the exchange of money refutes the claim of compulsion, or can the liberal concern for substantive freedom in labor relations translate into international standards? What working conditions render prostitution a per se unacceptably exploitative practice for children? Is it different for adults? Why or why not? What kinds of discrimination on the basis of sex or race are unacceptable? Does the demographic constitution of the market for sexual labor demonstrate such discrimination? If prostitution is one of women's best economic options, how does this shape other economic opportunities for women? Does female prostitution violate the equality ideal?

Jane E. Larson, *Prostitution, Labor, and Human Rights,* 37 U.C. DAVIS L. REV. 673, 698–99 (2004).

4. **Public education and construction of failure.** Cobb and Sennett were concerned primarily with the education and socialization of the sons of white working class "ethnic" immigrants. Other scholars have found that public education similarly sets up African American and Latino/a working class children, especially boys, to fail. For example, Theresa Glennon observes:

> First, African American boys are much more likely to be identified as disabled or delinquent than other children, including African American girls. Second, they are more likely than other children to be placed in educational, mental health, and juvenile justice programs that exert greater external control and deliver fewer services despite identified needs. Third, these negative experiences lead African American boys to stay away from or exit these institutional settings.

Theresa Glennon, *Knocking Against the Rocks: Evaluating Institutional Practices and the African American Boy,* 5 J. HEALTH CARE L. & POL'Y 10, 11 (2002). Glennon argues that these disparities are a result of racism.

Sociologist John Ogbu found another dynamic among African American children similar to that identified by Sennett and Cobb: black students both underperform and pressure one another to underperform by associating school success with "acting white." Signithia Fordham & John U. Ogbu, *Black Students' School Success: Coping with the "Burden of Acting White,"* 18 URB. REV. 176 (1986). Ogbu and Fordham's findings have been controversial in African American communities.

The Overworked American: The Unexpected Decline of Leisure

17–24 (1991).

■ JULIET B. SCHOR

Time squeeze has become big news. In summer 1990, the premiere episode of Jane Pauley's television show, "Real Life," highlighted a single father whose computer job was so demanding that he found himself at 2:00 A.M. dragging his child into the office. A Boston-area documentary featured the fourteen-to sixteen-hour workdays of a growing army of moonlighters. CBS's "Forty–Eight Hours" warned of the accelerating pace of life for everyone from high-tech business executives (for whom there are only two types of people—"the quick and the dead") to assembly workers at Japanese-owned automobile factories (where a car comes by every sixty seconds). Employees at fast-food restaurants, who serve in twelve seconds, report that the horns start honking if the food hasn't arrived in fifteen. Nineteen-year-olds work seventy-hour weeks, children are "penciled" into their parents' schedules, and second-graders are given "half an hour a day to unwind" from the pressure to get good grades so they can get into a good college. By the beginning of the 1990s, the time squeeze had become a national focus of attention, appearing in almost all the nation's major media outlets. * * *

The time squeeze surfaced with the young urban professional. These high achievers had jobs that required sixty, eighty, even a hundred hours a week. On Wall Street, they would regularly stay at the office until midnight or go months without a single day off. Work consumed their lives. And if they weren't working, they were networking. They power-lunched, power-exercised, and power-married. As the pace of life accelerated, time became an ever-scarcer commodity, so they used their money to buy more of it. Cooking was replaced by gourmet frozen foods from upscale delis. Eventually the "meal" started disappearing, in favor of "grazing." Those who could afford it bought other people's time, hiring surrogates to shop, write their checks, or even just change a light bulb. They cut back on sleep and postponed having children. ("Can you carry a baby in a briefcase?" queried one Wall Street executive when she was asked about having kids.)

High-powered people who spend long hours at their jobs are nothing new. Medical residents, top corporate management, and the self-employed have always had grueling schedules. But financiers used to keep bankers' hours, and lawyers had a leisured life. Now bankers work like doctors, and lawyers do the same. A former Bankers Trust executive remembers that "somebody would call an occasional meeting at 8 A.M. Then it became the regular 8 o'clock meeting. So there was the occasional 7 A.M. meeting.... It just kept spreading." On Wall Street, economic warfare replaced the clubhouse atmosphere—and the pressure forced the hours up. As women and new ethnic groups were admitted into the industry, competition for the plum positions heightened—and the hours went along. Twenty-two-year-olds wear beepers as they squeeze in an hour for lunch or jogging at the health club.

What happened on Wall Street was replicated throughout the country in one high-income occupation after another. Associates in law firms competed over who could log more billable hours. Workaholics set new standards of survival. Even America's sleepiest corporations started waking up; and when they did, the corporate hierarchies found themselves coming in to work a little earlier and leaving for home a little later. As many companies laid off white-collar people during the 1980s, those who remained did more for their monthly paycheck. A study of "downsizings" in auto-related companies in the Midwest found that nearly half of the two thousand managers polled said they were working harder than two years earlier.

At cutting-edge corporations, which emphasize commitment, initiative, and flexibility, the time demands are often the greatest. "People who work for me should have phones in their bathrooms," says the CEO from one aggressive American company. Recent research on managerial habits reveals that work has become positively absorbing. When a deadline approached in one corporation, "people who had been working twelve-hour days and Saturdays started to come in on Sunday, and instead of leaving at midnight, they would stay a few more hours. Some did not go home at all, and others had to look at their watches to remember what day it was." The recent growth in small businesses has also contributed to overwork. When Dolores Kordek started a dental insurance company, her strategy for survival was to work harder than the competition. So the office was open from 7 A.M. to 10 P.M. three hundred and sixty-five days a year. And she was virtually always in it.

This combination of retrenchment, economic competition, and innovative business management has raised hours substantially. One poll of senior executives found that weekly hours rose during the 1980s, and vacation time fell. Other surveys have yielded similar results. By the end of the decade, overwork at the upper echelons of the labor market had become endemic—and its scale was virtually unprecedented in living memory.

If the shortage of time had been confined to Wall Street or America's corporate boardrooms, it might have remained just a media curiosity. The number of people who work eighty hours a week and bring home—if they ever get there—a six-figure income is very small. But while the incomes of these rarefied individuals were out of reach, their schedules turned out to be downright common. As Wall Street waxed industrious, the longer schedules penetrated far down the corporate ladder, through middle management, into the secretarial pool, and even onto the factory floor itself. Millions of ordinary Americans fell victim to the shortage of time.

The most visible group has been women, who are coping with a double load—the traditional duties associated with home and children and their growing responsibility for earning a paycheck. With nearly two-thirds of adult women now employed, and a comparable fraction of mothers on the job, it's no surprise that many American women find themselves operating in overdrive. Many working mothers live a life of perpetual motion, effectively holding down two full-time jobs. They rise in the wee hours of the morning to begin the day with a few hours of laundry, cleaning, and other housework. Then they dress and feed the children and send them off to school. They themselves then travel to their jobs. The three-quarters of employed women with full-time positions then spend the next eight and a half hours in the workplace.

At the end of the official workday, it's back to the "second shift"—the duties of housewife and mother. Grocery shopping, picking up the children, and cooking dinner take up the next few hours. After dinner there's cleanup, possibly some additional housework, and, of course, more child care. Women describe themselves as "ragged," "bone-weary," "sinking in quicksand," and "busy every waking hour." For many, the workday rivals those for which the "satanic mills" of the Industrial Revolution grew justly infamous: twelve-or fourteen-hour stretches of labor. By the end of the decade, Ann Landers pronounced herself "awestruck at the number of women who work at their jobs and go home to another full-time job ... How do you do it?" she asked. Thousands of readers responded, with tales ranging from abandoned careers to near collapse. According to sociologist Arlie Hochschild of the University of California, working mothers are exhausted, even fixated on the topic of sleep. "They talked about how much they could 'get by on': ... six and a half, seven, seven and a half, less, more ... These women talked about sleep the way a hungry person talks about food."

By my calculations, the total working time of employed mothers now averages about 65 hours a week. Of course, many do far more than the average—such as mothers with young children, women in professional positions, or those whose wages are so low that they must hold down two jobs just to scrape by. These women will be working 70 to 80 hours a week. And my figures are extremely conservative: they are the lowest among existing studies. A Boston study found that employed mothers *average* over 80 hours of housework, child care, and employment. Two nationwide studies of white, married couples are comparable: in the first, the average week was 87 hours; in the second, it ranged from 76 to 89, depending on the age of the oldest child.

One might think that as women's working hours rose, husbands would compensate by spending less time on the job. But just the opposite has occurred. Men who work are also putting in longer hours. The 5:00 Dads of the 1950s and 1960s (those who were home for dinner and an evening with the family) are becoming an "endangered species." Thirty percent of men with children under fourteen report working fifty or more hours a week. And many of these 8:00 or 9:00 Dads aren't around on the weekends either. Thirty percent of them work Saturdays and/or Sundays at their regular employment. And many others use the weekends for taking on a second job.

A twenty-eight-year-old Massachusetts factory worker explains the bind many fathers are in: "Either I can spend time with my family or support them—not both." Overtime or a second job is financially compelling: "I can work 8–12 hours overtime a week at time and a half, and that's when the real money just starts to kick in.... If I don't work the OT my wife would have to work much longer hours to make up the differences, and our day care bill would double.... The trouble is, the little time I'm home I'm too tired to have any fun with them or be any real help around the house." Among white-collar employees the problem isn't paid overtime, but the regular hours. To get ahead, or even just to hold on to a position, long days may be virtually mandatory.

Overwork is also rampant among the nation's poorly paid workers. At $5, $6, or even $7 an hour, annual earnings before taxes and deductions range from $10,000 to $14,000. Soaring rents alone have been enough to put many of these low earners in financial jeopardy. For the more than one-third of all workers now earning hourly wages of $7 and below, the pressure to lengthen hours has been inexorable. Valerie Connor, a nursing-home worker in Hartford, explains that "you just can't make it on one job." She and many of her co-workers have been led to work two eight-hour shifts a day. According to an official of the Service Employees International Union in New England, nearly one-third of their nursing-home employees now hold two full-time jobs. Changes in the low end of the labor market have also played a role. Here is less full-time, stable employment. "Twenty hours here, thirty hours there, and twenty hours here. That's what it takes to get a real paycheck," says Domenic Bozzotto, president of Boston's hotel and restaurant workers union, whose members are drowning in a sea of work. Two-job families? Those were the good old days, he says. "We've got four-job families." The recent influx of immigrants has also raised hours. I.N. Yazbeck, an arrival from Lebanon, works ninety hours a week at three jobs. It's necessary, he says, for economic success.

This decline of leisure has been reported by the Harris Poll, which has received widespread attention. Harris finds that since 1973 free time has fallen nearly 40 percent—from a median figure of 26 hours a week to slightly under 17. Other surveys, such as the 1989 Decision Research Corporation Poll, also reveal a loss of leisure. Although these polls have serious methodological drawbacks, their findings are not far off the mark. A majority of working Americans—professionals, corporate management, "working" mothers, fathers, and lower-paid workers—*are* finding themselves with less and less leisure time.

Life.com

THE BERKELEY MONTHLY, October 1999.

■ CLIVE THOMPSON

The elevator door slides open and Jess slides in, looking slightly rumpled. Tara sizes her up.

"Didn't get much sleep last night?"

"You can tell?"

"Well, you're wearing the same clothes as yesterday."

Jess laughs. Her music show, Freq, broadcast live over the internet here at the new-media house Pseudo, went late last night and the staff wound up hanging around till dawn. Now it's 10:30 a.m. and she's back from breakfast to make some calls and set up meetings.

"At some point I'm gonna have to shower," she mutters as she wanders off to her desk.

Tara and I tour the studios, strolling through Pseudo's odd mix of high camp and high tech. The office is a study in chaos and energy, each room reflecting the peculiar pop-cultural animus of the twenty-somethings who work here. There's the room for the women's net shows, done up in late-'70s drag with a rainbow-colored bead-curtain entrance. There's a group of goateed musicians hanging out in one room, holding keyboards and a computer monitor. Who are they? "I have no idea," Tara says.

"Sorry," she apologizes at one point, yawning. "I'm a bit burnt out today."

I'm not surprised. In new media it's difficult to find anyone who can boast a full night's rest. Later in the day I visit a 23-year-old acquaintance at a website design firm across town and find him collapsed on a sofa in the staff room.

Late night? "Yeah." He's been setting up a database for a website that's set to go live in two days. The deadline looms and the client—a major corporation—is getting twitchy. Some deeply caffeinated all-nighters will be called for.

"It's intense but it's going pretty well," he says, his hair out of whack with a minor case of bed-head. "I figure I have another two days like this. But it's cool. It's a really cool project."

He pours himself a thick coffee in the well-stocked kitchen and heads back to his workstation, plopping down beside some two dozen other coders and designers clacking away at their keyboards as a stereo pumps out ambient techno in an endless loop. Most of them figure they'll be here until 4 in the morning.

Working till sunup, destroying your eyesight, playing Quake on the company lan, hanging out in a funky office with your dog: in the modern digital workplace this sort of stuff is de rigueur. Indeed, for young Turks in new media—software, website development or the amorphous zone of "content"—aggressively casual and freewheeling is the signature office style.

On the surface it has to do with making work seem a lot more fun and thus a lot less like work. It is, as it were, the master narrative of the New Work, which we could sketch out like this: young digital employees have thrown off the 9-to-5 straitjacket in which their parents so miserably toiled. No more suits, no more rigid corporate hierarchies, no more dull, repetitive tasks. Today work means getting to wear your Star Wars T-shirt, sport multiple piercings and hang out in an office with homey perks: massage-therapist visits, pets, wacky furniture, toys and lots of beer. The staff dines together and parties together. It works hard, sure, but it plays hard too, and usually at the same time. And the workers aren't chained to one job.

Instead they hop at will from company to company, forcing hapless employers to scramble after them, offering ever more perks and stock options to lure their portable, highly paid talents. These kids hold all the cards.

It's a story that has fascinated the media. Reporters covering the industry regularly marvel at the scenes of controlled chaos and pop-cultural riot. In Mountain View [California], Netscape staff members are willing to quit if they can't bring their dogs to work. *USA Today* once breathlessly noted that the office at Organic Online "has been the scene of a dance party, complete with disc jockeys, for 400 people."

Which is precisely the problem.

The studied hipness of new media is a rather devious cultural illusion. Those ultracool offices cover up a seldom-discussed truth: that the jobs themselves often demand intense work and devotion for relatively low pay and zero security. By making work more like play, employers neatly erase the division between the two, which ensures that their young employees will almost never leave the office.

High-tech employees hang out at work long after the city has gone to bed. They'll kill themselves over deadlines, putting in up to 80 hours a week. Then they'll smile and thank their lucky stars that they're part of the digital revolution, the cultural flashpoint of the '90s. For employers, of course, it's a sweet deal—you can't buy flexibility like that. As more than one worker has told me, a website design company can almost always hold a meeting at 2 o'clock on a Saturday afternoon because, well, everyone's there. Where else would they be?

New-media companies are notorious for employee burnout and nanosecond turnover. It's not surprising: given the insane hours, the payoffs are rather slim. We're hit relentlessly with media hype about digital workers' high pay, desirability and stock options. But none of these myths holds up under statistical scrutiny. The vast majority of new-media workers in New York, for example, make less than junior accountants, enjoy the job security of fast-food workers and have a laughably small chance of getting offered any stock anytime anywhere. As for programmers, most are paid surprisingly little and hurled overboard as soon as they hit their mid-30s.

Enamored of its distorted image, the digital workforce is reluctant to accept the facts. "People do not want to face reality," says Bill Lessard, a veteran of the industry who runs NetSlaves, a website that compiles true tales of new-media burnout. "Someone will tell you, 'Oh, I'm a producer.' But they're just a schmuck who's working 90 hours a week. You give these companies body and soul and you really get nothing back."

These workers are touted as the most renegade, the most entrepreneurial generation in years. Yet they are, in traditional labor terms, amazingly compliant. Chained to their keyboards, working far longer hours than they're paid for and blurring the boundaries between their jobs and their lives, digital employees paradoxically present the kind of servile workforce that would have pleased Henry Ford, Nelson Rockefeller and probably Chairman Mao.

When I visit Fred Kahl he's busy designing a computer game based on the TV cartoon "Space Ghost." I peer over his shoulder at the screen, where Fred is fiddling with a sequence: Space Ghost chasing the arch-villain Lokar, who is impersonating Santa Claus. In a few days this will air on the website of the Cartoon Network, one of the major clients of Funny Garbage, the new-media design firm that Kahl works for.

It's hard to deny that new-media workplaces are, aesthetically anyway, extremely pleasant places to be. Kahl shows me around Funny Garbage—a firm respected for its right-brained, creative web animations—and it's not unlike wandering through a gallery of '70s kitsch. Workstations are cluttered with retro-pop toys and icons. One of the company's founders, 33-year-old Peter Girardi, has three different video-game systems in his office.

This is not to suggest that everyone is horsing around. Over by the animation computers, three designers are hunkering down for a long haul, even though it's already past 5 o'clock on a Friday night. By 9, staff members will likely launch into a Quake tournament on the company lan. ("I had to stop," Kahl says. "I almost destroyed my wrists.") In this context, it's easy to see how work and life inexorably bleed into each other. It's also easy to see how new-media employers can capitalize on the confusion. For people involved in digital culture, a highly wired office—replete with digital toys and fueled by a T1 connection—can be a more inviting place to hang out than a cramped apartment or a bar or club.

In fact, sometimes work offers even better partying than a club.

One of Psuedo's longest-serving staff members, a 29-year-old programmer named Joey Fortuna, remembers arriving on his first day four years ago to find the office in a fantastic mess from a party held the night before. Pseudo CEO Josh Harris staggered in from his on-site apartment wearing nothing but boxer shorts and instantly set Fortuna to work, even though Fortuna had never written a line of code in his life.

To get up to speed on HTML, Fortuna—like most of the staff—put in months of 12-hour days. In 1996 he spent Christmas Day writing code for a video-publishing database. "It was just insane!" he says. "I was working all the time. I lived here. But I didn't mind. It was like a clubhouse."

He gestures around the loft, pointing to its kooky mix of high-and low-tech. "You know, it's ironic," he grins, "but in the last century this used to be a sweatshop."

If there's an archetypal success story in new media it's probably that of Jeff Dachis and Razorfish. In spring 1995, Dachis and his friend Craig Kanarick, both in their late 20s, founded the website design company in their living rooms. Last year they had 350 employees in eight offices and did $30 million in business.

Companies like Razorfish have built the mythos of gold-rush success in new media: start a firm in your garage, wow senior executives at Fortune 500 companies, then take occasional breaks from your PlayStation to watch the dough roll in. "The trappings of power have changed," wrote *Time* magazine in an October 1997 survey of the "cyber-elite."

But here too the hype outstrips the reality. True, there are dozens of fantastic entrepreneurial successes. But when you look at the statistics the New Work starts to look like an old story: low pay, no security and those who no longer suit the company profile pitched instantly overboard.

In 1997 the New York New Media Association did a study of the local scene. It discovered that high-tech jobs paid an average of $37,212. That's middling at best for a city as expensive as New York. It's also far outpaced by the average salaries in other media: advertising, $71,637; periodicals, $69,849; TV broadcasting, $85,938.

The churn rate in new-media jobs is amazingly high. The New York study found that almost half the work in new media is freelance or part time. More than two-thirds of all freelance contracts last fewer than six months, most are three-month stints. Part-time jobs are growing four-times faster than full-time positions.

In place of decent pay and regular work, new media offers the lure of instant wealth—the fabled stock options that turned the creators of Amazon.com or TheGlobe.com into overnight multimillionaires. It's a seductive tale, and those who have won the game have won huge. Berkeley's Adam Sah, who was in on the ground floor at Inktomi, cashed in some stocks when the company went public. The years of 400-hour months paid off. "It wasn't fun," he says, "but it did turn out all right for me."

Sah previously worked at Microsoft, which pretty much invented the stock-options trick, knowing that the lure of the market is one of the few things that will motivate coders to impale themselves upon unshippable products with unmeetable deadlines. "It's amazing what people will do for money," Sah laughs wryly.

The stock payoff, though, is about as chimerical as you can get. There are no stats on new-media stock cash-ins but high-tech hunters counsel their clients that the chance of getting lucrative options are slim.

"To cash in on stock you have to stick around for several years at a company," says Alex Santic, head of Silicon Valley Connections, one of the first headhunting firms to specialize in new media. "But few people really want to. They want to move on after a year. They get lured in by the promise of stock but rarely see it through." Indeed, as the New York new-media study found, the only folks who own substantial equity are management and founders—worker bees have a statistically insignificant slice of the pie.

Perhaps the most persistent myth of recent years, though, is that of the "programmer shortage." According to this tale, the geeks now run the show. There isn't enough programming talent to go around, so companies are fighting tooth and nail over warm bodies. Mainstream media have taken up the story like a mantra. "Business leaders say the shortage has reached near-crisis proportions," wrote the *Washington Post* in an article detailing—with a sort of horrified fascination—the incredible perks offered to lure programmers, from "signing bonuses like professional athletes" to $70-an-hour rates for temp work.

Again, the facts contradict the hype. Last year Norman Matloff, a professor of computer science at UC Davis, released one of the few studies ever done on the programmer job market. He surveyed the hiring practices of software and new-media firms and concluded that there was, in fact, no shortage of programmers. Companies were hiring only two to four percent of the people they interviewed, a rate far below that for other types of engineers.

Older programmers, meanwhile, are ruthlessly squeezed out. Age discrimination, Matloff says, is "amazingly rampant." He found that after age 35 and increasingly as they get older, programmers are ditched in favor of the fresh-scrubbed kids released each year from technical colleges. By their early 40s fewer than one-fifth of all trained programmers are still working in the field. One 47-year-old programmer Matloff talked to was fluent in C++, Perl, Unix and a host of other languages, but when he went looking for a new job he landed only two interviews in 15 months of searching. Another man had been programming since 1976. "I can't get so much as an interview," he told Matloff. "I now earn about $24,000 a year in retail sales and management."

When you look at the facts you begin to realize the incredible power of new-media workplace culture. It sells a lifestyle of liberation and autonomy that is wildly out of sync with reality. Then you begin to realize why those Quake marathons, those cappuccino machines in the staff kitchen and all those dogs at work are important. Absent decent pay and a commitment from your boss, maybe a game of Quake is the best you can get.

The Law and Economics of Critical Race Theory

112 YALE L.J. 1757, 1789–93, 1795–96, 1797–99, 1801–14 (2003) (reviewing CROSSROADS, DIRECTIONS, AND A NEW CRITICAL RACE THEORY (Francisco Valdes et al. eds., 2002)).

■ DEVON W. CARBADO & MITU GULATI

A starting point for thinking about workplace discrimination is to raise the question of whether today's workplace is buttressed by institutionalized racial norms. With respect to explicit racial norms, the answer is no: That would violate antidiscrimination law. But do implicit racial norms structure today's workplace culture? [Critical race theory, or CRT] answers this question affirmatively, pointing to workplace practices like English-only rules and grooming regulations (e.g., rules prohibiting employees from braiding their hair) that restrict the expression of particular identities and, in so doing, marginalize them.

There is, however, a subtle form of institutional discrimination to which CRT scholars have not paid attention. This discrimination derives from a commitment on the part of many employers, particularly employers who use teams to manage their workplace culture to achieve trust, fairness, and loyalty (TFL). Why? TFL reduces transaction costs. Empirical evidence suggests that the effectiveness of teams is enhanced when employers engender TFL among their employees. Employees who perceive that they are a part of a "TFL community" work hard, cooperate, police each other, and share valuable information. Based on this evidence, scholars have argued that law should be structured to facilitate the creation of TFL workplaces. In addition to its efficiency gains, TFL values seem normatively appealing.

TFL's normative surface appeal helps to explain why the institutional discrimination story we articulate below has not yet been told. Central to our story is not the fact that employers are invested in TFL but rather how they go about realizing that investment—by aggressively promoting homogeneity. Evidence suggests that, at least in the short term, a manager with a demographically homogeneous work team has a better chance of producing TFL than one with a diverse team. If, as is often suggested, managers focus primarily on short-term results, there is an incentive for managers to seek demographically homogeneous teams.

The relationship between the pursuit of demographic homogeneity and racial discrimination is direct. In short, workplaces organized to achieve homogeneity are likely to discriminate because homogeneity norms, by their very nature, reflect a commitment to sameness (favoring people perceived to be members of the in-group ("insiders")) and a rejection of difference (disfavoring people perceived to be members of the out-group ("outsiders")). Coupled with the fact that, within most professional settings, whites are insiders and nonwhites are outsiders, the relationship between discrimination and homogeneity becomes clear.

The foregoing suggests that race-neutral workplace norms institutionalize insider racial preference. Is this a reason for concern? The answer is not obviously yes. One might argue that, even to the extent that there are incentives for employers to create and maintain homogeneous workplaces, the threat of antidiscrimination sanctions undermines that incentive. Richard Epstein famously worried about exactly this effect of antidiscrimination law. According to Epstein, part of the problem with antidiscrimination law is that it compromises workplace efficiency by preventing employers from establishing homogeneous workplace cultures. One might conclude, then, that given the threat of legal sanctions, the institutionalized racism problem we have identified is theoretical—not real.

Moreover, there are institutional legitimacy concerns that militate against the establishment of homogenous workplaces. White-only work forces can create public relations problems. Perhaps not surprisingly, there is no employer-driven movement afoot to have antidiscrimination laws repealed because they prohibit employers from establishing demographically homogenous workplaces. To the contrary, even a cursory examination of the management and organizational behavior literature reveals (at least rhetorically) an institutional commitment to manage, and not to eliminate, heterogeneity. Thus, all seems well: Law prevents institutions from privileging homogeneity, and institutions perceive the pursuit of homogeneity to be problematic.

Our claim, however, is that all is not well. Neither antidiscrimination law nor the affirmative pursuit of diversity operates as a meaningful barrier to, or substantially undermines the incentives for employers to achieve, workplace homogeneity. Epstein need not worry. To be sure, the law prohibits blatant racial animus in hiring and promotion. But that is a minimal barrier to the managerial pursuit of racial homogeneity. To move from a phenotypic conception of race to a performative conception is to find that, to a significant extent, judges can (and, we surmise, do) apply antidiscrimination law to actually *protect* the pursuit of racial homogeneity. They do so by failing to capture employment discrimination based on *intraracial* distinctions—distinctions employers make among people within a particular racial group.

Driving these distinctions is a question about racial stereotypes and racial salience. Other things being equal, employers prefer nonwhites whose racial identity is not salient and whose identity performance is inconsistent with stereotypes about their racial group. In other words, employers screen for racial palatability. With respect to Asian Americans, for example, employers determine whether, notwithstanding phenotypic difference, a particular Asian American is (based on how she performs her identity) sufficiently like insiders to be successfully assimilated into a homogenized workplace.

To date, there are no Title VII cases that render a racial palatability discrimination claim cognizable. Thus, employers can make these kinds of intraracial distinctions with legal impunity. And to the extent employers engage in this practice, their associated institutional legitimacy remains intact because the practice anticipates and produces at least some workplace racial integration. Finally, because the racial diversity employers achieve by making intraracial distinctions is literally skin deep, it comfortably coexists with their commitment to homogeneity.

The foregoing sets forth a theory of institutional racism—that it is a function of an investment on the part of employers to realize the efficiency gains of homogeneity. Because many institutions operate under what we call a *diversity constraint*—a constraint that requires the firm to hire at least some nonwhites—employers will determine which nonwhites to hire on evidence of racial palatability. The more racially palatable employers perceive a potential employee to be, the less concerned they will be over the possibility that that potential employee will (racially) disrupt workplace homogeneity. * * *

B. *The Incentive for Employers To Pursue Homogeneity*
* * *

1. *Theories*

There are at least three theories suggesting that employers are motivated to pursue homogeneity: social identity theory, similarity-attraction theory, and statistical judgments theory.

Social identity theory suggests that people have an affinity for those they perceive to be part of their in-group. In concrete terms, people are more likely to demonstrate TFL (which, again, is shorthand for trust, fairness, and loyalty) to those they perceive to be members of their in-group. Conversely, they are more likely to discriminate against those they perceive to be members of an out-group. Race, being both socially salient and facially visible, is one of the primary categories along which people make initial in-group and out-group categorizations. One explanation is that people assume that those of a similar race are likely to share similar values and to have had similar experiences. As a result, racial outsiders are vulnerable to discrimination from their racial insider colleagues. To avoid this distrust and dislike (which will likely undermine workplace efficiency by increasing transaction costs), employers will want to hire people who are similar to insiders.

The similarity-attraction theory is largely analogous. It posits that people are attracted to those who are similar. The theory is that race is one of the primary categories used to determine similarity and that this similarity, in turn, translates into attraction. * * *

The final theory suggesting that employers are motivated to pursue homogeneity is statistical judgments theory. Most often attributed to economics (though also central to psychology), this theory claims that racial differences often activate *statistical judgments* about likely behavioral tendencies. These statistical judgments are a type of mental shortcut, a resource-saving device. For example, white workers may see a new black colleague as likely to be lazy, untrustworthy, disloyal (especially to her white colleagues), frequently angry (perhaps as a result of oversensitivity about race), and difficult to communicate with (due to her likely having different values, different interests, and different cultural and experiential points of reference). Under this theory, whether an insider-employer will hire a black person turns on the currency of the foregoing statistical judgments. The stronger the statistical judgment, the stronger the employer's perception that a prospective black employee will not fit into the institution.

These theories suggest that there is a disincentive for employers to hire outsiders and a corresponding incentive for employers to hire insiders. Difference engenders distrust, dislike, disconnection, disidentification, and disassociation. Each of these characteristics (and certainly all of them together) undermines a necessary condition for the effective operation of teams—cooperative behavior—and therefore increases the transaction costs of managing the workplace.

2. *Empirical Evidence*

   a. *The Basic Story*

In addition to the theoretical literature, there is empirical evidence predicting that racially heterogeneous teams are likely to be less effective than homogenous ones. Studies consistently show what the above theories suggest: Racial heterogeneity undermines trust and cooperation. Team members in heterogeneous teams tend not to communicate as well as team members in homogeneous teams. Turnover rates in heterogeneous teams are higher. And managerial attempts to spur innovation by diversifying their teams have "met with mixed success."

b. *The More Complicated Account*

Recent scholarship on diversity management suggests that the empirical story about workplace homogeneity may be more complicated than we have thus far described. The complication is that heterogeneity can operate as a double-edged sword. To appreciate how this is so, it is helpful to conceptualize heterogeneity/diversity as operating in a two-stage process. At stage one, superficial differences in terms of variables like race cause distrust, difficulties in communication, and a reluctance to cooperate. However, under the right conditions of intergroup contact—equal status, opportunities for self-revelation, egalitarian norms, and tasks that require cooperative interdependence—diverse team members can, at stage two, gain each other's trust, begin to see commonalities, work cooperatively, and realize the benefits of working as a diverse team. Central to this theory is the notion that there are meaningful things an employer can do at stage one—the initial contact stage—to facilitate cooperative behavior at stage two. * * *

C. *Summary*

There is theoretical and empirical evidence suggesting that employers are motivated to pursue homogeneity: Put simply, homogeneous workplaces facilitate trust, loyalty, and cooperative behavior. The story with respect to heterogeneous work teams is different. First, at an institutional level, heterogeneity is difficult and costly to manage. Second, the most cost-effective way for individual supervisors to manage heterogeneity is to "socialize away" outsider difference. Thus, it is more accurate to characterize this strategy as eliminating, rather than managing, heterogeneity. Third, even assuming that heterogeneity can be effectively managed, the benefits of a heterogeneous workplace are speculative, and they are realized primarily over the long term.

Acknowledging the homogeneity incentive is helpful to CRT in at least two ways. First, it provides critical race theorists with a different perspective on colorblindness. The homogeneity incentive exists because of the transaction costs of heterogeneity. Like colorblindness, then, the homogeneity incentive requires the submersion of racial difference. Second, the existence of the homogeneity incentive supports CRT's claim that an employer's preference for racial sameness won't always be motivated by racial animus. One of the most important ideas in CRT is that racism is not just a function of individual bad actors. From here, CRT advances one of two arguments: (1) that discrimination is unconscious and (2) that discrimination is institutional. The homogeneity incentive provides an additional base from which to theorize about the latter. It demonstrates that institutional discrimination can exist in the absence of racial animosity. * * *

IV. How Employers Respond to the Homogeneity Incentive

Given antidiscrimination laws and social norms disfavoring racial exclusivity, institutions are unlikely to respond to the homogeneity incentive by hiring only insiders. They will hire outsiders as well. The claim we advance is that employers will use specific mechanisms to screen outsiders for evidence of racial palatability. These mechanisms select "but for outsiders"—outsiders who, but for their racial phenotype, are very similar to the insiders—and they select against "essential outsiders"—outsiders whose personal characteristics are consistent with the image of the prototypical outsider. * * *

A. The "Race–Neutral" Response to the Homogeneity Incentive

1. The Basic Idea: Selection and Socialization

Broadly speaking, there are two mechanisms employers can use to respond to the homogeneity incentive: "selection" and "socializing" mechanisms. Selection mechanisms operate at the hiring and the promotion stages. Here, an employer screens individuals for particular characteristics that function as proxies for determining whether a given individual (1) is willing to be homogenized into the workplace culture *and* (2) has the capacity to do so. Socializing mechanisms, in turn, are used to initiate and integrate the individual into the workplace. In other words, socializing mechanisms are the rites of passage that structure a new employee's experiential travels through the workplace after selection mechanisms are used to bring her into the firm. Constituting this passage are numerous rituals through which the individual is expected to demonstrate her commitment to homogeneity. More particularly, she must effectively prove that the employer made the right selection decision. Due to space constraints, we do not elaborate further on socialization mechanisms. We focus on selection, identifying four selection mechanisms employers can use to screen potential employees for evidence of performative (and not simply phenotypic) homogeneity.

2. The Selection Mechanisms

Four interrelated selection mechanisms that we draw out of the theory and evidence on homogeneity are: similarity, comfort, differentiation, and respectable exoticism.

a. *Similarity*

This mechanism is intuitive. The question is whether the individual exhibits personal characteristics suggesting she is similar to employees already at the firm. The more an individual appears to be similar to existing employees, the more likely an employer is to conclude that the individual has the potential to be assimilated. The potential employee's response to standard interview questions can signal her potential for assimilation to employers. Consider, for example, Johnny, who is being considered for a mid-level associate position at an elite corporate law firm. A senior partner has asked Johnny to "tell us a little bit about yourself." Johnny's response includes the following:

> *I enjoy tennis and golf, though I confess that both need improvement. I like a good Gore Vidal novel; in fact, I'm in the process of rereading* Julian, *which, by the way, I highly recommend. I'm not a huge sports fan, but I try to make time to watch a good basketball game—usually with colleagues and friends. I wasn't always fond of theater, but two years ago my wife took me to see* The Tin Man, *and I've been sold on theater—both high and low—ever since. I enjoy Italian cinema, the old Fellini stuff as well as some of the more contemporary productions. And every so often, I truly enjoy a good B movie—not a B movie masquerading as an A movie, but a B movie that knows it's a B movie. I love going to the museum with my kids. We try to go twice a month. You'd be surprised at the interpretational skills of a six-year old.*

This response provides the employer with signals about Johnny's socialized identity, information that the employer can use to make a determination as to whether Johnny is sufficiently like the firm's existing employees. Johnny plays tennis and golf, the preferred sports of corporate America. The fact that both need improvement suggests that he is available to play both sports with his colleagues and not likely to be unduly competitive when he does so. In this way, both games can function as sites for socialization. Johnny's response also indicates that he is not an avid sports fan, but that he enjoys a good basketball game. Here, Johnny signals respectable (but not hyper-) masculinity and a willingness to participate in group-based spectator sport rituals. Johnny is married with kids, which reveals his heterosexuality and possibly a certain traditionalism. He appears to be cultured (he reads Gore Vidal, watches Italian cinema, attends the theater, and visits museums), but he is not overly elitist or pompous (he enjoys the occasional B movie and attends low-brow (and just barely high-brow) theater). Finally, the fact that Johnny's wife successfully socialized him into the theater, an experience that he was not predisposed to enjoy, suggests that he will likely not resist the firm's socialization efforts.

Not every institution will select for the foregoing qualities: Similarity selection mechanisms will vary from institution to institution. The point here is twofold: (1) Most employers will have a set of characteristics that they perceive to define their workplace, and (2) without much difficulty, employers can screen for these qualities in interviews.

b. *Comfort*

Related to similarity is comfort. Here, employers want to know whether incumbent employees will be comfortable working with the prospective hire. Again, they can select for comfort (or at least select against discomfort) by considering a prospective employee's response to standard interview questions. Stipulate once more that Johnny is interviewing for a job with an elite corporate law firm. The partner asks Johnny: "Tell us what kind of firm you're looking for." Johnny responds:

> *I am looking for a firm doing high-level, sophisticated corporate work. Quite frankly, most of the firms I am interviewing with seem to fall in that category—certainly your firm does. What becomes important for me, then, is firm culture. I am looking for a firm that values and*

respects difference. I guess I believe that people shouldn't have to lose themselves at work. They should be permitted to be who they are. I was happy to learn that your firm recently adopted a casual Friday policy.

I am also looking for a firm within which junior associates have a voice—that is, an opportunity to comment on the institutional governance of the firm, for example, the firm's billing, hiring, and pro bono policies. That sort of participation helps to make junior associates invested in the firm.

Employers could interpret Johnny's response in a number of ways. But if they are screening for comfort, a given employer may have concerns about whether Johnny "fits." Johnny's view is that individuals should be permitted to be themselves and that a firm should value difference. However, difference can be uncomfortable or discomforting. To employ what many would consider an extreme example, the firm would likely be uncomfortable with Johnny coming to work as a cross-dresser. If Johnny does cross dress, the firm would expect him to do so (if at all) outside of the workplace.

Recall that Johnny wants a voice in institutional governance and provides an indication of the kinds of issues he hopes to engage. Johnny's representations here might send a positive signal—specifically, that he wants to become a part of the firm. To the extent the employer is selecting for comfort, however, the employer could interpret Johnny's comments to suggest that he will likely make the firm uncomfortable about its hiring, pro bono, and billing practices, among other institutional governance matters.

c. *Differentiation*

Employers are most likely to utilize the differentiation mechanism when they perceive themselves to be making a "risky hire." Here, prospective employees are in a *category* that is presumed to be incapable of homogenization (or that is disinterested in socialization). Imagine that Johnny is seeking an entry-level job with a law firm. He is a third-year law student at State Law School, which is a third-tier law school. He is on law review and has an A-grade point average. His letters of recommendation are effusive; his writing sample is strong.

The firm has never hired a law student from State Law School, in part because the school is insufficiently elite and because most of the students at State Law School are from working-class backgrounds. The firm therefore assumes that these students are likely to have difficulty fitting into an elite corporate law firm. The firm might not be right for them (read: they might not be right for the firm). Given this concern, whether the employer hires Johnny will be a function of whether Johnny can differentiate himself from the category within which he is situated—that is, State law students. Consider the following exchange between Johnny and a senior partner.

Partner: Good of you to stop by. Come in and have a seat. It seems that I've left your resume elsewhere in the office. You wouldn't happen to have an extra copy, would you?

Johnny: Yes, in fact I do.

Partner: Oh yes ... I am beginning to remember this resume. I see that you went to Harvard undergrad and that you rowed crew. How did we do this year? I graduated Harvard in '75.

Johnny: We lost to Yale, second year in a row, no pun intended. I suppose if we're going to lose to any school, it ought to be Yale. Their heavyweight eight was selected to represent the country at the World Championships in London.

Partner: So you did really well at Harvard—Magna in history, 3.7 GPA, member of the debating team. I suspect that you had a lot of options when you applied to law school.

Johnny: I was fortunate to have a few. In addition to State, NYU, Columbia, and Michigan said yes. Harvard and Stanford placed me on a waiting list. Yale said no.

Partner: I didn't get into Yale, either. What's more, I've lived to tell the tale. You will, too. But, seriously, you had all these options. I'm curious as to how you made your decision.

Johnny: Well, to a considerable extent my decision was a financial one. I couldn't afford to attend any of the other schools. And I didn't want to burden my parents anymore than I had to. Besides, I hoped that if I distinguished myself at State, I would have many of the same opportunities as if I had attended, say, Michigan.

Partner: So, Johnny, tell me about how you're thinking about law firms. Big law firms are not for everyone, and as you know, we're a pretty big law firm.

Johnny: I had the good fortune of clerking for two summers at Bronton, Stevely & Kellog in Chicago.

Partner: Yes, yes, an excellent firm.

Johnny: I had a good time there. People got along well. They had interests similar to mine. I got the sense that the attorneys there felt that they were part of a larger community. Your firm describes itself in precisely that way. Most of my classmates run away from big firms. Why go through that haze, some ask?

Partner: They consider big firms a haze?

Johnny: Some do. Most simply believe that big firms treat individuals as fungible commodities. That's not my assumption but it is the predominant assumption on campus.

Partner: What's your view, then? Let me guess: You love big firms?

Johnny: Of course. Kidding aside, I'd say that, whether it's a big firm or a small firm, the question is really twofold: whether the individual is committed to becoming a part of a team and whether the firm provides him with the opportunity to play ball.

The foregoing reflects enough differentiation on Johnny's part to effectively remove him from, or at least situate him on the periphery of, the outsider group (again, students at State Law School). Presumably, few law students at State attended Harvard. Johnny's Harvard education is significant in at least three respects. First, it signifies Johnny's intellectual capacity. Second, the fact that Johnny graduated from Harvard (and rowed crew) suggests that he has the potential for socialization. Finally, Johnny's Harvard education places Johnny and the partner in a community that has significant cultural capital—the community of Harvard alumni. That the partner recognizes this shared community is evident in his question: "How did we do this year?"

Nor would many students at State have had the opportunity to attend NYU, Michigan, and Columbia or to clerk at an elite corporate law firm. Here, too, Johnny is different. Finally, Johnny is also different in terms of his strong academic performance and the fact that he does not have a bias against big-firm practice. In short, after completing the interview with Johnny, the partner could tell himself that, although, as a formal matter, Johnny belongs to the group of State Law students, in a substantive sense, he is different. It is this kind of information that the differentiation selection mechanism is designed to ascertain.

d. *Respectable Exoticism*

Certain differences do not threaten firm homogeneity. To the extent that a given difference is both exotic (not an awful lot of people are likely to have it) and respectable (the difference is not overdetermined by a negative social meaning), firms can commodify this difference to their advantage. Thus, while hiring too many immigrants might compromise a firm's commitment to homogeneity, hiring an immigrant of royal lineage might not produce that effect. Immigrant difference that is located in the context of royal identity can be marketed—for example, to employees who might feel special because they have a royal coworker.

Another example of respectable exoticism might be an ex-NBA player in a corporate context. Note, however, that while a firm's homogeneity might tolerate one such individual, it may not be able to tolerate several. The incentive for the employer to utilize the exotic difference selection perhaps is not as strong as the employer's incentive to utilize similarity, comfort, or differentiation. In this respect, it might be more accurate to say that a firm will not select against respectable exoticism than it would be to say that the firm will actively select for that characteristic.

B. *Explicitly Racializing the Discussion: Combining CRT Insights*

The preceding discussion does not identify the racial effects of selection mechanisms. These effects can be demonstrated by adopting CRT's methodology of racializing the analysis. To borrow from Jerome Culp, we "raise ... the race question" and, in the process, make a number of empirical assumptions about race. While we think the assumptions are plausible, the analysis is necessarily tentative and meant only to be illustrative of the type of analysis that might be performed.

1. *How Likely Is It That Johnny Will Be a Racial Minority?*

How likely is it that "Johnny" will be a racial minority? Consider, for example, the Johnny who is a student at State Law School. Recall that this Johnny attended Harvard College and rowed crew. Rowing crew often means that one attended an elite East Coast prep school, and the number of minorities who fit in this category will be small. Further, although Johnny is at State Law School, he had the option of attending first-tier law schools. Not many students of color at a third-tier law school will have had that opportunity. In short, few minorities will have the kind of cultural capital reflected in Johnny's background.

2. *Assuming That the Johnny at State Law School Is Black, Will He Be "Selected"?*

Our hypothetical assumes that an elite corporate firm would select a person like Johnny, notwithstanding the fact that Johnny does not fit the standard profile (that is, a person who has attended a first-tier law school). But if Johnny is black, this issue is far from clear. Few elite corporate firms hire blacks from schools other than those in the first-tier—more specifically, in the top ten. This may be (at least in part) due to two assumptions. The first is an assumption about affirmative action and intellectual competence—namely, that given race-based admission preferences, "smart blacks" should end up at first-tier schools. The second is an assumption about race and class—namely, that a black person at State Law School is likely to be working class and thus may have difficulty fitting into the law firm. While both assumptions can be rebutted, doing so would require an employer to engage in more intensive (read: more costly) screening of Johnny.

3. *As a General Matter, What Kind of Person of Color Is Johnny Likely to Be?*

Except for respectable exoticism, each of the selection mechanisms described above is designed to ascertain the extent to which a prospective employee is different from firm insiders. The outsiders likely to be the least different from the firm's insiders are those on (or who perform their identity as if they are on) the periphery of their outsider group identity. These "most peripheral outsiders" are likely to have grown up in predominantly white neighborhoods and to have attended elite (and predominantly white) high schools, colleges, and law schools. Employers can use these background characteristics as proxies for whether, and to what extent, outsider candidates will fit comfortably into a predominantly white workplace.

But there is a more direct method the employer can use to determine whether an outsider has the capacity to work within a homogenized workplace. There is evidence suggesting that particular types of outsiders are, from an employer's perspective, likely to cause fewer problems in the operation of a team dominated by insiders than are other types of outsiders. Racial outsiders who are "extroverted" and effective at "self-monitoring" are more likely to succeed than those who are not. Good self-monitors assess how others perceive them and adjust their behavior accordingly; extroverts project a strong and identifiable self-identity. Presumably, the reason these types of outsiders cause minimal disruption is that they actively engage in "impression management." That is, they are constantly interacting with others, sending signals about themselves, and reacting to the impressions that others have of them. An employer's selection decision likely will take account of how well outsiders manage impressions about their racial identity (that is, at least in part, how well they disprove racial stereotypes).

4. How Do People of Color Signal Racial Differentiation?

The point of differentiation strategies is to convey one of three ideas—that one does not identify as an outsider, that one is a different kind of outsider, or that what others think of outsiders is wrong. To convey the first idea, that one does not identify as an outsider, an employee would engage in disidentification or disassociation strategies—strategies that signal that the employee does not really identify with his outsider group. Imagine that, in the context of an interview with an elite firm, a partner says this to Johnny: "I have to tell you, Johnny, racial diversity at our firm is not good. We do our best. But the numbers are what they are—not pretty." That statement offers Johnny an "opportunity" to articulate his relationship to his outsider identity. To disidentify and disassociate, Johnny can say: "I appreciate your telling me this, but I am more interested in learning about how your firm cultivates and trains junior associates." Johnny's response could also reflect even stronger evidence of outsider disidentification and disassociation. He might have said: "I appreciate your telling me this, but I just don't believe in identity politics. Diversity is fine and good, but people are people." The point is that the earlier response is enough differentiation to suggest to the employer that Johnny is not a "race man."

To convey the second idea of differentiation, that one is a different kind of outsider, the outsider could adopt an individualized stereotype negation strategy. Here, the outsider would attempt to convey to the employer that stereotypes about his outsider identity do not apply to him. Imagine that the employer asks Johnny what he does with his spare time and Johnny responds: "Fishing, golfing, and catching up on foreign cinema." The employer could interpret this response to suggest that Johnny is not an ordinary black man (who, based on stereotypes, would have responded: "Watching basketball, playing basketball, and listening to hip-hop."). To the extent the employer does not perceive Johnny to be a black male prototype, the employer is less likely to attribute negative stereotypes of black men to Johnny.

Johnny can convey the final idea of differentiation—that others' assumptions about outsiders are wrong—through generalized stereotype negation. Under this strategy, Johnny attempts to persuade the employer that stereotypes about the employee's outsider group are inaccurate. This strategy is difficult and risky to perform when one is interviewing for a job. For instance, after articulating what he likes to do in his spare time (fishing, golfing, and catching up on foreign cinema), Johnny could add something like: "Not all black men like basketball. Moreover, most of the stereotypes about blacks are simply inaccurate. Consider, for example, crime...." It is unlikely that, in the context of an interview, Johnny would engage the employer in this way: The statement presupposes that the employer harbors stereotypes about blacks, a presupposition that could engender racial discomfort on the part of the employer ("This black guy thinks I am a racist."). Further, even if Johnny did make such a statement to the employer, it is unlikely that the employer would be persuaded by it. For generalized stereotype negation to work, there needs to be a level of trust, and sustained interaction, between the outsider and the employer.

Performing each of the foregoing differentiation strategies constitutes a form of work—identity work. Among other problems with this work, it can compromise one's sense of identity.

5. *What Are the Racial Community Costs of Differentiation Strategies?*

One of the problems with the first two differentiation strategies (disidentification/disassociation and individual stereotype negation) is that they are individually oriented. To the extent that an employee feels pressured to perform these strategies, he privileges his individual advancement over that of his group. Differentiation strategies are a response to an institutionalized problem—the employer's investment in homogeneity. So long as the homogeneity incentive drives employment decisions, there is little room for racial diversification. Society ends up with minimal (or token) outsider economic advancement into the workplace. The incentives for the outsider group, therefore, should be to engage in a collective struggle to change the system to tolerate (if not welcome) greater expression and representation of outsider identities. The first two differentiation strategies undermine that goal. They encourage outsiders to disidentify with, and disassociate from, the collective interests of the outsider group. In this sense, the problem with homogeneity is not simply that it drives employers to hire only certain kinds of outsiders, but also that the outsiders whom the employer hires are not likely to lift as they climb.

To summarize, the employer's pursuit of a homogenous workforce is likely to produce the following effects (subject to the assumptions made):

- Given the negative presumption that applies to the ability and willingness of outsiders to satisfy the homogeneity requirement (and the positive presumptions that apply to whites), the quantum of cultural capital (or the price of entry) that employers require of outsiders is likely to be higher than that for their white counterparts.
- Within the outsider community, only the elite are likely to possess the quantum of cultural capital necessary to gain entry. Employers seeking to satisfy the diversity constraint will affirmatively pursue this small subset of minorities.
- The strategies that an individual outsider employee is likely to pursue, such as differentiation, may hurt the collective cause of her minority group and compromise her sense of self. The collective cause

may be better served by a struggle to reduce and remove barriers, as opposed to a competition among outsiders for a few slots (and which requires outsider homogenization).

* * *

NOTES AND QUESTIONS

1. "Lean" production and new, ruthless economy. Changes in technology have permitted a steady rise in economic productivity for the United States in recent years. These changes, however, collectively have made labor much more insecure. William Greider discusses the case of labor unions and the manufacturing sector:

> Starting in the 1970s, U.S. companies gravitated toward a different strategy in which global price pressures were offset by extracting more from labor. Corporations discarded their long postwar truce with unions and began moving jobs, first to the low-wage South and then offshore. They closed factories and demanded wage contracts that depressed wages. They mobilized both political and economic power to weaken labor's bargaining position.
>
> American corporate managers might point out that they themselves were driven to these defensive actions by the global economic forces. The "virtuous circle" of the 1950s and 1960s had also been sustained by the existence of industrial oligopolies—a few big companies that dominated major sectors like autos, steel and aircraft and were powerful enough to set prices and wages in a clubby, arbitrary fashion. The rise of foreign producers, especially from Japan, broke up that comfortable arrangement forever.
>
> As firms shifted production to lower-wage workers, organized labor lost members and became steadily less able to discipline managements. The decline in wages was not confined to union members, however, but was more general. Retail sales workers, for instance, experienced a much sharper fall than manufacturing. In 1970, wages constituted 67 percent of all personal income in the United States, a ratio that had held constant for decades. By 1994, wages were less than 58 percent of total incomes. In 1960, wages were about 26 percent of total sales. By 1994, they were about 20 percent.

WILLIAM GREIDER, ONE WORLD, READY OR NOT: THE MANIC LOGIC OF GLOBAL CAPITALISM 77 (1997). Greider argues that these trends are symptomatic of a larger phenomenon: "wage arbitrage." Wage arbitrage "moves the production and jobs from a high-wage labor market to another where the labor is much cheaper. The producers thus reduce their costs and enhance profits by arbitraging these wage differences, usually selling their finished products back into the high-wage markets." *id.* at 57. Since labor is much less mobile than capital, wage arbitrage means the upper hand in bargaining power for capital in particular disputes. Unions, which are usually organized within national boundaries, become vulnerable to the threat of moving jobs to lower-wage countries.

2. **Law firms as internal labor markets.** For an extended application of economic theory to explain the hiring and promotion practices of large law firms, see David B. Wilkins & G. Mitu Gulati, *Reconceiving the Tournament of Lawyers: Tracking, Seeding, and Information Control in the Internal Labor Markets of Elite Law Firms*, 84 VA. L. REV. 1581 (1998).

3. **Winner-take-all markets.** Some economists argue that a new feature of contemporary labor markets is the existence of the "winner take all" market. In such markets there are many competitors for a very few extremely lucrative slots. The entertainment industry provides many examples: as reality shows like *American Idol* dramatically illustrate, the possibility of fame and fortune in the entertainment world draws many more people than could possibly succeed. As the economists argue, and as *American Idol* also illustrates, winner-take-all markets are socially wasteful because the possibility of extremely high rewards (coupled with the cognitive quirks identified by bounded rationality theory) draws people who would do better for themselves and the rest of society if they put their time and energy elsewhere. Winner-take-all markets also contribute to income inequality, since a very small number of players make a huge amount of money and the rest make very little. Robert Frank and Philip Cook argue that changes in tax policy, tort reform, health care finance, educational finance, and antitrust policy, among other reforms, could promote both efficiency and equity by reducing the spread and impact of winner-take-all markets. *See* ROBERT H. FRANK & PHILIP J. COOK, THE WINNER-TAKE-ALL SOCIETY 211–31 (1995).

4. **Women and emotional labor.** Arlie Russell Hochschild, in *The Managed Heart: Commercialization of Human Feeling* (20th anniversary edition 2003), argues that women in the workplace often face demands not placed on men, that they display certain kinds of emotions, usually cheeriness and nurturance. ARLIE RUSSELL HOCHSCHILD, THE MANAGED HEART: COMMERCIALIZATION OF HUMAN FEELING (20th anniv. ed. 2003). Thus, women may be asked to smile, will be expected to be peacemakers in workplace disputes, and are expected to defer to the emotional needs and desires of men. Hochschild argues that the requirement of emotional labor also tends to fall upon occupations that have been heavily feminized, such as secretaries and nurses, without regard to the sex of the people in those occupations. *See also* ARLIE RUSSELL HOCHSCHILD, COMMERCIALIZATION OF INTIMATE LIFE: NOTES FROM HOME AND WORK (2003). Does Carbado and Gulati's analysis suggest a similar burden of emotional labor on racial minorities in the workplace?

5. **Impression management.** Carbado and Gulati's analysis is indebted to the work of sociologist Erving Goffman, who coined the phrase "impression management" to describe how individuals attempt to control how they are seen by others, while those others in turn attempt to discern the "real" self behind the front. *See, e.g.*, Erving Goffman, *The Arts of Impression Management, in* THE PRESENTATION OF DELF IN EVERYDAY LIFE 208–37 (1959).

Goffman emphasizes that everyone in social life is constantly engaged in impression management, both in private and in public settings, and uses the metaphor of the dramatic performance throughout his analysis:

> In this report, the individual was divided by implication into two basic parts: he was viewed as a *performer*, a harried fabricator of impressions involved in the all-too-human task of staging a performance; he was viewed as a *character*, a figure, typically a fine one, whose spirit, strength, and other sterling qualities the performance was designed to evoke. The attributes of a performer and the attributes of a character are of a different order, quite basically so, yet both sets have their meaning in terms of the show that must go on. * * *
>
> A correctly staged and performed scene leads the audience to impute a self to a performed character, but this imputation—this self—is a *product* of a scene that comes off, and is not a *cause* of it. The self, then, as a performed character, is not an organic thing that has a specific location, whose fundamental fate is to be born, to mature, and to die; it is a dramatic effect arising diffusely from a scene that is presented, and the characteristic issue, the crucial concern, is whether it will be credited or discredited.

Id., at 252–53.

C. Class and Consumption

The Overspent American: Why We Want What We Don't Need
80–91 (1998).

■ Juliet B. Schor

While television has long been suspected as a promoter of consumer desire, there has been little hard evidence to support that view, at least for adult spending. After all, there's not an obvious connection. Many of the products advertised on television are everyday low-cost items such as aspirin, laundry detergent, and deodorant. Those TV ads are hardly a spur to excessive consumerism. Leaving aside other kinds of ads for the moment (for cars, diamonds, perfumes), there's another counter to the argument that television causes consumerism: TV is a *substitute* for spending. One of the few remaining free activities, TV is a popular alternative to costly recreational spending such as movies, concerts, and restaurants. If it causes us to spend, that effect must be powerful enough to overcome its propensity to save us money.

Apparently it is. My research shows that the more TV a person watches, the more he or she spends. The likely explanation for the link between television and spending is that what we see on TV inflates our sense of what's normal. The lifestyles depicted on television are far different from the average American's: with a few exceptions, TV characters are upper-middle-class, or even rich.

Studies by the consumer researchers Thomas O'Guinn and L.J. Schrum confirm this upward distortion. The more people watch television, the more they think American households have tennis courts, private planes, convertibles, car telephones, maids, and swimming pools. Heavy watchers also overestimate the portion of the population who are millionaires, have had cosmetic surgery, and belong to a private gym, as well as those suffering from dandruff, bladder control problems, gingivitis, athlete's foot, and hemorrhoids (the effect of all those ads for everyday products). What one watches also matters. Dramatic shows—both daytime soap operas and prime-time drama series—have a stronger impact on viewer perceptions than other kinds of programs (say news, sports, or weather).

Heavy watchers are not the only ones, however, who tend to overestimate standards of living. Almost everyone does. (And almost everyone watches TV.) In one study, ownership rates for twenty-two of twenty-seven consumer products were generally overstated. Your own financial position also matters. Television inflates standards for lower-, average-, and above-average-income students, but it does the reverse for really wealthy ones. (Among those raised in a financially rarefied atmosphere, TV is almost a reality check.) Social theories of consumption hold that the inflated sense of consumer norms promulgated by the media raises people's aspirations and leads them to buy more. In the words of one Los Angeles resident, commenting on this media tendency, "They try to portray that an upper-class lifestyle is normal and typical and that we should all have it."

Television also affects norms by giving us real information about how other people live and what they have. It allows us to be voyeurs, opening the door to the "private world" inside the homes and lives of others. * * *

Another piece of evidence for the TV-spending link is the apparent correlation between debt and excessive TV viewing. In the Merck Family Fund poll, the fraction responding that they "watch too much TV" rose steadily with indebtedness. More than half (56 percent) of all those who reported themselves "heavily" in debt also said they watched too much TV.

It is partly because of television that the top 20 percent of the income distribution, and even the top 5 percent within it, has become so important in setting and escalating consumption standards for more than just the people immediately below them. Television lets *everyone* see what these folks have and allows viewers to want it in concrete, product-specific ways. Let's not forget that television programming and movies are increasingly filled with product placements—the use of identifiable brands by characters. TV shows and movies are more and more like long-running ads. * * *

Part of what keeps the see-want-borrow-and-buy sequence going is lack of attention. Americans live with high levels of denial about their spending patterns. We spend more than we realize, hold more debt than we admit to, and ignore many of the moral conflicts surrounding our acquisitions. The importance of denial for dysfunctional consumers has been well documented. We've all heard the stories about people who drive around in cars full of unpaid credit card bills, who sneak into the guest room at 2:00 A.M. to make a QVC purchase, or who quietly slip off at lunchtime for a quick trip to the mall. What is not well understood is that the spending of many normal consumers is also predicated on denial. (How many times have you heard someone say, "Oh, I'm not materialistic, I'm just into books and CDs—and travel"?) * * *

Nowhere is denial so evident as with credit cards. Contrary to economists' usual portrayal of credit card debtors as fully rational consumers who use the cards to smooth out temporary shortfalls in income, the finding of the University of Maryland economist Larry Ausubel was that people greatly underestimate the amount of debt they hold on their cards—1992's actual $182 billion in debt was thought to be a mere $70 billion. Furthermore, most people do not expect to use their cards to borrow, but, of course, they do. Eighty percent end up paying finance charges within any given year, with just under half (47 percent) always holding unpaid balances.

Not paying attention to what we spend is also very common. How many of us really keep track of where the cash from the ATM goes? Most Americans don't budget. And they don't watch. Many "fritter," as this downshifter recalled: "All I know is at the end of the month I never had anything left. And so I have to say I spent it all. I don't know what I frittered away. I really don't know what I spent the money on." * * *

Finally, denial also helps us navigate the moral conflicts associated with consumption. Most of our cherished religious and ethical teachings condemn excessive spending, but we don't really know what that means. We have a sense that money is dirty and a nagging feeling that there must be something better to do with our hard-earned dollars than give them to Bloomingdale's. As our salaries and creature comforts expand, many of us keep alive our youthful fantasies of doing humanitarian work, continuing the inner dialogue between God and Mammon. Not looking *too* hard helps keep that inner conflict tolerable. Squarely facing the fact that you spent $6,000 on your wardrobe last year and gave less than one-third of that sum to charity is a lot harder than living with a vague sense that you need to start spending less on clothes and giving away more money. * * *

In many places, private school is becoming a part of the upper-middle- (and even middle-) class standard of living—a requisite element in the basic package. Parents worry that without it their children will fall behind. Fears about education become magnified because they tap into larger, more deep-seated anxieties. Class position seems to be at stake. And, of course, as the middle and upper-middle classes abandon the public schools, the class divisions widen. Public school becomes tainted with a lower-class image. As another mother in the Los Angeles study explained, the public schools work well for her "housekeeper's child," who will have language problems, but not for her children. "Our concern with the public schools is really the safety issue. I have blond-haired, blue-eyed children who are not very physical and not very aggressive, and I worry about interactions on playgrounds."

At the same time, these parents have to deal with the complications of schooling alongside the super-wealthy. The same woman who is afraid of the public school playgrounds also worries about her children being at the bottom of the economic ladder in their private school. "The wealth of these kids is just mind-boggling. You put them in an environment in which we cannot compete, nor do we *want* them to compete and have those kinds of values. I don't want them to come home and say, 'Why don't we live in a ten-bedroom house?'" * * *

We have no problem acknowledging the "conspicuous consumption" of the early twentieth century that [Thorstein] Veblen wrote about. Middle class Americans shake their heads at what inner-city youths do to obtain expensive sneakers or gold chains. We can even get passionate about the dangers of status symbols in the Third World. Many Americans boycotted Nestle for promoting infant formula, the often deadly status alternative to breast milk. (Nestle and other companies had women in "modern" white uniforms doling out free supplies of formula in hospitals, leading to sickness, malnutrition, and even death among "bottle babies.") Many Americans deplore the entry of soft drinks and fast-food outlets into poor countries because they contribute to comerciogenic malnutrition: the poor spend their few pesos on soft drinks or French fries, forgoing nutritious food and becoming sick in the process. On the lighter side, we can chuckle at Peruvian Indians carrying rocks painted like transistor radios, Chinese who keep the brand tags on their designer sunglasses, Brazilian shantytown dwellers with television antennae but no TV's, or the Papua New Guineans who substitute Pentel pens for boars' nose pieces. Third World status consumption seems straightforward, unambiguous in motive.

We have more trouble seeing the counterparts of these behaviors in the American middle class, and in ourselves.

No Scrubs

TLC, on FANMAIL, LA FACE (1999).

■ KEVIN BRIGGS, KANDI BURRUSS, TAMEKA COTTLE

A scrub is a guy that thinks he's fly
And is also known as a buster
Always talkin' about what he wants
And just sits on his broke ass
So (no)

I don't want your number (no)
I don't want to give you mine and (no)
I don't want to meet you nowhere (no)
I don't want none of your time and (no)

Chorus:
I don't want no scrub
A scrub is a guy that can't get no love from me
Hanging out the passenger side
Of his best friend's ride
Trying to holler at me
I don't want no scrub
A scrub is a guy that can't get no love from me
Hanging out the passenger side
Of his best friend's ride
Trying to holler at me

But a scrub is checkin' me
But his game is kinda weak
And I know that he cannot approach me
Cuz I'm lookin' like class and he's lookin' like trash
Can't get wit' no deadbeat ass
So (no)

I don't want your number (no)
I don't want to give you mine and (no)
I don't want to meet you nowhere (no)
I don't want none of your time (no)

Chorus
If you don't have a car and you're walking
Oh yes son I'm talking to you
If you live at home wit' your momma
Oh yes son I'm talking to you (baby)
If you have a shorty but you don't show love
Oh yes son I'm talking to you
Wanna get with me with no money
Oh no I don't want no (oh)

No scrub
No scrub (no no)
No scrub (no no no no no)
No scrub (no no)
No

* * *

Dress As Success

BEAUTY SECRETS: WOMEN AND THE POLITICS OF APPEARANCE 79–80, 83–85, 88–93 (1986).

■ WENDY CHAPKIS

Appearance talks, making statements about gender, sexuality, ethnicity and class. In a sexually, racially and economically divided society all those visual statements add up to an evaluation of power. Economic power, or class position, is easily suggested by a man's use of the standard business suit. An expensive tailored three-piece suit says authority and privilege quietly but unmistakeably. For a woman to get that kind of attention, she must speak up more loudly. Even dressed in designer everything and costly jewelry her appearance makes a less unambiguous statement than a man's $1,000 suit.

Traditionally, a woman dressed in money has been assumed to be making a statement not about herself, but about a man. Her expensive clothing was thought to signal to the world that her husband or other male provider was so wealthy he could afford a clearly useless luxury in the form of this female. In this Veblenesque* interpretation, the woman herself is relegated to the position of a passive object much like a clothes hanger in someone else's closet. While this may well explain a husband's rationale for paying the bills, conspicuous consumption has a special purpose in a wealthy woman's life, too. * * *

Not only has consuming been one of the few pursuits open to women of a certain class, but being dressed in money demonstrates to the viewing public that the woman's one all important investment—marriage—has paid off nicely. Woman to woman we know that the marriage contract is far from an agreement between peers. At least being well-dressed serves as the visual equivalent of a large pay check.

Women in the role of wife establish social position second hand. A wealthy husband provides access to power for the woman married to him. But this ascribed power has to be made visible. If he has it, you flaunt it— not merely to reflect well on him, but to protect yourself. Dressed in money, a woman looks like someone not to be trifled with despite her sex. She is clearly protected by someone with the ability to do the job.

Increasingly, though, women are finding a need to indicate *personal* financial authority through their dress. Many more women now are breadwinners than in the past. This change is due in part to the women's movement. However, perhaps even more important than feminism is rising male unemployment and inflation making a woman's paycheck indispensable. Higher divorce rates, too, have helped make female financial independence a necessity.

How a woman should indicate professional power through her appearance is still a subject of debate. But all those voices presuming to advise women on how to put together such an image seem to agree on two fundamental things. First, *looking* "successful" is more than half the battle in actually achieving professional success. And second, success is a formula not to be tinkered with—that is, women may now aspire to professional success but should not attempt to redefine it.

Both these precepts have a particular resonance for women. Haven't we always known that how we look is far more important than what we do or how we do it? And as interlopers in the man-made world of business, we

---

* Thorstein Veblen, author of *The Theory of the Leisure Class,* published in 1899.

tend toward gratitude if someone even takes the time to explain the rules of the game—we may feel in no position to try to change them. Success in these terms is intensely individual and conformity a useful strategy.

* * *

The carefully composed look of success is not without its fashion competition. New Wave culture and punk style are among the most radical forms of visual dissent. At a very minimum, punk is a statement about consumerism. At least initially, the fashion was put together from handmade or second hand clothing. Jewelry was to be found or created from inexpensive materials like rubber, plastic and cheap metals.

Punk has also been an explicit message on the state of the economy. If there is a possibility of a job interview in the near future, one probably won't choose a fluorescent green hair dye or a Mohawk haircut. But when unemployment becomes a predictable long-term condition, little is put at risk by looking outrageous. Radically transforming one's personal appearance can be an exercise of personal power in a life that feels out of control. While it may not be possible for an individual to change the reality of high unemployment, housing shortages and poverty, it is possible to transform one's body into a visual shout: "No, I do not accept the goodness of your goals and expectations. No, I will not help you feel secure in your choices. Do I look frightening? Do I look angry? Do I look dangerous? Do you still feel safe in thinking that the system works just fine? Think again."

Not surprisingly, it is not the Punk but the young urban professionals—the so-called Yuppies—who have become the darlings of contemporary media. Their aerobic bodies and expensive dress speak confidently of physical and economic health. The image is above all reassuring. The system works just fine if you play by the rules. We accept the goals and the methods and we will be among the winners.

Success as it is known in the contemporary corporate world is dependent on a division between winners and losers, with a built-in guarantee that more will fail than will be rewarded. Women have always been the structural losers in the system. To be a woman was to be slotted for the position of support staff, both professionally and personally. The reality remains that even today most women will not become senior executives. In fact, most women will not even marry senior executives. The majority of working women will remain on a parallel job ladder which ends in the position of executive secretary or senior administrative assistant.

As anyone with experience in the business world knows, these are the women who run the show, without whom many organizations would come to a standstill. Yet they will never have the money or the authority to accompany the responsibility.

As long as success remains an individual characteristic, only one name will go on the by-line, while research assistants will have to be satisfied with a thank you in the acknowledgements. Secretaries will continue to receive lunch invitations or roses once a year instead of colleague-to-colleague respect and recognition of their partnership in the business endeavor. And women who do make it to a position of recognized power will have to quickly switch class and gender allegiance. Too close an identification with the secretarial crowd, too much empathy with those who come up on the short end of the unequal division of rewards will only be detrimental to one's own climb toward success.

It is arguably an improvement if women as a group are no longer automatically relegated to subordinate positions. But only those who find Jeane Kirkpatrick and Margaret Thatcher shining examples of feminism will believe that this sort of individual success is the same thing as women's liberation.

* * *

In the early days of the contemporary women's movement, women created strategies of empowerment that focused on shared experience and collective labor. However, we also longed for the individual perques of authority and prestige. But we were operating in an economic structure that insured that while our efforts might allow some of us to "make it," all of us would not. Western industrial society is based on competition and scarcity; equality not of condition but of opportunity. Taking on male bastions of power like the corporate world and opening them up to women meant collectively breaking down the barriers to women's participation. We worked for and achieved legislation that guaranteed us access. But once we succeeded in opening the door, we stepped through and realized that the stairway to the top was narrow and already crowded.

Still, now that the opportunity was there, failure became evidence of personal inadequacy not a political problem. Nor was class (known in America as one's "background") a political concern—provided one knew how to hide it. An entire literature developed teaching the common woman how to reach uncommon heights by "applying" herself and dressing for the part. * * *

Once inside and part way up the corporate ladder, the need to disguise your origins becomes imperative. In order to become executive materials, you must look as if you come from executive stock—the upper middle class. Enter John T. Molloy and *Dress for Success*:

> We can increase [a woman's] chances of success in the business world; we can increase her chances of being a top executive; we can make her more attractive to various types of men.

Molloy believes at least as firmly as [Helen Gurley Brown, founder of *Cosmopolitan* magazine] that a woman's business success lies in her own hands. Failure, too, is a personal not a structural problem: "If you have to tell your boss not to send you for coffee, you must have already told him non-verbally that you were ready to go." He quotes "Two extremely successful women" to back him up on this; these women expressed the belief that "The reason most young women wouldn't succeed was because they didn't look like they wanted to succeed."

Dressed in the proper outfit and sporting the proper attitude, the political problem of sexism can be sidestepped. The trick is learning to *accept* reality, not trying to change it. "It is a stark reality that men dominate the power structure.... I am not suggesting that women dress to impress men simply because they are men [but rather because men have power] ... It is not sexism; it is realism."

In the chapter entitled "Does Your Background Hurt You," Molloy dismisses class as a political problem as neatly as he does sex. Women who intend to move into "The power ranks of American society" first must "learn the manners and mores of the inner circle. And the inner circle is most emphatically upper middle class." Not to worry; his advice is exceedingly specific:

> My research showed that a woman wearing a black raincoat is definitely not automatically categorized as lower middle class. Raincoats are important for women, but not as important as they are for men.... The country-tweed look is very upper middle class and highly recommended.... The blazer, by its very nature, is upper middle class; every woman should have at least one.... Office sweaters ... say lower middle class and loser. Don't wear lower middle class colors such as purple and gold.

Predictably, the colors that test best are "gray, medium range blue, beige, deep maroon, deep rust." And the colors to avoid are "most pastels, particularly pink and pale yellow, most shades of green, mustard, bright anything, any shade that would be considered exotic." What we end up with as acceptable colors in the business world are those commonly associated with men and with the white upper class. This look is then defined as "serious." Serious becomes a question of conformity not creative difference, of masculinity not femininity and of the bland over the exotic, i.e. the foreign or racially "deviant."

Racial difference is indeed problematic to success and must be minimized. The process begins with learning to lose any ethnic accent and avoiding exotic fashions. But people of color serious about success are also advised to do whatever possible to transform even their bodies. In African women's magazines, advertisements promote the skin lightner Clere:

> Clere for your own special beauty. We are a successful people and have to look successful. We use Clere for a lighter, smoother skin. Now, Clere will work its magic for you, and make you more beautiful and successful.

Of course, it is not only among dress for success advisors that one finds these prejudices. They just help make them respectable. Even among articulate critics of sexism and racism in contemporary society there is evidence that these standards have been internalized. * * *

The shift from full-time homemaking to double duty (working both for wages and in the home) has helped create a need for new symbols of identity. Women are discovering that they are expected to have not one, but several conflicting images: the wholesome mother, the coolly professional businesswoman and the sexy mistress. No wonder women turn to the magic of wardrobe and makeup to provide inspiration for their multiple selves:

"Springfever by Elizabeth Arden ... New make-up. New inspiration." "I can bring home the bacon, fry it up in a pan and never let you forget you're a man ... En Jolie" "Colors that inspire ... Let L'erin do the talking." You almost can hear the poor woman sigh "gladly."

The cosmetics industry has been carefully studying how best to make use of this bewildering set of demands made upon working women. Women's wages have been a mixed blessing for the beauty trade. In 1983, *Advertising Age*, an industry trade journal, noted with some alarm an increase in the number of women working outside the home:

> Today, 49% of America's mothers with children under six years old are employed as opposed to only 18% in 1960 ... Where women in this group once spent middays at the department store, they are now in the office.... Women who formerly had the time to sample and listen and spend money are no longer shoppers. Even when they do visit the store, they do so as buyers.

The subtle distinction between "shopping" and "buying," *Advertising Age* points out, is that the former implies leisure. This distinction seems to be borne out by figures on grocery store cosmetic sales (cheap and fast). In the U.S., they increased by 35 percent from 1980 to 1982.

Without the leisure to linger and shop, a woman may buy what is handy and in the process discover that what she is buying for convenience is not substantially different than the more expensive brand she used to carefully seek out. *Advertising Age* warns: "This is a dangerous conclusion for the industry."

And indeed after decades of constant growth, the beauty trade is now faced with a leveling off of sales and, in some cases, even a slight decline. Not all product lines have felt the squeeze, though. "Customers seem to be turning away from medium price products," the vice-president for marketing of one of America's largest cosmetic companies notes. "They are buying better goods or switching to generic, low-price products." * * *

Often the expensive and cheap products are not only produced by different divisions of the same conglomerate, but they are made of nearly identical ingredients. Even when we know this to be true, we often will buy the more expensive item because the fantasy it offers is more attractive. Psychologist Erika Freeman explains,

> An item that promises a fantasy by definition must be priced fantastically.... If a cream begins to sell at 50 cents it will not sell as well nor will it be considered as miraculous as a cream that sells for $30.
>
> * * *

Why do women buy costly beauty products that demonstrably have little purpose other than participation in a fantasy? The purchase of a new cosmetic, the decision to change the color or style of one's hair, the start of a new diet are the female equivalent of buying a lottery ticket. Maybe *you* will be the one whose life is transformed. Despite daily experience to the contrary, we continue to hope that maybe this time, maybe this product, will make a difference in our lives. And if it doesn't, it is still a relatively inexpensive way to visit the mysterious orient of Shiseido, the elite circle of Chanel, the smouldering, sensuous world of Dior. Everything that is so difficult to attain in real life is promised for the price of a new perfume or eye shadow.

NOTES AND QUESTIONS

1. **Thorstein Veblen and social meaning of consumption.** Thorstein Veblen [1857–1929] was an American economist whose work focused on the embeddedness of economic activity in a larger social world in which the desire for prestige in the eyes of others is as central as the desire for purely material gain. Two of the concepts he elaborated—"conspicuous consumption" and "pecuniary emulation"—illustrate this focus. Veblen argued that wealthy people desire to signal to others that they are wealthy, and that buying and displaying luxury goods is an important means by which this is done. Thus, "Conspicuous consumption is how the wealthy demonstrate their wealth, and thus their success in war or in business. By purchasing the finest houses, autos, suits, and shoes—all visible and public signs of financial success—they gain the respect and admiration of their peers and subordinates." Janet Knoedler, *Thorstein Veblen and the Predatory Nature of Contemporary Capitalism, in* INTRODUCTION TO POLITICAL ECONOMY 66 (Charles Sackrey & Geoffrey Schneider eds., 3d ed. 2002).

Veblen also argued that people in all economic classes make consumption decisions based not only on their rational desire for goods and services to make their life better, but out of envy of those who are more successful. This desire to be like and to be seen as like those with more money and social success he named "pecuniary emulation":

> [T]he standard of expenditure which commonly guides our efforts is not the average, ordinary expenditure already achieved; it is an ideal of consumption that lies just beyond our reach ... The motive is emulation—the stimulus of an invidious comparison which prompts us to outdo those with whom we are in the habit of classing ourselves ... [e]ach class envies and emulates the class next above it in the social scale, while it rarely compares itself with those below or with those who are considerably in advance.

THORSTEIN VEBLEN, THE THEORY OF THE LEISURE CLASS 81 (HOUGHTON MIFFLIN Co. 1973) (1899).

2. **Crisis of over-production and creation of desire.** Economic historians argue that after 1890, as modern forms of industrial production began to take shape and more and more mass-produced goods began to flood American markets, American business interests began a campaign to change consumption patterns away from patterns of thrift, self-denial, and self-reliance. As William Leach argues:

From the 1890s on, American corporate business, in league with key institutions, began the transformation of American society into a society preoccupied with consumption, with comfort and bodily well-being, with luxury, spending, and acquisition, with more goods this year than last, more next year than this. American consumer capitalism produced a culture almost violently hostile to the past and to tradition, a future-oriented culture of desire that confused the good life with goods. It was a culture that first appeared as an alternative culture—or as one moving largely against the grain of earlier traditions of republicanism and Christian virtue—and then unfolded to become the reigning culture of the United States. It was the culture that many people the world over soon came to see as *the* heart of American life.

WILLIAM LEACH, LAND OF DESIRE: MERCHANTS, POWER, AND THE RISE OF A NEW AMERICAN CULTURE, xiii (1993); *see also* STUART EWEN, CAPTAINS OF CONSCIOUSNESS: ADVERTISING AND THE SOCIAL ROOTS OF THE CONSUMER CULTURE (2001).

Consumer culture is partly a response to what Veblen identified as an incipient crisis within capitalist societies: the threat of overproduction, too many goods chasing too few buyers. As William Greider puts it:

As economist Thorstein Veblen taught several generations ago, the problem of capitalist enterprise is always the problem of supply: managing the production of goods in order to maximize profit and the return on invested capital. * * *

The great virtue of capitalism—the quality that always confounded socialist critics and defeated rival economic systems—is its ability to yield more from less. Its efficient organization of production strives to produce more goods from less input, whether the input is capital, labor or raw resources. Assuming markets are stable, the rising productivity increases the profit per unit, the yields that get distributed as returns to invested capital or as rising wages for labor or in lower product prices for consumers and, in the happiest circumstances, all three.

But this expanding potential to produce more goods also poses the enduring contradiction for capitalist enterprise: how to dispose of the surplus production. You can make more things, but can you sell them? An undisciplined expansion of productive capacity will be self-defeating, even dangerous for a firm, if all it accomplishes are continuing supply surpluses that degrade prices and undermine the rate of return. The problem of surplus capacity drives not only the competition among firms for market shares but also the imperative to discover new markets.

WILLIAM GREIDER, ONE WORLD, READY OR NOT: THE MANIC LOGIC OF GLOBAL CAPITALISM 44–45 (1997).

3. Branding and consumption. As the culture of consumption has matured, advertising strategies have changed as well. In the early 1990s, American corporations began to shift even more profoundly away from advertising what Karl Marx would have called the use-value of their products, to focus instead on using advertising to create an affective link between their products and the consumer's dreams and fantasies. This new technique relied on "branding," and the advertising of the brand rather than the product. As Naomi Klein observes:

> Overnight, "Brands, not products!" became the rallying cry for a marketing renaissance led by a new breed of companies that saw themselves as "meaning brokers" instead of product producers. What was changing was the idea of what—in both advertising and branding—was being sold. The old paradigm had it that all marketing was selling a product. In the new model, however, the product always takes a back seat to the real product, the brand, and the selling of the brand acquired an extra component that can only be described as spiritual.
> * * *
> On Marlboro Friday [a day in 1993 when Marlboro announced plans to dramatically reduce its prices in an attempt to compete with bargain cigarette brands], a line was drawn in the sand between the lowly price slashers and the high-concept brand builders. The brand builders conquered and a new consensus was born: the products that will flourish in the future will be the ones presented not as "commodities" but as concepts: the brand as experience, as lifestyle.

NAOMI KLEIN, NO LOGO: TAKING AIM AT THE BRAND BULLIES 21 (1999).

Does the ever-more-ephemeral link between products and the consumer's actual need for them threaten the pursuit of happiness?

Advertising At the Edge of the Apocalypse

Available at http://www.sutjhally.com/onlinepubs/onlinepubs_frame.html (n.d.)

■ SUT JHALLY

In this article I wish to make a simple claim: 20th century advertising is the most powerful and sustained system of propaganda in human history and its cumulative cultural effects, unless quickly checked, will be responsible for destroying the world as we know it. As it achieves this it will be responsible for the deaths of hundreds of thousands of non-western peoples and will prevent the peoples of the world from achieving true happiness. Simply stated, our survival as a species is dependent upon minimizing the threat from advertising and the commercial culture that has spawned it. I am stating my claims boldly at the outset so there can be no doubt as to what is at stake in our debates about the media and culture as we enter the new millennium.

COLONIZING CULTURE

Karl Marx, the pre-eminent analyst of 19th century industrial capitalism, wrote in 1867, in the very opening lines of *Capital* that: "The wealth of societies in which the capitalist mode of production prevails appears as an 'immense collection of commodities' ". * * * In seeking to initially distinguish his object of analysis from preceding societies, Marx referred to the way the society showed itself on a surface level and highlighted a *quantitative* dimension—the number of objects that humans interacted with in everyday life.

Indeed, no other society in history has been able to match the immense productive output of industrial capitalism. This feature colors the way in which the society presents itself—the way it *appears*. Objects are everywhere in capitalism. In this sense, capitalism is truly a revolutionary society, dramatically altering the very landscape of social life, in a way no other form of social organization had been able to achieve in such a short period of time. (In *The Communist Manifesto* Marx and Engels would coin the famous phrase "all that is solid melts into air" to highlight capitalism's unique dynamism.) It is this that strikes Marx as distinctive as he observes 19th century London. The starting point of his own critique therefore is not what he believes is the dominating agent of the society, *capital*, nor is it what he believes creates the value and wealth, *labor*—instead it is the *commodity*. From this surface appearance Marx then proceeds to peel away the outer skin of the society and to penetrate to the underlying essential structure that lies in the "hidden abode" of production.

It is not enough of course to only produce the "immense collection of commodities"—they must also be sold, so that further investment in production is feasible. Once produced commodities must go through the circuit of distribution, exchange and consumption, so that profit can be returned to the owners of capital and value can be "realized" again in a money form. If the circuit is not completed the system would collapse into stagnation and depression. Capitalism therefore has to ensure the sale of commodities on *pain of death*. In that sense the problem of capitalism is not mass production (which has been solved) but is instead the *problem of consumption*. That is why from the early years of this century it is more accurate to use the label "the consumer culture" to describe the western industrial market societies.

So central is consumption to its survival and growth that at the end of the 19th century industrial capitalism invented a unique new institution—the advertising industry—to ensure that the "immense accumulation of commodities" are converted back into a money form. The function of this new industry would be to recruit the best creative talent of the society and to create a culture in which desire and identity would be fused with commodities—to make the dead world of things come alive with human and social possibilities (what Marx would prophetically call the "fetishism of commodities"). And indeed there has never been a propaganda effort to match the effort of advertising in the 20th century. More thought, effort, creativity, time, and attention to detail has gone into the selling of the immense collection of commodities that any other campaign in human history to change public consciousness. One indication of this is [simple] the amount of money that has been exponentially expended on this effort. Today, in the United States alone, over $175 billion a year is spent to sell us things. This concentration of effort is unprecedented.

It should not be surprising that something this central and with so much being expended on it should become an important presence in social life. Indeed, commercial interests intent on maximizing the consumption of the immense collection of commodities have colonized more and more of the spaces of our culture. For instance, almost the entire media system (television and print) has been developed as a delivery system for marketers—its prime function is to produce audiences for sale to advertisers. Both the advertisements it carries, as well as the editorial matter that acts as a support for it, celebrate the consumer society. The movie system, at one time outside the direct influence of the broader marketing system, is now fully integrated into it through the strategies of licensing, tie-ins and product placements. The prime function of many Hollywood films today is to aid in the selling of the immense collection of commodities. As public funds are drained from the non-commercial cultural sector, art galleries, museums and symphonies bid for corporate sponsorship. Even those institutions thought to be outside of the market are being sucked in. High schools now sell the sides of their buses, the spaces of their hallways and the classroom time of their students to hawkers of candy bars, soft drinks and jeans. In New York City, sponsors are being sought for public playgrounds. In the contemporary world everything is sponsored by someone. The latest plans of Space Marketing Inc. call for rockets to deliver mile-wide Mylar billboards to compete with the sun and the moon for the attention of the earth's population.

With advertising messages on everything from fruit on supermarket shelves, to urinals, and to literally the space beneath our feet (Bamboo lingerie conducted a spray-paint pavement campaign in Manhattan telling consumers that "from here it looks likes you could use some new underwear"), it should not be surprising that many commentators now identify the realm of culture as simply an *adjunct* to the system of production and consumption.

Indeed so overwhelming has the commercial colonization of our culture become that it has created its own problems for marketers who now worry about how to ensure that their *individual* message stands out from the "clutter" and the "noise" of this busy environment. In that sense the main competition for marketers is not simply other brands in their product type, but all the other advertisers who are competing for the attention of an increasingly cynical audience which is doing all it can to avoid ads. In a strange paradox, as advertising takes over more and more space in the culture the job of the individual advertisers becomes much more difficult. Therefore even greater care and resources are poured into the creation of commercial messages—much greater care than the surrounding editorial matter designed to capture the attention of the audience. Indeed if we wanted to compare national television commercials to something equivalent, it [would be] the biggest budget movie blockbusters. Second by second, it costs more to produce the average network ad than a movie like *Jurassic Park*.

The twin results of these developments are that advertising is everywhere and huge amounts of money and creativity are expended upon them.

If Marx were writing today I believe that not only would he be struck by the presence of even more objects, but also by the ever-present "discourse through and about objects" that permeates the spaces of our public and private domains. * * * This commercial discourse is the *ground* on which we live, the space in which we learn to think, the *lens* through which we come to understand the world that surrounds us. In seeking to understand where we are headed as a society, an adequate analysis of this commercial environment is essential.

Seeking this understanding will involve clarifying what we mean by the power and effectiveness of ads, and of being able to pose the right question. For too long debate has been concentrated around the issue of whether ad campaigns create demand for a particular product. If you are Pepsi Cola, or Ford, or Anheuser Busch, then it may be the right question for your interests. But, if you are interested in the social power of advertising—the impact of advertising on society—then that is the wrong question.

The right question would ask about the *cultural* role of advertising, not its marketing role. Culture is the place and space where a society tells stories about itself, where values are articulated and expressed, where notions of good and evil, of morality and immorality, are defined. In our culture it is the stories of advertising that dominate the spaces that mediate this function. If human beings are essentially a storytelling species, then to study advertising is to examine the central storytelling mechanism of our society. The correct question to ask from this perspective, is not whether particular ads sell the products they are hawking, but what are the consistent stories that advertising spins as a whole about what is important in the world, about how to behave, about what is good and bad. Indeed, it is to ask what values does advertising consistently push.

Happiness

Every society has to tell a story about happiness, about how individuals can satisfy themselves and feel both subjectively and objectively good. The cultural system of advertising gives a very specific answer to that question for our society. *The way to happiness and satisfaction is through the consumption of objects through the marketplace.* Commodities will make us happy. * * * In one very [important sense] that is the consistent and explicit message of every single message within the system of market communication.

Neither the fact of advertising's colonization of the horizons of imagination or the pushing of a story about the centrality of goods to human satisfaction should surprise us. The immense collection of goods have to be consumed (and even more goods produced) and the story that is used to ensure this function is to equate goods with happiness. Insiders to the system have recognized this obvious fact for many years. Retail analyst Victor Liebow said, just after the second world war:

Our enormously productive economy ... demands that we make consumption our way of life, that we convert the buying and the selling of goods into rituals, that we seek our spiritual satisfaction, our ego satisfaction in commodities ... We need things consumed, burned up, worn out, replaced, and discarded at an ever increasing rate. * * *

So economic growth is justified not simply on the basis that it will provide employment (after all a host of alternative non-productive activities could also provide that) but because it will give us access to more things that will make us happy. This rationale for the existing system of ever-increasing production is told by advertising in the most compelling form possible. In fact it is this story, that human satisfaction is intimately connected to the provisions of the market, to economic growth, that is the major motivating force for social change as we start the 21st century.

The social upheavals of eastern Europe were pushed by this vision. As Gloria Steinhem described the East German transformation: "First we have a revolution then we go shopping." * * * The attractions of this vision in the Third World are not difficult to discern. When your reality is empty stomachs and empty shelves, no wonder the marketplace appears as the panacea for your problems. When your reality is hunger and despair it should not be surprising that the seductive images of desire and abundance emanating from the advertising system should be so influential in thinking about social and economic policy. Indeed not only happiness but political freedom itself is made possible by access to the immense collection of commodities. These are very powerful stories that equate happiness and freedom with consumption—and advertising is the main propaganda arm of this view.

The question that we need to pose at this stage (that is almost never asked) is, "Is it true?" Does happiness come from material things? Do we get happier as a society as we get richer, as our standard of living increases, as we have more access to the immense collection of objects? Obviously these are complex issues, but the general answer to these questions is "no."

* * *

In a series of surveys conducted in the United States starting in 1945 (labeled "the happiness surveys") researchers sought to examine the link between material wealth and subjective happiness, and concluded that, when examined both cross-culturally as well as historically in one society, there is a very *weak* correlation. Why should this be so?

When we examine this process more closely the conclusions appear to be less surprising than our intuitive perspective might suggest. In another series of surveys (the "quality of life surveys") people were asked about the kinds of things that are important to them—about what would constitute a good quality of life. The findings of this line of research indicate that if the elements of satisfaction were [divided up] into social values (love, family, friends) and material values (economic security and success) the former outranks the latter in terms of importance. What people say they really want out of life is: autonomy and control of life; good self-esteem; warm family relationships; tension-free leisure time; close and intimate friends; as well as romance and love. This is not to say that material values are not important. They form a necessary component of a good quality of life. But above a certain level of poverty and comfort, material things stop giving us the kind of satisfaction that the magical world of advertising insists they can deliver.

These conclusion[s] point to one of the great ironies of the market system. The market is good at providing those things that can be bought and sold and it pushed us—via advertising—in that direction. But the real sources of happiness—social relationships—are outside the capability of the marketplace to provide. The marketplace cannot provide love, it cannot provide real friendships, it cannot provide sociability. It can provide other material things and services—but they are not what makes us happy.

The advertising industry has known this since at least the 1920s and in fact have stopped trying to sell us things based on their material qualities alone. If we examine the advertising of the end of the 19th and first years of the 20th century, we would see that advertising talked a lot about the properties of commodities—what they did, how well they did it, etc. But starting in the 1920s advertising shifts to talking about the relationship of objects to the social life of people. It starts to connect commodities (the things they have to sell) with the powerful images of a deeply desired social life that people say they want.

No wonder then that advertising is so attractive to us, so powerful, so seductive. What it offers us are images of the real sources of human happiness—family life, romance and love, sexuality and pleasure, friendship and sociability, leisure and relaxation, independence and control of life. That is why advertising is so powerful, that is what is real about it. The cruel illusion of advertising however is in the way that it links those qualities to a place that by definition cannot provide it—the market and the immense collection of commodities. The falsity of advertising is not in the appeals it makes (which are very real) but in the answers it provides. We want love and friendship and sexuality—and advertising points the way to it through objects.

To reject or criticize advertising as false and manipulative misses the point. Ad executive Jerry Goodis puts it this way: "Advertising doesn't mirror how people are acting but how they are dreaming." * * * It taps into our real emotions and repackages them back to us connected to the world of things. What advertising really reflects in that sense is the dreamlife of the culture. Even saying this however simplifies a deeper process because advertisers do more than mirror our dreamlife—they help to create it. They translate our desires (for love, for family, for friendship, for adventure, for sex) into our dreams. Advertising is like a fantasy factory, taking our desire for human social contact and reconceiving it, reconceptualizing it, connecting it with the world of commodities and then translating into a form that can be communicated.

The great irony is that as advertising does this it draws us further away from what really has the capacity to satisfy us (meaningful human contact and relationships) to what does not (material things). In that sense advertising reduces our capacity to become happy by pushing us, cajoling us, to carry on in the direction of things. If we really wanted to create a world that reflected our desires then the consumer culture would not be it. It would look very different—a society that stressed and built the institutions that would foster social relationships, rather than endless material accumulation.

Advertising's role in channeling us in these fruitless directions is profound. In one sense, its function is [analogous] to the drug pusher on the street corner. As we try and break our addiction to things it is there, constantly offering us another "hit." By persistently pushing the idea of the good life being connected to products, and by colonizing every nook and cranny of the culture where alternative ideas could be raised, advertising is an important part of the creation of what Tibor Scitovsky * * * calls "the joyless economy." The great political challenge that emerges from this analysis is how to connect our real desires to a truly human world, rather than the dead world of the "immense collection of commodities."

"There is no such thing as 'society'"

A culture dominated by commercial messages that tells individuals that the way to happiness is through consuming objects bought in the marketplace gives a very particular answer to the question of "what is society?"—what is it that binds us together in some kind of collective way, what concerns or interests do we share? In fact, Margaret Thatcher, the former conservative British Prime Minister, gave the most succinct answer to this question from the viewpoint of the market. In perhaps her most (in)famous quote she announced: "There is no such thing as 'society'. There are just individuals and their families." According to Mrs. Thatcher, there is nothing solid we can call society—no group values, no collective interests—society is just a bunch of individuals acting on their own.

Indeed this is precisely how advertising talks to us. It addresses us not as members of society talking about collective issues, but as *individuals*. It talks about our individual needs and desires. It does not talk about those things we have to negotiate collectively, such as poverty, healthcare, housing and the homeless, the environment, etc.

The market appeals to the worst in us (greed, selfishness) and discourages what is the best about us (compassion, caring, and generosity).

Again this should not surprise us. In those societies where the marketplace dominates then what will be stressed is what the marketplace can deliver—and advertising is the main voice of the marketplace—so discussions of collective issues are pushed to the margins of the culture. They are not there in the center of the main system of communication that exists in the society. It is no accident that politically the market vision associated with neo-conservatives has come to dominate at exactly that time when advertising has been pushing the same values into every available space in the culture. The widespread disillusionment with "government" (and hence with thinking about issues in a collective manner) has found extremely fertile ground in the fields of commercial culture.

Unfortunately, we are now in a situation, both globally and domestically, where solutions to pressing nuclear and environmental problems will have to take a *collective* form. The marketplace cannot deal with the problems that face us at the turn of the millennium. For example it cannot deal with the threat of nuclear extermination that is still with us in the post-Cold War age. It cannot deal with global warming, the erosion of the ozone layer, or the depletion of our non-renewable resources. The effects of the way we do "business" are no longer localized, they are now global, and we will have to have international and collective ways of dealing with them. Individual action will not be enough. As the environmentalist slogan puts it "we all live downstream now."

Domestically, how do we find a way to tackle issues such as the nightmares of our inner cities, the ravages of poverty, the neglect of healthcare for the most vulnerable section of the population? How can we find a way to talk realistically and passionately of such problems within a culture where the central message is "don't worry, be happy." As Barbara Ehrenreich says:

> Television commercials offer solutions to hundreds of problems we didn't even know we had—from 'morning mouth' to shampoo build-up—but nowhere in the consumer culture do we find anyone offering us such mundane necessities as affordable health insurance, childcare, housing, or higher education. The flip side of the consumer spectacle ... is the starved and impoverished public sector. We have Teenage Mutant Ninja Turtles, but no way to feed and educate the one-fifth of American children who are growing up in poverty. We have dozens of varieties of breakfast cereal, and no help for the hungry. * * *

In that sense, advertising systematically relegates discussion of key societal issues to the peripheries of the culture and talks in powerful ways instead of individual desire, fantasy, pleasure and comfort.

Partly this is because of advertising's *monopolization* of cultural life. There is no space left for different types of discussion, no space at the center of the society where alternative values could be expressed. But it is also connected to the failure of those who care about collective issues to create alternative visions that can compete in any way with the commercial vision. The major alternatives offered to date have been a gray and dismal stateism. This occurred not only in the western societies but also in the former so called "socialist" societies of eastern Europe. These repressive societies never found a way to connect to people in any kind of pleasurable way, relegating issues of pleasure and individual expression to the non-essential and distracting aspects of social life. This indeed was the core of the failure of Communism in Eastern Europe. As Ehrenreich reminds us, not only was it unable to deliver the material goods, but it was unable to create a fully human "ideological retort to the powerful seductive messages of the capitalist consumer culture." * * * The problems are no less severe domestically:

> Everything enticing and appealing is located in the (thoroughly private) consumer spectacle. In contrast, the public sector looms as a realm devoid of erotic promise—the home of the IRS, the DMV, and other irritating, intrusive bureaucracies. Thus, though everyone wants national health insurance, and parental leave, few are moved to wage political struggles for them. 'Necessity' is not enough; we may have to find a way to glamorize the possibility of an activist public sector, and to glamorize the possibility of public activism. * * *

The imperative task for those who want to stress a different set of values is to make the struggle for social change fun and sexy. By that I do not mean that we have to use images of sexuality, but that we have to find a way of thinking about the struggle against poverty, against homelessness, for healthcare and child-care, to protect the environment, in terms of *pleasure and fun and happiness*.

To make this glamorization of collective issues possible will require that the present commercial monopoly of the channels of communication be broken in favor of a more democratic access where difficult discussion of important and relevant issues may be possible. While the situation may appear hopeless we should remind ourselves of how important capitalism deems its monopoly of the imagination to be. The campaigns of successive United States government against the Cuban revolution, and the obsession of our national security state with the Sandinista revolution in Nicaragua in the 1980s, demonstrates the importance that capitalism places on smashing the alternative model. Even as the United States government continues to support the most vicious, barbarous, brutal and murderous regimes around the world, it takes explicit aim at those governments that have tried to redistribute wealth to the most needy—who have been prioritized collective values over the values of selfishness and greed. The monopoly of the vision is vital and capitalism knows it.

The End of the World as We Know It

The consumer vision that is pushed by advertising and which is conquering the world is based fundamentally, as I argued before, on a notion of *economic growth*. Growth requires resources (both raw materials and energy) and there is a broad consensus among environmental scholars that the earth cannot sustain past levels of expansion based upon resource-intensive modes of economic activity, especially as more and more nations struggle to join the feeding trough.

The environmental crisis is complex and multilayered, cutting across both production and consumption issues. For instance just in terms of resource depletion, we know that we are rapidly exhausting what the earth can offer and that if the present growth and consumption trends continued unchecked, the limits to growth on the planet will be reached sometime within the next century. Industrial production uses up resources and energy at a rate that had never before even been imagined. Since 1950 the world's population has used up more of the earth's resources than all the generations that came before. * * * In 50 years we have matched the use of thousands of years. The west and especially Americans have used the most of these resources so we have a special responsibility for the approaching crisis. In another hundred years we will have exhausted the planet.

But even more than that even, we will have done irreparable damage to the environment on which we depend for everything. As environmental activist Barry Commoner says:

> The environment makes up a huge, enormously complex living machine that forms a thin dynamic layer on the earth's surface, and every human activity depends on the integrity and proper functioning of this machine.... This machine is our biological capital, the basic apparatus on which our total productivity depends. If we destroy it, our most advanced technology will become useless and any economic and political system that depends on it will flounder. The environmental crisis is a signal of the approaching catastrophe. * * *

The clearest indication of the way in which we produce is having an effect on the eco-sphere of the planet is the depletion of the ozone layer, which has dramatically increased the amount of ultraviolet radiation that is damaging or lethal to many life forms on the planet. In 1985 scientists discovered the existence of a huge hole in the ozone layer over the South Pole that is the size of the United States illustrating how the activities of humans are changing the very make-up of the earth. In his book *The End of Nature* Bill McKibben reminds us that "we have done this ourselves.... by driving our cars, building our factories, cutting down our forests, turning on air conditioners." * * * He writes that the history of the world is full of the most incredible events that changed the way we lived, but they are all dwarfed by what we have accomplished in the last 50 years.

> Man's efforts, even at their mightiest, were tiny compared with the size of the planet—the Roman Empire meant nothing to the Artic or the Amazon. But now, the way of life of one part of the world in one half-century is altering every inch and every hour of the globe.

The situation is so bad that the scientific community is desperately trying to get the attention of the rest of us to wake up to the danger. The Union of Concerned Scientists (representing 1700 of the world's leading scientists, including a majority of Nobel laureates in the sciences) recently issued this appeal:

> Human beings and the natural world are on a collision course. Human activities inflict harsh and irreversible damage on the environment and on critical resources. If not checked, many of our current practices put at serious risk the future that we wish for human society and the plant and animal kingdoms, and may so alter the living world that it will be unable to sustain life in the manner we know. Fundamental changes are urgent if we are to avoid the collision our present course will bring.

It is important to avoid the prediction of immediate catastrophe. We have already done a lot of damage but the real environmental crisis will not hit until some time in the middle of the next century. However to avoid that catastrophe we have to take action *now*. We have to put in place the steps that will save us in 70 years time.

The metaphor that best describes the task before us is of an oil tanker heading for a crash on the shore. Because of its momentum and size, to avoid crashing the oil tanker has to start turning well before it reaches the coast, anticipating [its] own momentum. If it starts turning too late it will smash into the coast. That is where the consumer society is right now. We have to make fundamental changes in the way we organize ourselves, in what we stress in our economy, if [we] want to avoid the catastrophe in 70 years time. We have to take action *now*.

In that sense the present generation has a unique responsibility in human history. It is literally up to us to save the world, to make the changes we need to make. If we do not, we will be in barbarism and savagery towards each other in 70 years time. We have to make short-term sacrifices. We have to give up [our non-essential appliances]. We especially have to rethink our relationship to the car. We have to make *real* changes—not just recycling but fundamental changes in how we live and produce. And we cannot do this individually, we have to do it collectively. We have to find the political will somehow to do this—and we may even be dead when its real effects will be felt. The vital issue is "how do we identify with that generation in the next century?" As the political philosopher Robert Heilbroner says:

> A crucial problem for the world of the future will be a concern for generations to come. Where will such concern arise? ... Contemporary industrial man, his appetite for the present whetted by the values of a high-consumption society and his attitude toward the future influenced by the prevailing canons of self-concern, has but a limited motivation to form such bonds. There are many who would sacrifice much for their children; fewer would do so for their grandchildren. * * *

Forming such bonds will be made even more difficult within our current context that stresses individual (not social) needs and the immediate situation (not the long-term). The advertising system will form *the ground* on which we think about the future of the human race, and there is nothing there that should give us any hope for the development of such a perspective. The time-frame of advertising is very short-term. It does not encourage us to think beyond the immediacy of present sensual experience. Indeed it may well be the case that as the advertising environment gets more and more crowded, with more and more of what advertisers label as "noise" threatening to drown out individual messages, the appeal will be made to levels of experience that cut through clutter, appealing immediately and deeply to very emotional states. Striking emotional imagery that grabs the "gut" instantly leaves no room for thinking about anything. Sexual imagery, especially in the age of AIDS where sex is being connected to death, will need to become even more powerful and immediate, to overcome any possible negative associations—indeed to remove us from the world of connotation and meaning construed *cognitively*. The value of a collective social future is one that does not, and will not, find expression within our commercially dominated culture. Indeed the prevailing values provide no incentive to develop bonds with future generations and there is a real sense of nihilism and despair about the future, and a closing of ranks against the outside.

Imagining a Different Future

Over a 100 years ago, Marx observed that there were two directions that capitalism could take: towards a democratic "socialism" or towards a brutal "barbarism". Both long-term and recent evidence would seem to indicate that the latter is where we are headed, unless alternative values quickly come to the fore.

Many people thought that the environmental crisis would be the linchpin for the lessening of international tensions as we recognized our interdependence and our collective security and future. But as the Persian Gulf War made clear, the New World Order will be based upon a struggle for scarce resources. Before the propaganda rationale shifted to the "struggle for freedom and democracy," George Bush reminded the American people that the troops were being dispatched to the Gulf to protect the resources that make possible "our way of life." An automobile culture and commodity-based culture such as ours is reliant upon sources of cheap oil. And if the cost of that is 100,000 dead Iraquis, well so be it. In such a scenario the peoples of the Third World will be seen as enemies who are making unreasonable claims on "our" resources. The future and the Third World can wait. Our commercial dominated cultural discourse reminds us powerfully everyday, we need *ours* and we need it *now*. In that sense the Gulf War is a preview of what is to come. As the world runs out of resources, the most powerful military sources will use that might to ensure access.

The destructive aspects of capitalism (its short-term nature, its denial of collective values, its stress on the material life), are starting to be recognized by some people who have made their fortunes through the market. The billionaire turned philanthropist George Soros * * * talks about what he calls "the capitalist threat"—and culturally speaking, advertising is the main voice of that threat. To the extent that it pushes us towards material things for satisfaction and away from the construction of social relationships, it pushes us down the road to increased economic production that is driving the coming environmental catastrophe. To the extent that it talks about our individual and private needs, it pushes discussion about collective issues to the margins. To the extent that it talks about the present only, it makes thinking about the future difficult. To the extent that it does all these things, then advertising becomes one of the major obstacles to our survival as a species.

Getting out of this situation, coming up with new ways to look at the world, will require enormous work, and one response may just be to enjoy the end of the world—one last great fling, the party to end all parties. The alternative response, to change the situation, to work for humane, collective long-term values, will require an effort of the most immense kind.

And there is evidence to be hopeful about the results of such an attempt. It is important to stress that creating and maintaining the present structure of the consumer culture takes enormous work and effort. The reason consumer ways of looking at the world predominate is because there are billions of dollars being spent on it every single day. The consumer culture is not simply erected and then forgotten. It has to be held in place by the activities of the ad industry, and increasingly the activities of the public relations industry. Capitalism has to try really hard to convince us about the value of the commercial vision. In some senses consumer capitalism is a house of cards, held together in a fragile way by immense effort, and it could just as soon melt away as hold together. It will depend if there are viable alternatives that will motivate people to believe in a different future, if there are other ideas as pleasurable, as powerful, as fun, as passionate with which people can identify.

I am reminded here of the work of Antonio Gramsci who coined the famous phrase, "pessimism of the intellect, optimism of the will." "Pessimism of the intellect" means recognizing the reality of our present circumstances, analyzing the vast forces arrayed against us, but insisting on the possibilities and the moral desirability of social change—that is "the optimism of the will," believing in human values that will be the inspiration for us to struggle for our survival

I do not want to be too Pollyannaish about the possibilities of social change. It is not just collective values that need to be struggled for, but collective values that recognize individual rights and individual creativity. There are many *repressive* collective movements already in existence—from our own home-grown Christian fundamentalists to the Islamic zealots of the Taliban in Afghanistan. The task is not easy. It means balancing and integrating different views of the world. As Ehrenreich writes:

> Can we envision a society which values—not "collectivity" with its dreary implications of conformity—but what I can only think to call *conviviality*, which could, potentially, be built right into the social infrastructure with opportunities, at all levels for rewarding, democratic participation? Can we envision a society that does not dismiss individualism, but truly values individual creative expression—including dissidence, debate, nonconformity, artistic experimentation, and in the larger sense, adventure ... the project remains what it has always been: to replace the consumer culture with a genuinely *human* culture.

* * *

The stakes are simply too high for us not to deal with the real and pressing problems that face [us as a] species—finding a progressive and humane collective solution to the global crisis and ensuring for our children and future generations a world fit for truly human habitation.

Uneasy Ryder! Jury Finds Winona Guilty in Shoplift Case

N.Y. DAILY NEWS, Nov. 6, 2002.

THE ASSOCIATED PRESS

BEVERLY HILLS, Calif.—Actress Winona Ryder was convicted Wednesday of stealing $5,500 worth of high-fashion merchandise from Saks Fifth Avenue last year.

The jury found the star of "Girl, Interrupted" guilty of felony grand theft and vandalism but cleared her of burglary.

She faces anywhere from probation to three years in prison. Sentencing is scheduled for Dec. 6.

Ryder showed no emotion as the verdict was announced. She kept her eyes on the jurors as they were asked whether the verdicts were accurate. They said yes.

She whispered to her attorney, Mark Geragos, took a drink of water and looked briefly toward her supporters in the audience.

The jury reached the verdict after 5 1/2 hours of deliberations over two days. The one count on which she was acquitted required a specific intent to go into the store to steal. District attorney's spokeswoman Sandi Gibbons said jurors often believe burglary is a crime of breaking and entering, but it does not require those circumstances.

"We're gratified with the verdicts," Gibbons added.

Ryder, a two-time Oscar nominee who marked her 31st birthday in the defendant's chair, was arrested Dec. 12 as she left the Beverly Hills store, her arms filled with packages.

Ryder did not testify during the two-week trial.

Prosecutors said Ryder came to Saks with larceny on her mind, bringing shopping bags, a garment bag and scissors to snip security tags off items.

"She came, she stole, she left. End of story," Deputy District Attorney Ann Rundle said. "Nowhere does it say people steal because they have to. People steal out of greed, envy, spite, because it's there or for the thrill."

Jurors were shown videotape of Ryder moving through the store laden with goods, and Saks security workers testified that after she was detained she apologetically told them a director had told her to shoplift to prepare for a movie role.

Her attorney denounced the security guards as liars even before the trial began.

At the start of her shopping trip, she paid more than $3,000 for a jacket and two blouses. The defense said Ryder believed the store would keep her account "open" while she shopped and would charge her later. But there was no evidence of an account.

In closing arguments Monday, Geragos suggested that the store, trying to avoid a lawsuit, conspired with employees to invent a story that would make Ryder appear guilty.

Geragos ridiculed the charge that Ryder vandalized merchandise by cutting holes in clothes when removing the security tags.

"This woman is known for her fashion sense," he said. "Was she going to start a new line of 'Winona wear' with holes in it?"

He carried a hair bow, which she allegedly had stolen, over to her, placed it on her head and said: "Can anyone see Ms. Ryder with this on top of her head? Does that make sense?"

Settlement talks between the defense and prosecution failed, but just before trial the district attorney's office agreed to dismiss a drug charge after a doctor said he had given her two pills found in her possession when she was arrested.

The 12-member jury included several people with Hollywood connections, including producer Peter Guber, who presided over Sony Entertainment Pictures when three successful Ryder films were made there.

Ryder has made some two-dozen films since 1986, including "Beetlejuice," "Heathers," "Mermaids," "Little Women," "The Age of Innocence," "Edward Scissorhands," "Bram Stoker's Dracula," "Reality Bites" and "Mr. Deeds."

She received her Academy Award nominations for "Little Women" (best actress) and for "The Age of Innocence" (supporting actress).

Ryder was raised by parents who were part of the counterculture revolution in the 1960s. Her godfather was LSD guru Timothy Leary.

In 1993, Ryder posted a $200,000 reward in the kidnap-murder case of a 12-year-old girl, Polly Klaas, in Petaluma, Calif., where the actress grew up. When Ryder was charged with shoplifting, Polly's father, Mark, came to legal proceedings to support her.

In recent years, Ryder has been featured frequently in fashion magazines. Her delicate beauty and waiflike persona were on display at the trial along with a wardrobe of appropriate trial clothes—dark sweaters and skirts, soft dresses and, on the climactic day of closing arguments, a cream silk suit with a pleated skirt and short jacket.

NOTES AND QUESTIONS

1. **Consumerism and capitalism.** Can capitalism survive without ever-expanding production and ever-expanding consumer demand? William Greider argues that a global crisis is on the way:

> The economic luxury hidden in the capitalist process is space—capitalism's ability to move on and re-create itself, abandoning the old for the new, creating and destroying production, while trailing a broad flume

of ruined natural assets in its wake. Because globalization has narrowed distances, the luxury has diminished visibly. It is now possible for people to glimpse what was always true: the wasteful nature of their own prosperity. So long as the consequences could be kept afar from the beneficiaries, no one had much incentive—neither producers nor consumers—to face the collective implications.

The brilliant possibility of "one world" is the emerging recognition that there is not going to be anyplace to hide. If Thailand becomes rich, where will it ship its toxic wastes? To Vietnam? To Africa? When every nation has industrialized, will they all dump their refuse in the ocean, as the so-called civilized societies now do? If the rain forests are shrinking, will someone invent machines to purify the air and generate rainfall? When the automobile conquers China, will the world be choking on the polluted atmosphere?

The economic dilemma embedded in these questions revolves around price: global producers are caught up in the desperate competition to reduce costs and prices to hold on to market share, yet the earth's imperative asks the economic system to achieve the opposite—to raise the price of goods so that consumers will begin paying the real production costs of their consumption. The marketplace (including most consumers) is naturally hostile to that imperative since it puts enterprises at immediate disadvantage unless all their competitors in the global system are required to accept the same pricing standards. There is at present no mechanism to achieve such harmony of purpose even if everyone agreed on its wisdom.

The social dilemma grows out of the same facts: If the collective interest requires a transformation of the industrial system's values, the poor will likely be injured more profoundly than the rich since they are the new entrants and least able to pay higher prices for consumption. The developing nations, after all, are emulating the rapacious practices they learned from the advanced economies and are understandably skeptical when high-minded reformers urge them not to repeat the same environmental mistakes—"mistakes" that have made Americans and Europeans quite wealthy. The environmental ethic proposes to alter the basic rules of capitalism at the very moment when some impoverished former colonies are at last enjoying the action.

WILLIAM GREIDER, ONE WORLD, READY OR NOT: THE MANIC LOGIC OF GLOBAL CAPITALISM 446–47 (1997).

2. Consumerism and fantasy. Can exhortations like Jhally's and Greider's stand up against the entwining of goods, the good life, fantasies, and dreams?

CHAPTER 3

DEFINING FAMILY

Introduction

The systematic application of economic theory to the complex zone of intimate, cultural, religious, and long term relationships that we call the family has had a checkered history. In macroeconomic theory, the economic implications of human fertility were explored by the eighteenth-century population economist, Thomas Malthus, who argued that the population would outstrip food supply, leading to rising poverty. This proposition was spelled out in his 1798 work, *An Essay on the Principle of Population,* in which he argued:

> Population, when unchecked, increases in a geometrical ratio. Subsistence only increases in an arithmetical ratio. A slight acquaintance with numbers will show the immensity of the first power compared to the second.

He also predicted that fertility would rise and fall in direct correlation with rising and falling incomes. When this early hypothesis was challenged by the dramatic decrease during the late-nineteenth and early-twentieth century in birthrates in industrialized countries with increasing incomes, Malthus's theories fell out of favor and economists of the era concluded that family decisionmaking was unsuited for useful macroeconomic theory.

In the 1960s, economist Gary Becker turned his attention to the microeconomic dynamics of family decision making. Relying on rational choice theory, once thought to be confined to the marketplace, Becker pursued an ambitious research agenda exploring the dynamics of economic activity within spheres of social interaction, in kinship relations, usually thought to be outside of the market domain. These included his seminal idea of measuring "human capital," investments in education, training, and other prerequisites to market competence.

In Becker's 1981 *Treatise on the Family,* work that is directly related to this chapter in which we consider the social norms and legal rules that define the family, he extended rational choice theory to family behavior, previously thought to be dominated by sentiment and irrationality. One famous application of this idea is the "Rotten Kid Theorem" (RKT). The core idea of the RKT is somewhat counterintuitive. The RKT posits that when parents invest altruistically in their children's early development and education, the children, no matter how selfish, will act to maximize the collective income of the entire family. Thus, the Rotten Kid Theorem introduces the concepts of interdependent preferences within a family system, and altruism. Both of these variables have a weak, if not nonexistent role in conventional microeconomic markets shaped by strangers. Needless to say, feminist economists have criticized both Becker's assumptions and conclusions.

In the cases that follow, we take up questions often put on the back burner of analysis in both family law and constitutional doctrine: What are the economic imperatives within living units that foster social cohesion for both individuals and society? Do legal rules incorporate social constructs about the "natural," pre-political norms of how a family should be configured? Does state intervention or refusal to intervene create economic incentives or disincentives for caring bonds that flow outside of conventional arrangements? Do legal rules privilege some family cultural practices over others, thus placing an economic burden on already disfavored groups? How are the tensions we referred to earlier between community, equality and individual rights resolved in these cases? Can Mrs. Moore's decision to provide housing for her grandchild be explained by Becker's rational choice theory?

A. Nuclear Family vs. Extended Family

Moore v. City of East Cleveland, Ohio

Supreme Court of the United States, 431 U.S. 494 (1977).

■ Mr. Justice Powell announced the judgment of the Court, and delivered an opinion in which Mr. Justice Brennan, Mr. Justice Marshall, and Mr. Justice Blackmun joined.

[In an earlier, related case, *Village of Belle Terre v. Boraas*, 416 U.S. 1 (1974), the Supreme Court rejected a challenge to the constitutionality of a zoning ordinance of the Village of Belle Terre, New York, restricting land use to one-family dwellings, and prohibiting occupancy of a dwelling by more than two unrelated persons as a "family," while permitting occupancy by any number of persons related by blood, adoption, or marriage. Justice Douglas, expressing the view of seven members of the court, held that the zoning ordinance (a) was not unconstitutional since it did not violate any right of interstate travel; (b) involved no procedural disparity inflicted on some but not on others; (c) involved no fundamental constitutional right, such as the rights of association or privacy; and (d) was reasonable and bore a rational relationship to a permissible state objective, thus not violating equal protection.

Justice Marshall's dissent argued that the challenged ordinance was unconstitutional. Marshall would have found that it unnecessarily burdened tenants' fundamental rights of association and privacy guaranteed by the First and Fourteenth Amendments. Marshall argued that since the village's legitimate interests in controlling land use and population density could be protected by limiting the number of occupants without discriminating on the basis of such occupants' constitutionally protected choices of life style.]

East Cleveland's housing ordinance, like many throughout the country, limits occupancy of a dwelling unit to members of a single family. § 1351.02.[1] But the ordinance contains an unusual and complicated definitional section that recognizes as a "family" only a few categories of related individuals. § 1341.08.[2] Because her family, living together in her home, fits none of those categories, appellant stands convicted of a criminal offense. The question in this case is whether the ordinance violates the Due Process Clause of the Fourteenth Amendment.

I

Appellant, Mrs. Inez Moore, lives in her East Cleveland home together with her son, Dale Moore, Sr., and her two grandsons, Dale, Jr., and John Moore, Jr. The two boys are first cousins rather than brothers; we are told that John came to live with his grandmother and with the elder and younger Dale Moore after his mother's death.

In early 1973, Mrs. Moore received a notice of violation from the city, stating that John was an "illegal occupant" and directing her to comply with the ordinance. When she failed to remove him from her home, the city filed a criminal charge. Mrs. Moore moved to dismiss, claiming that the ordinance was constitutionally invalid on its face. Her motion was overruled, and upon conviction she was sentenced to five days in jail and a $25 fine. The Ohio Court of Appeals affirmed after giving full consideration to her constitutional claims and the Ohio Supreme Court denied review. We noted probable jurisdiction of her appeal, 425 U.S. 949 (1976).

II

The city argues that our decision in *Village of Belle Terre v. Boraas, 416 U.S. 1 (1974)*, requires us to sustain the ordinance attacked here. Belle

---

1. All citations by section number refer to the Housing Code of the city of East Cleveland, Ohio.

2. Section 1341.08 (1966) provides:

" 'Family' means a number of individuals related to the nominal head of the household or to the spouse of the nominal head of the household living as a single housekeeping unit in a single dwelling unit, but limited to the following:

"(a) Husband or wife of the nominal head of the household.

"(b) Unmarried children of the nominal head of the household or of the spouse of the nominal head of the household, provided, however, that such unmarried children have no children residing with them.

"(c) Father or mother of the nominal head of the household or of the spouse of the nominal head of the household.

"(d) Notwithstanding the provisions of subsection (b) hereof, a family may include not more than one dependent married or unmarried child of the nominal head of the household or of the spouse of the nominal head of the household and the spouse and dependent children of such dependent child. For the purpose of this subsection, a dependent person is one who has more than fifty percent of his total support furnished for him by the nominal head of the household and the spouse of the nominal head of the household.

"(e) A family may consist of one individual."

Terre, like East Cleveland, imposed limits on the types of groups that could occupy a single dwelling unit. Applying the constitutional standard announced in this Court's leading land-use case, *Euclid v. Ambler Realty Co.*, 272 U.S. 365 (1926),[6] we sustained the Belle Terre ordinance on the ground that it bore a rational relationship to permissible state objectives.

But one overriding factor sets this case apart from *Belle Terre*. The ordinance there affected only *unrelated* individuals. It expressly allowed all who were related by "blood, adoption, or marriage" to live together, and in sustaining the ordinance we were careful to note that it promoted "family needs" and "family values." 416 U.S., at 9. East Cleveland, in contrast, has chosen to regulate the occupancy of its housing by slicing deeply into the family itself. This is no mere incidental result of the ordinance. On its face it selects certain categories of relatives who may live together and declares that others may not. In particular, it makes a crime of a grandmother's choice to live with her grandson in circumstances like those presented here.

When a city undertakes such intrusive regulation of the family, neither *Belle Terre* nor *Euclid* governs; the usual judicial deference to the legislature is inappropriate. "This Court has long recognized that freedom of personal choice in matters of marriage and family life is one of the liberties protected by the Due Process Clause of the Fourteenth Amendment." * * * A host of cases * * * have consistently acknowledged a "private realm of family life which the state cannot enter." * * * Of course, the family is not beyond regulation. * * * But when the government intrudes on choices concerning family living arrangements, this Court must examine carefully the importance of the governmental interests advanced and the extent to which they are served by the challenged regulation. * * *

When thus examined, this ordinance cannot survive. The city seeks to justify it as a means of preventing overcrowding, minimizing traffic and parking congestion, and avoiding an undue financial burden on East Cleveland's school system. Although these are legitimate goals, the ordinance before us serves them marginally, at best.[7] For example, the ordinance permits any family consisting only of husband, wife, and unmarried children to live together, even if the family contains a half dozen licensed drivers, each with his or her own car. At the same time it forbids an adult brother and sister to share a household, even if both faithfully use public

---

6. *Euclid* held that land-use regulations violate the Due Process Clause if they are "clearly arbitrary and unreasonable, having no substantial relation to the public health, safety, morals, or general welfare." 272 U.S., at 395. See *Nectow v. Cambridge*, 277 U.S. 183, 188 (1928). Later cases have emphasized that the general welfare is not to be narrowly understood; it embraces a broad range of governmental purposes. See *Berman v. Parker*, 348 U.S. 26 (1954). But our cases have not departed from the requirement that the government's chosen means must rationally further some legitimate state purpose.

7. It is significant that East Cleveland has another ordinance specifically addressed to the problem of overcrowding. See *United States Dept. of Agriculture v. Moreno*, 413 U.S. 528, 536–537 (1973). Section 1351.03 limits population density directly, tying the maximum permissible occupancy of a dwelling to the habitable floor area. Even if John, Jr., and his father both remain in Mrs. Moore's household, the family stays well within these limits.

transportation. The ordinance would permit a grandmother to live with a single dependent son and children, even if his school-age children number a dozen, yet it forces Mrs. Moore to find another dwelling for her grandson John, simply because of the presence of his uncle and cousin in the same household. We need not labor the point. Section 1341.08 has but a tenuous relation to alleviation of the conditions mentioned by the city.

III

The city would distinguish the cases based on *Meyer* and *Pierce*. It points out that none of them "gives grandmothers any fundamental rights with respect to grandsons," * * * and suggests that any constitutional right to live together as a family extends only to the nuclear family—essentially a couple and their dependent children.

To be sure, these cases did not expressly consider the family relationship presented here. They were immediately concerned with freedom of choice with respect to childbearing, * * * or with the rights of parents to the custody and companionship of their own children, *Stanley v. Illinois, supra,* or with traditional parental authority in matters of child rearing and education. *Yoder, Ginsberg, Pierce, Meyer, supra.* But unless we close our eyes to the basic reasons why certain rights associated with the family have been accorded shelter under the Fourteenth Amendment's Due Process Clause, we cannot avoid applying the force and rationale of these precedents to the family choice involved in this case.

Understanding those reasons requires careful attention to this Court's function under the Due Process Clause. Mr. Justice Harlan described it eloquently:

> "Due process has not been reduced to any formula; its content cannot be determined by reference to any code. The best that can be said is that through the course of this Court's decisions it has represented the balance which our Nation, built upon postulates of respect for the liberty of the individual, has struck between that liberty and the demands of organized society. If the supplying of content to this Constitutional concept has of necessity been a rational process, it certainly has not been one where judges have felt free to roam where unguided speculation might take them. The balance of which I speak is the balance struck by this country, having regard to what history teaches are the traditions from which it developed as well as the traditions from which it broke. That tradition is a living thing. A decision of this Court which radically departs from it could not long survive, while a decision which builds on what has survived is likely to be sound. No formula could serve as a substitute, in this area, for judgment and restraint."

> "... [T]he full scope of the liberty guaranteed by the Due Process Clause cannot be found in or limited by the precise terms of the specific guarantees elsewhere provided in the Constitution. This 'liberty' is not a series of isolated points pricked out in terms

of the taking of property; the freedom of speech, press, and religion; the right to keep and bear arms; the freedom from unreasonable searches and seizures; and so on. It is a rational continuum which, broadly speaking, includes a freedom from all substantial arbitrary impositions and purposeless restraints, ... and which also recognizes, what a reasonable and sensitive judgment must, that certain interests require particularly careful scrutiny of the state needs asserted to justify their abridgment." *Poe v. Ullman*, supra at 542–543 (dissenting opinion).

Substantive due process has at times been a treacherous field for this Court. There *are* risks when the judicial branch gives enhanced protection to certain substantive liberties without the guidance of the more specific provisions of the Bill of Rights. As the history of the *Lochner* era demonstrates, there is reason for concern lest the only limits to such judicial intervention become the predilections of those who happen at the time to be Members of this Court. That history counsels caution and restraint. But it does not counsel abandonment, nor does it require what the city urges here: cutting off any protection of family rights at the first convenient, if arbitrary boundary—the boundary of the nuclear family.

Appropriate limits on substantive due process come not from drawing arbitrary lines but rather from careful "respect for the teachings of history [and] solid recognition of the basic values that underlie our society." * * * Our decisions establish that the Constitution protects the sanctity of the family precisely because the institution of the family is deeply rooted in this Nation's history and tradition.[12] It is through the family that we inculcate and pass down many of our most cherished values, moral and cultural.

---

12. In *Wisconsin v. Yoder*, 406 U.S. 205 (1972), the Court rested its holding in part on the constitutional right of parents to assume the primary role in decisions concerning the rearing of their children. That right is recognized because it reflects a "strong tradition" founded on "the history and culture of Western civilization," and because the parental role "is now established beyond debate as an enduring American tradition." *id.*, at 232. In *Ginsberg v. New York*, 390 U.S. 629 (1968), the Court spoke of the same right as "basic in the structure of our society." *Id.*, at 639. *Griswold v. Connecticut, supra* struck down Connecticut's anticontraception statute. Three concurring Justices, relying on both the Ninth and Fourteenth Amendments, emphasized that "the traditional relation of the family" is "a relation as old and as fundamental as our entire civilization." 381 U.S., at 496 (Goldberg, J., joined by Warren, C.J., and BRENNAN, J., concurring). Speaking of the same statute as that involved in *Griswold*, Mr. Justice Harlan wrote, dissenting in *Poe v. Ullman*, 367 U.S. 497, 551–552 (1961):

"[H]ere we have not an intrusion into the home so much as on the life which characteristically has its place in the home.... The home derives its pre-eminence as the seat of family life. And the integrity of that life is something so fundamental that it has been found to draw to its protection the principles of more than one explicitly granted Constitutional right."

Although he agrees that the Due Process Clause has substantive content, MR. JUSTICE WHITE in dissent expresses the fear that our recourse to history and tradition will "broaden enormously the horizons of the Clause." *Post*, at 549–550. To the contrary, an approach grounded in history imposes limits on the judiciary that are more meaningful than any based on the abstract formula taken from *Palko v. Connecticut*, 302 U.S. 319 (1937), and apparently suggested as an alternative. Cf. *Duncan v. Louisiana, supra* at 149–150, n.14 (rejecting the *Palko* formula as the basis for deciding what procedural protections are required of a State, in favor of a

Ours is by no means a tradition limited to respect for the bonds uniting the members of the nuclear family. The tradition of uncles, aunts, cousins, and especially grandparents sharing a household along with parents and children has roots equally venerable and equally deserving of constitutional recognition.[14] Over the years millions of our citizens have grown up in just such an environment, and most, surely, have profited from it. Even if conditions of modern society have brought about a decline in extended family households, they have not erased the accumulated wisdom of civilization, gained over the centuries and honored throughout our history, that supports a larger conception of the family. Out of choice, necessity, or a sense of family responsibility, it has been common for close relatives to draw together and participate in the duties and the satisfactions of a common home. Decisions concerning child rearing, which *Yoder, Meyer, Pierce* and other cases have recognized as entitled to constitutional protection, long have been shared with grandparents or other relatives who occupy the same household—indeed who may take on major responsibility for the rearing of the children.[15] Especially in times of adversity, such as the death of a spouse or economic need, the broader family has tended to come together for mutual sustenance and to maintain or rebuild a secure home life. This is apparently what happened here.[16]

Whether or not such a household is established because of personal tragedy, the choice of relatives in this degree of kinship to live together may not lightly be denied by the State. *Pierce* struck down an Oregon law requiring all children to attend the State's public schools, holding that the Constitution "excludes any general power of the State to standardize its children by forcing them to accept instruction from public teachers only." 268 U.S., at 535. By the same token the Constitution prevents East Cleveland from standardizing its children—and its adults—by forcing all to live in certain narrowly defined family patterns.

Reversed.

---

historical approach based on the Anglo–American legal tradition). Indeed, the passage cited in Mr. Justice White's dissent as "most accurately reflect[ing] the thrust of prior decisions" on substantive due process, *post,* at 545, expressly points to history and tradition as the source for "supplying ... content to this Constitutional concept." *Poe v. Ullman, supra* at 542 (Harlan, J., dissenting).

14. See generally B. Yorburg, The Changing Family (1973); Bronfenbrenner, The Calamitous Decline of the American Family, Washington Post, Jan. 2, 1977, p. C1. Recent census reports bear out the importance of family patterns other than the prototypical nuclear family. In 1970, 26.5% of all families contained one or more members over 18 years of age, other than the head of household and spouse. U.S. Department of Commerce, 1970 Census of Population, vol. 1, pt. 1, Table 208. In 1960 the comparable figure was 26.1%. U.S. Department of Commerce, 1960 Census of Population, vol. 1, pt. 1, Table 187. Earlier data are not available.

15. Cf. *Prince v. Massachusetts,* 321 U.S. 158 (1944), which spoke broadly of family authority as against the State, in a case where the child was being reared by her aunt, not her natural parents.

16. We are told that the mother of John Moore, Jr., died when he was less than one year old. He, like uncounted others who have suffered a similar tragedy, then came to live with the grandmother to provide the infant with a substitute for his mother's care and to establish a more normal home environment. Brief for Appellant 25.

■ MR. JUSTICE BRENNAN, with whom MR. JUSTICE MARSHALL joins, concurring.

I join the plurality's opinion. I agree that the Constitution is not powerless to prevent East Cleveland from prosecuting as a criminal and jailing[1] a 63-year-old grandmother for refusing to expel from her home her now 10-year-old grandson who has lived with her and been brought up by her since his mother's death when he was less than a year old. I do not question that a municipality may constitutionally zone to alleviate noise and traffic congestion and to prevent overcrowded and unsafe living conditions, in short to enact reasonable land-use restrictions in furtherance of the legitimate objectives East Cleveland claims for its ordinance. But the zoning power is not a license for local communities to enact senseless and arbitrary restrictions which cut deeply into private areas of protected family life. East Cleveland may not constitutionally define "family" as essentially confined to parents and the parents' own children.[3] The plurality's opinion conclusively demonstrates that classifying family patterns in this eccentric way is not a rational means of achieving the ends East Cleveland claims for its ordinance, and further that the ordinance unconstitutionally abridges the "freedom of personal choice in matters of . . . family life [that] is one of the liberties protected by the Due Process Clause of the Fourteenth Amendment." *Cleveland Board of Education v. LaFleur*, 414 U.S. 632, 639–640 (1974). I write only to underscore the cultural myopia of the arbitrary boundary drawn by the East Cleveland ordinance in the light of the tradition of the American home that has been a feature of our society since our beginning as a Nation—the "tradition" in the plurality's words, "of uncles, aunts, cousins, and especially grandparents sharing a household along with parents and children. . . ." *Ante,* at 504. The line drawn by this ordinance displays a depressing insensitivity toward the economic and emotional needs of a very large part of our society.

In today's America, the "nuclear family" is the pattern so often found in much of white suburbia. J. Vander Zanden, Sociology: A Systematic Approach 322 (3d ed. 1975). The Constitution cannot be interpreted, however, to tolerate the imposition by government upon the rest of us of white suburbia's preference in patterns of family living. The "extended family" that provided generations of early Americans with social services and economic and emotional support in times of hardship, and was the

---

1. This is a criminal prosecution which resulted in the grandmother's conviction and sentence to prison and a fine. Section 1345.99 permits imprisonment of up to six months, and a fine of up to $1,000, for violation of any provision of the Housing Code. Each day such violation continues may, by the terms of this section, constitute a separate offense.

3. The East Cleveland ordinance defines "family" to include, in addition to the spouse of the "nominal head of the household," the couple's childless unmarried children, but only one dependent child (married or unmarried) having dependent children, and one parent of the nominal head of the household or of his or her spouse. Thus an "extended family" is authorized in only the most limited sense, and "family" is essentially confined to parents and their own children. Appellant grandmother was charged with violating the ordinance because John, Jr., lived with her at the same time her other grandson, Dale, Jr., was also living in the home; the latter is classified as an "unlicensed roomer" authorized by the ordinance to live in the house.

beachhead for successive waves of immigrants who populated our cities, remains not merely still a pervasive living pattern, but under the goad of brutal economic necessity, a prominent pattern—virtually a means of survival—for large numbers of the poor and deprived minorities of our society. For them compelled pooling of scant resources requires compelled sharing of a household.[5]

The "extended" form is especially familiar among black families.[6] We may suppose that this reflects the truism that black citizens, like generations of white immigrants before them, have been victims of economic and other disadvantages that would worsen if they were compelled to abandon extended, for nuclear, living patterns.[7] Even in husband and wife house-

---

5. See, *e.g.,* H. Gans, The Urban Villagers 45–73, 245–249 (1962).

"Perhaps the most important—or at least the most visible—difference between the classes is one of family structure. *The working class subculture* is distinguished by the dominant role of the family circle....

"The specific characteristics of the family circle may differ widely—from the collateral peer group form of the West Enders, to the hierarchical type of the Irish, or to the classical three-generation extended family.... What matters most—and distinguishes this subculture from others—is that there be a family circle which is wider than the nuclear family, and that all of the opportunities, temptations, and pressures of the larger society be evaluated in terms of how they affect the ongoing way of life that has been built around this circle." *Id.,* at 244–245 (emphasis in original).

6. Yorburg, *supra* n. 4, at 108. "Within the black lower-class it has been quite common for several generations, or parts of the kin, to live together under one roof. Often a maternal grandmother is the acknowledged head of this type of household which has given rise to the term 'matrifocal' to describe lower-class black family patterns." See J. Scanzoni, The Black Family in Modern Society 134 (1971); see also Anderson, The Pains and Pleasures of Old Black Folks, Ebony 123, 128–130 (Mar. 1973). See generally E. Frazier, The Negro Family in the United States (1939); Lewis, The Changing Negro Family, in E. Ginzberg, ed., The Nation's Children 108 (1960).

The extended family often plays an important role in the rearing of young black children whose parents must work. Many such children frequently "spend all of their growing-up years in the care of extended kin.... Often children are 'given' to their grandparents, who rear them to adulthood.... Many children normally grow up in a three-generation household and they absorb the influences of grandmother and grandfather as well as mother and father." J. Ladner, Tomorrow's Tomorrow: The Black Woman 60 (1972).

7. The extended family has many strengths not shared by the nuclear family.

"The case histories behind mounting rates of delinquency, addiction, crime, neurotic disabilities, mental illness, and senility in societies in which autonomous nuclear families prevail suggest that frequent failure to develop enduring family ties is a serious inadequacy for both individuals and societies." D. Blitsten, The World of the Family 256 (1963).

Extended families provide services and emotional support not always found in the nuclear family:

"The troubles of the nuclear family in industrial societies, generally, and in American society, particularly, stem largely from the inability of this type of family structure to provide certain of the services performed in the past by the extended family. Adequate health, education, and welfare provision, particularly for the two nonproductive generations in modern societies, the young and the old, is increasingly an insurmountable problem for the nuclear family. The unrelieved and sometimes unbearably intense parent-child relationship, where childrearing is not shared at least in part by others, and the loneliness of nuclear family units, increasingly turned in on themselves in contracted and relatively isolated settings, is another major problem." Yorburg, *supra* n. 4, at 194.

holds, 13% of black families compared with 3% of white families include relatives under 18 years old, in addition to the couple's own children.[8] In black households whose head is an elderly woman, as in this case, the contrast is even more striking: 48% of such black households, compared with 10% of counterpart white households, include related minor children not offspring of the head of the household.[9]

I do not wish to be understood as implying that East Cleveland's enforcement of its ordinance is motivated by a racially discriminatory purpose: The record of this case would not support that implication. But the prominence of other than nuclear families among ethnic and racial minority groups, including our black citizens, surely demonstrates that the "extended family" pattern remains a vital tenet of our society. It suffices that in prohibiting this pattern of family living as a means of achieving its objectives, appellee city has chosen a device that deeply intrudes into family associational rights that historically have been central, and today remain central, to a large proportion of our population.

Moreover, to sanction the drawing of the family line at the arbitrary boundary chosen by East Cleveland would surely conflict with prior decisions that protected "extended" family relationships. For the "private realm of family life which the state cannot enter," recognized as protected in *Prince v. Massachusetts*, 321 U.S. 158, 166 (1944), was the relationship of aunt and niece. And in *Pierce v. Society of Sisters*, 268 U.S. 510, 534–535 (1925), the protection held to have been unconstitutionally abridged was "the liberty of parents and *guardians* to direct the upbringing and education of children under their control" (emphasis added). See also *Wisconsin v. Yoder*, 406 U.S. 205, 232–233 (1972). Indeed, *Village of Belle Terre v. Boraas*, 416 U.S. 1 (1974), the case primarily relied upon by the appellee, actually supports the Court's decision. The Belle Terre ordinance barred only unrelated individuals from constituting a family in a single-family zone. The village took special care in its brief to emphasize that its ordinance did not in any manner inhibit the choice of *related* individuals to constitute a family, whether in the "nuclear" or "extended" form. This was because the village perceived that choice as one it was constitutionally powerless to inhibit. Its brief stated: "Whether it be the extended family of a more leisurely age or the nuclear family of today the role of the family in raising and training successive generations of the species makes it more important, we dare say, than any other social or legal institution.... *If any freedom not specifically mentioned in the Bill of Rights enjoys a 'preferred position' in the law it is most certainly the family."* (Emphasis supplied.) * * * The cited decisions recognized, as the plurality recognizes today, that the choice of the "extended family" pattern is within the "freedom of

---

8. R. Hill, The Strengths of Black Families 5 (1972).

9. *Id.,* at 5–6. It is estimated that at least 26% of black children live in other than husband-wife families, "including foster parents, the presence of other male or female relatives (grandfather or grandmother, older brother or sister, uncle or aunt), male or female nonrelatives, [or with] only *one* adult (usually mother) present...." Scanzoni, *supra* n. 6, at 44.

personal choice in matters of ... family life [that] is one of the liberties protected by the Due Process Clause of the Fourteenth Amendment." 414 U.S., at 639–640.

* * *

■ MR. JUSTICE STEVENS, concurring in the judgment.

In my judgment the critical question presented by this case is whether East Cleveland's housing ordinance is a permissible restriction on appellant's right to use her own property as she sees fit.

Long before the original States adopted the Constitution, the common law protected an owner's right to decide how best to use his own property. This basic right has always been limited by the law of nuisance which proscribes uses that impair the enjoyment of other property in the vicinity. But the question whether an individual owner's use could be further limited by a municipality's comprehensive zoning plan was not finally decided until this century.

The holding in *Euclid v. Ambler Realty Co.*, 272 U.S. 365, that a city could use its police power, not just to abate a specific use of property which proved offensive, but also to create and implement a comprehensive plan for the use of land in the community, vastly diminished the rights of individual property owners. It did not, however, totally extinguish those rights. On the contrary, that case expressly recognized that the broad zoning power must be exercised within constitutional limits.

In his opinion for the Court, Mr. Justice Sutherland fused the two express constitutional restrictions on any state interference with private property—that property shall not be taken without due process nor for a public purpose without just compensation—into a single standard: "[B]efore [a zoning] ordinance can be declared unconstitutional, [it must be shown to be] clearly arbitrary and unreasonable, *having no substantial relation to the public health, safety, morals, or general welfare.*" *Id.*, at 395 (emphasis added). This principle was applied in *Nectow v. Cambridge*, 277 U.S. 183; on the basis of a specific finding made by the state trial court that "the health, safety, convenience and general welfare of the inhabitants of the part of the city affected" would not be promoted by prohibiting the landowner's contemplated use, this Court held that the zoning ordinance as applied was unconstitutional. * * *

Litigation involving single-family zoning ordinances is common. Although there appear to be almost endless differences in the language used in these ordinances, they contain three principal types of restrictions. First, they define the kind of structure that may be erected on vacant land.[4]

---

4. As this Court recognized in *Euclid,* even residential apartments can have a negative impact on an area of single-family homes.

"[O]ften the apartment house is a mere parasite, constructed in order to take advantage of the open spaces and attractive surroundings created by [a single-family dwelling area].... [T]he coming of one apartment house is followed by others, interfering by their height and bulk with the free circulation of air and monopolizing the rays of the

Second, they require that a single-family home be occupied only by a "single housekeeping unit." Third, they often require that the housekeeping unit be made up of persons related by blood, adoption, or marriage, with certain limited exceptions.

Although the legitimacy of the first two types of restrictions is well settled, attempts to limit occupancy to related persons have not been successful. The state courts have recognized a valid community interest in preserving the stable character of residential neighborhoods which justifies a prohibition against transient occupancy. Nevertheless, in well-reasoned opinions, the courts of [several states] have permitted unrelated persons to occupy single-family residences notwithstanding an ordinance prohibiting, either expressly or implicitly, such occupancy.

These cases delineate the extent to which the state courts have allowed zoning ordinances to interfere with the right of a property owner to determine the internal composition of his household. The intrusion on that basic property right has not previously gone beyond the point where the ordinance defines a family to include only persons related by blood, marriage, or adoption. Indeed, as the cases in the margin demonstrate, state courts have not always allowed the intrusion to penetrate that far. The state decisions have upheld zoning ordinances which regulated the identity, as opposed to the number, of persons who may compose a household only to the extent that the ordinances require such households to remain nontransient, single-housekeeping units.

There appears to be no precedent for an ordinance which excludes any of an owner's relatives from the group of persons who may occupy his residence on a permanent basis. Nor does there appear to be any justification for such a restriction on an owner's use of his property. The city has failed totally to explain the need for a rule which would allow a homeowner to have two grandchildren live with her if they are brothers, but not if they are cousins. Since this ordinance has not been shown to have any "substantial relation to the public health, safety, morals, or general welfare" of the city of East Cleveland, and since it cuts so deeply into a fundamental right normally associated with the ownership of residential property—that of an owner to decide who may reside on his or her property—it must fall under the limited standard of review of zoning decisions which this Court preserved in *Euclid* and *Nectow*. Under that standard, East Cleveland's unprecedented ordinance constitutes a taking of property without due process and without just compensation.

sun which otherwise would fall upon the smaller homes, and bringing, as their necessary accompaniments, the distributing noises incident to increased traffic and business, and the occupation, by means of moving and parked automobiles, of larger portions of the streets, thus detracting from their safety and depriving children of the privilege of quiet and open spaces for play, enjoyed by those in more favored localities,—until, finally, the residential character of the neighborhood and its desirability as a place of detached residences are utterly destroyed. Under these circumstances, apartment houses, which in a different environment would be not only entirely unobjectionable but highly desirable, come very near to being nuisances." 272 U.S., at 394–395.

For these reasons, I concur in the Court's judgment.

■ Mr. Chief Justice Burger, with whom Mr. Justice Stewart and Mr. Justice White join, dissenting.

* * *

"... Courts are forced to add more clerks, more administrative personnel, to move cases faster and faster. They are losing ... time for reflection, time for the deliberate maturation of principles." [Department of Justice Committee on Revision of The Federal Judicial System, Report on the Needs of the Federal Courts 3–4 (1977).]

■ Mr. Justice Stewart, with whom Mr. Justice Rehnquist joins, dissenting.

* * *

The *Belle Terre* decision * * * disposes of the appellant's contentions to the extent they focus not on her blood relationships with her sons and grandsons but on more general notions about the "privacy of the home." Her suggestion that every person has a constitutional right permanently to share his residence with whomever he pleases, and that such choices are "beyond the province of legitimate governmental intrusion," amounts to the same argument that was made and found unpersuasive in *Belle Terre*.

To be sure, the ordinance involved in *Belle Terre* did not prevent blood relatives from occupying the same dwelling, and the Court's decision in that case does not, therefore, foreclose the appellant's arguments based specifically on the ties of kinship present in this case. Nonetheless, I would hold, for the reasons that follow, that the existence of those ties does not elevate either the appellant's claim of associational freedom or her claim of privacy to a level invoking constitutional protection.

* * *

The "association" in this case is not for any purpose relating to the promotion of speech, assembly, the press, or religion. And wherever the outer boundaries of constitutional protection of freedom of association may eventually turn out to be, they surely do not extend to those who assert no interest other than the gratification, convenience, and *economy* [emphasis added] of sharing the same residence.

* * *

The appellant also challenges the single-family occupancy ordinance on equal protection grounds. Her claim is that the city has drawn an arbitrary and irrational distinction between groups of people who may live together as a "family" and those who may not. While acknowledging the city's right to preclude more than one family from occupying a single-dwelling unit, the appellant argues that the purposes of the single-family occupancy law would be equally served by an ordinance that did not prevent her from sharing her residence with her two sons and their sons.

This argument misconceives the nature of the constitutional inquiry. In a case such as this one, where the challenged ordinance intrudes upon no substantively protected constitutional right, it is not the Court's business to decide whether its application in a particular case seems inequitable, or even absurd. The question is not whether some other ordinance, drafted more broadly, might have served the city's ends as well or almost as well. The task, rather, is to determine if East Cleveland's ordinance violates the Equal Protection Clause of the United States Constitution. And in performing that task, it must be borne in mind that "[w]e deal with economic and social legislation where legislatures have historically drawn lines which we respect against the charge of violation of the Equal Protection Clause if the law be ' "reasonable, not arbitrary" ' (quoting *Royster Guano Co. v. Virginia*, 253 U.S. 412, 415) and bears 'a rational relationship to a [permissible] state objective.' *Reed v. Reed*, 404 U.S. 71, 76." *Village of Belle Terre v. Boraas*, 416 U.S., at 8. "[E]very line drawn by a legislature leaves some out that might well have been included. That exercise of discretion, however, is a legislative, not a judicial, function." *Ibid.* (footnote omitted).[8]

Viewed in the light of these principles, I do not think East Cleveland's definition of "family" offends the Constitution. The city has undisputed power to ordain single-family residential occupancy. *Village of Belle Terre v. Boraas, supra; Euclid v. Ambler Realty Co.*, 272 U.S. 365. And that power plainly carries with it the power to say what a "family" is. * * *

* * *

For these reasons, I think the Ohio courts did not err in rejecting the appellant's constitutional claims. Accordingly, I respectfully dissent.

■ MR. JUSTICE WHITE, dissenting.

The Fourteenth Amendment forbids any State to "deprive any person of life, liberty, or property, without due process of law," or to "deny to any person within its jurisdiction the equal protection of the laws." Both provisions are invoked in this case in an attempt to invalidate a city zoning ordinance.

I

The emphasis of the Due Process Clause is on "process." * * * As Mr. Justice Harlan once observed, it has been "ably and insistently argued in response to what were felt to be abuses by this Court of its reviewing power," that the Due Process Clause should be limited "to a guarantee of procedural fairness." *Poe v. Ullman*, 367 U.S. 497, 540 (1961) (dissenting

---

8. The observation of Mr. Justice Holmes quoted in the *Belle Terre* opinion, 416 U.S., at 8 n. 5, bears repeating here.

"When a legal distinction is determined, as no one doubts that it may be, between night and day, childhood and maturity, or any other extremes, a point has to be fixed or a line has to be drawn, or gradually picked out by successive decisions, to mark where the change takes place. Looked at by itself without regard to the necessity behind it the line or point seems arbitrary. It might as well or nearly as well be a little more to one side or the other. But when it is seen that a line or point there must be, and that there is no mathematical or logical way of fixing it precisely, the decision of the legislature must be accepted unless we can say that it is very wide of any reasonable mark." *Louisville Gas Co. v. Coleman*, 277 U.S. 32, 41 (dissenting opinion).

opinion). These arguments had seemed "persuasive" to Justices Brandeis and Holmes, *Whitney v. California*, 274 U.S. 357, 373 (1927), but they recognized that the Due Process Clause, by virtue of case-to-case "judicial inclusion and exclusion," *Davidson v. New Orleans*, 96 U.S. 97, 104 (1878), had been construed to proscribe matters of substance, as well as inadequate procedures, and to protect from invasion by the States "all fundamental rights comprised within the term liberty." *Whitney v. California*, supra at 373.

* * *

Although the Court regularly proceeds on the assumption that the Due Process Clause has more than a procedural dimension, we must always bear in mind that the substantive content of the Clause is suggested neither by its language nor by preconstitutional history; that content is nothing more than the accumulated product of judicial interpretation of the Fifth and Fourteenth Amendments. This is not to suggest, at this point, that any of these cases should be overruled, or that the process by which they were decided was illegitimate or even unacceptable, but only to underline Mr. Justice Black's constant reminder to his colleagues that the Court has no license to invalidate legislation which it thinks merely arbitrary or unreasonable. And no one was more sensitive than Mr. Justice Harlan to any suggestion that his approach to the Due Process Clause would lead to judges "roaming at large in the constitutional field." *Griswold v. Connecticut, supra* at 502. No one proceeded with more caution than he did when the validity of state or federal legislation was challenged in the name of the Due Process Clause.

* * *

* * * Here the head of the household may house himself or herself and spouse, their parents, and any number of their unmarried children. A fourth generation may be represented by only one set of grandchildren and then only if born to a dependent child. The ordinance challenged by appellant prevents her from living with both sets of grandchildren only in East Cleveland, an area with a radius of three miles and a population of 40,000. Brief for Appellee 16 n. 1. The ordinance thus denies appellant the opportunity to live with all her grandchildren in this particular suburb; she is free to do so in other parts of the Cleveland metropolitan area. If there is power to maintain the character of a single-family neighborhood, as there surely is, some limit must be placed on the reach of the "family." Had it been our task to legislate, we might have approached the problem in a different manner than did the drafters of this ordinance; but I have no trouble in concluding that the normal goals of zoning regulation are present here and that the ordinance serves these goals by limiting, in identifiable circumstances, the number of people who can occupy a single household. The ordinance does not violate the Due Process Clause.

IV

For very similar reasons, the equal protection claim must fail, since it is not to be judged by the strict scrutiny standard employed when a fundamental interest or suspect classification is involved[.] * * * Rather, it is the generally applicable standard of *McGowan v. Maryland*, 366 U.S. 420, 425 (1961):

> "The constitutional safeguard [of the Equal Protection Clause] is offended only if the classification rests on grounds wholly irrelevant to the achievement of the State's objective. State legislatures are presumed to have acted within their constitutional power despite the fact that, in practice, their laws result in some inequality. A statutory discrimination will not be set aside if any state of facts reasonably may be conceived to justify it."

* * * Under this standard, it is not fatal if the purpose of the law is not articulated on its face, and there need be only a rational relation to the ascertained purpose.

On this basis, as already indicated, I have no trouble in discerning a rational justification for an ordinance that permits the head of a household to house one, but not two, dependent sons and their children.

Respectfully, therefore, I dissent and would affirm the judgment.

NOTES AND QUESTIONS

1. Teachings of history and sanctity of family. What limits can one expect to impose on the murky concepts of substantive due process as applied to government regulation of family life? Justice Powell, writing for the Court, thought that the "appropriate limits on due process come not from drawing arbitrary lines but rather from careful respect for the 'teachings of history [and] solid recognition of the basic values that underlie our society.'" *Moore*, supra at ___. See also Snyder v. Massachusetts, 291 U.S. 97, 105 (1934); Griswold v. Connecticut, 381 U.S. 479, 501 (1965) (Harlan, J., concurring). Powell goes on to say that the Court's "decisions establish that the Constitution protects the sanctity of the family precisely because the institution of the family is deeply rooted in this Nation's history and tradition." *Moore, supra* at 503.

Is there a cultural consensus about what the "teachings of history" are? Even if we could agree on the definition of the composition of the family, there remain important differences about the norms that should apply within the family system. Disputes about "family values" are a staple of divisive political campaigns today. Families certainly make intensely different decisions as to methods of discipline, breast feeding, intra-family privacy, individual space expectations, the sharing of bathrooms, young children's nakedness in the home, the appropriate age to begin dating, and the willingness of family to discuss biology and emotional components of human sexuality, just to name a few. *See* Gill Jagger & Caroline Wright, CHANGING FAMILY VALUES (eds., 1999).

Has Justice Powell assumed the existence of a stable, widely shared set of values about family in our very diverse society?

Is the model of deference to history likely to produce stagnant or dynamic approaches to constitutional interpretation of state restrictions on family preferences? What should be the role of the legal system in these intra-family debates? What is the role of economic analysis in Justice Powell's approach? What would Fran Olson's arguments about how the law should view the concepts of non-intervention, privacy, and the private/public distinction suggest about Powell's basis of reasoning (see chapter 1)?

2. Extended family vs. nuclear family. Justices Brennan and Marshall's concurrence focuses on the central role that the extended family has played for immigrant groups throughout American history, as well as African Americans today. The predominance of non-nuclear family structures in America, especially among ethnic and racial minority groups, suggests that the "extended family" pattern remains a vital tenet of our society. *See* ANDREW BILLINGSLEY, CLIMBING JACOB'S LADDER: THE ENDURING LEGACY OF AFRICAN-AMERICAN FAMILIES (1992); Ronald Angel & Marta Tienda, *Determinants of Extended Household Structure: Cultural Pattern or Economic Need?*, 87 AM. J. SOC. 1360 (1982). Under the reasoning in Brennan's concurrence, should associational forms which have been historically utilized by such populations in this country receive special protection?

If a minority group traditionally practiced polygamy in order to aid in pooling resources and to avoid the social problems associated with destitute widows and single motherhood, would Brennan's reasoning protect that group's definition of family? What about in the opposite case of polyandry? What about membership in a potentially criminal organization? *See* Linda Kelly, *Family Planning, American Style*, 52 ALA. L. REV. 943 (2001); Alison Harvison Young, *Reconceiving the Family: Challenging the Paradigm of the Exclusive Family*, 6 AM. U. J. GENDER & L. 505 (1998).

3. Drawing the line. What sociological theories are and could be employed by the Court to decide where to draw the line defining what is and is not a family? Are courts competent to make use of the often conflicting theories of social science research? Should people not related by blood have similar associational rights as the traditional family? *See* Smith v. Organization of Foster Families, 431 U.S. 816 (1977). What about unmarried parents? *See* Stanley v. Illinois, 405 U.S. 645 (1972). What about people engaging in casual sex? *See* FW/PBS, Inc. v. City of Dallas, 493 U.S. 215 (1990). How would economic theory shape this debate?

4. Strict scrutiny, rational basis, and *Moore v. East Cleveland*. At the time of *Moore v. East Cleveland*, Fourteenth Amendment Due Process analysis required that if a regulation excluded a suspect class of people, then that regulation must satisfy a "strict scrutiny" test. If the regulation did not discriminate against a suspect class, however, it needed only to pass a much more forgiving "rational basis" standard of review. Though the plurality opinion in *Moore* did not state that the ordinance in question should be subjected to strict scrutiny review, it does seem to be advocating more than a rational basis standard. Does *Moore* create another standard of review between strict scrutiny and rational relationship? If so, does the standard extend past the regulation of families? *See* Robert J. Hopperton,

The Presumption of Validity in American Land-Use Law: A Substitute for Analysis, A Source of Significant Confusion, 23 B.C. ENVTL. AFF. L. REV. 301 (1996).

5. Race, economics, and family definitions. Brennan and Marshall decry the "cultural myopia" of the plurality. In today's America, the "nuclear family" is the pattern so often found in much of white suburbia. The Constitution cannot be interpreted, however, to tolerate the imposition by government of white suburbia's preference in patterns of living. *See also* PEGGY COOPER DAVIS, NEGLECTED STORIES: THE CONSTITUTION AND FAMILY VALUES (1997); DOROTHY ROBERTS, KILLING THE BLACK BODIES (1998).

On the relevance of racial variation in patterns of family formation, the dissent of Justices Stewart and Rehnquist takes the opposite position than the plurality and concurring opinions:

> The opinion of MR. JUSTICE POWELL and MR. JUSTICE BRENNAN'S concurring opinion both emphasize the traditional importance of the extended family in American life. But I fail to understand why it follows that the residents of East Cleveland are constitutionally prevented from following what MR. JUSTICE BRENNAN calls the "pattern" of "white suburbia," even though that choice may reflect "cultural myopia." In point of fact, East Cleveland is a predominantly Negro community, with a Negro City Manager and City Commission.

Moore, supra at 537, n.7.

6. Additional reading. For an annotated catalog of cases and articles relating to the definition of "family" in zoning regulations and restrictive covenants, see James L. Rigelhaupt, Jr., *Annotation What Constitutes a "Family" Within Meaning of Zoning Regulation or Restrictive Covenant*, 71 A.L.R.3D 693 (2004). For a description of how housing codes can be used as tools for discrimination, see Ellen J. Pader, *CLUSTER VI: Class, Economics, and Social Rights: Space of Hate: Ethnicity, Architecture and Housing Discrimination*, 54 RUTGERS L. REV. 881 (2002). For an interesting proposal for defining family, see Angie Smolka, Note, *That's the Ticket: A New Way of Defining Family*, 10 CORNELL J. L. & PUB. POL'Y 629 (2001).

B. UNMARRIED HETEROSEXUAL COUPLES

Marvin v. Marvin
557 P.2d 106 (Cal. 1976).

■ JUSTICE TOBRINER delivered the opinion of the court.

During the past 15 years, there has been a substantial increase in the number of couples living together without marrying. Such nonmarital relationships lead to legal controversy when one partner dies or the couple separates. Courts of Appeal, faced with the task of determining property rights in such cases, have arrived at conflicting positions: two cases * * * have held that the Family Law Act (Civ. Code, § 4000 et seq.) requires division of the property according to community property principles, and one decision * * * has rejected that holding. We take this opportunity to resolve that controversy and to declare the principles which should govern distribution of property acquired in a nonmarital relationship.

We conclude: (1) The provisions of the Family Law Act do not govern the distribution of property acquired during a nonmarital relationship; such a relationship remains subject solely to judicial decision. (2) The courts should enforce express contracts between nonmarital partners except to the extent that the contract is explicitly founded on the consideration of meretricious sexual services. (3) In the absence of an express contract, the courts should inquire into the conduct of the parties to determine whether that conduct demonstrates an implied contract, agreement of partnership or joint venture, or some other tacit understanding between the parties. The courts may also employ the doctrine of quantum meruit, or equitable remedies such as constructive or resulting trusts, when warranted by the facts of the case.

In the instant case plaintiff and defendant lived together for seven years without marrying; all property acquired during this period was taken in defendant's name. When plaintiff sued to enforce a contract under which she was entitled to half the property and to support payments, the trial court granted judgment on the pleadings for defendant, thus leaving him with all property accumulated by the couple during their relationship. Since the trial court denied plaintiff a trial on the merits of her claim, its decision conflicts with the principles stated above, and must be reversed.

1. THE FACTUAL SETTING OF THIS APPEAL.

Since the trial court rendered judgment for defendant on the pleadings, we must accept the allegations of plaintiff's complaint as true, determining whether such allegations state, or can be amended to state, a cause of action. * * *

Plaintiff avers that in October of 1964 she and defendant "entered into an oral agreement" that while "the parties lived together they would combine their efforts and earnings and would share equally any and all property accumulated as a result of their efforts whether individual or combined." Furthermore, they agreed to "hold themselves out to the general public as husband and wife" and that "plaintiff would further render her services as a companion, homemaker, housekeeper and cook to ... defendant."

Shortly thereafter plaintiff agreed to "give up her lucrative career as an entertainer [and] singer" in order to "devote her full time to defendant ... as a companion, homemaker, housekeeper and cook;" in return defendant agreed to "provide for all of plaintiff's financial support and needs for the rest of her life."

Plaintiff alleges that she lived with defendant from October of 1964 through May of 1970 and fulfilled her obligations under the agreement.

During this period the parties as a result of their efforts and earnings acquired in defendant's name substantial real and personal property, including motion picture rights worth over $1 million. In May of 1970, however, defendant compelled plaintiff to leave his household. He continued to support plaintiff until November of 1971, but thereafter refused to provide further support.

On the basis of these allegations plaintiff asserts two causes of action. The first, for declaratory relief, asks the court to determine her contract and property rights; the second seeks to impose a constructive trust upon one half of the property acquired during the course of the relationship.

* * *

2. PLAINTIFF'S COMPLAINT STATES A CAUSE OF ACTION FOR BREACH OF AN EXPRESS CONTRACT.

* * * [W]e established the principle that nonmarital partners may lawfully contract concerning the ownership of property acquired during the relationship. * * * "If a man and woman [who are not married] live together as husband and wife under an agreement to pool their earnings and share equally in their joint accumulations, equity will protect the interests of each in such property."

In the case before us plaintiff, basing her cause of action in contract upon these precedents, maintains that the trial court erred in denying her a trial on the merits of her contention. Although that court did not specify the ground for its conclusion that plaintiff's contractual allegations stated no cause of action, defendant offers some four theories to sustain the ruling; we proceed to examine them.

Defendant first and principally relies on the contention that the alleged contract is so closely related to the supposed "immoral" character of the relationship between plaintiff and himself that the enforcement of the contract would violate public policy. He points to cases asserting that a contract between nonmarital partners is unenforceable if it is "involved in" an illicit relationship. * * * A review of the numerous California decisions concerning contracts between nonmarital partners, however, reveals that the courts have not employed such broad and uncertain standards to strike down contracts. The decisions instead disclose a narrower and more precise standard: a contract between nonmarital partners is unenforceable only *to the extent* that it *explicitly* rests upon the immoral and illicit consideration of meretricious sexual services.

In the first case to address this issue, *Trutalli v. Meraviglia* * * * the parties had lived together without marriage for 11 years and had raised two children. The man sued to quiet title to land he had purchased in his own name during this relationship; the woman defended by asserting an agreement to pool earnings and hold all property jointly. Rejecting the assertion of the illegality of the agreement, the court stated that "The fact that the parties to this action at the time they agreed to invest their earnings in property to be held jointly between them were living together in an unlawful relation, did not disqualify them from entering into a lawful agreement with each other, so long as such immoral relation was not made *a consideration* of their agreement." (Emphasis added.) * * *

In *Bridges v. Bridges, supra,* * * * both parties were in the process of obtaining divorces from their erstwhile respective spouses. The two parties agreed to live together, to share equally in property acquired, and to marry when their divorces became final. The man worked as a salesman and used his savings to purchase properties. The woman kept house, cared for seven children, three from each former marriage and one from the nonmarital relationship, and helped construct improvements on the properties. When they separated, without marrying, the court awarded the woman one-half the value of the property. Rejecting the man's contention that the contract was illegal, the court stated that: "Nowhere is it expressly testified to by anyone that there was anything in the agreement for the pooling of assets and the sharing of accumulations that contemplated meretricious relations as any part of the consideration or as any object of the agreement." * * *

* * * Numerous other cases have upheld enforcement of agreements between nonmarital partners in factual settings essentially indistinguishable from the present case.

* * * Although the past decisions hover over the issue in the somewhat wispy form of the figures of a Chagall painting, we can abstract from those decisions a clear and simple rule. The fact that a man and woman live together without marriage, and engage in a sexual relationship, does not in itself invalidate agreements between them relating to their earnings, property, or expenses. Neither is such an agreement invalid merely because the parties may have contemplated the creation or continuation of a nonmarital relationship when they entered into it. Agreements between nonmarital partners fail only to the extent that they rest upon a consideration of meretricious sexual services. Thus the rule asserted by defendant, that a contract fails if it is "involved in" or made "in contemplation" of a nonmarital relationship, cannot be reconciled with the decisions.

The three cases cited by defendant which have *declined* to enforce contracts between nonmarital partners involved consideration that *was* expressly founded upon an illicit sexual services. In *Hill v. Estate of Westbrook,* * * * the woman promised to keep house for the man, to live with him as man and wife, and to bear his children; the man promised to provide for her in his will, but died without doing so. Reversing a judgment for the woman based on the reasonable value of her services, the Court of Appeal stated that "the action is predicated upon a claim which seeks, among other things, the reasonable value of living with decedent in meretricious relationship and bearing him two children.... The law does not award compensation for living with a man as a concubine and bearing him children.... As the judgment is at least in part, for the value of the claimed services for which recovery cannot be had, it must be reversed." * * * Upon retrial, the trial court found that it could not sever the contract and place an independent value upon the legitimate services performed by claimant. We therefore affirmed a judgment for the estate. * * *

In the only other cited decision refusing to enforce a contract, * * * the contract "was based on the consideration that the parties live together as husband and wife." * * * Viewing the contract as calling for adultery, the court held it illegal.[6]

The decisions in the *Hill* and *Updeck* cases thus demonstrate that a contract between nonmarital partners, even if expressly made in contemplation of a common living arrangement, is invalid only if sexual acts form an inseparable part of the consideration for the agreement. In sum, a court will not enforce a contract for the pooling of property and earnings if it is explicitly and inseparably based upon services as a paramour. The Court of Appeal opinion in *Hill*, however, indicates that even if sexual services are part of the contractual consideration, any *severable* portion of the contract supported by independent consideration will still be enforced.

The principle that a contract between nonmarital partners will be enforced unless expressly and inseparably based upon an illicit consideration of sexual services not only represents the distillation of the decisional law, but also offers a far more precise and workable standard than that advocated by defendant.

* * * Similarly, in the present case a standard which inquires whether an agreement is "involved" in or "contemplates" a nonmarital relationship is vague and unworkable. Virtually all agreements between nonmarital partners can be said to be "involved" in some sense in the fact of their mutual sexual relationship, or to "contemplate" the existence of that relationship. Thus defendant's proposed standards, if taken literally, might invalidate all agreements between nonmarital partners, a result no one favors. Moreover, those standards offer no basis to distinguish between valid and invalid agreements. By looking not to such uncertain tests, but only to the consideration underlying the agreement, we provide the parties and the courts with a practical guide to determine when an agreement between nonmarital partners should be enforced.

* * * In summary, we base our opinion on the principle that adults who voluntarily live together and engage in sexual relations are nonetheless as competent as any other persons to contract respecting their earnings and property rights. Of course, they cannot lawfully contract to pay for the performance of sexual services, for such a contract is, in essence, an

---

6. Although not cited by defendant, the only California precedent which supports his position is *Heaps v. Toy* * * * In that case the woman promised to leave her job, to refrain from marriage, to be a companion to the man, and to make a permanent home for him; he agreed to support the woman and her child for life. The Court of Appeal held the agreement invalid as a contract in restraint of marriage (Civ. Code, § 1676) and, alternatively, as "contrary to good morals" (Civ. Code, § 1607). The opinion does not state that sexual relations formed any part of the consideration for the contract, nor explain how—unless the contract called for sexual relations—the woman's employment as a companion and housekeeper could be contrary to good morals.

The alternative holding in *Heaps v. Toy, supra,* finding the contract in that case contrary to good morals, is inconsistent with the numerous California decisions upholding contracts between nonmarital partners when such contracts are not founded upon an illicit consideration, and is therefore disapproved.

agreement for prostitution and unlawful for that reason. But they may agree to pool their earnings and to hold all property acquired during the relationship in accord with the law governing community property; conversely they may agree that each partner's earnings and the property acquired from those earnings remains the separate property of the earning partner.[10] So long as the agreement does not rest upon illicit meretricious consideration, the parties may order their economic affairs as they choose, and no policy precludes the courts from enforcing such agreements.

In the present instance, plaintiff alleges that the parties agreed to pool their earnings, that they contracted to share equally in all property acquired, and that defendant agreed to support plaintiff. The terms of the contract as alleged do not rest upon any unlawful consideration. We therefore conclude that the complaint furnishes a suitable basis upon which the trial court can render declaratory relief. * * * The trial court consequently erred in granting defendant's motion for judgment on the pleadings.

3. * * *

As we have noted, both causes of action in plaintiff's complaint allege an express contract; neither assert any basis for relief independent from the contract. In *In re Marriage of Cary*, * * * however, the Court of Appeal held that, in view of the policy of the Family Law Act, property accumulated by nonmarital partners in an actual family relationship should be divided equally. Upon examining the *Cary* opinion, the parties to the present case realized that plaintiff's alleged relationship with defendant might arguably support a cause of action independent of any express contract between the parties. The parties have therefore briefed and discussed the issue of the property rights of a nonmarital partner in the absence of an express contract. Although our conclusion that plaintiff's complaint states a cause of action based on an express contract alone compels us to reverse the judgment for defendant, resolution of the *Cary* issue will serve both to guide the parties upon retrial and to resolve a conflict presently manifest in published Court of Appeal decisions.

Both plaintiff and defendant stand in broad agreement that the law should be fashioned to carry out the reasonable expectations of the parties. Plaintiff, however, presents the following contentions: that the decisions prior to *Cary* rest upon implicit and erroneous notions of punishing a party for his or her guilt in entering into a nonmarital relationship, that such decisions result in an inequitable distribution of property accumulated during the relationship, and that *Cary* correctly held that the enactment of the Family Law Act in 1970 overturned those prior decisions. Defendant in response maintains that the prior decisions merely applied common law principles of contract and property to persons who have deliberately elected

---

10. A great variety of other arrangements are possible. The parties might keep their earnings and property separate, but agree to compensate one party for services which benefit the other. They may choose to pool only part of their earnings and property, to form a partnership or joint venture, or to hold property acquired as joint tenants or tenants in common, or agree to any other such arrangement. * * *

to remain outside the bounds of the community property system.[11] *Cary*, defendant contends, erred in holding that the Family Law Act vitiated the force of the prior precedents.

* * * This failure of the courts to recognize an action by a nonmarital partner based upon implied contract, or to grant an equitable remedy, contrasts with the judicial treatment of the putative spouse. Prior to the enactment of the Family Law Act, no statute granted rights to a putative spouse.[13] The courts accordingly fashioned a variety of remedies by judicial decision. Some cases permitted the putative spouse to recover half the property on a theory that the conduct of the parties implied an agreement of partnership or joint venture. * * * Others permitted the spouse to recover the reasonable value of rendered services, less the value of support received. * * * Finally, decisions affirmed the power of a court to employ equitable principles to achieve a fair division of property acquired during putative marriage. * * *

Thus in summary, the cases prior to *Cary* exhibited a schizophrenic inconsistency. By enforcing an express contract between nonmarital partners unless it rested upon an unlawful consideration, the courts applied a common law principle as to contracts. Yet the courts disregarded the common law principle that holds that implied contracts can arise from the conduct of the parties.[16] Refusing to enforce such contracts, the courts spoke of leaving the parties "in the position in which they had placed themselves" * * * just as if they were guilty parties *in pari delicto*.

11. We note that a deliberate decision to avoid the strictures of the community property system is not the only reason that couples live together without marriage. Some couples may wish to avoid the permanent commitment that marriage implies, yet be willing to share equally any property acquired during the relationship; others may fear the loss of pension, welfare, or tax benefits resulting from marriage * * * Others may engage in the relationship as a possible prelude to marriage. In lower socio-economic groups the difficulty and expense of dissolving a former marriage often leads couples to choose a nonmarital relationship; many unmarried couples may also incorrectly believe that the doctrine of common law marriage prevails in California, and thus that they are in fact married. Consequently we conclude that the mere fact that a couple have not participated in a valid marriage ceremony cannot serve as a basis for a court's inference that the couple intend to keep their earnings and property separate and independent; the parties' intention can only be ascertained by a more searching inquiry into the nature of their relationship.

13. The Family Law Act, in Civil Code section 4452, classifies property acquired during a putative marriage as "'quasi-marital property,'" and requires that such property be divided upon dissolution of the marriage in accord with Civil Code section 4800.

16. "Contracts may be express or implied. These terms however do not denote different kinds of contracts, but have reference to the evidence by which the agreement between the parties is shown. If the agreement is shown by the direct words of the parties, spoken or written, the contract is said to be an express one. But if such agreement can only be shown by the acts and conduct of the parties, interpreted in the light of the subject matter and of the surrounding circumstances, then the contract is an implied one." * * * Thus, as Justice Schauer observed in *Desny v. Wilder* * * * in a sense all contracts made in fact, as distinguished from quasi-contractual obligations, are express contracts, differing only in the manner in which the assent of the parties is expressed and proved. * * *

Justice Curtis noted this inconsistency in his dissenting opinion in *Vallera*, pointing out that "if an express agreement will be enforced, there is no legal or just reason why an implied agreement to share the property cannot be enforced." * * * And in *Keene v. Keene* * * * Justice Peters observed that if the man and woman "were not illegally living together . . . it would be a plain business relationship and a contract would be implied."

* * *

Still another inconsistency in the prior cases arises from their treatment of property accumulated through joint effort. To the extent that a partner had contributed *funds* or *property*, the cases held that the partner obtains a proportionate share in the acquisition, despite the lack of legal standing of the relationship. * * * Yet courts have refused to recognize just such an interest based upon the contribution of *services*. As Justice Curtis points out "Unless it can be argued that a woman's services as cook, housekeeper, and homemaker are valueless, it would seem logical that if, when she contributes money to the purchase of property, her interest will be protected, then when she contributes her services in the home, her interest in property accumulated should be protected." * * *

Thus as of 1973, the time of the filing of *In re Marriage of Cary* * * * the cases apparently held that a nonmarital partner who rendered services in the absence of express contract could assert no right to property acquired during the relationship. The facts of *Cary* demonstrated the unfairness of that rule.

Janet and Paul Cary had lived together, unmarried, for more than eight years. They held themselves out to friends and family as husband and wife, reared four children, purchased a home and other property, obtained credit, filed joint income tax returns, and otherwise conducted themselves as though they were married. Paul worked outside the home, and Janet generally cared for the house and children.

In 1971 Paul petitioned for "nullity of the marriage." Following a hearing on that petition, the trial court awarded Janet half the property acquired during the relationship, although all such property was traceable to Paul's earnings. The Court of Appeal affirmed the award.

Reviewing the prior decisions which had denied relief to the homemaking partner, the Court of Appeal reasoned that those decisions rested upon a policy of punishing persons guilty of cohabitation without marriage. The Family Law Act, the court observed, aimed to eliminate fault or guilt as a basis for dividing marital property. But once fault or guilt is excluded, the court reasoned, nothing distinguishes the property rights of a nonmarital "spouse" from those of a putative spouse. Since the latter is entitled to half the " 'quasi marital property' " (Civ. Code, § 4452), the Court of Appeal concluded that, giving effect to the policy of the Family Law Act, a nonmarital cohabitator should also be entitled to half the property accumulated during an "actual family relationship." * * *

* * *

* * * The argument that granting remedies to the nonmarital partners would discourage marriage must fail; as *Cary* pointed out, "with equal or greater force the point might be made that the pre–1970 rule was calculated to cause the income-producing partner to avoid marriage and thus retain the benefit of all of his or her accumulated earnings." * * * Although we recognize the well-established public policy to foster and promote the institution of marriage * * * perpetuation of judicial rules which result in an inequitable distribution of property accumulated during a nonmarital relationship is neither a just nor an effective way of carrying out that policy.

In summary, we believe that the prevalence of nonmarital relationships in modern society and the social acceptance of them, marks this as a time when our courts should by no means apply the doctrine of the unlawfulness of the so-called meretricious relationship to the instant case. As we have explained, the nonenforceability of agreements expressly providing for meretricious conduct rested upon the fact that such conduct, as the word suggests, pertained to and encompassed prostitution. To equate the nonmarital relationship of today to such a subject matter is to do violence to an accepted and wholly different practice.

We are aware that many young couples live together without the solemnization of marriage, in order to make sure that they can successfully later undertake marriage. This trial period, preliminary to marriage, serves as some assurance that the marriage will not subsequently end in dissolution to the harm of both parties. We are aware, as we have stated, of the pervasiveness of nonmarital relationships in other situations.

The mores of the society have indeed changed so radically in regard to cohabitation that we cannot impose a standard based on alleged moral considerations that have apparently been so widely abandoned by so many. Lest we be misunderstood, however, we take this occasion to point out that the structure of society itself largely depends upon the institution of marriage, and nothing we have said in this opinion should be taken to derogate from that institution. The joining of the man and woman in marriage is at once the most socially productive and individually fulfilling relationship that one can enjoy in the course of a lifetime.

We conclude that the judicial barriers that may stand in the way of a policy based upon the fulfillment of the reasonable expectations of the parties to a nonmarital relationship should be removed. As we have explained, the courts now hold that express agreements will be enforced unless they rest on an unlawful meretricious consideration. We add that in the absence of an express agreement, the courts may look to a variety of other remedies in order to protect the parties' lawful expectations.[24]

---

24. We do not seek to resurrect the doctrine of common law marriage, which was abolished in California by statute in 1895. * * * Thus we do not hold that plaintiff and defendant were "married," nor do we extend to plaintiff the rights which the Family Law Act grants valid or putative spouses; we hold only that she has the same rights to enforce contracts and to assert her equitable interest

The courts may inquire into the conduct of the parties to determine whether that conduct demonstrates an implied contract or implied agreement of partnership or joint venture * * * or some other tacit understanding between the parties. The courts may, when appropriate, employ principles of constructive trust * * * or resulting trust * * *. Finally, a nonmarital partner may recover in quantum meruit for the reasonable value of household services rendered less the reasonable value of support received if he can show that he rendered services with the expectation of monetary reward. * * *[25]

Since we have determined that plaintiff's complaint states a cause of action for breach of an express contract, and, as we have explained, can be amended to state a cause of action independent of allegations of express contract,[26] we must conclude that the trial court erred in granting defendant a judgment on the pleadings.

The judgment is reversed and the cause remanded for further proceedings consistent with the views expressed herein.[27]

■ MR. JUSTICE CLARK, concurring in part and dissenting in part.

The majority opinion properly permit recovery on the basis of either express or implied in fact agreement between the parties. These being the issues presented, their resolution requires reversal of the judgment. Here, the opinion should stop.

This court should not attempt to determine all anticipated rights, duties and remedies within every meretricious relationship—particularly in vague terms. Rather, these complex issues should be determined as each arises in a concrete case.

* * *

The general sweep of the majority opinion raises but fails to answer several questions. First, because the Legislature specifically excluded some parties to a meretricious relationship from the equal division rule of Civil Code section 4452, is this court now free to create an equal division rule? Second, upon termination of the relationship, is it equitable to impose the economic obligations of lawful spouses on meretricious parties when the latter may have rejected matrimony to avoid such obligations? Third, does not application of equitable principles—necessitating examination of the conduct of the parties—violate the spirit of the Family Law Act of 1969, designed to eliminate the bitterness and acrimony resulting from the

in property acquired through her effort as does any other unmarried person.

25. Our opinion does not preclude the evolution of additional equitable remedies to protect the expectations of the parties to a nonmarital relationship in cases in which existing remedies prove inadequate; the suitability of such remedies may be determined in later cases in light of the factual setting in which they arise.

26. We do not pass upon the question whether, in the absence of an express or implied contractual obligation, a party to a nonmarital relationship is entitled to support payments from the other party after the relationship terminates.

27. We wish to commend the parties and amici for the exceptional quality of the briefs and argument in this case.

former fault system in divorce? Fourth, will not application of equitable principles reimpose upon trial courts the unmanageable burden of arbitrating domestic disputes? Fifth, will not a quantum meruit system of compensation for services—discounted by benefits received—place meretricious spouses in a better position than lawful spouses? Sixth, if a quantum meruit system is to be allowed, does fairness not require inclusion of all services and all benefits regardless of how difficult the evaluation?

When the parties to a meretricious relationship show by express or implied in fact agreement they intend to create mutual obligations, the courts should enforce the agreement. However, in the absence of agreement, we should stop and consider the ramifications before creating economic obligations which may violate legislative intent, contravene the intention of the parties, and surely generate undue burdens on our trial courts.

By judicial overreach, the majority perform a nunc pro tunc marriage, dissolve it, and distribute its property on terms never contemplated by the parties, case law or the Legislature.

NOTES AND QUESTIONS

1. **The choice to marry.** Rational Choice Theory relies on the assumption that humans have goals and sets of hierarchically ordered preferences or "utilities." In making a choice between one behavior and another, humans will weigh the utility of the behavior against its costs, including the utility of alternate behaviors and the cost of selecting this behavior over another in terms of utility foregone. In an efficient transaction between two parties, the goal is presumably to increase utility for at least one party without sacrificing utility for either party. *See* MICHAEL ALLINGHAM, RATIONAL CHOICE (1999). How do the arguments of Rational Choice Theory apply to *Marvin v. Marvin*? What are the utilities and costs of opting not to marry and instead choosing to contract as the plaintiff in *Marvin* claims? Has utility been maximized in this transaction, given the foregone utility of the alternate behavior of marriage? *See* Margaret F. Brinig, *Unmarried Partners and the Legacy of* Marvin v. Marvin: *The Influence of* Marvin v. Marvin *on Housework during Marriage*, 76 NOTRE DAME L. REV. 1311 (2001). Which sex is most likely to receive the primary benefit of the express and implied contract rules? *See* Debra S. Betteridge, Note, *Inequality in Marital Liabilities: The Need for Equal Protection When Modifying the Necessaries Doctrine*, 17 U. MICH. J.L. REFORM 43 (1983). Are important differences in the transaction costs likely to arise from the enforcement of the express and implied contract theories?

2. **History and tradition?** Is the court ignoring legal, cultural, and religious arguments in deciding that parties who are eligible to marry but who choose not to should not be given the economic benefits of marriage? Does the court disregard the "history and tradition" of rewarding compliance with the social and legal norms of marriage? *See* Carol Weisbrod,

Gender-Based Analyses of World Religions and the Law: Universals and Particulars: A Comment on Women's Human Rights and Religious Marriage Contracts, 9 S. CAL. REV. L. & WOMEN'S STUD. 77 (1999). What is the role of cultural change and what framework of analysis did this court rely upon to assess the relevance of these changes to its decision in this case? How do the rationales employed by the court in *Marvin* relate to those employed in *Moore v. East Cleveland*?

3. **Bargaining.** How would you expect the pre-cohabitation bargaining dynamic to be affected by this decision? How do differences in gender correspond to differences in bargaining power? *See* Elizabeth G. Anderson, *Women and Contracts: No New Deal,* 88 MICH. L. REV. 1792 (1990). Is there any way for a couple to cohabit without automatically pooling their assets, short of writing an extremely unromantic contract explicitly separating their assets? *See* Jennifer K. Robbennolt & Monica Kirkpatrick Johnson, *Therapeutic Jurisprudence: Legal Planning for Unmarried Committed Partners: Empirical Lessons for a Preventive and Therapeutic Approach,* 41 ARIZ. L. REV. 417 (1999). How does the rule announced in *Marvin* affect the cultural and economic status of the parties? Furthermore, does this rule provide disincentives for parties who have a strong competitive position in the marriage market because of beauty, wealth, or social status to ever marry? *See* Amy L. Wax, *Bargaining in the Shadow of the Market: Is There a Future for Egalitarian Marriage?*, 84 VA. L. REV. 509 (1998).

4. **Meretricious consideration and prostitution.** The holding of *Marvin* is limited to the extent that it does not mandate the enforcement of contracts which are made expressly in consideration of sexual services. Given that the courts, as a rule, do not examine the adequacy of consideration, does the court's decision in *Marvin* open the door to legalized prostitution? If a prostitute were to say to a client, "Those pants don't look good on you, let's get them off," would that "fashion advice" qualify as separate consideration and thus render a contract between prostitute and client enforceable under *Marvin*? What is the implication of the court referring to the relationship of two unwed cohabitants as "meretricious," defined as "of, relating to, or befitting a prostitute; having the character of a prostitute" or "showily or superficially attractive but having in reality no value or integrity." OXFORD ENGLISH DICTIONARY (drafted. 2001), *available at* www.oed.com.

5. **Common law marriage.** From 1920 to 1930, Charlotte Fixel-Erlanger and Abraham Lincoln Erlanger lived together. Charlotte abandoned her career as an actress to support Abraham and take care of his house. Charlotte and Abraham never married and, when Abraham died in 1930, Charlotte was left out of his will. However, in 1932, after a three-month trial, Charlotte was given rights in Abraham's estate as his common-law wife. *In re Estate of Erlanger,* 145 Misc. 1, 259 N.Y.S. 610 (N.Y. Surr. Ct. 1932). Does *Marvin* do anything more than sanction adultery? Is *Marvin* the beginning of common-law polygamy?

6. **Additional reading.** For more information on the law of cohabitation, see generally Ariela R. Dubler, *Wifely Behavior: A Legal History of Acting*

Married, 100 COLUM. L. REV. 957 (2000); Katherine C. Gordon, Note, *The Necessity and Enforcement of Cohabitation Agreements: When Strings Will Attach and How to Prevent Them a State Survey*, 37 BRANDEIS L.J. 245 (1998/1999). For more information on associational rights and marriage, see generally Symposium, *Liberty and Marriage-Baehr and Beyond: Due Process in 1998*, 12 BYU J. PUB. L. 253 (1998); David A. Anderson, Note, *Jail, Jail, The Gang's All Here: Senate Crime Bill Section 521, The Criminal Street Gang Provision*, 36 B.C. L. REV. 527 (1995). For information on how *Marvin* extends to same sex couples, see Sharmila Roy Grossman, Comment, *The Illusory Rights of* Marvin v. Marvin *for the Same-Sex Couple versus the Preferable Canadian Alternative—*M. v. H., 38 CAL. W. L. REV. 547 (2002).

C. SAME-SEX COUPLES

Whorton v. Dillingham
248 Cal.Rptr. 405 (Cal. Ct. App. 1988).

■ JUDGE WORK delivered the opinion of the court.

Donnis G. Whorton appeals a judgment dismissing his action against Benjamin F. Dillingham III after the court sustained a demurrer without leave to amend. Whorton claims property rights based on an oral cohabiters' agreement with which he fully complied but which Dillingham breached after approximately seven years. The trial court found the pleadings showed the contract was unenforceable as expressly and inseparably based on sexual services. We conclude Whorton has alleged consideration for the purported contract substantially independent of sexual services, and reverse the judgment.

I

On appeal from a judgment of dismissal arising from the sustaining of a demurrer, we accept the facts pleaded in the complaint as true. *(Noguera v. N. Monterey County Unified Sch. Dist.* (1980) 106 Cal. App. 3d 64, 66, 164 Cal. Rptr. 808.)

The alleged facts include the following. At the time the parties began dating and entered into a homosexual relationship, Whorton was studying to obtain his Associate in Arts degree, intending to enroll in a four-year college and obtain a Bachelor of Arts degree. When the parties began living together in 1977, they orally agreed that Whorton's exclusive, full-time occupation was to be Dillingham's chauffeur, bodyguard, social and business secretary, partner and counselor in real estate investments, and to appear on his behalf when requested. Whorton was to render labor, skills, and personal services for the benefit of Dillingham's business and investment endeavors. Additionally, Whorton was to be Dillingham's constant companion, confidant, traveling and social companion, and lover, to terminate his schooling upon obtaining his Associate in Arts degree, and to make no investment without first consulting Dillingham.

In consideration of Whorton's promises, Dillingham was to give him a one-half equity interest in all real estate acquired in their joint names, and in all property thereafter acquired by Dillingham. Dillingham agreed to financially support Whorton for life, and to open bank accounts, maintain a positive balance in those accounts, grant Whorton invasionary powers to savings accounts held in Dillingham's name, and permit Whorton to charge on Dillingham's personal accounts. Dillingham was also to engage in a homosexual relationship with Whorton. Importantly, for the purpose of our analysis, the parties specifically agreed that any portion of the agreement found to be legally unenforceable was severable and the balance of the provisions would remain in full force and effect.

Whorton allegedly complied with all terms of the oral agreement until 1984 when Dillingham barred him from his premises. Dillingham now refuses to perform his part of the contract by giving Whorton the promised consideration for the business services rendered.

II

Adults who voluntarily live together and engage in sexual relations are competent to contract respecting their earnings and property rights. Such contracts will be enforced "unless expressly and inseparably based upon an illicit consideration of sexual services...." *(Marvin v. Marvin* (1976) 18 Cal. 3d 660, 672 [134 Cal. Rptr. 815, 557 P.2d 106].) One cannot lawfully contract to pay for the performance of sexual services since such an agreement is in essence a bargain for prostitution. (*Id.* at p. 674, 134 Cal.Rptr. 815, 557 P.2d 106, 134 Cal. Rptr. 815, 557 P.2d 106.)

A standard which inquires whether an agreement involves or contemplates a sexual relationship is vague and unworkable because virtually all agreements between nonmarital (and certainly, marital) cohabiters involve or contemplate a mutual sexual relationship. Further, a compact is not totally invalid merely because the parties may have contemplated creating or continuing a sexual relationship, but is invalid only to the extent it rests upon a consideration of sexual services. (*Id.* at pp. 670–671, 134 Cal. Rptr. 815, 557 P.2d 106.) Thus, "even if sexual services are part of the contractual consideration, any *severable* portion of the contract supported by independent consideration will still be enforced." (*Id.* at p. 672, 134 Cal. Rptr. 815, 557 P.2d 106.) For instance, contracting parties may make a variety of arrangements regarding their property rights—i.e., agree to pool their earnings and to hold all property in accord with the law governing community property, or to treat monetary earnings and property as separate property of the earning partner, or to keep property separate but compensate one party for services which benefit the other, or to pool only a part of their earnings and property, etc. (*Id.* at p. 674, fn. 10, 134 Cal. Rptr. 815, 557 P.2d 106.) "So long as the agreement does not rest upon illicit meretricious consideration, the parties may order their economic affairs as they choose, and no policy precludes the courts from enforcing such agreements." (*id.* at p. 674, 134 Cal. Rptr. 815, 557 P.2d 106.)

Regarding the issue of what constitutes adequate consideration, *Marvin* notes "[a] promise to perform homemaking services is, of course, a lawful and adequate consideration for a contract...." (*Id.* at p. 670, fn. 5, 134 Cal. Rptr. 815, 557 P.2d 106.) *Marvin* expressly rejects the argument that the partner seeking to enforce the contract must have contributed either property or services additional to ordinary homemaking services. (*Ibid.*)

In *Marvin*, the plaintiff alleged the parties orally agreed that while they lived together they would combine their efforts and earnings and would share equally all property accumulated as a result of their efforts, that they would hold themselves out to the general public as husband and wife, that plaintiff would render services as companion, homemaker, housekeeper and cook, that plaintiff would give up her career in order to provide these services full-time, and that in return defendant would provide for all of plaintiff's financial support for the rest of her life. (*Id.* at p. 666.) The court stated:

> "... plaintiff alleges that the parties agreed to pool their earnings, that they contracted to share equally in all property acquired, and that defendant agreed to support plaintiff. The terms of the contract as alleged do not rest upon any unlawful consideration." (*Id.* at pp. 674–675, 134 Cal. Rptr. 815, 557 P.2d 106.)

The holding in *Marvin* suggests the court determined that the contract before it did not *expressly* include sexual services as part of the consideration, and thus, it did not need to reach the issue of whether there were severable portions of the contract supported by independent consideration. The only reference to sexual services in *Marvin's* alleged facts was that the parties agreed to hold themselves out to the public as husband and wife, which apparently the court did not interpret as expressly indicating sexual services were part of the consideration. (See *Alderson v. Alderson* (1986) 180 Cal. App. 3d 450, 462–464, 225 Cal. Rptr. 610 [even though couple engaged in sexual relations and plaintiff perceived this as part of her "role," no evidence that implied agreement between the parties explicitly rested upon a consideration of meretricious sexual services].)

III

Unlike the facts of *Marvin*, here the parties' sexual relationship was an express, rather than implied, part of the consideration for their contract. The contract cannot be enforced to the extent it is dependent on sexual services for consideration, and the complaint does not state a cause of action to the extent it asks for damages from the termination of the sexual relationship.

The issue here is whether the sexual component of the consideration is severable from the remaining portions of the contract.[1] We reiterate the

---

1. Dillingham does not assert *Marvin* is inapplicable to same-sex partners, and we see no legal basis to make a distinction.

guiding language of *Marvin v. Marvin, supra* 18 Cal. 3d at page 672, 134 Cal. Rptr. 815, 557 P.2d 106 "[E]ven if sexual services are part of the contractual consideration, any *severable* portion of the contract supported by independent consideration will still be enforced." One test for determining the enforceability of a contract having both lawful and unlawful factors for consideration is stated in the Restatement Second of Contracts, section 183, "If the parties' performances can be apportioned into corresponding pairs of part performances so that the parts of each pair are properly regarded as agreed equivalents and one pair is not offensive to public policy, that portion of the agreement is enforceable by a party who did not engage in serious misconduct." (See also Civ. Code, § 1599: "Where a contract has several distinct objects, of which one at least is lawful, and one at least is unlawful, in whole or in part, the contract is void as to the latter and valid as to the rest.")

Tyranski v. Piggins (1973) 44 Mich. App. 570, 205 N.W.2d 595, 596–597, evaluates the issue of severability as follows:

> "Professor Corbin and the drafters of the Restatement of Contracts both write that while bargains in whole or in part in consideration of an illicit relationship are unenforceable, agreements between parties to such a relationship with respect to money or property will be enforced if the agreement is independent of the illicit relationship.
>
> "Neither these authorities nor the large body of case law in other jurisdictions ... articulate a guideline for determining when the consideration will be regarded as 'independent' and when it is so coupled with the meretricious acts that the agreement will not be enforced. A pattern does, however, emerge upon reading the cases.
>
> "Neither party to a meretricious relationship acquires, by reason of cohabitation alone, rights in the property accumulations of the other during the period of the relationship. But where there is an express agreement to accumulate or transfer property following a relationship of some permanence and *an additional consideration in the form of either money or of services, the courts tend to find an independent consideration.*
>
> "Thus, a plaintiff who can show an actual contribution of money, pursuant to an agreement to pool assets and share accumulations, will usually prevail. Services, such as cooking meals, laundering clothes, 'caring' for the decedent through sickness, have been found to be adequate and independent considerations in cases where there was an express agreement." (Fns. omitted; italics added.)[2]

---

2. In *Tyranski v. Piggins, supra* 205 N.W.2d at pages 596–597, the plaintiff cleaned the house, did the marketing, cooked the food, did the decedent's personal laundry, acted as his hostess, cared for him when he was sick, and contributed money towards the purchase of a house in which the unmarried

Of particular significance is the decision in *Latham v. Latham* (1976) 274 Ore. 421, 547 P.2d 144. In *Latham*, the court overruled a demurrer where complainant pleaded an agreement to live with defendant, to care for, and to furnish him with all the amenities of married life. The court recognized the alleged agreement specifically included the sexual services implicit in cohabitation. (*id.* 547 P.2d at p. 145.) Thus, as here, the sexual aspect of the agreement appeared on the face of the complaint. In overruling a demurrer based on public policy, the court stated it was not validating an agreement in which sexual intercourse was the only or primary consideration, but only one of the factors incident to the burdens and amenities of married life. (*id.* 547 P.2d at p. 147.)

Thus, the crux of our analysis is whether Whorton's complaint negates as a matter of law, a trier of fact finding he made contributions, apart from sexual services, which provided independent consideration for Dillingham's alleged promises pertaining to financial support and property rights. The services which plaintiff alleges he agreed to and did provide included being a chauffeur, bodyguard, secretary, and partner and counselor in real estate investments. If provided, these services are of monetary value, and the type for which one would expect to be compensated unless there is evidence of a contrary intent. Thus, they are properly characterized as consideration independent of the sexual aspect of the relationship. By way of comparison, such services as being a constant companion and confidant are not the type which are usually monetarily compensated nor considered to have a "value" for purposes of contract consideration, and, absent peculiar circumstances, would likely be considered so intertwined with the sexual relationship as to be inseparable. (Cf. *Walters v. Calderon* (1972) 25 Cal. App. 3d 863, 873, 102 Cal. Rptr. 89 [love and affection do not constitute valuable consideration necessary to support validity of contractual promise].)

We hold that Whorton—based on allegations he provided Dillingham with services of a chauffeur, bodyguard, secretary, and business partner—has stated a cause of action arising from a contract supported by consideration independent of sexual services. Further, by itemizing the mutual promises to engage in sexual activity, Whorton has not precluded the trier of fact from finding those promises are the consideration for each other and independent of the bargained for consideration for Whorton's employment.

We believe our holding does not conflict with that in *Jones v. Daly* (1981) 122 Cal. App. 3d 500, 508, 176 Cal. Rptr. 130, where services provided by the complaining homosexual partner were limited to "lover, companion, homemaker, traveling companion, housekeeper and cook...." The court there found the pleadings unequivocally established that plaintiff's rendition of sex and other services naturally flowing from sexual cohabitation was an inseparable part of the consideration for the so-called cohabitor's agreement. The court stated:

> plaintiff and the decedent resided. The court held it was proper to enforce the parties' express agreement to convey the house, which was held in the name of the decedent, to the plaintiff.

"According to the allegations of the complaint, the agreement provided that the parties would share equally the earnings and property accumulated as a result of their efforts while they lived together and that Daly would support plaintiff for the rest of his life. *Neither the property sharing nor the support provision of the agreement rests upon plaintiff's acting as Daly's traveling companion, housekeeper or cook as distinguished from acting as his lover.* The latter service forms an inseparable part of the consideration for the agreement and renders it unenforceable in its entirety." (*Jones v. Daly, supra* 122 Cal. App. 3d at p. 509, 176 Cal. Rptr. 130 italics added.)

Jones is factually different in that the complaining party did not allege contracting to provide services apart from those normally incident to the state of cohabitation itself. Further, Jones's complaint stated the agreement was premised on that they "would hold themselves out to the public at large as cohabiting mates...." (*Id.* at p. 505, 176 Cal. Rptr. 130.) In contrast, Whorton's complaint separately itemizes services contracted for as companion, chauffeur, bodyguard, secretary, partner and business counselor. These, except for companion, are significantly different than those household duties normally attendant to nonbusiness cohabitation and are those for which monetary compensation ordinarily would be anticipated.[5] Accepting Whorton's allegations as true, we cannot say as a matter of law any illegal portion of the contract is not severable so as to leave the balance valid and enforceable, especially where it is alleged the parties contemplated such a result when entering into their agreement.

IV

Statute of frauds

Dillingham asserts the oral agreement is invalid under the statute of frauds, requiring agreements not to be performed within one year or for the sale of an interest in real property to be written. (Civ. Code, § 1624, subds. (a) and (c).) In *Marvin v. Marvin, supra* 18 Cal. 3d at page 674, footnote 10, 134 Cal. Rptr. 815, 557 P.2d 106, the court noted in cases involving agreements between nonmarital partners, the majority of the agreements were oral and the courts have expressly rejected defenses grounded upon the statute of frauds.

Marvin cites *Cline v. Festersen* (1954) 128 Cal. App. 2d 380, 386, 275 P.2d 149. In *Cline*, the court rejected a statute of frauds argument on the basis of estoppel, reasoning that the nonmarital partner seeking to obtain her promised share of the property had trusted and worked for many years in reliance on the promise, and her partner had never repudiated the agreement. *Cline* relies on the principle that the doctrine of estoppel to

---

5. Most of the numerous cases cited in *Marvin* where nonmarital cohabiters' oral agreements to pool earnings were upheld involved contributions other than normal homemaking services. However, *Marvin* states homemaking services alone are lawful consideration. (*Marvin v. Marvin, supra* 18 Cal. 3d, p. 670, fn. 5; see also *Watkins v. Watkins* (1983) 143 Cal. App. 3d 651, 655, 192 Cal. Rptr. 54.)

assert the statute of frauds should be applied to prevent fraud and unconscionable injury that would result from refusal to enforce oral contracts in certain circumstances—i.e., after one party has been induced by the other seriously to change position in reliance on the contract, or when unjust enrichment would result if a party who has received the benefits of the other's performance were allowed to rely upon the statute. (*Id.* at p. 387, 275 P.2d 149).

Whorton alleges he stopped his education earlier than planned to assist Dillingham in his business ventures in exchange for promises of support and sharing of accumulated property. These facts are sufficient to estop Dillingham from raising the statute of frauds by way of demurrer to bar enforcement of the contract.

Statute of limitations

Dillingham meritlessly asserts the action is barred by the statute of limitations.

The general rule is that a cause of action for breach of contract accrues at the time of breach. (See 3 Witkin, Cal. Procedure (3d ed. 1985) Actions, § 375, p. 402.) A *Marvin*-type contract is breached when one partner terminates the relationship. (*Estate of Fincher* (1981) 119 Cal. App. 3d 343, 352, 174 Cal. Rptr. 18.) The statute of limitations for an action upon a contract not founded on a writing is two years. (Code Civ. Proc., § 339, subd. 1.) The complaint states the breach occurred "on or about the latter part of 1984." The complaint was filed in June 1986. The complaint on its face does not show the contract cause of action is barred by the statute of limitations.

For the same reasons, the complaint on its face does not show the three-year fraud limitation has expired.[6]

Additionally, a cause of action based on equitable grounds is not barred, for which the statute of limitations is four years. (*Nelson v. Nevel* (1984) 154 Cal. App. 3d 132, 140–141, 201 Cal. Rptr. 93; Code Civ. Proc., § 343; see generally *Marvin v. Marvin*, supra 18 Cal. 3d at p. 684, fn. 25, 134 Cal. Rptr. 815, 557 P.2d 106.)

Terminable at will

Finally, Dillingham contends that under *Labor Code section 2922*, the contract was terminable at will.[7] That section has no applicability to the issues here. This case does not involve an employment contract within the purview of the Labor Code, but rather a cohabiters' agreement regarding

---

6. The caption of the complaint does not refer to fraud, stating: "Complaint for damages for breach of express oral contract; breach of implied in fact contract; to impress a constructive trust; for declaratory relief; and for injunctive relief." However, the body of the complaint states facts in support of, and refers to, a fraud cause of action.

7. Labor Code section 2922 states: "An employment, having no specified term, may be terminated at the will of either party on notice to the other. Employment for a specified term means an employment for a period greater than one month."

how two nonmarital partners have agreed to regulate their economic affairs. Of course, one partner has a right to end the relationship, and the only issue is whether the facts support a monetary and/or property award to one of the partners.

* * *

Domestic Partner Ordinance Quashed: Atlanta to Appeal in Second Defeat

ATLANTA J. & CONST., Jan. 1, 1997 at D2.

■ BILL RANKIN

A Fulton County judge Tuesday struck down Atlanta's domestic partnership ordinance, the second try by the city to extend insurance benefits to live-in partners of city employees.

The city is attempting "to incorporate a 'family relationship' it has created, domestic partners, into the definition of a dependent," Superior Court Judge Isaac Jenrette said. This "is now inconsistent with state law."

The city will appeal the ruling, said Nick Gold, spokesman for Mayor Bill Campbell. Six city employees have signed up for the domestic partnership benefits, he said.

"Georgia law is clear—no matter how the city manipulates the language of its ordinance, domestic partners are neither 'family' nor 'dependents,'" said Atlanta lawyer David Reed, who argued the case for the conservative Southeastern Legal Foundation. "The taxpayers and families of Georgia have had enough of this nonsense."

Foundation lawyers have said the ordinance was an unconstitutional attempt by the city to encourage homosexuality and was a waste of taxpayers' money.

The foundation filed the lawsuit Sept. 10, the same day the U.S. Senate approved a bill denying recognition of same-sex marriages. The lawsuit challenged an ordinance passed by the City Council to authorize insurance benefits to the unmarried, live-in partners of city employees.

The new provision is a revised version of a 1993 city ordinance granting benefits for domestic partners. The Georgia Supreme Court struck down that ordinance in 1995, saying the city "exceeded its power ... by recognizing domestic partners as 'a family relationship.'" The court noted that the state uses several definitions for "dependents" when allowing insurance benefits and "domestic partners do not meet any of these statutory definitions."

On Tuesday, Jenrette said the city's new ordinance is fatally flawed for the same reasons.

Teresa Nelson, executive director of the Georgia chapter of the American Civil Liberties Union, expressed disappointment at the ruling.

"There are a number of individuals who have no dependents who are city employees, and they have shared the burden for the coverage of those employees who have dependents," Nelson said. "For those who are in partnership relationships, whether they are heterosexual or homosexual, their dependents have been denied that coverage. The city's ordinance is not a statement of morality. It is a statement of equality."

But Matthew Glavin, president of the Southeast Legal Foundation, said the City Council should realize this is not something it has the authority to do.

"If the City Council or the mayor want this kind of ordinance, they should march up the street to the state Legislature and convince it to change the law to include domestic partners," he said. "Unless they do that, anything they do will be unconstitutional, and we will stop them at every attempt."

NOTES AND QUESTIONS

1. Limits of consideration for homosexual couples. The Court in this case held that "Whorton—based on allegations he provided Dillingham with services of a chauffeur, bodyguard, secretary, and business partner—has stated a cause of action arising from a contract supported by consideration independent of sexual services." Of course, none of those services were provided in *Marvin*, though the services that were provided in *Marvin*—keeping house, functioning as a companion, etc. were also present in *Whorton*. Why, then, would the court choose to focus on these tasks to find consideration, and what are the implications of that decision? *See, e.g.,* Jones v. Daly, 176 Cal.Rptr. 130 (Cal. App. 1981).

2. Impact of *Whorton v. Dillingham*. Is *Whorton* a victory for homosexual rights? After all, the case is specifically premised on the idea of an express contract being enforced even though it was partially based on sexual consideration. Since this holding is completely orientation-neutral, why should *Whorton v. Dillingham* be considered significant? If it is a victory, how far does it extend? *See* Sharmila Roy Grossman, Comment, *The Illusory Rights of* Marvin v. Marvin *for the Same-Sex Couple Versus the Preferable Canadian Alternative*—M. v. H., 38 Cal. W. L. Rev. 547, 557 (2002). If homosexual couples are allowed to enter valid marriages in the state in which they reside, does the *Marvin v. Marvin* rationale apply?

3. Additional reading. For additional information on domestic partner ordinances, see generally, Jonathan Andrew Hein, *Caring for the Evolving American Family: Cohabiting Partners and Employer Sponsored Health Care*, 30 N.M. L. Rev. 19 (2000); Debbie Zielinski, Note, *Domestic Partnership Benefits: Why not Offer Them to Same-Sex Partners and Unmarried Opposite Sex Partners*, 13 J.L. & Health 281 (1998–99); William V. Vetter, *Restrictions on Equal Treatment of Unmarried Domestic Partners*, 5 B.U. Pub. Int. L.J. 1 (1995).

D. Sex Between Consenting Adults

Lawrence v. Texas

Supreme Court of the United States, 539 U.S. 558 (2003).

■ JUSTICE KENNEDY delivered the opinion of the Court.

Liberty protects the person from unwarranted government intrusions into a dwelling or other private places. In our tradition the State is not omnipresent in the home. And there are other spheres of our lives and existence, outside the home, where the State should not be a dominant presence. Freedom extends beyond spatial bounds. Liberty presumes an autonomy of self that includes freedom of thought, belief, expression, and certain intimate conduct. The instant case involves liberty of the person both in its spatial and more transcendent dimensions.

I

The question before the Court is the validity of a Texas statute making it a crime for two persons of the same sex to engage in certain intimate sexual conduct.

In Houston, Texas, officers of the Harris County Police Department were dispatched to a private residence in response to a reported weapons disturbance. They entered an apartment where one of the petitioners, John Geddes Lawrence, resided. The right of the police to enter does not seem to have been questioned. The officers observed Lawrence and another man, Tyron Garner, engaging in a sexual act. The two petitioners were arrested, held in custody over night, and charged and convicted before a Justice of the Peace * * * [of] "deviate sexual intercourse, namely anal sex, with a member of the same sex (man)." App. to Pet. for Cert. 127a, 139a. The applicable state law is Tex. Penal Code Ann. § 21.06(a) (2003). It provides: "A person commits an offense if he engages in deviate sexual intercourse with another individual of the same sex." * * *

* * *

We granted certiorari, 537 U.S. 1044 (2002), to consider three questions:

"1. Whether Petitioners' criminal convictions under the Texas 'Homosexual Conduct' law—which criminalizes sexual intimacy by same-sex couples, but not identical behavior by different-sex couples—violate the Fourteenth Amendment guarantee of equal protection of laws?

"2. Whether Petitioners' criminal convictions for adult consensual sexual intimacy in the home violate their vital interests in liberty and privacy protected by the Due Process Clause of the Fourteenth Amendment?

"3. Whether Bowers v. Hardwick, 478 U.S. 186 (1986), should be overruled?" Pet. for Cert. i.

* * *

II

We conclude the case should be resolved by determining whether the petitioners were free as adults to engage in the private conduct in the exercise of their liberty under the Due Process Clause of the Fourteenth Amendment to the Constitution. For this inquiry we deem it necessary to reconsider the Court's holding in *Bowers*.

There are broad statements of the substantive reach of liberty under the Due Process Clause in earlier cases, * * * but the most pertinent beginning point is our decision in *Griswold v. Connecticut*, 381 U.S. 479 (1965).

In *Griswold* the Court invalidated a state law prohibiting the use of drugs or devices of contraception and counseling or aiding and abetting the use of contraceptives. The Court described the protected interest as a right to privacy and placed emphasis on the marriage relation and the protected space of the marital bedroom. *Id.*, at 485.

After *Griswold* it was established that the right to make certain decisions regarding sexual conduct extends beyond the marital relationship. In *Eisenstadt v. Baird*, 405 U.S. 438 (1972), the Court invalidated a law prohibiting the distribution of contraceptives to unmarried persons. The case was decided under the Equal Protection Clause, *id.*, at 454; but with respect to unmarried persons, the Court went on to state the fundamental proposition that the law impaired the exercise of their personal rights, *ibid*. It quoted from the statement of the Court of Appeals finding the law to be in conflict with fundamental human rights, and it followed with this statement of its own:

> "It is true that in *Griswold* the right of privacy in question inhered in the marital relationship.... If the right of privacy means anything, it is the right of the *individual*, married or single, to be free from unwarranted governmental intrusion into matters so fundamentally affecting a person as the decision whether to bear or beget a child." *Id.*, at 453.

The opinions in *Griswold* and *Eisenstadt* were part of the background for the decision in *Roe v. Wade*, 410 U.S. 113 (1973). As is well known, the case involved a challenge to the Texas law prohibiting abortions, but the laws of other States were affected as well. Although the Court held the woman's rights were not absolute, her right to elect an abortion did have real and substantial protection as an exercise of her liberty under the Due Process Clause. The Court cited cases that protect spatial freedom and cases that go well beyond it. *Roe* recognized the right of a woman to make certain fundamental decisions affecting her destiny and confirmed once more that the protection of liberty under the Due Process Clause has a substantive dimension of fundamental significance in defining the rights of the person.

In *Carey v. Population Services Int'l*, 431 U.S. 678 (1977), the Court confronted a New York law forbidding sale or distribution of contraceptive devices to persons under 16 years of age. Although there was no single opinion for the Court, the law was invalidated. Both *Eisenstadt* and *Carey*, as well as the holding and rationale in *Roe*, confirmed that the reasoning of *Griswold* could not be confined to the protection of rights of married adults. This was the state of the law with respect to some of the most relevant cases when the Court considered *Bowers* v. *Hardwick*.

The facts in *Bowers* had some similarities to the instant case. A police officer, whose right to enter seems not to have been in question, observed Hardwick, in his own bedroom, engaging in intimate sexual conduct with another adult male. The conduct was in violation of a Georgia statute making it a criminal offense to engage in sodomy. One difference between the two cases is that the Georgia statute prohibited the conduct whether or not the participants were of the same sex, while the Texas statute, as we have seen, applies only to participants of the same sex. Hardwick was not prosecuted, but he brought an action in federal court to declare the state statute invalid. He alleged he was a practicing homosexual and that the criminal prohibition violated rights guaranteed to him by the Constitution. The Court, in an opinion by Justice White, sustained the Georgia law. * * *

The Court began its substantive discussion in *Bowers* as follows: "The issue presented is whether the Federal Constitution confers a fundamental right upon homosexuals to engage in sodomy and hence invalidates the laws of the many States that still make such conduct illegal and have done so for a very long time." *Id.*, at 190. That statement, we now conclude, discloses the Court's own failure to appreciate the extent of the liberty at stake. To say that the issue in *Bowers* was simply the right to engage in certain sexual conduct demeans the claim the individual put forward, just as it would demean a married couple were it to be said marriage is simply about the right to have sexual intercourse. The laws involved in *Bowers* and here are, to be sure, statutes that purport to do no more than prohibit a particular sexual act. Their penalties and purposes, though, have more far-reaching consequences, touching upon the most private human conduct, sexual behavior, and in the most private of places, the home. The statutes do seek to control a personal relationship that, whether or not entitled to formal recognition in the law, is within the liberty of persons to choose without being punished as criminals.

This, as a general rule, should counsel against attempts by the State, or a court, to define the meaning of the relationship or to set its boundaries absent injury to a person or abuse of an institution the law protects. It suffices for us to acknowledge that adults may choose to enter upon this relationship in the confines of their homes and their own private lives and still retain their dignity as free persons. When sexuality finds overt expression in intimate conduct with another person, the conduct can be but one element in a personal bond that is more enduring. The liberty protected by the Constitution allows homosexual persons the right to make this choice.

Having misapprehended the claim of liberty there presented to it, and thus stating the claim to be whether there is a fundamental right to engage in consensual sodomy, the *Bowers* Court said: "Proscriptions against that conduct have ancient roots." *Id.*, at 192. In academic writings, and in many of the scholarly *amicus* briefs filed to assist the Court in this case, there are fundamental criticisms of the historical premises relied upon by the majority and concurring opinions in *Bowers.* * * * We need not enter this debate in the attempt to reach a definitive historical judgment, but the following considerations counsel against adopting the definitive conclusions upon which *Bowers* placed such reliance.

At the outset it should be noted that there is no longstanding history in this country of laws directed at homosexual conduct as a distinct matter. Beginning in colonial times there were prohibitions of sodomy derived from the English criminal laws passed in the first instance by the Reformation Parliament of 1533. The English prohibition was understood to include relations between men and women as well as relations between men and men. See, *e.g., King v. Wiseman*, 92 Eng. Rep. 774, 775 (K. B. 1718) (interpreting "mankind" in Act of 1533 as including women and girls). Nineteenth-century commentators similarly read American sodomy, buggery, and crime-against-nature statutes as criminalizing certain relations between men and women and between men and men. See, *e.g.,* 2 J. Bishop, Criminal Law § 1028 (1858); 2 J. Chitty, Criminal Law 47–50 (5th Am. ed. 1847); R. Desty, A Compendium of American Criminal Law 143 (1882); J. May, The Law of Crimes § 203 (2d ed. 1893). The absence of legal prohibitions focusing on homosexual conduct may be explained in part by noting that according to some scholars the concept of the homosexual as a distinct category of person did not emerge until the late 19th century. See, *e.g.,* J. Katz, The Invention of Heterosexuality 10 (1995); J. D'Emilio & E. Freedman, Intimate Matters: A History of Sexuality in America 121 (2d ed. 1997) ("The modern terms *homosexuality* and *heterosexuality* do not apply to an era that had not yet articulated these distinctions"). Thus early American sodomy laws were not directed at homosexuals as such but instead sought to prohibit nonprocreative sexual activity more generally. This does not suggest approval of homosexual conduct. It does tend to show that this particular form of conduct was not thought of as a separate category from like conduct between heterosexual persons.

Laws prohibiting sodomy do not seem to have been enforced against consenting adults acting in private. A substantial number of sodomy prosecutions and convictions for which there are surviving records were for predatory acts against those who could not or did not consent, as in the case of a minor or the victim of an assault. As to these, one purpose for the prohibitions was to ensure there would be no lack of coverage if a predator committed a sexual assault that did not constitute rape as defined by the criminal law. Thus the model sodomy indictments presented in a 19th-century treatise, see 2 Chitty, *supra* at 49, addressed the predatory acts of an adult man against a minor girl or minor boy. Instead of targeting relations between consenting adults in private, 19th-century sodomy prosecutions typically involved relations between men and minor girls or minor boys, relations between adults involving force, relations between adults implicating disparity in status, or relations between men and animals.

* * * The longstanding criminal prohibition of homosexual sodomy upon which the *Bowers* decision placed such reliance is as consistent with a general condemnation of nonprocreative sex as it is with an established tradition of prosecuting acts because of their homosexual character.

The policy of punishing consenting adults for private acts was not much discussed in the early legal literature. We can infer that one reason for this was the very private nature of the conduct. Despite the absence of prosecutions, there may have been periods in which there was public criticism of homosexuals as such and an insistence that the criminal laws be enforced to discourage their practices. But far from possessing "ancient roots," *Bowers*, 478 U.S., at 192, American laws targeting same-sex couples did not develop until the last third of the 20th century. * * *

It was not until the 1970's that any State singled out same-sex relations for criminal prosecution, and only nine States have done so. * * * Post-*Bowers* even some of these States did not adhere to the policy of suppressing homosexual conduct. Over the course of the last decades, States with same-sex prohibitions have moved toward abolishing them. * * *

In summary, the historical grounds relied upon in *Bowers* are more complex than the majority opinion and the concurring opinion by Chief Justice Burger indicate. Their historical premises are not without doubt and, at the very least, are overstated.

It must be acknowledged, of course, that the Court in *Bowers* was making the broader point that for centuries there have been powerful voices to condemn homosexual conduct as immoral. The condemnation has been shaped by religious beliefs, conceptions of right and acceptable behavior, and respect for the traditional family. For many persons these are not trivial concerns but profound and deep convictions accepted as ethical and moral principles to which they aspire and which thus determine the course of their lives. These considerations do not answer the question before us, however. The issue is whether the majority may use the power of the State to enforce these views on the whole society through operation of the criminal law. "Our obligation is to define the liberty of all, not to mandate our own moral code." *Planned Parenthood of Southeastern Pa. v. Casey*, 505 U.S. 833, 850 (1992).

Chief Justice Burger joined the opinion for the Court in *Bowers* and further explained his views as follows: "Decisions of individuals relating to homosexual conduct have been subject to state intervention throughout the history of Western civilization. Condemnation of those practices is firmly rooted in Judeao–Christian moral and ethical standards." 478 U.S., at 196. As with Justice White's assumptions about history, scholarship casts some doubt on the sweeping nature of the statement by Chief Justice Burger as it pertains to private homosexual conduct between consenting adults. See, *e.g.,* Eskridge, Hardwick and Historiography, 1999 U. Ill. L. Rev. 631, 656. In all events we think that our laws and traditions in the past half century are of most relevance here. These references show an emerging awareness that liberty gives substantial protection to adult persons in deciding how to conduct their private lives in matters pertaining to sex. "History and tradition are the starting point but not in all cases the ending point of the substantive due process inquiry." *County of Sacramento v. Lewis*, 523 U.S. 833, 857 (1998) (KENNEDY, J., concurring).

* * *

In *Bowers* the Court referred to the fact that before 1961 all 50 States had outlawed sodomy, and that at the time of the Court's decision 24 States and the District of Columbia had sodomy laws. 478 U.S., at 192–193. Justice Powell pointed out that these prohibitions often were being ignored, however. Georgia, for instance, had not sought to enforce its law for decades. Id., at 197–198, n. 2 ("The history of nonenforcement suggests the moribund character today of laws criminalizing this type of private, consensual conduct").

The sweeping references by Chief Justice Burger to the history of Western civilization and to Judeo–Christian moral and ethical standards did not take account of other authorities pointing in an opposite direction. A committee advising the British Parliament recommended in 1957 repeal of laws punishing homosexual conduct. The Wolfenden Report: Report of the Committee on Homosexual Offenses and Prostitution (1963). Parliament enacted the substance of those recommendations 10 years later. Sexual Offences Act 1967, § 1.

Of even more importance, almost five years before *Bowers* was decided the European Court of Human Rights considered a case with parallels to *Bowers* and to today's case. * * * The court held that the laws proscribing [consenting homosexual] conduct were invalid under the European Convention on Human Rights. *Dudgeon v. United Kingdom*, 45 Eur. Ct. H. R. (1981) P52. Authoritative in all countries that are members of the Council of Europe (21 nations then, 45 nations now), the decision is at odds with the premise in *Bowers* that the claim put forward was insubstantial in our Western civilization.

In our own constitutional system the deficiencies in *Bowers* became even more apparent in the years following its announcement. The 25 States with laws prohibiting the relevant conduct referenced in the *Bowers* decision are reduced now to 13, of which 4 enforce their laws only against homosexual conduct. In those States where sodomy is still proscribed, whether for same-sex or heterosexual conduct, there is a pattern of nonenforcement with respect to consenting adults acting in private. The State of Texas admitted in 1994 that as of that date it had not prosecuted anyone under those circumstances. *State v. Morales*, 869 S.W.2d 941, 943 .

Two principal cases decided after *Bowers* cast its holding into even more doubt. In *Planned Parenthood of Southeastern Pa. v. Casey*, 505 U.S. 833 (1992), the Court reaffirmed the substantive force of the liberty protected by the Due Process Clause. The *Casey* decision again confirmed that our laws and tradition afford constitutional protection to personal decisions relating to marriage, procreation, contraception, family relationships, child rearing, and education. *Id.*, at 851. In explaining the respect the Constitution demands for the autonomy of the person in making these choices, we stated as follows:

> "These matters, involving the most intimate and personal choices a person may make in a lifetime, choices central to personal dignity and autonomy, are central to the liberty protected by the *Fourteenth Amendment*. At the heart of liberty is the right to define one's own concept of existence, of meaning, of the universe, and of the mystery of human life. Beliefs about these matters could not define the attributes of personhood were they formed under compulsion of the State." *Ibid.*

Persons in a homosexual relationship may seek autonomy for these purposes, just as heterosexual persons do. The decision in *Bowers* would deny them this right.

The second post-*Bowers* case of principal relevance is *Romer v. Evans*, 517 U.S. 620, (1996). There the Court struck down class-based legislation directed at homosexuals as a violation of the Equal Protection Clause. *Romer* invalidated an amendment to Colorado's constitution which named as a solitary class persons who were homosexuals, lesbians, or bisexual either by "orientation, conduct, practices or relationships," *id.*, at 624 (internal quotation marks omitted), and deprived them of protection under state antidiscrimination laws. We concluded that the provision was "born of animosity toward the class of persons affected" and further that it had no rational relation to a legitimate governmental purpose. *Id.*, at 634.

* * *

Equality of treatment and the due process right to demand respect for conduct protected by the substantive guarantee of liberty are linked in important respects, and a decision on the latter point advances both interests. If protected conduct is made criminal and the law which does so remains unexamined for its substantive validity, its stigma might remain even if it were not enforceable as drawn for equal protection reasons. When homosexual conduct is made criminal by the law of the State, that declaration in and of itself is an invitation to subject homosexual persons to discrimination both in the public and in the private spheres. The central holding of *Bowers* has been brought in question by this case, and it should be addressed. Its continuance as precedent demeans the lives of homosexual persons.

The stigma this criminal statute imposes, moreover, is not trivial. The offense, to be sure, is but a class C misdemeanor, a minor offense in the Texas legal system. Still, it remains a criminal offense with all that imports for the dignity of the persons charged. The petitioners will bear on their record the history of their criminal convictions. * * * We are advised that if Texas convicted an adult for private, consensual homosexual conduct under the statute here in question the convicted person would come within the [sexual-offender] registration laws of a least four States were he or she to be subject to their jurisdiction. * * * This underscores the consequential nature of the punishment and the state-sponsored condemnation attendant to the criminal prohibition. Furthermore, the Texas criminal conviction carries with it the other collateral consequences always following a conviction, such as notations on job application forms, to mention but one example.

* * *

* * * The right the petitioners seek in this case has been accepted as an integral part of human freedom in many other countries. There has been no showing that in this country the governmental interest in circumscribing personal choice is somehow more legitimate or urgent.

The doctrine of *stare decisis* is essential to the respect accorded to the judgments of the Court and to the stability of the law. It is not, however, an inexorable command. *Payne v. Tennessee*, 501 U.S. 808, 828 (1991) ("*Stare decisis* is not an inexorable command; rather, it 'is a principle of policy and not a mechanical formula of adherence to the latest decision'") (quoting *Helvering v. Hallock*, 309 U.S. 106, 119 (1940)). In *Casey* we noted that when a Court is asked to overrule a precedent recognizing a constitutional liberty interest, individual or societal reliance on the existence of that liberty cautions with particular strength against reversing course. 505 U.S., at 855–856; see also *id.*, at 844 ("Liberty finds no refuge in a jurisprudence of doubt"). The holding in *Bowers*, however, has not induced detrimental reliance comparable to some instances where recognized individual rights are involved. Indeed, there has been no individual or societal reliance on *Bowers* of the sort that could counsel against overturning its holding once there are compelling reasons to do so. *Bowers* itself causes uncertainty, for the precedents before and after its issuance contradict its central holding.

The rationale of *Bowers* does not withstand careful analysis. In his dissenting opinion in *Bowers* JUSTICE STEVENS came to these conclusions:

> "Our prior cases make two propositions abundantly clear. First, the fact that the governing majority in a State has traditionally viewed a particular practice as immoral is not a sufficient reason for upholding a law prohibiting the practice; neither history nor tradition could save a law prohibiting miscegenation from constitutional attack. Second, individual decisions by married persons, concerning the intimacies of their physical relationship, even when not intended to produce offspring, are a form of "liberty" protected by the Due Process Clause of the Fourteenth Amendment. Moreover, this protection extends to intimate choices by unmarried as well as married persons." 478 U.S., at 216 (footnotes and citations omitted).

JUSTICE STEVENS' analysis, in our view, should have been controlling in *Bowers* and should control here.

* * *

The present case does not involve minors. It does not involve persons who might be injured or coerced or who are situated in relationships where consent might not easily be refused. It does not involve public conduct or prostitution. It does not involve whether the government must give formal recognition to any relationship that homosexual persons seek to enter. The case does involve two adults who, with full and mutual consent from each other, engaged in sexual practices common to a homosexual lifestyle. The petitioners are entitled to respect for their private lives. The State cannot demean their existence or control their destiny by making their private sexual conduct a crime. Their right to liberty under the Due Process Clause gives them the full right to engage in their conduct without intervention of the government. "It is a promise of the Constitution that there is a realm of personal liberty which the government may not enter." *Casey, supra* at 847. The Texas statute furthers no legitimate state interest which can justify its intrusion into the personal and private life of the individual.

Had those who drew and ratified the Due Process Clauses of the Fifth Amendment or the Fourteenth Amendment known the components of liberty in its manifold possibilities, they might have been more specific. They did not presume to have this insight. They knew times can blind us to certain truths and later generations can see that laws once thought necessary and proper in fact serve only to oppress. As the Constitution endures, persons in every generation can invoke its principles in their own search for greater freedom.

[Reversed.]

It is so ordered.

■ JUSTICE O'CONNOR, concurring in the judgment.

The Court today overrules *Bowers v. Hardwick*, 478 U.S. 186 (1986). I joined *Bowers*, and do not join the Court in overruling it. Nevertheless, I agree with the Court that Texas' statute banning same-sex sodomy is unconstitutional. See Tex. Penal Code Ann. § 21.06 (2003). Rather than relying on the substantive component of the Fourteenth Amendment's Due Process Clause, as the Court does, I base my conclusion on the Fourteenth Amendment's Equal Protection Clause.

The Equal Protection Clause of the Fourteenth Amendment "is essentially a direction that all persons similarly situated should be treated alike." *Cleburne v. Cleburne Living Center, Inc.*, 473 U.S. 432, 439 (1985); see also *Plyler v. Doe*, 457 U.S. 202 (1982). Under our rational basis standard of review, "legislation is presumed to be valid and will be sustained if the classification drawn by the statute is rationally related to a legitimate state interest." *Cleburne v. Cleburne Living Center, supra* at 440; see also *Department of Agriculture v. Moreno*, 413 U.S. 528, 534 (1973); *Romer v. Evans*, 517 U.S. 620, 632–633 (1996); *Nordlinger v. Hahn*, 505 U.S. 1, 11–12 (1992).

* * * We have consistently held * * * that some objectives, such as "a bare ... desire to harm a politically unpopular group," are not legitimate state interests. *Department of Agriculture v. Moreno, supra* at 534. See also *Cleburne v. Cleburne Living Center, supra* at 446–447; *Romer v. Evans, supra* at 632. When a law exhibits such a desire to harm a politically unpopular group, we have applied a more searching form of rational basis review to strike down such laws under the Equal Protection Clause.

* * *

The statute at issue here makes sodomy a crime only if a person "engages in deviate sexual intercourse with another individual of the same sex." Tex. Penal Code Ann. § 21.06(a) (2003). Sodomy between opposite-sex partners, however, is not a crime in Texas. That is, Texas treats the same conduct differently based solely on the participants. Those harmed by this law are people who have a same-sex sexual orientation and thus are more likely to engage in behavior prohibited by § 21.06.

The Texas statute makes homosexuals unequal in the eyes of the law by making particular conduct—and only that conduct—subject to criminal sanction. * * * [W]hile the penalty imposed on petitioners in this case was relatively minor, the consequences of conviction are not. As the Court notes, see *ante*, at 15, petitioners' convictions, if upheld, would disqualify them from or restrict their ability to engage in a variety of professions, including medicine, athletic training, and interior design. * * * Indeed, were petitioners to move to one of four States, their convictions would require them to register as sex offenders to local law enforcement. * * *

And the effect of Texas' sodomy law is not just limited to the threat of prosecution or consequence of conviction. Texas' sodomy law brands all homosexuals as criminals, thereby making it more difficult for homosexuals to be treated in the same manner as everyone else. Indeed, Texas itself has previously acknowledged the collateral effects of the law, stipulating in a prior challenge to this action that the law "legally sanctions discrimination against [homosexuals] in a variety of ways unrelated to the criminal law," including in the areas of "employment, family issues, and housing." *State v. Morales*, 826 S.W.2d 201, 203 (Tex. App. 1992).

Texas attempts to justify its law, and the effects of the law, by arguing that the statute satisfies rational basis review because it furthers the legitimate governmental interest of the promotion of morality. * * *

This case raises a different issue than *Bowers*: whether, under the *Equal Protection Clause*, moral disapproval is a legitimate state interest to justify by itself a statute that bans homosexual sodomy, but not heterosexual sodomy. It is not. Moral disapproval of this group, like a bare desire to harm the group, is an interest that is insufficient to satisfy rational basis review under the Equal Protection Clause. See, *e.g., Department of Agriculture v. Moreno, supra* at 534; *Romer v. Evans*, 517 U.S., at 634–635. Indeed, we have never held that moral disapproval, without any other asserted state interest, is a sufficient rationale under the Equal Protection Clause to justify a law that discriminates among groups of persons.

* * *

Whether a sodomy law that is neutral both in effect and application, see *Yick Wo v. Hopkins*, 118 U.S. 356, 30 L. Ed. 220, 6 S. Ct. 1064 (1886), would violate the substantive component of the Due Process Clause is an issue that need not be decided today. I am confident, however, that so long as the Equal Protection Clause requires a sodomy law to apply equally to the private consensual conduct of homosexuals and heterosexuals alike, such a law would not long stand in our democratic society. * * *

A law branding one class of persons as criminal solely based on the State's moral disapproval of that class and the conduct associated with that class runs contrary to the values of the Constitution and the Equal Protection Clause, under any standard of review. I therefore concur in the Court's judgment that Texas' sodomy law banning "deviate sexual intercourse" between consenting adults of the same sex, but not between consenting adults of different sexes, is unconstitutional.

■ JUSTICE SCALIA, with whom THE CHIEF JUSTICE and JUSTICE THOMAS join, dissenting.

"Liberty finds no refuge in a jurisprudence of doubt." *Planned Parenthood of Southeastern Pa. v. Casey*, 505 U.S. 833, 844, 120 L. Ed. 2d 674, 112 S. Ct. 2791 (1992). That was the Court's sententious response, barely more than a decade ago, to those seeking to overrule *Roe v. Wade*, 410 U.S. 113, 35 L. Ed. 2d 147, 93 S. Ct. 705 (1973). The Court's response today, to those who have engaged in a 17-year crusade to overrule *Bowers v. Hardwick*, 478 U.S. 186, 92 L. Ed. 2d 140, 106 S. Ct. 2841 (1986), is very different. The need for stability and certainty presents no barrier.

Most of the rest of today's opinion has no relevance to its actual holding—that the Texas statute "furthers no legitimate state interest which can justify" its application to petitioners under rational-basis review. *Ante*, at 18 (overruling *Bowers* to the extent it sustained Georgia's anti-sodomy statute under the rational-basis test). Though there is discussion of "fundamental propositions," *ante*, at 4, and "fundamental decisions," *ibid.* nowhere does the Court's opinion declare that homosexual sodomy is a "fundamental right" under the Due Process Clause; nor does it subject the Texas law to the standard of review that would be appropriate (strict scrutiny) if homosexual sodomy *were* a "fundamental right." Thus, while overruling the *outcome* of *Bowers*, the Court leaves strangely untouched its central legal conclusion: "Respondent would have us announce ... a fundamental right to engage in homosexual sodomy. This we are quite unwilling to do." 478 U.S., at 191. Instead the Court simply describes petitioners' conduct as "an exercise of their liberty"—which it undoubtedly is—and proceeds to apply an unheard-of form of rational-basis review that will have far-reaching implications beyond this case. *Ante*, at 3.

* * *

Today's approach to *stare decisis* invites us to overrule an erroneously decided precedent (including an "intensely divisive" decision) *if:* (1) its foundations have been "eroded" by subsequent decisions, *ante*, at 15; (2) it has been subject to "substantial and continuing" criticism, *ibid.*; and (3) it has not induced "individual or societal reliance" that counsels against overturning, *ante*, at 16. The problem is that *Roe* itself—which today's majority surely has no disposition to overrule—satisfies these conditions to at least the same degree as *Bowers*.

* * *

I do not quarrel with the Court's claim that *Romer v. Evans*, 517 U.S. 620, 134 L. Ed. 2d 855, 116 S. Ct. 1620 (1996), "eroded" the "foundations" of *Bowers*' rational-basis holding. See *Romer, supra* at 640–643 (SCALIA, J., dissenting). But *Roe* and *Casey* have been equally "eroded" by *Washington v. Glucksberg*, 521 U.S. 702, 721, 138 L. Ed. 2d 772, 117 S. Ct. 2258, 117 S. Ct. 2302 (1997), which held that *only* fundamental rights which are " 'deeply rooted in this Nation's history and tradition' " qualify for anything other than rational basis scrutiny under the doctrine of "substantive due process." *Roe* and *Casey*, of course, subjected the restriction of abortion to heightened scrutiny without even attempting to establish that the freedom to abort *was* rooted in this Nation's tradition.

* * * *Bowers*, the Court says, has been subject to "substantial and continuing [criticism], disapproving of its reasoning in all respects, not just as to its historical assumptions." *Ante*, at 15. * * * Of course, *Roe* too (and by extension *Casey*) had been (and still is) subject to unrelenting criticism, including criticism from the two commentators cited by the Court today. See Fried, *supra* at 75 ("Roe was a prime example of twisted judging"); Posner, *supra* at 337 ("[The Court's] opinion in *Roe* . . . fails to measure up to professional expectations regarding judicial opinions"); Posner, Judicial Opinion Writing, 62 U. Chi. L. Rev. 1421, 1434 (1995) (describing the opinion in *Roe* as an "embarrassing performanc[e]").

* * * It seems to me that the "societal reliance" on the principles confirmed in *Bowers* and discarded today has been overwhelming. Countless judicial decisions and legislative enactments have relied on the ancient proposition that a governing majority's belief that certain sexual behavior is "immoral and unacceptable" constitutes a rational basis for regulation. * * * State laws against bigamy, same-sex marriage, adult incest, prostitution, masturbation, adultery, fornication, bestiality, and obscenity are likewise sustainable only in light of *Bowers*' validation of laws based on moral choices. Every single one of these laws is called into question by today's decision; the Court makes no effort to cabin the scope of its decision to exclude them from its holding. * * * The impossibility of distinguishing homosexuality from other traditional "morals" offenses is precisely why *Bowers* rejected the rational-basis challenge. "The law," it said, "is constantly based on notions of morality, and if all laws representing essentially moral choices are to be invalidated under the Due Process Clause, the courts will be very busy indeed." 478 U.S., at 196.

What a massive disruption of the current social order, therefore, the overruling of *Bowers* entails. * * *

Texas Penal Code Ann. § 21.06(a) (2003) undoubtedly imposes constraints on liberty. So do laws prohibiting prostitution, recreational use of heroin, and, for that matter, working more than 60 hours per week in a bakery. But there is no right to "liberty" under the Due Process Clause, though today's opinion repeatedly makes that claim. * * * The Fourteenth Amendment *expressly allows* States to deprive their citizens of "liberty," *so long as "due process of law" is provided[.]*

Our opinions applying the doctrine known as "substantive due process" hold that the Due Process Clause prohibits States from infringing *fundamental* liberty interests, unless the infringement is narrowly tailored to serve a compelling state interest. *Washington v. Glucksberg*, 521 U.S., at 721. We have held repeatedly, in cases the Court today does not overrule, that *only* fundamental rights qualify for this so-called "heightened scrutiny" protection—that is, rights which are " 'deeply rooted in this Nation's history and tradition,' " *ibid.* See *Reno v. Flores*, 507 U.S. 292, 303 (1993) * * * *United States v. Salerno*, 481 U.S. 739, 751 (1987) * * * See also *Michael H. v. Gerald D.*, 491 U.S. 110, 122 (1989) * * * *Moore v. East Cleveland*, 431 U.S. 494, 503 (1977) (plurality opinion); *Meyer v. Nebraska*, 262 U.S. 390, 399 (1923) * * * All other liberty interests may be abridged or abrogated pursuant to a validly enacted state law if that law is rationally related to a legitimate state interest.

Bowers held * * * that criminal prohibitions of homosexual sodomy are not subject to heightened scrutiny because they do not implicate a "fundamental right" under the Due Process Clause, 478 U.S., at 191–194. * * *

The Court today does not overrule this holding. Not once does it describe homosexual sodomy as a "fundamental right" or a "fundamental liberty interest," nor does it subject the Texas statute to strict scrutiny. Instead, having failed to establish that the right to homosexual sodomy is " 'deeply rooted in this Nation's history and tradition,' " the Court concludes that the application of Texas's statute to petitioners' conduct fails the rational-basis test, and overrules *Bowers*' holding to the contrary, see *id.*, at 196. * * *

* * *

It is (as *Bowers* recognized) entirely irrelevant whether the laws in our long national tradition criminalizing homosexual sodomy were "directed at homosexual conduct as a distinct matter." *Ante*, at 7. Whether homosexual sodomy was prohibited by a law targeted at same-sex sexual relations or by a more general law prohibiting both homosexual and heterosexual sodomy, the only relevant point is that it *was* criminalized—which suffices to establish that homosexual sodomy is not a right "deeply rooted in our Nation's history and tradition." The Court today agrees that homosexual sodomy was criminalized and thus does not dispute the facts on which *Bowers actually* relied.

* * * [T]he Court makes the claim, again unsupported by any citations, that "[l]aws prohibiting sodomy do not seem to have been enforced against consenting adults acting in private." *Ante*, at 8. The key qualifier here is "acting in private"—since the Court admits that sodomy laws *were* enforced against consenting adults (although the Court contends that prosecutions were "infrequent," *ante*, at 9). I do not know what "acting in private" means; surely consensual sodomy, like heterosexual intercourse, is rarely performed on stage. If all the Court means by "acting in private" is "on private premises, with the doors closed and windows covered," it is entirely unsurprising that evidence of enforcement would be hard to come by. (Imagine the circumstances that would enable a search warrant to be obtained for a residence on the ground that there was probable cause to believe that consensual sodomy was then and there occurring.) Surely that lack of evidence would not sustain the proposition that consensual sodomy on private premises with the doors closed and windows covered was regarded as a "fundamental right," even though all other consensual sodomy was criminalized. * * *

* * *

[A]n "emerging awareness" is by definition not "deeply rooted in this Nation's history and traditions," as we have said "fundamental right" status requires. Constitutional entitlements do not spring into existence because some States choose to lessen or eliminate criminal sanctions on certain behavior. Much less do they spring into existence, as the Court seems to believe, because *foreign nations* decriminalize conduct. The *Bowers* majority opinion *never* relied on "values we share with a wider civilization," *ante*, at 16, but rather rejected the claimed right to sodomy on the ground that such a right was not " 'deeply rooted in *this Nation's* history and tradition,' " 478 U.S., at 193–194 (emphasis added). * * *

* * *

The Texas statute undeniably seeks to further the belief of its citizens that certain forms of sexual behavior are "immoral and unacceptable," *Bowers, supra* at 196—the same interest furthered by criminal laws against fornication, bigamy, adultery, adult incest, bestiality, and obscenity. *Bowers* held that this *was* a legitimate state interest. The Court today reaches the opposite conclusion. The Texas statute, it says, "furthers *no legitimate state interest* which can justify its intrusion into the personal and private life of the individual," *ante*, at 18 (emphasis added). * * * This effectively decrees the end of all morals legislation. If, as the Court asserts, the promotion of majoritarian sexual morality is not even a *legitimate* state interest, none of the above-mentioned laws can survive rational-basis review.

* * *

[As for JUSTICE O'Connor's Equal Protection Clause analysis, m]en and women, heterosexuals and homosexuals, are all subject to [the statute's] prohibition of deviate sexual intercourse with someone of the same sex. To be sure, § 21.06 does distinguish between the sexes insofar as concerns the partner with whom the sexual acts are performed: men can violate the law only with other men, and women only with other women. But this cannot itself be a denial of equal protection, since it is precisely the same distinction regarding partner that is drawn in state laws prohibiting marriage with someone of the same sex while permitting marriage with someone of the opposite sex.

* * * A racially discriminatory purpose is always sufficient to subject a law to strict scrutiny, even a facially neutral law that makes no mention of race. See *Washington v. Davis*, 426 U.S. 229, 241–242 (1976). No purpose to discriminate against men or women as a class can be gleaned from the Texas law, so rational-basis review applies. That review is readily satisfied here by the same rational basis that satisfied it in *Bowers*—society's belief that certain forms of sexual behavior are "immoral and unacceptable," 478 U.S., at 196. This is the same justification that supports many other laws regulating sexual behavior that make a distinction based upon the identity of the partner—for example, laws against adultery, fornication, and adult incest, and laws refusing to recognize homosexual marriage.

JUSTICE O'CONNOR argues that the discrimination in this law which must be justified is not its discrimination with regard to the sex of the partner but its discrimination with regard to the sexual proclivity of the principal actor.

"While it is true that the law applies only to conduct, the conduct targeted by this law is conduct that is closely correlated with being homosexual. Under such circumstances, Texas' sodomy law is targeted at more than conduct. It is instead directed toward gay persons as a class." *Ante*, at 5.

Of course the same could be said of any law. A law against public nudity targets "the conduct that is closely correlated with being a nudist," and hence "is targeted at more than conduct"; it is "directed toward nudists as a class." But be that as it may. Even if the Texas law *does* deny equal protection to "homosexuals as a class," that denial *still* does not need to be justified by anything more than a rational basis, which our cases show is satisfied by the enforcement of traditional notions of sexual morality.

* * *

Today's opinion is the product of a Court, which is the product of a law-profession culture, that has largely signed on to the so-called homosexual agenda, by which I mean the agenda promoted by some homosexual activists directed at eliminating the moral opprobrium that has traditionally attached to homosexual conduct. * * *

One of the most revealing statements in today's opinion is the Court's grim warning that the criminalization of homosexual conduct is "an invitation to subject homosexual persons to discrimination both in the public and in the private spheres." *Ante*, at 14. It is clear from this that the Court has taken sides in the culture war, departing from its role of assuring, as neutral observer, that the democratic rules of engagement are observed. Many Americans do not want persons who openly engage in homosexual conduct as partners in their business, as scoutmasters for their children, as teachers in their children's schools, or as boarders in their home. They view this as protecting themselves and their families from a lifestyle that they believe to be immoral and destructive. The Court views it as "discrimination" which it is the function of our judgments to deter. So imbued is the Court with the law profession's anti-anti-homosexual culture, that it is seemingly unaware that the attitudes of that culture are not obviously "mainstream[.]" * * *

* * * [P]ersuading one's fellow citizens is one thing, and imposing one's views in absence of democratic majority will is something else. I would no more *require* a State to criminalize homosexual acts—or, for that matter, display *any* moral disapprobation of them—than I would *forbid* it to do so. What Texas has chosen to do is well within the range of traditional democratic action, and its hand should not be stayed through the invention of a brand-new "constitutional right" by a Court that is impatient of democratic change. It is indeed true that "later generations can see that laws once thought necessary and proper in fact serve only to oppress," *ante*, at 18; and when that happens, later generations can repeal those laws. But it is the premise of our system that those judgments are to be made by the people, and not imposed by a governing caste that knows best.

* * *

■ JUSTICE THOMAS, dissenting.

I join JUSTICE SCALIA'S dissenting opinion. I write separately to note that the law before the Court today "is ... uncommonly silly." *Griswold v. Connecticut*, 381 U.S. 479, 527 (1965) (Stewart, J., dissenting). If I were a member of the Texas Legislature, I would vote to repeal it. Punishing someone for expressing his sexual preference through noncommercial consensual conduct with another adult does not appear to be a worthy way to expend valuable law enforcement resources.

Notwithstanding this, I recognize that as a member of this Court I am not empowered to help petitioners and others similarly situated. My duty, rather, is to "decide cases 'agreeably to the Constitution and laws of the United States.'" *Id.*, at 530. And, just like Justice Stewart, I "can find [neither in the Bill of Rights nor any other part of the Constitution a] general right of privacy," *ibid.*, or as the Court terms it today, the "liberty of the person both in its spatial and more transcendent dimensions," *ante*, at 1.

NOTES AND QUESTIONS

1. ***Moore* in context of *Lawrence*.** The plurality opinion in *Moore* relied on the primary place that the extended family has traditionally occupied in United States history. This reasoning is similar to that used in *Bowers v. Hardwick*, 478 U.S. 186 (1986), where a history and tradition of intolerance for homosexual conduct was used to support an anti-sodomy law. However, now that *Lawrence v. Texas*, 539 U.S. 558 (2003) has overruled *Bowers*, is the history and tradition argument which was invoked by the plurality in *Moore* on shaky ground? See David M. Wagner, *Hints, Not Holdings: Use of Precedent in* Lawrence v. Texas, 18 BYU J. PUB. L. 681 (2004); Susan

Austin Blazier, Note, *The Irrational Use of Rational Basis Review in Lawrence v. Texas*, 26 CAMPBELL L. REV. 21 (2004).

2. Justice O'Connor's concurrence.

   a. Domestic partners and O'Connor's concurrence in *Lawrence*. In her concurring opinion in *Lawrence v. Texas*, 539 U.S. 558 (2003) (O'Connor, J., concurring), Justice O'Connor notes that the conduct targeted by the Texas sodomy law was "closely correlated with being homosexual," and that this contributed to her decision that that law violated the equal protection clause. Under that rationale, it would seem that the state law that forbids recognition of domestic partners as dependants would also violate the equal protection clause, given that, as long as homosexuals are not allowed to marry, they will be forced into domestic partnership arrangements. Does this mean, under O'Connor's equal protection argument, that the state would be required to extend positive benefits (like domestic partner benefits) to homosexuals if those benefits are extended to heterosexuals?

   In May 1992, MCA Corporation announced that it would provide health benefits to employees' same-sex partners, but not heterosexual domestic partners. William V. Vetter, *Restrictions on Equal Treatment of Unmarried Domestic Partners*, 5 B.U. PUB. INT. L.J. 1, 3 (1995). Is this asymmetric treatment of same-sex and opposite domestic partnerships discriminatory, or is some level of asymmetry necessary in order to compensate for the asymmetry in marriage laws between same-sex and opposite-sex couples?

   b. Heterosexual domestic partnership. Domestic partnership arrangements are certainly not limited to same-sex couples. Would the "correlated with" approach O'Conner uses to equal protection sweep too broadly and end up refuting legislative intent by requiring domestic partner benefits for all cohabiting couples? However, if you reject a "correlated with" approach to equal protection, what would prevent a legislature from enacting a law which fell much more heavily on some disfavored group but had an ostensibly neutral purpose, like promoting marriage?

3. Morality as a state interest. Justice Scalia's dissent is longer than the opinion of the court itself, yet in eleven pages of dissent, he devotes only two paragraphs to the majority opinion, and those two paragraphs merely observe that no other society has decreed that morality is a sufficient basis for the enactment of a law. Does this mean that Scalia believes that enforcing public morality should be considered a legitimate state interest? *See* TracyLee Schimelfenig, Note, *Recognition of the Rights of Homosexuals: Implications of* Lawrence v. Texas, 40 CAL. W. L. REV. 149, 158–59 (2003). If that is the case, under Scalia's philosophy, can any law *ever* fail a rational basis review, since, presumably, the public elected the legislature and the legislature writes laws that are consistent with the social norms of the society that elected them? In other words, if morality alone is a legitimate state interest, is there anything left of due process?

4. Silly laws and legitimate state interests. Justice Thomas' dissent begins by stating that the Texas anti-sodomy law is "uncommonly silly." Given that Justice Thomas does not believe that enforcing this law is a "worthy" use of government resources, how can he support the idea that it survives a due process attack for lacking a rational relation to a legitimate state interest? Is Thomas' version of due process something closer to "a silly relation to an unworthy government interest?" See Kris Franklin, *Homophobia and the "Matthew Shepard Effect": In* Lawrence v. Texas, 48 N.Y.L. Sch. L. Rev. 657, 667 at n.51 (2004).

5. **The limits of *Lawrence*.** The holding of the court in this case is that "[t]he Texas statute furthers no legitimate state interest which can justify its intrusion into the personal and private life of the individual." However, this holding raises an interesting question: is the Texas statute unconstitutional because it furthers no legitimate state interest, or because it intrudes into the private life of the individual? If the former is true, then it would seem that all morals-based legislation is illegitimate and, unless it has some ancillary benefits, will most likely be struck down. If the latter is the case, *Lawrence* is a much more limited victory for gay rights, essentially stating that individuals have the right to be homosexual in their bedrooms, but nowhere else. See Wagner, *supra* at 236, n.1.

6. **Response of the church to changing social norms.** In response to the decision in *Lawrence v. Texas*, televangelist Pat Robertson issued a national call for Christians to pray for the retirement of Justices O'Connor, Stevens, and Ginsburg. Interview by Paula Zahn with Pat Robertson, *Pat Robertson: Pray For Justices to Retire*, July 17, 2003, *available at* http://www.cnn.com/2003/LAW/07/17/cnna.robertson/. Additionally, the Catholic Church has issued a statement condemning homosexual marriage. Victor L. Simpson, *Vatican Issues Offensive on Gay Marriages*, Associated Press, July 28, 2003.

7. **Additional reading.** For additional information on morality laws, see generally Peter M. Cicchino, *Reason and the Rule of Law: Should Bare Assertions of "Public Morality" Qualify as Legitimate Government Interests for the Purposes of Equal Protection Review?*, 87 Geo. L.J. 139 (1998); Steve Sheppard, *The State Interest in the Good Citizen: Constitutional Balance Between the Citizen and the Perfectionist State*, 45 Hastings L.J. 969 (1994). For a look at existing methods of gaining state recognition of same-sex marriages, see Phyllis Randolph Frye & Alyson Dodi Meiselman, *Same-Sex Marriages Have Existed Legally in the United States for a Long Time Now*, 64 Alb. L. Rev. 1031 (2001). For an overview of the evolving definition of family with respect to same-sex unions, see Paula Ettelbrick, *Domestic Partnership, Civil Unions, or Marriage: One Size Does Not Fit All*, 64 Alb. L. Rev. 905 (2001).

E. A Family Based on Same Sex Marriage

Goodridge v. Department of Public Health
798 N.E.2d 941 (Mass. 2003).

■ Marshall, C.J.

Marriage is a vital social institution. The exclusive commitment of two individuals to each other nurtures love and mutual support; it brings stability to our society. For those who choose to marry, and for their children, marriage provides an abundance of legal, financial, and social benefits. In return it imposes weighty legal, financial, and social obligations. The question before us is whether, consistent with the Massachusetts Constitution, the Commonwealth may deny the protections, benefits, and obligations conferred by civil marriage to two individuals of the same sex who wish to marry. We conclude that it may not. The Massachusetts Constitution affirms the dignity and equality of all individuals. It forbids the creation of second-class citizens. In reaching our conclusion we have given full deference to the arguments made by the Commonwealth. But it has failed to identify any constitutionally adequate reason for denying civil marriage to same-sex couples.

We are mindful that our decision marks a change in the history of our marriage law. Many people hold deep-seated religious, moral, and ethical convictions that marriage should be limited to the union of one man and one woman, and that homosexual conduct is immoral. Many hold equally strong religious, moral, and ethical convictions that same-sex couples are entitled to be married, and that homosexual persons should be treated no differently than their heterosexual neighbors. Neither view answers the question before us. * * *

[In *Lawrence*,] the Court affirmed that the core concept of common human dignity protected by the Fourteenth Amendment to the United States Constitution precludes government intrusion into the deeply personal realms of consensual adult expressions of intimacy and one's choice of an intimate partner. The Court also reaffirmed the central role that decisions whether to marry or have children bear in shaping one's identity. * * *

Barred access to the protections, benefits, and obligations of civil marriage, a person who enters into an intimate, exclusive union with another of the same sex is arbitrarily deprived of membership in one of our community's most rewarding and cherished institutions. That exclusion is incompatible with the constitutional principles of respect for individual autonomy and equality under law.

I

The plaintiffs are fourteen individuals from five Massachusetts counties. * * *

In March and April, 2001, each of the plaintiff couples attempted to obtain a marriage license from a city or town clerk's office. * * * In each case, the clerk either refused to accept the notice of intention to marry or denied a marriage license to the couple on the ground that Massachusetts does not recognize same-sex marriage. Because obtaining a marriage license is a necessary prerequisite to civil marriage in Massachusetts, denying marriage licenses to the plaintiffs was tantamount to denying them access to civil marriage itself, with its appurtenant social and legal protections, benefits, and obligations.

[The District Court ruled in favor of the defendants, concluding "prohibiting same-sex marriage rationally furthers the Legislature's legitimate interest in safeguarding the 'primary purpose' of marriage, 'procreation.'"]

* * *

III

A

The larger question is whether, as the department claims, government action that bars same-sex couples from civil marriage constitutes a legitimate exercise of the State's authority to regulate conduct, or whether, as the plaintiffs claim, this categorical marriage exclusion violates the Massachusetts Constitution. We have recognized the long-standing statutory understanding, derived from the common law, that "marriage" means the lawful union of a woman and a man. But that history cannot and does not foreclose the constitutional question.

The plaintiffs' claim that the marriage restriction violates the Massachusetts Constitution can be analyzed in two ways. Does it offend the Constitution's guarantees of equality before the law? Or do the liberty and due process provisions of the Massachusetts Constitution secure the plaintiffs' right to marry their chosen partner? In matters implicating marriage, family life, and the upbringing of children, the two constitutional concepts frequently overlap, as they do here. * * *

We begin by considering the nature of civil marriage itself. Simply put, the government creates civil marriage. In Massachusetts, civil marriage is, and since pre-Colonial days has been, precisely what its name implies: a wholly secular institution. * * *

Civil marriage is created and regulated through exercise of the police power. * * * In broad terms, it is the Legislature's power to enact rules to regulate conduct, to the extent that such laws are "necessary to secure the health, safety, good order, comfort, or general welfare of the community."
* * *

Without question, civil marriage enhances the "welfare of the community." It is a "social institution of the highest importance." * * * Civil marriage anchors an ordered society by encouraging stable relationships over transient ones. It is central to the way the Commonwealth identifies individuals, provides for the orderly distribution of property, ensures that children and adults are cared for and supported whenever possible from private rather than public funds, and tracks important epidemiological and demographic data.

Marriage also bestows enormous private and social advantages on those who choose to marry. Civil marriage is at once a deeply personal commitment to another human being and a highly public celebration of the ideals of mutuality, companionship, intimacy, fidelity, and family. * * *

Tangible as well as intangible benefits flow from marriage. The marriage license grants valuable property rights to those who meet the entry requirements, and who agree to what might otherwise be a burdensome degree of government regulation of their activities. * * *

The benefits accessible only by way of a marriage license are enormous, touching nearly every aspect of life and death. The department states that "hundreds of statutes" are related to marriage and to marital benefits. With no attempt to be comprehensive, we note that some of the statutory benefits conferred by the Legislature on those who enter into civil marriage include, as to property [including: joint Massachusetts income tax filing, automatic rights to inherit the property of a deceased spouse who does not leave a will, and entitlement to wages owed to a deceased employee].

* * *

Where a married couple has children, their children are also directly or indirectly, but no less auspiciously, the recipients of the special legal and economic protections obtained by civil marriage. Notwithstanding the Commonwealth's strong public policy to abolish legal distinctions between marital and nonmarital children in providing for the support and care of minors, * * * the fact remains that marital children reap a measure of family stability and economic security based on their parents' legally privileged status that is largely inaccessible, or not as readily accessible, to nonmarital children. Some of these benefits are social, such as the enhanced approval that still attends the status of being a marital child. Others are material, such as the greater ease of access to family-based State and Federal benefits that attend the presumptions of one's parentage.

It is undoubtedly for these concrete reasons, as well as for its intimately personal significance, that civil marriage has long been termed a "civil right." * * *

Without the right to marry—or more properly, the right to choose to marry—one is excluded from the full range of human experience and denied full protection of the laws for one's "avowed commitment to an intimate and lasting human relationship." * * * Because civil marriage is central to the lives of individuals and the welfare of the community, our laws assiduously protect the individual's right to marry against undue government incursion. Laws may not "interfere directly and substantially with the right to marry." * * *

B

For decades, indeed centuries, in much of this country (including Massachusetts) no lawful marriage was possible between white and black Americans. That long history availed not when the Supreme Court of California held in 1948 that a legislative prohibition against interracial marriage violated the due process and equality guarantees of the Fourteenth Amendment, *Perez v. Sharp*, * * * or when, nineteen years later, the United States Supreme Court also held that a statutory bar to interracial marriage violated the Fourteenth Amendment, *Loving v. Virginia*, * * * As both *Perez* and *Loving* make clear, the right to marry means little if it does not include the right to marry the person of one's choice, subject to appropriate government restrictions in the interests of public health, safety, and welfare. * * * As it did in *Perez* and *Loving,* history must yield to a more fully developed understanding of the invidious quality of the discrimination. * * *

The individual liberty and equality safeguards of the Massachusetts Constitution protect both "freedom from" unwarranted government intrusion into protected spheres of life and "freedom to" partake in benefits created by the State for the common good. * * * Both freedoms are involved here. Whether and whom to marry, how to express sexual intimacy, and whether and how to establish a family—these are among the most basic of every individual's liberty and due process rights. * * * And central to personal freedom and security is the assurance that the laws will apply equally to persons in similar situations. "Absolute equality before the law is a fundamental principle of our own Constitution." * * * The liberty interest in choosing whether and whom to marry would be hollow if the Commonwealth could, without sufficient justification, foreclose an individual from freely choosing the person with whom to share an exclusive commitment in the unique institution of civil marriage.

* * *

The department posits three legislative rationales for prohibiting same-sex couples from marrying: (1) providing a "favorable setting for procreation"; (2) ensuring the optimal setting for child rearing, which the department defines as "a two-parent family with one parent of each sex"; and (3) preserving scarce State and private financial resources. We consider each in turn.

The judge in the Superior Court endorsed the first rationale, holding that "the state's interest in regulating marriage is based on the traditional concept that marriage's primary purpose is procreation." This is incorrect. Our laws of civil marriage do not privilege procreative heterosexual intercourse between married people above every other form of adult intimacy and every other means of creating a family. * * * People who have never consummated their marriage, and never plan to, may be and stay married. * * * While it is certainly true that many, perhaps most, married couples have children together (assisted or unassisted), it is the exclusive and permanent commitment of the marriage partners to one another, not the begetting of children, that is the sine qua non of civil marriage.

Moreover, the Commonwealth affirmatively facilitates bringing children into a family regardless of whether the intended parent is married or unmarried, whether the child is adopted or born into a family, whether assistive technology was used to conceive the child, and whether the parent or her partner is heterosexual, homosexual, or bisexual. If procreation were a necessary component of civil marriage, our statutes would draw a tighter circle around the permissible bounds of nonmarital child bearing and the creation of families by noncoital means. The attempt to isolate procreation as "the source of a fundamental right to marry," * * * overlooks the integrated way in which courts have examined the complex and overlapping realms of personal autonomy, marriage, family life, and child rearing. Our jurisprudence recognizes that, in these nuanced and fundamentally private areas of life, such a narrow focus is inappropriate.

* * *

The department's first stated rationale, equating marriage with unassisted heterosexual procreation, shades imperceptibly into its second: that confining marriage to opposite-sex couples ensures that children are raised in the "optimal" setting. Protecting the welfare of children is a paramount State policy. Restricting marriage to opposite-sex couples, however, cannot plausibly further this policy. * * * The "best interests of the child" standard does not turn on a parent's sexual orientation or marital status.
* * *

The department has offered no evidence that forbidding marriage to people of the same sex will increase the number of couples choosing to enter into opposite-sex marriages in order to have and raise children. There is thus no rational relationship between the marriage statute and the Commonwealth's proffered goal of protecting the "optimal" child rearing unit. Moreover, the department readily concedes that people in same-sex couples may be "excellent" parents. These couples (including four of the plaintiff couples) have children for the reasons others do—to love them, to care for them, to nurture them. But the task of child rearing for same-sex couples is made infinitely harder by their status as outliers to the marriage laws. * * * Given the wide range of public benefits reserved only for married couples, we do not credit the department's contention that the absence of access to civil marriage amounts to little more than an inconvenience to same-sex couples and their children. Excluding same-sex couples from civil marriage will not make children of opposite-sex marriages more secure, but it does prevent children of same-sex couples from enjoying the immeasurable advantages that flow from the assurance of "a stable family structure in which children will be reared, educated, and socialized." * * *

The third rationale advanced by the department is that limiting marriage to opposite-sex couples furthers the Legislature's interest in conserving scarce State and private financial resources. The marriage restriction is rational, it argues, because the General Court logically could assume that same-sex couples are more financially independent than married couples and thus less needy of public marital benefits, such as tax advantages, or private marital benefits, such as employer-financed health plans that include spouses in their coverage.

An absolute statutory ban on same-sex marriage bears no rational relationship to the goal of economy. First, the department's conclusory generalization—that same-sex couples are less financially dependent on each other than opposite-sex couples—ignores that many same-sex couples, such as many of the plaintiffs in this case, have children and other dependents (here, aged parents) in their care. The department does not contend, nor could it, that these dependents are less needy or deserving than the dependents of married couples. Second, Massachusetts marriage laws do not condition receipt of public and private financial benefits to married individuals on a demonstration of financial dependence on each other; the benefits are available to married couples regardless of whether they mingle their finances or actually depend on each other for support.

* * *

It has been argued that, due to the State's strong interest in the institution of marriage as a stabilizing social structure, only the Legislature can control and define its boundaries. * * * The Massachusetts Constitution requires that legislation meet certain criteria and not extend beyond certain limits. It is the function of courts to determine whether these criteria are met and whether these limits are exceeded. In most instances, these limits are defined by whether a rational basis exists to conclude that legislation will bring about a rational result. The Legislature in the first instance, and the courts in the last instance, must ascertain whether such a rational basis exists. To label the court's role as usurping that of the Legislature, * * * is to misunderstand the nature and purpose of judicial review. We owe great deference to the Legislature to decide social and policy issues, but it is the traditional and settled role of courts to decide constitutional issues.

* * *

The history of constitutional law "is the story of the extension of constitutional rights and protections to people once ignored or excluded." * * * As a public institution and a right of fundamental importance, civil marriage is an evolving paradigm. * * * Marriage has survived [many] transformations, and we have no doubt that marriage will continue to be a vibrant and revered institution.

* * *

- [GREANEY, J. concurred in the opinion]
- [SPINA, J. and SOSMAN, J. dissented, with CORDY, JJ. joining both opinions].
- CORDY, J. (dissenting, with whom Spina and Sosman, JJ., join).

* * *

Civil marriage is the institutional mechanism by which societies have sanctioned and recognized particular family structures, and the institution of marriage has existed as one of the fundamental organizing principles of human society. * * * Marriage has not been merely a contractual arrangement for legally defining the private relationship between two individuals (although that is certainly part of any marriage). Rather, on an institutional level, marriage is the "very basis of the whole fabric of civilized society," * * * and it serves many important political, economic, social, educational, procreational, and personal functions.

Paramount among its many important functions, the institution of marriage has systematically provided for the regulation of heterosexual behavior, brought order to the resulting procreation, and ensured a stable family structure in which children will be reared, educated, and socialized. * * * Admittedly, heterosexual intercourse, procreation, and child care are not necessarily conjoined (particularly in the modern age of widespread effective contraception and supportive social welfare programs), but an orderly society requires some mechanism for coping with the fact that sexual intercourse commonly results in pregnancy and childbirth. The institution of marriage is that mechanism.

The institution of marriage provides the important legal and normative link between heterosexual intercourse and procreation on the one hand and family responsibilities on the other. * * * The alternative, a society without the institution of marriage, in which heterosexual intercourse, procreation, and child care are largely disconnected processes, would be chaotic.

The marital family is also the foremost setting for the education and socialization of children. Children learn about the world and their place in it primarily from those who raise them, and those children eventually grow up to exert some influence, great or small, positive or negative, on society. The institution of marriage encourages parents to remain committed to each other and to their children as they grow, thereby encouraging a stable venue for the education and socialization of children. * * *

It is difficult to imagine a State purpose more important and legitimate than ensuring, promoting, and supporting an optimal social structure within which to bear and raise children. At the very least, the marriage statute continues to serve this important State purpose. * * *

Taking all of this available information into account, the Legislature could rationally conclude that a family environment with married opposite-sex parents remains the optimal social structure in which to bear children, and that the raising of children by same-sex couples, who by definition cannot be the two sole biological parents of a child and cannot provide children with a parental authority figure of each gender, presents an alternative structure for child rearing that has not yet proved itself beyond reasonable scientific dispute to be as optimal as the biologically based marriage norm. * * *

NOTES AND QUESTIONS

1. **Economic framework for same sex marriage.**

    a. **Orderly distribution of property, private support for children's care.**

    "It is central to the way the Commonwealth identifies individuals, provides for the orderly distribution of property, ensures that children and adults are cared for and supported whenever possible from private rather than public funds..."

    b. **Property rights to those who choose to marry.**

    "The marriage license grants valuable property rights to those who meet the entry requirements, and who agree to what might otherwise be a burdensome degree of government regulation of their activities."

2. **Justifications for ban on same sex marriage.**

    a. Providing a "favorable setting for procreation"

    b. Ensuring the optimal setting for child rearing, which the department defines as "a two-parent family with one parent of each sex"

    c. Preserving scarce state and private financial resources

Which of the above listed rationales for banning same-sex marriage are based upon libertarian arguments for limited government and maximum personal autonomy?

3. Neo-classical economics and same sex marriage. Libertarian economist Milton Friedman has argued that there were four duties of government: (1) to protect citizens from military invasion, (2) to protect citizens from violence by fellow citizens, (3) to create and maintain the public works infrastructure and (4) to provide for "irresponsibles." Does a state or federal ban on same-sex marriage fit into any of these categories?

What position would you guess Milton and Rose Friedman take in the same-sex marriage debates? Would their position be consistent with economic libertarianism? If not, what rationale would they give for any inconsistency?

4. Queer theory arguments against same sex marriage? Can you imagine what the arguments of gay advocates might be against same sex marriage? For a representative selection of such arguments, see WILLIAM H. ESKRIDGE & NAN D. HUNTER, *Families We Choose, in* SEXUALITY, GENDER AND THE LAW 1008–99 (2d ed. 2004), (featuring gay argument and counter arguments for same sex marriage).

Paula Ettelbrick argues that:

> "Marriage runs contrary to two of the primary goals of the lesbian and gay movement: the affirmation of gay identity and culture and the validation of many forms of relationships.... At this point in time, making legal marriage for lesbian and gay couples a priority would set an agenda of gaining rights for a few, but would do nothing to correct power imbalances between those who are married (whether gay or straight) and those who are not. Thus justice would not be gained.... Being queer means pushing the parameters of sex, sexuality, and family, and in the process transforming the very fabric of society.... The thought of emphasizing our sameness to married heterosexuals in order to obtain this 'right' terrifies me. It rips away the very heart and soul of what I believe it is to be a lesbian in this world. It robs me of the opportunity to make a difference. We end up mimicking all that is bad about the institution of marriage in our effort to appear to be the same as straight couples."

Id. at 1098 (excerpted from Paula Ettelbrick, *Since When is Marriage a Path to Liberation*, OUTLOOK, Autumn 1989, at 8–12).

CHAPTER 4

CULTURE AND IDENTITY

Introduction

The assumptions of conventional economic theory largely ignore questions of race, class, or other variables that affect individual identity. The rational actor of economics is assumed to be, like the reasonable person of law, a male member of the dominant culture. This assumption allows the values and perspectives of the dominant groups to serve as a crude surrogate for a more refined understanding of other perspectives.

The major consequence of omitting identity from economic reasoning is that economic theory has been unable to provide effective tools for diagnosing some of the most critical issues of economic inequality. This omission is present in both theoretical models and empirical research assumptions. The "thin" accounts of how race, gender, and other identity variables play a role in creating economic distribution are now being vigorously challenged by more robust models that for the first time are explicitly concerned with the economic impact of identity.

In 2003, George Akerlof, a Nobel laureate in economics, and Rachel Kranton, a professor of economics, introduced an important model of economic behavior that explicitly addresses critical questions of race, class and other identity factors and their relationship to the distribution of economic resources.

In this chapter, we begin with Akerlof and Kranton's model that offers a persuasive account of identity and culture in the sphere of economic activity. Next, we take up the insights of social norm theory, which draws upon modern sociological theory and turns attention to the dynamics of social group interaction. Finally, we look at race itself, a major identity variable. In this section, we explore the two competing theories about race and economics, and we look at law professor Ian Ayres' pathbreaking empirical study of evidence of pervasive racial discrimination in the market for the second-largest consumer retail purchase: new cars. Ayres has extended his empirical studies of racial discrimination to include transactions as varied as kidney transplants, taxi tipping practices, and bail setting. From these investigations he has argued, with some success in actual litigation, for a more sensitive test of the disparate impact theory of racial discrimination. Ayres' view does not require proof of discriminatory intent, and relies instead upon statistical disparities that show discriminatory impact upon subordinated groups.

A. Culture and Identity

Economics and Identity
115 Q. J. Econ. 715 (2000).

George A. Akerlof and Rachel E. Kranton

This paper considers how identity, a person's sense of self, affects economic outcomes. We incorporate the psychology and sociology of identity into an economic model of behavior. In the utility function we propose, identity is associated with different social categories and how people in these categories should behave. We then construct a simple game-theoretic model showing how identity can affect individual interactions. The paper adapts these models to gender discrimination in the workplace, the economics of poverty and social exclusion, and the household division of labor. In each case, the inclusion of identity substantively changes conclusions of previous economic analysis.

I. Introduction

This paper introduces identity—a person's sense of self—into economic analysis. Identity can account for many phenomena that current economics cannot well explain. It can comfortably resolve, for example, why some women oppose "women's rights," as seen in microcosm when Betty Friedan was ostracized by fellow suburban housewives for writing *The Feminine Mystique*. Other problems such as ethnic and racial conflict, discrimination, intractable labor disputes, and separatist politics all invite an identity-based analysis. Because of its explanatory power, numerous scholars in psychology, sociology, political science, anthropology, and history have adopted identity as a central concept. This paper shows how identity can be brought into economic analysis, allowing a new view of many economic problems.

We incorporate identity into a general model of behavior and then demonstrate how identity influences economic outcomes. Specifically, we consider gender discrimination in the labor market, the household division of labor, and the economics of social exclusion and poverty. In each case, our analysis yields predictions, supported by existing evidence, that are different from those of existing economic models. The Conclusion indicates many other realms where identity almost surely matters.

Our identity model of behavior begins with social difference. Gender, a universally familiar aspect of identity, illustrates. There are two abstract social categories, "man" and "woman." These categories are associated with different ideal physical attributes and prescribed behaviors. Everyone in the population is assigned a gender category, as either a "man" or a "woman." Following the behavioral prescriptions for one's gender affirms one's self-image, or identity, as a "man" or as a "woman." Violating the prescriptions evokes anxiety and discomfort in oneself and in others. Gender identity, then, changes the "payoffs" from different actions.

This modeling of identity is informed by a vast body of research on the salience of social categories for human behavior and interaction. We present in the next section a series of examples of identity-related behavior. These examples, and other evidence, indicate that (1) people have identity-based payoffs derived from their own actions; (2) people have identity-based payoffs derived from others' actions; (3) third parties can generate persistent changes in these payoffs; and (4) some people may choose their identity, but choice may be proscribed for others.

The concept of identity expands economic analysis for at least four corresponding reasons.

First, identity can explain behavior that appears detrimental. People behave in ways that would be considered maladaptive or even self-destructive by those with other identities. The reason for this behavior may be to bolster a sense of self or to salve a diminished self-image.

Second, identity underlies a new type of externality. One person's actions can have meaning for and evoke responses in others. Gender again affords an example. A dress is a symbol of femininity. If a man wears a dress, this may threaten the identity of other men. There is an externality, and further externalities result if these men make some response.

Third, identity reveals a new way that preferences can be changed. Notions of identity evolve within a society and some in the society have incentives to manipulate them. Obvious examples occur in advertising (e.g., Marlboro ads). As we shall explore, there are many other cases, including public policies, where changing social categories and associated prescriptions affects economic outcomes.

Fourth, because identity is fundamental to behavior, choice of identity may be the most important "economic" decision people make. Individuals may—more or less consciously—choose who they want to be. Limits on this choice may also be the most important determinant of an individual's economic well-being. Previous economic analyses of, for example, poverty, labor supply, and schooling have not considered these possibilities. * * *

B. *Psychology and Experiments on Group Identification*

The prominence of identity in psychology suggests that economists should consider identity as an argument in utility functions. Psychologists have long posited a self or "ego" as a primary force of individual behavior. They have further associated an individual's sense of self to the social setting; identity is bound to social categories; and individuals identify with people in some categories and differentiate themselves from those in others.

While experiments in social psychology do not show the existence of a "self" or this identification per se, they do demonstrate that even arbitrary social categorizations affect behavior. Consider the Robbers Cave experiment. In its initial week, two groups of boys at a summer camp in Oklahoma were kept apart. During this period, the boys developed norms of behavior and identities as belonging to *their* group. When they met for a tournament in the second week, the eleven-year-old equivalent of war broke out, with name-calling, stereotyping, and fighting. Later experiments show that competition is not necessary for group identification and even the most minimal group assignment can affect behavior. "Groups" form by nothing more than random assignment of subjects to labels, such as even or odd. Subjects are more likely to give rewards to those with the same label than to those with other labels, even when choices are anonymous and have no impact on own payoffs. Subjects also have higher opinions of members of their own group.

Our modeling of identity exactly parallels these experiments. In the experiments ... there are social categories; there is an assignment of subjects to those social categories; finally, subjects have in mind some form of assignment-related prescriptions, else rewards would not depend on group assignment.

C. *Examples of Identity–Related Behavior*

We next present a set of "real-world" examples of four different ways, outlined in the introduction and formalized in our utility function, that identity may influence behavior.

Our *first* set demonstrates that people have identity-related payoffs from their own actions. The impact of an action a_j on *utility* U_j depends in part on its effect on identity I_j.

Self-Mutilation. The first of these examples is perhaps the most dramatic: people mutilate their own or their children's bodies as an expression of identity. Tattooing, body-piercing (ear, nose, navel, etc.), hair conking, self-starvation, steroid abuse, plastic surgery, and male and female circumcision all yield physical markers of belonging to more or less explicit social categories and groups. In terms of our utility function, these practices transform an individual's physical characteristics to match an ideal. The mutilation may occur because people believe it leads to pecuniary rewards and interactions such as marriage. But the tenacity and defense of these practices indicate the extent to which belonging relies on ritual, and people have internalized measures of beauty and virtue.

Gender and Occupations. Female trial lawyer, male nurse, woman Marine—all conjure contradictions. Why? Because trial lawyers are viewed as masculine, nurses as feminine, and a Marine as the ultimate man. People in these occupations but of the opposite sex often have ambiguous feelings about their work. In terms of our utility function, an individual's actions do not correspond to gender prescriptions of behavior. A revealing study in this regard is Pierce's [1995] participant-observer research on the legal profession. Female lawyers thought of themselves as women, yet being a good lawyer meant acting like a man. Lawyers were told in training sessions to act like "Rambo" and to "take no prisoners." In the office, trial attorneys who did not "win big" were described as "having no balls." Intimidation of witnesses was "macho blasts against the other side." A Christmas skit about two partners dramatized the gender conflict:

[O]ne secretary dressed up as Rachel and another dressed up as Michael. The secretary portraying Michael ... ran around the stage barking orders and singing, "I'm Michael Bond, I'm such a busy man. I'm such a busy man." The other secretary followed suit by barking orders and singing. "I'm Rachel Rosen, I'm such a busy man, I mean woman. I'm such a busy man, I mean woman...." Michael responded to the spoof in stride.... Rachel, on the other hand, was very upset [Pierce, 1995, p. 130].

Female lawyers expressed their ambivalence in many discussions. "Candace," another partner, told Pierce: "I had forgotten how much anger I've buried over the years about what happened to the woman who became a lawyer ... To be a lawyer, somewhere along the way, I made a decision that it meant acting like a man. To do that I squeezed the female part of me into a box, put on the lid, and tucked it away" [Pierce 1995, p. 134].

Alumni Giving. Charitable contributions may yield a "warm glow" [Andreoni 1989], but how do people choose one organization over another? Charity to the organization with the highest marginal return would maximize its economic impact. Yet, at least for higher education, contributions may well reflect identity. Graduates give to *their own* alma mater. Alumni giving could enhance the value of a degree by maintaining an institution's reputation. But this explanation suffers from the collective action problem. And it does not account for student loyalty and identification with an institution, as expressed in such lyrics as "For God, for country, and for Yale."

Mountaineering. Why do people climb mountains? Loewenstein [1998] argues that facing the extreme discomfort and danger of mountaineering enhances an individual's sense of self.

Our *second* set of examples demonstrates that people have identity-related payoffs from others' actions. The effect of an action a_j on utility includes an impact on I_j.

Gender and Occupations. A woman working in a "man's" job may make male colleagues feel less like "men." To allay these feelings, they may act to affirm their masculinity and act against female coworkers. In her study of coal handlers in a power plant, Padavic [1991] interpreted the behavior of her male coworkers in this way. On one occasion, they picked her up, tossed her back and forth, and attempted to push her onto the coal conveyer belt (jokingly, of course). In the case of another worker, no one trained her, no one helped her, and when she asked for help, she was refused assistance that would have been routine for male coworkers.

To further assay the reasons for such behavior, we took a random-sample telephone survey relating a vignette about a female carpenter at a construction company who was "baited and teased" by a male coworker. We see in Table I that among the six possible explanations, 84 percent of the respondents said it was "somewhat likely," "likely," or "very likely" that the male worker behaved in this way because he felt less masculine. This explanation was one of the most popular, and more than three-quarters of the respondents thought that a woman in a man's job "frequently" or "almost always" faces such treatment.

Manhood and Insult. For a man, an action may be viewed as an insult which, if left unanswered, impugns his masculinity. As in the example above, an action a_{-j} impacts I_j, which may be countered by an action a_j. Psychologists Nisbett and Cohn [1996] have detected such identity concerns in experiments at the University of Michigan. These experiments, they argue, reveal remnants of the white antebellum Southern "culture of honor" in disparate reactions to insult of males from the U. S. South and North. Their experiments involved variations of the following scenario: an associate of the experimenters bumped subjects in the hallway as they made their way to the experiment. Rather than apologizing, the associate called the subject "asshole." Insulted Southerners were more likely than insulted Northerners and control Southerners to fill in subsequent word-completion tests with aggressive words (for example, g-un rather than f-un), and had raised cortisol levels.

TABLE I

Vignette Concerning Harassment and Evaluation of Possible Explanations

Vignette: Paul is a carpenter for a construction company. The company has just hired Christine, its first female carpenter, for 3 dollars *less* per hour than it pays Paul and the other carpenters. On Christine's first day of work, Paul and two of his coworkers bait and tease Christine, making it difficult for her to do her job.

Try to imagine why Paul behaved as he did. Rate each of the following explanations for Paul's behavior as not-at-all likely, not likely, somewhat likely, likely, or very likely.

Explanation	Fraction somewhat likely, likely, or very likely[a,b]	Average Score[c]
Paul put Christine down because he is afraid that by hiring a woman the company can lower his wage.	.36 (.06)	2.5 (.12)
Paul put Christine down because he does not feel that it is fair that Christine is getting a lower wage.	.13 (.04)	1.7 (.12)
Paul put Christine down because he feels less masculine when a woman is doing the same job.	.84 (.04)	3.4 (.12)
Paul put Christine down because he feels he and his friends will not be able to joke around if a woman is present.	.84 (.04)	3.6 (.12)
Paul put Christine down because he is afraid that other men will tease him if a woman is doing the same job.	.76 (.05)	3.3 (.13)
Paul put Christine down because he is afraid that people will think that his	.64 (.06)	2.9 (.12)

Explanation	Fraction likely, likely, or very likely[a,b]	Average Score[c]
requires less skill if a woman is doing the same job.		
Paul put Christine down because he is afraid that if he does not, then his male coworkers will start to tease him.	.80 (.05)	3.4 (.13)
Paul put Christine down because he feels that it is wrong for women to work in a man's job.	.77 (.05)	3.2 (.14)

a. Sample size is 70 households. Households were selected randomly from the Fremont, CA phonebook.
b. Standard errors are in parentheses.
c. Average with not-at-all likely = 1, not likely = 2, somewhat likely = 3, likely = 4, very likely = 5.

Most revealing that the insult affected identity, insulted Southerners were also more likely to fear that the experimenter had a low opinion of their masculinity. They will probably never meet the experimenter or the hallway accomplice again; their encounter in the experiment is otherwise anonymous. Their concern about the experimenter then can only be a concern about how they feel about themselves, about their own sense of identity, as perceived through the "mirror of the opinions and expectations of others" [Gleitman 1996, p. 343]. We see the same psychology in other examples.

Changing Groups or Violating Prescriptions. Because of j's *identification* with others, it may affect j's identity when another person in j's social category violates prescriptions or becomes a different person. A common response is scorn and ostracism, which distances oneself from the maverick and affirms one's own self-image. Such behavior occurs daily in school playgrounds, where children who behave differently are mocked and taunted. Those who seek upward mobility are often teased by their peers, as in *A Hope in the Unseen* [Suskind 1998], which describes Cedric Jennings' progress from one of Washington's most blighted high schools to Brown University. The book opens with Cedric in the high-school chemistry lab, escaping the catcalls of the crowd at an awards assembly. Those who try to change social categories and prescriptions may face similar derision because the change may devalue others' identity, as for the housewives in Betty Friedan's suburb.

Our *third* set of examples demonstrates that to some extent people choose their identity; that is, c_j may be partially a choice. Many women in the United States can choose either to be a career woman or a housewife (see Gerson [1986]). Parents often choose a school—public versus private, secular versus parochial—to influence a child's self-image, identification with others, and behavior. The choice of where to live at college can both reflect and change how students think of themselves. Fraternities, sororities, African–American, or other "theme"-oriented dorms are all associated with social groups, self-images, and prescribed behavior. The list can continue. The choice for an immigrant to become a citizen is not only a change in legal status but a change in identity. The decision is thus often fraught with ambivalence, anxiety, and even guilt.

Identity "choice," however, is very often limited. In a society with racial and ethnic categories, for example, those with nondistinguishing physical features may be able to "pass" as a member of another group. But others will be constrained by their appearance, voice, or accent.

Our *fourth* set of examples demonstrates the creation and manipulation of social categories **C** and prescriptions **P**.

Advertising. Advertising is an obvious attempt to manipulate prescriptions. Marlboro and Virginia Slims advertisements, for example, promote an image of the ideal man or woman complete with the right cigarette.

Professional and Graduate Schools. Graduate and professional programs try to mold students' behavior through a change in identity. As a "one-L" Harvard Law School student said: " 'They are turning me into someone else. They're making me different' " [Turow 1977, p. 73]. In medicine, theology, the military, and the doctorate, a title is added to a graduate's name, suggesting the change in person.

Political Identity. Politics is often a battle over identity. Rather than take preferences as given, political leaders and activists often strive to change a population's preferences through a change in identity or prescriptions. Again, examples abound. Fascist and populist leaders are infamous for their rhetoric fostering racial and ethnic divisions, with tragic consequences. Symbolic acts and transformed identities spur revolutions. The ringing of the Liberty Bell called on the colonists' identities as Americans. Gandhi's Salt March sparked an Indian national identity. The French Revolution changed subjects into *citizens*, and the Russian Revolution turned them into *comrades*.

III. Economics and Identity: A Prototype Model

In this section we construct a prototype model of economic interaction in a world where identity is based on social difference. In addition to the usual tastes, utility from actions will also depend on identity. Identity will depend on two social categories—Green and Red—and the correspondence of own and others' actions to behavioral prescriptions for their category.

A. A Prototype Model

We begin with standard economic motivations for behavior. There are two possible activities, Activity One and Activity Two. There is a population of individuals each of whom has a taste for either Activity One or Two. If a person with a taste for Activity One (Two) undertakes Activity One (Two), she earns utility V. An individual who chooses the activity that does not match her taste earns zero utility. In a standard model of utility maximization, each person would engage in the activity corresponding to her taste.

We next construct identity-based preferences. We suppose that there are two social categories, Green and Red. We assume the simplest division of the population into categories; all persons think of themselves and others as Green. We add simple behavioral prescriptions: a Green should engage in Activity One (in contrast to Reds who engage in Activity Two). Anyone who chooses Activity Two is not a "true" Green—she would lose her Green identity. This loss in identity entails a reduction in utility of I_s, where the subscript s stands for "self." In addition, there are identity externalities. If an i and j are paired, Activity Two on the part of i diminishes j's Green identity. j has a loss in utility I_o, where the subscript o denotes "other." After i has committed Activity Two, j may "respond." The response restores j's identity at a cost c, while entailing a loss to i in amount L.

Figure I represents an interaction between an individual with a taste for Activity One ("Person One") and an individual with a taste for Activity Two ("Person Two"). Person One chooses an activity first.

This model can be expressed by ideas central to the psychodynamic theory of personality, found in almost any psychology text. In personality development, psychologists agree on the importance of *internalization* of rules for behavior. Freud called this process the development of the *superego*. Modern scholars disagree with Freud on the importance of psychosexual factors in an individual's development, but they agree on the importance of *anxiety* that a person experiences when she violates her internalized rules. One's *identity*, or *ego*, or *self*, must be constantly "defended against anxiety in order to limit disruption and maintain a sense of unity" [Thomas 1996, p. 284]. In terms of our model, Person Two's internalization of prescriptions causes her to suffer a loss in utility of I_s if she chooses Activity Two. To avoid this anxiety, she may refrain from that activity.

Identification is a critical part of this internalization process: a person learns a set of values (prescriptions) such that her actions should conform with the behavior of some people and contrast with that of others. If Person One has internalized prescriptions via such identifications, another person's violation of the prescriptions will cause anxiety for Person One. In our model, this anxiety is modeled as a loss in utility of I_o. Person One's response, in our language, restores her identity, and in terms of the psychology textbook relieves her anxiety and maintains her sense of unity. Person One no longer loses I_o, although she does incur c.

* * *

IV. IDENTITY, GENDER AND ECONOMICS IN THE WORKPLACE

An identity theory of gender in the workplace expands the economic analysis of occupational segregation. As recently as 1970, two-thirds of the United States' female or male labor force would have had to switch jobs to achieve occupational parity. This measure of occupational segregation remained virtually unchanged since the beginning of the century. Yet, in twenty years, from 1970 to 1990, this figure declined to 53 percent. An identity model points to changes in societal notions of male and female as a major cause.

The model we propose captures the "auras of gender" [Goldin 1990a] that have pervaded the labor market. Occupations are associated with the social categories "man" and "woman," and individual payoffs from different types of work reflect these gender associations. This model can explain patterns of occupational segregation that have eluded previous models. It also directly captures the consequences of the women's movement and affords a new economic interpretation of sex discrimination law.

Identity also provides a microfoundation for earlier models. The "distaste" of men for working with women, as in the crudest adaptations of racial discrimination models [Becker 1971; Arrow 1972], can be understood as due to loss in male identity when women work in a man's job. Similarly women's assumed lower desire for labor force participation (as in Mincer and Polachek [1974], Bulow and Summers [1986], and Lazear and Rosen [1990]) can be understood as the result of their identity as homemakers.

A. *The Model*

There are two social categories, "men" and "women," with prescriptions of appropriate activities for each. A firm wishes to hire labor to perform a task. By the initial prescriptions, this task is appropriate only for men; it is a "man's job." Relative to a "woman's job," women lose identity in amount I_s by performing such work. In this situation, male coworkers suffer a loss I_o. They may relieve their anxiety by taking action against women coworkers, reducing everyone's productivity.

To avoid these productivity losses, the firm may change gender-job associations at a cost. The firm is likely to create a "woman's job" alongside the "man's job," rather than render the whole task gender neutral, when a new job description can piggyback on existing notions of male and female. A well-known historical example illustrates. In the nineteenth century, Horace Mann (as Secretary of Education for Massachusetts) transformed elementary school teaching into a woman's job, arguing that women were "more mild and gentle," "of purer morals," with "stronger parental impulses." Secondary school teaching and school administration remained jobs for men.

The model also indicates why gender-job associations may persist. If associations are sector-wide or economy-wide, and not firm-specific, perfectly competitive firms will underinvest in new job categories. Benefits would accrue to other firms. In the absence of market power or technological change, a shift in social attitudes and legal intervention would be necessary for changes in employment patterns.

The model easily extends to the decision to participate in the labor force. If women's identity is enhanced by work inside the home, they will have lower labor force attachment than men. Historically, female labor force participation rates, relative to male rates, have been both lower and more cyclically variable.

B. *Implications for Labor Market Outcomes*

This identity model explains employment patterns arising from associations between gender and type of work. These patterns go beyond what can be explained by women's assumed lower labor force attachment as in Mincer and Polachek [1974], where women work in occupations that require little investment in firm-specific human capital.

In our model, women will dominate jobs whose requirements match construed female attributes and inferior social status; men eschew them. Historically, three occupations illustrate: secretaries (97.8 percent female in 1970) have often been called "office wives," and elements of sexuality are inscribed in the working relationship (boss = male, secretary = female) [MacKinnon 1979; Pringle 1988]. Secretaries are expected to serve their bosses, with deference, and to be attentive to their personal needs [Davies 1982; Kanter 1977; Pierce 1996]. Elementary school teachers (83.9 percent female), in contrast to secondary school teachers (49.6 percent female), are supposed to care for young children. Nurses (97.3 percent female) are supposed to be tender and care for patients, as well as be deferential to doctors [Fisher 1995; Williams 1989].

In our model, women do not enter male professions because of gender associations. Historically, many male professions have required similar levels of education and training to female professions and could have been amenable to part-time and intermittent work. Contrast nursing and teaching with accounting and law. All require college degrees and certification, and sometimes have tenure and experience-based pay. Only the very top of these professions have required continuity in employment and full-time work.

Rhetoric surrounding job shifts from male to female further demonstrates the salience of gender-job associations. The recruitment of women into "men's jobs" during World War II, for example, was accompanied by official propaganda and popular literature picturing women taking on factory work without loss of femininity [Milkman 1987; Honey 1984; Pierson 1986]. In addition, the jobs were portrayed as temporary; only the wartime emergency excused the violation of the usual gender prescriptions.

C. Effects of the Women's Movement

The model gives a theoretical structure for how the women's movement may have impacted the labor market. The movement's goals included reshaping societal notions of femininity (and masculinity) and removing gender associations from tasks, both in the home and in the workplace. In the model, such changes would decrease women's gains (men's losses) in identity from homemaking, and decrease the identity loss I_s of women (men) working in traditionally men's (women's) jobs, as well as the accompanying externalities I_o. These shifts would increase women's labor force participation and lead to a convergence of male and female job tenure rates. More women (men) would work in previously male (female) jobs.

All these outcomes are observed coincidental with and following the women's movement. Gender-job associations diminished, reflected in changes in language (e.g., firemen became firefighters). In 1998 the median job tenure of employed women over 25 was 0.4 years lower than that of men; in 1968 that gap had been 3.3 years. Changes in sex composition within occupations accounted for the major share of decline in occupational segregation from 1970–1990 [Blau, Simpson, and Anderson, 1998]. Of the 45 three-digit Census occupations that were 0.0 percent female in 1970, only one (supervisors: brickmasons, stonemasons, and tile setters), was less than 1 percent female twenty years later. Many incursions of females into male-dominated professions were very large. Consider again accounting and law. In 1970 (1990) females were 24.6 (52.7) percent of auditors and accountants, and 4.5 (24.5) percent of lawyers. Not only did the proportion of women in men's jobs increase, but so did the proportion of men in women's jobs (albeit much less dramatically). Of the triumvirate of explanations for such increases—technology, endowments, and tastes—elimination makes tastes the leading suspect, since there was no dramatic change in technology or endowments that would have caused such increased mixing on the job. Legal initiatives discussed next reflect such changes in tastes.

D. Gender–Job Associations and Sex Discrimination Law

Legal interpretations of sex discrimination correspond to earlier economic models as well as our own. Title VII of the Civil Rights Act of 1964 makes it unlawful for an employer to discriminate "against any individual ... with respect to ... compensation, terms, conditions of employment" or "to [adversely] limit, segregate, or classify his employees ... because of ... sex." At its most basic, this law prohibits a discriminatory exercise of "tastes" against women (analogous to Becker [1971] and Arrow [1972]). Courts also interpret Title VII as outlawing statistical discrimination by sex or criteria correlated with sex, even when women on average lack a desirable job qualification. Discriminatory hiring because of women's presumed lower workplace attachment, as in Lazear and Rosen [1990], was precisely the issue addressed in *Phillips v. Martin-Marietta*.

Our model, where sex discrimination occurs because jobs have gender associations, corresponds to a wider interpretation of Title VII. This interpretation is at the forefront of current legal debate and is supported by a number of precedents. In *Diaz v. Pan American World Airways*, the Court outlawed sex bans in hiring. The airline originally pleaded for their prohibition of male flight attendants because women were better at "the nonmechanical aspects of the job." But this association of gender with the job was disallowed on appeal since feminine traits were deemed irrelevant to the "primary function or services offered" (cited in MacKinnon [1979, p. 180]). *Price Waterhouse v. Hopkins* set a precedent for workers already hired. The plaintiff had been denied a partnership after negative evaluations for her masculine deportment. The Supreme Court ruled that "an employer who objects to aggressiveness in women but whose positions require this trait places women in an intolerable and impermissible Catch 22" (cited in Wurzburg and Klonoff [1997, p. 182]). Cases have also involved harassment of women working in men's jobs as, in the terminology of our model, male coworkers protect themselves from loss of identity I_o. *Berkman v. City of New York* reinstated a firefighter who had been dismissed because of substandard work performance. The Court ruled that the interference and harassment by her male coworkers made it impossible for her to perform her job adequately [Schultz 1998, p. 1770]. This expansive interpretation of a "hostile work environment," a category of sexual harassment which is in turn a category of sex discrimination, has been exceptional. Judges have viewed sexual desire as an essential element of sexual harassment. However, Schultz [1998] and Franke [1995] argue that any harassment derived from gender prescriptions has discriminatory implications (as depicted in our model) and are thus violations of Title VII.

V. Identity and the Economics of Exclusion and Poverty

This section will consider identity and behavior in poor and socially excluded communities. In an adaptation of the previous model of Greens and Reds, people belonging to poor, socially excluded groups will choose their identity. Greens identify with the dominant culture, while those with Red identity reject it and the subordinate position assigned to those of their "race," class, or ethnicity. From the point of view of those with Green identities, Reds are often making bad economic decisions; they might even be described as engaging in self-destructive behavior. Taking drugs, joining a gang, and becoming pregnant at a young age are possible signs of a Red identity. This aspect of behavior has not been explored in previous models, but it is implicit in Wilson's account of black ghetto poverty [1987, 1996]. It also is implicit in every study that finds significant dummy variables for "race," after adjustment for other measures of socioeconomic status. The Green/Red model of this section offers an explanation for the significance of such dummy variables. Furthermore, it yields a less monolithic view of poverty than current economic theories that emphasize conformity (e.g., Akerlof [1997] and Brock and Durlauf [1995]).

A. *Motivation for Model*

Our model reflects the many ethnographic accounts of "oppositional" identities in poor neighborhoods. MacLeod's [1987] study of teenagers in a Boston area housing project, for example, contrasts the murderous and alcoholic Hallway Hangers to their obedient and athletic peers, the Brothers. In *Learning to Labour* Willis [1977] describes the antagonism between the unruly "lads" and the dutiful "earholes" in a working-class English secondary school. Similarly, Whyte's [1943] description of Boston's Italian North End circa 1940 contrasts the Corner Boys to the College Boys. Yet earlier, turn-of-the century accounts of the Irish in the United States contrast the "lace curtain" Irish of poor districts to their neighbors (see, e.g., Miller [1985]).

Our model further evokes the psychological effects of social exclusion in the colonial experience analyzed by Bhabha [1983] and Fanon [1967], and in the context of African–Americans in the United States by Anderson [1990], Baldwin [1962], Clark [1965], DuBois [1965], Frazier [1957], Hannerz [1969], Rainwater [1970], Wilson [1987, 1996], and others. In these settings, individuals from particular groups can never fully fit the ideal type, the ideal "Green," of the dominant culture. Some in excluded groups may try to "pass" or integrate with the dominant group, but they do so with ambivalence and limited success. A series of autobiographies tells of the pain and anger of discovering that one is not really "Green." Former *New York Times* editor Mel Watkins [1998] titles the chapter on his freshman year at Colgate as "stranger in a strange land." Gandhi [1966], Fanon [1967], Fulwood [1996], Staples [1994], and Rodriguez [1982] all relate strikingly similar experiences of perceived or real rejection and alienation. This social exclusion may create a conflict: how to work within the dominant culture without betraying oneself. As Jill Nelson [1993, p. 10] explains her exhaustion after a long day of interviewing for a job at *The Washington Post*:

> I've also been doing the standard Negro balancing act when it comes to dealing with white folks, which involves sufficiently blurring the edges of my being so that they don't feel intimidated, while simultaneously holding on to my integrity. There is a thin line between Uncle-Tomming and Mau-Mauing. To fall off that line can mean disaster. On one side lies employment and self-hatred; on the other, the equally dubious honor of unemployment with integrity.

These reactions, it must be emphasized, reflect how dominant groups define themselves by the exclusion of others. The creation and evolution of such social differences are the subject of much historical research. Said [1978] documents the emergence of the Western idea of the "Oriental," a concept that had significant implications for colonialism. In the United States Roediger [1991] and other historians show how workers of European descent in the nineteenth century increasingly were defined as "white." Prior to Emancipation, this identity evoked the contrast between white freedom and African-American enslavement. In the model we construct, the key interaction is between such social differences and the adoption of oppositional identities by those in excluded groups.

Lack of economic opportunity may also contribute to the choice of an oppositional identity. Wilson [1987, 1996] underscores the relation between the decline in remunerative unskilled jobs, the loss of self-respect by men who cannot support their families, and the rise in inner city crime and drug abuse. This process is illustrated in microcosm by "Richard" in *Tally's Corner* [Liebow 1967]. Unable to find decent-paying work, he abandoned his family and joined Tally's group of idlers on the street corner. By adopting a different identity, Richard no longer suffered the guilt of a failed provider.

Red activities have negative pecuniary externalities. Richard's wife and children had to find alternative means of support. The prime goal of the "lads" in Willis' secondary school was to get a "laff," through vandalism, picking fights, and returning drunk to school from the local pub. Running a school with lads is difficult. The situation corresponds to the externalities in Benabou's [1993, 1996] models of high schooling costs in poor neighborhoods. Further externalities accrue from drug dealing, crime, and other "pathological" behavior. In our model, there are also identity-based externalities. A Red is angered by a Green's complicity with the dominant culture, while a Green is angered by a Red's "breaking the rules." Again consider Willis' lads and earholes. As the lads define themselves in contrast to the earholes, the earholes define themselves in contrast to the lads. The earholes are even more proestablishment than the teachers—feeling that the teachers should be stricter. The lads, in turn, bait the earholes. This situation is just one (relatively tame) example of how interaction between the two groups generates antagonism on both sides.

B. Identity Model of Poverty and Social Exclusion

As in the prototype model, there are two activities, One and Two. Activity One can be thought of as "working" and Activity Two as "not working." There is a large community, normalized to size one, of individuals. The economic return to Activity One for individual i is v_i which we assume is uniformly distributed between zero and one, to reflect heterogeneity in the population and to ensure interior solutions. The economic return to Activity Two is normalized to zero.

As for identity, there are two social categories, Green and Red. A Green suffers a loss in identity r, representing the extent to which someone from this community is not accepted by the dominant group in society. Those with the less adaptive Red identity do not suffer this loss. Behavioral prescriptions say that Greens (Reds) should engage in Activity One (Two). Thus, a Green (Red) loses identity from Activity Two (One) in amount I^G_s ($I^R_s il$). Because Reds reject the dominant Green culture, they are also likely to have lower economic returns to Activity One than Greens. A Red individual i will only earn $v_i - a$ from Activity One, as well as suffer the loss I^R_s. There are also identity externalities when Greens and Reds meet. A Green (Red) suffers a loss I^G_o (I^R_o). In addition, Reds who have chosen Activity Two impose a pecuniary externality k on those who have chosen Activity One.

Each person i chooses an identity and activity, given the choices of everyone else in the community. We assume that people cannot modify their identity or activity for each individual encounter. Rather, individuals choose an identity and activity to maximize expected payoffs, given the probabilities of encounters with Greens who choose Activity One, Greens who choose Two, Reds who choose One, and Reds who choose Two.

* * *

D. Further Lessons from the Model

The model and its solution also afford interpretations of policies designed to reduce poverty and the effects of social exclusion.

First, the model indicates why residential Job Corps programs may succeed while other training programs fail [Stanley, Katz, and Krueger 1998]. According to the model, taking trainees out of their neighborhoods would eliminate, at least for a time, the negative effects of interaction with those with Red identities. Moreover, being in a different location may reduce a trainee's direct loss r from being Green and pursuing Activity One. That is, this loss may be both individual-specific and situational, and leaving a poor neighborhood is likely to generate a lower r than otherwise.

In a somewhat controlled experiment, the U.S. government tried to save money with JOBSTART, which preserved many of the features of Job Corps except the expensive housing of trainees. Follow-up studies of JOBSTART show little or no improvement in employment or earnings.

Second, the model affords an interpretation of different education initiatives for minority students. Like Job Corps, the Central Park East Secondary School (CPESS) in East Harlem may succeed because it separates Green students from Red students. Students, for example, must apply to the school, indicating their and their parents' willingness to adopt its rules (see Fliegel [1993] and Meier [1995] for this and other details). Another interpretation of CPESS and other successes (e.g., Comer [1980] in New Haven) parallels the logic of the all-Red equilibrium where some people nonetheless pursue Activity One. The schools take measures to reduce the loss in identity of Red students, I^R_s, in activities such as learning Standard English. Delpit's [1995] award-winning book *Other People's Children* proposes numerous ways to reduce the alienation that minority students may experience in school.

Finally, the model illuminates a set of issues in the affirmative action debate. Much of this debate concerns the success or failure of specific programs (see, e.g., Dickens and Kane [1996]). Yet, more is at stake. The rhetoric and symbolism of affirmative action may affect the level of social exclusion r. On the one hand, Loury [1995] argues that portraying African-Americans as victims, a portrayal necessary to retain affirmative action programs, is costly to blacks. In terms of the model, such rhetoric will increase r and the adoption of Red identities. On the other hand, affirmative action will decrease r, to the extent it is seen as an apology for previous discrimination and an invitation for black admission to the dominant culture. Reversal of affirmative action would negate this effect. To cite a recent example, our analysis suggests that removing affirmative action admissions criteria at the University of California and University of Texas Law Schools could have behavioral implications that far exceed the impact on applicants.

The identity model of exclusion, then, explains why legal equality may not be enough to eliminate racial disparities. If African-Americans choose to be Red because of exclusion and if whites perpetuate such exclusions, even in legal ways, there can be a permanent equilibrium of racial inequality. The negative externalities and their consequences, however, would disappear when the community is fully integrated into the dominant culture, so that $r = \mathbf{a} = 0$, and everyone in the community adopts a Green identity. This, of course, is the American ideal of the melting pot, or the new ideal of a mosaic where difference can be maintained within the dominant culture.

VI. IDENTITY AND THE ECONOMICS OF THE HOUSEHOLD

An identity model of the household, unlike previous models, predicts an asymmetric division of labor between husbands and wives. Theories based on comparative advantage (e.g., Becker [1965] and Mincer [1962]) predict that whoever works more outside the home will work less inside the home, whether it be the husband or the wife. Yet, the data we present below indicate a gender asymmetry. When a wife works more hours outside the home, she still undertakes a larger share of the housework.

Hochschild's [1990] study *The Second Shift* reveals the details of such asymmetries. One of the couples in her study found an ingenious way to share the housework. "Evan Holt," a furniture salesman, took care of the lower half of the house (i.e., the basement and his tools). His wife "Nancy," a full-time licensed social worker, took care of the upper half. She took care of the child. He took care of the dog.

Quantitative evidence from Hochschild's sample and our data analysis suggest that the Holts conform to a national pattern. Figure III shows the low average of husbands' share of housework and its low elasticity with respect to their share of outside work hours. The figure plots shares of housework reported by married men in the Panel Study of Income Dynamics, as computed from answers to the question(s): "About how much time do you (your wife) spend on housework in an average week? I mean time spent cooking, cleaning, and doing other work around the house?" The intent of the question was to exclude child care. The figure plots men's share of housework as a fourth-order polynomial of their share of outside hours, for households by age of youngest child. When men do all the outside work, they contribute on average about 10 percent of housework. But as their share of outside work falls, their share of housework rises to no more than 37 percent. As shown in the figure the presence of children of different ages makes a small difference to the function. Similar results obtain when the independent variable is shares of income rather than shares of outside work hours.

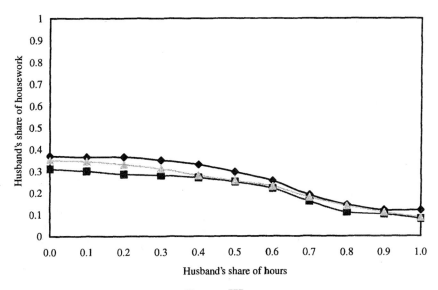

FIGURE III
Husband's Share of Housework versus Their Share of Outside Work Hours

Existing theories do not predict this asymmetry. Consider the following variant based on comparative advantage. Husband and wife both have the same utility function, which is increasing in quantity of a household public good that derives from their joint labor. Utility is decreasing in own labor inputs in outside and home production. We assume equal bargaining power, so that each marriage partner enjoys the same level of utility. With this framework, returns to specialization explain the observed division of labor when a wife has a comparative advantage in home production. Women who put in less than half of the outside work hours put in more than half the housework, as seen in the right-hand side of the graph of Figure III. But this model is inconsistent with the left-hand side of the graph.

Identity considerations can explain the high shares of housework of wives who undertake a large share of outside work hours. Add to the above model two social categories, "men" and "women." Prescriptions dictate that "men" should not do "women's work" in the home and "men" should earn more than their wives. Hochschild's interviews suggest that many men, and some women, hold these prescriptions. In the amended model, the husband loses identity when he does housework and when his wife earns more than half the household income. Equality of utility is restored when the wife undertakes more housework than her husband. Hochschild reports that in the "Tanagawa" household, for example, "Nina" earned more than half the family income, but she worked more than "Peter" at home to assuage his unease with the situation. Eventually, she quit her job.

VII. Conclusion

This paper considers how identity affects economic outcomes. Following major themes in psychology and sociology, identity in our models is based on social difference. A person's sense of self is associated with different social categories and how people in these categories should behave. This simple extension of the utility function could greatly expand our understanding of economic outcomes. In a world of social difference, one of the most important economic decisions that an individual makes may be the type of person to be. Limits on this choice would also be critical determinants of economic behavior, opportunity, and well-being.

Identity affects economic behavior in our models through four avenues. First, identity changes the payoffs from one's own actions. We capture this possibility by a value I_s in our models. In our study of gender in the workplace, for example, a woman working in a "man's" job suffers a loss in utility, affecting the labor supply. Second, identity changes the payoffs of others' actions. We capture this externality by a value I_o in our models. A "Red" in our poverty model, for example, is harmed by a member of his own community who complies with the dominant culture. Third, the choice, or lack thereof, of different identities affects an individual's economic behavior. In our poverty model, while individuals could choose between

Green or Red, they could never be a "true" Green. The greater the extent of this social exclusion, the greater the possibility of equilibria in which individuals eschew remunerative activities. Finally, the social categories and behavioral prescriptions can be changed, affecting identity-based preferences. This possibility expanded the scope of employment policy in our model of gender in the workplace and of education policy in our study of social exclusion.

This paper has only scratched the surface of the economic implications of identity. A first tack in future research would be continued analysis of particular settings. Identity is likely to affect economic outcomes, for example, in areas of political economy, organizational behavior, demography, the economics of language, violence, education, consumption and savings behavior, retirement decisions, and labor relations. As in this paper, models that incorporate well-documented existing social categories and prescriptions could yield new results. A second tack in this agenda is comparative, examining identity across space and time. Researchers, for example, could consider why notions of "class" or "race" vary across countries; why might gender and racial integration vary across industries; what might explain the rise and fall of ethnic tensions. Such comparative studies would be a fruitful way to explore the formation of identity-based preferences.

In peroration, this paper explores how to incorporate identity into economic models of behavior. Many standard psychological and sociological concepts—*self-image, ideal type, in-group and out-group, social category, identification, anxiety, self-destruction, self-realization, situation*—fit naturally in our framework, allowing an expanded analysis of economic outcomes. This framework is then perhaps one way to incorporate many different nonpecuniary motivations for behavior into economic reasoning, with considerable generality and a common theme.

Identity in Mashpee

THE PREDICAMENT OF CULTURE: TWENTIETH-CENTURY ETHNOGRAPHY, LITERATURE, AND ART 277–346 (1988).

JAMES CLIFFORD

In August 1976 the Mashpee Wampanoag Tribal Council, Inc., sued in federal court for possession of about 16,000 acres of land constituting three-quarters of Mashpee, "Cape Cod's Indian Town." (The township of Mashpee extends inland from the Cape's southern shore, facing Martha's Vineyard, between Falmouth and Barnstable.) An unprecedented trial ensued whose purpose was not to settle the question of land ownership but rather to determine whether the group calling itself the Mashpee Tribe was in fact an Indian tribe, and the same tribe that in the mid-nineteenth century had lost its lands through a series of contested legislative acts.

The Mashpee suit was one of a group of land-claim actions filed in the late 1960s and 1970s, a relatively favorable period for redress of Native American grievances in the courts. Other claims were being initiated by the Gay Head Wampanoag Tribe on Martha's Vineyard; the Narragansets of Charlestown, Rhode Island; Western Pequots, Schaghticokes, and Mohegans in Connecticut; and Oneidas, St. Regis Mohawks, and Cayugas in New York. The Mashpee action was similar in conception to a much-publicized suit by the Passamaquoddy and Penobscot tribes laying claim to a large portion of the state of Maine. Their suit, after initial successes in Federal District Court, direct intervention from President Jimmy Carter, and five years of hard negotiation, resulted in a favorable out-of-court settlement. The tribes received $81.5 million and the authority to acquire 300,000 acres with Indian Country status.

The legal basis of the Penobscot-Passamaquoddy suit, as conceived by their attorney, Thomas Tureen, was the Non-Intercourse Act of 1790. This paternalist legislation, designed to protect tribal groups from spoliation by unscrupulous whites, declared that alienation of Indian lands could be legally accomplished only with permission of Congress. The act had never been rescinded, although throughout the nineteenth century it was often honored in the breach. When in the 1970s Indian groups appealed to the Non-Intercourse Act, they were attempting, in effect, to reverse more than a century of attacks on Indian lands. The alienations had been particularly severe for eastern groups, whose claim to collective land was often unclear. When court decisions confirmed that the Non–Intercourse Act applied to non-reservation Indians, the way was opened for suits, like those of the Maine tribes, claiming that nearly two centuries of Indian land transfers, even ordinary purchases, were invalid since they had been made without permission of Congress.

Although the Mashpee claim was similar to the Maine Indians', there were crucial differences. The Passamaquoddy and Penobscot were generally recognized Indian tribes with distinct communities and clear aboriginal roots in the area. The Mashpee plaintiffs represented most of the nonwhite inhabitants of what, for over three centuries, had been known as an "Indian town" on Cape Cod; but their institutions of tribal government had long been elusive, especially during the century and a half preceding the suit. Moreover, since about 1800 the Massachusett language had ceased to be commonly spoken in Mashpee. The town was at first largely Presbyterian then Baptist in its public religion. Over the centuries inhabitants had intermarried with other Indian groups, whites, blacks, Hessian deserters from the British Army during the Revolutionary War, Cape Verde islanders. The inhabitants of Mashpee were active in the economy and society of modern Massachusetts. They were businessmen, schoolteachers, fishermen, domestic workers, small contractors. Could these people of Indian ancestry file suit as the Mashpee Tribe that had, they claimed, been despoiled of collectively held lands during the mid-nineteenth century? This was the question a federal judge posed to a Boston jury. Only if they answered yes could the matter proceed to a land-claim trial.

The forty-one days of testimony that unfolded in Federal District Court during the late fall of 1977 bore the name *Mashpee Tribe v. New Seabury et al.*, shorthand for a complex, multipartied dispute. Mashpee Tribe referred to the plaintiffs, the Mashpee Wampanoag Tribal Council, Inc., described by its members as an arm of the Mashpee Tribe. A team of lawyers from the Native American Rights Fund, a nonprofit advocacy group, prepared their suit. Its chief architects were Thomas Tureen and Barry Margolin. In court the plaintiffs' case was argued by the trial lawyer Lawrence Shubow, with assistance from Tureen, Margolin, Ann Gilmore, and Moshe Genauer. New Seabury et al. referred to the New Seabury Corporation (a large development company), the Town of Mashpee (representing over a hundred individual landowners), and various other classes of defendant (insurance companies, businesses, property owners). The case for the defense was argued by James St. Clair (Richard Nixon's Watergate attorney) of the large Boston firm Hale and Dorr, and Allan Van Gestel of Goodwin, Proctor, and Hoar. They were assisted by a team of eight other lawyers.

The presence of the Town of Mashpee among the defendants requires explanation. It was not until 1869 that the community living in Mashpee was accorded formal township status. From 1869 until 1964 the town government was overwhelmingly in the hands of Indians. During this period every selectman but one was an Indian or married to an Indian. Genealogical evidence presented at the trial showed that the families of town officers were closely interrelated. No one contested the fact that before the 1960s Mashpee was governed by Indians. The disagreement was over whether they governed as an "Indian tribe."

This basic demographic and political situation, which had not altered drastically for over three centuries, was revolutionized during the early 1960s. Before then census figures showed a population in Mashpee fluctuating in the neighborhood of 350 Indians and "negroes," "coloreds," or "mulattoes" (the official categories shifted), and 100 or fewer whites. A reliable count of 1859, which served as a benchmark in the trial, listed only one white resident. After 1960 for the first time white were recorded in the majority and by 1970 whites outnumbered Indians and other people of color by 982 to 306. By 1968 two of the town's selectmen were whites, the third Indian. This proportion was in effect at the time of the lawsuit. Mashpee's white selectmen voted that the town should legally represent the non-Indian majority of property holders who were threatened by the land claim.

"Cape Cod's Indian Town" had finally been discovered. For centuries a backwater and a curiosity, in the 1950s and 1960s Mashpee became desirable as a site for retirement, vacation homes, condominiums, and luxury developments. Fast roads now made it accessible as a bedroom and weekend suburb of Boston. The new influx of money and jobs was first welcomed by many of Mashpee's Indian residents, including some of the leaders of the land-claim suit. They took advantage of the new situation. The town government, still run by Indians, enjoyed a surge in tax revenues. But when local government passed out of Indian control, perhaps for good, and as the scale of development increased, many Indians began to feel qualms. What they had taken for granted—that this was their town—no longer held true. Large tracts of undeveloped land formerly open for hunting and fishing were suddenly ringed with "No Trespassing" signs. The New Seabury development, on a choice stretch of coastline, with its two golf courses and expansionist plans, seemed particularly egregious. Tensions between traditional residents and newcomers increased, finally leading to the suit, filed with the support of most, but not all, of the Indians in Mashpee. The land claim, while focusing on a loss of property in the nineteenth century, was actually an attempt to regain control of a town that had slipped from Indian hands very recently.

Earl Mills

Earl Mills has taught high school in the Falmouth Public School system for over twenty-five years. Between 1952 and 1967 he lived in Falmouth, ten miles from Mashpee. Mills has taught physical education, health, and social studies. He advises the student council and directs various other extracurricular activities.

In Mashpee he shares ownership of the town's best restaurant with his ex-wife, Shirley. He is its principal cook.

Since the mid-fifties Mills has held the title of Chief Flying Eagle of the Mashpee Wampanoag Tribe.

On the witness stand he is earnest, engaging, very much the coach or Boy Scout leader. Forty-eight years old, trim, athletic-looking, he wears a striped necktie, blue blazer, loafers.

Mills recalls his youth in Mashpee during the thirties and forties. He was never as good a hunter as his brother, Elwood, so he often skipped the frequent hunting trips. Early on he asked questions and read books. He questioned his grandmother, "the strong arm" behind his uncle (who had held the formal title of chief and was "a drifter"), and also his mother, the treasurer and tax collector of the town, "the strong arm behind me."

In the thirties, Mills recalls, some townspeople wore regalia occasionally, and a few spoke a little Indian dialect. He remembers the festive atmosphere of a close community—selling corn at town meetings, the yearly beach outings, the annual herring run.

As a child he was shown the location of "Indian taverns." These were not drinking places, according to Mills, but just places where paths crossed. You would pick up a stick, spit on it, and throw it on a heap to appease spirits in the area.

Mills says he can still identify two "Indian taverns," but most have long since been cleared away because the sticks, piled high, were a fire hazard.

This is the extent of the Indian rituals Mills reports. Raised a Baptist, he does not now consider himself a Christian; but he believes in a creator, "something greater than me."

Mills says that when he inquired after Indian artifacts, especially the traditional Mashpee plaited baskets, he was told by his father that "those fellows up around Cambridge must've taken them" (a reference probably to the Harvard Anthropology Department). His father showed him how to plait bark baskets, a skill he had acquired as a young man from Eben Queppish, a master basket maker in Mashpee.

Mills recalls that as a boy he made fun of the old-timers, including the medicine man of the period, William James.

In Falmouth High School Mills excelled in athletics. ("You had to be a scrapper to make it.") Sports were a road to confidence in a threatening environment. Outside of school, like his father and other Mashpee Indians, he served as a guide for hunting and fishing parties in the region.

Q.: "How was your youth different from that of any small-town youth?"

A.: "We were different. We knew we were different. We were told we were different."

Only in the late forties did Mills learn Indian dancing—in the army. On a lonely evening during basic training at Fort Dix two comrades, a Montana Chippewa and a New York Iroquois, performed their dances. Mills was chagrined to admit that he knew none himself.

Earl Mills tells about his five children-four by his first wife, who is part Navajo, and one by his second wife, who is Caucasian. The eldest, Roxanne, is married to a Choctaw. Earl Jr. (called "Chiefy") lives in Falmouth and in recent years has become a champion drummer at various Indian gatherings and powwows. Shelly, also a fine drummer, attends Native American festivals all over the Northeast. Robert lives on Commonwealth Avenue in Boston. "He's into quill work, leather work, skins." Nancy, the child of Mills's second marriage, is now six years old. She does Indian dances. Her parents agree that she is a Wampanoag.

Mills explains his duties as tribal chief. He teaches beadwork, leatherwork, and basketry in Mashpee. Overall his job is to be a mediator, to keep his people "on balance."

Under questioning he cannot or will not give any specific examples of his mediations. Mills tells how in the late fifties and early sixties he and three whites formed a committee to restore the Old Indian Meeting House in Mashpee. The meeting house, which had fallen into disrepair, had for many years been the most visible symbol of Indian life in the town.

During the fifties there had been a tribal constitution of some sort (the document is introduced into evidence), but Mills testifies that the tribe did not follow the constitution as written. Tribal meetings were held irregularly, with notice passed by word of mouth. (Where, St. Clair asks on cross-examination, are the minutes for these purported tribal meetings?)

In the early seventies, Mills says, he attended a grant-writing seminar at Dartmouth College, along with Amelia Bingham, a state employee (sister of John Peters, the tribal medicine man, and Russell Peters, chairman of the Tribal Council, Inc.). Mills says he had little originally to do with the land suit. As chief he simply approved the action of the incorporated body on behalf of the tribe. It was discussed in his restaurant kitchen.

Earl Mills testifies that he respects John Peters. The two of them represent the Mashpee traditionalist wing. The modernists, he says, people like Russell Peters, are the legal arm of the tribe and represent its interests in dealings with the government, the courts, and foundations.

St. Clair's questions portray Chief Flying Eagle as an opportunist following rather than leading his people. They reveal that Mills's traditional authority was recently challenged by Russell Peters and others who wanted to sell beer at the annual Mashpee powwow, a festival attended by a considerable number of tourists and other outsiders. Over the chief's objections beer was sold. St. Clair harps on this evidence of lack of leadership. Rebuttals follow, concerning different tribal responsibilities and roles. There are references to President Carter's inability to control the (beer-related) behavior of his brother, Billy.

On the stand Chief Flying Eagle often sounds like a social studies teacher; his speech is larded with pat anecdotes and homilies.

Only once, toward the end of his testimony, does he do something unexpected. Asked whether he often wears Indian regalia, Mills answers no, only at powwows. Then he suddenly lugs at his necktie, pulling two thin strings of beads from under his shirt. One, he says, is turquoise, from the Southwest. The other small strand was a gift from his father.

Many people in the courtroom are surprised by this apparently spontaneous revelation—surprised and, as Mills stuffs the beads back into his shirt and fumbles to readjust his tie, a little embarrassed.

Images

At the end of the trial Federal Judge Walter J. Skinner posed a number of specific questions to the jurors concerning tribal status at certain dates in Mashpee history; but throughout the proceedings broader questions of Indian identity and power permeated the courtroom. Although the land claim was formally not at issue, the lawyers for New Seabury et al. sometimes seemed to be playing on a new nightmare. At the door of your suburban house a stranger in a business suit appears. He says he is a Native American. Your land has been illegally acquired generations ago, and you must relinquish your home. The stranger refers you to his lawyer.

Such fears, the threat of a "giveaway" of private lands, were much exploited by politicians and the press in the Penobscot-Passamaquoddy negotiations. Actually small holdings by private citizens were never in danger; only large tracts of undeveloped land held by timber companies and the state were in question. In Mashpee the plaintiffs reduced their claim to eleven thousand acres, formally excluding all private homes and lots up to an acre in size. Large-scale development, not small ownership, was manifestly the target; but their opponents refused pretrial compromises and the kinds of negotiation that had led to settlement of the Maine dispute.

According to Thomas Tureen the sorts of land claims pursued in Maine, Mashpee, Gay Head, and Charlestown were always drastically circumscribed. At that historical moment the courts were relatively open to Native American claims, a situation unlikely to last. In a decision of 1985 permitting Oneida, Mohawk, and Cayuga Non-Intercourse Act suits the Supreme Court made it abundantly clear, in Tureen's words, "that Indians are dealing with the magnanimity of a rich and powerful nation, one that is not about to divest itself or its non-Indian citizens of large acreage in the name of its own laws." In short, the United States will permit Indians a measure of recompense through the law—indeed, it has done so to an extent far greater than any other nation in a comparable situation—but it ultimately makes the rules and arbitrates the game. (Tureen 1985:147; also Barsh and Henderson 1980:289–293).

Seen in this light, the Mashpee trial was simply a clarification of the rules in an ongoing struggle between parties of greatly unequal power. But beneath the explicit fear of white citizens losing their homes because of an obscure past injustice, a troubling uncertainty was finding its way into the dominant image of Indians in America. The plaintiffs in the Non-Intercourse Act suits had power. In Maine politicians lost office over the issue, and the Mashpee case made national headlines for several months. Scandalously, it now paid to be Indian. Acting aggressively, tribal groups were doing sophisticated, "nontraditional" things. All over the country they were becoming involved in a variety of businesses, some claiming exemption from state regulation. To many whites it was comprehensible for Northwest Coast tribes to demand traditional salmon-fishing privileges; but for tribes to run high-stakes bingo games in violation of state laws was not.

Indians had long filled a pathetic imaginative space for the dominant culture; they were always survivors, noble or wretched. Their cultures had been steadily eroding, at best hanging on in museumlike reservations. Native American societies could not by definition be dynamic, inventive, or expansive. Indians were lovingly remembered in Edward Curtis' sepia photographs as proud, beautiful, and "vanishing." But Curtis, we now know, carried props, costumes, and wigs, frequently dressing up his models. The image he recorded was carefully staged (Lyman 1982). In Boston Federal Court a jury of white citizens would be confronted by a collection of highly ambiguous images. Could a group of four women and eight men (no minorities) be made to believe in the persistent "Indian" existence of the Mashpee plaintiffs without costumes and props? This question surrounded and infused the trial's technical focus on whether a particular form of political-cultural organization called a tribe had existed continuously in Mashpee since the sixteenth century.

The image of Mashpee Indians, like that of several other eastern groups such as the Lumbee and the Ramapough, was complicated **by** issues of race (Blu 1980; Cohen 1974). Significant intermarriage **with** blacks had occurred since the mid-eighteenth century, and the Mashpee were, at times, widely identified as "colored." In court the defense occasionally suggested that they were really blacks rather than Native Americans. Like the

Lumbee (and, less successfully, the Ramapough) the Mashpee plaintiffs had struggled to distinguish themselves from other minorities and ethnic groups, asserting tribal status based on a distinctive political-cultural history. In court they were not helped by the fact that few of them looked strongly "Indian." Some could pass for black, others for white.

* * *

Borderlines

Mashpee Indians suffered the fate of many small Native American groups who remained in the original thirteen states. They were not accorded the reservations and sovereign status (steadily eroded) of tribes west of the Mississippi. Certain of the eastern communities, such as the Seneca and the Seminoles, occupied generally recognized tribal lands. Others—the Lumbee, for example—possessed no collective lands but clustered in discrete regions, maintaining kinship ties, traditions, and sporadic tribal institutions. In all cases the boundaries of the community were permeable. There was intermarriage and routine migration in and out of the tribal center—sometimes seasonal, sometimes longer term. Aboriginal languages were much diminished, often entirely lost. Religious life was diverse—sometimes Christian (with a distinctive twist), sometimes a transformed tradition such as the Iroquois Longhouse Religion. Moral and spiritual values were often Native American amalgams compounded from both local traditions and pan-Indian sources. For example the ritual and regalia at New England powwows now reflect Sioux and other western tribal influences; in the 1920s the feathered "war bonnet" made its appearance among Wampanoag leaders. Eastern Indians generally lived in closer proximity to white (or black) society and in smaller groups than their western reservation counterparts. In the face of intense pressure some eastern communities have managed to acquire official federal recognition as tribes, others not. During the past two decades the rate of applications has risen dramatically.

Within this diversity of local histories and institutional arrangements the long-term residents of Mashpee occupied a gray area, at least in the eyes of the surrounding society and the law. The Indian identity of the Penobscot and Passamaquoddy was never seriously challenged, even though they had not been federally recognized and had lost or adapted many of their traditions. The Mashpee were more problematic. Partisans of their land claim, such as Paul Brodeur (1985), tend to accept without question the right of the tribal council, incorporated in 1974, to sue on behalf of a group that had lost its lands in the mid-nineteenth century. They see the question of tribal status as a legal red herring, or worse, a calculated ploy to deny the tribe its birthright. However procrustian and colonial in origin the legal definition of tribe, there was nonetheless a real issue at stake in the trial. Although tribal status and Indian identity have long been vague and politically constituted, not just anyone with some native blood or claim to adoption or shared tradition can be an Indian; and not just any Native American group can decide to be a tribe and sue for lost collective lands.

Indians in Mashpee owned no tribal lands (other than fifty-five acres acquired just before the trial). They had no surviving language, no clearly distinct religion, no blatant political structure. Their kinship was much diluted. Yet they did have a place and a reputation. For centuries Mashpee had been recognized as an Indian town. Its boundaries had not changed since 1665, when the land was formally deeded to a group called the South Sea Indians by the neighboring leaders Tookonchasun and Weepquish. The Mashpee plaintiffs of 1977 could offer as evidence surviving pieces of Native American tradition and political structures that seemed to have come and gone. They could also point to a sporadic history of Indian revivals continuing into the present.

The Mashpee were a borderline case. In the course of their peculiar litigation certain underlying structures governing the recognition of identity and difference became visible. Looked at one way, they were Indian, seen another way, they were not. Powerful ways of *looking* thus became inescapably problematic. The trial was less a search for the facts of Mashpee Indian culture and history than it was an experiment in translation—part of a long historical conflict and negotiation of "Indian" and "American" identities.

◆

I offer vignettes of persons and events in the courtroom that are obviously composed and condensed. Testimony evoked in a page or two may run to hundreds of pages in the transcript. Some witnesses were on the stand for several days. Moreover, real testimony almost never ends the way my vignettes do; it trails off in the quibbles and corrections of redirect and recross-examination. While I have included for comparison a verbatim excerpt from the transcript, I have generally followed my courtroom notes, checked against the record, and have not hesitated to rearrange, select, and highlight. Where quotation marks appear, the statement is a fairly exact quotation; the rest is paraphrase.

Overall, if the witnesses seem flat and somewhat elusive, the effect is intentional. Using the usual rhetorical techniques, I could have given a more intimate sense of peoples' personalities or of what they were really trying to express; but I have preferred to keep my distance. A courtroom is more like a theater than a confessional.

Mistrustful of transparent accounts, I want mine to manifest some of its frames and angles, its wavelengths.

* * *

History I

The case against the plaintiffs was straightforward: there never had been an Indian tribe in Mashpee. The community was a creation of the colonial encounter, a collection of disparate Indians and other minorities who sought over the years to become full citizens of the Commonwealth of Massachusetts and of the Republic. Decimated by disease, converted to Christianity, desirous of freedom from paternalistic state tutelage, the people of mixed Indian descent in Mashpee were progressively assimilated into American society. Their Indian identity had been lost, over and over, since the mid-seventeenth century.[2]

The plague. When the English Pilgrims arrived at Plymouth in 1620, they found a region devastated by a disease brought by white seamen. The settlers walked into empty Indian villages and planted in already cleared fields. The region was seriously underpopulated. In the years that followed Puritan leaders like Myles Standish pressed steadily to limit Indian territories and to establish clear "properties" for the growing number of newcomers. Misunderstandings inevitably ensued: for example whites claimed to own unoccupied land that had been ceded to them for temporary use.

Richard Bourne of Sandwich, a farmer near what is now Mashpee Pond and a tenant on Indian lands, studied the language of his landlords and soon became an effective mediator between the societies. He was friendly to the area's inhabitants, remnants of earlier groups, who came to be called South Sea Indians by the settlers to the north. He believed that they needed protection; becoming their advocate, he negotiated formal title to a large tract adjoining his farm (which in the meantime he had managed to purchase). His ally in these transactions was Paupmunnuck, a leader of the nearby Cotachesset.

Bourne's "South Sea Indian Plantation" was to become a refuge for Christian converts, for as white power increased, it became increasingly dangerous for Indians to live around Cape Cod unless they came together as a community of "praying Indians." Under Bourne's tutelage the Mashpee plantation was a center for the first Indian church on the Cape, organized in 1666.

Thus Mashpee was originally an artificial community, never a tribe. It was created from Indian survivors in an area between the traditional sachemdoms of Manomet and Nauset—the former centered on the present town of Bourne at the Cape's western edge, the latter near its tip.

Conversion to Christianity. Badly disorganized after the plague and confronted by a growing number of determined settlers, the Cape Cod Indians made accommodations. Live and let live was not the Puritan way, especially once their power had been consolidated. Tensions and conflicts

---

2. The two "histories" that follow represent the best brief interpretive accounts I could construct of the contending versions of Mashpee's past. They draw selectively on the expert testimony presented at the trial—testimony much too long, complex, and contested to summarize adequately. The overall shape of the two accounts reflects the summation provided at the end of the testimony by each side's principle attorney. "History I" owes a good deal to Francis Hutchins' book *Mashpee: The Story of Cape Cod's Indian Town* (1979). This book takes a somewhat more moderate position than the courtroom testimony on which it is based. "History II" owes something to the general approach of James Axtell's book *The European and the Indian* (1981). Axtell was a witness for the plaintiffs.

grew, leading to war in 1675 with the forces of the Wampanoag Supreme Sachem Metacomet ("King Philip"). After Metacomet's defeat Indians who sympathized with him were expelled from their lands. Many, including some who had remained neutral, were sold into slavery.

The price for living on ancestral lands in eastern New England was cooperation with white society. The Mashpee, under Bourne's tutelage became model Christians. By 1674 ninety Mashpee inhabitants were counted as baptized, and twenty-seven were admitted to full communion. The "praying Indians" were entering a new life. They stopped consulting "powwows" (medicine men, in seventeenth-century usage); they respected the Sabbath and other holy days, severed ties with "pagans," altered child-rearing practices, dressed in new ways, washed differently. The changes were gradual but telling. They reflected not only a tactical accommodation but also a new belief, born of defeat, that the powerful white ways must be superior. When Bourne died in 1682, his successor as protestant minister was an Indian, Simon Popmonet, son of Bourne's old ally Paupmunnuck. This was a further sign that the Indians were willingly giving up their old ways for the new faith.

"Plantation" status. Once the South Sea Indian Plantation had been established, its inhabitants' claim to their land rested on a written deed and on English law rather than on any aboriginal sovereignty. Like other "plantations" in New England, the community at Mashpee was a joint-ownership arrangement by a group of "proprietors." Under English law proprietors were licensed to develop a vacant portion of land, reserving part for commons, part for the church, and part for individual holdings. All transfers of land were to be approved collectively. This plantation-proprietory form, as applied to early Cape Cod settlements such as Sandwich and Barnstable, was intended to evolve quickly into a township where freemen held individual private property and were represented in the General Court of the colony. The white plantations around Mashpee did evolve directly into towns. From the late seventeenth century on their common lands were converted into private individual holdings in fee simple. Mashpee followed the same course, but more slowly. As late as 1830 its lands were the joint property of proprietors.

For complex historical reasons Mashpee's progress toward full citizenship lagged almost two centuries behind that of its neighbors. An enduring prejudice against Indians, and their supposed lack of "civility" certainly played a part, for during the early and mid-eighteenth century the Indian plantation was governed in humiliating ways by white "guardians." Nonetheless, development toward autonomy, while delayed, did occur. In 1763, after a direct appeal to King George III, Mashpee won the right to incorporation as a district, a step on the road to township status and a liberation from oppressive meddling by white outsiders. Then, beginning in 1834 and culminating in 1870, a series of acts of the Massachusetts legislature changed the Mashpee plantation into an incorporated town. Its inhabitants had overcome the prejudice and paternalism that had so long hemmed them in. They were now full-fledged citizens of Massachusetts.

Taking the colonists' side. From early on the Indian inhabitants of Mashpee gave signs of active identification with the new white society. During King Philip's War a certain Captain Amos, probably a Nauset from near Sandwich, led a group of Indians against Metacomet. Amos became a prominent inhabitant of Mashpee after the conflict ended. A century later the district of Mashpee sent a contingent to fight in the Revolutionary War against the British, a commitment of troops even greater than that of the surrounding white towns. Reliable accounts estimate that about half the adult male population died in the war. A Mashpee Indian, Joshua Pocknet, served at Valley Forge with George Washington. At these critical moments, therefore, the descendants of the South Sea Indians showed something more than simple acquiescence under colonial rule. Their enthusiastic patriotism strongly suggests that they had identified with white society, relinquishing any sense of a separate tribal political identity.

Intermarriage. Mashpee's population showed two significant periods of expansion. During the 1660s and 1670s there had been an influx of Indians from elsewhere on the Cape. Then after a century of relative equilibrium the population rose again in the 1760s and 1770s. Census figures are inexact and subject to interpretation, but it seems clear that before 1760 the principal newcomers were a steady trickle of New England Indians: Wampanoags from Gay Head and Herring Pond, Narragansets and Mohicans from Connecticut, Long Island Montauks. Immigration was restrained by the tutelage of outside "guardians," some of whom had an interest in keeping Mashpee small so that "unused" Indian lands could be made available for whites. After 1763, however, the newly incorporated district opened its borders to a variety of new settlers. A few whites entered by marriage but maintained a separate legal status. Their progeny, if one parent was Indian, could become proprietors. A least one white man "went native," living in a wigwam—just as the Indian residents of Mashpee were abandoning the last of theirs. Four Hessian mercenaries stayed on after the Revolutionary War and married Mashpee women. It is recorded that they accepted Indian manners.

The 1776 census counted fourteen "negroes" in a total population of 341. Significant intermarriage with freed black slaves occurred in this period, but it is difficult to say how much since common parlance, reflected in the census, sometimes mixed diverse peoples of brownish skin color in categories such as "Indian," "mulatto," or "negro." Intermarriage between blacks and Indians was encouraged by a common social marginality and by a relative shortage of men among the Indians and of women among the blacks. The local racial mix also included Cape Verde islanders and exotic imports resulting from the employment of Mashpee men in the far-flung sailing trades and women in domestic service: a Mexican and an Indian from Bombay are mentioned in the written sources.

By 1789 Mashpee's white minister, the Reverend Gideon Hawley, had become so concerned about Mashpee being overrun by blacks and foreigners that he engineered a return to plantation status, with himself as guardian of the town's threatened authenticity. This return to a restrictive paternalism was a setback for Mashpee's ability to grow and develop into a distinctive, independent nonwhite community. It was not until the 1840s, after a long conflict with Hawley's successor, the Reverend Phineas Fish, that local leaders finally rid themselves of outside tutelage. The struggle for citizenship had been slowed but not stopped. By the time of the final transition from plantation to township status in the four decades after 1830 the American citizens of Mashpee had become a complex mix—"colored" in contemporary parlance—that included several American Indian, black, and foreign ingredients.

Mashpee becomes a town. In 1834, following a popular rebellion against the outside authority of the Presbyterian minister Fish, district status was again accorded by the Massachusetts General Court. The Mashpee were no longer wards of the state and, like other towns, were governed by three elected selectmen. But full citizenship did not follow, largely because the proprietors of Mashpee wished to preserve traditional restraints on the sale of lands to outsiders. Leaders such as Daniel Amos argued that many inhabitants of Mashpee were not yet ready for the responsibilities of citizenship and unrestricted property rights. They might sell their lands irresponsibly or be maneuvered into debt; the community would be invaded and broken up. In practice the entailment on property did not seal off Mashpee from growth. To qualify as a landowner one had to trace ancestry to at least one Indian proprietor; and by the mid-nineteenth century quite a few individuals around the Cape could make this claim. In 1841–42, at the urging of Indian entrepreneurs such as Solomon Attaquin, who had returned to Mashpee with the end of state tutelage, most of the district's common lands were divided among its individual proprietors—men, women, and children. Lands could now be freely bought and sold, but still only among proprietors.

This progress did not go uncontested. Mashpee was divided among those who, like Attaquin—self-made men reflecting the era's dominant laissez-faire capitalist ethos—wanted to move quickly to remove all barriers to individual initiative and others who wanted to move more slowly or who saw in the old plantation entailments a guarantee of community integrity. In 1868 matters finally came to a head. A petition to the General Court from two of Mashpee's three selectmen and twenty-nine residents requested an end to all land-sale restrictions and the granting of full state and federal voting rights. This petition was promptly countered by a "remonstrance" signed by the third selectman and fifty-seven Mashpee residents urging that the district's status not be altered. A public hearing was called to air the differing views.

The hearing, which took place in early 1869, marks a crucial turning point in Mashpee history. Records of its disagreements offer a rare access to a diversity of local voices and opinions. Those who spoke in favor of the proposed changes evoked centuries of degrading state tutelage and second-class status. It was time, they said, for Mashpee inhabitants to be full citizens, to stand on their own. If this meant that some would fail or be displaced from their lands, so be it. They spoke also of the commercial advantages to the region of making portions of its land available for outside capital investment. Representatives of Mashpee's "colored non-proprietors" (a status that gave certain mulattoes and blacks all rights of proprietorship except title to land) also favored the changes in legal status. As valued members of the community they felt the restriction on landholding to be an insult and a reminder of an inferior condition they had in every other respect left behind.

Others opposed the changes. They argued that the influx of outside capital would be a very mixed blessing, and without the present protections many who were not wealthy and wise to the ways of business would soon be displaced. They would find themselves, in the words of one speaker, "ducking and dodging from one city to another, and gain no residence." Some proprietors did not think the right to vote in state and federal elections worth the risk; the present system, providing real control over Mashpee's government, seemed sufficient to local needs. The Reverend Joseph Amos ("Blind Joe" Amos), the community's most influential spiritual voice and leader of a successful Indian Baptist movement three decades earlier, opposed the changes. He said that another generation of preparation was needed before the proposed step could safely be taken. Solomon Attaquin, who owned the Hotel Attaquin, a renowned hunting lodge in Mashpee, spoke for abandoning the district's special status. He evoked a lifelong dream of full citizenship and equality, a dream shared with others in the community. Those who had worked long and hard for this day should not have to die without gaining the status of free men in the commonwealth and the nation.

A vote was taken. Eighteen favored participation in federal and state elections, eighteen were opposed. The removal of land restrictions was sharply rejected, twenty-six to fourteen. Despite this vote by a minority of the total population the recorded discussions clearly showed a consensus in favor of ultimately ending Mashpee's special status, with disagreements only on the timing. The Massachusetts General Court, recognizing this fact and more impressed by Mashpee's "progressive" voices, in 1870 formally abolished the status of "Mashpee proprietor." All lands were henceforth held in fee simple with no restrictions on alienation. All residents, whatever their ancestry, now enjoyed equal status before the law. The transfer of town lands to outsiders began immediately.

This turning point marked the end of Mashpee's distinctive institutional status stemming from its Indian past. Though the community was divided on the change, the most dynamic, forward-looking leaders favored it; whatever their hesitations on timing, community members willingly embraced their future as Massachusetts and United States citizens.

Assimilation. During the years between 1670 and the 1920s Indians throughout the nation were forced to abandon tribal organizations and to become individual citizen-farmers, workers, and businessmen. This was the period of the Dawes Act with its extensive land-allotment projects west of the Mississippi. Not until the twenties was there much evidence anywhere of tribal dynamism. Mashpee residents continued to live as before, working as hunting and fishing guides, servants, and laborers in various trades. The town remained a backwater. To find steady work people often had to move to nearby towns or even farther afield. The historical record contains little evidence of any distinctly Indian life in Mashpee before the Wampanoag revival movements of the twenties. The town apparently did not undergo any major demographic or social changes and remained a rather cohesive community of long-term residents, most of whom were of varying degrees of Indian descent. Significantly, between 1905 and 1960 the category "Indian" disappeared from Mashpee's federal census records. The more than two hundred individuals who had previously been so classified were now listed as either "colored" (distinct from "negro") or "other." Only in 1970 would they again be called Indian. In the eyes of the state the majority of Mashpee's inhabitants were simply Americans of color.

Some of these Americans participated in the founding of the Wampanoag Nation in the late twenties. At that time various more-or-less theatrical revivals of Indian institutions were under way. People in Mashpee showed interest, but the daily life and government of the town were not materially affected. The Wampanoags did not, like many other Indian groups in the thirties, take advantage of the turnaround in policy at John Collier's Bureau of Indian Affairs (BIA) to reorganize themselves as a federally recognized "tribal" unit. The new sense of Indianness around Mashpee was a matter of county fairlike powwows, costumes, and folkloric dances.

The individuals of Indian ancestry from Mashpee who filed suit in 1976 were American citizens similar to Irish-or Italian–Americans with strong ethnic attachments. Individuals such as Earl Mills and John and Russell Peters had simply taken advantage of the latest wave of pan-Indian revivalism and the prospect of financial gain to constitute themselves as a Mashpee Tribe. Mashpee's distinctive history was in fact a story of Indian–Christian remnants who over the centuries had repeatedly given up their customs and sovereignty. Theirs had been a long, hard struggle for equality and respect in a multiethnic America.

Vicky M. Costa

Vicky Costa is seventeen years old; her father is Portuguese, her mother Indian. She considers herself an Indian. She looks like any American teenager.

Q.: How do you know you're an Indian? A.: My mother told me.

She speaks softly. Judge Skinner asks her to speak up so the court can hear. "Think of yourself shouting across a field to those people," indicating the jury, "over there." (The "field" is a courtroom cluttered with lawyers tables, papers, documents, items of evidence.)

Vicky Costa does not shout, and everyone listens closely. She tells about the values she is currently learning in Mashpee: "To walk on Mother Earth in balance, and to respect every living thing."

Q.: How often do you dance? A.: All the time. Q.: When did you dance most recently? A.: Last night.

She describes her Indian dancing. She says she first learned at a powwow "a long time ago." Now she attends powwows regularly.

She names the dances: animal names, "blanket dance," "fancy dance." In the "round dance" they turn and dance to the good and bad spirit, moving in both directions so neither of the spirits will be offended. Is there music? Singing? Just the round-dance song. The purpose of the animal dances? To imitate the animals, mocking them. To thank the Creator for that animal.

(The mood in these questions and answers is conversational, quiet. Is it partly because this time Ann Gilmore of the plaintiffs' trial team is conducting the examination? It is one of the rare moments in the trial when a woman speaks directly with another woman. For whatever reasons the prevailing sense of contest and performance is gone.)

Costa testifies that she has been studying what she calls the "Wampanoag language" for one-and-a-half years. She says that as a girl she had to go to the Baptist church but now believes in Indian values.

On cross-examination she assents to hostile questions with the devastating American teenage shrug: "Yeah... yeah... yeah..."

History II

The case against the Mashpee plaintiffs was based on a reading of Cape Cod history. Documents were gathered, interpreted, and arranged in a coherent sequence. The story emerged of a small mixed community fighting for equality and citizenship while abandoning, by choice or coercion, most of its aboriginal heritage. But a different, also coherent, story was constructed by the plaintiffs, drawing on the same documentary record. In this account the residents of Mashpee had managed to keep alive a core of Indian identity over three centuries against enormous odds. They had done so in supple, sometimes surreptitious ways, always attempting to control, not reject, outside influences.

The plague. Aboriginally the concept of tribe has little meaning. The "political" institutions of Native American groups before contact with Europeans varied widely. Cape Cod Indian groupings seem to have been flexible, with significant movement across territories. Communities formed and reformed. In this context it is unclear whether the elders of local villages or sachems or supreme sachems should be identified as "tribal" leaders. These individuals had supreme power in some situations, limited authority in others. The plague was a disaster, but it did not decimate the Cape to the extent that it did the Plymouth area. In any event the response of the survivors at Mashpee, regrouping to form a cohesive unit, was a traditional political response, albeit to an unusual emergency. Written sources reflect only the views of whites, such as the evangelist Bourne, who saw his "praying Indians" paternalistically as passive remnants. The intentions of leaders such as Paupmunnuck and his kin are not recorded.

Thus it is anachronistic to say that the community gathered at what would later be called Mashpee was not a tribe. It is well known that the political institutions of many bona fide American Indian "tribes" actually emerged during the nineteenth and twentieth centuries in response to white expectations and power. Neat analytic categories such as "political organization," "kinship," "religion," and "economy" do not reflect Indian ways of seeing things. The simple fact remains that Bourne's South Sea Indian Plantation was a discrete community of Cape Cod Indians living on traditional Indian land—an arrangement that, through many modifications, survived until the mid-twentieth century.

Conversion to Christianity. Accounts of conversion as a process of "giving up old ways" or "choosing a new path" usually reflect a wishful evangelism rather than the more complex realities of cultural change, resistance, and translation. Recent ethnohistorical scholarship has tended to show that Native Americans' response to Christianity was syncretic over the long run, almost never a radical either-or choice. Moreover, in situations of drastically unequal power, as on Puritan Cape Cod, one should expect the familiar response of colonized persons: outward agreement and inner resistance.

The disruptions caused by disease, trade, and military conquest were extreme. All Indian societies had to adjust, and they developed varying strategies for doing so. Some passed through revitalization movements in the late eighteenth and early nineteenth centuries, led by messianic figures: the Delaware Prophet or Handsome Lake. These movements incorporated Christian features in a new "traditional" religion. Other groups renewed native culture by using Christianity for their own purposes. The white man's religion could be added on to traditional deities and rites. Beliefs that appeared contradictory to Puritan evangelists coexisted in daily life. Native American religions are generally more tolerant, pragmatic, and inclusive than Christianity, a strongly evangelical, exclusive faith.

This is not to say that groups such as the South Sea Indians did not embrace Christianity in good faith or find there a source of spiritual strength. It is only to caution against the either-or logic of conversion as seen by the outsiders whose accounts dominate the written record. The gain of Christian beliefs did not necessarily mean the loss of Indian spirituality. It is easy to be impressed by surface transformations of clothing and public behavior and to forget that continuous kin ties and life on a familiar piece of land also carry potent "religious" values.

Adopting Christianity in Mashpee was not merely a survival strategy in an intolerant, hostile environment. The faith of the "praying Indians" kept a distinctly indigenous cast. Beginning with Richard Bourne's successor, Simon Popmonet, Indian ministers in Mashpee preached in Massachusett, a practice that continued throughout the eighteenth century. When white missionaries were imposed from outside, they were forced to use some Massachusett or to compromise, like Gideon Hawley, who conducted bilingual services in tandem with a respected Indian pastor, Solomon Briant. Moreover, the historical record before 1850 is filled with conflict between authoritarian missionaries and Indian church members. Hawley, who served from 1757 to 1807, progressively alienated his parishioners, especially after Solomon Briant's death in 1775. His successor, Phineas Fish, lost virtually all local support and in 1840, after a protracted struggle, was physically ejected from the Old Indian Meeting House by irate Indian Christians.

Baptist revivalism had already won over most of the congregation, a change tied to a political assertion of Indian power. As in many nativist revitalization movements, an Indian outsider took a leading role—in this case William Apes, a young Pequot Baptist preacher. Blind Joe Amos had already acquired a larger following for his all-Indian Baptist meetings than the Congregationalist minister, Fish.

The situation was volatile. Apes, a firebrand with a vision of united action by "colored" peoples against white oppressors, stimulated a Masphee "Declaration of Independence" in 1833 on behalf of a sovereign Mashpee Tribe. (This was one of the few times before the twentieth century that the word tribe appears in the historical record.) The effect of the declaration and of the political maneuvers that ensued was to wrest control of the town's religion from the outsider Fish, reclaiming the Meeting House and funds from Harvard University supporting Indian Christianity for the majority faith, which was now Baptist. Mashpee returned to district status, free of outside governors.

Over the centuries Indians in Mashpee fought to keep control first of their Presbyterian and then their Baptist institutions. Religion was a political as well as a spiritual issue. Well into the 1950s the New England Baptist Convention habitually referred to Mashpee as "our Indian church." The exact nature of Mashpee Christian belief and practice over the centuries is obscure. The historical record does not inform us, for example, of exactly what took place in Blind Joe Amos' insurgent Baptist services during the 1830s; but even the partial written record makes it clear that Christianity in Mashpee, symbolized by the Old Indian Meeting House, was a site of local power and of resistance to outsiders. At recurring intervals it was a focus of openly Indian, or "tribal," power.

"Plantation" Status. Leaders of the South Sea Indians probably recognized, with Bourne, that title to land under white law was needed if it was not to be despoiled by an aggressive colonization; but seventeenth-century English proprietory forms did not unduly restrict their ability to function as an Indian community. Collective ownership of land, with individual use rights, could be maintained. The legal status that to some appeared an impediment to progress in fact protected the traditional life ways of Indian proprietors.

Although eastern Indians were not accorded reservation lands, Mashpee's plantation status created a de facto reservation. Unlike all its neighbors Mashpee did not quickly become a town but had the status forced on it in 1869. The plantation was widely considered to be Indian land held collectively in a distinctive manner. The reasons for keeping Mashpee "backward," a pupil of the state, were often racist and paternalist; but from the viewpoint of a small group struggling to maintain its collective identify, the proprietorship arrangement was an effective way of having legal status while also maintaining a difference. While there was internal disagreement at times, the majority of Mashpee proprietors consistently favored keeping the plantation land system. This was changed only by legislative fiat in 1969, against their expressed wishes. Until then an "archaic" status had been effectively used to preserve Indian lands in a collective form through rapidly changing times. The land claim suit aimed to restore a situation illegally altered by the Massachusetts legislature.

Taking the colonists' side. The fact that some South Sea Indians fought against Metacomet in King Philip's War does not prove that they were abandoning their Indian sovereignty or independence. More did not fight, and the motivations of those who did are a matter of speculation. There was nothing new about Indians making war on other Indians. Moreover they may have had little choice. Puritan authorities were on the warpath, and even "loyal" Indians were punished during and after the war by loss of lands and slavery.

As for the war against England, again we should be wary of imputing motives. The Mashpee Indians who served in the Revolutionary Army may not have done so primarily as "American" patriots. They were, among other things, rebelling against the authority of their missionary Hawley, an ardent Tory. Moreover, as Indian status has evolved in the United States, it has been legally recognized that the privileges of citizenship (including the decision to unite in war against a common enemy) do not contradict other arrangements establishing special group identity and status. One can be fully a citizen and fully an Indian.

To expect Cape Cod Indians to hold themselves apart from the historical currents and conflicts of the dominant society would be to ask them to commit suicide. Survival in changing circumstances meant participation, wherever possible on their own terms. Staying separate or uninvolved would be to yield to the dangerous fantasies of protectors, like Hawley, who worked to keep the Mashpee pure—and under his tutelage. The inhabitants of Mashpee again and again resisted this restrictive "authenticity." The record confirms that they wanted integrity but never isolation.

Intermarriage. There was a good deal of racial mixing In Mashpee, but the exact extent is hard to determine, given the shifting categories of different censuses and doubts about how race was actually measured. Mashpee was a refuge for misfits, refugees, and marginal groups. At certain times a natural alliance against dominant white society formed between the town's Indian "survivors" and newly freed blacks. The crucial issue is whether the core Indian community absorbed the outsiders or were themselves absorbed in the American melting pot.

Historical evidence supports the former conclusion. Since whites and people of color who settled in Mashpee during the eighteenth and most of the nineteenth centuries could not become proprietors, this limited the influx; non-Indians remained a significant but small minority. Children with one Indian parent could become full community members. Intermarriage frequently occurred, and thus the purity of Indian blood was much diluted; but the legal and social structure consistently favored Indian identification. With land entailment and the maintenance of close kin ties among property holders a core was maintained. In any event blood is a debatable measure of identity, and to arrive at quotas for determining "tribal" status is always a problematic exercise. There are federally recognized tribes as mixed as the Mashpee, and organized Indian groups vary widely in the amount of traceable ancestry they actually require for membership.

Ethnohistorical studies show that in New England mixing of different communities was common well before the Pilgrims' arrival. Adoption was frequent, and it was customary to capture and incorporate opponents in war. Indians were in this respect color blind. In colonial times a large number of white captives stayed with their captors, adopting Indian ways, some even becoming chiefs. Mashpee's later openness to outsiders—as long as the newcomers intermarried and conformed to Indian ways—was a continuation of an aboriginal tradition, not a loss of distinct identity.

In 1859, after more than a century of intermarriage and sporadic population growth (the dilution of Indian stock lamented by the missionary Hawley), a detailed report by the commissioner for Indian affairs, John Earle, offered a census of the "Mashpee Tribe" that included 371 "natives" and 32 "foreigners." The latter were people living on the land without proprietary rights and not lineal descendants of Indians. They were described as "Africans" and "colored." Only one "white" was listed. The names of "natives" listed on the 1859 census served in the trial as a benchmark of continuous "tribal" kinship ties.

Mashpee becomes a town. There is strong documentary evidence that most of the proprietors between 1834 and 1869 wanted to hold on to Mashpee's special land restrictions. Commissioner Earle asserts this in his report. "Progressives" such as Attaquin were more vocal, and their testimony thus receives more weight in the record than the less articulate majority who in 1869 voted decisively against township status. Spokesmen (note how few female voices are "heard" by history, although the role of women at the center of community life was undoubtedly crucial) such as Blind Joe Amos and his brother Daniel urged postponing the transition. They argued that most people in Mashpee were too "immature," not "ready" to dispose of their land individually. Give us just one more generation, Daniel Amos asked in the 1830s. His brother asked the same thing in the late 1860s. What do these arguments signify?

For those who see Mashpee's "development" and assimilation as inevitable, such statements require no interpretation: they simply show that even the traditionalists in Mashpee were ready eventually to give up their special status. But this is to assume the historical outcome. The Indian proprietors of Mashpee valued community integrity and possessed effective public and informal leadership. They had shown much strength and initiative in dealing with their various "protectors." The early historical record reveals a steady stream of petitions—1748, 1753, 1760—on behalf of the "poor Indians of Mashpee called the South Sea Indians" protesting abuses by the agents appointed to watch over them. More recently they had successfully asserted their autonomy against the missionaries Hawley and Fish. They were hardly "immature." Yet throughout the mid-nineteenth century Mashpee proprietors temporized, hesitated in the face of an "inevitable" progress. Their ability to protect their community from the coercions and enticements of white society was evidently precious to them.

The modified plantation status they had secured in 1834 gave them a way of keeping collective control over land and immigration while not isolating the community from interaction with the surrounding society. Even the "allotment" of lands sanctioned at that time reproduced an aboriginal land arrangement. Parcels were traditionally given to families for exclusive use while ultimate collective ownership was maintained. (In 1834, moreover, three thousand acres were formally kept as common land.) Continuing entailments on land sales outside the community guaranteed a flexible nineteenth-century tribalism. In this context public arguments about Mashpee's "immaturity" should be seen as ways of addressing an outside audience, the Massachusetts General Court, which still thought of the plantation as a ward of the state and which had already decided and again would arbitrarily decide its fate. It would be impolitic in addressing this body to say that Mashpee rejected full township status in the name of a distinctive vision of Indian community and citizenship. An argument for delay couched in paternalist rhetoric was more likely to succeed.

This interpretation of the debates in 1869 is at least as plausible as a literal reading of the recorded public utterances. Mashpee, like Indian communities throughout their recent history, was split between modernists and traditionalists. The traditionalists prevailed in the vote, but the modernists swayed the authorities. In changing Mashpee's land entailment the legislature violated both simple democracy and, the Federal Non-Intercourse Act of 1790. But even the forced change—although it ultimately brought much land into non-Indian hands—was not fatal. The Mashpee Indians used their new imposed status as they had their former one. For almost a century local government was kept firmly in the hands of a closely interrelated group of town officers. Mashpee remained "Cape Cod's Indian Town."

Assimilation. The Mashpee Indians did not "assimilate." The term's linear, either-or connotations cannot account for revivalism and for changes in the cultural and political climate between 1869 and 1960. There have been better and worse times in the United States to be publicly Indian. The late nineteenth and early twentieth centuries were among the worst. Government policy strongly favored tribal termination and the dispersal of collective lands. It was not until the late 1920s that the failure of allotment schemes was recognized and a "New Indian Policy" instituted at the BIA that favored tribal reorganization. If there is little evidence in the historical record of "tribal" life in Mashpee between 1869 and 1920, it is no surprise. Many groups all over the nation that would emerge later as tribes kept a low profile during these years. Mashpee seemed to be simply a sleepy town run by Indians, known for its good hunting and fishing. There was no political need or any wider context for them to display their Indianness in spectacular ways. Everyone knew who they were. A few attended the Carlisle Indian School in Pennsylvania during this period. Traditional myths and stories were told around kitchen tables; the piles of sticks at Mashpee's "Indian taverns" or "sacrifice heaps" grew into enormous mounds; life close to the land went on.

The history of Indian tribes in the United States has been punctuated by revival movements. The 1920s saw the organization of the Wampanoag Nation, with various explicit tribal institutions including a supreme sachem and a renewed interest in more public Indian displays: dances, regalia, powwows, and the like. As in all revitalization movements "outside" influences from other Indian groups played a major role. Eben Queppish, who had once ridden with Buffalo Bill's Wild West Show, taught traditional basket making and on demand donned his Sioux war bonnet. Individuals from Mashpee participated in nationally known groups such as the Thunderbird Indian Dancers. The effects of these revivals were largely cultural. There was little need for political reorganization in Mashpee, for the town was still governed by an unchallenged Indian majority. Political reorganization of a more explicit "tribal" structure would occur during a later revivalist period, the ferment spurred by the loss of town control after 1968.

Like other tribal groups the Mashpee have been opportunists, taking advantage of propitious historical contexts and undergoing external influences. They have survived as Indians because they have *not* conformed to white stereotypes. They have lived since aboriginal times in a traditional locale. They have maintained their own hybrid faith. Over the centuries they have controlled the rate of intermarriage and have fought for the political autonomy of their community. Explicitly tribal political structures have sometimes been visible to the outside world, as in 1833, the 1920s, and the 1970s, but for the most part these structures have been informal. Often the "tribe" in Mashpee was simply people deciding things by consensus in kitchens or at larger ad hoc gatherings where no records were kept. The chief in Mashpee, when there was one, shared authority with a variety of respected leaders, women and men. Politics was not hierarchical and did not need much in the way of institutional forms. The "tribe" in Mashpee was simply shared Indian kinship, place, history and a long struggle for integrity without isolation. Sometimes the Baptist parish served as an arm of the tribe; so did the town government. When the Mashpee Wampanoag Tribal Council, Inc. filed suit in 1976, it did so as a new legal arm of the tribe.

* * *

◆

The jurors were sequestered, accompanied by a large pile of documents. After twenty-one hours of deliberation they emerged with a verdict:

Did the proprietors of Mashpee, together with their spouses and children, constitute an Indian tribe on any of the following dates:

July 22, 1790? No.
March 31, 1834? Yes.
March 3, 1842? Yes.

June 23, 1869? No.
May 28, 1870? No.

Did the plaintiff groups, as identified by the plaintiff's witnesses, constitute an Indian tribe as of August 26, 1976? No.

If the people living in Mashpee constituted an Indian tribe or nation on any of the dates prior to August 26, 1976, did they continuously exist as a tribe or nation from such date or dates up to and including August 26, 1976? No.

◆

The verdict was a clear setback for the Indians' suit. But as a statement about their tribal history it was far from clear. Judge Skinner, after hearing arguments, finally decided that despite its ambiguity—the apparent emergence of a tribe in 1834—the jury's reply was a denial of the required tribal continuity. His dismissal of the suit has since been upheld on appeal.

The verdict remains, however, a curious and problematic outcome. We can only speculate on what happened in the jury room—the obscure chemistry of unanimity. What was done with the pile of historical documents during the twenty-one hours of discussion? Did the jurors search for a false precision? Asked to consider specific dates, did they conscientiously search the record for evidence of tribal institutions, for mention of the word *tribe*? If so, their literalism was nonetheless different from that encouraged by the particularist history of the defense, for the jury found that Mashpee Indians were inconsistently a tribe. Violating the judge's instructions, they found that a tribe first did not, then did, then did not again exist in Mashpee. Historical particularism does not by itself yield coherent developments or stories. Entities appear and disappear in the record.

The jurors' response contained an element of subversion. In effect it suggested that the trial's questions had been wrongly posed. Asked to apply consistent criteria of tribal existence over three centuries of intense change and disruption, the jury did so and came up with an inconsistent verdict.

Afterthoughts

The court behaved like a philosopher who wanted to know positively whether a cat was on the mat in Mashpee. I found myself seeing a Cheshire cat now a head, now a tail, eyes, ears, nothing at all, in various combinations. The Mashpee "tribe" had a way of going and coming; but something was persistently, if not continuously, there.

The testimony I heard convinced me that organized Indian life had been going on in Mashpee for the past 350 years. Moreover a significant revival and reinvention of tribal identity was clearly in process. I concluded that since the ability to act collectively as Indians is currently bound up with tribal status, the Indians living in Mashpee and those who return regularly should be recognized as a "tribe."

Whether land improperly alienated after 1869 should be transferred to them, how much, and by what means was a separate issue. I was, and am, less clear on this matter. A wholesale transfer of property would in any case be politically unthinkable. Some negotiation and repurchase arrangement—such as that in Maine involving local, state, and federal governments—could eventually establish a tribal land base in some portion of Mashpee. But that, for the moment, is speculation. In the short run the outcome of the trial was a setback for Wampanoag tribal dynamism.

In Boston Federal Court, Cape Cod Indians could not be seen for what they were and are. Modern Indian lives—lived within and against the dominant culture and state—are not captured by categories like tribe or identity. The plaintiffs could not prevail in court because their discourse and that of their attorneys and experts was inevitably compromised. It was constrained not simply by the law, with its peculiar rules, but by powerful assumptions and categories underlying the common sense that supported the law.

Among the underlying assumptions and categories compromising the Indians' case three stand out: (1) the idea of cultural wholeness and structure, (2) the hierarchical distinction between oral and literate forms of knowledge, and (3) the narrative continuity of history and identity.

The idea of cultural wholeness and structure. Although the trial was formally about "tribal" status, its scope was significantly wider. The *Montoya* definition of tribe, featuring race, territory, community and government, did not specifically mention "cultural" identity. The culture concept in its broad anthropological definition was still new in 1901; but the relatively loose *Montoya* definition reflected this emerging notion of a multifaceted, whole way of life, determined neither by biology nor politics. By 1978 the modern notion of culture was part of the trial's common sense.

In the courtroom an enormous amount of testimony from both sides debated the authenticity of Indian culture in Mashpee. Often this seemed to have become the crucial point of contention. Had the Mashpee lost their distinct way of life? Had they assimilated? In his summation for the plaintiffs Lawrence Shubow took time to define the term culture anthropologically, distinguishing it from the "ballet and top hat" conception. Closely paraphrasing E. B. Tylor's classic formula of 1871, he presented culture as a group's total body of behavior. He said that it included how people eat as well as how they think. Using the anthropological definition, he argued that ecology, the special feeling for hunting and fishing in Mashpee, the herring eaten every year, spitting on a stick at an "Indian tavern," these and many other unremarkable daily elements were integral parts of a whole, ongoing way of life.

It is easy to see why the plaintiffs focused on Indian culture in Mashpee. Culture, since it includes so much, was less easily disproven than tribal status. But even so broadly defined, the culture concept posed problems for the plaintiffs. It was too closely tied to assumptions of organic form and development. In the eighteenth century culture meant simply "a tending to natural growth." By the end of the nineteenth century the word could be applied not only to gardens and well-developed individuals but to whole societies. Whether it was the elitist singular version of a Matthew Arnold or the plural, lower-case concept of an emerging ethnography, the term retained its bias toward wholeness, continuity, and growth. Indian culture in Mashpee might be made up of unexpected everyday elements, but it had in the last analysis to cohere, its elements fitting together like the parts of a body. The culture concept accommodates internal diversity and an "organic" division of roles but not sharp contradictions, mutations, or emergences. It has difficulty with a medicine man who at one time feels a deep respect for Mother Earth and at another plans a radical real estate subdivision. It sees tribal "traditionalists" and "moderns" as representing aspects of a linear development, one looking back, the other forward. It cannot see them as, contending or alternating futures.

Groups negotiating their identity in contexts of domination and exchange persist, patch themselves together in ways different from a living organism. A community, unlike a body, can lose a central "organ" and not die. All the critical elements of identity are in specific conditions replaceable: language, land, blood, leadership, religion. Recognized, viable tribes exist in which any one or even most of these elements are missing, replaced, or largely transformed.

The idea of culture carries with it an expectation of roots, of a stable, territorialized existence. Weatherhead (1980:10–11) shows how the *Montoya* definition of tribe was designed to distinguish settled, peaceful Indian groups from mobile, marauding "bands." This political and military distinction of 1901 between tribe and band was debated again, in technical, anthropological terms, during the Mashpee trial. How rooted or settled should one expect "tribal" Native Americans to be—aboriginally, in specific contact periods, and now in highly mobile twentieth century America? Common notions of culture persistently bias the answer toward rooting rather than travel.

Moreover the culture idea, tied as it is to assumptions about natural growth and life, does not tolerate radical breaks in historical continuity. Cultures, we often hear, "die." But how many cultures pronounced dead or dying by anthropologists and other authorities have, like Curtis' "vanishing race" or Africa's diverse Christians, found new ways to be different? Metaphors of continuity and "survival" do not account for complex historical processes of appropriation, compromise, subversion, masking, invention, and revival. These processes inform the activity of a people not living alone but "reckoning itself among the nations." The Indians at Mashpee made and remade themselves through specific alliances, negotiations, and struggles. It is just as problematic to say that their way of life "survived" as to say that it "died" and was "reborn."

The related institutions of culture and tribe are historical inventions, tendentious and changing. They do not designate stable realities that exist aboriginally "prior to" the colonial clash of societies and powerful representations. The history of Mashpee is not one of unbroken tribal institutions or cultural traditions. It is a long, relational struggle to maintain and recreate identities that began when an English-speaking Indian traveler, Squanto, greeted the Pilgrims at Plymouth. The struggle was still going on three-and-a-half centuries later in Boston Federal Court, and it continues as the "Mashpee Tribe" prepares a new petition, this time for recognition from the Department of the Interior.

The hierarchical distinction between oral and literate. The Mashpee trial was a contest between oral and literate forms of knowledge. In the end the written archive had more value than the evidence of oral tradition, the memories of witnesses, and the intersubjective practice of fieldwork. In the courtroom how could one give value to an undocumented "tribal" life largely invisible (or unheard) in the surviving record?

As the trial progressed the disjuncture of oral and literate modes sharpened. The proceedings had been theatrical, full of contending voices and personalities, but they ended with a historian's methodical recitation of particulars. In the early portions of the trial the jurors had been asked to piece together and imagine a tribal life that showed recurring vitality but no unimpeachable essence or institutional core. Indianness in Mashpee often seemed improvised, ad hoc. The jury heard many wishful, incomplete memories of childhood events and debatable versions of recent happenings. In what may be called the "oral-ethnographic" parts of the trial many—too many—voices contended, in its "documentary" ending too few. A historian's seamless monologue was followed by attorneys' highly composed summations, two fully documented stories. There was no way to give voice to the silences in these histories, to choose the unrecorded.

The court imposed a literalist epistemology. Both sides searched the historical records for the presence or absence of the word and institution *tribe*. In this epistemology Indian identity could not be a real yet essentially contested phenomenon. It had to exist or not exist as an objective documentary fact persisting through time. Yet oral societies—or more accurately oral domains within a dominant literacy—leave only sporadic and misleading traces. Most of what is central to their existence is never written. Thus until recently nearly everything most characteristically Indian in Mashpee would have gone unrecorded. The surviving facts are largely the records of missionaries, government agents, outsiders. In the rare instances when Indians wrote—petitions, deeds, letters of complaint—it was to address white authorities and legal structures. Their voices were adapted to an imposed context. The same is true even in the rare cases in which a range of local *voices* was recorded, for example the public debates of 1869 on township status.

History feeds on what finds its way into a limited textual record. A historian needs constant skepticism and a willingness to read imaginatively, "against" the sources, to divine what is not represented in the accumulated selection of the archive. Ultimately, however, even the most imaginative history is tied to standards of textual proof. Anthropology, although it is also deeply formed and empowered by writing, remains closer to orality. Fieldwork—interested people talking with and being interpreted by an interested observer—cannot claim to be "documentary" in the way history can. For even though the origin of evidence in an archive may be just as circumstantial and subjective as that in a field journal, it enjoys a different value: archival data has been found, not produced, by a scholar using it "after the fact."

The distinction between historical and ethnographic practices depends on that between literate and oral modes of knowledge. History is thought to rest on past—documentary, archival—selections of texts. Ethnography is based on present—oral, experiential, observational—evidence. Although many historians and ethnographers are currently working to attenuate, even erase this opposition, it runs deeper than a mere disciplinary division of labor, for it resonates with the established (some would say metaphysical) dichotomy of oral and literate worlds as well as with the pervasive habit in the West of sharply distinguishing synchronic from diachronic, structure from change. As Marshall Sahlins (1985) has argued, these assumptions keep us from seeing how collective structures, tribal or cultural, reproduce themselves historically by risking themselves in novel conditions. Their wholeness is as much a matter of reinvention and encounter as it is of continuity and survival.

The narrative continuity of history and identity. Judge Skinner instructed the jury to decide whether the Indians of Mashpee had continuously constituted a tribe prior to filing suit in 1976. For the land claim to go forward the same tribal group had to have existed, without radical interruption, from at least the eighteenth century. The court's common sense was that the plaintiffs' identity must be demonstrated as an unbroken narrative, whether of survival or change. Both attorneys in their summations duly complied.

St. Clair's story of a long struggle for participation in plural American society and Shubow's "epic of survival and continuity" had in common a linear teleology. Both ruled out the possibility of a group existing discontinuously, keeping open multiple paths, being both Indian and American.

An either-or logic applied. St. Clair argued that there had never been a tribe in Mashpee, only individual Indian Americans who had repeatedly opted for white society. His story of progress toward citizenship assumed a steady movement away from native tradition. Identity as an American meant giving up a strong claim to tribal political integrity in favor of ethnic status within a national whole. Life as an American meant death as an Indian. Conversely Shubow's Mashpee had "survived" as a living tribe and culture from aboriginal times; but the historical record often contradicted his claim, and he sometimes strained to assert continuity. The plaintiffs could not admit that Indians in Mashpee had lost, even voluntarily abandoned, crucial aspects of their tradition while at the same time pointing to evidence over the centuries of reinvented "Indianness." They could not show tribal institutions as relational and political, coming and going in response to changing federal and state policies and the surrounding ideological climate. An identity could not die and come back to life. To recreate a culture that had been lost was, by definition of the court, inauthentic.

But is any part of a tradition lost if it can be remembered, even generations later, caught up in a present dynamism and made to symbolize a possible future?

The Mashpee were trapped by the stories that could be told about them. In this trial "the facts" did not speak for themselves. Tribal life had to be emplotted, told as a coherent narrative. In fact only a few basic stories are told, over and over, about Native Americans and other "tribal" peoples. These societies are always either dying or surviving, assimilating or resisting. Caught between a local past and a global future, they either hold on to their separateness or "enter the modern world." The latter entry—tragic or triumphant—is always a step toward a global future defined by technological progress, national and international cultural relations. Are there other possible stories?

Until recently the "history" accorded to tribal peoples has always been a Western history. They may refuse it, embrace it, be devastated by it, changed by it. But the familiar paths of tribal death, survival, assimilation, or resistance do not catch the specific ambivalences of life in places like Mashpee over four centuries of defeat, renewal, political negotiation, and cultural innovation. Moreover most societies that suddenly "enter the modern world" have already been in touch with it for centuries.

The Mashpee trial seemed to reveal people who were sometimes separate and "Indian," sometimes assimilated and "American." Their history was a series of cultural and political transactions, not all-or-nothing conversions or resistances. Indians in Mashpee lived and acted between cultures in a series of ad hoc engagements. No one in Boston Federal Court, expert or layperson, stood at the end point of this historical series, even though the stories of continuity and change they told implied that they did. These stories and the trial itself were episodes, turns in the ongoing engagement. Seen from a standpoint not of finality (survival or assimilation) but of emergence, Indian life in Mashpee would not flow in a single current.

Interpreting the direction or meaning of the historical "record" always depends on present possibilities. When the future is open, so is the meaning of the past. Did Indian religion or tribal institutions disappear in the late nineteenth century? Or did they go underground? In a present context of serious revival they went underground; otherwise they disappeared. No continuous narrative or clear outcome accounts for Mashpee's deeply contested identity and direction. Nor can a single development weave together the branching paths of its past, the dead ends and hesitations that, with a newly conceived future, suddenly become prefigurations.

◆

(Hesitations. In 1869 Blind Joe Amos and the majority of Mashpee proprietors agreed that they were not yet ready to become citizens of

Massachusetts, separate entrepreneurs with individual control over their lands. They held back, declining a "progressive" step imposed by the legislature. Was it from backwardness? Confusion? Fear? Or something else: an alternate vision? A different voice?

What Susan Howe (1985) has written about a woman—Emily Dickinson, working during the same decade from another place of New England "isolation"—echoes strangely the Indian predicament: the problem of finding a different way through capitalist America.

> HESITATE from the Latin, meaning to stick. Stammer. To hold back in doubt, have difficulty speaking. "*He* may pause but *he* must not hesitate"—Ruskin. Hesitation circled back and surrounded everyone in that confident age of aggressive industrial expansion and brutal Empire building. Hesitation and Separation. The Civil War had split America in two. *He* might pause, *She* hesitated. Sexual, racial, and geographical separation are at the heart of Definition. Tragic and eternal dichotomy—if we concern ourselves with the deepest Reality, is this world of the imagination the same for men and women? What voice when we hesitate and are silent is moving to meet us? (p. 22)

In 1869 Joe Amos and the others did not go on record as resisting full citizenship. Separation and dichotomy were not their agenda: they were already more than half-caught up in a new America. It is important to distinguish hesitation from resistance, for hesitation need not oppose or acquiesce in the dominant course. It can be an alert waiting, thinking, anticipating of historical possibilities. Along with the history of resistances we need a history of hesitations.)

Stories of cultural contact and change have been structured by a pervasive dichotomy: absorption by the other *or* resistance to the other. A fear of lost identity, a Puritan taboo on mixing beliefs and bodies, hangs over the process. Yet what if identity is conceived not as a boundary to be maintained but as a nexus of relations and transactions actively engaging a subject? The story or stories of interaction must then be more complex, less linear and teleological. What changes when the subject of "history" is no longer Western? How do stories of contact, resistance, and assimilation appear from the standpoint of groups in which exchange rather than identity is the fundamental value to be sustained? Events are always mediated by local cultural structures. By focusing on the peripheral places, the neglected "islands of history" In Sahlins' words, "we ... multiply our conceptions of history by the diversity of structures. Suddenly there are all kinds of new things to consider" (1985:72).

In the diversity of local histories—like that of Mashpee—we find distinctive processes and directions. The channeled, inevitable flow of events begins to loop, waver, and fork. In 1830, for example, was the proprietary status of the Mashpee Indians an eroded "survival" from archaic English law, a social form destined to disappear? Or by the nineteenth century had it become a specific invention, a novel way to live on Indian land in modern America, a possible future? Neither story is false; both can be amply documented from the historical record. To say that the strange "tribal" integrity of the Mashpee Plantation was destined to disappear is to accept the history of the victors. But the suit filed a century later was an attempt to reopen this foregone conclusion. Mashpee's semiautonomous plantation, a specific mix of individual citizenship and collective entailment, now appeared not as a historical dead end but as a precursor of reinvented tribalism. No return to a pure Wampanoag tradition was at issue, but rather a reinterpretation of Mashpee's contested history in order to act—with other Indian groups—powerfully, in an impure present-becoming-future.

Whatever the trial's outcome "tribal" life had once again become powerful in Mashpee. Only a literal, backward-looking sense of authenticity (one no group would willingly apply to itself, only to others) could deny this emergent reality. The Wampanoag Supreme Sachem, Elsworth Oakley, commented after the verdict: "How can a white majority decide on whether we are a tribe? We know who we are."

The future of Native American life on Cape Cod after the setback in court is uncertain.

◆

The years immediately following the verdict were marked by disarray in Mashpee. An anticipated petition to the Department of the Interior for tribal status was slow to emerge. During this period the Bureau of Indian Affairs standardized its procedure for recognition claims, following criteria similar to those required by the court in *Mashpee v. New Seabury et al.* (Weatherhead 1980:17). The Indians in Mashpee watched with misgivings the progress of a petition by their fellow Wampanoags at Gay Head. In 1986 the petition was turned down in a preliminary finding. Government experts cited an insufficient degree of community specificity over the years and a loss of tribal political authority after Gay Head became a township in 1870. Gay Head's history was similar to Mashpee's.

Appealing the preliminary finding, the Native American Rights Fund presented additional evidence, compiled by Jack Campisi, of continuing social networks among Gay Head Indians and of a line of tribal authority after 1870. On February 8, 1987, for the first time ever the Bureau of Indian Affairs reversed a negative preliminary finding. The Gay Head Wampanoags were given full tribal recognition.

Quotations from a Native American Rights Fund press release:

Henry Sockbeson, the Penobscot attorney representing the tribe: "This decision means that the Gay Head will be able to settle their land claim within a few months. Under the terms of the settlement the Tribe will receive approximately 250 acres of land that can be developed. We anticipate that they will use it for housing and economic development."

Gladys Widdiss, chairperson of the Wampanoag Tribal Council of Gay Head, Inc.: "I am delighted. This now means that the Tribe can function in a formally recognized manner. Our status as a tribe can no longer be in doubt. Recognition means that our survival as a tribe for generations to come is assured."

Jack Campisi and Native American Rights Fund attorneys are working on Mashpee's petition.

TWO SNAPSHOTS

Mrs. Pells is an Indian born in Mashpee. She is seventy-one years old, now living eighteen miles away near the Bourne Bridge, and is an active member of the Tribal Council, Inc. She is dignified, slow-speaking.

She shows an enlarged photograph of her grandmother, Rebecca Hammond, Blind Joe Amos' daughter.

She has been a member of the Mashpee Wampanoag tribe "since birth."

She testifies that she lived in New York between 1928 and 1972 where she was active in a number of Native American organizations. During the 1940s she was secretary of the "American Indian Thunderbird Dancers." Most of the dancers did not originate in Massachusetts, and only one of the dancers was from Cape Cod.

◆

"Chiefy" Mills is Earl Mills's teenage son. He says he knows he is an Indian because his father told him. He likes to hunt and hang around with his cousins in Mashpee. A champion drummer, he participates often in Native American gatherings around New England. Recently he was among the young people arrested at a camping retreat held to promote Indian consciousness on the fifty-five acres of tribal land in Mashpee.

* * *

Whiteness as Property
106 Harv. L. Rev. 1707 (June 1993).

Cheryl I. Harris

Issues regarding race and racial identity as well as questions pertaining to property rights and ownership have been prominent in much public discourse in the United States. In this article, Professor Harris contributes to this discussion by positing that racial identity and property are deeply interrelated concepts. Professor Harris examines how whiteness, initially constructed as a form of racial identity, evolved into a form of property, historically and presently acknowledged and protected in American law. Professor Harris traces the origins of whiteness as property in the parallel systems of domination of Black and Native American peoples out of which were created racially contingent forms of property and property rights. Following the period of slavery and conquest, whiteness became the basis of racialized privilege—a type of status in which white racial identity provided the basis for allocating societal benefits both private and public in character.

These arrangements were ratified and legitimated in law as a type of status property. Even as legal segregation was overturned, whiteness as property continued to serve as a barrier to effective change as the system of racial classification operated to protect entrenched power.

Next, Professor Harris examines how the concept of whiteness as property persists in current perceptions of racial identity, in the law's misperception of group identity and in the Court's reasoning and decisions in the arena of affirmative action. Professor Harris concludes by arguing that distortions in affirmative action doctrine can only be addressed by confronting and exposing the property interest in whiteness and by acknowledging the distributive justification and function of affirmative action as central to that task.

> she walked into forbidden worlds
>
> impaled on the weapon of her own pale skin
>
> she was a sentinel
>
> at impromptu planning sessions
>
> of her own destruction . . .
>
> Cheryl I. Harris, *poem for alma*[1]

[P]etitioner was a citizen of the United States and a resident of the state of Louisiana of mixed descent, in the proportion of seven eighths Caucasian and one eighth African blood; that the mixture of colored blood was not discernible in him, and that he was entitled to every recognition, right, privilege and immunity secured to the citizens of the United States of the white race by its Constitution and laws . . . and thereupon entered a passenger train and took possession of a vacant seat in a coach where passengers of the white race were accommodated.

Plessy v. Ferguson[2]

I. INTRODUCTION

In the 1930s, some years after my mother's family became part of the great river of Black migration that flowed north, my Mississippi-born grandmother was confronted with the harsh matter of economic survival for herself and her two daughters. Having separated from my grandfather, who himself was trapped on the fringes of economic marginality, she took one long hard look at her choices and presented herself for employment at a major retail store in Chicago's central business district. This decision would have been unremarkable for a white woman in similar circumstances, but for my grandmother, it was an act of both great daring and self-denial, for in so doing she was presenting herself as a white woman. In the parlance of racist America, she was "passing."

---

[1]. Cheryl I. Harris, *poem for alma* (1990) (unpublished poem, on file at the Harvard Law School Library).

[2]. 163 U.S. 537, 538 (1896).

Her fair skin, straight hair, and aquiline features had not spared her from the life of sharecropping into which she had been born in anywhere/nowhere, Mississippi—the outskirts of Yazoo City. But in the burgeoning landscape of urban America, anonymity was possible for a Black person with "white" features. She was transgressing boundaries, crossing borders, spinning on margins, traveling between dualities of Manichean space, rigidly bifurcated into light/dark, good/bad, white/Black. No longer immediately identifiable as "Lula's daughter," she could thus enter the white world, albeit on a false passport, not merely passing, but *tres*passing.

Every day my grandmother rose from her bed in her house in a Black enclave on the south side of Chicago, sent her children off to a Black school, boarded a bus full of Black passengers, and rode to work. No one at her job ever asked if she was Black; the question was unthinkable. By virtue of the employment practices of the "fine establishment" in which she worked, she could not have been. Catering to the upper-middle class, understated tastes required that Blacks not be allowed.

She quietly went about her clerical tasks, not once revealing her true identity. She listened to the women with whom she worked discuss their worries—their children's illnesses, their husbands' disappointments, their boyfriends' infidelities—all of the mundane yet critical things that made up their lives. She came to know them but they did not know her, for my grandmother occupied a completely different place. That place—where white supremacy and economic domination meet—was unknown turf to her white co-workers. They remained oblivious to the worlds within worlds that existed just beyond the edge of their awareness and yet were present in their very midst.

Each evening, my grandmother, tired and worn, retraced her steps home, laid aside her mask, and reentered herself. Day in and day out, she made herself invisible, then visible again, for a price too inconsequential to do more than barely sustain her family and at a cost too precious to conceive. She left the job some years later, finding the strain too much to bear.

From time to time, as I later sat with her, she would recollect that period, and the cloud of some painful memory would pass across her face. Her voice would remain subdued, as if to contain the still remembered tension. On rare occasions she would wince, recalling some particularly racist comment made in her presence because of her presumed, shared group affiliation. Whatever retort might have been called for had been suppressed long before it reached her lips, for the price of her family's well-being was her silence. Accepting the risk of self-annihilation was the only way to survive.

Although she never would have stated it this way, the clear and ringing denunciations of racism she delivered from her chair when advanced arthritis had rendered her unable to work were informed by those experiences. The fact that self-denial had been a logical choice and had made her complicit in her own oppression at times fed the fire in her eyes when she confronted some daily outrage inflicted on Black people. Later, these painful memories forged her total identification with the civil rights movement. Learning about the world at her knee as I did, these experiences also came to inform my outlook and my understanding of the world.

My grandmother's story is far from unique. Indeed, there are many who crossed the color line never to return. Passing is well-known among Black people in the United States and is a feature of race subordination in all societies structured on white supremacy. Notwithstanding the purported benefits of Black heritage in an era of affirmative action, passing is not an obsolete phenomenon that has slipped into history.

The persistence of passing is related to the historical and continuing pattern of white racial domination and economic exploitation that has given passing a certain economic logic. It was a given to my grandmother that being white automatically ensured higher economic returns in the short term, as well as greater economic, political, and social security in the long run. Becoming white meant gaining access to a whole set of public and private privileges that materially and permanently guaranteed basic subsistence needs and, therefore, survival. Becoming white increased the possibility of controlling critical aspects of one's life rather than being the object of others' domination.

My grandmother's story illustrates the valorization of whiteness as treasured property in a society structured on racial caste. In ways so embedded that it is rarely apparent, the set of assumptions, privileges, and benefits that accompany the status of being white have become a valuable asset that whites sought to protect and that those who passed sought to attain—by fraud if necessary. Whites have come to expect and rely on these benefits, and over time these expectations have been affirmed, legitimated, and protected by the law. Even though the law is neither uniform nor explicit in all instances, in protecting settled expectations based on white privilege, American law has recognized a property interest in whiteness that, although unacknowledged, now forms the background against which legal disputes are framed, argued, and adjudicated.

My Article investigates the relationships between concepts of race and property and reflects on how rights in property are contingent on, intertwined with, and conflated with race. Through this entangled relationship between race and property, historical forms of domination have evolved to reproduce subordination in the present. * * * I examine the emergence of whiteness as property and trace the evolution of whiteness from color to race to status to property as a progression historically rooted in white supremacy and economic hegemony over Black and Native American peoples. The origins of whiteness as property lie in the parallel systems of domination of Black and Native American peoples out of which were created racially contingent forms of property and property rights. I further argue that whiteness shares the critical characteristics of property even as the meaning of property has changed over time. In particular, whiteness and property share a common premise—a conceptual nucleus—of a right to exclude. This conceptual nucleus has proven to be a powerful center around which whiteness as property has taken shape. Following the period of slavery and conquest, white identity became the basis of racialized privilege that was ratified and legitimated in law as a type of status property. After legalized segregation was overturned, whiteness as property evolved into a more modern form through the law's ratification of the settled expectations of relative white privilege as a legitimate and natural baseline.

[I examine] the two forms of whiteness as property—status property and modern property—that are the submerged text of two paradigmatic cases on the race question in American law, *Plessy v. Ferguson* and *Brown v. Board of Education*. As legal history, they illustrate an important transition from old to new forms of whiteness as property. Although these cases take opposite interpretive stances regarding the constitutional legitimacy of legalized racial segregation, the property interest in whiteness was transformed, but not discarded, in the Court's new equal protection jurisprudence.

[I then consider] the persistence of whiteness as property. I first examine how subordination is reinstituted through modern conceptions of race and identity embraced in law. Whiteness as property has taken on more subtle forms, but retains its core characteristic—the legal legitimation of expectations of power and control that enshrine the status quo as a neutral baseline, while masking the maintenance of white privilege and domination. I further identify the property interest in whiteness as the unspoken center of current polarities around the issue of affirmative action. As a legacy of slavery and de jure and de facto race segregation, the concept of a protectable property interest in whiteness permeates affirmative action doctrine in a manner illustrated by the reasoning of three important affirmative action cases—*Regents of the University of California v. Bakke, City of Richmond v. J. A. Croson & Co.,* and *Wygant v. Jackson Board of Education.*

* * *, I offer preliminary thoughts on a way out of the conundrum created by protecting whiteness as a property interest. I suggest that affirmative action, properly conceived and reconstructed, would de-legitimate the property interest in whiteness. I do not offer here a complete reformulation of affirmative action, but suggest that focusing on the distortions created by the property interest in whiteness would provoke different questions and open alternative perspectives on the affirmative action debate. The inability to see affirmative action as more than a search for the "blameworthy" among "innocent" individuals is tied to the inability to see the property interest in whiteness. Thus reconstructed, affirmative action would challenge the characterization of the unfettered right to exclude as a legitimate aspect of identity and property.

II. THE CONSTRUCTION OF RACE AND THE EMERGENCE OF WHITENESS AS PROPERTY

The racialization of identity and the racial subordination of Blacks and Native Americans provided the ideological basis for slavery and conquest. Although the systems of oppression of Blacks and Native Americans differed in form—the former involving the seizure and appropriation of labor, the latter entailing the seizure and appropriation of land—undergirding both was a racialized conception of property implemented by force and ratified by law.

The origins of property rights in the United States are rooted in racial domination. Even in the early years of the country, it was not the concept of race alone that operated to oppress Blacks and Indians; rather, it was the *interaction* between conceptions of race and property that played a critical role in establishing and maintaining racial and economic subordination.

The hyper-exploitation of Black labor was accomplished by treating Black people themselves as objects of property. Race and property were thus conflated by establishing a form of property contingent on race—only Blacks were subjugated as slaves and treated as property. Similarly, the conquest, removal, and extermination of Native American life and culture were ratified by conferring and acknowledging the property rights of whites in Native American land. Only white possession and occupation of land was validated and therefore privileged as a basis for property rights. These distinct forms of exploitation each contributed in varying ways to the construction of whiteness as property.

A. *Forms of Racialized Property: Relationships Between Slavery, Race, and Property*

1. *The Convergence of Racial and Legal Status.*—Although the early colonists were cognizant of race, racial lines were neither consistently nor sharply delineated among or within all social groups. Captured Africans sold in the Americas were distinguished from the population of indentured or bond servants—"unfree" white labor—but it was not an irrebuttable presumption that all Africans were "slaves" or that slavery was the only appropriate status for them. The distinction between African and white indentured labor grew, however, as decreasing terms of service were introduced for white bond servants. Simultaneously, the demand for labor intensified, resulting in a greater reliance on African labor and a rapid increase in the number of Africans imported into the colonies.

The construction of white identity and the ideology of racial hierarchy also were intimately tied to the evolution and expansion of the system of chattel slavery. The further entrenchment of plantation slavery was in part an answer to a social crisis produced by the eroding capacity of the landed class to control the white labor population. The dominant paradigm of social relations, however, was that, although not all Africans were slaves, virtually all slaves were not white. It was their racial otherness that came to justify the subordinated status of Blacks. The result was a classification system that "key[ed] official rules of descent to national origin" so that "[m]embership in the new social category of 'Negro' became itself sufficient justification for enslaveability." Although the cause of the increasing gap between the status of African and white labor is contested by historians, it is clear that "[t]he economic and political interests defending Black slavery were far more powerful than those defending indentured servitude."

By the 1660s, the especially degraded status of Blacks as chattel slaves was recognized by law. Between 1680 and 1682, the first slave codes appeared, codifying the extreme deprivations of liberty already existing in social practice. Many laws parceled out differential treatment based on racial categories: Blacks were not permitted to travel without permits, to own property, to assemble publicly, or to own weapons; nor were they to be educated. Racial identity was further merged with stratified social and legal status: "Black" racial identity marked who was subject to enslavement; "white" racial identity marked who was "free" or, at minimum, not a slave. The ideological and rhetorical move from "slave" and "free" to "Black" and "white" as polar constructs marked an important step in the social construction of race.

2. *Implications for Property.*—The social relations that produced racial identity as a justification for slavery also had implications for the conceptualization of property. This result was predictable, as the institution of slavery, lying at the very core of economic relations, was bound up with the idea of property. Through slavery, race and economic domination were fused.

Slavery produced a peculiar, mixed category of property and humanity—a hybrid possessing inherent instabilities that were reflected in its treatment and ratification by the law. The dual and contradictory character of slaves as property and persons was exemplified in the Representation Clause of the Constitution. Representation in the House of Representatives was apportioned on the basis of population computed by counting all persons and "three-fifths of all other persons"—slaves. Gouveneur Morris's remarks before the Constitutional Convention posed the essential question: "Upon what principle is it that slaves shall be computed in the representation? Are they men? Then make them Citizens & let them vote? Are they property? Why then is no other property included?"

The cruel tension between property and humanity was also reflected in the law's legitimation of the use of Blackwomen's bodies as a means of increasing property. In 1662, the Virginia colonial assembly provided that "[c]hildren got by an Englishman upon a Negro woman shall be bond or free according to the condition of the mother...." In reversing the usual common law presumption that the status of the child was determined by the father, the rule facilitated the reproduction of one's own labor force. Because the children of Blackwomen assumed the status of their mother, slaves were bred through Blackwomen's bodies. The economic significance of this form of exploitation of female slaves should not be underestimated. Despite Thomas Jefferson's belief that slavery should be abolished, like other slaveholders, he viewed slaves as economic assets, noting that their value could be realized more efficiently from breeding than from labor. A letter he wrote in 1805 stated: "I consider the labor of a breeding woman as no object, and that a child raised every 2 years is of more profit than the crop of the best laboring man."

Even though there was some unease in slave law, reflective of the mixed status of slaves as humans and property, the critical nature of social relations under slavery was the commodification of human beings. Productive relations in early American society included varying forms of sale of labor capacity, many of which were highly oppressive; but slavery was distinguished from other forms of labor servitude by its permanency and the total commodification attendant to the status of the slave. Slavery as a legal institution treated slaves as property that could be transferred, assigned, inherited, or posted as collateral. For example, in *Johnson v. Butler,* the plaintiff sued the defendant for failing to pay a debt of $496 on a specified date. Because the covenant had called for payment of the debt in "money or negroes," the plaintiff contended that the defendant's tender of one negro only, although valued by the parties at an amount equivalent to the debt, could not discharge the debt. The court agreed with the plaintiff. This use of Africans as a stand-in for actual currency highlights the degree to which slavery "propertized" human life.

Because the "presumption of freedom [arose] from color [white]" and the "black color of the race [raised] the presumption of slavery," whiteness became a shield from slavery, a highly volatile and unstable form of property. In the form adopted in the United States, slavery made human beings market-alienable and in so doing, subjected human life and personhood—that which is most valuable—to the ultimate devaluation. Because whites could not be enslaved or held as slaves, the racial line between white and Black was extremely critical; it became a line of protection and demarcation from the potential threat of commodification, and it determined the allocation of the benefits and burdens of this form of property. White identity and whiteness were sources of privilege and protection; their absence meant being the object of property.

Slavery as a system of property facilitated the merger of white identity and property. Because the system of slavery was contingent on and conflated with racial identity, it became crucial to be "white," to be identified as white, to have the property of being white. Whiteness was the characteristic, the attribute, the property of free human beings.

B. Forms of Racialized Property: Relationships Between Native American Land Seizure, Race, and Property

Slavery linked the privilege of whites to the subordination of Blacks through a legal regime that attempted the conversion of Blacks into objects of property. Similarly, the settlement and seizure of Native American land supported white privilege through a system of property rights in land in which the "race" of the Native Americans rendered their first possession rights invisible and justified conquest. This racist formulation embedded the fact of white privilege into the very definition of property, marking another stage in the evolution of the property interest in whiteness. Possession—the act necessary to lay the basis for rights in property—was defined to include only the cultural practices of whites. This definition laid the foundation for the idea that whiteness—that which whites alone possess—is valuable and is property.

Although the Indians were the first occupants and possessors of the land of the New World, their racial and cultural otherness allowed this fact to be reinterpreted and ultimately erased as a basis for asserting rights in land. Because the land had been left in its natural state, untilled and unmarked by human hands, it was "waste" and, therefore, the appropriate object of settlement and appropriation. Thus, the possession maintained by the Indians was not "true" possession and could safely be ignored. This interpretation of the rule of first possession effectively rendered the rights of first possessors contingent on the race of the possessor. Only particular forms of possession—those that were characteristic of white settlement—would be recognized and legitimated. Indian forms of possession were perceived to be too ambiguous and unclear.

The conquest and occupation of Indian land was wrapped in the rule of law. The law provided not only a defense of conquest and colonization, but also a naturalized regime of rights and disabilities, power and disadvantage that flowed from it, so that no further justifications or rationalizations were required. A key decision defending the right of conquest was *Johnson and Graham's Lessee v. M'Intosh,* in which both parties to the action claimed the same land through title descendant from different Indian tribes. The issue specifically presented was not merely whether Indians had the power to convey title, but to whom the conveyance could be made—to individuals or to the government that "discovered" land. In holding that Indians could only convey to the latter, the Court reasoned that Indian title was subordinate to the absolute title of the sovereign that was achieved by conquest because "[c]onquest gives a title which the Courts of the conqueror cannot deny...." If property is understood as a delegation of sovereign power—the product of the power of the state—then a fair reading of history reveals the racial oppression of Indians inherent in the American regime of property.

In *Johnson* and similar cases, courts established whiteness as a prerequisite to the exercise of enforceable property rights. Not all first possession or labor gave rise to property rights; rather, the rules of first possession and labor as a basis for property rights were qualified by race. This fact infused whiteness with significance and value because it was solely through being white that property could be acquired and secured under law. Only whites possessed whiteness, a highly valued and exclusive form of property.

C. Critical Characteristics of Property and Whiteness

The legal legacy of slavery and of the seizure of land from Native American peoples is not merely a regime of property law that is (mis)informed by racist and ethnocentric themes. Rather, the law has established and protected an actual property interest in whiteness itself, which shares the critical characteristics of property and accords with the many and varied theoretical descriptions of property.

Although by popular usage property describes "things" owned by persons, or the rights of persons with respect to a thing, the concept of property prevalent among most theorists, even prior to the twentieth century, is that property may "consist[] of rights in 'things' that are intangible, or whose existence is a matter of legal definition." Property is thus said to be a right, not a thing, characterized as metaphysical, not physical. The theoretical bases and conceptual descriptions of property rights are varied, ranging from first possessor rules, to creation of value, to Lockean labor theory, to personality theory, to utilitarian theory. However disparate, these formulations of property clearly illustrate the extent to which property rights and interests embrace much more than land and personality. Thus, the fact that whiteness is not a "physical" entity does not remove it from the realm of property.

Whiteness is not simply and solely a legally recognized property interest. It is simultaneously an aspect of self-identity and of personhood, and its relation to the law of property is complex. Whiteness has functioned as self-identity in the domain of the intrinsic, personal, and psychological; as reputation in the interstices between internal and external identity; and, as property in the extrinsic, public, and legal realms. According whiteness actual legal status converted an aspect of identity into an external object of property, moving whiteness from privileged identity to a vested interest. The law's construction of whiteness defined and affirmed critical aspects of identity (who is white); of privilege (what benefits accrue to that status); and, of property (what *legal* entitlements arise from that status). Whiteness at various times signifies and is deployed as identity, status, and property, sometimes singularly, sometimes in tandem.

1. Whiteness as a Traditional Form of Property.—Whiteness fits the broad historical concept of property described by classical theorists. In James Madison's view, for example, property "embraces every thing to which a man may attach a value and have a right," referring to all of a person's legal rights. Property as conceived in the founding era

> included not only external objects and people's relationships to them, but also all of those human rights, liberties, powers, and immunities that are important for human well-being, including: freedom of expression, freedom of conscience, freedom from bodily harm, and free and equal opportunities to use personal faculties.

Whiteness defined the legal status of a person as slave or free. White identity conferred tangible and economically valuable benefits and was jealously guarded as a valued possession, allowed only to those who met a strict standard of proof. Whiteness—the right to white identity as embraced by the law—is property if by property one means all of a person's legal rights.

Other traditional theories of property emphasize that the "natural" character of property is derivative of custom, contrary to the notion that property is the product of a delegation of sovereign power. This "bottom up" theory holds that the law of property merely codifies existing customs and social relations. Under that view, government-created rights such as social welfare payments cannot constitute legitimate property interests because they are positivistic in nature. Other theorists have challenged this conception, and argued that even the most basic of "customary" property rights—the rule of first possession, for example—is dependent on its acceptance or rejection in particular instances by the government. Citing custom as a source of property law begs the central question: whose custom?

Rather than remaining within the bipolar confines of custom or command, it is crucial to recognize the dynamic and multifaceted relationship among custom, command, and law, as well as the extent to which positionality determines how each may be experienced and understood. Indian custom was obliterated by force and replaced with the regimes of common law that embodied the customs of the conquerors. The assumption of American law as it related to Native Americans was that conquest *did* give rise to sovereignty. Indians experienced the property laws of the colonizers and the emergent American nation as acts of violence perpetuated by the exercise of power and ratified through the rule of law. At the same time, these laws were perceived as custom and "common sense" by the colonizers. The Founders, for instance, so thoroughly embraced Lockean labor theory as the basis for a right of acquisition because it affirmed the right of the New World settlers to settle on and acquire the frontier. It confirmed and ratified their experience.

The law's interpretation of those encounters between whites and Native Americans not only inflicted vastly different results on them, but also established a pattern—a *custom*—of valorizing whiteness. As the forms of racialized property were perfected, the value and protection extended to whiteness increased. Regardless of which theory of property one adopts, the concept of whiteness—established by centuries of custom (illegitimate custom, but custom nonetheless) and codified by law—may be understood as a property interest.

2. *Modern Views of Property as Defining Social Relations.*—Although property in the classical sense refers to everything that is valued and to which a person has a right, the modern concept of property focuses on its function and the social relations reflected therein. In this sense, modern property doctrine emphasizes the more contingent nature of property and has been the basis for the argument that property rights should be expanded.

Modern theories of property reject the assumption that property is "objectively definable or identifiable, apart from social context." Charles Reich's ground-breaking work, *The New Property*, was an early effort to focus on the function of property and note the changing social relations reflected and constructed by new forms of property derived from the government. Property in this broader sense encompassed jobs, entitlements, occupational licenses, contracts, subsidies, and indeed a whole host of intangibles that are the product of labor, time, and creativity, such as intellectual property, business goodwill, and enhanced earning potential from graduate degrees. Notwithstanding the dilution of new property since *Goldberg v. Kelly* and its progeny as well as continued attacks on the concept, the legacy of new property infuses the concept of property with questions of power, selection, and allocation. Reich's argument that property is not a natural right but a construction by society resonates in current theories of property that describe the allocation of property rights as a series of choices. This construction directs attention toward issues of relative power and social relations inherent in any definition of property.

3. *Property and Expectations.*—"Property is nothing but the basis of expectation," according to Bentham, "consist[ing] in an established expectation, in the persuasion of being able to draw such and such advantage from the thing possessed." The relationship between expectations and property remains highly significant, as the law "has recognized and protected even the expectation of rights as actual legal property." This theory does not suggest that all value or all expectations give rise to property, but those expectations in tangible or intangible things that are valued and protected by the law are property.

In fact, the difficulty lies not in identifying expectations as a part of property, but in distinguishing which expectations are reasonable and therefore merit the protection of the law as property. Although the existence of certain property rights may seem self-evident and the protection of certain expectations may seem essential for social stability, property is a legal construct by which selected private interests are protected and upheld. In creating property "rights," the law draws boundaries and enforces or reorders existing regimes of power. The inequalities that are produced and reproduced are not givens or inevitabilities, but rather are conscious selections regarding the structuring of social relations. In this sense, it is contended that property rights and interests are not "natural," but are "creation[s] of law."

In a society structured on racial subordination, white privilege became an expectation and, to apply Margaret Radin's concept, whiteness became the quintessential property for personhood. The law constructed "whiteness" as an objective fact, although in reality it is an ideological proposition imposed through subordination. This move is the central feature of "reification": "Its basis is that a relation between people takes on the character of a thing and thus acquires a 'phantom objectivity,' an autonomy that seems so strictly rational and all-embracing as to conceal every trace of its fundamental nature: the relation between people." Whiteness was an "object" over which continued control was—and is—expected. The protection of these expectations is central because, as Radin notes: "If an object you now control is bound up in your future plans or in your anticipation of your future self, and it is partly these plans for your own continuity that make you a person, then your personhood depends on the realization of these expectations."

Because the law recognized and protected expectations grounded in white privilege (albeit not explicitly in all instances), these expectations became tantamount to property that could not permissibly be intruded upon without consent. As the law explicitly ratified those expectations in continued privilege or extended ongoing protection to those illegitimate expectations by failing to expose or to radically disturb them, the dominant and subordinate positions within the racial hierarchy were reified in law.

When the law recognizes, either implicitly or explicitly, the settled expectations of whites built on the privileges and benefits produced by white supremacy, it acknowledges and reinforces a property interest in whiteness that reproduces Black subordination.

4. *The Property Functions of Whiteness.*—In addition to the theoretical descriptions of property, whiteness also meets the functional criteria of property. Specifically, the law has accorded "holders" of whiteness the same privileges and benefits accorded holders of other types of property. The liberal view of property is that it includes the exclusive rights of possession, use, and disposition. Its attributes are the right to transfer or alienability, the right to use and enjoyment, and the right to exclude others. Even when examined against this limited view, whiteness conforms to the general contours of property. It may be a "bad" form of property, but it is property nonetheless.

(a) Rights of Disposition.—Property rights are traditionally described as fully alienable. Because fundamental personal rights are commonly understood to be inalienable, it is problematic to view them as property interests. However, as Margaret Radin notes, "inalienability" is not a transparent term; it has multiple meanings that refer to interests that are non-salable, non-transferable, or non-market-alienable. The common core of inalienability is the negation of the possibility of separation of an entitlement, right, or attribute from its holder.

Classical theories of property identified alienability as a requisite aspect of property; thus, that which is inalienable cannot be property. As the major exponent of this view, Mill argued that public offices, monopoly privileges, and human beings—all of which were or should have been inalienable—should not be considered property at all. Under this account, if inalienability inheres in the concept of property, then whiteness, incapable of being transferred or alienated either inside or outside the market, would fail to meet a criterion of property.

As Radin notes, however, even under the classical view, alienability of certain property was limited. Mill also advocated certain restraints on alienation in connection with property rights in land and probably other natural resources. In fact, the law has recognized various kinds of inalienable property. For example, entitlements of the regulatory and welfare states, such as transfer payments and government licenses, are inalienable; yet they have been conceptualized and treated as property by law. Although this "new property" has been criticized as being improper—that is, not appropriately cast as property—the principal objection has been based on its alleged lack of productive capacity, not its inalienability.

The law has also acknowledged forms of inalienable property derived from nongovernmental sources. In the context of divorce, courts have held that professional degrees or licenses held by one party and financed by the labor of the other is marital property whose value is subject to allocation by the court. A medical or law degree is not alienable either in the market or by voluntary transfer. Nevertheless, it is included as property when dissolving a legal relationship.

Indeed, Radin argues that, as a deterrent to the dehumanization of universal commodification, market-inalienability may be justified to protect property important to the person and to safeguard human flourishing. She suggests that non-commodification or market-inalienability of personal property or those things essential to human flourishing is necessary to guard against the objectification of human beings. To avoid that danger, "we must cease thinking that market alienability is inherent in the concept of property." Following this logic, then, the inalienability of whiteness should not preclude the consideration of whiteness as property. Paradoxically, its inalienability may be more indicative of its perceived enhanced value, rather than its disqualification as property.

(b) Right to Use and Enjoyment.—Possession of property includes the rights of use and enjoyment. If these rights are essential aspects of property, it is because "the problem of property in political philosophy dissolves into ... questions of the will and the way in which we use the things of this world." As whiteness is simultaneously an aspect of identity and a property interest, it is something that can both be experienced and deployed as a resource. Whiteness can move from being a passive characteristic as an aspect of identity to an active entity that—like other types of property—is used to fulfill the will and to exercise power. The state's official recognition of a racial identity that subordinated Blacks and of privileged rights in property based on race elevated whiteness from a passive attribute to an object of law and a resource deployable at the social, political, and institutional level to maintain control. Thus, a white person "used and enjoyed" whiteness whenever she took advantage of the privileges accorded white people simply by virtue of their whiteness—when she exercised any number of rights reserved for the holders of whiteness. Whiteness as the embodiment of white privilege transcended mere belief or preference; it became usable property, the subject of the law's regard and protection. In this respect whiteness, as an active property, has been used and enjoyed.

(c) Reputation and Status Property.—In constructing whiteness as property, the ideological move was to conceptualize white racial identity as an external thing in a constitutive sense—an "object [] or resource [] necessary to be a person." This move was accomplished in large measure by recognizing the reputational interest in being regarded as white as a thing of significant value, which like other reputational interests, was intrinsically bound up with identity and personhood. The reputation of being white was treated as a species of property, or something in which a property interest could be asserted. In this context, whiteness was a form of status property.

The conception of reputation as property found its origins in early concepts of property that encompassed things (such as land and personalty), income (such as revenues from leases, mortgages, and patent monopolies), and one's life, liberty, and labor. Thus, Locke's famous pronouncement, "every man has a 'property' in his own 'person,'" undergirded the assertion that one's physical self was one's property. From this premise, one's labor, "the work of his hands," combined with those things found in the common to form property over which one could exercise ownership, control, and dominion. The idea of self-ownership, then, was particularly fertile ground for the idea that reputation, as an aspect of identity earned through effort, was similarly property. Moreover, the loss of reputation was capable of being valued in the market.

The direct manifestation of the law's legitimation of whiteness as reputation is revealed in the well-established doctrine that to call a white person "Black" is to defame her. Although many of the cases were decided in an era when the social and legal stratification of whites and Blacks was more absolute, as late as 1957 the principle was reaffirmed, notwithstanding significant changes in the legal and political status of Blacks. As one court noted, "there is still to be considered the social distinction existing between the races," and the allegation was likely to cause injury. A Black person, however, could not sue for defamation if she was called "white." Because the law expressed and reinforced the social hierarchy as it existed, it was presumed that no harm could flow from such a reversal.

Private identity based on racial hierarchy was legitimated as public identity in law, even after the end of slavery and the formal end of legal race segregation. Whiteness as interpersonal hierarchy was recognized externally as race reputation. Thus, whiteness as public reputation and personal property was affirmed.

(d) The Absolute Right to Exclude.—Many theorists have traditionally conceptualized property to include the exclusive rights of use, disposition, and possession, with possession embracing the absolute right to exclude. The right to exclude was the central principle, too, of whiteness as identity, for mainly whiteness has been characterized, not by an inherent unifying characteristic, but by the exclusion of others deemed to be "not white." The possessors of whiteness were granted the legal right to exclude others from the privileges inhering in whiteness; whiteness became an exclusive club whose membership was closely and grudgingly guarded. The courts played an active role in enforcing this right to exclude—determining who was or was not white enough to enjoy the privileges accompanying whiteness. In that sense, the courts protected whiteness as any other form of property.

Moreover, as it emerged, the concept of whiteness was premised on white supremacy rather than mere difference. "White" was defined and constructed in ways that increased its value by reinforcing its exclusivity. Indeed, just as whiteness as property embraced the right to exclude, whiteness as a theoretical construct evolved for the very purpose of racial exclusion. Thus, the concept of whiteness is built on both exclusion and racial subjugation. This fact was particularly evident during the period of the most rigid racial exclusion, as whiteness signified racial privilege and took the form of status property.

At the individual level, recognizing oneself as "white" necessarily assumes premises based on white supremacy: It assumes that Black ancestry in any degree, extending to generations far removed, automatically disqualifies claims to white identity, thereby privileging "white" as unadulterated, exclusive, and rare. Inherent in the concept of "being white" was the right to own or hold whiteness to the exclusion and subordination of Blacks. Because "[i]dentity is ... continuously being constituted through social interactions," the assigned political, economic, and social inferiority of Blacks necessarily shaped white identity. In the commonly held popular view, the presence of Black "blood"—including the infamous "one-drop"— consigned a person to being "Black" and evoked the "metaphor ... of purity and contamination" in which Black blood is a contaminant and white racial identity is pure. Recognizing or identifying oneself as white is thus a claim of racial purity, an assertion that one is free of any taint of Black blood. The law has played a critical role in legitimating this claim.

D. White Legal Identity: The Law's Acceptance and Legitimation of Whiteness as Property

The law assumed the crucial task of racial classification, and accepted and embraced the then-current theories of race as biological fact. This core precept of race as a physically defined reality allowed the law to fulfill an essential function—to "parcel out social standing according to race" and to facilitate systematic discrimination by articulating "seemingly precise definitions of racial group membership." This allocation of race and rights continued a century after the abolition of slavery.

The law relied on bounded, objective, and scientific definitions of race—what Neil Gotanda has called "historical race"—to construct whiteness as not merely race, but race plus privilege. By making race determinant and the product of rationality and science, dominant and subordinate positions within the racial hierarchy were disguised as the product of natural law and biology rather than as naked preferences. Whiteness as racialized privilege was then legitimated by science and was embraced in legal doctrine as "objective fact."

Case law that attempted to define race frequently struggled over the precise fractional amount of Black "blood"—traceable Black ancestry—that would defeat a claim to whiteness. Although the courts applied varying fractional formulas in different jurisdictions to define "Black" or, in the terms of the day, "Negro" or "colored," the law uniformly accepted the rule of hypodescent—racial identity was governed by blood, and white was preferred.

This legal assumption of race as blood-borne was predicated on the pseudo-sciences of eugenics and craniology that saw their major development during the eighteenth and nineteenth centuries. The legal definition of race was the "objective" test propounded by racist theorists of the day who described race to be immutable, scientific, biologically determined—an unsullied fact of the blood rather than a volatile and violently imposed regime of racial hierarchy.

In adjudicating who was "white," courts sometimes noted that, by physical characteristics, the individual whose racial identity was at issue appeared to be white and, in fact, had been regarded as white in the community. Yet if an individual's blood was tainted, she could not claim to be "white" as the law understood, regardless of the fact that phenotypically she may have been completely indistinguishable from a white person, may have lived as a white person, and have descended from a family that lived as whites. Although socially accepted as white, she could not *legally* be white. Blood as "objective fact" dominated over appearance and social acceptance, which were socially fluid and subjective measures.

But, in fact, "blood" was no more objective than that which the law dismissed as subjective and unreliable. The acceptance of the fiction that the racial ancestry could be determined with the degree of precision called for by the relevant standards or definitions rested on false assumptions that racial categories of prior ancestors had been accurately reported, that those reporting in the past shared the definitions currently in use, and that racial purity actually existed in the United States. Ignoring these considerations, the law established rules that extended equal treatment to those of the "same blood," albeit of different complexions, because it was acknowledged that, "[t]here are white men as dark as mulattoes, and there are pure-blooded albino Africans as white as the whitest Saxons."

The standards were designed to accomplish what mere observation could not: "That even Blacks who did not look Black were kept in their place." Although the line of demarcation between Black and white varied from rules that classified as Black a person containing "any drop of Black blood," to more liberal rules that defined persons with a preponderance of white blood to be white, the courts universally accepted the notion that white status was something of value that could be accorded only to those persons whose proofs established their whiteness as defined by the law. Because legal recognition of a person as white carried material benefits, "false" or inadequately supported claims were denied like any other unsubstantiated claim to a property interest. Only those who could lay "legitimate" claims to whiteness could be legally recognized as "white," because allowing physical attributes, social acceptance, or self-identification to determine whiteness would diminish its value and destroy the underlying presumption of exclusivity. In effect, the courts erected legal "No Trespassing" signs.

In the realm of *social* relations, racial recognition in the United States is thus an act of race subordination. In the realm of *legal* relations, judicial definition of racial identity based on white supremacy reproduced that race subordination at the institutional level. In transforming white to whiteness, the law masked the ideological content of racial definition and the exercise of power required to maintain it: "It convert[ed] [an] abstract concept into [an] entity."

1. *Whiteness as Racialized Privilege.*—The material benefits of racial exclusion and subjugation functioned, in the labor context, to stifle class tensions among whites. White workers perceived that they had more in common with the bourgeoisie than with fellow workers who were Black. Thus, W. E. B. Du Bois's classic historical study of race and class, *Black Reconstruction,* noted that, for the evolving white working class, race

identification became crucial to the ways that it thought of itself and conceived its interests. There were, he suggested, obvious material benefits, at least in the short term, to the decision of white workers to define themselves by their whiteness: their wages far exceeded those of Blacks and were high even in comparison with world standards. Moreover, even when the white working class did not collect increased pay as part of white privilege, there were real advantages not paid in direct income: whiteness still yielded what Du Bois termed a "public and psychological wage" vital to white workers. Thus, Du Bois noted:

> They [whites] were given public deference ... because they were white. They were admitted freely with all classes of white people, to public functions, to public parks.... The police were drawn from their ranks, and the courts, dependent on their votes, treated them with ... leniency.... Their vote selected public officials, and while this had small effect upon the economic situation, it had great effect on their personal treatment.... White schoolhouses were the best in the community, and conspicuously placed, and they cost anywhere from twice to ten times as much per capita as the colored schools.

The central feature of the convergence of "white" and "worker" lay in the fact that racial status and privilege could ameliorate and assist in "evad[ing] rather than confront[ing] [class] exploitation." Although not accorded the privileges of the ruling class, in both the North and South, white workers could accept their lower class position in the hierarchy "by fashioning identities as 'not slaves' and as 'not Blacks.'" Whiteness produced—and was reproduced by—the social advantage that accompanied it.

Whiteness was also central to national identity and to the republican project. The amalgamation of various European strains into an American identity was facilitated by an oppositional definition of Black as "other." As Hacker suggests, fundamentally, the question was not so much "who is white," *but* "who may be considered white," as the historical pattern was that various immigrant groups of different ethnic origins were accepted into a white identity shaped around Anglo–American norms. Current members then "ponder[ed] whether they want[ed] or need[ed] new members as well as the proper pace of new admissions into this exclusive club." Through minstrel shows in which white actors masquerading in blackface played out racist stereotypes, the popular culture put the Black at "'solo spot centerstage, providing a relational model in contrast to which masses of Americans could establish a positive and superior sense of identity[,]' ... [an identity] ... established by an infinitely manipulable negation comparing whites with a construct of a socially defenseless group."

It is important to note the effect of this hypervaluation of whiteness. Owning white identity as property affirmed the self-identity and liberty of whites and, conversely, denied the self-identity and liberty of Blacks. The attempts to lay claim to whiteness through "passing" painfully illustrate the effects of the law's recognition of whiteness. The embrace of a lie, undertaken by my grandmother and the thousands like her, could occur only when oppression makes self-denial and the obliteration of identity rational and, in significant measure, beneficial. The economic coercion of white supremacy on self-definition nullifies any suggestion that passing is a logical exercise of liberty or self-identity. The decision to pass as white was not a choice, if by that word one means voluntariness or lack of compulsion. The fact of race subordination was coercive and circumscribed the liberty to self-define. Self-determination of identity was not a right for all people, but a privilege accorded on the basis of race. The effect of protecting whiteness at law was to devalue those who were not white by coercing them to deny their identity in order to survive.

2. *Whiteness, Rights, and National Identity.*—The concept of whiteness was carefully protected because so much was contingent upon it. Whiteness conferred on its owners aspects of citizenship that were all the more valued because they were denied to others. Indeed, the very fact of citizenship itself was linked to white racial identity. The Naturalization Act of 1790 restricted citizenship to persons who resided in the United States for two years, who could establish their good character in court, and who were "white." Moreover, the trajectory of expanding democratic rights for whites was accompanied by the contraction of the rights of Blacks in an ever deepening cycle of oppression. The franchise, for example, was broadened to extend voting rights to unpropertied white men at the same time that Black voters were specifically disenfranchised, arguably shifting the property required for voting from land to whiteness. This racialized version of republicanism—this Herrenvolk republicanism—constrained any vision of democracy from addressing the class hierarchies adverse to many who considered themselves white.

The inherent contradiction between the bondage of Blacks and republican rhetoric that championed the freedom of all men was resolved by positing that Blacks were different. The laws did not mandate that Blacks be accorded equality under the law because nature—not man, not power, not violence—had determined their degraded status. Rights were for those who had the capacity to exercise them, a capacity denoted by racial identity. This conception of rights was contingent on race—on whether one could claim whiteness—a form of property. This articulation of rights that were contingent on property ownership was a familiar paradigm, as similar requirements had been imposed on the franchise in the early part of the republic.

For the first two hundred years of the country's existence, the system of racialized privilege in both the public and private spheres carried through this linkage of rights and inequality, and rights and property. Whiteness as property was the critical core of a system that affirmed the hierarchical relations between white and Black.

* * *

IV. THE PERSISTENCE OF WHITENESS AS PROPERTY

In the modern period, neither the problems attendant to assigning racial identities nor those accompanying the recognition of whiteness have disappeared. Nor has whiteness as property. Whiteness as property continues to perpetuate racial subordination through the courts' definitions of group identity and through the courts' discourse and doctrine on affirmative action. The exclusion of subordinated "others" was and remains a central part of the property interest in whiteness and, indeed, is part of the protection that the court extends to whites' settled expectations of continued privilege.

The essential character of whiteness as property remains manifest in two critical areas of the law and, as in the past, operates to oppress Native Americans and Blacks in similar ways, although in different arenas. This Part first examines the persistence of whiteness as valued social identity; then exposes whiteness as property in the law's treatment of the question of group identity, as the case of the Mashpee Indians illustrates; and finally, exposes the presence of whiteness as property in affirmative action doctrine.

A. The Persistence of Whiteness as Valued Social Identity

Even as the capacity of whiteness to deliver is arguably diminished by the elimination of rigid racial stratifications, whiteness continues to be perceived as materially significant. Because real power and wealth never have been accessible to more than a narrowly defined ruling elite, for many whites the benefits of whiteness as property, in the absence of legislated privilege, may have been reduced to a claim of relative privilege only in comparison to people of color. Nevertheless, whiteness retains its value as a "consolation prize": it does not mean that all whites will win, but simply that they will not lose, if losing is defined as being on the bottom of the social and economic hierarchy—the position to which Blacks have been consigned.

Andrew Hacker, in his 1992 book *Two Nations,* recounts the results of a recent exercise that probed the value of whiteness according to the perceptions of whites. The study asked a group of white students how much money they would seek if they were changed from white to Black. "Most seemed to feel that it would not be out of place to ask for $50 million, or $1 million for each coming black year." Whether this figure represents an accurate amortization of the societal cost of being Black in the United States, it is clear that whiteness is still perceived to be valuable. The wages of whiteness are available to all whites regardless of class position, even to those whites who are without power, money, or influence. Whiteness, the characteristic that distinguishes them from Blacks, serves as compensation even to those who lack material wealth. It is the relative political advantages extended to whites, rather than actual economic gains, that are crucial to white workers. Thus, as Kimberlé Crenshaw points out, whites have an actual stake in racism. Because Blacks are held to be inferior, although no longer on the basis of science as antecedent determinant, but by virtue of their position at the bottom, it allows whites—all whites—to "include themselves in the dominant circle. [Although most whites] hold no real power, [all can claim] their privileged racial identity."

White workers often identify primarily as white rather than as workers because it is through their whiteness that they are afforded access to a host of public, private, and psychological benefits. It is through the concept of whiteness that class consciousness among white workers is subordinated and attention is diverted from class oppression.

Although dominant societal norms have embraced the idea of fairness and nondiscrimination, removal of privilege and antisubordination principles are actively rejected or at best ambiguously received because expectations of white privilege are bound up with what is considered essential for self-realization. Among whites, the idea persists that their whiteness is meaningful. Whiteness is an aspect of racial identity surely, but it is much more; it remains a concept based on relations of power, a social construct predicated on white dominance and Black subordination.

B. *Subordination Through Denial of Group Identity*

Whiteness as property is also constituted through the reification of expectations in the continued right of white-dominated institutions to control the legal meaning of group identity. This reification manifests itself in the law's dialectical misuse of the concept of group identity as it pertains to racially subordinated peoples. The law has recognized and codified racial group identity as an instrumentality of exclusion and exploitation; however, it has refused to recognize group identity when asserted by racially oppressed groups as a basis for affirming or claiming rights. The law's approach to group identity reproduces subordination, in the past through "race-ing" a group—that is, by assigning a racial identity that equated with inferior status, and in the present by erasing racial group identity.

In part, the law's denial of the existence of racial groups is predicated not only on the rejection of the ongoing presence of the past, but is also grounded on a basic tenet of liberalism—that constitutional protections inhere in individuals, not groups. As informed by the Lockean notion of the social contract, the autonomous, free-will of the individual is central. Indeed, it is the individual who, in concert with other individuals, elects to enter into political society and to form a state of limited powers. This philosophical view of society is closely aligned with the antidiscrimination principle—the idea being that equality mandates only the equal treatment of individuals under the law. Within this framework, the idea of the social group has no place.

Although the law's determination of any "fact," including that of group identity, is not infinitely flexible, its studied ignorance of the issue of racial group identity insures wrong results by assuming a pseudo-objective posture that does not permit it to hear the complex dialogue concerning the identity question, particularly as it pertains to historically dominated groups.

Instead, the law holds to the basic premise that definition from above can be fair to those below, that beneficiaries of racially conferred privilege have the right to establish norms for those who have historically been oppressed pursuant to those norms, and that race is not historically contingent. Although the substance of race definitions has changed, what persists is the expectation of white-controlled institutions in the continued right to determine meaning—the reified privilege of power—that reconstitutes the property interest in whiteness in contemporary form.

In undertaking any definition of race as group identity, there are implicit and explicit normative underpinnings that must be taken into account. The "riddle of identity" is not answered by a "search for essences" or essential discoverable truth, nor by a search for mere "descriptions and re-descriptions." Instead, when handling the complex issue of group identity, we should look to "purposes and effects, consequences and functions." The questions pertaining to definitions of race then are not principally biological or genetic, but social and political: what must be addressed is who is defining, how is the definition constructed, and why is the definition being propounded. Because definition is so often a central part of domination, critical thinking about these issues must precede and adjoin any definition. The law has not attended to these questions. Instead, identity of "the other" is still objectified, the complex, negotiated quality of identity is ignored, and the impact of inequitable power on identity is masked. These problems are illustrated in the land claim suit brought by the Mashpee, a Massachusetts Indian tribe.

In *Mashpee Tribe v. Town of Mashpee,* the Mashpee sued to recover land that several Indians had conveyed to non-Indians in violation of a statute that barred alienation of tribal land to non-Indians without the approval of the federal government. In order to recover possession of the land, the Mashpee were required to prove that they were a tribe at the time of the conveyance. Although the trial judge admitted to some preliminary confusion about the appropriate definition of "tribe," he ultimately accepted the standard articulated in prior case law that defined tribe as "a body of Indians of the same or similar race, united in a community under one leadership or government, and inhabiting a particular though sometimes ill-defined territory." The Mashpee were held not to be a tribe at the time the suit was filed, so that their claim to land rights based on group identity were rejected.

The Mashpee's experience was filtered, sifted, and ultimately rendered incoherent through this externally constituted definition of tribe that incorporated outside criteria regarding race, leadership, territory, and community. The fact that the Mashpee had intermingled with Europeans, runaway slaves, and other Indian tribes signified to the jury and to the court that they had lost their tribal identity.

But for the Mashpee, blood was not the measure of identity: their identity as a group was manifested for centuries by their continued relationship to the land of the Mashpee; their consciousness and embrace of difference, even when it was against their interest; and, their awareness and preservation of cultural traditions. Nevertheless, under the court's standard, the tribe was "incapable of *legal* self-definition." Fundamentally, then, the external imposition of definition maintained the social equilibrium that was severely challenged by the Mashpee land claims.

The Mashpee case presents new variations on old themes of race and property. Previous reified definitions of race compelled abandonment of racial identity in exchange for economic and social privilege. Under the operative racial hierarchy, passing is the ultimate assimilationist move—the submergence of a subordinate cultural identity in favor of dominant identity, assumed to achieve better societal fit within prevailing norms. The modern definition of "tribe" achieved similar results by misinterpreting the Mashpee's adaptation to be assimilation. The Mashpee absorbed and managed, rather than rejected and suppressed, outsiders; yet the court erased their identity, assuming that, by virtue of intermingling with other races, the Mashpee's identity as a people had been subsumed. The Mashpee were not "passing," but were legally determined to have "passed"—no longer to have distinct identity. This erasure was predicated on the assumption that what is done from necessity under conditions of established hierarchies of domination and subordination is a voluntary surrender for gain.

Beyond the immediate outcome of the case lies the deeper problem posed by the hierarchy of the rules themselves and the continued retention by white-controlled institutions of exclusive control over definitions as they pertain to the identity and history of dominated peoples. Although the law will always represent the exercise of state power in enforcing its choices, the violence done to the Mashpee and other oppressed groups results from the law's refusal to acknowledge the negotiated quality of identity. Whiteness as property assumes the form of the exclusive right to determine rules; it asserts that, against a framework of racial dominance and unequal power, fairness can result from a property rule, or indeed any other rule, that imposes an entirely externally constituted definition of group identity. Reality belies this presumption. In *Plessy*, the Court affirmed the right of the state to define who was white, obliterating aspects of social acceptance and self-identification as sources of validation and identity. The Mashpee were similarly divested of their identity through the state's exclusive retention of control over meaning in ways that reinforced group oppression. When group identity is a predicate for exclusion or disadvantage, the law has acknowledged it; when it is a predicate for resistance or a claim of right to be free from subordination, the law determines it to be illusory. This determinist approach to group identity reproduces racial subordination and reaffirms whiteness as property.

C. *Subjugation Through Affirmative Action Doctrine*

The assumption that whiteness is a property interest entitled to protection is an idea born of systematic white supremacy and nurtured over the years, not only by the law of slavery and "Jim Crow," but also by the more recent decisions and rationales of the Supreme Court concerning affirmative action. In examining both the nature of the affirmative action debate and the legal analysis applied in three Supreme Court cases involving affirmative action—*Regents of University of California v. Bakke, City of Richmond v. J. A. Croson Co.*, and *Wygant v. Jackson Board of Education*, it is evident that the protection of the property interest in whiteness still lies at the core of judicial and popular reasoning.

* * *

VI. CONCLUSION

Whiteness as property has carried and produced a heavy legacy. It is a ghost that has haunted the political and legal domains in which claims for justice have been inadequately addressed for far too long. Only rarely declaring its presence, it has warped efforts to remediate racial exploitation. It has blinded society to the systems of domination that work against so many by retaining an unvarying focus on vestiges of systemic racialized privilege that subordinates those perceived as a particularized few—the "others." It has thwarted not only conceptions of racial justice but also conceptions of property that embrace more equitable possibilities. In protecting the property interest in whiteness, property is assumed to be no more than the right to prohibit infringement on settled expectations, ignoring countervailing equitable claims that are predicated on a right to inclusion. It is long past time to put the property interest in whiteness to rest. Affirmative action can assist in that task. Affirmative action, if properly conceived and implemented, is not only consistent with norms of equality, but is essential to shedding the legacy of oppression.

NOTES AND QUESTIONS

1. Identity, economics, and multiculturalism. If, as this article seems to imply, non-market-oriented identities will invariably arise in response to economic discrimination, does that mean that economic developments that tend to reduce the incidence of such non-market identities are desirable as a means of reducing discrimination? Would the aggressively paternalistic practices that led to the partial assimilation of the Mashpee tribe discussed on pages 276–277 be viewed as desirable practices because they reduce the incidence of the "Red" identity? What about even more intrusive measures such as taking children away from "Red" parents so that they can be raised in a "Green" environment?

2. Akerlof, Kranton and McAdams. The identity payoff model presented in this paper, and the group-status production model presented by McAdams, *infra* at 325, both attempt to explain the persistence of economic inequality when classical economic theory states that the free market should eliminate discrimination. However, while the goals of the two papers might be similar, their approaches are quite different. First, McAdams' approach is group based; all individuals are looked upon as basically the same, with differences created by quasi-market forces. By contrast, the model presented by Akerlof and Kranton focuses on individuals and assumes that, even in the absence of markets, some individuals would have a predisposition to be "Red" while others would be "Green." Additionally, McAdams sees discrimination as the result of self-interested behavior on the part of the majority, while Akerlof and Kranton see identity differentiation as arising partially as a survival strategy by the minority. Given these differences between the two explanations for discrimination, is there any way that the Akerlof–Kranton and McAdams positions can be reconciled?

3. Different identities or different settings? Are the "Red" and "Green" cultures of the Akerlof-Kranton model necessarily representative of different identities, or could they be thought of more accurately as different manifestations of the same identity when faced with different circumstances? When Malcolm X began hustling, his mentor gave him the following advice: "[g]et here early ... everything in place ... you never need to waste motion." ALEX HALEY & MALCOLM X, THE AUTOBIOGRAPHY OF MALCOLM X 46 (1965). When Malcolm X became a more successful drug dealer he demonstrated considerable capitalist acumen. He reinvested his profits into his business, developed rational strategies for dealing with law enforcement and entered new markets when government regulation became too tight. *Id.* at 99–102. Given the effort and business skills required to succeed as a hustler, as well as Malcolm X's success when he was able to find non-criminal employment with the Nation of Islam, does it seem more likely that Malcolm's "Red" identity was different from a mainstream "Green" identity, or that it was simply a "Green" identity expressing itself in "Red" surroundings?

4. Definition of tribe. This case was presented as a contest between history and anthropology, with history winning in the end. However, aren't broad historical and anthropological definitions of the word tribe ultimately beside the point? Shouldn't the definition of tribe be that used by the drafters of the Non-Intercourse Act?

5. Performative identity. The Indians of Mashpee lost their case because they didn't behave in a way that comported with the jury's view of how an Indian tribe should act, thus their performative identity was not that of a tribe. Isn't this a rather odd way to structure a lawsuit? Modern anti-discrimination laws generally take the opposite approach: the more a minority has assimilated into mainstream culture, the greater chance that minority has of winning an anti-discrimination claim. Devon W. Carbado & Mitu Gulati, *The Law and Economics of Critical Race Theory: Crossroads, Directions, and a New Critical Race Theory*, 112 YALE L.J. 1757, 1822 (2003) (book review). Why is it that in this case, assimilation was (from the standpoint of the outcome of the suit) a bad thing? Does a legal regime which encourages rejection of mainstream culture provide perverse incentives from an anti-discrimination viewpoint?

6. The point of all this. How did the disposition of this case effect the "tribe?" According to the plaintiffs, the tribe was based on culture, shared traditions, kinship, and other intangible bonds. Would those bonds have been strengthened if the "tribe" had won its suit? Would they have been diluted by the effects of a large settlement? Since the "tribe" was not simply an amalgam of individuals, could it possibly have been aided in any way by a positive verdict? Is it more likely that the "tribe" would have been destroyed by the ascendancy of Tribal Council, Inc., which was organized specifically to provide a structure for interaction with the non-tribal world? Would victory for the corporation have helped the "tribe" of Mashpee?

7. **Taint of whiteness.** According to Professor Harris, "[a]t the individual level, recognizing oneself as 'white' necessarily assumes premises based on white supremacy ... privileging 'white' as unadulterated, exclusive, and rare." *Supra* p. 310. Is it constructive to tar all people who recognize themselves as white with the implication of white supremacy? It would seem likely that recognition of the social power of whiteness is necessary in order to try to eliminate discrimination against blacks. How, under Professor Harris' conception of whiteness as property, is it possible for a white person to work against racism, when by acknowledging the social privileges accorded to whiteness, white people assume the premises of white supremacy?

8. **Neutrality of affirmative action.** Professor Harris asserts that, "[b]ecause affirmative action can only be implemented through conscious intervention and requires constant monitoring and reevaluation, it does not function behind a mask of neutrality in the realm beyond scrutiny." Of course, chattel slavery was also implemented through conscious intervention and required constant monitoring and reevaluation (not to mention terroristic violence). The same is true of Jim Crow segregation. Does this mean that segregation and slavery did not function to distort white expectations because they did not "function behind a mask of neutrality?" Further, how could any meaningful affirmative action program not change black expectations? Will expectations not change if affirmative action is effective and reliable? Is Professor Harris arguing that blacks can never be beneficiaries of racism in the future because they have been its victims in the past?

9. **Additional reading.** For a non-technical perspective on economics and identity, see Gerald D. Jaynes, *Identity and Economic Performance*, 568 ANNALS AM. ACAD. POL. & SOC. SCI. 128 (2000). For an interesting description of an interaction between cultures, see *Ann Southerland, Complexities of U.S. Law and Gypsy Identity*, 45 AM. J. COMP. L. 393 (1997). For additional information on anthropological issues in the courts, see generally Larry Cata Backer, *Chroniclers in the Field of Cultural Production: Courts, Law and the Interpretive Process*, 20 B.C. THIRD WORLD L.J. 291 (2000); Glen Stohr, Comment, *The Repercussions of Orality in Federal Indian Law*, 31 ARIZ. ST. L.J. 679 (1999). For additional information on Indian tribes in the courts, see generally Jennifer L. Tomsen, Note, *"Traditional" Resource Uses and Activities: Articulating Values and Examining Conflicts in Alaska*, 19 ALASKA L. REV. 167 (2002); Neu Jessup Newton, *Sovereignty and the Native American Nation: Memory and Misrepresentation: Representing Crazy Horse*, 27 CONN. L. REV. 1003 (1995). For additional information on the Mashpee case, see Gerald Torres & Kathryn Milun, *Frontier of Legal Thought III: Translating Yonnondio by Precedent and Evidence: The Mashpee Indian Case*, 1990 DUKE L.J. 625 (1990). For an approach to white privilege outside of the property framework, see Sylvia A. Law, *White*

Privilege and Affirmative Action, 32 AKRON L. REV. 603 (1999). For an article that, notwithstanding Harris, espouses the idea of Blackness as property, see Jim Chen, *Affirmative Action: Diversity of Opinions: Embryonic Thoughts on Racial Identity as New Property*, 68 U. COLO. L. REV. 1123 (1997). For a Marxist approach to identity as property, see e. christi cunningham, *Identity Markets*, 45 HOW. L.J. 491 (2002). For an analysis of whiteness as property explored through a fictionalized dialogue with a space alien, see Derrick Bell, *Xerces and the Affirmative Action Mystique*, 57 GEO. WASH. L. REV. 1595 (1989).

B. RACIAL DISCRIMINATION: TWO COMPETING THEORIES AND EMPIRICAL EVIDENCE OF DISPARATE RACIAL IMPACT

A major dispute between scholars who are interested in the problem of persistent racial discrimination is whether the market can be expected to provide a self-correction for racial discrimination that locks members of racial minorities out of participation in basic transactions and therefore wealth accumulation. We return to economics Nobel laureate, Gary Becker for his economic model which treats racial discrimination like any other private preference that can be expressed as a "taste" with monetary value in the marketplace. Legal scholar Richard McAdams draws on sociological theories of group status production to offer an alternative view of the mechanisms fueling persistent racial discrimination. Legal scholar and economist Ian Ayres enters this debate with a powerful new tool: empirical studies of actual marketplace racial dynamics in important transactions.

1. A RATIONAL CHOICE THEORY OF RACIAL DISCRIMINATION IN THE MARKETPLACE

The Forces Determining Discrimination in the Market Place

THE ECONOMICS OF DISCRIMINATION 13–18 (2d ed. 1971).

GARY BECKER

In the socio-psychological literature on this subject one individual is said to discriminate against (or in favor of) another if his behavior toward the latter is not motivated by an "objective" consideration of fact. It is difficult to use this definition in distinguishing a violation of objective facts from an expression of tastes or values. For example, discrimination and prejudice are not usually said to occur when someone prefers looking at a glamorous Hollywood actress rather than at some other woman; yet they are said to occur when he prefers living next to whites rather than Negroes. At best calling just one of these actions "discrimination" requires making subtle and rather secondary distinctions. Fortunately, it is not necessary to get involved in these more philosophical issues. It is possible to give an unambiguous definition of discrimination in the market place and yet get at the essence of what is usually called discrimination.

1. THE ANALYTICAL FRAMEWORK

Money, commonly used as a measuring rod, will also serve as a measure of discrimination. If an individual has a "taste for discrimination," he must act *as if* he were willing to pay something either directly or in the form of a reduced income, to be associated with some persons instead of others. When actual discrimination occurs, he must, in fact, either pay or forfeit income for this privilege. This simple way of looking at the matter gets at the essence of prejudice and discrimination.

Social scientists tend to organize their discussion of discrimination in the market place according to their disciplines. To the sociologist, different levels of discrimination against a particular group are associated with different levels of social and physical "distance" from that group or with different levels of socioeconomic status; the psychologist classifies individuals by their personality types, believing that this is the most useful organizational principle. The breakdown used here is most familiar to the economist and differs from both of these: all persons who contribute to production in the same way, e.g., by the rent of capital or the sale of labor services, are put into one group, with each group forming a separate "factor of production." The breakdown by economic productivity turns out to be a particularly fruitful one, since it emphasizes phenomena that have long been neglected in literature on discrimination.

By using the concept of a *discrimination coefficient* (this will be abbreviated to "DC"), it is possible to give a definition of a "taste for discrimination" that is parallel for different factors of production, employers, and consumers. The *money* costs of a transaction do not always completely measure *net* costs, and a DC acts as a bridge between money and net costs. Suppose an *employer* were faced with the money wage rate π of a particular factor; he is assumed to act as $\pi(1 + d_i)$ were the net wage rate, with di as his DC against this factor. An *employee*, offered the money wage rate π_i for working with this factor, acts as if $\pi(1-d_j)$ were the *net* wage rate, with dj as his DC against this factor. A *consumer*, faced with a unit money of p for the commodity "produced" by this factor, acts as if the net price were $p(1 + d_k)$ with dk as his DC against this factor. In all three instances a DC gives the percentage by which either money costs or money returns are changed in going from money to net magnitudes: the employer uses it to estimate his net wage costs, the employee his net wage rate, and the consumer the net price of a commodity.

A DC represents a non-pecuniary element in certain kinds of transactions, and it is positive or negative, depending upon whether the non-pecuniary element is considered "good" or "bad." Discrimination is commonly associated with *dis*utility caused by contact with some individuals and this interpretation is followed here. Since this implies that d_i, d_j, and d_k are all greater than zero, to the employer this coefficient represents a non-monetary cost of production, to the employer a non-monetary cost of employment, and to the consumer a non-monetary cost of consumption. "Nepotism" rather than "discrimination" would occur if they were less than zero, and they would then represent non-monetary returns of production, employment, and consumption to the employer, employee, and consumer, respectively.

The quantities πd_i, $\pi j d_j$, and pd_k are the exact money equivalents of these non-monetary costs; for given wage rates and prices, these money equivalents are larger, the larger di, dj, and dk are. Since a DC can take on any value between zero and plus infinity, tastes for discrimination can also vary continuously within this range. This quantitative representation of a taste for discrimination provides the means for empirically estimating the quantitative importance of discrimination.

2. TASTES FOR DISCRIMINATION

The magnitude of a taste for discrimination differs from person to person, and many investigators have directed their energies toward discovering the variables that are most responsible for these differences. I also attempt to isolate and estimate the quantitative importance of some of these variables; the following discussion briefly describes several variables that receive attention in subsequent chapters.

The discrimination by an individual against a particular group (to be called N) depends on the social and physical distance between them and on their relative socioeconomic status. If he works with N in production, it may also depend on their substitutability in production. The relative number of N in the society at large also may be very important: it has been argued that an increase in the numerical importance of a minority group increases the prejudice against them, since the majority begins to fear their growing power; on the other hand, some argue that greater numbers bring greater knowledge and that leads to a decline in prejudice. Closely related to this variable are the frequency and regularity of "contact" with N in different establishments and firms.

According to our earlier definition, if someone has a "taste for discrimination," he must act *as if* he were willing to forfeit income in order to avoid certain transactions; it is necessary to be aware of the emphasis on the words "as if." An employer may refuse to hire Negroes solely because he erroneously underestimates their economic efficiency. His behavior is discriminatory not because he is prejudiced against them but because his is ignorant of their true efficiency. Ignorance may be quickly eliminated by the spread of knowledge, while a prejudice (i.e. preference) is relatively independent of knowledge. This distinction is essential for understanding the motivation of many organizations, since they either explicitly or implicitly assume that discrimination can be eliminated by a wholesale spread of knowledge.

Since a taste for discrimination incorporates both prejudice and ignorance, the amount of knowledge available must be included as a determinant of tastes. Another proximate determinant is geographical and chronological location: discrimination may vary from country to country, from region to region within a country, from rural to urban areas within a region, and from one time period to another. Finally, tastes may differ simply because of differences in personality.

3. MARKET DISCRIMINATION

Suppose there are two groups, designated by W and N, with members of W being perfect substitutes in production for members of N. In the absence of discrimination and nepotism and if the labor market were perfectly competitive, the equilibrium wage rate of W would equal that of N. Discrimination could cause these wage rates to differ; the market discrimination coefficient between W and N (this will be abbreviated "MDC") is defined as the proportional difference between these wage rates. If π_w and π_n represent the equilibrium wage rates of W and N, respectively, then

$$MDC = \pi_w - \pi_n \, \pi_w -$$

If W and N are imperfect substitutes, they may receive different wage rates even in the absence of discrimination. A more general definition of the MDC sets it equal to the difference between the ratio of W's and N's wage rate with and without discrimination. In the special case of perfect substitutes, this reduces to the simpler definition given previously, because

$$\pi_w^\circ \text{ would equal } \pi_n^\circ$$

It should be obvious that the magnitude of the MDC depends on the magnitude of individual DC's. Unfortunately, it is often implicitly assumed that it depends only on them; the arguments proceed as if a knowledge of the determinants of tastes was sufficient for a complete understanding of market discrimination. This procedure is erroneous; many variables in addition to tastes take prominent roles in determining market discrimination, and, indeed, tastes sometimes play a minor part. The abundant light thrown on the other variables by the tools of economic analysis has probably been the major insight gained from using them.

The MDC does depend in an important way on each individual's DC; however, merely to use some measure of the average DC does not suffice. The complete distribution of DC's among individuals must be made explicit because the size of the MDC is partly related to individual *differences* in tastes. It also depends on the relative importance of competition and monopoly in the labor and product markets, since this partly determines the weight assigned by the market to different DC's. The economic and quantitative importance of N was mentioned as one determinant of tastes for discrimination; this variable is also an independent determinant of market discrimination. This independent effect operates through the number of N relative to W and the cost of N per unit of output relative to the total cost per unit of output. Both may be important, although for somewhat different reasons, in determining the weight assigned by the market to different DC's. Reorganizing production through the substitution of one factor for another is a means of avoiding discrimination; the amount of substitution available is determined by the production function.

The MDC is a direct function of these variables and an indirect function of other variables through their effect on tastes. Our knowledge of the economic aspects of discrimination will be considered satisfactory only when these relationships are known exactly. In subsequent chapters I present the results of my own attempts to close some gaps in this knowledge.

* * *

2. A Sociological Theory Of Racial Discrimination In The Marketplace

Cooperation and Conflict: The Economics of Group Status Production and Race Discrimination
108 Harv. L. Rev. 1003 (1995).

Richard H. McAdams

In Shakespeare's history of King Henry V, when the time comes for the young King to ready his troops to battle a much larger French force at Agincourt, he delivers a stirring speech that many regard as a masterpiece of inspirational rhetoric. Rejecting his advisor's lament for more men, he responds: "No, my fair cousin:/ If we are marked to die, we are enow/ To do our country loss: and if to live,/ The fewer men, the greater share of honour." The King proclaims his personal desire for honor, offers safe passage back to England for those who do not wish to fight, and then describes how those who stay will be celebrated on future anniversaries of this day of battle, known as the Feast of St. Crispian:

> And Crispin Crispian shall ne'er go by,
>
> From this day to the ending of the world,
>
> But we in it shall be remembered;
>
> We few, we happy few, we band of brothers:
>
> For he to-day that sheds his blood with me
>
> Shall be my brother....
>
> And gentlemen in England, now a-bed,
>
> Shall think themselves accursed they were not here;
>
> And hold their manhoods cheap, whiles any speaks
>
> That fought with us upon Saint Crispin's day.

For those of us who strive to be hard-headed theorists of human behavior, and who use economics and game theory to reveal the consequences of legal rules, our initial response to this speech is likely to be: "What a disaster." The King and his soldiers are about to risk their lives.

Yet he denies wanting more men though additional troops would obviously better their odds of surviving and winning. Such a non sequitur can only raise doubts about the clarity of Henry's thinking, which in turn can only increase the chances that his officers will question his commands. And, one might ask, what are the meaning and value of "honor" and "brotherhood"? If Henry wishes to motivate his men, a better strategy would be to spell out the potential material benefits (perhaps promising them more pay) or to remind them of the serious penalties for breaking their promise to fight. Offering to pay their way home, after the enhanced risk of loss has caused Henry's troops to regret their decision to join him in France, is sheer insanity. Finally, those "gentlemen in England now a-bed" will likely count themselves lucky for the opportunity to free-ride on a victory. After all, most of the benefits of victory—the general peace and prosperity of England—cannot be withheld from those who do not fight.

Economics, especially "law and economics," prides itself on the universal application of its method. Yet a theory of human motivation that did not grasp the meaning and power of this speech would be seriously flawed. Military leaders are among the more pragmatic and hard-headed people around and would likely scoff at this economic analysis of Henry's speech. Military rhetoric frequently appeals to honor and brotherhood. If such words prod men and women to risk their lives, one can only imagine how much greater is the power of such words relative to smaller material sacrifices. Consider, for example, the possible economic consequences of the following words:

> Standing in the presence of this multitude, sobered with the responsibility of the message I deliver to the young men of the South, I declare that the truth above all others to be worn unsullied and sacred in your hearts, to be surrendered to no force, sold for no price, compromised in no necessity, but cherished and defended as the covenant of your prosperity, and the pledge of peace to your children, is that the white race must dominate forever in the South, because it is the white race, and superior to that race by which its supremacy is threatened.

A principal purpose of this Article is to illuminate the economic power of this white supremacist oration by Henry Grady and of Henry V's justly celebrated speech, as well as to examine the precise parallel between the two.

Each speech appeals to *group* interests, *group* loyalty, and *group* identity. The ubiquity of social groups says something of their importance: groups include not just firms, trade associations, and families, but groups based on demographic traits such as race, gender, or age, and those based on membership, such as fraternities or sororities, amateur sports teams, gangs, the Rotary or Elks Clubs, or private lunch clubs. Undoubtedly, some or all of these groups, like the firm, serve the individual's interest by minimizing the transaction costs she incurs while acting to satisfy her preference for whatever interest or function the group facilitates. But that explanation offers no insight into the meaning or power of the speeches of Henry V and Henry Grady.

This Article offers an economic theory to explain why individuals make material sacrifices for group welfare. My thesis is that a material view of human motivation underestimates both the level of cooperation that groups elicit from their members and the level of conflict that groups elicit from each other. A single group dynamic connects these added increments of cooperation and conflict: groups achieve solidarity and elicit loyalty beyond what economic analysis conventionally predicts, but solidarity and loyalty within groups lead predictably, if not inevitably, to competition and conflict between groups. The connection is the desire for esteem or status. Groups use intra-group status rewards as a non-material means of gaining material sacrifice from members, but the attendant desire for inter-group status causes inter-group conflict. This theory explains the power of King Henry's speech, which appeals to the individual's identification with the group ("we band of brothers") and effectively describes the status reward by contrasting other members of the group (those gentlemen left in England) who will not share in it. At the same time, the war itself was the product of England's desire for esteem and status—more specifically, Henry's desire for honor—which can only be achieved by conquering France.

This two-fold importance of status is essential to a genuine understanding of race discrimination, which has eluded economics. Discrimination is a means by which social groups produce status for their members, but pivotal to understanding this form of inter-group *conflict* is the role that status plays in generating the intra-group *cooperation* necessary to make discrimination effective. Absent the desire for intra-group status, selfish individuals would not make the material sacrifices that discrimination requires. In this context, Henry Grady's racist speech is an economically explicable (if unusually candid) means of enlisting white troops in the ongoing status warfare, urging them to "compromise[ ] in no [material] necessity" the process of discriminating against, and thereby subordinating, the blacks whose inferior position produces a status gain for whites. The rhetoric helps establish a norm of white behavior, the abrogation of which will lower the in-group status of non-conforming whites.

Race discrimination is the best and most important illustration of what I view as a more general phenomenon of intra-group cooperation and inter-group conflict. Before discussing race, however, I must articulate the general theory—to establish empirically that, because of concern for status, cooperation arises within groups and conflict occurs between groups. Part I sets forth puzzling instances of intra-group cooperation in experimental "dilemma" situations and elsewhere, which are not explained by existing economic theory but are well explained by concern for the esteem of other group members. Part I then proposes a model that describes how "esteem payments" afford groups a novel means of solving their collective action problems and, finally, how this same mechanism leads inevitably to inter-group status conflict. Part II considers the particular problem of race discrimination—the deficiencies in existing economic theory, the superior ability of a status-production model to explain many race-related phenomena, and the implications of such a model. In particular, if race discrimination is a means of producing group status—if groups are engaged in a form of status "warfare"—then discrimination presents the same case for government prohibition that exists for more traditional government restraints on force and fraud.

I. Explaining "Excess" Cooperation and Conflict: An Economic Theory of Social Groups

Current economic theory fails to predict the prevalence of cooperation and conflict in human affairs. Considerable evidence supports David Hume's observation that "[w]hen men are once inlisted on opposite sides, they contract an affection to the persons with whom they are united, and an animosity against their antagonists: And these passions they often transmit to their posterity." Economics has been slow to address the function of social groups and the means by which they engender levels of loyalty and hostility in apparent defiance of conventional notions of material selfishness. But the psychic motivations that explain these "passions"—and the resulting intra-group cooperation and inter-group conflict—are reconcilable with rational self-interest.

This Part presents the modern evidence that supports Hume's claim. Initially, section A examines the empirical evidence that people cooperate beyond conventionally predicted levels. This "excess" cooperation is explained neither by sophisticated rational choice mechanisms such as reciprocity, nor by unselfish motives such as altruism. Instead, the experimental data indicate that cooperation is related to group membership. Section B advances a theory to account for this data: individuals who seek to maximize the esteem they receive from others have selfish reasons to contribute to group status. Two concepts of "group" are advanced: one defined externally by common characteristics observable by third-parties, and one defined internally by relationships among the members. In each case, there are selfish but non-pecuniary reasons for cooperating with one's group members. Finally, section C suggests reasons that the very mechanisms that increase cooperation within groups also increase conflict between groups, and considers evidence that such status-based "excess" conflict exists.

A. The Empirical Evidence of "Excess" Cooperation

To understand conflict among social groups, we must first understand how groups elicit cooperation from their members. Game theorists study the strategic interactions of individuals, and their most compelling contribution is their description of the difficulties groups face in procuring the cooperation of members. In contrast to Adam Smith's "invisible hand," which guides society to desirable outcomes though individuals are selfishly motivated, game theory describes "collective action problems"—situations in which individually rational decisions lead to sub-optimal collective outcomes. The classic example is the prisoner's dilemma, but the basic problem exists in more complex situations with more than two parties: each individual faces a choice essentially between cooperation and defection, where the dominant strategy for each individual is defection, but where mutual defection is worse for everyone than mutual cooperation. The interest in studying such "games" is generated by the belief that they represent a fundamental feature of social life. Whether it is the undersupply of "public goods," the overconsumption of common resources, or related difficulties, the problem of collective action is commonly offered as a rationale for government regulation. Conversely, many private economic practices can best be understood as mechanisms for solving collective action problems.

The focus of this section and the next is a particular mechanism for solving collective action problems commonly ignored by legal economists: groups achieve cooperation by allocating intra-group status. To persuade the skeptical that the desire for esteem exists and is necessary to explain important examples of cooperation, I could begin with a number of real-world examples of group cooperation. It is difficult, however, to distinguish subtle motivations in complex, uncontrolled events. Some might plausibly assert that, for any number of reasons, the individual's pecuniary self-interest in such examples happens to conform to the group interest. Others, including some critics of economic analysis, would argue that cooperation indicates the existence, not of a selfish interest in status, but of genuine altruism. Given these difficulties, I turn first to laboratory experiments, which can control for alternative motivations for cooperation.

1. Dilemma Experiments: Evidence of Non-Material Motivations for Cooperation.—Since the 1950s, social scientists have conducted experiments with the prisoner's dilemma game, its multi-party variants, public goods problems, and common resource problems. In each test, experimenters structure monetary payoffs to make defection or free-riding the dominant strategy. Despite the logical force of the monetarily dominant strategy, researchers have not found uniform defection. Many individuals defect, but a significant proportion—one-quarter to two-thirds—chooses to cooperate. After more than two thousand social dilemma experiments, one of the "generally accepted" conclusions is that, when pecuniary incentives appear to compel defection, "many subjects do *not* defect." For those who employ game theory to predict the consequences of legal rules, this residuum of cooperation demands explanation.

One immediate and material explanation is *reciprocity*. When future interactions are likely, reciprocity is possible, and defection may no longer be the dominant strategy. One reciprocal strategy is "tit-for-tat," in which one begins by cooperating and then responds in future rounds by doing whatever the other player did in the previous round. Considerable evidence demonstrates the success of tit-for-tat in preventing mutual defection in iterated prisoner's dilemmas.

Reciprocity does not, however, explain the cooperation observed in the dilemma experiments discussed above. Reciprocity requires future interaction in which players can reciprocate past decisions. Theorists still predict mutual defection for "one-shot" prisoner's dilemmas. Yet a large number of the empirical tests of collective action problems were intentionally designed as "one-shot" games to exclude the opportunity for reciprocity, and these tests have repeatedly found significant amounts of cooperation. In the very circumstance in which there is no material reason to cooperate, there is the undeniable fact of cooperation. Thus, however powerful reciprocity may be in some contexts, a significant residual level of cooperation remains unexplained.

One might note, finally, that the material stakes in these experiments typically involve only a few dollars or less. Though higher stakes might cause people to free-ride, the question is what explains subjects' consistent failure to free-ride when low material stakes suggest they should. After all, entire industries arise to capture stakes of a similar size; what seems low in isolation is vast when aggregated over a large population. Whether we can say the same of the motivations causing this residual cooperation requires us first to discover what those motivations are.

2. Dilemma Experiments: Evidence of Non–Altruistic Motivations for Cooperation.—Critics and reformers of economic modeling have pointed to the dilemma experiments described above as proof of altruism or a commitment to principles of fairness. Yet a full review of the psychological research on collective dilemmas refutes this thesis. Some sense of "group identity," rather than altruism or fairness, explains the variations in cooperation researchers have observed. Of particular note are studies revealing that individuals cooperate more frequently in dilemma games than do groups of individuals and studies revealing that discussion increases the level of cooperation in dilemma games.

First, many prisoner's dilemma studies have contrasted games between individual subjects with games between groups of subjects. Holding the payoffs constant, these studies consistently find significantly more cooperation when individuals play individuals than when teams play teams. One study, for example, found that three-person groups defected an average of 8.73 times in twenty rounds, compared to an average of 1.8 defections out of twenty when individuals played each other. This individual-group "discontinuity" is consistent with research finding that the formation of a purely experimental "group" can elicit a bias in favor of in-group members, against out-group members, or both. Psychologists discovered this when they set out to create a base line in which individuals would have no reason to favor their own group. To their surprise, whenever subjects were divided into groups, people consistently evaluated members of their own group more favorably than members of other groups. Summarizing this effect, one pair of researchers stated that "mere awareness of the presence of an out-group is sufficient to provoke intergroup competitive or discriminatory responses on the part of the in-group."

Additional confirmation of the importance of groups is provided by dilemma experiments in which researchers elicited differences in cooperation by symbolically invoking "real-world" group memberships. In one study, psychologists observed significantly more cooperation from subjects sharing a common resource when they told the subjects that they were being evaluated as a single group against groups not then a part of the experiment (for example, college students versus non-students) than when they told the subjects that they were being evaluated as members of one of two subgroups in the experiment (for example, psychology majors versus economics majors).

These studies appear to confirm David Hume's insight that individuals "have such a propensity to divide into personal factions, that the smallest appearance of real difference will produce them." The experimenter's arbitrary division of subjects into groups is sufficient to "factionalize" them, causing more competitive behavior between groups than between individuals and favoritism for members of one's own "group." Neither a general concern for the welfare of others nor a concern for fairness explains why subjects were so much less cooperative with other subjects whom the experimenter placed in a different group.

The second body of studies that challenge the altruism-fairness explanation are those involving discussion. Repeated study shows that permitting communication between the subjects in a prisoner's dilemma situation dramatically increases the level of cooperation; indeed, discussion as much as doubles cooperation rates. Yet "in none of these experiments does group discussion change the fact of defection's dominance"; given the structure of the experiments, there is no reason for any threat or promise to be credible.

To explain this puzzle, researchers varied the conditions of discussion in multi-party prisoner's dilemmas. In one study, the experimenters randomly divided subjects into two groups and placed each group in a separate room. The experimenters permitted ten minutes of discussion in half the groups and no discussion in the others. In addition, half the groups were told that their decisions would affect the payoff for their own group, while the other half were told that their decisions would determine the payoff for the other group and, conversely, that the decisions of the other group would determine the payoff for their group. The results were striking. When subjects believed their decisions would affect the payoffs of members of their own group, discussion increased cooperation from thirty-four percent to sixty-nine percent. But when subjects believed that their decisions affected payoffs for the *other* group, discussion slightly reduced cooperation. The researchers concluded that "discussion does *not* enhance contribution when beneficiaries are strangers." Of course, *all* of these subjects were "strangers" to each other in the sense that they had never met before the experiment and were randomly assigned to the different groups. Yet with ten minutes of discussion about their upcoming decisions, they were, in an important economic sense, no longer strangers. Limited discussion was sufficient to dramatically increase cooperation if and only if the discussants were the beneficiaries of the cooperation.

These findings further demonstrate that altruism and fairness do not fully explain excess cooperation in the prisoner's dilemma. If discussion invoked a general concern for others or for fairness, it should not matter that the beneficiaries are arbitrarily placed in another room. Instead, discussion seems to permit formation of a group identity that creates a special reason for discussants to cooperate. In the transcripts of the subjects' pre-decision discussion, people frequently referred to what "we"—the members of the group—should do. Moreover, where one group knew that its decisions would affect only the other group, there were "frequent statements that the best results would occur if we all keep and they all give to us." The motive seems to fall far short of altruism or fairness. The kind of speech that so effectively increases cooperation tends to be an appeal not to principle, but to solidarity. Thus, successful inspirational rhetoric—like Henry Grady's racist speech—is often centered around repeated invocations of an "us against them" image.

3. *Cooperation Outside the Laboratory: Further Evidence That Groups Matter.*—Although laboratory experiments more easily control for alternative explanations, it is also appropriate to consider two real-world collective action problems: social protest and war. Although law and economics scholars have criticized Title VII, none has attempted to explain why individual blacks participated in the civil rights protests that led to its enactment. Social protests—such as marches, boycotts, and "sit-ins"—are costly to the individual. Although a group may benefit from collective protest, the gains will likely be enjoyed by all members of the group, regardless of whether they participated in the protest. Thus, social movements are rife with collective action problems, which usually prevents such movements from forming or succeeding. Posing this problem, Dennis Chong inquires how the civil rights movement of the 1950s and 1960s succeeded in mobilizing considerable collective action. Given the violence of white resisters, Chong rejects the possibility that material rewards explain the participation, recounting instead the importance of social incentives within small, pre-existing groups such as black churches.

Consider also the high-stakes collective action problems in war. If all soldiers attempt to free-ride on the combat efforts of others, the result is a rout. S.L.A. Marshall argues forcefully that, for the bulk of soldiers, the only thing that stops them from fleeing in the face of fire is the *opinion* of those with whom the soldiers have formed social ties. Marshall's evaluation is based on the fighting effectiveness of "battle stragglers," soldiers separated from their fighting unit who temporarily join an unfamiliar company. He found that individual stragglers had almost no "combat value" in a new unit, while small squads of stragglers "tended to fight as vigorously as any element:"

> Within the group increments the men were still fighting alongside old friends, and though they were now joined to a new parent body, they were under the same compulsion to keep face and share in the common defense. The individual stragglers were simply responding to the first law of nature which began to apply irresistibly the moment they were separated from the company of men whom they knew and who knew them.

Even in the face of death—high stakes indeed—individuals cooperate not merely to secure material rewards, but also to preserve the opinion that group members hold of them. This, of course, is the very dynamic King Henry manipulates in his St. Crispian speech.

B. *Economic Explanations of "Excess" Cooperation: The Production of Inter-Group and Intra-Group Status*

If neither material self-interest nor altruism explains the residuum of cooperation, what can? And why does the level of cooperation vary so significantly with the manner in which individuals are categorized by group? This section proposes an answer: group-based status production. In the experiments discussed above, individuals behave selfishly, not altruistically, but their selfish end is the production of the non-material good of esteem. If individuals seek such non-material ends, members of social groups have another means of solving collective action problems—by allocating esteem to induce members to make contributions to group welfare. Once we add esteem consequences to the material payoffs of individual decisions in such settings, we can explain both the fact and the nature of residual cooperation.

This section argues that human beings seek esteem from others; in aggregate terms, they seek social status. Individuals derive status from groups in two ways: first, individuals gain esteem from strangers based on visible group memberships; and second, within a socially connected group, individuals are especially concerned with the esteem of fellow members. In each case, though for different reasons, status production creates a non-material incentive for group cooperation.

1. The Individual Preference for Esteem and Status.—If one assumes that individuals behave rationally, the only explanation for the subjects' behavior in the experiments discussed in Part I.A is that the subjects receive benefits from cooperation, or avoid costs from defection, that are not part of the formal, pecuniary payoff structure of the game. One simple way of explaining the cooperation is that the benefit they receive is the esteem of their fellow game-players.

In an earlier article, I described the pervasiveness and power of what I called "negative relative preferences—preferences for approaching or surpassing the consumption level of others." In particular, I offered evidence that people care greatly about achieving a relative social rank or social status. What one gains by attaining "status," however, is merely a state of mind—the opinion of others in society—that one is particularly worthy in some way. To understand "excess" cooperation, we should start with precisely this point: that one of the "basic pleasures" people seek in life is the esteem of others.

That people care what others think of them is a parsimonious explanation of many phenomena. The desire for esteem explains, for example, why people are obsessed with the impression their goods make on others. The desire for esteem also underlies the common emotion of embarrassment: individuals feel a momentary but acute pain from loss of esteem at having others observe their missteps or indiscretions. And this desire for esteem helps explain the well-established finding that individuals conform dramatically in the face of a group judgment. Even when there is no material cost to disagreement, individuals appear to fear that dissent will adversely affect how others view them.

Given this behavior, it is not implausible to say that some individuals would cooperate in what is nominally a prisoner's dilemma solely to preserve the minimal esteem strangers (in that community) normally feel for one another. Individuals add the "esteem rewards" and "esteem penalties" to the material payoffs and choose accordingly. Esteem concerns may change the total payoffs enough to make cooperation rational.

2. *Members of "Shared-Trait" Groups Cooperate to Produce Inter-Group Status.*—To explain the dilemma experiments adequately, an esteem theory must also explain why the level of cooperation varies with "group identity" measures. The concept of "shared-trait groups" explains the existence and variation in the level of cooperation observed in the experiments. By "shared-trait" group, I mean a collection of individuals who have in common some readily observable feature. In American society, people can roughly agree on how to group individuals—for example, by age, by language, or by physical characteristics we refer to as "race." In each case, on the basis of casual observation, one can determine reasonably well whether individuals fall within the category.

Observable traits are important because, when individuals encounter a stranger, they have no other basis for making an esteem judgment. If individuals feel particularly high or low esteem for others with the same trait, they tend to extend that judgment to the stranger. I am not describing irrational prejudice, but a simple application of the economics of information. Given the scarcity of information, it is rational to use cheaper information—proxies—to infer the existence of more expensive, individualized information. The economics literature describes the use of proxies for making decisions of material consequence (such as employment), but proxies can also be used for the allocation of status. Shared-trait group membership is a proxy people use for granting or withholding esteem to individuals they do not know personally.

The use of observable traits as proxies gives individuals a reason to care about the esteem-generating behavior of those with whom they share an observable trait. If an individual shares a trait with others, she expects strangers to extend her the esteem they have for the group that shares the trait. If these third-party observers know only an individual's putative group membership, the individual expects them to judge her entirely on the basis of that membership. She therefore has a selfish concern that the group be highly esteemed in comparison to other groups. Even though the "members" of a group may not know or feel any affinity for each other, third-party categorization gives these members a reason to care about the group's status.

This proxy effect provides a parsimonious explanation of the variation in cooperation observed in the experiments reviewed above: in the laboratory, the experimenter is the third party who categorizes individuals. Any set of subjects the experimenter designates as constituting a group has a "shared trait" for purposes of the experiment. The subjects know that the researcher is observing and evaluating them as members of the group she created. In collective action experiments, the only means of distinguishing successful from unsuccessful groups is the extent to which the group cooperates and achieves the best collective result. Subjects in such experiments may earn additional benefits for cooperating or face additional costs for defecting—thus, esteem consequences may make cooperation a rational strategy.

Further, in the prisoner's dilemma studies, individuals playing the game against individuals cooperated at higher levels than teams playing the same game against teams. With team-play, individuals expect that the esteem they receive depends on the success of the arbitrarily created groups to which they belong. The proxy effect works to raise the payoff of defecting when the other team cooperates (the one way of "beating" the other team) and to lower the payoff of cooperating when the other team defects (thereby "losing"). With individual play, however, either there is no cognizable "group," or the group contains both of the subjects in the game. Thus any proxy effect works toward cooperation. If subjects understand that the experimenter will have other pairs play the game, they may imagine themselves being evaluated as a pair against other pairs, which raises the payoff of mutual cooperation (the best "pair" outcome) and lowers the payoff of mutual defection (the worst "pair" outcome).

To the experiments previously reviewed, we may now add studies on relative deprivation as a cause of social protest. Relative deprivation refers to the fact that individuals react strongly to deprivation when others have what they lack. "Psychologists hypothesize that a central component of people's angry feelings over deprivation is a comparison between themselves and others who have the desired thing." Numerous studies have demonstrated the importance of comparison with others to feelings of relative deprivation and to behavior motivated by such feelings. Most important, many of these studies find that attitudes about inter-group comparisons predict participation in social protest, whereas attitudes about interpersonal comparisons do not. People are more likely to protest when they feel that the group to which they belong is relatively deprived than when they simply feel that they as individuals are relatively deprived.

In sum, laboratory experiments show that, even when the group is an entirely arbitrary construct, individuals seek to acquire esteem from "nongroup" members by raising the status of what, in the eyes of those nongroup members, is the individuals' group. Outside the laboratory, concern with how one's shared-trait group is regarded also motivates significant action.

3. Members of "Socially Connected" Groups Cooperate to Produce Intra-Group Status.—A second, more conventional understanding of the group posits that the members are, in some manner, socially connected. These socially connected groups are comprised of people who know each other, the paradigm cases being families, networks of friends, or social clubs. Such groups have two noteworthy features, each of which contributes to the group's ability to overcome collective action problems: individuals tend to care especially about the esteem of their fellow group members, and individuals tend to grant esteem to members who contribute to group welfare.

The first feature of socially connected groups is that individuals tend to value the esteem of fellow group members more than they value the esteem of non-members. If we care what others think of us, we care more intensely the more well-informed an opinion is; those with whom we have frequent interaction—group members—know us best. Moreover, the dilemma experiments in which the simple act of discussion generated greater cooperation among discussants indicate that even minimal social connection can significantly increase the concern for the esteem of another. In addition, the very reason many social groups exist is that the members share some skill, trait, or interest; members tend to value the esteem of in-group members more than outsiders because members share a sense of what skills or traits are worth possessing. Finally, there is a self-reinforcing aspect to the concern for intra-group status: we tend to value most the opinion of those we esteem highly, and we prefer to belong to social groups including such people.

Given the especially high concern for esteem from socially connected group members, we can better understand high-stakes cooperation in the collective action problems presented by social protest and war. Military and social protest groups elicit cooperation by rewarding members with esteem or prestige based on how much they contribute to the group's welfare. Yet even if people *seek* intra-group esteem, the question remains why individual group members *provide* intra-group esteem to those who contribute to group welfare. The second noteworthy feature of socially connected groups is that members readily provide esteem to those who benefit the group; even without a central authority, members tend not to free-ride completely on the "esteem payments" of other members.

People provide esteem to members who benefit the group because, up to a point, thinking well of others is not a cost. To the contrary, esteeming others is a valuable "consumption good." A person deprived of this good—who finds no one in the world worth esteeming—is far less happy than one who has located a small collection of worthy souls. Nor is an individual who esteems twenty others necessarily poorer than someone who esteems only ten others to the same degree. To the extent that esteem is not costly, there is no reason to free-ride by withholding esteem from others. Instead, group members tend to allocate esteem in a way that brings them some return by rewarding those who contribute materially to group welfare and, at a secondary level, by rewarding those who allocate esteem in a manner that benefits the group. Imagine, as an analogy, that people have a kind of currency that is useless except for making group members feel better. It would be irrational to keep the currency or to distribute it randomly; one might as well provide it as a reward for those who contribute to group welfare and withhold it to punish those who do not.

Departing briefly from an economic description of human behavior, I can state the point in more realistic psychological terms. "Thinking well of others" is often reflexive rather than deliberate. People who might free-ride on material payments tend not to free-ride on esteem "payments" because they reflexively admire and respect those who benefit the group. Imagine, for example, a chessmaster, a person who not only intensely studies the game, but also socializes predominantly with others who do the same. Taking egoism seriously means that this person will consider chess-playing ability to be an important measure by which others can be judged. Individuals elevate the importance of those traits or skills that they possess. This process helps the individual secure self-esteem. But a consequence of thinking that a particular trait is desirable is to esteem *others* who possess the trait and to esteem them in relation to how much of the trait they possess. It is neither plausible nor coherent for the chessmaster to withhold esteem from other people who excel in chess. Barring an overshadowing negative trait, an individual will more or less *automatically* esteem others who have the traits the individual most values in herself, or the traits the individual would most like to acquire for herself.

Frequently, people reflexively esteem traits or behaviors that increase the welfare of the group. A player's success at chess tournaments raises the prestige of the chess club to which she belongs and earns her esteem within the club. A soldier whose skill or effort saves the lives of his fellow squad members earns their esteem. Moreover, if one who is known to value a particular trait withholds esteem from those who possess it, she risks appearing envious and losing the esteem of others. Especially within a group of people who desire a particular trait, refusing to esteem the trait (or at least to appear to esteem it) calls into question the dissenter's commitment to or understanding of shared values. Of course, some members may nonetheless be envious and refuse to provide esteem. But since esteem is at least partially reflexive, there is less than complete free-riding in allocating esteem, and the group can achieve a significant level of coordination.

Sociological evidence supports the theory that socially connected groups allocate esteem to overcome collective action problems. Socially connected groups, as I have defined them, consist of relatively small numbers of people who know each other. Sociologists have long been interested in how, within larger groups in society, "norms" arise as an important decentralized mechanism of social control. Esteem allocation, it turns out, provides the necessary micro-level explanation for social norms; the functioning of social norms, in turn, demonstrates the full power of intra-group cooperation.

Although economically inclined theorists have mostly ignored norms, one important exception is Robert Ellickson. *In Order Without Law*, Ellickson summarizes and supplements the empirical literature on the success of norms in regulating individual behavior. Ellickson's empirical contribution is his study of norms that govern the resolution of various disputes over livestock between neighbors in Shasta County, California. Like other social norms that arise within "close-knit groups," the Shasta County norms are a means of enhancing group welfare. The norms are a non-legal means by which the group facilitates desirable collective action. To some degree, what Ellickson and others identify as efficient norms are enforced by reciprocity between neighbors who expect to interact indefinitely, and the norms are therefore explicable in material terms. But the unique contribution norms make to cooperation—the additional power of norms beyond reciprocity—is third-party enforcement. What Ellickson has in mind are sanctions administered not by the immediate "victim" of a norm violation, but by "friends, relatives, gossips, vigilantes, and other nonhierarchical third-party enforcers." Third parties sanction—by gossip, scorn, ostracism, or physical retaliation—those who violate the norms or informal rules of the group.

My point, however, is that this informal third-party enforcement cannot exist without the desire for esteem. There is no material incentive to obey norms unless there is a material cost attached to violating them. There is no material cost associated with violation unless someone imposes a material penalty. And there is no material incentive for others to bear the cost of inflicting such a penalty; after all, norm-enforcement is, for the group, a public good, and like all public goods, faces the problem of free-riding. Ellickson says that there is a secondary enforcement norm that compels people to punish those who violate norms and that those who fail to do so will also be sanctioned. But then the question arises why anyone would bear the cost of sanctioning those who failed to sanction a substantive norm violator. As Jon Elster argues, "People do not frown upon others when they fail to sanction people who fail to sanction people who fail to sanction people who fail to sanction a norm violation." As one moves away from the original norm violation, "the cost of receiving disapproval falls rapidly to zero." Yet if the cost of refusing to enforce a norm at any level falls to zero, there is no reason for anyone to enforce the norm, and hence no reason for anyone to follow the norm.

A concern for esteem as an end in itself, however, is sufficient to defend norm enforcement against the infinite regress Elster describes. Elster's argument assumes that mechanisms like gossip, scorn, and ostracism work only to signal who is to be subject to material sanctions and are only as effective as those material sanctions. But if disapproval *itself* exerts a real force, then the gossip, scorn, and ostracism are themselves sufficient to enforce norms; they punish the violator by lowering the esteem she receives from the community. In addition to this direct support, the desire for esteem may produce a secondary enforcement norm that requires material sanctions for violators of the primary norm. To avoid esteem punishment, individuals may have to bear some cost incurred by imposing material sanctions on norm violators. Thus, the considerable body of evidence that shows that social norms govern behavior further supports the significance of esteem motives, especially within socially connected groups.

In sum, individuals care particularly for esteem within socially connected groups. Even without a central authority, individuals tend to provide esteem to those who contribute to the welfare of such groups, and this process of esteem allocation facilitates wider social norms that bring about further cooperation. Of course, group members will still free-ride when their desire for material well-being outweighs their desire for intra-group status, but esteem allocation will ameliorate, if not eliminate, collective action problems.

C. *The Consequences of Intra–Group Cooperation: Inter–Group Conflict*

Intra-group cooperation increases inter-group conflict. Status is both an additional *means* of ensuring intra-group cooperation and a new *end* of intra-group cooperation, and it contributes in both ways to conflict between groups. Given that social groups often conflict over material resources, the desire for intra-group status means that group members will cooperate more effectively in such disputes, which ensures that groups will be more effective "combatants" whenever material conflict arises. More important, the very mechanism that facilitates greater intra-group cooperation will ensure a new form of conflict: competition for *inter-group* status. This latter result is the unfortunate and inevitable connection between cooperation and conflict.

Groups sometimes engage in zero-sum competition with other groups. A classic example is lobbying. When interest groups pursue what economists call "rent-seeking" legislation, such as farm subsidies and tax "loopholes," they seek merely to transfer resources from one group to another. Cartels similarly seek to extract the profits of non-competitive pricing from consumers. For lobbying groups and cartels, individual contributions to the group's rent-seeking endeavor tend to be undersupplied; selfish members free-ride on the efforts of other members. But the cooperation secured by intra-group status production means that individuals contribute more heavily than they otherwise would toward their group's effort to win a conflict.

Indeed, intra-group esteem production, and social norms based on such esteem, may provide the only explanations for the success of very large groups in lobbying despite powerful incentives for individuals to free-ride. Judge Richard Posner has conceded some uncertainty, for example, in explaining how farmers cooperate in legislative activities. I propose that the answer is the same for farmers as it is for the ranchers Ellickson studied in Shasta County. Although the occupational status of farmers or ranchers is not as observable as, for example, their race, it is one of the first things strangers detect about them. And within a geographic area, farmers and ranchers tend to be socially connected. Thus, farmers and ranchers have an interest in the status generally accorded their occupation and a means of inducing contributions to that status. Intra-group esteem allocation elicits material contributions to group material welfare, such as monetary contributions to lobbying efforts. For individual farmers and ranchers, the amount contributed may be small, but multiplication by a large number produces considerable political clout.

There is a second reason intra-group esteem allocation increases group conflict. Individuals compete for esteem. One arena of competition is *group* status competition, in which individuals seek to produce status for themselves by raising the status of their groups. Under certain conditions, status is zero-sum, so that satisfaction of the status preferences of one group's members necessarily means non-satisfaction of the status preferences of another group's members.

In another article, I detailed the conditions under which relative preferences "inherently" conflict—that is, the circumstances under which the relative position is genuinely zero-sum. Although I focused there primarily on individual status-seeking, those conditions exist for social groups when members of different groups seek incompatible positions for their groups along some common, observable, and reasonably objective dimension. When these conditions do not hold, group status production is socially benign. But the conditions do hold, for example, when groups compare themselves along the "common dimension" of generalized social status and seek a position of superiority on that scale. Under such circumstances, social status is entirely relative. Investment in such zero-sum competition is therefore socially wasteful; the extent of the investment measures the size of the inefficiency. In particular, note the social waste of an obvious group optimizing strategy: *one way to raise the status of one's group is to invest in lowering the status of other groups.* Thus, the desire for esteem may lead to "subordination" as groups attempt to sabotage each other's general social position.

The status theory of cooperation and conflict may now be summarized. First, individuals seek, as an end, the esteem of others; in aggregate terms, they seek social status. Second, because socially connected group members are a key source of esteem, individuals will make material sacrifices on behalf of the group to gain intra-group status. Conversely, the group will reward such status to those who contribute to its welfare. Third, because another source of status is the larger society beyond one's social groups, one measure of group welfare is its status within society. Consequently, groups will use intra-group status "payments" to encourage members to contribute materially to inter-group status. Finally, because general social status is relative, one group can raise its inter-group status by lowering the status of other groups.

* * *

The novelty of these otherwise non-instrumental beliefs is that the normal economic correctives to false belief formation do not apply. For expressive purposes, a "good" belief is not necessarily an accurate belief, but rather one that is pleasurable to express. Of course, even if a category of beliefs serves only expressive ends, there are some constraints on belief formation. Our cognitive mechanisms may make it difficult for us to believe certain things that are manifestly contradicted by experience. Moreover, we may not experience the full pleasure of expressing our beliefs if others find them palpably false in an uninteresting way.

Most important for our purposes, however, is the constraint of self-esteem. Some beliefs are more pleasant than others. For expressive purposes, people are more likely to adopt beliefs that enhance, rather than degrade, their self-esteem. If the issue is the talent of a celebrity, for example, a person is more likely to think highly of the celebrity if, through some connection—having attended the same school, for example—the celebrity's talent will enhance the individual's self-esteem. If esteem can influence expressive belief formation in this manner, esteem can also affect conventionally instrumental beliefs—beliefs concerning how best to satisfy one's preferences. As long as the gain in esteem from the bias toward esteem-producing beliefs is larger than any instrumental loss from the bias, then such a bias serves the individual's overall interests. There is considerable evidence to support this claim: research shows, for example, that people tend systematically to overevaluate their own performance and characteristics. Such a bias may even be essential to mental well-being. Self-evaluation is clearly an instrumental belief—one needs to know what one's talents and abilities are—yet the need for self-esteem is sufficient to create some deviation from strictly impartial beliefs about oneself.

If esteem production favorably biases one's self-evaluations, esteem production may also cause a positive bias toward the social groups to which one belongs. One may gain pleasure from believing positive things about one's groups. Moreover, groups will reward status to those who hold beliefs that are conducive to group welfare. A favorable bias regarding group members may strengthen intra-group cooperation by increasing the apparent material advantage available from transacting with members rather than non-members.

But groups may encourage and reward beliefs more complex than simple bias. For example, although he does not explain how belief distortion occurs, Richard Posner has invoked such distortion to explain how certain cartels solve collective action problems. According to Posner, the distinguishing feature of certain successful cartels—which he terms "guilds"—is their having an "ideology." A guild is a social as well as an economic institution in which members have adopted a common "personal morality" of loyalty, conformity, and craftsmanship, and which has achieved a certain "mystique" involving the idealization of quality over quantity. The "mutually reinforcing combination" of this morality and mystique comprises "the *ideology* of guild production," which serves the "the self-interest of producers in the cartelization of production."

Posner appears to mean that guild members convince themselves that the public interest is served by the restrictions on market entry and production necessary to cartelize an industry. This analysis implies that a principled concern for the public good has some force in motivating behavior, so that cartel members would be even more likely to free-ride if they realized that cartel pricing is contrary to the public interest. Ideology, however, turns the moral force against free-riding. An ideological commitment to quality allows the guild member to believe that conduct that would undermine the cartel—lowering quality and expanding output—would harm the public. Self-interested self-deception thus serves the cartel's long run interests by curbing the individual's impulse to free-ride on the restraint of others.

Return now to racial beliefs. In Posner's terms, negative stereotypes are part of a racial "guild's" efforts to monopolize production of esteem. Even for beliefs that serve an instrumental purpose (such as evaluating potential employees), the desire for esteem will cause an individual to adopt distorted beliefs about racial groups as long as the esteem benefit exceeds the instrumental cost. Consequently, the status-production model can explain differences in voting behavior between blacks and whites. A person may gain esteem by believing positive things about political candidates from her own group and, at least in a relative sense, negative things about politicians of other races. If people do not vote for instrumental reasons, there is no instrumental check on the accuracy of these beliefs. A small bias may suffice to explain a significant difference in voting behavior because, for different racial groups, the bias works in opposite directions.

If one assumes that this analysis correctly explains the existence and direction of racial bias, the question remains how to explain the *evolution* of white attitudes regarding race. Recall that status production commonly involves the denial that one's motive is status production. When one seeks to gain status by lowering the status of others, it is all the more important to deny that one is degrading others in order to look better by comparison. Consequently, "guild ideology" never acknowledges its self-serving nature. Members of Posner's representative guild do not openly declare, even among themselves, that they desire to restrain competition in order to charge higher prices and earn monopoly profits. Similarly, whites never explain their discriminatory behavior as serving the function of status production. Even in the Jim Crow South, whites attempted to justify segregation not by reference to naked self-interest but by claims that blacks were inherently inferior, that blacks preferred segregation, or that segregation somehow reflected the natural order of things. Toward this end, the Jim Crow doctrine of "separate but equal" was ideal. Separation was a means of expressing contempt; the pretense of equality served to deny the status motivation.

When proponents of a status-driven ideology can no longer confidently deny the status motivation of their beliefs, the ideology fails and proponents must search for another ideology. This insight may explain the evolution of white attitudes toward segregation. Although the exact causal strands are difficult to disentangle, events leading up to and including the modern civil rights movement undermined the ability of whites to believe that their existing racial beliefs were anything other than a self-serving ideology. World War II provided one ideological shock, as revulsion to Nazi claims of racial superiority was difficult to square with rationalization of southern racial practices. Rising levels of black education and job skills put a material strain on racial ideology by raising the attractiveness of black labor and thus the cost of absolute racial exclusion. I suspect the most immediate cause of ideological breakdown occurred during the civil rights movement, when photographs captured segregation extremists using violent means, often against women and children, to suppress peaceful protests. Violence against peaceful demonstrators was, even for some southern supporters of Jim Crow, irrefutable evidence that whites were not (at least morally) superior, that blacks were indisputably unhappy with segregation, and that segregation was not a naturally ordained moral order. One of the constraints I have suggested for non-instrumental beliefs is "palpable falsity"; the events of the 1950s and 1960s made salient to whites the falsity of the belief that intentional racial segregation is something other than selfishly hurtful.

Whatever the causal mechanism, many whites have come genuinely to believe that segregation is wrong. This shift does not mean, however, that a psychological veil of prejudice has simply been lifted from their eyes. The expressive beliefs whites adopt about race can no longer be of the crude form needed to justify segregation, but the quest for the production of status continues. Having abandoned the older ideology, whites still tend to oppose policies and candidates that would increase the social status of blacks. Whites can give up old, extreme stereotypes and still embrace negative views of blacks. Unless one consciously scrutinizes the statistical validity of one's generalizations about other groups—an unlikely scenario—even false stereotypes will rarely be *palpably* false. Thus, one may acknowledge the good faith and intellectual integrity of conservative arguments on political issues concerning race—like busing, affirmative action, and welfare—and still worry that the same status-maximizing bias that first rationalized slavery and then segregation infects much of the public thinking on these matters. It is more pleasant to believe that one lives in a society in which everyone (or at least everyone else) is being treated as well as she deserves, that past transgressions have been righted, and that fairness and justice require no further sacrifice. The evolution of white attitudes, therefore, reflects an ideological adjustment to status production under changed circumstances. The final descriptive virtue of the status-production theory is that it offers some insight into this otherwise puzzling evolution of white attitudes.

C. *Implications of the Status Production Model of Discrimination*

The associational model of discrimination has two key implications: market competition will erode discrimination and, partly for that reason, prohibiting race discrimination is inefficient. The status-production model leads to different conclusions on both points.

1. The Persistence of Race Discrimination.—Becker drew an analogy between race discrimination and transportation costs, both of which increase the cost of certain trades. It is uncontroversial that, other things being equal, those who can minimize transportation costs achieve a competitive advantage over those who cannot. If the analogy with discrimination is sound, we should also expect that whites with less intense tastes for discrimination will enjoy a competitive advantage over those with more intense tastes and will tend to dominate a competitive market.

Under the status-production model, discrimination is not the result of costs that discriminators incur from contact with members of other groups, but is a means of producing status. The discriminator does bear a cost in discriminating—forgoing otherwise beneficial trade with the objects of the discrimination—but that cost is an *investment* in the production of status. As long as such investments are cost-effective for the discriminator, the status-production model predicts that race discrimination will persist in the face of market competition. Consequently, the transportation analogy is inapt. Discrimination may exist in a competitive equilibrium for at least three reasons: the power of discriminatory social norms; the existence of reciprocity between whites; and, under certain circumstances, the effect of esteem-producing racial biases. I will examine each of these in turn.

(a) The Stability of Discriminatory Norms.—This section presents a theory of discriminatory social norms. I begin with George Akerlof's economic theory of a racial caste system. I then raise and respond to two key objections to Akerlof's theory—that it does not explain why anyone enforces the caste-based norms, and that it does not capture the complexities of modern American society. I conclude that, despite market competition, status production can support a stable system of discriminatory norms.

Akerlof has provided an explanation for the resiliency of the discriminatory customs of a caste society. It is the essence of a caste-system, Akerlof says, that "any transaction that breaks the caste taboos changes the subsequent behavior of uninvolved parties" who may act to punish the caste-breaker. Third party reactions change the calculus for those who have not internalized the norm:

> Those who fail to follow, or even to enforce the caste customs do not gain the profits of the successful arbitrageur but instead suffer the stigma of the outcaste. If the punishment of becoming an outcaste is predicted to be sufficiently severe, the system of caste is held in equilibrium irrespective of individual tastes, by economic incentives; the predictions of the caste system become a self-fulfilling prophecy.

Thus, Akerlof applies to race discrimination the same view of social norm enforcement that Ellickson has applied to property law—because people boycott norm breakers, it often pays to follow norms.

This insight would be trivial, however, if it only applied when *everyone* in society was willing to boycott those who break the caste rules. Surely a few individuals will always be willing to deal with social outcasts (such as other social outcasts or near outcasts). One could argue that, as long as the number of people willing to violate the discriminatory norms exceeds the number of people targeted by the norm, violators need suffer no harm. Further, one might predict that if a few people violate the norm intially, their violation will weaken the norm and induce other violations to follow, eventually leading to the norm's complete unraveling.

Akerlof responds to these arguments with a simple point that depends merely on the existence of transaction costs. Suppose there are search costs for firms seeking buyers or sellers; because of imperfect information about the existence and reputation of buyers and sellers, firms cannot instantly replace existing trading partners but must incur costs inversely proportional to the number of potential trading partners in the relevant geographic market. Under these circumstances, assuming that there are any parties who will boycott "innovators" (those who violate discriminatory norms), the innovators necessarily incur higher search costs in finding trading partners. Thus, each boycotter raises the likely search costs the innovator will incur before locating a trading partner. Further, when the innovator locates a non-boycotter, its higher search costs will place it "in a weaker bargaining position, since the cost of failing to make a trade is greater to [it] than to noninnovators." If the costs of innovation are higher than the benefits, the discriminatory norm will be stable in a competitive market.

There are, however, weaknesses in Akerlof's explanation. First, Akerlof simply posits that some discriminators will boycott those who fail to follow the discriminatory norm. He offers no explanation of why these boycotters are willing to bear such costs. The status-production model does offer such an explanation. The model shows how individuals gain from adhering to and enforcing certain norms, why the kind of norms individuals benefit from enforcing include norms of discrimination, and why the groups for which this process is frequently employed are racial groups. As I argued above, individuals within racial groups benefit from raising the status of their shared traits. One means of contributing to one's racial status is by subordinating members of other races. With sufficient overlap between racial and socially connected groups, whites have a status benefit to exploit and the cooperative means to exploit it.

Consider, however, a second possible weakness in Akerlof's model. A simple caste society is an appropriate starting point, but American society is more complex. Unquestionably, a norm exists against racial discrimination (or at least against certain forms of racial discrimination), and some whites, as well as blacks, boycott those who overtly discriminate. Given this reality, one might reject the Akerlof caste model.

Yet, even with blacks and some whites "counter-boycotting" discriminators, the equilibrium may entail significant discrimination. Discriminators will bear a cost when targeted for a counter-boycott (or other sanction), but unless that cost exceeds the cost that discriminators create for non-discriminators, it will pay to continue discriminating. The relative costs depend largely on the relative size and economic power of the two groups. Because whites constitute a large majority and possess disproportionate wealth, the costs from white boycotts is likely to exceed the costs from black counter-boycotts. At some point, the participation by a sufficient number of whites in the counter-boycott would tip the balance the other way, but this outcome seems unlikely. First, one cannot infer from the fact that opponents of discrimination are more vocal today—when discrimination in various forms is illegal—that white opponents of discrimination exceed supporters. Second, those who rely on the power of white counter-boycotts rely on the force of moral principle (or altruism) to overcome the selfish force of status production. Under existing theory, selfishness is thought to undermine discrimination. But given the status productivity of discrimination, the power of selfishness suggests the more pessimistic outcome.

One might object that discriminatory norms do not exist if any whites are willing to act against them. That some whites will boycott discriminators merely reflects, however, the fact that American whites do not constitute a single group. "Whites" include various ethnic, religious, political, regional, and class subgroups. How much a particular subgroup invests in subordination as a means of producing status will depend on what its various status options are. Low-status whites have fewer options and tend to discriminate more than high-status whites. Further, white condemnation of the blatant racial discrimination common in an earlier era is consistent with a more subtle discriminatory norm. Subordination works only as long as one can deny that one is acting for the purpose of producing status. Whites are less able to deny this function of racial derogation now than in the past; consequently, overt discrimination is no longer as productive of status as it once was. Just as a "nouveau riche" may undermine her own status by engaging in ostentatious and wasteful consumption, a "redneck" or bigot undermines her own status by expressing contempt solely on the basis of race. But, there is still status in wealth if one displays it more deftly, with the appearance of not calculating to make a display. Likewise, there is status to be gained from race discrimination of a more subtle form, especially when one can plausibly deplore its more flagrant manifestations.

One might nevertheless assert that there are significant numbers of whites who oppose even subtle forms of discrimination. One interpretation of this behavior is that high-status whites who condemn low-status whites for their discrimination may gain more by distinguishing themselves from other whites than by investing in the subordination of blacks or other minorities. In fact, certain classes of whites may enjoy free-riding on the status that other whites secure and then further increase their status by subordinating those whites for being discriminatory. A second, more sanguine interpretation begins with Ellickson's claim that norms tend to be efficient, at least from the perspective of the group in which they arise. Ellickson does not discuss norms that span a group as large as an entire society, but a weaker concern for the esteem of strangers might give rise to norms between strangers. If a weak counter-norm arises against discrimination, perhaps it is because discrimination is inefficient from the perspective of the entire society. But because the norm arises at a different and more diffuse level, it can exist alongside more powerful discriminatory norms that arise within or between socially connected groups.

Becker's model does not contemplate the existence of discriminatory social norms. Thus, I cannot be certain how he would respond to the claim I make here. But Robert Cooter, who embraces Becker's prediction that competition will drive out discrimination, does consider social norms. Cooter argues that the proper economic model for discrimination is that of a cartel and that during the Jim Crow era, southern whites advanced their material ends by using law to gain monopoly power in various markets. Like all cartels, whites faced the inherent problem of instability—that is, the incentive for each member to cheat. Cooter agrees that discriminatory social norms countered the incentives to free-ride, but asserts that the effectiveness of the norms probably depended on their being supported by

Jim Crow legislation. Thus, Cooter expresses the conventional economic skepticism that the norms that supported the white "cartel" could survive absent such legal restrictions. The material incentives in an unfettered market, in his view, provide a strong lure for individuals to defect from the group enterprise.

The theory of intra-group cooperation and inter-group conflict offers a reason for thinking otherwise. Cooter's skepticism about the independent strength of social norms would be well-founded if the only ends that individuals seek are material. Indeed, I argued previously that social norms add nothing to our understanding of cooperation beyond what can be explained by reciprocity unless people value the esteem of others as an end in itself. Therefore Cooter's argument might be right if the only purpose of the white cartel were to advance the material ends of whites and the only means of inducing cooperation were material rewards. The whole thrust of the status-production model, however, is that the cartel-like behavior of whites serves to maximize the non-material end of status production (the cartel seeks to monopolize social status) and that the cartel employs the non-material means of intra-group status rewards and punishments. If this fundamental point is right, then social norms can support discrimination notwithstanding market competition.

Nevertheless, Cooter's basic insight is quite helpful. Whites do act like a cartel. But whites are more accurately described as the subset of cartels that Posner calls "guilds," that is, cartels with "social cohesiveness." Based on a morality emphasizing loyalty and conformity, these guilds have an "ideology"—a set of beliefs that serves to inhibit free-riding—specifically that blacks tend to be inferior, that whites should not interact with blacks in certain ways, and that whites must "stick together." Posner contends that farmers and lawyers—very large industrial groups—manage to cooperate in legislative lobbying efforts despite incentives to free-ride. Racial groups may similarly succeed. For reasons explained above, the more observable the trait that links a group of people, the more status members have to gain by cooperating and the greater the reason to expect such groups to become socially connected as a means of achieving cooperation. Given that race is more observable than these industrial affinities, there is reason to believe racial groups can better succeed in overcoming their collective action problems despite their large size.

Consider, then, a new economic analogy for race discrimination: not transportation costs, but an analogy to the acquisition of a public reputation. An entrepreneur donates a large sum of money to a local museum, or a corporate president agrees to sponsor a marathon. No doubt, the economically inclined theorist would assert that such behavior occurs not because it serves an individual's "taste" for fame, but because it produces greater profits for entrepreneurs and firms by bolstering their reputation or name recognition. I suspect the main force behind this view, however, is nothing as contingent as empirical data on the profitability of such donations, but an inference that economic actors would not give money away unless it was productive to do so. I merely argue for a similar inference with respect to race discrimination. Discrimination exists because it is productive for its practitioners.

(b) Reciprocity as a Basis for Market Discrimination.—There is a second reason to believe that race discrimination will persist in the face of market competition. Becker's theory does not argue that market competition erodes social discrimination. Yet because social interaction facilitates more commercial reciprocity, social discrimination may cause persistent "market" discrimination.

According to Axelrod's analysis of iterated prisoner's dilemmas, it often pays to seek cooperation through a reciprocal strategy such as tit-for-tat when there is sufficient likelihood of future interaction with another. Axelrod emphasizes that the more likely future interactions are, the more likely it is that those who employ reciprocal strategies will prosper. Thus, to increase the prospects of cooperation with a particular individual, Axelrod advises (consciously) increasing the durability and frequency of interactions with that individual. One time-honored means of implementing Axelrod's strategy is to pursue social interaction with the group of individuals with whom one wishes to cooperate. When prospective business partners eat, talk, or play together, they are not merely acquiring information about each other. Social interaction also supports reciprocity; by joining a social group, one increases the likelihood of future interaction with members of the group. Most important, social interactions may themselves be relatively inexpensive but might increase the chance of cooperation's emerging in a business or market setting, where the benefits of cooperation are greater. Joining a country club, a "businessman's"club, or a particular neighborhood may "lock" one into a particular social group, raising one's ability to cooperate with members in non-social settings.

We can now understand more fully the power of discriminatory norms. Even in the absence of a social norm that restrains market trading with other racial groups, social norms could significantly impede such trades. A norm limited to preventing social contacts with members of another race is sufficient to harm such members economically. Since social contacts affect the probability of reciprocity, the absence of such contacts places the isolated individual or the disfavored group at a comparative disadvantage in economic trades. Consequently, norm-based discrimination in one setting, such as social clubs or housing, may cause discrimination in other settings, such as business or employment. Social clubs that exclude women and minorities thus cause them more harm than simply denying them information about, and the chance to become known to, market players. They deny them the opportunity to make reciprocity work.

(c) The Power of Esteem-Producing Racial Biases.—A final factor that contributes to the persistence of discrimination is racially biased beliefs or stereotypes. As noted above, discriminatory norms invoke rationalization mechanisms; discriminators prefer to have reasons for discriminating other than a bare interest in status production. Indeed, because status production is inconsistent with an overt strategy of subordination, it is important that discriminators have an explanation—an "ideology"—apart from status

production. Such an explanation can most easily take the form of negative stereotypes—that the failure of blacks to succeed is their own fault, due to their own shortcomings in ability, integrity, or dependability. This ideology buttresses discriminatory norms. Whatever the social cost of violating the norm, biased evaluations of blacks make it appear that the material benefits of norm violation are less than they are. Self-deception prevents cheating that would undermine the cartel.

Indeed, even if there were no discriminatory social norms, ideologically based racial stereotypes might sustain a stable level of discrimination. One might argue, to the contrary, that absent norms, market competition would discipline whites whose evaluations of blacks were biased. If some white employers fail to perceive black workers accurately, for example, they will lose a competitive advantage to more discerning whites. Yet there is one condition under which stereotypes alone will sustain discrimination—when the material costs of one's miscalculation is zero. In the employment setting, for example, the employer may believe in some cases that the applicants are essentially "tied," that is, they appear to have equal marginal productivities. A white employer would suffer no harm from the decision to hire a white applicant who was tied with a black applicant. Of course, given the white employer's ideology, the employer may not actually perceive the two candidates as being equal, but rather will think that the white candidate is better. The point, however, is that there will be no market correction for such a perception; having white job applicants win all "ties" is a market equilibrium. The question remains how frequently such ties occur in the real world—an interesting empirical question that I, like opponents of Title VII, leave to be answered by others. I simply note that, if such ties were frequent, stereotyping could itself add to the persistence of race discrimination.

In sum, the status-production model provides three reasons to suppose that race discrimination will survive market competition: the power of discriminatory social norms; the existence of reciprocity between whites; and, under certain circumstances, the effect of esteem-producing racial biases.

2. *The Efficiency of Anti-Discrimination Laws.*—Many legal economists have contended that federal anti-discrimination laws are efficient only to the extent that they nullify state laws mandating discrimination. These theorists view such laws as inefficient when they prohibit private discrimination because their only function is to frustrate discriminatory preferences. But the new descriptive theory I propose requires a rethinking of this normative claim. The status-production model views anti-discrimination laws as potentially correcting a market failure in which individuals invest in essentially confiscatory behavior. That discrimination is a market failure would not itself prove that government action is desirable. We must consider whether the regulation can correct the failure and whether the benefits of such intervention exceed the costs.

(*a*) *Discrimination as Market Failure: The Theft Analogy.*—Welfare economics provides a justification for laws that prohibit theft (and other forms of force and fraud) that is not dependent on discounting the gains to the thief (or other criminals). Even assuming that the transfer accomplished by theft itself causes no wealth loss, because the thief gains what the owner loses, a system that permits theft "results in a very substantial diversion of resources to fields where they essentially offset each other, and produce no positive product." In other words, absent laws against theft, individuals must expend resources merely to protect their property from seizure. They will also forgo certain wealth-creating activities to protect what they already have and because it may be too costly to protect some forms of wealth from theft. In response, the thief invests in gaining tools and knowledge to circumvent anti-theft practices and technology. These dynamic reactions to the risk of theft result in deadweight losses to society. Less is produced, and part of what is produced (burglar alarms and burglars' tools) provides no greater satisfaction of an individual's preferences, but merely helps the individual to retain or confiscate goods that will satisfy preferences. The net effect is to decrease wealth. The same argument applies for laws against violence. It is, of course, Thomas Hobbes's justification for the state: that the only alternative, the "warre ... of every man, against every man," is worse.

It follows from the status-production model that a society without discrimination laws permits an unfettered status war of "every group against every group." What is striking about Richard Epstein's *Forbidden Grounds*, which argues for the repeal of laws that prohibit employment discrimination, is not so much his controversial claim that the only role of government is to prevent force or fraud, but that he never considers how laws against race discrimination may fall precisely within this libertarian principle. Status "warfare" may not be as violent as literal combat, but the term is more than just a metaphor. Hobbes identifies competition for honor as one of the three causes of war; he warns that violent conflict results from attempted subordination. Similarly, Hume warned of the tendency of factions to produce "the fiercest animosities." Competition for group status has generated much of America's history of interracial violence, as when whites lynched blacks to preserve their social position or when blacks retaliated against repeated acts of derogation and dishonor.

Of course, laws prohibit such violence. But even with such laws, unregulated status competition mirrors the inefficiency of a regime without laws prohibiting theft. First, racial status preferences inherently conflict. Race discrimination exists because members of (at least) one race seek for their group a status position that is incompatible with the position sought by members of one or more other groups. Even when only one group seeks superiority, if the other group seeks equality, the struggle for social status is zero sum. Consequently, the appropriation of status by subordinating behavior is, like theft, a mere wealth transfer; the gain to the discriminator is at least matched by the loss to the victim. Second, this form of transfer—using discrimination as a mechanism of subordination—generates extremely high costs. By definition, the discriminator makes a material sacrifice (giving up an otherwise favorable trade or engaging in costly behavior) as a means of lowering the status of the victim. The size of the material sacrifice measures the investment that the discriminator makes in status appropriation. This investment determines the initial cost of the process of racial group status production.

But that is not the whole story. As I noted at the outset of this Part, economic analysis of discrimination strikes many non-economists as barren because it fails to acknowledge the full benefit to its practitioners or the full harm to its victims. The status-production model takes as its central premise that whites gain status by discriminating against blacks. To determine the full extent of the investment in, and therefore the costs of, status competition, we must consider the full range of status defense mechanisms employed by victims of discrimination. Such defense mechanisms include the sometimes desperate reactions of those who live as targets of discrimination. These reactions represent further investment in status production and increase the wastefulness of the unregulated process, much like added investment in theft-protection devices constitute waste in a society without theft laws. Of course, the psychological mechanisms at work are vastly more complex. I will attempt merely a brief summary of the reactions within the framework of the status-production model.

First, enraged victims may respond in kind by attempting to disparage and subordinate the original discriminator. Such behavior may take the form of discrimination, which means the victim also makes a wasteful material sacrifice for the sake of status. The victim may, however, lack the opportunity or wealth to respond in kind and may seek a cheaper means of disparagement such as an insult. Violence is the extreme form of such an insult; it inflicts the loss of dignity inherent in an intentional deprivation of bodily integrity. Even if an African American counters with some means other than violence, the original subordinator may resort to violence to ensure the effectiveness of the original insult and to counter any responsive insult. Hobbes identified this escalation over dishonor as a primary source of war.

A second response is to seek to regain status by subordinating someone *other* than the original discriminator. If whites present too difficult a target, other minority groups may be within reach. Thus, the long and unpleasant history of status competition between minority groups exemplifies a predictable response to subordination. The original victim may also focus on vulnerable members of her own group, such as women or those of a different economic class. Evidence suggests, for example, that African Americans discriminate against one another on the basis of the relative lightness or darkness of their skin. Finally, because the original victim may lack any non-violent means of responding to discrimination, some of what appears to be "senseless violence" among discrimination victims may actually be a rational attempt to produce status by subordinating others.

The victim's responses are not limited to subordinating others. The victim may also withdraw from competition—by which status is generally determined—by adopting beliefs that such competitions are without merit. When a subordinated subgroup fails according to the prevailing cultural values, its members may decide to reject those values completely. For example, minorities facing discrimination may decide, rather than be judged by standards of academic or economic success, that education or employment is an overrated "white" value. Like the processes of rationalization, the belief that academics is unimportant may preserve self-esteem; however, such a belief may prove destructive in the long run because it depresses efficient investment in human capital.

Finally, a victim of subordination may wholeheartedly adopt the beliefs of the subordinators, including those that members of her group are deserving of their low status. Such a response might seem unlikely; however, for some it may be easier to accept a lower status with the belief that such a role is natural and proper than to live out such a role every day believing it is arbitrarily imposed. The result, however, is a form of self-loathing.

In sum, many of the effects of discrimination, well-explored in other disciplines, should be of central concern to an economic assessment of the system of race discrimination. In many cases, these effects represent investments that the victims make in defending their status. Combined with the investments made by the original discriminators, these resources represent the deadweight loss of race discrimination. Consequently, considerable evidence demonstrates that race discrimination is a grossly inefficient market failure.

(b) An Efficiency Argument for Anti-Discrimination Laws.—As with laws against theft, the benefit of prohibiting a form of discrimination is to prevent the wasteful investment of resources in such discrimination. When laws prohibit theft, the primary alternative by which the former thief can make material gains is to engage in lawful, productive activity. The argument for laws that prohibit subordination as a means of acquiring status is exactly parallel: by raising the costs of subordination, such laws induce people to switch to socially productive, or at least socially benign, means of acquiring status (either at an individual or a group level). Subordination is not the only means of group status production, and intergroup status production is not the only means of gaining esteem.

A possible distinction from theft, however, is the availability of equally wasteful substitutes to blatant discrimination. A group with a disproportionately large share of political power, economic wealth, and symbols of status will have at its disposal a number of alternative means of subordinating a minority group. Prohibiting one form of subordinating behavior may simply cause a shift to an equally wasteful form of acquiring status. Such a concern, however, may be overstated. After all, common law larceny initially required a trespass in the taking and thus exempted what we now think of as embezzlement and fraud. Even though thieves were free to switch to non-trespassory means of confiscation, the initial prohibition was nonetheless efficient. The opportunities remaining were more limited and costly; a complete substitution would not occur. The same argument can be made for prohibiting private discrimination in certain key areas, such as employment and housing. These forms of discrimination probably represent the most productive means of subordination and therefore induce the greatest "investment" by whites. As I previously pointed out, employment discrimination offers for whites a double insult to blacks: not only the insult inherent in shunning someone, but also the consequence of lowering black income in a society that accords status to wealth. Similarly, excluding blacks from neighborhoods is not only a very public symbol of subordination, but also denies them the material benefits of reciprocity that may arise among neighbors. Effectively prohibiting employment and housing discrimination would deprive whites of their most productive private means of subordination and would thereby lower the resources invested in this wasteful confiscatory activity.

Second, anti-discrimination laws may lower the investment in status confiscation by increasing the incidence of "cross-membership." *Ceteris paribus*, an individual prefers subordinating a group to which she does not belong to subordinating a group to which she does belong. An individual always bears a cost from subordination of her own group and that cost gives her an incentive to avoid such behavior. In fact, an individual who is a member of group *A* and group *B* might find it in her interest to invest in efforts to prevent members of group *A* from seeking to subordinate group *B*. Therefore, the more "cross-membership" between two groups, the fewer the resources that will be invested by the two groups in subordinating each other.

Laws forbidding race discrimination may increase the occurrence of cross-membership and thereby undermine the effectiveness of racial subordination as a status strategy. Race has been and remains highly correlated with other demographic factors. If a white individual lives in an all-white neighborhood, attends an all-white school, works in an all-white firm, worships at an all-white church, belongs to an all-white amateur sports league, and patronizes all-white hobby clubs, she will never face the problem of cross-membership. If, however, anti-discrimination laws were to integrate neighborhoods, schools, firms, and private clubs, more whites would find themselves in a position in which racial minorities belong to some of *their* groups. Consequently, racial subordination would lower the status of these integrated groups. One response will be for whites to flee the groups that become integrated, but if the costs are too high, as when the law integrates a number of social groups at the same time, the effect might be to lower the effectiveness of racial subordination as a status strategy for many whites.

Finally, anti-discrimination laws may serve to correct the market failure of discrimination by undermining the credibility of rationalizations for discrimination. Several commentators have noted that the law shapes preferences, and that Title VII and other civil rights laws may have reduced the preference for discrimination. The status-production model explains this evolution not as a change in the taste for discrimination, but as a change in the productive capacity of certain forms of subordination. Individuals who seek status require some rationalization for their behavior. Admitting that one seeks to subordinate others for the sake of status conflicts with obtaining such status. Law affects the credibility of any alternative explanation. Take Posner's example of a guild that survives on an ideology of quality to justify restrictions on competition. Consider the long-term effect Posner's critique might have on such ideology were it sufficiently publicized. Exposing the naked self-interest behind platitudes of public concern erodes their effectiveness.

Law is more crude than an intellectual critique, yet it is inherently more public, and can carry more weight. When Jim Crow laws mandated certain forms of segregation, whites confidently spoke of segregation as the natural order of things; when the laws forbade segregation, discriminatory whites had a greater difficulty believing their own ideology. Rationalizations can be fragile things; sometimes they require that dissent be held to a minimum. In the South and elsewhere, Title VII constituted a very powerful "dissent," an indication that a large number, perhaps a majority, of Americans no longer believed the explanations of discrimination. If people care about esteem, the law can change behavior merely by signaling on what grounds the majority will henceforth give and withhold esteem.

In sum, law may correct the market failure of discrimination in three ways: by raising the costs and lowering the productive returns of certain forms of subordination; by increasing the racial diversity of socially connected groups, which raises selfish resistance to the subordination strategy; and by symbolizing a consensus that the rationalizations for the subordination strategy are, in fact, mere rationalizations. Whether such laws are efficient depends on the magnitude of these benefits relative to the administrative and opportunity costs of the system that adjudicates discrimination claims. But under the status-production model, the efficiency question is, like it is for the prohibition of theft, an empirical one; one can no longer simply assert that laws prohibiting satisfaction of discriminatory preferences are presumptively inefficient.

One might inquire about the implications of the status-production model of discrimination for affirmative action. In what may seem like an evasion, I believe the model provides no clear answer for affirmative action, but does reveal the consequential tensions the policy represents. The "cross-membership" effect of anti-discrimination laws provides a theoretical foundation for the claim that affirmative action serves to combat discrimination more effectively than a mere non-discrimination policy. Indeed, the benefit of cross-membership might justify a very aggressive affirmative action program. The utility of integrating social groups by race is not limited by any principle of past wrongful discrimination. The status-production model indicates that we can reduce investment in future status subordination by decreasing racial stratification in society.

Conversely, affirmative action creates a "common fate" for those of the same race and thus raises the salience of race. As critics of affirmative action have claimed, this fact may cause whites to identify themselves more fully with their race. The status-production model adds this insight: raising the salience of race may increase the return from racial subordination and enhance the power of whites to elicit intra-group cooperation for the remaining avenues of racial subordination. Affirmative action likely has already had this effect, which offsets the positive effects of cross-membership. However difficult it is to ascertain the present net effect, the more important and difficult question is what the future effects will be. Affirmative action has, so far, done little to integrate effectively American society. Therefore, we have no reason to expect the positive consequences of that policy to have emerged. In the end, the status-production model reveals what I think we knew already: affirmative action is an investment in which we bear certain costs today for the hope of a greater return tomorrow. The model illuminates, but does not resolve, the empirical question of whether the future benefits will outweigh the present costs.

III. Conclusion

Groups inherently tend to elicit a level of cooperation from their members and to incur a level of conflict with other groups. The cooperation, in fact, facilitates the conflict. Intra-group esteem allocation permits groups to overcome certain collective action problems that would otherwise make conflict impossible. At the same time, the desire for esteem provides a new objective of group conflict—competition over social status.

What I have termed the theory of intra-group cooperation and inter-group conflict is merely the logical extension of three other steps in political and economic theory. First, Hobbes, among others, justified the state as necessary to avoid perpetual conflict in the state of nature; thus the state's role is to facilitate peaceful cooperation. Second, economists have persuasively contended that certain forms of peaceful cooperation, such as price-fixing, are detrimental to society. Consequently, the government should act in such cases to prevent cooperation. Third, Ellickson, among others, has written that groups use social norms to solve collective action problems without the centralized coercive power of the state, namely to bring about a cooperative "order without law." The next step, I propose, is to recognize that significant instances of this decentralized cooperation will inevitably be socially destructive and, therefore, that government should obstruct these forms of cooperation. Groups inherently tend to use their powers of decentralized cooperation to produce status through the socially wasteful process of subordination. As with cartels, cooperation in such cases is a social threat that justifies state action.

Aside from these general political implications, the theory of intra-group cooperation and inter-group conflict illuminates the complex problem of race discrimination. Status production explains both the historic and contemporary contours of race discrimination far better than the prevailing associational model of discrimination. Understanding race discrimination as a means of producing status helps us explain its tenacity in the face of market competition and reveals, within an economic model, the full costs of the practice of discrimination. The effort to gain status by taking status away from others, and the responsive measures this effort elicits, are socially wasteful in the same way that confiscation of material property is wasteful. The inefficiency in the system of status competition is measured by the investments each group makes in gaining or protecting its status.

Prohibiting the more productive forms of investments can reduce the wastefulness of such actions even if it does not eliminate it.

In criticizing the associational preference model of discrimination, I focused intensively on a single form of discrimination—racial discrimination—and within that category, exclusively on discrimination against African Americans. The points I made in this context, however, apply to other forms of racial and ethnic discrimination. When substantial overlap exists between groups that share publicly observable traits and groups that are socially connected, the theory predicts substantial investment in status production, including the subordination of other groups. With more than two racial and ethnic groups, greater opportunity exists for movement in social position, and there is, therefore, reason to expect greater investment in maintaining or improving status.

* * * * *

Groups matter. Groups form for simple informational reasons, as economics describes in considerable detail: to minimize the transaction costs people incur in the course of satisfying their preferences. Yet the formation of groups has another consequence. People have a loyalty to groups that goes beyond what serves their narrow pecuniary self-interest. I have sought to explain that solidarity in self-interested terms; doing so requires an expanded understanding of self-interest that includes a powerful desire for esteem and status. Given the ubiquity of groups, this broader social science perspective on their function should prove useful in understanding legal issues beyond racial discrimination. For now, I have argued for a sober appreciation that solidarity for some often means enmity for others.

NOTES AND QUESTIONS

1. Comparing Rational Choice Theory with Group Status Production Theory. Is it possible to compare the Becker and McAdams Models? What are the starting assumptions of each piece? Does McAdams accept any part of the rational choice heuristic?

2. Groups vs. individuals. One possible difference between the Becker and McAdams models is how they treat groups. McAdams is primarily concerned with the operation of intergroup processes for enforcing subordination. In contrast, Becker treats the individual as the central unit of measuring preferences for discrimination. Becker does, however, note that "it has been argued that an increase in the numerical importance of a minority group increases the prejudice against them, since the majority begins to fear their growing power; on the other hand, some argue that greater numbers bring greater knowledge and that leads to a decline in prejudice." To what use does Becker's theory of discrimination put this observation about group size?

3. Racial discrimination, the moral argument. If racial discrimination is simply a preference with exactly the same entitlement to expression in the marketplace as a taste for strawberry ice cream, how does rational choice distinguish between morally repugnant choices (child pornography) and morally neutral choices? Does rational choice theory require a normative view of racial discrimination to work?

Becker observes that: "[f]or example, discrimination and prejudice are not usually said to occur when someone prefers looking at a glamorous Hollywood actress rather than at some other woman; yet they are said to occur when he prefers living next to whites rather than Negroes. At best, calling just one of these actions 'discrimination' requires making subtle and rather secondary distinctions. Fortunately, it is not necessary to get involved in these more philosophical issues."

4. Adam Smith and Group Status Production Theory. Recall that Adam Smith argued, self interest, modified by benevolence born of conscience, or the influence of the moral spectator are the primary motivations for human economic behavior. Now, compare Smith to McAdams' thesis "that a material view of human motivation underestimates both the level of cooperation that groups elicit from their members and the level of conflict that groups elicit from each other. A single group dynamic connects these added increments of cooperation and conflict: groups achieve solidarity and elicit loyalty beyond what economic analysis conventionally predicts, but solidarity and loyalty within groups lead predictably, if not inevitably, to competition and conflict between groups. The connection is the desire for esteem or status. Groups use intra-group status rewards as a non-material means of gaining material sacrifice from members, but the attendant desire for inter-group status causes inter-group conflict."

---

3. AN EMPIRICAL STUDY OF RACIAL DISCRIMINATION

Fair Driving: Gender and Race Discrimination in Retail Car Negotiations

104 Harv. L. Rev. 817 (1991).

Ian Ayres

> *The struggle to eradicate discrimination on the basis of race and gender has a long history in American law. Based on the widely held belief that such discrimination will occur only in markets in which racial or gender animus distorts competition, regulatory efforts have been limited to areas in which interpersonal relations are significant and ongoing, such as housing and employment. In this Article, Professor Ayres offers empirical evidence that seriously challenges faith in the*

ability of competitive market forces to eliminate racial and gender discrimination in other markets. His Chicago based research demonstrates that retail car dealerships systematically offered substantially better prices on identical cars to white men than they did to blacks and women. Professor Ayres details the nature and startling degree of the discrimination his testers encountered and evaluates various theoretical explanations for their disparate treatment. Based on his conclusions, Professor Ayres explores routes by which "fair driving" plaintiffs might bring suits against dealerships and mechanisms through which regulators might effectively rid the retail car market of such discrimination.

[The] civil rights laws of the 1960s prohibit race and gender discrimination in the handful of markets—employment, housing, and public accommodations—in which discrimination was perceived to be particularly acute. In recent years, lawsuits have increasingly presented claims of more subtle and subjective forms of discrimination within these protected markets. Both legislators and commentators, however, have largely ignored the possibility of discrimination in the much broader range of markets left uncovered by civil rights laws. Housing and employment may be the two most important markets in which people participate, but women and racial minorities may also be susceptible to discrimination when spending billions of dollars on other goods and services. Of these unprotected markets, the market for new cars is particularly ripe for scrutiny because, for most Americans, new car purchases represent their largest consumer investment after buying a home. In 1986, for example, more than $100 billion was spent on new cars in the United States.

This Article examines whether the process of negotiating for a new car disadvantages women and minorities. More than 180 independent negotiations at ninety dealerships were conducted in the Chicago area to examine how dealerships bargain. Testers of different races and genders entered new car dealerships separately and bargained to buy a new car, using a uniform negotiation strategy. The study tests whether automobile retailers react differently to this uniform strategy when potential buyers differ only by gender or race.

The tests reveal that white males receive significantly better prices than blacks and women. As detailed below, white women had to pay forty percent higher markups than white men; black men had to pay more than twice the markup, and black women had to pay more than three times the markup of white male testers. Moreover, the study reveals that testers of different race and gender are subjected to several forms of nonprice discrimination. Specifically, testers were systematically steered to salespeople of their own race and gender (who then gave them worse deals) and were asked different questions and told about different qualities of the car.

At the outset it is difficult to choose how, linguistically, to characterize the results that black and female testers were treated differently from white male testers using the same bargaining strategy. The term "discrimination," although surely a literal characterization, unfortunately connotes to many the notion of animus (even though in antitrust, for example, "price discrimination" is not taken to imply any hatred by sellers). "Disparate treatment," in contrast, connotes to others a strictly technical legal meaning developed in civil rights case law. For the moment, the terms "discrimination" and "disparate treatment" are both used to refer to the result that sellers' conduct was race-and gender-dependent; sellers took race and gender into account and treated differently testers who were otherwise similarly situated. These terms are not meant to imply that salespeople harbored any animus based on race or gender.

In recent years, the Supreme Court has struggled in the employment context to enunciate workable evidentiary standards to govern claims of subtle and possibly unconscious forms of discrimination. Although the 1960s civil rights laws do not reach retail car sales, the finding that car retailers bargain differently with different races might give rise to disparate treatment suits under 42 U.S.C. §§ 1981 and 1982, which originated in the 1866 Civil Rights Act. The test results, by focusing on an unexplored manifestation of disparate treatment, push us to define more clearly what constitutes discrimination generally.

Furthermore, the results highlight a gaping hole in our civil rights laws regarding gender discrimination. Although sections 1981 and 1982 prohibit racial discrimination in contracting and the sale of real and personal property, no federal laws bar intentional discrimination on the basis of gender in the sale of most goods or services. The civil rights laws of the 1960s fail to fill this gap, leaving unregulated a legion of markets in which women contract. Put simply, car dealers can legally charge more or refuse to sell to someone *because* she is a woman. Intentional gender (or race) discrimination of this kind might alternatively be attacked as an "unfair or deceptive" trade practice under state and federal consumer protection laws. In the end, however, courts might perceive that the quintessentially individualized and idiosyncratic nature of negotiation places such disparate treatment entirely outside the purview of either the civil rights or consumer protection laws.

The goal of Congress in passing the Civil Rights Act of 1866 was to guarantee that "a dollar in the hands of a Negro will purchase the same thing as a dollar in the hands of a white man." The standard argument against enacting civil rights laws has been grounded in the conviction that the impersonal forces of market competition will limit race and gender discrimination to the traditionally protected markets, in which there is significant interpersonal contact. Yet the results of this study give lie to such an unquestioning faith in competition: in stark contrast to congressional objectives, this Article indicates that blacks and women simply cannot buy the same car for the same price as can white men using identical bargaining strategies. The price dispersion engendered by the bargaining process implicates basic notions of equity and indicates that the scope of the civil rights laws has been underinclusive. The process of bargaining, already inefficient in many ways, becomes all the more problematic when it works to the detriment of traditionally disadvantaged members of our society.

Part I of this Article describes how the tests of race and gender discrimination were conducted. Part II reports the results of the tests. An analysis of disparate treatment in price, sales tactics, and steering is combined with a regression analysis focusing on the determinants of final offers. Part III explores theoretical explanations of the results. Animus-based theories of disparate treatment are compared with theories of statistical discrimination and tested against the results of the study. Particular attention is paid to the role of competition at both the wholesale and retail level in limiting and channeling the form of race and gender discrimination. Finally, Part IV explores the legal implications of the study. This Part considers whether and how "fair driving" plaintiffs could legally challenge this disparate treatment under consumer protection laws and sections 1981 and 1982. The Article concludes by considering the need for legal reform.

I. METHODOLOGY OF THE TEST

To test whether there is disparate treatment by car retailers on the basis of race or gender, pairs of consumers/testers (for example, a white male and a black female) used the same bargaining strategy in negotiating at new car dealerships. A white male tester was included in each pair of testers. The white male results provide a bench-mark against which to measure the disparate treatment of the non-"whitemale" tester. Three consumer pairs (black female and white male, black male and white male, and white female and white male) conducted approximately 180 tests at ninety Chicago dealerships.

Each tester followed a bargaining script designed to frame the bargaining in purely distributional terms: the only issue to be negotiated was the price. The script instructed the testers to focus quickly on buying a particular car, and testers offered to provide their own financing. The testers elicited an initial price from the dealers and then, after waiting five minutes, the testers responded with an initial counteroffer that equalled an estimate of the dealer's marginal cost. After the tester's initial counteroffer, the salesperson could do one of three things: (1) attempt to accept the tester's offer, (2) refuse to bargain further, or (3) make a lower offer. If the salesperson attempted to accept the tester's offer or refused to bargain further, the test was over (and the tester left the dealership). If the salesperson responded by making a lower offer, the script instructed the tester to wait five minutes and to split the difference. After the tester split the difference, the salesperson again had the same three choices, and the rounds of bargaining continued until the salesperson accepted a tester offer or refused to bargain further. Testers jotted down each offer and counteroffer, as well as options on the car and the sticker price. Upon leaving the dealership, the testers completed a survey recording information about the test.

This design produced results that permit two tests for discrimination. The first, "short test" of discrimination simply compares the dealer's response to the testers' initial question, "How much would I have to pay to buy this car?" The "long test" of discrimination, on the other hand, compares instead the final offers given to testers after the multiple rounds of concessionary bargaining. By focusing on the initial offer, the short test is well controlled because salespeople had little information from which to draw inferences. By focusing on the final offer, the long test isolates more closely the price a real consumer would pay, but it increases the risk that individual differences among the testers influenced the results.

In order to minimize the possibility of non-uniform bargaining, particular attention was paid to issues of experimental control. A major goal of the study was to choose uniform testers and to train them to behave in a standardized manner. Testers were chosen to satisfy the following criteria for uniformity:

1. *Age*: All testers were twenty-four to twenty-eight years old.
2. *Education*: All testers had three or four years of college education.
3. *Dress*: All testers were dressed similarly during the negotiations. Testers wore casual "yuppie" sportswear: the men wore polo or buttondown shirts, slacks, and loafers; the women wore straight skirts, blouses, minimal make-up, and flats.
4. *Economic Class*: Testers volunteered that they could finance the car themselves.
5. *Occupation*: If asked by a salesperson, each tester said that he or she was a young urban professional (for example, a systems analyst for First Chicago Bank).
6. *Address*: If asked by the salesperson, each tester gave a fake name and an address for an upper-class, Chicago neighborhood (Streeterville).
7. *Attractiveness*: Applicants were subjectively ranked for average attractiveness.

The testers were trained for two days before visiting the dealerships. The training included not only memorizing the tester script, but also participating in mock negotiations designed to help testers gain confidence and learn how to negotiate and answer questions uniformly. The training emphasized uniformity in cadence and inflection of tester response. In addition to spoken uniformity, the study sought to achieve tester uniformity in non-verbal behavior.

* * *

Readers should focus, therefore, not merely on statistical significance but also on the *amount* of the reported discrimination. Although perfect control of such complex bargaining is impossible, the amounts of discrimination reported in the next Part cannot be plausibly explained by idiosyncratic divergence from uniform bargaining.

II. RESULTS OF THE TEST

The results from the tester surveys provide a rich database for investigating how salespeople bargain and whether they treat testers of a different race or gender differently. This Part presents the results of these tests in three sections. The first section reports disparate treatment regarding the prices that dealerships were willing to offer the testers. This section includes an analysis of both initial and final offers as well as refusals to bargain and differences in the bargaining paths (the sequence of offers made in succeeding rounds). In the second section, nonprice dimensions of the bargaining process are analyzed. The tests reveal that salespeople asked testers different types of questions and used different tactics in attempting to sell the cars. Finally, the third section uses multivariate regression analysis to analyze the determinants of the final offers. The regressions reveal a fairly sophisticated seller strategy. In particular, the size of final offers is sensitive not only to the race and gender of both the tester and the salesperson, but also to the information revealed by the tester in the course of bargaining.

A. Price Discrimination

1. *Final Offers.*—The final offer of each test was the lowest price offered by a dealer after the multiple rounds of bargaining. By comparing these final offers with independent estimates of dealer cost, it was possible to calculate the dealer profit associated with each final offer (final offer minus dealer cost). For a sample of 165 tester visits, the average dealer profits for the different classes of tester are presented in Table 1.

TABLE 1: AVERAGE DEALER PROFIT FOR FINAL OFFERS	
White Male	$ 362
White Female	504
Black Male	783
Black Female	1237

Black female testers were asked to pay over three times the markup of white male testers, and black male testers were asked to pay over twice the white male markup. Moreover, race and gender discrimination were synergistic or "superadditive": the discrimination against the black female tester was greater than the combined discrimination against both the white female and the black male tester.

The reliability of these results is buttressed by an analysis of the relative unimportance of individual effects. The average dealer profits on the non-"white male" testers were statistically different from the average profits on the white males at a five percent significance level. The average profits for the three individual white males were, however, not significantly different from each other. This last result lends support to the proposition that the idiosyncratic characteristics of at least the white male testers did not affect the results.

* * *

Dealer discrimination in early rounds will cause disparate concessions by testers that may preclude equal treatment in final rounds. The possibility that early offers matter, however, is not an embarrassment of design.

Bargainers engage in time consuming initial rounds of bargaining because they individually believe that these rounds will affect the final price. The tests provide strong evidence that if consumers use the same "split the difference" strategy, they will receive different final offers that are determined by their race and gender. * * *

2. *Initial Offers.*—This study also constructed a test of disparate treatment on the basis of the initial offers sellers made to the testers. * * *

The average dealer profit on offers made to white female testers was not significantly different from the average profit on offers made to white male testers. Sellers, however, offered both black males and black females significantly higher prices: sellers asked black males to pay almost twice the markups they charged white males, and they asked black females to pay two and one-half times that markup.

TABLE 2: AVERAGE DEALER PROFIT FOR FINAL OFFERS	
White Male	$ 818
White Female	829
Black Male	1534
Black Female	2169

3. *Willingness to Bargain.*—Another potentially important form of disparate treatment concerns the sellers' willingness to bargain. Consumers are hurt if the sellers either refuse to bargain or force the consumers to spend more time bargaining to achieve the same price. An analysis of the number of bargaining rounds reveals that the average number of rounds for different types of testers did not differ significantly, as shown in Table 3. The amount of time black male and white female testers spent bargaining (both total and per round) was not statistically longer than the amount spent by white male testers. Although black female testers clearly had to pay the most for cars, it was not because dealers refused to spend time bargaining with them. * * *

TABLE 3: DIFFERENCES IN ROUNDS			
	Average Number of Rounds	Average Length of Test (Minutes)	Average Length per Round (Minutes)
White Male	2.43	35.8	14.8
White Female	2.21	32.9	14.9
Black Male	2.32	49.1	21.2
Black Female	3.08	34.6	11.2

* * *

B. Nonprice Discrimination

The study also examined other ways in which sellers may have treated the testers differently. Although these other types of disparate treatment do not directly concern the sales price, they could facilitate price discrimination. Moreover, these comparisons suggest something about the racial and sexual perceptions that determine the behavior of salespeople.

1. Customer Steering.—As designed, the script allowed dealerships to steer testers to different types of salespeople or different types of cars. The script instructed testers to go to the center of the showroom and wait for a salesperson to approach them. The salespeople chose the tester, so that the testers could be steered to salespeople of a particular race or gender. In the sample of 119 encounters, sellers paired with testers as reported in Table 4.

The salesperson's race and gender was not randomly distributed across testers. Instead, sellers steered testers to persons of their own race and gender: white male sellers were more likely to serve white male testers; white female sellers were more likely to serve white female testers; and black male sellers were more likely to serve black testers.

	TABLE 4: STEERING TO PARTICULAR TYPES OF SALESPEOPLE		
	Seller Type Percentages		
	White Male	White Female	Black Male
All testers	83.2%	7.5%	9.3%
White Male	89.5	3.5	7.0
White Female	71.4	19.1	9.5
Black Male	83.4	5.5	11.1
Black Female	82.6	4.3	13.1

In addition, the study was designed to uncover a second type of dealer steering. Upon entering the dealership, the testers told the salesperson that they were interested in buying a certain car model with certain options and then allowed the salesperson to show them specific cars. However, no statistically significant disparate treatment was found. The test results reveal that dealers did not systematically steer different types of testers to cars of different cost.

2. Disparate Questioning.—The testers recorded how often they were asked specific types of questions. Statistical tests were then conducted to evaluate whether sellers asked non-"white male" testers particular questions significantly more or less often than white male testers. These tests indicate the following:

Sellers asked black female testers *more* often about their occupation, about financing, and whether they were married. Sellers asked black female testers *less* often whether they had been to other dealerships and whether they had offers from other dealers.

Sellers asked black male testers *less* often if they would like to test drive the car, whether they had been to other dealerships, and whether they had offers from other dealers.

Sellers asked white female testers *more* often whether they had been to other dealerships. Sellers asked white female testers *less* often what price they would be willing to pay.

These differences may indicate ways that dealers try to sort consumers in order to price discriminate effectively. For example, the fact that salespeople asked black testers less often about whether they had been to other dealerships (or had other offers) may indicate that salespeople do not think that interdealer competition is as much of a threat with black customers as with white customers. Because the price that sellers are willing to offer any customer may be sensitive to that customer's responses, the disparity among who is questioned may facilitate a seller's attempt to price discriminate.

3. Disparate Sales Tactics.—The testers also recorded the different tactics that the salespeople used in trying to sell the car. Test statistics were calculated to evaluate whether particular sales tactics were used significantly more or less often with white male testers than with non-"white male" testers. These tests indicate the following:

Salespeople tried to sell black female testers *more* often on gas mileage, the color of the car, dependability, and comfort, and asked them more often to sign purchase orders.

Salespeople tried to sell white female testers more often on gas mileage, the color of the car, and dependability.

With black male testers, salespeople *more* often offered the sticker price as the initial offer and forced the tester to elicit an initial offer from the seller. Salespeople asked black male testers to sign a purchase order less often.

These tests suggest that salespeople believe women are more concerned with gas mileage, color, and dependability than are men. The tests also indicate that salespeople try to "sucker" black males into buying at the sticker price by offering the sticker price or refusing to make an initial offer until asked.

4. Cost Revelation.—The script also elicited information about the dealers' willingness to reveal their marginal cost to consumers. In half of the bargaining sessions, the testers were told to ask the seller (at the end of the test) what the dealer had paid the car manufacturer. Thirty-five per cent of the sellers represented a specific dollar cost in response to the testers' inquiries. These disclosures, however, were not evenly distributed across the tester groups. Disaggregated by tester type, the disclosure rates indicate that salespeople were less willing to disclose cost data to black testers, especially black female testers, as presented in Table 5.

TABLE 5: DISCLOSURE OF COST DATA	
Tester Type	Percentage of Salespeople Disclosing Cost Figure
All Testers	35%
White Male	47
White Female	42
Black Male	25
Black Female	0

Instead of disclosing their cost information to black testers, the salespeople were more likely to dissemble and claim that they did not know the car's cost. To the extent that such cost disclosure is valuable, the failure to disclose costs to black testers undermines their ability to bargain as effectively as white testers and thus facilitates price discrimination based on race.

Based on this sample, however, it is unclear whether such disclosure would actually put white testers at a competitive advantage. When the seller did reveal his cost, the represented cost was substantially higher than independent estimates of seller cost for the same models, as seen in Table 6. Thus, although salespeople are more likely to disclose cost figures to white testers, they systematically overstate their costs. The greatest misrepresentations were made to white female testers.

* * *

Although the individual interaction variables are not statistically significant, the regressions indicate that the linear constraints in Model Two are binding. * * *

TABLE 6: SELLER MISREPRESENTATION OF COST DATA	
	Average Misrepresentation
White Male Tester	$ 849
White Female Tester	1046
Black Male Tester	752
Black Female Tester	—

White male testers received best deals from white female sellers.

White female testers received best deals from black male sellers.

Black male testers received best deals from white female sellers.

Black female testers received best deals from white male sellers.

The social psychology literature would not suggest this result to be expected. Several studies, for example, have shown that parties tend to bargain more cooperatively with an opponent of their own race and gender than with a person of a different race or gender. The interaction effects revealed in Model Three (although not statistically significant) suggest, however, that salespeople may try to take strategic advantage of consumers' perceptions. This result is especially plausible when combined with the earlier finding that testers were systematically steered to salespeople of the same race and gender. The data thus paints a clear picture: sellers steered testers to salespeople of their own race and gender, who then proceeded to give them the worst deals.

III. Toward a Theoretical Explanation

The preceding Part detailed race and gender discrimination that was not only statistically significant but also surprisingly pronounced. This Part explores possible explanations for why dealers would discriminate in this manner. Only with an accurate understanding of the reasons for dealer behavior can regulators hope to determine what, if any, governmental intervention can effectively protect black and female customers. With this goal in mind, this Part examines two broad theories of discrimination: animus-based theories and theories of statistical discrimination.

A. Animus–Based Theories of Discrimination

Animus theories of discrimination posit that a certain group is treated differently because that group is disliked or hated. A variety of market participants can interject animus into a market. A dealership, for example, might charge blacks more because the dealership dislikes blacks, because the dealership's employees dislike blacks, or because the dealership's other customers dislike blacks. As originally formulated by Gary Becker, these sources of bigotry could force sellers to charge blacks higher prices as an animus-compensating tax.

The source of bigotry might partially determine the specific form that animus-based discrimination takes. For example, in the fair housing context, consumer animus has led to steering and refusals to bargain. In the "fair driving" context, employee animus against blacks or women might cause salespeople to bargain frivolously. Because testers visited the dealerships during the least busy times of the day, bigoted dealers—with nothing better to do with their time—might have gained satisfaction in frustrating or wasting the time of women or blacks. Finally, the testers also might have experienced "role-based" bigotry: dealers might have discriminated against buyers who acted in ways that diverged from the dealer's expectation. Female testers could have faced prejudice for speaking with "a male voice"; black testers could have faced prejudice for not "staying in their place." In sum, the animus of various market participants can manifest itself as disparate treatment not only in the prices offered but also in other aspects of seller behavior.

* * *

C. A Tentative Explanation

1. Statistical Discrimination as an Explanation for Dealer Behavior.—The preceding discussion presented three broad theories of discrimination: animus-based, cost-based, and revenue-based. The fair driving tests, like their fair housing analogues, were designed primarily to identify the existence of disparate treatment—not to determine its cause. As a result, ancillary evidence must be used to determine which of the three competing theories best explains seller behavior. Although more study is warranted, it appears that the revenue-based theory best explains the discrimination that the testers encountered.

The cost-based theories of statistical discrimination are perhaps the weakest. The testers' script was explicitly structured to eliminate cost-based differences among the testers. The testers volunteered that they did not need financing—a potentially major source of disparate dealer cost. Notwithstanding these uniform representations, it is possible that the dealers inferred residual differences among the tester types. As an empirical matter, however, differences in net dealership cost simply do not explain why black female testers paid over three times the markup of white male testers. Moreover, on a cost-based theory, the observed seller inferences about profits from ancillary sales might predict a different pattern of disparate treatment.

Animus theories find more support in the data. The testers, for example, recorded several instances of overtly sexist and racist language by sellers. Nonetheless, animus theories do not appear to explain the magnitude of the discrimination. For example, under a theory of salesperson animus, the seller required a higher price from black females as compensation for having to deal with a black customer whom the seller disliked. The data would then imply that the dealer-required compensation must have been an implausible $900 per hour.

Consumer-based animus also fails to explain adequately disparate treatment by sellers. First, each class of testers received its best treatment from salespeople of a different race and gender and, in many cases, the worst treatment from salespeople of the same race and gender. For example, although all salespeople discriminated against black male testers, black salesmen gave them their worst deals. This result runs counter to the standard notion that a person's bigotry is usually directed at another race. Second, the amount of price discrimination black testers encountered at all dealerships did not vary with the racial makeup of the dealership's customer base. One-third of Chicago dealerships are located in neighborhoods with a greater than ninety percent black population, yet the offers these dealerships made to black testers did not differ from offers black testers received elsewhere. If disparate treatment were caused by white consumers' dislike of blacks, there should be less discrimination by sellers in neighborhoods where most consumers are black. Because the data do not confirm this prediction, the animus theory seems an unlikely explanation for the disparate treatment. Finally, consumer animus is inconsistent with observed salesperson behavior: salespeople did not attempt to reduce the length of bargaining sessions with the non-"white male" testers. If disparate treatment of black consumers were caused by sellers' concern for white consumers' desire not to associate with blacks, dealerships should have discouraged black consumers from bargaining for lengthy periods.

Although any conclusions based on this evidence must remain tentative, the case for revenue-based statistical discrimination is strongest. Despite the large amount of randomness (or unexplained variance) in bargaining outcomes, the dealerships seem to display a great deal of sophistication in bargaining. The systematic steering of customers to salespeople who charge them higher markups may be evidence of revenue-based statistical discrimination. Salespeople of the consumer's race and gender may, for example, be better able to infer that consumer's willingness to pay—and thus more finely tune the price discrimination.

* * *

Yet the conundrum persists as to why race and gender would be proxies for consumers' firm-specific reservation price that disfavor women and blacks. Even accepting that firm-specific willingness to pay is more a function of search costs than of ability to pay, why would blacks and women be disfavored? George Stigler has predicted that consumers with high opportunity costs will search less for a particular good than those consumers with lower opportunity costs. Because white males earn more on average than other tester types, under Stigler's theory a dealer should rationally infer that white males search less than members of other race and gender classes. If race and gender serve as proxies for dealer-specific willingness to pay, these proxies would seem to lead sellers to charge higher prices to white males, and not the lower prices revealed by this study.

Nevertheless, group differences in search costs, information, and aversion to bargaining may explain why profit-maximizing dealers charge white males less. The caricatured assertion that white males have higher opportunity costs (because they forgo higher wages when searching) ignores other effects that on balance may make it more difficult for blacks and women to search for a car. For example, white males may have a greater ability to take time off from work or family responsibilities to search for a car. Moreover, blacks are less likely to have a trade-in car with which to search when purchasing a new car. If, on net, blacks and women experience higher search costs than do white males, revenue-based statistical discrimination might lead dealers to make lower offers to white males. Knowing that blacks and women tend to incur higher search costs, a dealer could "safely" charge members of those groups higher prices, because the dealer would effectively have less competition for members of those groups from other dealers. White men may also have superior access to information about the car market. A large proportion of white men know that automobiles can be purchased for less than the sticker price, and white men may more easily be able to discover the customary size of negotiated discounts from the sticker price.

* * *

2. *The Reinforcing Role of Dealer Competition.*—Many commentators have argued that competition among sellers will tend to eliminate certain forms of race and gender discrimination against buyers. The following discussion examines how market competition among dealerships may in fact reinforce the opportunities for statistical discrimination.

As a first intuition, competition should quickly eliminate revenue-based statistical discrimination, slowly eliminate animus-based discrimination, and never eliminate cost-based statistical discrimination. Competition should quickly eliminate revenue-based discrimination because rival dealers would immediately move to undercut any supra-competitive prices offered to high-valuing car buyers. Competition should slowly eliminate animus discrimination because bigoted sellers would be at a competitive disadvantage and so would eventually be driven out of the market. By contrast, competition should not eliminate cost-based statistical discrimination because no dealer would have a market-based incentive to offer prices that fall below the best estimates of that dealer's actual costs.

The preceding analysis, however, tentatively suggested just the opposite causal ordering. Cost-based statistical discrimination is the least plausible explanation, and revenue-based statistical discrimination is the most plausible. The simple competitive story thus poses a major challenge to the assertion that revenue-based statistical discrimination caused the disparate treatment. In a large city such as Chicago, with hundreds of car dealerships, how could rival dealerships successfully charge individual consumers significantly more than dealership marginal costs?

* * *

The dealers' reliance on high-markup buyers lends additional credibility to the notion that dealership disparate treatment of consumers might be a form of revenue-based statistical discrimination. The dealers' search for high-markup buyers may be tailored to focus on specific racial or gender groups. In their quest to locate high-markup buyers, dealers are not guided by the amount that the *average* black woman is willing to pay. Rather, they focus on the proportion of black women who are willing to pay close to the sticker price. Even a small difference in the percentage of high-markup buyers represented by consumers of any one race or gender class may lead to large differences in the way dealers treat that entire class. Thus, the previous explanations of racial- or gender-based differences in search costs, information, or aversion to bargaining need not be true for the average members of a consumer group in order for those differences to generate significant amounts of revenue-based disparate treatment. The Consumer Federation of America recently completed a survey which revealed that thirty-seven percent of consumers do not understand that the sticker price is negotiable. These responses varied greatly across both race and gender. Sixty-one percent of black consumers surveyed did not realize that the sticker price is negotiable, whereas only thirty-one percent of white consumers made this error. This fact by itself could easily explain dramatic disparate treatment by sellers. Profit maximizing dealers may rationally quote higher prices to blacks even if the average black consumer in fact has a lower willingness to pay.

In sum, although simple economic theory suggests that dealer competition should quickly eliminate price dispersion, dealers in the market for new cars nevertheless sell the same car for different prices. Highly concentrated profits give dealers incentives to search for high-markup buyers through the process of bargaining. In particular, the dealers' search for high-markup buyers may reinforce incentives to discriminate on the basis of race or gender. The concentration of profits is a central pathology of retail car sales and one to which we will return below.

IV. Legal Implications

The results of the bargaining tests show that car dealerships treat black and female testers differently than they do white men who use the same bargaining strategy. Whether these findings constitute actionable racial or gender discrimination in a traditional legal sense, however, is a separate matter. The differential treatment of consumers might be seen as a natural consequence of any bargaining process. Market economies sanction such treatment by allowing sellers to pursue high-markup sales through a variety of bargaining methods. The pre-contractual interplay between a potential buyer and seller may seem, in some sense, outside the purview of the law.

This Part argues, however, that the findings presented in this Article constitute compelling evidence of unlawful racial and gender discrimination under both the civil rights and consumer protection laws. In particular, the following section explores whether the car sellers' dealings with black testers constitute unlawful disparate treatment violative of sections 1981 and 1982. Such a claim does not necessarily imply that sellers dislike black or female customers—only that sellers take their customers' race and gender into account when deciding how to bargain. Section B then proposes legal reforms to strengthen sections 1981 and 1982 and to extend their coverage to currently unprotected groups.

A. Liability Under Sections 1981 and 1982

Sections 1981 and 1982 mandate that all people shall have the same rights "to make and enforce contracts" and to "purchase ... personal property," respectively, "as is enjoyed by white citizens." Although a racial discrimination suit has never been brought against a retail car dealership under section 1981 or section 1982, there seems little doubt that one or both these laws covers discrimination relating to retail car price bargaining between private parties. In *Jones v. Alfred H. Mayer Co.*, the Supreme Court emphatically stated that section 1982 (and by implication section 1981) applies to acts of private discrimination. Since *Jones*, courts have applied these sections' prohibitions of private discrimination to contexts similar to retail car price bargaining.

Even if car dealership bargaining falls within the scope of sections 1981 and 1982, a fair driving plaintiff would have a number of hurdles to overcome in winning a claim under these statutes. The substantive legal standard under sections 1981 and 1982 is straightforward: plaintiffs claiming disparate treatment must prove that the defendant intentionally discriminated against them and caused them an identifiable injury. Although the Supreme Court has stated that intentional discrimination "can *in some situations* be inferred from the mere fact of differences in treatment," no civil rights case has ever concluded that a showing of disparate treatment was insufficient to establish intentional discrimination. Thus, it appears that courts will find intentional discrimination whenever the defendant's conduct was conditioned on the plaintiff's race. To establish liability in this context, the typical fair driving plaintiff would need to show that the specific car dealer with whom he or she had bargained considered the plaintiff's race in deciding how to bargain.

On the other hand, because of the difficulties in obtaining direct proof that a defendant's conduct was race-dependent, the law has developed a method for allocating the burdens of proof under sections 1981 and 1982 that in effect allows intent to be inferred from indirect evidence. In particular, courts hearing section 1981 or 1982 claims have imported from the title VII context the shifting burdens of proof scheme articulated in *McDonnell Douglas v. Green*.

Applying the *McDonnell Douglas* reasoning to fair driving suits, the plaintiff bears the initial burden of establishing disparate treatment: that sellers took race into account when deciding how to bargain. If the plaintiff can establish a prima facie violation of section 1981 or section 1982, a burden of production shifts to the defendant "to articulate some legitimate, nondiscriminatory reason" for its differential behavior. Finally, if the defendant can offer such a reason, the burden shifts back to the plaintiff to show that the defendant's response is a mere "pretext."

A black tester from the present study who wanted to make out a successful prima facie case against a particular dealership would have to persuade the court of two things. First, she would have to persuade the court that the study was sufficiently controlled—that is, that she and the white tester visiting the defendant's car dealership appeared similar in every objective respect except for the color of their skin. If courts' attitudes in housing cases under sections 1981 and 1982 are any indication, the fair driving tests conducted in this study were more than sufficiently controlled. Although the typical fair housing test is similarly controlled with respect to timing of the tests, it is less controlled with respect to verbal and nonverbal conduct than was the testing in this study.

Second, fair driving plaintiffs would have to persuade the court that the instances of differential treatment are sufficiently numerous so that the results can not be explained by chance. Again, analogy to the fair housing context suggests that the results of one pair of well controlled testers should suffice. Under this standard, the present study could theoretically give rise to dozens of actionable instances of discrimination against individual dealers.

Although comparisons with the fair housing context are generally apposite, courts may be much more reluctant to find the existence of prima facie cases in the fair driving context because society has differing presumptions about the pervasiveness of the two kinds of discrimination. The long and ongoing history of housing discrimination in the United States is so well known and well documented that courts may require relatively less proof. Discrimination in car negotiations may have a similarly long and deep-seated history, but the size and nature of such discrimination may be masked by the processes of bargaining. As a result, a court hearing a fair driving claim may require that the tests be that much more controlled, that the disparity of treatment be that much greater, or that there be that many more instances of disparate treatment by the same dealer.

Once a court finds that a fair driving plaintiff has made out a prima facie case of disparate treatment, the burden shifts to the defendant-dealer to articulate a legitimate, nondiscriminatory explanation for why it treated white buyers and black buyers differently. If the defendant does not directly rebut the plaintiff's evidence of disparate treatment, it might put forward two distinct arguments that the disparate treatment was not "intentional" discrimination. First, the dealer may argue that the disparate treatment was unintentional because the dealer's motive was to make money, not to harm black people. Under this theory, the dealer might openly admit that its behavior flowed from consciously drawn, economically rational inferences based on the race of prospective buyers—revenue-based inferences, for example, about the proportion of blacks willing to pay a higher markup. It is, however, precisely these sorts of inferences—inferences based on the color of a person's skin—that sections 1981 and 1982 do not countenance. As Judge Posner recently held, "[d]iscrimination may be instrumental to a goal not itself discriminatory, just as murder may be instrumental to a goal not itself murderous (such as money); it is not any less—it is, indeed, more clearly—discriminatory on that account."

Alternatively, defendants might claim that their disparate treatment was unintentional in the sense that they were not conscious of it. The D.C. Circuit rejected this argument in *Hopkins v. Price Waterhouse*:

> [Plaintiff demonstrated] that she was treated less favorably than male candidates because of her sex. This is sufficient to establish discriminatory motive; the fact that some or all of the partners at Price Waterhouse may have been unaware of that motivation, even within themselves, neither alters the fact of its existence nor excuses it.

Once a plaintiff has proven that a defendant has treated blacks differently from identically situated whites, it is fair and reasonable to conclude as a matter of law that the dealer at some level of consciousness must have been aware of the testers' race. Such a legal inference conforms with our common moral intuition that a dealer who must consciously decide what initial price to offer every customer who walks through the door must be aware of the skin color of those to whom it consistently offers a higher initial price. Thus, so long as the fair driving plaintiff can persuade the factfinder that sellers treated similarly situated blacks differently from whites, the disparate treatment discussed in this Article violates sections 1981 and 1982.

B. *Legal Reform*

1. Modernizing Civil Rights Laws.—Lawmakers could respond to bargaining discrimination by expanding the current coverage of the civil rights and consumer protection laws. Most important, Congress could amend sections 1981 and 1982 to extend to women (and other protected classes) the right to be free from discrimination in contracting to buy and sell services as well as goods. Modernized versions of sections 1981 and 1982 could also allow plaintiffs to bring disparate impact suits, currently actionable under title VII, which require no showing of intent. Disparate impact litigation would allow suits to challenge the bargaining practices of sellers that are facially neutral (in the sense that they do not consciously take a buyer's race or gender into account) but have significant discriminatory effects. In sum, creating an additional roman numeraled civil rights "title" to cover the sale of goods and services would provide a remedy for the kinds of discrimination examined in this Article.

Although this Article has argued that the sellers' search for high-markup consumers causes sellers to discriminate against blacks and women, the proposal to extend civil rights protection to the sale of all goods and services is based on the notion that racial and gender-based disparate treatment may well exist in a broader variety of markets. The problem of disparate treatment in new car sales has been perpetuated by the fact that the bargaining process conceals from black and female consumers the prices received by their white male counterparts. Without such information, blacks and women cannot directly learn of disparate treatment. Black and female consumers may also be deprived of this crucial bench-mark in retail markets in which bargaining does not occur. Although uniform stated-pricing eliminates the potential for gender or race discrimination in pricing for most goods, such discrimination may still exist along such different dimensions as product or service quality. Again, although blacks and women can gather information about how other retailers treat them, they face difficulty in learning how retailers treat white men.

The 1960s civil rights laws outlawed discrimination in those markets—most notably housing and employment—in which conspicuous accessible bench-marks disclosed disparate treatment. But the absence of a manifest bench-mark does not imply the absence of discrimination; there is no reason to think that animus or statistical causes of discrimination manifest themselves only in markets in which interracial comparisons of treatment can be readily made. Indeed, as various overt forms of discrimination have become illegal, more subtle and covert manifestations have often replaced them. This Article seeks fundamentally to expand the domain of the civil rights inquiry.

2. *Reinvigorating Consumer Protection Laws.*—State and federal governments might also attempt to enforce more rigorously consumer protection laws to reduce the type of discrimination revealed in this Article. Indeed, recent Supreme Court decisions hostile to civil rights suits suggest the wisdom of pursuing a remedy under consumer protection laws. In *Patterson v. McLean Credit Union*, for example, the Court, although refusing to apply section 1981 to what it considered "postformation conduct," suggested instead that the victims of discrimination turn to traditional contractual remedies. To the extent that consumer protection laws codify common law remedies such as fraud and duress, they may provide a viable alternative to civil rights remedies. Thus, although consumer protection laws have not yet been used to attack racial disparate treatment as a "deceptive" misrepresentation, this history does not preclude more extensive governmental intervention in the future.

The Federal Trade Commission (FTC) Act and the numerous baby FTC acts passed by the individual states outlaw the use of "unfair or deceptive" trading practices. Utilizing such acts to reach discrimination in bargaining for a new car purchase will require a reconceptualization of what we consider unfair or deceptive. Attacking sellers' disparate treatment in bargaining as being "deceptive" strikes at closely held beliefs about what is appropriate in the normal course of negotiations. The complexity of these beliefs is demonstrated by contrasting the effect of seller misrepresentation in the context of car sales with seller misrepresentation in housing sales. Fair housing cases often gain their moral authority from the egregious nature of seller misrepresentations such as "the apartment is no longer available." In the retail car bargaining context, however, some forms of misrepresentation are broadly accepted. Few would believe, for example, that a seller would be held liable for misrepresenting "I can't reduce the price any further"—even if the seller did reduce the price for another consumer. Seller misrepresentation is present in both the housing market and in the new car market. The distinction in our response turns, if at all, on which types of misrepresentation we deem acceptable.

Nevertheless, consumer protection laws do provide a framework for attacking disparate treatment in bargaining. Courts have construed consumer protection statutes to prohibit implied as well as express misrepresentation. Courts could attack disparate treatment in negotiations for new cars by finding an implied representation that the dealer would not treat black consumers differently from white consumers. In other words, courts may preserve the "essence" of bargaining—by conceding that all consumers should expect inconsistent and unpredictable treatment at the hands of car dealers—but refuse to sanction "discrimination" by rejecting regimes in which the unpredictable behavior is in fact predicated on race or gender.

Such a finding would be completely consistent with freedom of contract. Sellers could avoid making this implicit representation by expressly reserving the right to bargain differently with customers of different races. A judicial or legislative finding of an implicit representation of no racial disparate treatment would simply be "filling a gap" in the parties' contract. Finding an implied representation of no racial disparate treatment is at least as reasonable as finding an implied representation that sellers reserve the right to treat different races differently: few explicit contracts would ever opt for the latter provision. Once lawmakers established a default rule of no disparate treatment, plaintiffs bringing implied misrepresentation cases would then face the same burden as traditional section 1981 plaintiffs: the burden of demonstrating disparate treatment.

The Supreme Court's decision in *Patterson v. McLean Credit Union* strongly supports this analysis. In restricting civil rights protection under section 1981 to discrimination in the formation of a contract, the *Patterson* Court suggested that victims of discrimination should turn to traditional contractual remedies: racial harassment "amounting to a breach of contract under state law is precisely what the language of § 1981 does not cover. That is because, in such a case . . . the plaintiff is free to enforce the terms of the contract in state court." Although the contract at issue was silent as to whether post-formation discrimination was permissible, the court implied that nondiscrimination provisions could be read into state contract remedies. Following the *Patterson* rationale, finding an implicit representation not to treat consumers differently in bargaining because of their race or gender would offer a free market alternative to civil rights interventionism.

3. *Structural Reforms.*—The expansion of traditional civil rights and consumer protection laws is unlikely to completely eliminate disparate treatment in bargaining based on race or gender. Victims of disparate bargaining treatment will most likely be restricted to suing individual dealerships—instead of manufacturers or groups of dealerships. Even if plaintiffs bring class actions and courts consistently grant testers standing to sue, the piecemeal approach of such suits, combined with the protracted nature of litigation, is unlikely to be sufficient to deter race- and gender-dependent behavior.

In light of these conditions, policymakers might consider structural reforms to improve the workings of the market. Structural changes should grow out of specific causal theories of disparate treatment in order quickly and effectively to erase such treatment. For example, if animus is inducing price discrimination, a law that outlawed price discrimination might induce some sellers to refuse to bargain. However, if the disparate treatment is caused by inferences about different consumer demand, then outlawing price discrimination should not generate such refusals. Simply put, to formulate effective intervention, policymakers must understand why sellers discriminate.

The earlier analysis of competition suggested that high-markup customers (and the ensuing concentration of profits) are a central cause of dealer price discrimination. As a result, if policymakers can find a way to reduce significantly the profits on these sucker sales, the manner in which dealerships conduct the retail sale of *all* cars would become dramatically more competitive. Without the pathological effects of highly concentrated profits, dealers would no longer have an incentive to force consumers to expend real and psychic resources in bargaining.

Policymakers could use three different strategies to eliminate high-markup sales. Most directly, courts could strengthen current notions of substantive unconscionability to prohibit high-markup sales. This strategy, however, is unlikely to occur: courts in the past have shown extreme reluctance to distinguish conscionable from unconscionable markups. Although courts voided contracts for unconscionable markups in two well-known cases, *Frostifresh Corp. v. Reynoso* and *American Home Improvement v. MacIver*, few courts since the early 1960s have reached similar holdings. The likelihood of courts taking the dramatic step of expanding this rarely used doctrine becomes even smaller in light of the special nature of bargaining for retail cars and society's solicitude toward such bargaining.

As a second regulatory strategy, policymakers might restrict the amount of price dispersion permissible in the car market. Regulators might, for example, allow dealerships to engage in bargaining, but void sales with markups that are more than twenty percent above the average markup. Unlike direct unconscionability regulation, firms would retain the freedom to set the average markup for any one model as high as the market would bear but would be prohibited from selling similar cars at significantly different prices. At its most extreme, this form of regulation would prohibit bargaining and mandate that dealerships sell at advertised prices. Restraining price dispersion is an attractive form of regulation because it might benefit all would-be car buyers. If the number of high-markup sales is reduced, sellers may find that bargaining (and the transaction costs that it imposes on all consumers) is no longer profitable. Once high-markup consumers are protected, sellers may no longer subject their low-markup consumers to costly and unpleasant bargaining.

Finally and least intrusively, regulators might reduce the number of sales with disparately high markups by mandating various types of disclosure from dealerships to consumers. Dealerships, for example, might be required to reveal the average price for which each make of car is sold. Knowing that the dealership is attempting to charge $3000 more than the average price would allow high-markup consumers to protect themselves. Alternatively, regulation might force dealerships to reveal the size of the markup on each individual transaction. Clay Miller and I have argued elsewhere that markup disclosure could improve both the equity and efficiency of retail car sales: "markup revelation would truncate the bargaining process at each dealership. The possibility of hoodwinking uninformed buyers into purchasing at a high markup would diminish as the excessive profits would be directly revealed."

In sum, mandating disclosure and restraining price dispersion are plausible strategies to reduce the importance that dealerships place on high-markup sales. A central prediction of this Article is that at some point reducing the concentration of dealership profits would rationalize dealership competition by giving individual dealerships an incentive to opt for high-volume, stated-price selling strategies. The relatively unintrusive nature of disclosure and price-dispersion regulation makes them politically and administratively more viable.

Before choosing a strategy to eliminate price dispersion, policy-makers should determine whether a single price equilibrium is "sustainable": that is, whether competitive dealerships that charge a single price could break even and thus survive price dispersion. In markets with high fixed costs, if sellers were required (directly or indirectly through disclosure) to charge a single price, competition might drive that price to a level below sellers' average cost. Such markets have "hollow cores" (because the "core" set of viable single-price equilibriums is empty or "hollow").

If the retail car market has a hollow core, government intervention to eliminate price dispersion would tend to drive dealerships from the market. In such markets, high-markup sales help dealers cover their fixed costs. In the airline industry, for example, the high-markup sales to business travelers may be necessary to meet industry fixed costs. Indeed, business travelers may benefit from the presence of lower-price tourist fares because "cheap" seats defray part of these fixed costs. If regulation eliminated price dispersion and mandated a single fare per route, business travelers might have to pay higher prices than under the current regime. Tourist travelers would stop buying, and the airline would then pass its fixed costs along to the smaller group of business travelers.

Regulator concerns should be allayed, however, because the retail car market does not resemble hollow core markets. Retail car dealerships do not experience significant high fixed costs (especially when compared to many other single price markets such as the market for electronic appliances and stereo equipment). Moreover, it is implausible that white males would (like tourist travelers) stop purchasing in a single price equilibrium. Mandating a single fare for airlines might lead to an inflated price that only businesspeople could afford, but mandating a single price for automobiles would not leave blacks and females alone to shoulder even higher proportions of the retailers' fixed costs.

Although this discussion of potential regulatory strategies is impressionistic, at the very least it suggests that regulators have a variety of choices beyond traditional civil rights and consumer protection remedies to attack the inequalities uncovered in this Article. Naturally, implementing one of these structural interventions would impose enforcement costs that must be weighed against the benefits of regulation. Dealers may attempt to circumvent such regulations in several ways. Nevertheless, in evaluating the efficacy of structural changes, policymakers should pay particular attention to the concentration of profits and the prevalence of high-markup sales.

V. Conclusion

The negotiation of contracts occupies a mysterious and somewhat mythical position in the law and in our society. In *The Wealth of Nations*, Adam Smith opined that people have a natural propensity to "truck and barter" over the sale of goods. Law-and-economic scholars at times extend this insight, suggesting that people will tend to negotiate whenever resources are misallocated: if I want to sit on a crowded subway, I will negotiate with the other passengers for a seat.

Common experience indicates, however, that many people in the United States are averse to bargaining. The frustration that many consumers experience in bargaining for a car is largely attributable to the ludicrously inefficient manner in which cars are marketed. Although Smith and others attach almost mythic qualities to the process of bargaining, this Article has thrown the equity and efficiency of car negotiations into question. The process of retail car negotiations becomes even more problematic when traditionally disadvantaged members of our society effectively pay a bargaining tax whenever they purchase a new car.

Earlier this year, I asked a car dealer during an interview whether the bulk of his profits were concentrated in a few sales. He told me that his dealership made a substantial number of both "sucker" and "non-sucker" sales. He added: "My cousin, however, owns a dealer-ship in a black neighborhood. He doesn't sell nearly as many [cars], but he hits an awful lot of home runs. You know, sometimes it seems like the people that can least afford it have to pay the most." Although it is dangerous to extrapolate from the results of a single study, the amounts of discrimination uncovered, if representative of a larger phenomenon, are truly astounding. A $500 overcharge per car means that blacks annually pay $150 million more for new cars than they would if they were white males. There are substantial reasons to uncover *and eliminate* such discrimination.

For further reading, *see also* Peter Siegelman, *Gender and Race Discrimination in Retail Car Negotiations, in* PERVASIVE PREJUDICE?: UNCONVENTIONAL EVIDENCE OF RACE AND GENDER DISCRIMINATION 19 (Ian Ayres ed., 2001).

CHAPTER 5

CASH AND CARRY

A. THE UNDERGROUND ECONOMY

The "underground" or "informal" economy roughly consists of the total of all economic transactions minus those transactions that are in compliance with applicable government regulations. This economy can include both transactions where just *full* compliance with the law is avoided, such as in Martha Shirk's article in this chapter about domestic help, or transactions directly prohibited by the law, such as in the other articles in this chapter about the drug trade and prostitution.[a] The underground economy in the United States can include everything from the waiter who neglects to report all of his tip income, to the doctor who takes cash on the side for weekend visits, to the unlicensed street vendor who sells knockoff goods on the sidewalks of a major city.[b] In extreme situations, the underground economy—sometimes referred to as the "black market"—may actually satisfy more of the citizens' basic needs for housing, clothing, food, and the like than the formal economy.[c]

Defining exactly what the boundary is between the informal and formal economies, however, can have significant cultural and legal implications by distorting the data on which the government relies to control the economy.[d] The Internal Revenue Service, for instance, excludes the value of household labor, such as childcare done by family members or do-it-yourself activities around the house, from its calculations of income.[e] National economic welfare, furthermore, is measured by looking at annual reported income and its relation to the poverty line. But, because the income from underground economies is consistently not reported or underreported, using only reported income as a measure of poverty mixes the truly poor with those who have a much higher standard of living as a result of the underground economy.[f]

But what leads to the creation of underground economies in the first place? In some cases, informal economies arise to respond to a market failure created by a government prohibition on an activity seen as immoral

---

a. *See* George L. Priest, *The Ambiguous Moral Foundations of the Underground Economy*, 103 YALE L.J. 2259, 2259 (1994).

b. Richard A. Epstein, *The Moral and Practical Dilemmas of the Underground Economy*, 103 YALE L.J. 2157, 2157, 2164 (1994).

c. *See* Priest, *supra* at 2268–70.

d. *Id.* at 2259.

e. *See* Morton Paglin, *The Underground Economy: New Estimates from Household Income and Expenditure Surveys*, 103 YALE L.J 2239, 2244–45 (1994).

f. *Id.* at 2250–51.

or undesired.[g] In other cases, they arise because of a governmental inability to provide a particular good or service in a way that is responsive to the demands of the citizenry.[h] And in still other cases, the underground economy rises up because the regulations surrounding certain economic transactions seem unjust or unfair, or their enforcement is seen as arbitrary.[i] As a result, individuals turn away from the formal economy to attempt to correct these problems.

Despite the negative implications of calling these systems "underground" economies, such structures can provide real benefits. Informal economic activity can significantly increase the standard of living for some of the poorest in a population, provide otherwise unavailable or inefficiently distributed goods and services which may be necessary for survival, and even provide work opportunities for those excluded from the formal economy by discrimination.[j] But, on the other hand, a large underground economy may undermine the stability and responsibility of the government institutions that control the economy, and such economies may also be seen as fundamentally dishonest.[k] Furthermore, unregulated underground economies also deprive the state of tax revenues that could otherwise be used for public services and can lead to sweatshop conditions and risks to the general welfare.[l] What do the following articles contribute to the underground-economy discourse?

Cashing in on Domestic Help[a]

ST. LOUIS POST-DISPATCH, Feb. 15, 1993, at 1C.

■ MARTHA SHIRK

To my mind, the most stunning revelation from the Zoe Baird controversy has been the apparent lack of interest of many Americans in the lives of the maids and baby sitters they employ in their homes.

The Internal Revenue Service says that only one out of four families with domestic workers contributes to the Social Security system for their employees, as required by law. Among the scofflaws, we've learned recently, are Secretary of Commerce Ron Brown, former attorney general nominee Zoe Baird and at least a half-dozen members of Congress.

Ask around, and you'll find that most of your neighbors and colleagues aren't paying into the Social Security system for their domestic help.

Chances are, you aren't either.

g. *See* Epstein, *supra* at 2158–59.

h. Priest, *supra* at 2271.

i. *See* Epstein, *supra* at 2162–63.

j. *See* Priest, *supra* at 2272–73.

k. *See* Priest, *supra* at 2260.

l. *See* Lora Jo Foo, *The Vulnerable and Exploitable Workforce and the Need for Strengthening Worker Protective Legislation*, 103 YALE L.J 2179, 2179–80 (1994).

a. For further discussion of the racial, national, and class dimensions of the U.S. domestic labor market, see chapter 2.

For the most part, employers cite one of two reasons for not complying with the law:

They don't know they're supposed to.

Their domestic workers don't want them to.

Few would admit that one of their motivations is the savings to themselves.

For instance, for my $50-a-half-day housecleaner, I pay $7.50 a week, or almost $400 a year, to make sure she's covered by Social Security. (The law requires the employer to pay only half that much, but I cover her legally required contribution, too.)

OK, you say, but it's not because of greed that you don't do it. It's because your maid, or your baby sitter, would quit if you did. She wants to be paid in cash, with no deductions.

It's true that their employees' resistance keeps a lot of employers from paying by the book. Some people do domestic work to supplement their welfare benefits, which, in Missouri anyway, provide only a third of the amount the federal government says a family needs to survive above the poverty level.

If they reported their income from domestic work, they'd lose part or all of their welfare checks, and they might lose Medicaid coverage for their children as well.

But a lot of household workers insist on cash, with no deductions, simply because they lack information about the consequences, which are considerable.

In the first place, if a worker is paid in cash, she's probably not filing a federal income tax return. That means that she can't claim the Earned Income Credit, a tax credit authorized by Congress to shore up the incomes of America's poorest families.

The IRS believes that 2 million eligible families failed to claim the Earned Income Credit last year, simply because they didn't realize they could. (Almost 14 million families did, becoming $11.3 billion richer—about $807 a family—as a result.)

The woman to whom I pay $50 a week will get an Earned Income Credit of $520 this year.

The tragedy for her is that she could be getting an earned income credit of $1,384, in one lump sum, if just two of her four other employers weren't paying her under the table. That's more money than she's managed to save in 20 years, the beginning of a nice little nest.

And what about 25 years from now, when it comes time for a household worker to retire? She's out of luck if her employers haven't contributed to the Social Security system for her. Social Security is not an entitlement. You have to pay into the system for at least 10 years—or have been married to someone who did—to draw benefits.

My housecleaner isn't going to be entitled to much of a retirement check 25 years from now if I'm the only employer who contributes to Social Security for her.

Most likely, my housecleaner, and yours, will end up among the 40 percent of elderly American women who live in or near poverty. She'll probably have to apply for SSI—Supplementary Security Income—which will put only $434 into her pocketbook each month.

I use the feminine pronoun here for a reason: Most household workers are women.

And as with many economic issues, this is one where race and gender converge. A higher proportion of black women than white women make their livings doing domestic work. By not taking care of their household employees' Social Security payments, many Americans are discriminating disproportionately against African-Americans, as well as against women.

Even at retirement, the lifelong disparities in income between men and women and whites and blacks persist. The median income in 1989 for black women over 65 was only $4,494, compared with $7,655 for over-65 white women. (Men over 65 had a median annual income of $13,107.)

It's something to think about the next time you pay your maid cash, under the table.

And if compassion doesn't make you do the right thing, maybe self-interest will.

At your employee's request, the IRS can come after you 25 years from now for back contributions—with interest and penalties.

NOTES AND QUESTIONS

1. **Nannygate and the Zoë Baird problem.** In 1993, President Clinton nominated Zoë Baird for Attorney General during the first days of his presidency. Support from the public and from the Senate for Baird's confirmation, however, quickly faded: Baird and her husband, it turned out, had hired an illegal-immigrant Peruvian couple to serve as their chauffer and children's nanny and neglected to pay Social Security taxes on the couple's wages. The public uproar surrounding what eventually became known as "Nannygate" effectively led to the withdrawal of Baird's nomination and cost her the position. The American public, it seemed, was unsympathetic to the troubles of a woman worth $2.3 million. *See* Gwen Ifill, *Settling In: Anatomy of a Doomed Nomination; The Baird Appointment: In Trouble From the Start, Then a Firestorm*, N.Y. TIMES, Jan. 23, 1993, at A8.

President Clinton's next nominee for Attorney General, Kimba Woods, also failed to pass inspection when she was asked if she had "a Zoë Baird problem," even though she had legally employed an alien as a babysitter and properly filed all her taxes. Following Zoë Baird, asking whether or not a particular nominee had hired immigrant nannies became standard during confirmation hearings:

> It was also the question that helped pluck the childless and unmarried Janet Reno from relative obscurity to become the President's nominee for the job. No kids, no nanny, no Zoe Baird problem. Reno, 54, who appears to be well qualified for the post, doesn't even have an immigrant gardener: she mows her own lawn.

Claudia Wallis, *The Lessons of Nannygate*, TIME MAG., Feb. 22, 1993, at 76. Clinton's top officials, including Vice President Al Gore, Labor Secretary Robert Reich, and U.S. Trade Representative Mickey Cantor were all asked if they had hired illegal aliens. J. Jennings Moss & Carleton R. Bryant, *Domestic Help a Taxing Issue*, WASH. TIMES, Feb. 8, 1993, at A1.

To be fair, Zoë Baird's acts were not criminal. Though, technically, undocumented alien workers are not allowed to start working until they receive their green cards, Baird and her husband, a professor at Yale Law School, reported the hiring to the Immigration and Naturalization Service and obtained a letter from the INS saying that it was aware of the situation and, that as long as Baird helped the couple obtain necessary documentation, there would be no problem. In addition, Baird did not pay taxes for the Peruvian couple because she was informed by a lawyer, albeit incorrectly, that the Internal Revenue Service would not accept payment until the workers were properly documented. STEPHEN L. CARTER, THE CONFIRMATION MESS 23–28 (1994). In January 1993, Baird and her husband made a lump-sum payment of the taxes due. Neither the failure to pay taxes nor the hiring of illegal immigrants is a criminal offense. Employers of illegal immigrants, though rarely prosecuted, are liable only for civil penalties, including fines of up to $3,000. David Johnston, *Clinton's Choice for Justice Dept. Hired Illegal Aliens for Household*, N.Y. TIMES, Jan. 14, 1993, at A1. And yet, support for Baird's confirmation became suddenly non-existent. Should the hiring of illegal immigrants be criminally punishable? Is what happened to Zoë Baird an example of the arbitrary enforcement of regulations that can lead to underground economies in the first place?

2. Nanny tax. At the time of Zoë Baird's confirmation hearings, federal statutes enacted over four decades earlier governing household employees mandated certain reporting and withholding requirements for household employers who paid their household employees more than $50 every three months. The law was sharply criticized as being outdated, however, especially since, given the right circumstances, it frequently applied to the casual, teenaged, neighborhood baby-sitter that many families of all economic backgrounds hire to occasionally watch their children. A year-and-a-half after Zoë Baird, Congress passed the Social Security Domestic Employment Reform Act of 1994, changing the threshold to $1,000 annually. Given individual state laws and the statutes enforced by the Department of Labor and the Immigration and Naturalization Service, however, this threshold increase has had little effect on reporting requirements. CHAD R. TURNER, THE NANNY TAX vii (1997).

3. **Need for childcare.** Zoë Baird was criticized primarily because she could afford to make other childcare arrangements without breaking the law. However, not only the very wealthy are avoiding immigration and taxation laws for the sake of childcare, though many may not be able to afford *in-home* childcare. Nearly two-thirds of American women with school-age children work and require some sort of childcare arrangement. Moreover, nearly 60 percent of married men with children in America have working wives. At the time of Nannygate, only one in four people who employed household help paid the Social Security taxes required. Wallis, *supra*. In single-parent or two-working-parent homes, how does the Nanny Tax affect the parent's quality of life and ability to work in the marketplace?

4. **Benefits now or later?** Martha Shirk's article suggests that "[s]ome people do domestic work to supplement their welfare benefits, which, in Missouri anyway, provide only a third of the amount the federal government says a family needs to survive above the poverty level." She also suggests that reporting the domestic work income might decrease the amount of money the domestic worker was able to receive from welfare, while not reporting means that they won't receive an Earned Income Credit or Social Security Benefits in old age. For a family at or below the poverty line, which is worse? Is avoiding taxes merely short-sighted, or could it be necessary for immediate survival? Then again, Shirk makes the point that the Earned Income Credit would give her domestic "more money than she's managed to save in 20 years." Given Thomas Shapiro's research on intergenerational wealth, what effect could this wealth accumulation have on the nanny's own children?

5. **Outsourcing.** In a two-parent home, a mother or father who stays out of the work force to raise the children is not paid for his or her labor, though that parent effectively does the same work as a nanny or housekeeper. As a result, the parent does not receive income, nor does he or she pay the Social Security taxes that ensure future benefits. Is it ultimately more efficient to hire a nanny regardless of the employer's financial status in order to allow the parent to enter the market to obtain greater retirement benefits?

6. **Domestic workers and the public/private distinction.** Because domestic work was traditionally done by housewives for no pay, it has been considered of little or no economic value. Considered part of the private sphere, domestic work is largely unregulated, while the regulations that do exist largely go unenforced. Given Critical Feminist Theory and Frances Olsen's suggestion that the public/private distinction is unsustainable, how does and how should the law regulate the hired domestic worker, who performs private, household work in the public marketplace? How does the reform of the Nanny Tax "protect[] the interests of the propertied class employers who benefit from the public-private distinction?" *See* Taunya Lovell Banks, *Toward a Global Critical Feminist Vision: Domestic Work and the Nanny Tax Debate*, 3 J. GENDER RACE & JUST. 1, 6–9 (1999); *see also*

Peggie R. Smith, *Regulating Paid Household Work: Class, Gender, Race and Agendas of Reform*, 48 AM. U. L. REV. 851 (1999).

7. **Nanny gendering.** Could not Zoë Baird's husband, Yale Law Professor Paul Gewirtz, have stayed at home and raised the couple's children, given Baird's published annual salary of $507,000? How does the naturalized assumption that women are the caretakers of children interact with the increase of women in the marketplace? Are laws that make it more difficult for families to hire domestic workers discriminatory against women in those families where women want to work? Are those same laws discriminatory against the poor, female domestic worker? *See* Banks, *supra* at 8–9.

8. **Title, race, and national origin.** Banks argues that "[t]he term 'domestic worker' invokes the historic image of a native-born Black women, the mammy, an 'ideological construct of the plantation's faithful household servant and the South's most perfect slave.'" She argues further that the "term 'nanny' invokes the image of a 'foreign' woman" and summons "'vastly sentimentalized notions ... that a typical nanny came to change the diapers and stayed on for the weddings.'" *Id.* at 18–19. How do these terms, as Banks argues, "erase[] the most negative connotations of in-home childcare—low wage work often performed by non-white women in a potentially exploitative environment," and how does the use of such terms influence the debate about the Nanny Tax? *See id.* at 18–24. How do these terms simultaneously mask and highlight the class and racial differences between employer and employee? Given the Critical Legal Theorist's tenet that law and language are indeterminate, is there a better term to use, or are all the terms used for domestic work meant to gloss over the negative aspects of the job?

9. **Non-neutrality of immigration law.** In 1990, Congress limited the number of foreign "unskilled workers" that could receive permits to work in the United States to 10,000. Included in this category of occupations that require fewer than two years of experience was domestic help such as housekeepers and nannies. Given that most immigrants to the U.S. are women and that most domestic workers are also women, is this seemingly neutral immigration policy discriminatory against women? Furthermore, does it discriminate against the American woman in the workforce by decreasing the supply of child caretakers in the United States? *See* Joan Fitzpatrick, *The Gender Discrimination of U.S. Immigration Policy*, 9 YALE J.L. & FEMINISM 23, 23–37 (1997).

The Diamonds As a Business Enterprise

THE GANG AS AN AMERICAN ENTERPRISE 91–116 (1992).

■ FELIX M. PADILLA

* * *

Several major questions will be considered in the examination. What are the reasons for the gang becoming a business organization? What does the gang look like as an entrepreneurial establishment? That is, what are its defining characteristics as a business enterprise? Which cultural elements are used by youngsters for cementing and reinforcing business relations among themselves? What is the gang's occupational structure? How does the gang generate income for maintaining itself as a business establishment?

* * *

The history of the Diamonds dates back approximately twenty years, a relatively short period compared to other Latino youth gangs in Chicago. At first the Diamonds were a musical group, playing their music on street corners in the neighborhood and in local neighborhood nightclubs. Some members believe that in about 1971 a member of the musical group was mistaken for a gang member and was killed by a gunshot fired by a youngster from an opposition gang. This incident sparked the reorganization of the group into a violent criminal youth gang. And for a period of about six years after that the Diamonds were on a course of vengeance and retaliation, provoking intergang fights with other groups.

Spike, a thirty-year member of the Diamonds, who is still very active in the gang, provides a clear description of the early days: "We were a band, and we would play to pass the time, you know, or in some gigs in the neighborhood. This was not one of your well-known professional bands, but we did OK. We were just a bunch of guys who would get together to have fun, to play music in the hood, you know—out on the streets. You know, we were doing the same thing that other people were doing at the park or in basements, except that we were in our hood. Then the band started to attract followers, people from the neighborhood that liked the music, and they would be there all the time. These people were like body guards, you know, to make sure the band was safe. So the group started growing, and then, all of a sudden, there was talk about forming the group into a gang, so some of them decided to do it. These were the followers and not the band. I don't know what was the problem with some of these guys; maybe one of them had a run-in with the opposition. But, anyway, it was about this time when one of the band players got shot. So, from here on they decided to become a gang and keep the name of the Diamonds, you know, the name of the band. And for a long time they were hard-core, you know— these guys were mean motherfuckers. You couldn't go by the neighborhood because they were shooting at everybody. It was really bad. It was worse than what these guys are doing today. There were times we would have these wars with the opposition, and we go out to the park, the two gangs, with bats, clubs, guns, and shit, and just have it out right there. It was crazy. I can tell you of about ten guys from our side who died from gang fights. Some of the fights were right here because the opposition would drive by shooting at us. Some of our guys got killed right here."

During most of this early period the membership of the Diamonds was quite small; the organization had not expanded and divided itself into sections. Gang members' involvement in drugs—in particular, marijuana—was essentially for their own recreational use. The Diamonds had yet to become a profit-making business enterprise. In some instances, a member would purchase a relatively sizable amount of marijuana and sell to others in the gang. Sometimes money was collected to purchase a quantity of marijuana, which would be equally distributed among contributing members, again, most of the drug was for personal and, at times, social use. As indicated by Spike, while describing the early days of the gang, "We would just get high a lot. It seemed that everybody was doing drugs at that time. It's not like today where people are trying to prevent drug use. No, before there used to be stories about movie stars smoking reefer and doing coke, and they were cool and bad. Doctors were doing drugs; attorneys were doing drugs. I tell you, everybody was doing it. So, we started doing it, too. There were the fights between us and some other gangs—that's another thing we used to do. But, besides that, we would be drinking beer and doing drugs. We were not selling drugs at this time. What we did was to buy the drugs and use them ourselves. We still did not know enough to go into business. We didn't know where to sell them, expect for to our friends, who were already one of us."

Then, in the late 1970s, a major change occurred in the operational structure of the Diamonds. It began to take on a businesslike character. No longer were retaliative, violent behavior against opposition gangs and reefer smoking the mainstays of the organization. Money-making through drug dealing came to represent the gang's emerging chief function. Although a great deal of gangbanging persisted as the Diamonds and enemy gangs maintained ongoing feuds, overall the gang embraced and carried out a program that was built around money-making activities.

Why did the Diamonds undergo this change during this particular period? Which factors and conditions were responsible for the transformation?

Controlled Substance Act

"I remember this older guy from the neighborhood who wanted me to sell for him. He asked several of us to be his dealers. He was offering good money, but I was afraid. I didn't know what he was about. We knew that he was doing something because all these people used to come to his house all the time. Hey, like some of us guys sometimes went to him to cop some smokes for us. He was offering us some good money. He said that we could work for him and that he was going to take care of us. He was even talking about cars; you know, if you do real good and if you're reliable, you know, all of that shit, that he would buy us a beamer [BMW]. And that we would not have to worry again about buying smokes because we would have it all the time. But since he had never dealt with us before and then all of sudden he wanted us to work for him, I was scared. I said no to the buy, I couldn't trust the cat."

What Carmelo is describing is in larger terms an event that had a major influence on the business development of the gang—namely, a piece of legislation: the Illinois Controlled Substance Act, which was passed in 1971 and carried heavy criminal penalties for adult heroin and cocaine dealers. The bill called for mandatory twenty-year prison sentences for drug peddling offenders eighteen years and older.

Well aware that juveniles could always beat the penalties of the newly instituted law, those adults who for the most part had controlled drug distribution and dealing up to this point began enlisting some of the youngsters from the Diamonds as well as from other gangs to work the street blocks and corners of particular neighborhoods. Some youngsters, like Carmelo, refused the job offers, while others agreed to them. It did not take some these youngsters or leaders of the gang very long to realize, however, that they could profit substantially by controlling neighborhood drug dealing. In other words, these young people began to ask the question "If this is our neighborhood and people are using it to make money, why can't we develop our own business?"

And indeed, they did. Gang leaders began reorganizing the structure of the Diamonds into a wholesale enterprise or investment; the organization became a business establishment. It now purchased wholesale merchandise itself and hired its own members, especially the younger ones, to retail the street level. Since the Diamonds viewed themselves as landlords of several *puntos* in the neighborhood (literally translated, the word *punto* stands for "points," but here it refers to street corners), the only missing ingredient for developing a business operation was the necessary capital with which to purchase large amounts of drugs for extracting a profit.

* * *

Not one individual within the Diamonds organization possessed the necessary capital for purchasing large enough quantities of drugs for turning a profit. No single member had the money necessary for establishing himself as the sole owner or shareholder of the corporation. Therefore, some members began pooling their money: Sometimes two or three of the older members (usually the leaders, or chiefs) would "go into business"; at other times the group of investors was larger. On other occasions leaders would command all members to make an investment of a certain minimum amount (along with the lines of passing the hat) and would use this sum for purchasing the necessary amount of drugs with which to start the business. And in still other situations leaders of the gang would simply take and use the dues money for the purchase of large amounts of drugs.

Spike recounts this initial stage in the business development of the Diamonds: "At first it was real tough because we didn't have any cash. So, we would try different ways to raise enough to make a profit. You know, we would all chip in; you know there was no hassle about the money or stuff like that. We wanted the business to get off the ground, you know, make it work because we didn't have nothing for us. This was going to be something that was going to be ours, you know, for us. And once we got going we took control. But at first it was real difficult. And then we had to make sure that people did not spend gang money on themselves. So, it took a little while to get going. But we knew that there was a lot of money to be made in this business. This was a business made for us; it was something like it was sent by God. It was a business that we could do straight from the neighborhoods that we controlled and knew real well. How could you go wrong?"

To the question, "Who controlled the money made from dealing?" Spike answered, "It always was the chief or mainheads. They were the leaders. They had earned their position, and we respected them, and we had a lot of trust in them. So when we paid dues we knew that it was our money, but, in fact, it was the gang's money. And, since the chiefs and mainheads were the leaders, it was the same as the gang. That's how we used to see it then."

* * *

Perceptions of Conventional Work

Youngsters' images of "traditional" jobs were perhaps the leading force that helped to transform the gang into a business venture. These young men began turning to the gang in search of employment opportunities, believing that available conventional work would not sufficiently provide the kinds of material goods they wished to secure. Some of the more common assessments I heard about conventional work available for Latino youth are captured in the following two expressions:

> There are some jobs that people can still find, but who wants them? They don't pay. I want a job that can support me. I want a job that I could use my talents—speaking, communicating, selling, and a definite goal that I'd be working toward as far as money is concerned.

> We were just tired of factory jobs. We were supposed to go to school and receive an education. For what? To be employed in factory jobs? We were tired of that. At the same time we were watching these other guys making a lot of money, so we said, "Hey, let's follow these guys. Let's do what they were doing."

These remarks also allow us to gain insight into the pessimistic outlook these young people have developed toward job prospects in the regular economy. Members of the Diamonds have become increasingly convinced that the jobs available to them are essentially meaningless, far from representing the vehicles necessary for overcoming societal barriers to upward mobility. Although these youngsters have been socialized with a view in the conventional cultural course to achieving material success, they refuse to buy into its official means. That is, they do not agree to accept the "American achievement ideology" representative of middle-class norms and shown by Horowitz (1983), Kornblum (1985), and others to be widely supported by ethnic and racial minority parents and teenagers. The ideology stresses that success in school leads to the attainment of managerial and professional jobs, which, in turn, pave the way for social and economic advancement. The youngsters' own school experiences and occasional contacts with the job market—as well as their observations of the frustrating and often futile efforts by some adults around them to achieve social advancement through menial, dead-end jobs—combine to serve as overwhelming evidence that the American achievement ideology does not necessarily apply to them. In brief, these young men do not believe in the power of education to be the "great equalizer," nor do they see existing "legitimate work" as capable of leading them to a successful, meaningful life.

The views of these young people point out the poignant paradox between having culturally defined goals and ineffective but socially legitimate means for achieving them, indicated by sociologist Robert Merton several decades ago and since confirmed by researchers and scholars writing on gangs, youth, and employment (Vigil 1988; Kornblum 1987; Horowitz 1983; Moore 1978; Cloward and Ohlin 1960). The contradiction lies in the absence of avenues and resources necessary for securing the rewards that society most values and which it purports to offer its members.

The decision by members of the Diamonds to accept participation in the gang is informed by their assessments of the lack of available opportunities in the regular economy but also by their high level of aspirations. Rather than arising as a deliberate violation of middle-class aspirations, the gang represents a "counter-organization," a response geared to fulfilling the standards of the larger society. The transformation of the gang into a business enterprise was sparked by the will to change, to alter those forces of domination weighing heavily upon its members' lives. In effect, what these youngsters did was reconstruct the "criminal" gang into a income-generating business operation—an alternate form of employment with which they could hope to "make it" in U.S. society. In the words of Spike, "We grew up at a time when people were making money and making it quick. You know, we saw on television people getting rich overnight. You had the professional athletes—these are the guys who are supposed to have natural talents, you know. That's a lot of bullshit. It's true these guys were taking steroids. You had all these reports about how these athletes were pumping iron and taking steroids so they could sell their bodies and so people could pay to watch them. That's one thing we saw. Then we saw, you know, you had the white-collar criminals—you know, those guys who are just like us but never get caught, except that everybody knows that they are crooks. You had all these guys becoming filthy rich. And what do you think that's going to tell us? Shit, it didn't tell me to and get a job at McDonalds and save my nickels and dimes. Who the fuck was doing it that way? Who the fuck is saving nickels and dimes today? You have kids coming up to you today and asking you for a buck, not for a nickel or a dime or a quarter. Where do they see this shit? You tell me. I wasn't going to save my nickels and dimes. That certainly wasn't going to be me because I would still be waiting, and I would be the only one waiting. Things are not done like that anymore. So, we decided to turn to what we have, and that was us."

"Some of us fucked up. We didn't make it. I'm thirty years old, and I'm still out here hustling everyday. But that's because certain things didn't work out the way that I wanted. I'm not going to make excuses for my mistakes. But you know what? I'm going to continue because there are many people like me, people who have jobs, people who are making only enough to pay the rent, and then they come out here or go into other kinds of illegal business because they know that what society says and gives them are two different things."

Social and Cultural Components of the Ethnic Enterprise

What are the distinguishing characteristics of the gang which enable it to function as a business organization—a type of establishment necessarily built around a great deal of trust and commitment, which allow it to generate and sustain consistent and dependable social relations and monetary gains? That is, which social and cultural elements did the youngsters use for organizing the gang into a reliable money-making enterprise?

In the same way that the family unit teaches its young the norms, skills, values, beliefs, and traditions of the larger society, the gang has developed its own culture, including its own myths, norms, values and ways of communicating and reinforcing them. At the heart of the gang culture is a collective ideology that serves as the basis for realizing the overall welfare of all the members. For the gang collectivism is the major determinant of its efficient development as a business operation. The members' responses to their shared conditions and circumstances are collective in the sense that they lead to partnership, therefore uniting many individuals.

For the members of the Diamonds collectivism translates into an ideology of strength. These young men share the belief that their capacity to make a living or improve their life chances can only be realized through a "collective front." In Coco's view, "We are a group, a community, a family—we have to learn to live together. If we separate, we will never have a chance. We need each other even to make sure that we have a spot for selling our supply. You know, there is people around here, like some opposition, that want to take over your *negocio* [business]. And they think that they can do this very easy. So we stick together, and that makes other people thing twice about trying to take over what is yours. In our case, the opposition has never tried messing with our hood, and that's because they know it's protected real good by us fellas."

Rafael echoes Coco's interpretation of collectivism: "Together we have the numbers. We have protection. My business is his business because we protect our interests together. So we talk about our thing—it's nobody's thing; rather, it's our thing. I think that one of the first things we learn when we start off is to feel like a group or a family. That means that we have to share and we have to protect each other and whatever belongs to us." In effect, though gang members can (and in some cases do) pursue individual financial gains, their business ventures are made possible because of the gang, and their individual work is geared to enhancing the common good and to pursuing collective ends.

The collectivist nature of the gang can he said to be an extension of the traditional Puerto Rican family. In Puerto Rican immigrant society, as well as in other societies from which ethnic and racial groups in the United

States originated, the family served as the cornerstone of the culture, defining and determining individual and social behavior. Ties between families were cemented by the establishment of *compadrazco* [godparent-godchild] relationships. Relatives by blood and ceremonial ties as well as friends of the family were linked together in an intricate network of reciprocal obligation. Individuals who suffered misfortunes were aided by relatives and friends, and when these individuals had reestablished themselves they shared their good fortunes with those who had helped them.

* * *

In addition to its stemming directly from Puerto Rican family tradition, ethnic solidarity served as another fundamental cultural element, used by the youngsters for cementing their business relations. As Puerto Ricans, they expressed feelings of a fundamental tie (blood, or kinship, solidarity), believed to represent a major unifying force. Of course, this organic bond, in turn, provided the basis for trust. One explanation about the correlation between ethnicity and group solidarity was offered by Rafael: "The fact that I knew that what I liked was at another person's house—they would talk to me about things like, 'We're going to listen to Salsa music, we're going to have *arroz con candules* [rice and potpies] and some other stuff—I would get more attracted to that than to other things. That brought us more together. And that's how things are with other people from other nationalities. Polish people—have you been over where they have all the stores not far from here? Well, they have their own neighborhood and groups, you know, like they do their own thing together. So, we do our thing together, too, as one people. We have our hood, our own Latin stores and the business we do in our gang works because we are the same people. We trust each other because we understand what we are all about."

* * *

It is clear that the collectivist, communitarian underpinning of the gang was also buttressed by a base of local consumers. Their willingness to become faithful customers, to continuously purchase available goods—drugs and stolen merchandise—is viewed by those in the gang as an indication of a sort of surrogate membership in the gang. Additionally, customers protect gang members working as street-level dealers by agreeing to withhold information when interrogated by police officers and other law enforcement agents. These customers become, in the opinion of one youngster, "one of us." Flaco elaborated on this point: "People from the neighborhood know that they can get smoke, caine, and other things from us. It's risky going to other places. They don't know what those other people be about. So they protect us because they feel secure with us. And we are safe with them. So, we think of them as part of the business."

These various sources of collective behavior are thought to have played a leading role in cementing the Diamond's business structure. The significance of collectivism for gang members can also be gleaned from their views about the idea of individualism. These youngsters do not agree with the view that the exercise of individual effort in pursuit of economic and social mobility applies to them. To them individualism means placing oneself in a precarious position: How can they survive without one another? They are fully aware that they do not possess the traditional resources, such as money and high levels of formal education, used by members of the middle class to negotiate and advance their individual life chances.

To them individual behavior leads to obliteration. Tony makes the claim that "by ourselves we are nobody." He says, "We can be had without no problem. I'm always with my partners because when you're by yourself you are easy prey. You are going to fall the bottom of the barrel because, well, who's going to be there for you? So, if people come to you as a bunch, then we need to create our bunch." Other of Tony's remarks are just as straightforward: "This is not a game that you can win by yourself. If you want to win, you do it as a team. We call ourselves a family, but, you know, when you really think about it we're also a team. And, if you want to lose, play alone. Most of our guys who fall, they fall because they sometimes do things without thinking. Sometimes just do stupid things. Myself, I have gotten busted by the police several times because I was alone. I couldn't see them coming. When you're with your boys you have more eyes to check out what's going on—you can see the cops; you can see the opposition. But when you are by yourself sometimes you feel scared, and you know there is so much you see and so much you can do. In the Diamonds we teach the young guys; we practice how to be together all the time. We think that that's our strength. Other people have money. We have each other."

One other major reason for rejecting the individualist stance is that these young people recognize that success in U.S. society, which is structured around the concept of individualism, has one major interpretative implication: As success honors those who have achieved it, failure (and economic failure in particular) stigmatizes those who suffer it. The system, thus, makes those who have "failed" the objects of criticism and scorn. It can also imply that one's inadequacies in the social system are based upon innate deficiency; failure thus evokes pity and concern. The emphasis on the individual in gauging success and failure in U.S. society is unacceptable as far as these young men are concerned. For this reason they see collectivism as a way of giving gang members a special sense of purpose—the driving force with which to pursue economic and social success.

* * *

NOTES AND QUESTIONS

1. Illinois Controlled Substance Act. The Illinois Controlled Substance Act, 720 Ill. Comp. Stat. 570/510 et seq. (2002 & Supp. 2003), was intended to effectively remove certain substances from the marketplace. Does this Act fall under one of Milton Freidman's four duties of government? In what ways do the Diamonds's business enterprise respond to the market failure created by the act? Does criminalizing a substance or activity simply invite a market response such as the one seen here? Is this act, by strengthening the criminal penalties for its violation, attempting to restructure the market by increasing the risk premium of dealing in those goods it makes illicit? Can it effectively do so?

2. **Gang as government.** In what ways do the Diamonds function as a micro-level government for those in their neighborhood? Does the system of drug trade among gang members function as a system of taxation? How does the Diamonds's business enterprise redistribute wealth? Is the micro-government a more efficient method of wealth redistribution than taxing the drug trade and redistributing wealth through the centralized governments of the United States?

3. **Criminal law approach to the gang problem.** Liza Vertinsky argues that, because American criminal law is essentially "transaction-based," where the wrongdoer is punished only for the harm attributable to his own, individual conduct, it is ineffective at controlling organized criminal activities. LIZA VERTINSKY, A LAW AND ECONOMICS APPROACH TO CRIMINAL GANGS 2 (1999). Where multiple actors are involved, proof of the act (*actus reus*) and intent (*mens rea*) are more difficult to establish for the specific individual charged. Furthermore, the organizations will likely have their own systems in place to diffuse responsibility for group activity among many, if not all, of their members, as well as incentive systems that offset the deterrent effect of governmental enforcement policies. *See id.* at 178–80. Vertinsky argues instead for a more "enterprise-based," law and economics approach, focusing on how the group as a whole functions as an economic system. *Id.* at 2–5. What might the policies following this approach look like? Does tort law provide any suggestions? *See id.* at 67–87. What are the potential problems with implementing more "enterprise-based" enforcement policies that might not be as problematic in tort law? How might Becker's rational choice paradigm be overly simplistic in the face of gang organization?

4. **Gangs and the racism-oppression thesis.** The racism-oppression thesis suggests that American race relations and ethnic conflict, as well as both majority and minority perceptions of race and oppression, leads to the formation of highly racially-homogenized gangs. *See* GEORGE W. KNOX, AN INTRODUCTION TO GANGS 75 (1994). How does the homogenization of neighborhoods along racial lines contribute to the formation of gangs? How does the organization of gangs along racial lines lead to "bias crimes"? How does the functioning of gangs as vehicles of ethnic conflict promote racial and economic inequality? *See id.* at 74–96. Furthermore, is legislating to minimize the "patterns of ethnic conflict and competition in America, the social structure and institutionalized patterns or race relations, the accommodation of poor and minority group members to an affluent society, and the individual experiences, patterns of enduring racial conflict, and perceptions of racism and oppression" a better solution than the Illinois Controlled Substance Act? *Id.* at 75. Assuming the racism-oppression thesis is correct, how can wealth redistribution affect the formation of gangs? (*See* Thomas Shapiro's work in chapter 1.)

5. **Cheap labor below minimum wage.** A study of the monthly financial records of a drug-selling gang showed that although the average hourly wage for the gang members who were involved in the drug trade reached up to $11, the hourly wage for street-level drug dealers was less than minimum wage. Furthermore, the gang's largest non-wage expenditure was tribute to higher levels of the gang. While the gang leader made between $50,000 to $130,000 annually in income, "foot-soldiers" typically made less than $200 per year. However, the average hourly wage for the gang far exceeded the legitimate market wage available to those foot-soldiers, who could rarely expect to make more than minimum wage. For a foot-soldier, then, can participation in the gang be an economically rational decision? Stephen D. Levitt & Sudhir Alladi Venkatesh, *An Economic Analysis of a Drug–Selling Gang's Finances*, NATIONAL BUREAU OF ECONOMIC RESEARCH, WORKING PAPER 6592, 1–19 (1998), available at http://www.nber.org/papers/w6592.

"Measuring Impact of Crack Cocaine"

"There are three primary reasons why crack may have been so devastating to the Black community. First street gangs, which already controlled outdoor spaces, became the logical sellers of crack. Second, the increased returns associated with drug dealing attracted young Black males to gangs and may have reduced educational investment. Third, a large fraction of crack users were young women." STEVEN D. LEVITT & STEPHEN J. DUBNER, FREAKONOMICS: A ROGUE ECONOMIST EXPLORES THE HIDDEN SIDE OF EVERYTHING (2005) at (8–9).

Note on the Financial Pyramid of a Chicago Gang

Net monthly profit accruing to leader $8,500

Combined wages paid to three officers $2,100

Combined wages paid to foot soldiers $7,400

Total monthly gang wages (excluding leader) $9,500

The total monthly gang wages totals only $1,000 more than the net profits accrued to the leader excluding any side money the leader earns. The combination of danger and low profits suggests that low ranking gang members would reject crack dealing, but the hopes of reaching the top of the pyramid are often too high for them to resist. *Id.*

Carole, *Interview with Barbara*, in SEX WORK: WRITINGS BY WOMEN IN THE SEX INDUSTRY

166–74 (Frédérique Delacoste & Pricilla Alexander eds., 1987).

■ FRÉDÉRIQUE DELACOSTE & PRISCILLA ALEXANDER, EDS.

Barbara is a thirty-nine year old woman. She's worked with prostitutes' rights groups and lives in Richmond, California. I interviewed her in her home, which she shares with her daughter, mother and sister.

Carole: How long have you worked as a prostitute?

Barbara: I've been a prostitute for seventeen or eighteen years.

Carole: Where have you worked?

Barbara: Basically California. I've also worked in Alaska, Washington, Hawaii, and Nevada. I've worked on the streets and in the casinos in Nevada. But I don't work the streets anymore. What I do now is really not prostitution, it's domination. I still charge for it and still like doing it. If I could work on the streets I would, but the police make it too dangerous. They arrest you a lot so that you have to spend all your earnings to get out of jail. And then, they make you work in dark corners; you can't work out in the open for any amount of time. They come along and say, "Move on, move on." Basically, that's why I don't work the streets anymore. I'm older, too, but I think if the police didn't bother me and if it was legal, I'd be working the streets still. It's much easier and you don't have to play the boyfriend-girlfriend routine, you know, and it's quicker! (*She laughs.*) If you get a guy off the streets, it usually lasts about twenty minutes. The whole date, from there to the apartment and back.

Carole: What are your experiences with police arrests? Are tricks ever arrested?

Barbara: They never arrest johns. One time, I can remember in particular when they arrested me and four other women in San Francisco. There were five guys there and instead of arresting them, they made them testify in the trial against us.

Carole: Is that typical?

Barbara: That's typical, yes. If they catch you with the guy, no matter what the guy says, they won't arrest him. One time I can remember I was arrested and I was with a guy when the police pulled up behind us. I told him, "Look, don't say nothing, you know, just tell them, hey, I'm talking to you because as long as you don't say anything, I won't." Well, he freaked out and told the police, "Yeah, she solicited me for X amount of money," and they let him go. They wanted him to testify against me, but he didn't. The guy was into domination. At that time I didn't know what domination was, but he wanted me to whip him and beat him, and he wanted me to put him under a table and just do my commands, do whatever I told him to do. I thought he was crazy, but I also didn't know it was domination. (*She laughs.*) I knew he wasn't going to the court, because if he'd come to trial, I would have told everything. They finally dismissed the case, but I had to go to court at least five times.

And the case was not a case. I mean, the guy had actively solicited me. But I had to pay the cost. I had to bail out of jail and make five court appearances.

Carole: How many times have you been arrested?

Barbara: To be honest, I don't know. At least thirty, probably closer to fifty.

Carole: What kind of violent experiences have taken place in your work?

Barbara: Well, I don't know if this is violent or not. To me, it was. It was the first time I was arrested in San Francisco. I was with a girl. I didn't know her. She had two guys with her. She said they wanted to date her, so we walked around to the place that we were supposed to date at, and we find out that the guys were policemen. So the police said, "You're under arrest," and he said, "Bitch, if you make a move, I'll knock you down in the streets right now. Do you hear me?" I said, "I'm not going to do anything," and he said, "Did you hear me bitch?" You know, he screamed and hollered at me.

Carole: This was in San Francisco?

Barbara: Yes, the San Francisco police.

Carole: Have you been raped while working?

Barbara: Yes. The first year. I was working in Oakland. This guy pulled up to me. He was a young black guy, and he told me that he had a friend who had fifty dollars, but who was too ashamed to come in the area. He said he would take me to the guy. At the time, I didn't know any better and I was loaded on reds, so I went with him. He was supposed to take me to this hotel, but he pulled up in this remote area. And when he pulled off, he grabbed my purse and told me, "Bitch, give me all your money." I told him I wasn't going to give him anything. Okay, since then I've learned that you don't fight back. But I fought back that night. He wound up taking my purse and my coat. I wore wigs then, and he took my wig. He took everything. That was the only time something like that really happened ... and I don't blame the guy. I blame myself for it because I was loaded on reds, because I should have known better in the first place, and, believe me, after that I have. That's about the most violent thing that has happened to me.

Carole: So, he didn't rape you?

Barbara: Well, yes, he did. He raped me. But the rape part was nothing. I mean, the devastating part to me was him taking everything I had. He did rape me ... the rape was nothing. You know, he screwed for about twenty minutes, not even that long, maybe about fifteen. That part doesn't really stick with me because that wasn't the devastating part. Everything after that was.

Carole: When that happened, you didn't want to go to the police?

Barbara: I didn't even think about going to the police at all, you know. At that time I was so young. I was twenty-one. I had just started working. I thought because I was a prostitute, how dare I go to the police....

Carole: Was it because you didn't want them to know you were a prostitute?

Barbara: Well, yes. But at that time I didn't think I had any rights. And, I was loaded, too. I figured I'd be in just as much trouble as this guy would be.

Carole: Were you ever raped again while working?

Barbara: I've had them try. It's just that that's the only time anyone's succeeded. I had this guy one time. I was in Emeryville. He pulled up to me and told me he wanted to date me.

I got in his car and we drove like we were going to my apartment. All of a sudden, he pulled over and said, "I don't have any money and you're going to fuck me right now." I said, "In the front seat?" He had a small knife, it was real small, like a pen knife, and he said, "Get in the back seat." So I got in the back seat. And I said, "Look, whatever you want to do, just do it. I won't fight at all, there won't be any trouble." He started dating me and I kept on being so nice. I'd say, "Oh, and you have to put on a rubber." (*She laughs.*) I was just real sweet. He couldn't stand it. He started dating me, he started screwing me and he pushed me out of the car. I think he really wanted me to fight and jump with him. And I wasn't violent at all—"Okay, you want some, fine I understand, just don't mess up my dress, don't mess up my hair." (*She laughs.*) He didn't want anything to do with me because I wouldn't fight him.

One time I was in Alaska. This guy pulled up and when he pulled up I knew that it wasn't someone I should go with, but it was cold. We were in Anchorage, and in Anchorage you have to work on the streets. They won't let you work in any of the hotels or bars. They harass you some on the streets, but you can still work. It was freezing that night and this guy pulled up and he looked wrong, but I went with him anyway. So I'm on my way to the apartment and two blocks before we get there he grabs me. Well, I had some hair spray, those little aqua-net hair sprays, they make good mace. I took it and sprayed it in his face and it sort of blinded him. Then I just got out of the car.

* * *

Carole: Have police officers tried to get sexual favors from you?

Barbara: Several times. But not as bad as the other girls. Once two other girls and I were sharing an apartment and the landlord decided to call the police and tell them were working out of it. He flagged down this police. Well, I knew the guy flagged down and he was really good. One time, he'd seen me turning a car date, doing a blow job in a car, and he didn't do anything on that occasion. And there were a couple of other times, too. Then after about four times, he told me that I owed him a date. He told me if didn't want to go to jail, I should give him something. I said, "Well, I can't do that, I'm a prostitute, and if I do that you're gonna pay me." He wound up giving me a dollar and seventy cents. I didn't mind because I would much rather have dated him for a dollar and seventy cents then go to jail.

I've heard that happening many times. With vice officers, too. Most of the times I hear about it they're trying to scare the girls into something, you know. It's like, if you date me then I'll keep all the rest of the policemen away from you, or I'll tell you who all the police are.

Carole: Do you think it's better for the prostitutes not to give them anything?

Barbara: For me it was always better if I didn't date them. It's like dating a bartender. If you're in a place and he wants you then he'll keep letting you be there until he gets you. Then after he gets you, he won't want to see you anymore. And so that's what I did with the bartender and cops, too. I'd tease them and play like I was going to—"I can't do it right now, you remind me of a trick; you're too nice a guy." But I've dated a lot of police. Lots of them. I didn't know until afterwards.

Carole: It was during their off-hours?

Barbara: I don't know if it was or not. They said they weren't working, but they showed their badges and stuff afterwards. One cop said he wanted his money back. I said, "Bull." I wasn't afraid of him. I knew that if he told people he'd get in more trouble than I would.

Carole: I've also heard a lot more black prostitutes are arrested than white prostitutes, and that black prostitutes are kept in jail longer. Is that true?

Barbara: That's true. I can barely remember any white girls who were in jail with me in Oakland. The black girl has a much harder time on everything. She'll get kicked out of a hotel much faster than a white girl. A white girl, if she's got any kind of class about her, can work anywhere. Whereas if you're black, if you do anything wrong at all, like getting up to go to a guy in a bar when he calls you over instead of making him come over to you, they can kick you. If you're black, they kick you out faster. In Las Vegas, they arrested a lot of white prostitutes, but at first there *were* only white prostitutes.

Carole: A San Francisco study by Mimi Silbert, PhD, of the Delancey Street Foundation, of two hundred street prostitutes revealed that two-thirds had been raped or forced to do things they didn't want to do. What do you think of those numbers?

Barbara: It sounds too high, and I've known quite a few prostitutes. See, people want to downgrade prostitutes and they think that guys can just take advantage of them. But most of the time the prostitutes set the rules. Johns go where we want them to go. We run everything. They pay you first, they come to your place, they wash, they must use a rubber. People think that the tricks call out the rules but I don't know what girls they talked to. Now junkies work totally differently from prostitutes who are not junkies. And they get hurt more.

Carole: Barbara, why did you first get into prostitution?

Barbara: I did it for the money. That was the only reason I got into it. I couldn't find a job that paid more than minimum wage, whatever it was at the time, two dollars and thirty-five cents. I had two children. I had no way of supporting them besides being on welfare. I was always working two jobs but with the one or two jobs I could still barely pay rent.

Carole: At this point, how difficult would it be for you to leave prostitution if you want to?

Barbara: It would be hard. I'm not into prostitution right now. I'm into domination. But if I wanted to leave both of them alone it would be very difficult because my mother stays here with me, and my sister and my daughter. My sister and my daughter have jobs that don't pay much and my mother is on social security, so I'm the breadwinner, have to pay the rent, help take care of them. And I have to care of myself, too.

Carole: What kinds of things would you change about prostitution if you could?

Barbara: First, I'd make it legal. Lots of prostitutes feel they're guilty when they're arrested and that they don't have any rights. I'd like prostitutes to train prostitutes to change that so they don't think that they have to have pimps. If a woman wants a pimp, that's her business, she should be allowed one. But if she doesn't want one, I don't think that she should have one. I'd make it so that prostitutes had a place where they could work. If they wanted to work the streets I'd make it so that they could. I'd make it so the police would do other things besides bother prostitutes. So many times I was harassed by policemen and they'd say: "It's much easier coming here and talking with you because you're not going to do anything to me."

I was in Amsterdam last year. We had a Forum. A lot of the girls were telling me how bad it was even though they have places to work out of. At first, you know, I went along with them and said, "Yeah, I understand," but then I went down to the red light district, and if I had had a red light district when I was a prostitute, I would have loved it. They have little store fronts, and they sit in the window. Some girls wear hardly anything, some are dressed regular. The guy comes up and if he wants you, he knocks on the door. You've got your bodyguard in there in case anybody wants to go off or anybody's drunk or whatever. Now, I don't think we'd have to be limited that way. The women in Amsterdam complained that this was the only place they could work. I think that women should be able to work where they want to. They also complained that if they got a regular job in addition to the prostitution, they had to tell people that they were prostitutes. I think that's totally wrong. I don't think that I should be stigmatized if I want to sell my body.

Carole: So, that was their main complaint, that they had to stay in one area?

Barbara: Yeah. And that the landlords charged them an arm and a quarter. That if they wanted to get out of it, or just take a part-time job, they had to say they were prostitutes. Still, if we had that much! Some of the women who were with us said, "Yeah, but that's horrible—they're standing there like cows and they're taking them out like cattle." Well, fine, but I'd much rather have guys come to me than go to them. (*She laughs*.) And most prostitutes would.

* * *

Carole: Why do you think that prostitution is kept illegal in the United States?

Barbara: Because they're stupid and lazy. The politicians don't want to figure out a way to get the money, they're afraid that prostitutes will cheat and they won't get enough tax money. And men don't want women to have control over anything. Men want to run everything. Especially white middle class businessmen. They can get away with anything and they know they can.

Carole: What other things would you do, if prostitution was decriminalized?

Barbara: Well, a lot of violence would not happen if it wasn't a crime. Men take advantage of women, true enough, but if the girls were more organized and knew more, then they wouldn't let the guys take advantage of them. Beatings and robbings might not be if women would just stick together. There are so many things I could tell prostitutes so that they'd be protected but if I did that now, I'd be committing a felony because I'd be training a prostitute. It's also conspiracy to tell a girl that someone is a policeman. There are so many laws they can use on you. It's completely sickening to me. Just sitting on this bed could probably be illegal. (*Laughter*)

* * *

Carole: If you could have other work options that paid better than the minimum wage, might you leave prostitution?

Barbara: Prostitution is something I'd like to do on my own terms when I felt like doing it. What I mean is that I wouldn't want to do it all the time. I'd go out maybe twice a week instead of five, six times. I think I'd continue because I like the power I have with men. I like making them do whatever I want them to do. But it gets stressful too. You have to be on your toes. But there's so much money in it. And there's a power thing in making them pay for it and in deciding whether or not I'm going to date them. If I want to be nice to you, that's my choice, and if I want to be a straight up bitch, I can do that too. That's my choice.

Phyllis Luman Metal, *One for Ripley's, in* Sex Works: Writings by Women in the Sex Industry

119–21 (Frédérique Delacoste & Priscilla Alexander eds., 1987).

■ Phyllis Luman Metal

Well, my dear, I must admit your story seems somewhat unusual ... quite unusual as a matter of fact. I would never imagine a woman would begin being a prostitute at the age of fifty-five. I think that's one for Ripley's, if you don't mind me saying so. I guess I thought of prostitution as something unfortunate young girls got talked into by unscrupulous men. That was my impression. But to get into it at that age and of your own free will, although it does seem there was some financial pressure.... Still, there must have been something else you could have done. Tell me, what did you feel about it? Were you overwhelmed by guilt?

No, I was not. It was a hell of a lot better than marriage. And I tried that five times.

Well, I just don't understand. You seem quite normal. You are an attractive woman, of good family, well brought up. The men you married must have been monsters. But five of them? Something just does not fit.

Well . . . I found it very liberating to be a prostitute, and the men must have found it liberating too, for they were much better lovers than my husbands. They seemed to feel free with me and I with them. Why are you so upset? You don't think sex is wrong do you?

Well, no, I don't think sex is wrong between two consenting adults.

You don't think it's wrong to earn a living, for a woman to earn a living that is?

Why no my dear, of course not. Women have jobs now, all sorts of jobs, married or unmarried.

Well then, why is it wrong to get paid for sex? You must be getting upset about putting the two together.

It would be like selling your organs. Some part of your body.

Well, what about selling blood? That doesn't seem to bother you.

Well, that is to save lives.

True, but you would be amazed at how desperate some of the men are to have sex in the way they need to have sex, and how uptight they are about telling their wives about what they need. And then there are always the guys who are between relationships, or can't seem to get anything going.

Well, my dear, the whole subject is quite confusing. Why don't we just go to a hotel and have some relaxation.

Are you willing to pay me?

Well now, we are good friends. You wouldn't charge me would you?

Do you treat your patients who are your friends for nothing? My body is my source of livelihood. I have upkeep to be available and appealing.

I just wouldn't feel right about paying you. It would spoil it for me. I think you should give it to me.

Sorry. We can be good friends, but forget the sex then. When I first charged for it, I hade much more self respect and self worth than I ever had before. I felt appreciated. When I was a wife I was expected to do a lot of shit work and service my husbands and their desire, not mine. I felt used and abused. No trick ever broke my ribs like my husband did. No trick ever took all my money and left me when it was all gone—another husband did that. No trick ever urged me to neglect my children to accommodate him. No trick ever threw a bunch of in-laws who made my life miserable at me. No trick ever came home drunk every night like one of my husbands did. And I always had money, which I did not when I was married. And I never got a venereal disease. And something else. I got to know people of all nationalities in a way I never could have otherwise. My customers in Paris were from all nations. They were Swiss, British, German, Norwegian, Italian, Spanish, French, Syrian, Berber, Algerian, Senegalese, Saudi, Iranian, Japanese. I felt like a citizen of the world. Prostitution made me feel that all of us on the planet were one family.

Well, my dear it is all very interesting. But I am sure you are an anomaly. I can't believe this is how it usually goes. There is something wrong about it. What would happen to the family if it were legal?

I think it is much more prevalent and accepted in Catholic countries where the family is much stronger than here.

Well, my dear, let's have a drink and talk about something else. There are so many aspects to you. You have such a varied life. This surely isn't that important to you. Why don't you just forget about it? I think you just like to take up controversial issues for causes. You just like the role of being a social reformer. What in the world do you have in common with all those girls who stand on corners? They can't do anything else. Don't tell me you are a feminist.

NOTES AND QUESTIONS

1. Sex work in the economically just society. How does economic inequality contribute to prostitution? Do the overt practices of exchanging dowries and arranging marriages for economic gain in some societies, and the less overt determinations of who pays for dates, weddings, and engagement rings reinforce economic inequality and contribute to prostitution? *See* Priscilla Alexander, *Prostitution: Still a Difficult Issue for Feminists*, in SEX WORK, *supra* at 190–92. How do the dangers of prostitution, including violence and sexually transmitted diseases, reduce the economic viability of women in the workforce and perpetuate economic inequality? Is prostitution a way for those who lack the social skills, attractiveness, or life situation that might prohibit them from competing in the non-monetized sex market of dating, marriage, and one-night stands to gain access to the type of sexual interaction they desire? *See* HELEN REYNOLDS, THE ECONOMICS OF PROSTITUTION 189–90 (1986).

Liz Highleyman, also known as Mistress Veronika Frost, suggests that "[f]rom and anticapitalist perspective, sex work is perhaps the ultimate expression of worker ownership of the means of production, as expressed in the slogan 'my body is my business,' as a person's body is the one asset that cannot be taken away from them." Liz Highleyman, *Professional Dominance: Power, Money, and Identity, in* WHORES AND OTHER FEMINISTS 148 (Jill Nagle ed., 1997). She further suggests that, although it is true that some sex workers are badly exploited and hate their work, "body labor" in the form of sex work should not be taken away from those that lack the educational and infrastructural resources necessary for "mind labor" until alternatives are available. *Id.* at 149. If alternative job choices pay less, is paying a prostitute for sex not the most efficient use of her human resources? *See* REYNOLDS, *supra* at 190. Are prohibitions on the sex industry an exercise in capitalistic dominance? In an economically just society, would the sex industry still exist? *See* Highleyman, *supra* at 148–49.

2. Gender and "exploitation." Female prostitutes are traditionally regarded as victimized, degrading to all women, and in need of rescue from their circumstances. Is there anything *inherently* exploitative about adults engaging in consensual sex for money, or is it only after the actors in a sex-for-money exchange are gendered as female and male that the practice becomes seemingly exploitative? In a gay sex-for-money exchange, "[w]hose erect penis represents the 'weaker sex'?" *See* Julian Marlowe, *It's Different for Boys, in* WHORES AND OTHER FEMINISTS, *supra* at 141–44.

3. Prostitution and civil rights. Are prostitutes being systematically deprived of their civil rights? Does prostitution violate the Thirteenth Amendment's prohibition on slavery? *See* Catherine A. Mackinnon, *Prostitution and Civil Rights, in* APPLICATIONS OF FEMINIST LEGAL THEORY TO WOMEN'S LIVES 226–227 (D. Kelley Weisberg ed., 1996). Frequently, female prostitutes are arrested while the soliciting customers, usually men, are let go with a citation or a warning. *Id.* at 224. Does this violate the Equal Protection Clause of the Fourteenth Amendment? *See* People v. Superior Court of Alameda County, 138 Cal.Rptr. 66, 562 P.2d 1315 (Cal. 1977). What about the fact that police usually send men out to solicit prostitutes, resulting in a higher percentage of women arrested than men? Mackinnon, *supra* at 224.

4. Sex work and stigma. How does the fear of being stigmatized as a "whore" interact with the economics of sex work? Does it discourage participation in the sex trade, or merely "provoke and permit violence against prostitute, and ensure poor working conditions and the inability of many sex workers to move on to other kinds of work without lying about their experience?" Alexander, *supra* at 185.

*

COPYRIGHT PERMISSIONS & FURTHER ACKNOWLEDGMENTS

Ackerman, Bruce & Alstott, Anne, *Your Stake in America*, 41 Ariz. L. Rev. 249, 249–261 (1999). Copyright © 1999 by Bruce Ackerman, Ann Alstott and the Arizona Law Review. Reprinted with permission of the Arizona Law Review in the format Textbook via the Copyright Clearance Center.

Akerlof, George A. & Kranton, Rachel E., *Economics and Identity*, 115 Q.J. of Econ. 715 (Aug. 2000). Copyright © 2000 by the Quarterly Journal of Economics. Reprinted by permission of The MIT Press.

Amott, Teresa L. & Matthei, Julie A., *Race Gender & Work: A Multicultural Economic History of Women in the United States* 63–64, 70–72, 73, 194–95 (1991) (excerpts from chapter 4 "The Soul of the *Tierra Madre*: Chicano Women" and chapter 7 "Climbing Gold Mountain: Asian American Women"). Copyright © 1991 by Teresa L. Amott, Julie A. Matthei and South End Press. Reprinted by permission of South End Press.

Associated Press, *Uneasy Rider! Jury Finds Wynona Guilty in Shoplift Case*, N.Y. Daily News, Nov. 6, 2002. Copyright © 2002 by the Associated Press. Reprinted by permission.

Ayres, Ian, *Fair Driving and Race Discrimination in Retail Car Negotiations*, 104 Harv. L. Rev. 817 (1991). Copyright © 1991 by the Harvard Law Review Association. Reprinted by permission.

Becker, Gary S., *The Forces Determining Discrimination in the Market Place*, in *The Economics of Discrimination* 13–18 (2d. ed. 1971). Copyright © 1971 by The University of Chicago Press and Gary S. Becker. Reprinted by permission.

Brooks, David, *The Sticky Ladder*, N.Y. Times, Jan. 25, 2005, at A19. Copyright © 2005 by the New York Times Publishing Company. Reprinted by permission.

Chapkis, Wendy, *Dress as Success*, in *Beauty Secrets: Women and the Politics of Appearance* 79–80, 83–85, 88–93 (1986). Copyright © 1986 by Wendy Chapkis and South End Press. Reprinted by permission.

Clifford, James, *Identity in Mashpee*, in The Predicament of Culture: Twentieth-Century Ethnography, Literature, and Art 277–346 (1988). "Identity in Mashpee" reprinted by permission of the publisher of THE PREDICAMENT OF CULTURE: TWENTIETH–CENTURY ETHNOGRAPHY, LITERATURE, AND ART by James Clifford, pp. 277–346, Cambridge, Mass.: Harvard University Press, Copyright © 1988 by the President and Fellows of Harvard College.

Dash, Leon, *Just Trying to Survive*, in Rosa Lee: A Mother and Her Family in Urban America 39 47 (1996). Copyright © 1996 Leon Dash and Basic Books, a subdivision of Harper Collins Publishing. Reprinted by permission of Harper Collins Publishing.

Featherstone, Liza, *Down and Out in Discount America*, TheNation.Com, *available at* http://thenation.com/doc.mhtml?i=20050103

&s=featherstone (posted Dec. 16, 2004) (last visited Mar. 6, 2005). Copyright © 2004 by Liza Featherstone and TheNation.Com. Reprinted by permission from the January 3, 2005 issue of *The Nation*. For subscription information, call 1-800-333-8536. Portions of each week's Nation magazine can be accessed at http://www.thenation.com.

Harris, Cheryl I., *Whiteness as Property*, 106 HARV. L. REV. 1707 (1993). Copyright © 1993 by the Harvard Law Review Association and Cheryl I. Harris. Reprinted by permission of the Harvard Law Review Association.

Jhally, Sut, *Advertising at the Edge of the Apocalypse*, available at http://www.sutjhally.com/onlinepubs/onlinepubs_frame.html. Copyright © by Sut Jhally. Reprinted by permission.

Krueger, Alan B., *Economic Scene: The Apple Falls Close to the Tree, Even in the Land of Opportunity*, N.Y. TIMES, Nov. 14, 2002, at C01. Copyright © 2002 by Alan B. Krueger and The New York Times Publishing Company. Reprinted by permission of The New York Times Publishing Company.

Krugman, Paul, *For Richer*, N.Y. TIMES, Oct. 20, 2002, at s.6, p.62. Copyright © 2002 by Paul Krugman and The New York Times Publishing Company. Reprinted by permission of The New York Times Publishing Company.

Krugman, Paul, *The Sons Also Rise*, N.Y. TIMES, Nov. 22, 2002, at A.27. Copyright © 2002 by Paul Krugman and The New York Times Publishing Company. Reprinted by permission of The New York Times Publishing Company.

Malamud, Deborah C., *Class Based Affirmative Action: Lessons and Caveats*, 74 TEX. L. REV. 1847 (1996). Copyright © 1996 by Deborah C. Malamud and the University of Texas Law Review. Reprinted by permission of the University of Texas Law Review and Deborah C. Malamud.

Mathematics, Words and Music by Dante Beze and Christopher Martin © 1999 EMI BLACKWOOD MUSIC INC., EMPIRE INTERNATIONAL, MEDINA SOUND MUSIC, EMI APRIL MUSIC INC., and GIFTED PEARL MUSIC. All Rights for EMPIRE INTERNATIONAL and MEDINA SOUND MUSIC Controlled and Administered by EMI BLACKWOOD MUSIC INC. All Rights for GIFTED PEARL MUSIC Controlled and Administered by EMI APRIL MUSIC INC. All Rights Reserved. International Copyright Secured. Used by Permission.

McAdams, Richard, *Cooperation and Conflict: The Economics of Group Status Production and Race Discrimination*, 108 HARV. L. REV. 1003 (1995). Copyright © 1995 by Richard McAdams and the Harvard Law Review Association. Reprinted by permission of the Harvard Law Review Association.

Metal, Phyllis Luman, *One for Ripley's*, in SEX WORK: WRITINGS BY WOMEN IN THE SEX INDUSTRY 119-21 (Frederique Delacoste & Priscilla Alexander eds., 1987). Copyright © 1987 by Phyllis Luman Metal and The Cleis Press. Reprinted by permission of The Cleis Press.

Miller, Robert J., *Economic Development in Indian Country: Will Capitalism or Socialism Succeed?*, 80 OREG. L. REV. 757 (2001). Copyright © 2001 by Robert J. Miller and the Oregon Law Review. Reprinted by permission in the format Textbook via the Copyright Clearance Center.

Morin, Richard, *The Price of Segregation—Unconventional Wisdom: New Facts from the Social Sciences*, WASH. POST, Dec. 28, 1997, at C05. Copyright © 1997 by Richard Morin and the Washington Post Writer's Group. Reprinted by permission in the format Textbook via the Copyright Clearance Center.

No Scrubs, Words and Music by Kandi L. Burruss, Tameka Cottle and Kevin Brigs, © 1999 EMI APRIL MUSIC INC., AIR CONTROL MUSIC, KANDACY MUSIC, TINY TAM MUSIC, SHEK'EM DOWN MUSIC, HITCO-MUSIC SOUTH, WARNER-TAMERLANE PUBLISHING CORP., PEPPER DRIVE MUSIC, WB MUSIC CORP. and TONY MERCEDES MUSIC. All Rights for AIR CONTROL MUSIC, KANDACY MUSIC and TINY TAM MUSIC Controlled and Administered by EMI APRIL MUSIC INC. All Rights for PEPPER DRIVE MUSIC Controlled and Administered by WARNER-TAMERLANE PUBLISHING CORP. All Rights for TONY MERCEDES MUSIC Controlled and Administered by WB MUSIC CORP. All Rights Reserved. International Copyright Secured. Used by Permission.

Oliver, Melvin L. & Shapiro, Thomas M., *Wealth and Inequality in America*, in Black Wealth/White Wealth: New Perspectives on Racial Inequality 53–90 (1997). Copyright © by Melvin Oliver, Thomas Shapiro, and Routledge Taylor and Francis Group. Reprinted by permission of Routledge.

Padilla, Felix M., *The Diamonds as a Business Enterprise*, in THE GANG AS AN AMERICAN ENTERPRISE 90–116 (1992). Copyright © 1992 by Felix Padilla and Rutgers University Press. Reprinted by permission of the Rutgers University Press.

Pear, Robert, *Number of People Living in Poverty Increases in U.S.*, N.Y. TIMES, Sept. 25, 2002, at A01. Copyright © 2002 by Robert Pear and The New York Times Publishing Company. Reprinted by permission of the New York Times Publishing Company

Rankin, Bill, *Domestic Partner Ordinance Quashed: Atlanta to Appeal in Second Defeat*, Atlanta J. Const., Jan. 1, 1997, at D02. Copyright © 1997 by Bill Rankin and the Atlanta Journal-Constitution. Reprinted by permission in the format Textbook via the Copyright Clearance Center.

Romero, Mary, *Nanny Diaries and Other Stories: Imagining Immigrant Women's Labor in the Social Reproduction of American Families*, 52 DEPAUL L. REV. 809, 809, 813, 814–22, 832–47 (2003). Copyright © 2003 by Mary Romero and the DePaul Law Review. Reprinted by permission.

Schor, Juliet B., *The Unexpected decline of Leisure*, in The OVERWORKED AMERICAN 17–24 (1998). From THE OVERSPENT AMERICAN by JULIET SCHOR. Copyright © 1998 by Juliet Schor. Reprinted by permission of Basic Books, a member of Perseus Books, L.L.C.

Sennet, Richard & Cobb, Jonathan, *The Hidden Injuries of Class* 78–87 (1972). From THE HIDDEN INJURIES OF CLASS by Richard Sennet and Jonathan Cobb, copyright © 1972 by Richard Sennet and Jonathan Cobb. Used by permission of Alfred A. Knopf, a division of Random House, Inc.

Shapiro, Thomas, *The Hidden Cost of Being African American* 183–200 (2004). Copyright © 2004 by Thomas Shapiro and the Oxford University Press. Reprinted by permission in the format Textbook via the Copyright Clearance Center.

Shipler, David K., *The Working Poor: Invisible in America* 39–44, 50, 64–67 (2004). Copyright © 2004 by David K. Shipler and Vintage Books. From THE WORKING POOR: INVISIBLE IN AMERICA by David Shipler, copyright © 2004 by David K. Shipler. Used by permission of Vintage Books, a division of Random House, Inc.

Shirk, Martha, *Cashing in on Domestic Help*, St. Louis Post-Dispatch, Feb. 15, 1993, at 1C. Copyright © 1993 by Martha Shirk and the St. Louis Post–Dispatch. Reprinted by permission in the format Textbook via the Copyright Clearance Center.

Waldron, Jeremy, *Homelessness and the Issue of Freedom*, 39 UCLA L. Rev. 295, 299–302 (1991). Copyright © 1991 by Jeremy Waldron and the UCLA Law Review. Reprinted by permission of Jeremy Waldron.

INDEX

References are to pages

ADVERTISING
Generally, 155
Branding and consumption, 167
Cultural effects, 167
Society, effects on, 173

AFFIRMATIVE ACTION
Class-based, 2
Legacy preferences, 68
Negative effects, 355
Neutrality of, 320
Status production model of racial discrimination, 355
Subjugation through, 318
Whiteness as property interest, 318

AGE DISCRIMINATION
High tech industry, 140

ANTI–SUBORDINATION THEORY
Group identification, denial of, 315

ASIAN–AMERICAN RIGHTS
Generally, 35

BEHAVIOR
Identity model of, 248

BELIEF DISTORTION
Generally, 341

BOYCOTTS
Counter-boycott sanctions, 346
Racial discrimination remedies
Generally, 345
Boycott enforcement, 346

BRANDING
Consumption and, 167

BULIMIA
Identity-related behavior, 250

CAPITALISM
Consumption and, 167
Surplus production problems, 166

CHECK CASHING SERVICES
Generally, 112

CHICANO RIGHTS
Generally, 34

CHILD CARE
Family structure and, 244
Globalization of, 117
Immigrant domestic workers, 115
Nanny gendering, 386
Nannygate, 384
Working parents, 134

CIRCUMCISION
Identity-related behavior, 250

CIVIL RIGHTS LAWS
Car dealership pricing discrimination, empirical study, 358
Efficiency of, 350, 352

CLASS
Generally, 1 et seq.
Affirmative action
Class-based, 2
American Dream, 14
Appearance, 160
Bonded labor as slavery, 129
Categorical models, 12
Colonized and immigrant minorities, 15
Consciousness and, 12
Consumption, class and
Generally, 155
Conspicuous consumption, 158, 165
Dress as success, 160
Measures of consumption, 10
Decreasing economic mobility, 37
Defining, 2
Dress as success, 160
Economic individualism, 2
Executive compensation, growth of, 44, 48
Experiences in class society, 83 et seq.
Gender issues, 13
Globalization, effects of, 47
Globalization and marginalized labor classes, 128
Group vs individual class mobility, 15
Hidden injuries, 124
Homelessness, 93
Immigrant groups, 15
Income inequality, 24
Income vs occupational measures, 9
Individualism, economic, 2
Information technology, effects of, 47
Intergenerational effects

411

CLASS—Cont'd
Intergenerational effects—Cont'd
    Generally, 3, 36 et seq.
    Legacy-based college advantages, 68
    Racial implications, 53, 62
    Widening gap between rich and poor, 42
Legal system ideals, 1
Life in class society, 83 et seq.
Marginalized labor classes, globalization and, 128
Marxist class theory, 2, 7
Middle class
    Decline of, 42
    Ideals, 1, 14
    Stagnation, 71
Narratives, 86, 92, 98, 113, 124
Occupation-based class analysis, 7
Poor and, 1
Professionals, 7
Public school funding systems, 16
Race and, 13
Relational models, 12
Segregation and property values, 64, 67
Slavery, bonded labor, 129
Social nature of, 3
Stagnation of middle class, 71
Status-class, 2
Three-class analysis, 71
Underclass and culture of poverty, 97
Upper-middle class, 38

CLASSIC MARKET THEORY
Adam Smith
    Group status production model of racial discrimination, 357

COEFFICIENT OF DISCRIMINATION (DC)
Generally, 322

COMMODIFICATION
Reproductive labor, 113, 119
Sex work and human trafficking, 130

CONSTITUTIONAL LAW
Contraception, laws regulating, 222
Due process, substantive, 188
Legacy preferences, equal protection challenges, 69
Morality and constitutionality, 237
Public school funding systems, 16
Rational basis review, 199, 234
Sexual behavior, criminal laws regulating, 220
Strict scrutiny
    Generally, 199, 234
Substantive due process, 188
Zoning and land planning, 186

CONSUMER PROTECTION
Car dealership pricing discrimination, empirical study, 358
Usury, 112

CONSUMPTION
Advertising, 155

CONSUMPTION—Cont'd
Branding and, 167
Buying vs shopping, 164
Capitalism and, 167
Class and
    Generally, 155
    Dress as success, 160
Comerciogenic malnutrition, 158
Conspicuous, 158, 165
Dress as success, 160
Envy-based decisions, 165
Globalization and, 182
Malnutrition, comerciogenic, 158
Moral conflicts, 157
Narratives, 158
Norms, expectations as to, 156
Pecuniary emulation, 165
Poverty markets, 112
Shopping vs buying, 164
Society, effects of consumerism on, 173
Surplus production problems, 166
Television and, 155

CRITICAL RACE THEORY (CRT)
Implicit racial norms, 140
Law and economics of, 140
Workplace discrimination, 140

CULTURE AND IDENTITY
    Generally, 247, 247 et seq.
Affirmative action, negative effects, 355
Behavior, identity-related, 250
Behavior models, economic outcomes based on, 248
Bulimia, 250
Circumcision, 250
Classical economic theory, rational actor assumptions of, 247
Dominant culture assumptions, 247
Economic behavior and identity, 265
Gender and occupation, 250, 255
Group identification
    Generally, 250
    Subordination through denial of, 315
Hair conking, 250
Household models, 263
Indian tribes, identification to, 266, 317
Inter- and intra-group status, 333, 336
Male assumptions, 247
Occupation, gender and, 250, 255
Performative identity, 320
Piercing, 250
Plastic surgery, 250
Political identity, 254
Poverty and, 259
Preferences, identity-based, 255
Psychology studies, 249
Psychosexual, 255
Racial discrimination, status and, 325, 327
Racial identity
    Generally, 296
Rational actor assumptions of classical economic theory, 247
School choice, 254

CULTURE AND IDENTITY—Cont'd
Self-mutilation phenomena, 250
Self-starvation, 250
Slavery, race and, 303
Steroid abuse, 250
Subordination through denial of group identification, 315
Superego, 255
Tattooing, 250
Whiteness as property, 296, 320

DEFINITIONS AND ACRONYMS
Belief distortion, 341
Class, definitional problems, 2
DC, 322
Discrimination, definitional problems, 322, 359
Discrimination coefficient (DC), 322
Disparate treatment, 359
Family, definitional problems, 4, 183 et seq.
Historical race, 310
Homogeneity incentive, 141
Household, 4
Impression management, 155
MDC, 324
NBER, 66
NFA, 55
NW, 54
Performative identity, 320
Racial discrimination, 322
RKT, 183
SCF, 56
SIPP, 54
Status-class, 2
TFL, 141
Underclass, 97
Wealth, 54

DISCRIMINATION
Asian immigrants, 35
Car dealership pricing, empirical study, 358
Coefficient of discrimination (DC), 322
Disparate racial impact, 321
Dress codes, 140
Efficiency of civil rights laws, 350, 352
English-only rules, 140
Grooming policies, 140
Group status production theory
    Generally, 325
    Adam Smith and, 357
    Rational choice theory compared, 357
Homogeneity incentive, 141, 145
Market failure, discrimination as, 350
Moral arguments, 357
Prejudice and discrimination, 322, 357
Public school funding systems, 16
Punk styles, 161
Sociological theories of racial discrimination, 325
Status production model
    Generally, 333, 344
    Affirmative action and, 355
Team system, 141
TFL workplaces, 141

DISCRIMINATION—Cont'd
Trust, fairness, and loyalty (TFL) management, 141

DISPARATE TREATMENT
Generally, 359
Car dealership pricing, empirical study, 358

DIVORCE
Palimony, 200

DOMESTIC LABOR
Immigrant women, subordination of, 120
Nanny gendering, 386
Nannygate, 383
Non-neutrality of immigration law, 386
Sexual harassment, 122
Stereotypes, 386
Tax withholding, 384

DOMESTIC PARTNERS
Adultery, 211
Contractual relationships, 211
Employment benefits, 219
Heterosexual, 200, 237
Meretriciousness, 211, 213
Morality and constitutionality, 237
Palimony, 200
Prostitution and, 211, 213
Same-sex couples, 212

DRESS, HAIR, GROOMING, AND APPEARANCE
Class and appearance, 160
Discrimination, 140
Dress as success, 160
Dress codes, 140
Gender discrimination, 160
Grooming regulations, 140
Hair styles
    Conking, 250
    Identity-related behavior, 250
Piercing, 250
Punk, 161
Tattooing, 250

ECONOMIC MODELS, PRINCIPLES, AND THEORIES
Behavior, economic models of, 248
Culture and economic models of behavior, 248
Formal and informal economies, 380
Group status production theory of racial discrimination
    Generally, 325
    Adam Smith and, 357
    Rational choice theory compared, 357
Identity and affect on economic outcomes, 248
Identity economic models of behavior, 248
Individualism, economic, 2
Malthusianism, 183
Net financial assets (NFA), 55, 60
Net worth (NW), 54
Racial discrimination, taste characterization, 321

ECONOMIC MODELS, PRINCIPLES, AND THEORIES—Cont'd
Redistribution of wealth, 72
Rotten Kid Theorem, 183
Self, sense of and affect on economic outcomes, 248
Stakeholding redistribution of wealth, 72
Status production model of racial discrimination
    Generally, 344
    Affirmative action and, 355
Surveys of Consumer Finances (SCF), 56
Taste characterization of racial discrimination, 321
Trickle-down economics, 71

EDUCATION
Constitutional challenges to school funding systems, 16
Identity and school choice, 254
Legacy preferences
    Equal protection challenges, 69
    Wealth and inequality, intergenerational effects, 68
Narrative, 124
Public school funding, constitutional challenges, 16
Racism in schools, 131

ENGLISH–ONLY RULES
Immigration, 140

FAMILIES
    Generally, 183 et seq.
Blood vs associational rights, 199
Choosing marriage, 210
Common law marriage, 211
Criminal laws regulating sexual behavior, 220
Employment benefits for domestic partners, 219
Estate taxes and intergenerational wealth and inequality, 69
Extended families, 184, 199
Four-job families, 135
Historical norms, 198, 210
Household distinguished, 4
Intergenerational effects of wealth and inequality
    Generally, 36 et seq.
    Estate taxes, 69
    Home ownership, effect of, 58
    Industrialization and wealth inequality, 56
    Legacy-based college advantages, 68
    Racial implications, 53, 62
    Widening gap between rich and poor, 42
Legacy-based college advantages, intergenerational effects, 68
Moonlighting and single parents, 132
Nuclear and extended families, 184, 199
Polygamy and polyandry, 199
Rotten Kid Theorem, 183
Same-sex couples as, 212
Single parents, 132

FAMILIES—Cont'd
Single-family occupancy laws, 184
Stereotypes
    Domestic labor, 386
    Nanny gendering, 386
Traditional norms, 210
Two-job families, 135
Unmarried heterosexual couples, 200, 237
Working parents, 132
Working parents and housekeepers, 385
Zoning laws and extended families, 184

FORTY ACRES AND A MULE
Generally, 30

GAME THEORY
Prisoners' dilemma, 330

GANGS
Business activities by, 386
Criminal proscriptions, 395
Governmental functions, 395
Racism-oppression thesis, 395

GAY MEN
Queer theory, 246
Queer theory arguments against marriage, 246

GENDER DISCRIMINATION
Car dealership pricing, empirical study, 358
Dress as success, 160
Emotional labor demands, 154
Housework stereotypes, 386
Immigrant women, subordination of, 120
Occupation, gender and, 250, 255
Reproductive labor, 113, 120
Sex work and human trafficking, 130
Sex workers, exploitation, 405
Working poor, 107, 111

GLOBALIZATION
Branding and consumption, 167
Child care workers, 117
Consumerism, implications of globalization of, 182
Domestic service, 120
Human trafficking, 130
Labor unions, decline of, 153
Lean production systems, 153
Marginalized labor classes, 128
Off-shoring, 153
Sex work and human trafficking, 130

GROSS NATIONAL PRODUCT (GNP)
Standard of living distinguished, 51

HOMELESSNESS
    Generally, 93
Criminal justice policy, 98

HOUSEHOLD
Family distinguished, 4

HOUSEWORK
Domestic worker's narrative, 113
Identity, household models, 263

HOUSEWORK—Cont'd
Immigrant women, subordination of, 120
Stereotypes, 386
Working parents and housekeepers, 385

HOUSING AND HOMES
Class distinctions
    Homelessness, 93
Culture and identity, household models, 263
Homelessness
    Generally, 93
    Criminal justice policy, 98
Households, 4
Intergenerational effects of home ownership, 58
Wealth and inequality implications of home ownership, 58

IMMIGRATION LAW AND POLICY
Asian immigrations, 35
Class, immigrant groups, 15
Colonized and immigrant minorities, 15
Domestic labor
    Stereotypes, 386
    Subordination of immigrant women in, 120
English-only rules, 140
Federation for American Immigration Reform (FAIR), 123
Globalization and marginalized labor classes, 128
Marginalized labor classes, globalization and, 128
Nannygate, 383
Non-neutrality of immigration law, 386
Stereotypes
    Domestic labor, 386
Visas, domestic worker, 122

IMPRESSION MANAGEMENT
Generally, 155

INCOME
Wealth and income inequalities, 24, 54, 66

INDIANS
Generally, 24
Assimilation, 279
Displacement of, cultural otherness and, 303
Tribal identification, 266, 317

INDIVIDUALISM, ECONOMIC
Generally, 2

INTENT TO DISCRIMINATE
Disparate racial impact, 321
Disparate treatment as intentional or unintentional, 373

LABOR UNIONS
Decline of, 153

LAW AND ECONOMICS SCHOOL
Belief distortion, 341
Prisoners' dilemma, 330

LEGACY PREFERENCES
Generally, 68

LEISURE
Narratives, 135
Workaholism, 132

LENDERS
Usury, 112

LESBIANS
Queer theory, 246

LIBERTARIANISM
Same-sex marriage, 246

MALTHUSIANISM
Generally, 183

MARKET FAILURE
Discrimination as, 350
Underground economy and, 381

MARKETS AND MARKET THEORIES
Underground economies, 381

MARRIAGE
Adultery, 211
Choosing, 210
Common law, 211
Palimony, 200
Queer theory, 246
Same-sex couples, 212, 238
Unmarried heterosexual couples, 200, 237

MARXISM
Class theory, 2, 7
Consumption and capitalism, 167, 178

NARRATIVES
Class society, life in, 86, 92, 98, 113, 124
Consumption, 158
Domestic workers, 113
Education in underfunded schools, 124
Gangs as business organizations, 388
High tech workplace, 135
Homogeneity incentive, 146
Invisibility of working poor, 98
Leisure and workaholism, 135
Sex workers, 396
Sexual harassment, 252
Stereotypes, 251
TFL management, 143
Underground economy, 388
Working poor, 98

NEUTRALITY
Affirmative action contradictions, 320
Immigration law, non-neutrality of, 386

NEW DEAL
Undoing of, 47

OCCUPATION
Gender and, 250, 255

PALIMONY
Generally, 200

PIERCING
Identity-related behavior, 250

PLASTIC SURGERY
Identity-related behavior, 250

POLITICS
Identity, political, 254

POVERTY AND POOR PEOPLE
Bonded labor as slavery, 129
Census data, 83
Check cashing services, 112
Consumerism and markets in poverty, 112
Crime and poverty, 86, 98
Experiences in class society, 83 et seq.
Gangs as business organizations, 388
Gender discrimination, 107, 111
Globalization and marginalized labor classes, 128
Health care, 112
Homelessness, 93
Human trafficking, 130
Identity and poverty, 259
Immigrant women, subordination of, 120
Invisibility of working poor, 98
Life in class society, 83 et seq.
Malnutrition, comerciogenic, 158
Marginalized labor classes, globalization and, 128
Markets in poverty, 112
Moneylenders, 112
Moonlighting, 132
Narratives, 86, 92, 98, 113, 124
Prison industrial complex, 97
Race and poverty, 84
Sex work and human trafficking, 130
Underclass and culture of poverty, 97
Usury, 112
Welfare and working poor, 98

PREFERENCES
Racial discrimination, taste characterization, 321

PREJUDICE
Discrimination and, 322, 357

PRISONERS' DILEMMA
Game theory tools, 330

PRIVACY RIGHTS
Contraception, laws regulating, 222
Sexual behavior, criminal laws regulating, 220

PRIVATIZATION
Voucher systems, 80

PROPERTY AND PROPERTY RIGHTS
Whiteness as, 296, 320

PUBLIC/PRIVATE DICHOTOMY
Underground economy, 385, 386

QUEER THEORY
Marriage, 246

RACE
Historical race, 310
Identity, racial
    Generally, 296
Poverty and race, 84
Slavery and, 303
Whiteness as property, 296, 320

RACIAL DISCRIMINATION
    Generally, 321, 321 et seq.
Belief distortion, 341
Boycott enforcement, 345, 346
Boycott sanctions, 346
Car dealership pricing, empirical study, 358
Counter-boycott sanctions, 346
Critical race theory and workplace discrimination, 140
Definition, 322
Discrimination coefficient (DC), 322
Efficiency of civil rights laws, 350, 352
Esteem-producing racial biases, power of, 349
Group status production theory
    Generally, 325
    Adam Smith and, 357
    Rational choice theory compared, 357
Implicit racial norms, 140
Inter- and intra-group status, 333, 336
Intergenerational economic mobility, effects of, 53, 62
Market failure, discrimination as, 350
MDC, 324
Moral arguments, 357
Prejudice and discrimination, 322, 357
Sociological theories, 325
Status and, 327
Status production model
    Generally, 333, 344
    Affirmative action and, 355
Strict scrutiny of laws, 234
Taste characterization, 321
Tax policy, racial impacts, 70
Workplace discrimination, critical race theory and, 140

RACISM
Domestic labor stereotypes, 386
Education, disadvantaged, 131
Esteem-producing racial biases, power of, 349
Gangs and racism-oppression thesis, 395
Homogeneity incentive, 141, 145
Implicit racial norms, 140
Segregation and property values, 64, 67

RATIONAL ACTOR ASSUMPTION
Culture and identity assumptions, 247
Identity and culture assumptions, 247

RATIONAL CHOICE THEORY
Group status production theory compared, 357

REDISTRIBUTION OF WEALTH
Stakeholding, 72

REPARATIONS
    Generally, 82

REPARATIONS—Cont'd
African American, 82

REPRODUCTIVE LABOR
Commodification, 113, 119

ROTTEN KID THEOREM
Generally, 183

SAME–SEX MARRIAGE
Generally, 212, 238
Libertarianism, 246
Queer theory, 246

SEGREGATION
Property value effects on, 64, 67

SELF–MUTILATION PHENOMENA
Identity-related behavior, 250

SELF–STARVATION
Identity related behavior, 250

SEX WORKERS
Civil rights for prostitutes, 405
Exploitation, 405
Narrative, 396
Stigmatization, 405
Underground economy, sex industry and, 396, 404

SEXUAL HARASSMENT
Generally, 259
Domestic workers, 122
Immigrant workers, 117
Narrative, 252

SEXUAL ORIENTATION DISCRIMINATION
Criminal laws regulating sexual behavior, 220
Same-sex couples, 212
Same-sex marriage, 238

SHOPLIFTING
Generally, 86, 180

SLAVERY
Bonded labor, 129
Human trafficking, 130
Prostitution and civil rights, 405
Race and, 303

SOCIOLOGICAL THEORIES
Racial discrimination, 325

STATUS
Group status production theory of racial discrimination
Generally, 325
Adam Smith and, 357
Rational choice theory compared, 357

STEREOTYPES
Domestic labor, 386
Nanny gendering, 386
Narratives, 251
Occupation, gender and, 250, 255

STEROID ABUSE
Identity-related behavior, 250

SURVEY OF INCOME AND PROGRAM PARTICIPATION (SIPP)
Generally, 54

SURVEYS OF CONSUMER FINANCES (SCF)
Generally, 56

TATTOOING
Identity-related behavior, 250

TAX POLICY
Domestic labor, 384
Estate taxes and intergenerational wealth and inequality, 69
Progressive tax systems, 70
Racial impacts, 70
Trickle-down economics, 71

TRICKLE–DOWN ECONOMICS
Generally, 71

UNDERGROUND ECONOMY
Generally, 380 et seq.
Benefits of, 381
Domestic workers, 380
Formal and informal economies, 380
Gangs as business organizations, 386
Housework, 385
Market failures and, 381
Nannygate, 383
Narratives, 388
Public/private distinction, 385, 386
Sex industry, 396, 404

USURY
Generally, 112

VALUE AND VALUES
GNP and standard of living, 51

WEALTH AND INEQUALITY
Generally, 1 et seq.
African American reparations, 82
Asian-American rights, 35
Black rights, 29
Chicano rights, 34
Decreasing economic mobility, 37
Defining wealth, 54
Economic individualism, 2
Estate taxes, intergenerational effects, 69
Executive compensation, growth of, 44, 48
Forty Acres and a Mule, 30
Gangs as business organizations, 388
Globalization, effects of, 47
GNP and standard of living, 51
Home ownership and intergenerational wealth, 58
Homelessness, 93
Income inequality, 24
Income vs wealth, 24, 54, 66
Indian rights, 24
Individualism, economic, 2
Industrialization and wealth inequality, 56

WEALTH AND INEQUALITY—Cont'd
Information technology, effects of, 47
Interaction among elements of economic inequality, 12
Intergenerational effects
    Generally, 36 et seq.
    Estate taxes, 69
    Home ownership, effect of, 58
    Industrialization and wealth inequality, 56
    Legacy-based college advantages, 68
    Racial implications, 53, 62
    Widening gap between rich and poor, 42
Legacy-based college advantages, intergenerational effects, 68
Legal system ideal of classlessness, 1
Measuring economic inequality, 3
Middle class as ideal, 1, 14
Net financial assets (NFA), 55, 60
Net worth (NW), 54
Poor and classlessness ideal, 1
Professionals, 7
Public school funding systems, 16
Sex industry, 396, 404
Survey of Income and Program Participation (SIPP), 54
Surveys of Consumer Finances (SCF), 56

WEALTH AND INEQUALITY—Cont'd
Widening gap between rich and poor, 42

WELFARE RIGHTS
Economic individualism, 2
Income inequality, 24
Individualism, economic, 2
Legal system ideal of classlessness, 1
Working poor, 98

WORKAHOLISM
    Generally, 132
Narratives, 135

WORKING POOR
Child care, 134
Gender discrimination, 107, 111
Health care, 112
Invisibility of working poor, 98
Narrative, 98
Narratives, 98
Overtime vs family obligations, 132
Welfare rights, 98

ZONING AND LAND PLANNING
Constitutionality, 186
Extended families, 184
Single-family occupancy, 184

†